The Palgrave International Handbook of Higher Education
Policy and Governance

The Palgrave International Handbook of Higher Education Policy and Governance

Edited by

Jeroen Huisman
Ghent University, Belgium

Harry de Boer
University of Twente, the Netherlands

David D. Dill
University of North Carolina at Chapel Hill, USA

Manuel Souto-Otero
Cardiff University, UK

First published 2015 by
PALGRAVE MACMILLAN

Palgrave Macmillan in the UK is an imprint of Macmillan Publishers Limited,
registered in England, company number 785998, of Houndmills, Basingstoke,
Hampshire RG21 6XS.

Palgrave Macmillan in the US is a division of St Martin's Press LLC,
175 Fifth Avenue, New York, NY 10010.

Palgrave Macmillan is the global academic imprint of the above companies
and has companies and representatives throughout the world.

Palgrave® and Macmillan® are registered trademarks in the United States,
the United Kingdom, Europe and other countries.

ISBN 978–1–137–45616–8

This book is printed on paper suitable for recycling and made from fully
managed and sustained forest sources. Logging, pulping and manufacturing
processes are expected to conform to the environmental regulations of the
country of origin.

A catalogue record for this book is available from the British Library.

Library of Congress Cataloging-in-Publication Data
The Palgrave international handbook of higher education policy and
    governance / edited by Jeroen Huisman, Harry de Boer, David D. Dill.
        pages   cm
    ISBN 978–1–137–45616–8 (hardback)
    1. Higher education and state.   2. Education, Higher—Administration.
    I. Huisman, Jeroen.   II. Boer, Harry de, 1962–   III. Dill, David D., 1940–
    LC171.P35 2015
    379—dc23   2015019591

Contents

Part I Concepts, Theories and Methods

Figures and Tables

Figures

Tables

Preface

As a field of study, higher education is receiving increasing attention from scholars, not only from the community of what Teichler (2000) terms theme-based and applied higher education researchers who traditionally have seen this field as their turf, but also increasingly from scholars who are strongly embedded in the social sciences disciplines and that have started to discover that higher education is a 'suitable' field to test their theories or to explore concepts and phenomena of their interest. The Bologna Process is a case in point, in that political scientists have used this phenomenon in higher education to explore aspects such as multi-level governance and Europeanization. In addition, management scholars appear to engage more and more with issues that play out in higher education, such as leadership, marketing and organizational change.

In one way or another, one could argue, all higher education themes that have been investigated so far are related to policy and/or governance. This is not surprising, for in many higher education systems, governmental policies are still a major driver for change and dynamics taking place in higher education systems and their organizations. Whether one discusses access to higher education, global rankings of higher education institutions or quality assurance, ultimately questions are raised – and should be raised – about the role that governments play. Who is responsible for setting the rules for the game, for holding institutions – public and private – responsible for their outcomes and performances, for fair access and so on? If it is, in the end, not the government that is directly responsible, governments eventually have – implicitly or explicitly – a significant role in deciding on who will be responsible.

A couple of decades ago, a focus on higher education policy would have sufficed, but we argue that it is now important to broaden up and include governance issues when looking at higher education. In a context in which governments were in the driving seat, a focus on policy seemed warranted. Policy should, in this context, be understood as the (political) decisions for implementing courses of action to reach certain societal objectives (see, e.g., Cochran and Malone, 1995), with policy instruments figuring as the tools of these courses of action (see Chapter 3 by van Vught and De Boer). But as several scholars – from political sciences and public administration – have argued, looking at policy solely would narrow our perspective on the issues at stake. Undeniably, stakeholders beyond governments are playing an increasingly important role in higher education (as they do in other [semi-]public and even in private sectors), and other mechanisms – including those of the market – have gradually been introduced. Enter governance, defined as 'a change in the meaning of government, referring to a new process of governing; or a changed condition of ordered rule; or the new method by which society is governed' (Rhodes, 1996, pp. 652–653, see also Chapter 2 by Reale and Primeri).

This Handbook aims to present the state-of-the-art research on higher education policy and governance. It brings together key conceptual, theoretical and methodological insights and contains contributions on topics that figure prominently on governmental and other stakeholders' agendas, such as funding, research and development, gender and graduate employment.

A few caveats must be kept in mind when reading this volume, one of which we explicitly would like to address in this editorial introduction. As for any handbook, there is not sufficient space to address all salient concepts, methods and themes. Readers may wonder why certain themes and theories have been addressed and others ignored. This partly goes back to the way we took up this challenging project, through an open call for contributions. We tried to make our selection of chapters as representative as possible, also bearing in mind geographical coverage of the themes. That call was, after an initial selection of solid proposals, complemented with some explicit invitations to contributions. In all, we think we offer a rather comprehensive set of 30 chapters that address a vast range of exciting concepts, methods and themes. The concepts addressed are those that dominate the current discourse and debates on higher education, and the themes relate to overarching topics that are equally salient and pertain to enduring governance challenges.

Acknowledging the above caveat, it is even more important to celebrate the rich diversity that lurks behind the overall idea of higher education policy and governance. Embarking on the project, we thought that it made sense to distinguish concepts, methods and themes. We still think it does but emphasize the blurring boundaries between them. We were aware that a watertight distinction between concepts and theories, for instance, may be untenable, in that they are inextricably connected: theories use concepts, although some higher education concepts are 'theory light'. Similarly, it was not always easy to distinguish themes from theories: Is regionalism a theme or a theory (Chapter 20 by Chou and Ravinet)? But other demarcation challenges loomed. Should one see the network approach (Chapter 12 by Shields) as a method or should it have been included under the section addressing concepts? And, is institutional research (Chapter 11 by Webber and Calderon) a specific method or a theme?

If we look behind the functionalistic division, there is even more variety. Some themes are much more 'mature' than others. Chapter 29 (by Burke and Kuo) and Chapter 30 (by O'Connor, Carvalho, Vabø and Cardoso) show that considerable attention has been paid to inequalities in higher education over the past decades, whereas Chapter 19 (by Fevolden and Tømte) makes clear that research, despite a tradition of investigating online learning, has only started to scratch the surface when it comes to exploring new developments like open educational resources. The distinction between mature and less mature themes coincides to some extent with whether a significant body of literature has developed, leading to a robust understanding of the phenomenon. In a similar way, we see less and more mature theories, concepts and methods. Policy instruments go back a while (Chapter 3 leads us back to the seminal work on policy instruments of the 1950s), whereas the idea of multi-level governance (Chapter 5 by Fumasoli) is much more recent. In that sense, presenting the state of the art is a significant challenge. Therefore, in this Handbook, chapters can be conceived of as stock-taking exercises, showing the reader what we know and do not know (yet), whereas in other chapters it seemed more appropriate to introduce and explore relevant underlying concepts. Some themes lend themselves easier than others for developing a particular theoretical perspective or for giving input in terms of a new or revised research agenda. A final point regarding variety – not unimportantly in light of our comment on higher education as a growing field – is that we are pleased to see that chapters have been contributed by seasoned scholars and as well by a new generation of higher education scholars.

As said, the objective of our endeavour was to compose a broad overview of the current state of higher education and governance studies to inform and inspire those interested in the field. It has been an interesting and rewarding journey, and we are confident that this objective has been reached, but obviously success and failure are in the eyes of the beholder!

References

Cochran, C. E. and E. F. Malone (1995) *Public Policy: Perspectives and Choices* (New York: McGraw-Hill).

Rhodes, R. A. W. (1996) 'The new governance: governing without government', *Political Studies*, 44(4), 652–667.

Teichler, U. (2000) 'Higher education research and its institutional basis', in S. Schwarz and U. Teichler (eds) *The Institutional Basis of Higher Education Research. Experiences and Perspectives* (pp. 13–24) (Dordrecht: Kluwer).

Contributors

Alberto Amaral is Professor Emeritus at the University of Porto, Portugal, and President of the Portuguese Agency for the Assessment and Accreditation of Higher Education (A3ES). He has been the chair of the board of Consortium of Higher Education Researchers (CHER) and is a member of IAUP, EAIR, SRHE, SCUP and IMHE. He is editor and co-editor of several books, including *Governing Higher Education: National Perspectives on Institutional Governance* (2002), *The Higher Education Managerial Revolution?* (2003), *Markets in Higher Education: Rhetoric or Reality?* (2004), *Reform and Change in Higher Education* (2005), *From Governance to Identity* (2008), *European Integration and the Governance of Higher Education and Research* (2009) and *Higher Education in Portugal 1974–2009 – A Nation, a Generation* (2012). His recent articles have appeared in *Higher Education, Quality in Higher Education, Tertiary Education and Management, Higher Education Quarterly, Higher Education Policy, Higher Education in Europe* and *European Journal of Education.*

Sophia Arkoudis is Associate Professor of Higher Education at the Melbourne Centre for the Study of Higher Education, University of Melbourne, Australia. Her research interests broadly focus on the quality of the student experience in higher education and include English-language teaching and assessment in higher education, graduate employability, academic workforce and internationalizing the curriculum. Her recent work includes papers on internationalization in *Teaching in Higher Education*, on academic workforce in *Higher Education* and a co-authored book on English-language standards in higher education.

Chi Baik is Senior Lecturer in Higher Education at the Melbourne Centre for the Study of Higher Education, University of Melbourne, Australia. Her research interests include higher education policy, internationalization, university curriculum and student experience, and she has recently published papers on these topics. She is a co-director of two national projects related to professionalizing university teaching, curriculum innovation and student experience and has been a chief investigator in several large national projects on the internationalization of higher education.

Elizabeth Balbachevsky is an associate professor at the Department of Political Science, University of São Paulo, Brazil; Deputy Director of the University of São Paulo's Center for Public Policy Research (Núcleo de Pesquisa de Políticas Públicas – NUPPs-USP); and a fellow at the Laboratory of Studies in Higher

Education, State University of Campinas, Brazil. Her main research interests are governance and institutional development of higher education institutions and higher education and science policies in a comparative perspective. Her publications include 'Academic Research and Advanced Training: Building Up Research Universities in Brazil' in *Latin America's New Knowledge Economy: Higher Education, Government and International Collaboration* (edited by Balan, 2013) and 'Brazil: Diverse Experience in Institutional Governance in the Public and Private Sectors' in *Changing Governance and Management in Higher Education: The Perspectives of Academy* (edited by Locke and colleagues, 2011).

Harry de Boer is a senior research associate at the Center for Higher Education Policy Studies (CHEPS), University of Twente, the Netherlands. Within the field of higher education, he specializes in government university relationships, steering models, policy analysis, institutional governance, leadership and management, and strategic planning. In his field of expertise, he participated in international and national research and consultancy projects (e.g. for the European Commission, *Deutsche Forschungsgemeinschaft*, Dutch and Norwegian ministries of education and national advisory bodies). He has been lecturing several higher education and public administration courses at the University of Twente, as well as in international higher education programmes and management training courses. In 2008, he was a visiting Erasmus Mundus scholar at the University of New England in Australia, and from 2005 he is on the editorial board of *Higher Education Quarterly*.

Fabiana Barros de Barros is a PhD candidate at the LH Martin Institute, University of Melbourne, Australia. She holds a Master's in Higher Education, jointly awarded by the universities of Oslo, Tampere and Aveiro at Norway, Finland and Portugal, respectively. She has several years of professional experience in fundraising and project management, focusing on building management capacity at universities. She has been a trainee of the European Commission at CORDIS, Luxembourg. She is an alumni and active member of the Erasmus Mundus Students and Alumni Association. Her research interests include governance, leadership and management of research, particularly at collaborative Centres of Excellence, research policy and funding instruments, knowledge production and scientific networks. Her recent publications include a master's thesis on the impact of the Innovation Law upon the management of Brazilian universities and contributions to the Organisation for Economic Co-operation and Development (OECD) IHERD (Innovation, Research and Higher Education for Development) programme's report on centres of excellence as a tool for capacity-building, featuring Australia as a case study.

Emiko Blalock is a graduate assistant and doctoral student at Higher, Adult, and Lifelong Education (HALE) programme at Michigan State University, USA. Previous to her position at Michigan, she was at Seattle University, USA, as an instructor and member of the advisory committee for non-profit management and leadership programme. Her research interests include curriculum development for emerging fields of study, organizational change and curriculum reform, and faculty issues in US higher education.

Bruno Broucker is a postdoctoral researcher and lecturer at the Public Governance Institute, University of Leuven (KU Leuven), Belgium. He is an expert in public management and public governance, including change management, leadership and human resource management in the public sector. Over the last ten years, he has been involved with several public sector research projects regarding educational effectiveness and knowledge transfer, change management, reforms in the federal Belgian judicial system, workload measurement and quality measurement. Between 2010 and 2013, he was affiliated to the KU Leuven's Education Policy and Quality Department as an expert and policy advisor for higher education. His research interests span change management, leadership, higher education policy and governance, Big Data governance and open government. His most recent publications include articles in *Teaching Public Administration* and the *European Educational Research Journal*.

Penny Jane Burke is Global Innovation Chair of Equity and Co-Director of the Centre of Excellence of Equity in Higher Education, University of Newcastle, Australia. She is also Professor of Education at Roehampton University, London, where she is Co-founder and Director of the Paulo Freire Institute-UK (PFI-UK) and Research in Inequalities, Societies and Education (RISE). She has published extensively in the field of equity in higher education, including *Accessing Education Effectively Widening Participation* (2002), *The Right to Higher Education: Beyond Widening Participation* (2012) and *Reconceptualising Lifelong Learning: Feminist Interventions* (with Sue Jackson, 2007). She is the co-convenor of Access and Widening Participation Network for the Society for Research in Higher Education (SRHE), editor of *Teaching in Higher Education* and a member of SRHE's governing council and publication committee. She has held the posts of Professor of Education at the University of Sussex and Reader in Education at the Institute of Education, University of London.

Yuzhuo Cai is a senior lecturer and an adjunct professor at the Higher Education Group (HEG), School of Management, University of Tampere, Finland, and was the acting professor of the unit during August 2013–July 2014. He is also a guest professor at the Institute of International and Comparative Education, Beijing Normal University, China. He is one of the two founding members of the Chinese Education Research and Exchange Centre at the University of Tampere, the first centre specializing in Chinese education research and education cooperation with China in Continental Europe. He is the co-convener of the Thematic Research Group on 'Entrepreneurial Universities' in the Triple Helix Association, Italy. His main teaching and research areas are organization theory, higher education policy and management, internationalization of higher education and innovation studies, with extensive publications in these fields.

Angel J. Calderon is the principal advisor of planning and research at RMIT University, Australia. Previously, he was manager of Statistical Services at Monash University, Australia. He has worked as a journalist and foreign correspondent in several countries. He was co-editor of the *Journal of Higher Education Policy and Management* (2001–2007) and the *Journal of Institutional Research in Australasia* (1998–2001). His research interests include higher education policy, international education, impacts of trade liberalization on educational services, emerging markets, graduate outcomes and satisfaction, benchmarking and university rankings. He has co-edited (with Karen Webber, 2015) a book on institutional research and planning in higher education.

Sónia Cardoso is a researcher at the Centre for Research in Higher Education Policies (CIPES), Portugal, and at the Research and Analysis Office of A3ES. She is a referee for *Assessment and Evaluation in Higher Education, Quality Assurance in Education* and *Tertiary Education and Management*. Her research interests are quality assurance, higher education students and professionals (academics and non-academics) and gender. Her recent publications include articles in *Educational Assessment, Evaluation and Accountability, Higher Education, Studies in Higher Education* and *European Journal of Education*.

Teresa Carvalho is a senior researcher at CIPES and an assistant professor in the Department of Social, Political and Territorial Sciences, University of Aveiro, Portugal. Her research interests are reforms in the public sector, higher education policy, higher education governance, professions, professionalism and gender issues. She has been a coordinator of the European Sociological Association Network of the Sociology of Professions (RN19) since 2013. Her research findings on the New Public Management and the sociology of professions and academic careers have appeared in *Higher Education, Higher Education Quarterly, Higher Education Policy* and *Minerva*. She has co-edited the book *Professionalism, Managerialism and Reform in Higher Education and the Health Services* (with Rui Santiago).

Joakim Caspersen is a senior researcher at Nordic Institute for Studies in Innovation, Research and Education (NIFU) in Oslo, Norway, and at Norwegian

University of Technology and Science (NTNU) in Trondheim, Norway. His main research interests are sociological analyses of the relationship between quality in higher education and labour market qualification, particularly within the professions. His latest publications examine the introduction of learning outcomes in higher education in Norway as part of international reform movements such as the Bologna Process and the development of qualifications frameworks. He has also examined the statistical relationship between different measurements of learning outcomes and how these are related to disciplinary profiles.

Meng-Hsuan Chou is Nanyang Assistant Professor in Public Policy and Global Affairs at Nanyang Technological University (NTU), Singapore, an associate fellow at the EU Centre Singapore and the academic coordinator for The Academic Association for Contemporary European Studies (UACES) collaborative research network in the European Research Area. Prior to joining NTU in 2013, she was a postdoctoral fellow at ARENA Centre for European Studies, University of Oslo. She has researched at Chatham House, London, and Centre for European Policy Studies, Brussels, and was a visiting scholar at Stanford University and the Université libre de Bruxelles (Free University of Brussels). She holds a PhD from Cambridge, an MPhil in European Politics and Society from Oxford and a Master's in European Public Policy from Leiden. Her research interests lie at the intersection of regionalism, public policy and international relations and include knowledge policy cooperation and all dimensions of human mobility (trafficking and talent migration). Her publications include articles in, inter alia, the *Journal of European Public Policy* and *PS: Political Science & Politics*.

Fadia Dakka was recently awarded a doctorate by the Faculty of Social Sciences and Law, University of Bristol, UK, where she holds a teaching position in the School for Policy Studies. She teaches courses such as Comparative and International Social Policy and Social Policy and the Welfare State: Theoretical Perspectives. Her doctoral thesis investigated discourses and strategies on institutional competition, differentiation and convergence in English higher education. Her research interests focus on higher education policy and governance, institutional/organizational changes in higher education, the political economy of (higher) education transformation and comparative social policy in a globalizing context. Her teaching interests include political philosophy, social theory, sociology of higher education and international relations.

Kurt De Wit is Head of Data Management Unit of the Education Policy Department at KU Leuven in Belgium. He carries out institutional research on students and education and monitors national and European higher education policy. He also serves on the Executive Council of the Flemish Sociological Association and was editor-in-chief (2010–2013) of its peer-reviewed journal. His current research interests include education innovation policy in higher education, the role of ICT in university students, international rankings of higher education institutions, governance and funding of higher education and the development of the network society and its consequences for higher education. His most recent publications include articles in *Computers and Education, Education and Information Technologies* and the *European Educational Research Journal*.

David D. Dill is Professor Emeritus of Public Policy at the University of North Carolina, Chapel Hill. He has been a visiting research fellow at the University of Manchester Business School, a visiting fellow at Wolfson College, Cambridge University, a visiting professor at CHEPS, University of Twente, and a visiting professor at the European University Institute in Florence, Italy. His research interests include public policy analysis, the regulation of academic quality and research policy. His most recent books are *National Innovation and the Academic Research Enterprise: Public Policy in Global Perspective* (with Frans A. van Vught); *Public Policy for Academic Quality: Analyses of Innovative Policy Instruments* (with Maarja Beerkens); and *Public Vices, Private Virtues? Assessing the Effects of Marketization in Higher Education* (with Pedro Teixeira). He serves as Director of the Research Program on Public Policy for Academic Quality in the Department of Public Policy, the University of North Carolina.

Sara Diogo is a PhD student at the University of Aveiro and CIPES, Portugal, and at the Finnish Institute for Educational Research, University of Jyväskylä, Finland. Her doctoral work focuses on policy changes in Portuguese and Finnish higher education systems. Her research interests include higher education governance and management, higher education policy and internationalization. Her publications include articles in *Higher Education Management and Policy Journal, Journal of the European Higher Education Area, European Journal of Higher Education* and in the recently established journal *Working Papers in Higher Education Studies*.

James S. Fairweather is Professor of Higher, Adult, and Lifelong Education at the Department of Educational Administration, Michigan State University, USA. His research focuses on faculty roles and rewards, higher education policy and reforming STEM (science, technology, education and mathematics) education. He is the author of *Faculty Work and Public Trust*. Recently, he and his colleagues on the National Academy of Sciences' committee on Disciplinary-Based Educational Research published the principal summative work on the status of postsecondary STEM education in the United States. He serves the American Association of Universities Undergraduate STEM Education Initiative as a co-principal investigator. He received the Career Research Award from the American Educational Research Association – Division J. He is also the recipient of a Fulbright Scholarship and was twice awarded an Erasmus Mundus Professorship. He holds a PhD in Higher Education from Stanford University.

Arne M. Fevolden is a postdoctoral researcher at the Centre for Technology, Innovation and Culture (TIK), University of Oslo, and a senior researcher at NIFU. He holds a Master's in Economic Sociology and a PhD in Innovation Studies from the University of Oslo. Much of his research is concerned with the information and communications industry. His doctoral dissertation focuses on innovation and capacity utilization in the information and communications industry, and his more recent research has looked at transition paths in the computer industry and the development of massive open online courses (MOOCs) and e-learning. In addition to studying the information and communications industry, he has also carried out research on the defence industry and the renewable energy sector.

Nicoline Frølich is Head of Research in Studies in Higher Education and a research professor at NIFU, Norway. She is a member of the executive committee of EAIR and a peer reviewer of several journals. Her research interests include higher education policy, higher education governance, organizational change in higher education and internationalization. She has published papers on higher education learning outcomes and strategic change in European universities.

Tatiana Fumasoli is a researcher and lecturer at the Department of Education, University of Oslo. Her research interests lie on university management focusing on the role of political and social actors in higher education governance and policy. Her work has appeared, among others, in Higher Education, Minerva, Higher Education Policy, International Journal of Public Administration, and with Springer and Palgrave Macmillan.

Yuan Gao is a PhD candidate at Melbourne Centre for the Study of Higher Education (MCSHE), University of Melbourne, Australia. Previously, she was a programme manager in the International Office of Nankai University, China. She obtained an MEd with distinction from the University of Bristol and an honours Bachelor's degree from Peking University, China. She has served as research consultant for several projects, including the recent 'Asian Humanities' project for the Australian Academy of Humanities and 'STEM: Country Comparison' project for the Australian Council of Learned Academies (ACOLA), contributing two special country reports on STEM system in China and Taiwan. Her research interests include globalization and internationalization of higher education, STEM education and Chinese diaspora in Australia. Her recent works include papers on constructing and measuring university internationalization in the *Journal of Studies in International Education* and *Higher Education* and two chapters in the newly launched book *The Age of STEM: Educational Policy and Practice in Science, Technology, Engineering and Mathematics across the World.*

Leo Goedegebuure is a professor and director at the LH Martin Institute for Tertiary Education Leadership and Management, University of Melbourne, Australia. From 2005 to 2009, he was an associate professor in the School of Business, Economics and Public Policy at the University of New England and a member of its Centre for Higher Education Management and Policy (CHEMP). Prior to moving to Australia in 2005, he was Executive Director of CHEPS at the University of Twente. His research and capacity-building interests span the areas of governance and management, both at the systems and institutional level, the future of the academic workforce and system institutional diversity. Recent publications include a cross-country analysis of academic job satisfaction, profiling diversity of Australian universities and strategies for re-conceptualizing Australia's future workforce.

Lee Harvey has been researching higher education issues since the early 1990s. He was a professor at Copenhagen Business School until 31 December 2010. Prior to that, he established and was also the director of both the Centre for Research into Quality at the University of Central England, Birmingham, and the Centre for Research and Evaluation at Sheffield Hallam University, UK. He was also Director of Research at the Higher Education Academy (HEA), UK. He has an extensive experience in social research as a research methodologist and social philosopher. He has a teaching qualification alongside his Master's in Information Technology and PhD in Sociology. His recent research areas are research methodology; higher education policy; quality, quality assurance and quality culture; employability; student feedback; learning and teaching; and diversity and funding. He has published widely, with more than 35 books and research monographs and more than 120 articles in international journals, books and compendiums. He has been a quality advisor to institutions across the world.

Jeroen Huisman is Professor of Higher Education at the Centre for Higher Education Governance Ghent (CHEGG), Department of Sociology, Ghent University, Belgium. He was a researcher at CHEPS, University of Twente (1991–2005), and Professor of Higher Education Management, University of Bath, UK (2005–2013). He is editor of the journal *Higher Education Policy*, co-editor of the Routledge/SRHE Higher Education book series, co-editor of *Theory and Method in Higher Education Research* (with Malcolm Tight) and a member of the editorial board of several higher education journals. His research interests are higher education policy, higher education governance, organizational change in higher education and internationalization and Europeanization. His recent works include papers on organizational image and identity in *Studies in Higher Education* and *Higher Education Research and Development* and an edited book on salient issues in contemporary higher education research (with Jenni Case).

Ben Jongbloed is a senior research associate at Center for Higher Education Policy Studies (CHEPS), University of Twente, the Netherlands. He studied econometrics at the University of Groningen, the Netherlands, and holds a PhD from the University of Twente. He has published widely on governance and resource allocation issues in higher education and was involved in several national and international research projects. He is co-editing a book on massification in higher education and completing articles on hybridization in universities, on research funding and on performance-based funding. He is involved in the implementation of a multidimensional ranking of universities worldwide (U-Multirank) and in a research project looking at policies and indicators for student completion. For the Netherlands' Ministry of Education, he supports the review committee overseeing the system of performance contracts for Dutch universities.

Roger King is a visiting professor at the School of Management, University of Bath, and a research associate at the Centre for the Analysis of Risk and Regulation, London School of Economics and Political Science. He is also a member of the UK Westminster Higher Education Commission and was co-chair of its 'Inquiry into the Regulation of Higher Education' (report published in October 2013 by PolicyConnect, London). Previously, he was Vice-Chancellor of the University of Lincoln (1989–2001) and the founding chair of the Institute for Learning and Teaching in Higher Education (1998–2001), which is now the Higher Education Academy. He is the author of *Governing Universities Globally: Organizations, Regulation and Rankings* (2009) and was co-editor (with Simon Marginson and Rajani Naidoo) of the *Handbook on Globalization and Higher Education* (2011) and *The Globalization of Higher Education* (2013). He has published extensively on higher education regulation, risk, governance and globalization, both in academic journals and in other outlets.

Fumi Kitagawa is Lecturer in Entrepreneurship and Innovation at the University of Edinburgh Business School, UK. Her previous academic and policy research appointments include Manchester Business School at the University of Manchester, Graduate School of Education at the University of Bristol, the Centre for Innovation and Research in the Learning Economies (CIRCLE) at Lund University in Sweden and the Higher Education Research Unit at the National Institute of Educational Policy Research in Tokyo, Japan. She has researched the role of higher education in national and regional innovation processes extensively, drawing on science and technology policy studies, research policy and higher education studies. She has been involved in a number of international projects, working with the OECD and the European Commission. She holds a PhD in Urban and Regional Studies from the University of Birmingham and an MBA in Higher Education Management from the Institute of Education, University of London.

Jussi Kivistö is a university lecturer and an adjunct professor at HEG, University of Tampere, Finland. His research interests are related to funding of higher education, higher education governance and higher education policy. Internationally, he has published several book chapters in edited books, focusing specifically on higher education funding and governance. His most recent articles have appeared in *Tertiary Education and Management*, *Journal of Higher Education Policy and Management* and *Journal of Studies in International Education*.

Manja Klemenčič is Lecturer in Sociology of Higher Education at the Department of Sociology, Faculty of Arts and Sciences, Harvard University, Cambridge, MA. She researches, teaches, advises and consults in the area of international and comparative higher education, with particular interest in contemporary higher education reforms and student experience and engagement, teaching and learning, institutional research and internationalization. She is editor-in-chief of *European Journal of Higher Education*, thematic editor of the section 'Elite and Mass Higher Education in the 21st Century' of the *International Encyclopedia of Higher Education Systems and Institutions*, co-editor of the book series *Understanding Student Experience in Higher Education* and serves on the governing board of Consortium of Higher Education Researchers (CHER).

Yu-Ching Kuo is a postdoctoral research fellow based at the Science and Technology Policy Research and Information Center, National Applied Research Laboratories, Taiwan. She provides research assistance in supporting the Taiwanese government's science and technology (S&T) development plan, specifically exploring the roles that higher education can play in facilitating science innovation and technology development. Her recent research has focused on the areas of widening participations and fair access policies, international higher education policy regime, embedding societal demands in S&T policy mechanism and misalignments between the supply and demand for skilled human resources. Her recent publications include *Entrepreneurial Identities of International Students at UK Business Schools* and the report *S&T Input and Performance in Brazil* (in Chinese).

Benedetto Lepori holds a PhD in Communication Sciences from the University of Lugano, Switzerland. He is head of the research group on management and performance of research and higher education institutions in the Centre of Organisational Research (CORe) of the Faculty of Economics. He has broad experience in the field of S&T indicators, research policy and research funding and higher education governance and funding. He is coordinating the European Commission's 'European Tertiary Education Register' project and was a partner of the European Science Foundation's 'Transforming Universities in Europe' project. His main work in the field of higher education deals with diversity of higher education systems, the working of binary systems, university funding and governance. He has published extensively on these subjects in *Organization Studies, Research Policy, Studies in Higher Education, Higher Education* and *Scientometrics*.

Amy Y. Li is a doctoral candidate in the Department of Educational Leadership, Policy, and Organizations, College of Education, University of Washington. She has participated in the CREST programme, an IES pre-doctoral training fellowship. Her research interest is in higher education finance policy. She studies state spending on higher education; student financial aid; and performance funding policy adoption, implementation and impacts. Her recent projects include a study on Washington community colleges' responses to performance funding; research on the current state of performance funding for the Bill and Melinda Gates Foundation; and event history analyses of state funding cuts and policy innovations.

António Magalhães is an associate professor at the Faculty of Psychology and Education Sciences, University of Porto, Portugal, where he is acting Head of the Education Department. He is also a senior researcher at CIPES, Porto. His expertise lies in education policy analysis, namely on the relationship between the state and higher education system and institutions. He has been developing national and international projects and has been publishing on these issues. His recent publications have appeared in *Higher Education, Higher Education Policy* and *Higher Education Quarterly*.

Cheryl A. Matherly is Vice Provost of Global Education and Applied Assistant Professor of Education at the University of Tulsa (TU), USA. She is the former Assistant Dean of Students for Career and International Education at Rice University in Houston, Texas. She has written extensively on the impact of globalization on the employment of college graduates. She is also conducting research as part of a National Science Foundation-funded grant on workplace competencies of science and engineering graduates. She teaches in the TU graduate programme in courses on current issues in higher education, comparative and international education and history of American education. She holds an EdD from the University of Houston, an MS in Education from Indiana University at Bloomington and a BA in English and Political Science from the University of New Mexico.

V. Lynn Meek is a professorial fellow and Foundation Director at the LH Martin Institute, University of Melbourne, Australia. He was previously a professor and director of the CHEMP at the University of New England. Having completed a PhD in Sociology of Higher Education at the University of Cambridge, he has more than three decades of experience researching higher education policy issues. Specific research interests include governance and management, research management, diversification of higher education institutions and systems, institutional amalgamations, organizational change and the comparative study of higher education systems. He has attracted numerous competitive research grants and is regularly invited to address international conferences. He has published more than 30 books and monographs and numerous scholarly articles and book chapters. He is on the editorial board of several international journals and book series, is the editor-in-chief of the journal *Studies in Higher Education* and has worked with international agencies such as UNESCO and the OECD.

Pat O'Connor is Professor of Sociology and Social Policy at the University of Limerick, Ireland. She was the first woman to be appointed as full professor there in 1997 and the first woman to become a faculty dean in 2000. Previously, she worked at Waterford Institute of Technology, Ireland, and she was a researcher at Bedford and Royal Holloway College, London; at the National Institute for Social Work, London; and at the Economic and Social Research Institute, Dublin. Her research interests are in the gendering of higher education; organizational cultures; excellence, leadership and management; and organizational change, masculinities and power. She is currently involved in an EU-funded Framework 7 project, FESTA (2012–2017). Her latest book is *Management and Gender in Higher Education* (2014). Recent articles include those on excellence in *Studies in Higher Education* and on university leadership and management in special issues of *Higher Education Research and Development* and *Gender and Education.*

Alan Pettigrew is an Honorary Professorial fellow at the LH Martin Institute, University of Melbourne, Australia. He holds a PhD from the University of Sydney and was Vice-Chancellor and CEO of the University of New England from 2006 to 2009. He was the inaugural CEO of the National Health and Medical Research Council (NHMRC) of Australia and a member of the Australian government's Cooperative Research Centres Committee. He is a member of the

Council of the QIMR Berghofer Medical Research Institute and is chair of the board of the Illawarra Health and Medical Research Institute. He has been an advisor to the Chief Scientist of Australia and is a consultant to universities, research centres and international organizations such as the World Bank and the OECD on issues such as leadership and management in higher education and research. Recent publications include a typology of knowledge and skills requirements for effective research and innovation management and a paper for the Office of the Chief Scientist on Australia's Position in the World of Science, Technology and Innovation.

Thomas Pfeffer is a researcher, lecturer and consultant at the Department for Migration and Globalisation, Danube University Krems, Austria. He was a researcher at the Institute for Science Communication and Higher Education Research at University of Klagenfurt, Austria (1997–2014), and a policy expert at the Center for Teaching and Learning at the University of Vienna (2008–2009). He gained much experience not only in international comparative research but also in organizational development projects. His main research interests are higher education policy and organizational development, information and communication technology (ICT) in research and higher education, social systems theory and systemic research methods, as well as migration and globalization. His recent works include papers on institutionalized procedures for the recognition of foreign qualifications, on diversity in the recruitment practices of employing organizations, on academic media literacy and the impact of digital media on the organization of research and higher education, and on the global university system.

Rómulo Pinheiro is Associate Professor of Public Policy and Management at the University of Agder, Norway. He is also a senior associate researcher at Agderforskning and a visiting professor at the universities of Tampere, Finland, and Danube Krems, Austria, as well as an affiliate member of the ExCID research group and the HEDDA consortium, both based at the University of Oslo. His research interests are located at the intersection of the fields of public policy and administration, organizational studies, regional science and innovation studies and higher education studies. His recent work includes cross-sectorial (health and higher education) and cross-country (Nordics, BRICS, Europe, etc.) comparative studies in areas such as access and participation into higher education, stakeholder governance, high participation systems, mergers, the role of universities in the economy and so forth. His publications have appeared in *Studies in Higher Education, European Journal of Higher Education, Public Organization Review, Cambridge Journal of Regions, Economy and Society and City* and *Culture and Society.*

Emilia Primeri is a research fellow at IRCRES CNR (Research Institute on Sustainable Economic Growth of the National Research Council, formerly CERIS CNR), Italy, and has participated in several European and national research projects (EC-JOREP on Joint and Open Programmes; Prest-ENCE: From Prestige to Excellence in higher education ANR-FR; EC RTD Tool on ERA Indicators). She is involved in the EC-UNISTUDY for the analysis of universities engagement in the European Union's Framework Programmes (EUFPs) and in the EUFP projects IMPACT-EV and RISIS. Her main research interests concern policies for higher education and governance systems, evaluation of public research, the study of features and impact of joint programming at the EU level and of opening of national R&D programmes. Her recent works include papers on indicators for the setting up of national R&D programmes in *Research Evaluation* (2014) and book chapters on early career researchers' training and academic prestige (2014) and on Italian university system reform (2014).

Pauline Ravinet is Assistant Professor of Political Science at CERAPS, Université Lille 2 and an associate fellow at the Center for Sociology of Organizations, Sciences Po, France. Her PhD research has focused on the emergence and governance of the European higher education area. During 2008–2009, she researched European governance mechanisms in education, higher education and research as a post-doctoral at the Université Libre de Bruxelles and was a participant to a Franco-Norwegian project (Sciences Po/University of Oslo). She is the co-editor of *Dictionnaire des politiques publiques* (2004) and has authored articles and chapters on the Bologna Process in several journals and edited books. She is also working on the project 'Higher Education Regionalism', comparing higher education regional initiatives on different continents.

Emanuela Reale is a senior researcher of science policy at IRCRES CNR, Italy. She is Head of the Research Unit 'Organization and sustainability of the large systems of contemporary societies' of IRCRES CNR located in Rome and has been working as a principal investigator in several international research projects. She is a board member of the European Network of Indicator Designers (ENID) and CHER, and Vice President of the European Forum for Research and Policy Studies (EU-SPRI). Her research interests are higher education policy and governance, organizational change in higher education, funding and evaluation of higher education and research institutions, processes of integration and Europeanization of higher education. Her recent works include papers on methodological challenges in comparative studies in *Higher Education*, on logics of integration in transnational research programmes in *Research Policy* and on responsible research innovation and the governance of science (EU SiS-RRI Stocktaking, forthcoming).

Robin Shields is Senior Lecturer in Higher Education Management at the University of Bath, UK. His research applies innovative research methods to better understand the globalization of education. In his recent work, he has used social network analysis to examine changing flows in international student mobility and social media networks between higher education institutions. He has received research grants from the HEA, the Leadership Foundation for Higher Education, the Economic and Social Research Council and the Dutch Ministry for Foreign Affairs; he has also received the George Bereday Award from the Comparative and International Education Society. He is the author of *Globalization and International Education* (2013).

Manuel Souto-Otero is Senior Lecturer in Education Policy at the School of Social Sciences, Cardiff University, UK. He has published widely in the area of higher education policy, internationalization and student mobility and on the links between higher education and the labour market. His research has been funded by the Directorate-General of Education and Culture of the European Commission, the European Parliament, the Joint Research Centre of the European Commission, the European Youth Forum, the HEA and national ministries for education in Spain and the United Kingdom, among other bodies. He has also acted as a consultant for the OECD and UNESCO. His most recent book *Evaluating European Education Policy-Making* was published by Palgrave Macmillan in 2015.

Rudolf Stichweh is the Dahrendorf Professor for "Theory of Modern Society" and the director of the 'Forum Internationale Wissenschaft' at the University of Bonn. He studied Sociology and Philosophy in Berlin and Bielefeld. He has worked at the Max-Planck-Institut für Gesellschaftsforschung, Köln (1985–1989); the Maison des Sciences de l'Homme, Paris (1987); Max-Planck-Institut für europäische Rechtsgeschichte, Frankfurt (1989–1994); University of Bielefeld, Bielefeld (1994–2003); and University of Lucerne, Luzern (2003–2012). He was also the rector of the University of Lucerne (2006–2010) and a visiting professor at Princeton University and the University of Lucerne. He is a member of the North Rhine-Westphalian Academy of Sciences, Humanities and the Arts, Germany. His research fields are theory of world society, sociocultural evolution and functional differentiation, sociology of science and universities, sociology of the stranger and systems theory. His recent books include *Wissenschaft, Universität, Professionen* (2nd ed., 2013); *Inklusion und Exklusion: Studien zur Gesellschaftstheorie* (2nd ed., 2015); and *Theorie der Weltgesellschaft* (forthcoming).

Malcolm Tight is Professor of Higher Education at Lancaster University, UK. Previously, he was Professor of Higher Education at the University of Warwick and has also worked at Birkbeck College London and the Open University, UK. He is editor of *Assessment and Evaluation in Higher Education, International Perspectives on Higher Education Research* and *Tertiary Education and Management*, and co-editor of the book series *Theory and Method in Higher Education Research*. His current research interests focus on mapping the field of higher education research internationally through the meta-analysis of publications. Key recent publications include *Researching Higher Education* and *The Development of Higher Education in the United Kingdom since 1945*.

Martin J. Tillman is President of Global Career Compass, an international consulting practice focused on global workforce trends and the impact of education abroad experiences on student career development. He is former Associate Director of Career Services at the Paul H. Nitze at the School of Advanced International Studies, Johns Hopkins University, Washington, DC. He has served as a US State Department's Speaker Specialist on the role of career service offices in the transition of students to the workforce in Tbilisi in Georgia and Harare in Zimbabwe. He has authored the chapter 'Employer Perspectives on International Education' in *The SAGE Handbook of International Higher Education* (2012). He is a contributor of book reviews and essays (1994–2014) to the NAFSA: Association of International Education's magazine *International Educator*. He was cited as a pedagogical pioneer in cross-cultural education and service learning in the book *Service-Learning: A Movement's Pioneers Reflect on Its Origins, Practice, and Future* (by Timothy K. Stanton). His blog Global Career Compass is read in 94 nations.

Cathrine E. Tømte is a research professor at NIFU, where she is responsible for research activities related to ICT and education. She has for years worked with issues related to digital literacy and e-learning, both nationally and internationally. She specializes in formal and informal learning, learning environments, online learning, teacher professional development along with interdisciplinary research on ICT and education. She has also worked as a researcher at the Norwegian Center for ICT in Education (2006–2009) and seconded the OECD project 'The New Millennium Learners' (2008–2009). She holds a PhD in Digital Communication in Organizations from NTNU. Her latest publications include a paper on online learning and teacher training in *Computers & Education* (with Ann-Britt Enochsson, Ulf Buskqvist and Asbjørn Kårstein) and a chapter on the emergence of MOOCs in an edited book on e-learning as a socio-cultural system (with Arne Fevolden and Dorothy Olsen).

Agnete Vabø is a research professor at NIFU in Oslo. She holds a PhD in Sociology from the University of Bergen, Norway. She has published numerous reports and articles on change in higher education with a particular focus on the academic profession, organization and governance in higher education. She is currently directing and co-directing large Nordic comparative research projects investigating recruitment patterns and organizational change in higher education. Her recent works include articles on gender, quality and internationalization in higher education.

Frans van Vught is a policy advisor at the European Commission and president of the Netherlands House for Education and Research in Brussels. He is a co-project leader of U-Multirank, the multidimensional and user-driven global higher education ranking tool. He was president and rector of the University of Twente (1997–2005) and founding director of CHEPS (1984–1997). He is the author of 30 books and more than 250 articles on higher education policy, higher education management and innovation strategies. He is an honorary professorial fellow at the universities of Melbourne and Twente and holds several honorary doctorates. Recent publications include *National Innovation and the Academic Research Enterprise* (with David Dill, 2010) and *Multidimensional Ranking* (with Frank Ziegele, 2012).

Anne C. van Wageningen is an assistant professor at the Department of European Studies, Faculty of Humanities, University of Amsterdam, the Netherlands. He obtained his doctorate from the University of Twente in 2003. His research interests include constitutional aspects of European integration, in particular the constitutional aspects of European higher education law and the European higher education area. His articles have appeared in *Tijdschrift voor Onderwijsrecht en Onderwijsbeleid*, and *Nederlands tijdschrift voor onderwijsrecht*, and *Higher Education Policy*. His recent works include papers on higher education, citizenship and state formation and papers on national policy change as a result of case law of the Court of Justice of the European Union.

Amélia Veiga is a researcher at CIPES and at A3ES, Portugal. Her main research interests lie in higher education policy analysis, in particular governing and governance in higher education, European integration, internationalization and globalization of higher education. She has been involved in national and international projects on these matters. Her recent works include papers on differentiated integration (with António Magalhães and Alberto Amaral) and on the impact of Bologna Process at the institutional level under a comparative perspective.

Gerald Wangenge-Ouma is Director of Institutional Planning at the University of Pretoria, South Africa. Previously, he was Associate Professor of Higher Education Studies and coordinated the Higher Education Master's in Africa programme at the University of the Western Cape, South Africa. His research interests are financing higher education, higher education policy and higher education and development. His recent works include papers on tuition fees and private higher education in *Higher Education* and *European Journal of Education* and book chapters on incentives for knowledge production (with Agnes Lutomiah and Patricio Langa) and diaspora linkages and knowledge production. He has served on several ministerial task teams on various aspects of higher education in South Africa and sits on the editorial boards of several journals. He holds a PhD in Higher Education Studies from the University of Cape Town, South Africa.

Karen L. Webber is an associate professor in the Institute of Higher Education at the University of Georgia (UGA), USA. Prior to her current position, she was interim associate provost for institutional effectiveness at UGA, and worked in institutional research offices for about 20 years. Her areas of research include the examination of factors that contribute to institutional effectiveness, institutional research and the careers of higher education faculty. She teaches graduate-level courses on research in higher education, institutional research and introduction to the US national datasets. Her recent publications include an analysis of graduate student educational debt, gender differences in doctoral recipients' salaries, career effects of postdoctoral research and a co-edited book (with Angel Calderon) on the globalization of institutional research and planning in higher education.

Don F. Westerheijden is a senior research associate at the CHEPS at the University of Twente, where he coordinates research on quality management and is involved in the coordination and supervision of PhD students. His areas of interest include quality assurance in higher education in the Netherlands and Europe, its impacts, as well as university rankings. Around 1993, he co-developed the Institutional Evaluation Programme of the European University Association in Brussels. He led the independent assessment of the Bologna Process in 2009/2010. His recent publications include 'Next Generations, Catwalks, Random Walks and Arms Races: conceptualising the Development of Quality Assurance Schemes' (with Stensaker, Rosa and Corbett, 2014) in *European Journal of Education*; 'Employability of Professional Bachelors from an International Perspective (with Kolster, 2014); and 'Quality Assurance in the European Policy Arena' (with Enders, 2014) in *Policy and Society*.

James Williams is a senior researcher at the Social Research and Evaluation Unit, School of Social Sciences, Birmingham City University, UK. He is an associate editor of the international journal *Quality in Higher Education*. His research interests include quality in higher education, student feedback mechanisms, history of higher education, cultural history and aspects of social exclusion. Recent works include a chapter on student feedback in *Using Data to Improve Higher Education* (edited by Menon et al., 2014) and a chapter on public art of universities in *The Physical University: Contours of Space and Place in Higher Education* (edited by Paul Temple, 2014).

Inga Zalyevska is a graduate student in the Erasmus Mundus programme 'Research and Innovation in Higher Education' based at the University of Applied Sciences Osnabrück, Germany, and Danube University Krems, Austria. Her current research interests focus on applications of the agency theory to understand informational asymmetries in university–enterprise partnerships and accreditation.

William Zumeta is Professor of Public Policy and Higher Education at the University of Washington in Seattle. He holds a PhD in Public Policy from the University of California, Berkeley, and has previously taught at the University of British Columbia, Vancouver, and University of California, Los Angeles. He is a fellow of the TIAA-CREF Institute, New York, and from 2005 to 2011 was a senior fellow at the National Center for Public Policy and Higher Education, USA. He served as president of the Association for the Study of Higher Education at Las Vegas, USA, in 2009–2010. His research centres on higher education policy and finance, including accountability policies. He also teaches and writes about policies regarding transitions from secondary to post-secondary education and about policies involving private higher education. Recent publications include articles in *The American Behavioral Scientist, The Annals of Political and Social Science* and *Journal of Comparative Policy Analysis*.

Part I
Concepts, Theories and Methods

1
Higher Education: The Nature of the Beast

James S. Fairweather and Emiko Blalock

In this chapter, from a macro perspective, we lay out the historical bases for institutions and systems of higher education, discuss the policy challenges facing higher education today and lay the groundwork for subsequent chapters that examine the organizational, administrative and policy responses to these challenges by institutions and systems of higher education. We pay particular attention to three interdependent and universal policy themes – access, quality and cost – and the triumph in higher education of the pursuit of prestige.

From their beginning, institutions of higher education, of all types and locations, have tried to balance external responsiveness to meet societal needs with internally driven collegial systems guided by norms such as academic freedom, where decisions about student accomplishments, curricula and hiring new faculty members are within the purview of the professoriate (Birnbaum, 1988; Geiger, 2015). This balancing act holds true more or less irrespective of the characterization of national higher education systems: from ministry-led to market-driven, from elite to mass higher education, from having a colonial history to being a colonial power, from systems with selective admissions and prestigious faculties to systems with open access (Ashby, 1974; Clark, 1972; Kerr, 1982; Maassen, 2012). Even institutions and systems deemed the most removed from societal pressures – the 'ivory towers' (Knorr-Cetina, 1999) or, in Slaughter and Leslie's (2004) terms, the institutions least influenced by academic capitalism – often fulfil important societal requirements such as preparing the next generation of leaders in various occupations and generating important research. The modern interconnected global economy with its concomitant emphasis on human capital through more and better education has made this balancing act more complex and fragile (Duderstadt, 2007).

The internal structures of universities reflect both the external/internal dynamics and the distinct operating functions of academic institutions. Similar to any government agency or business, higher education institutions rely on bureaucratic structures to manage functions such as finance and facilities.

In contrast, the academic side of these institutions is better characterized as a loosely coupled system (Orton and Weick, 1990) where distinct professional units – departments, schools, colleges – operate collegially but independently within an overall shared institutional context typically designed to govern decisions made about students (admissions, academic progress, degree-granting) and the faculty (hiring, promotion, tenure) (Birnbaum, 1988). Even in top-down, ministry-based systems, most of the decisions about academic work are left to the judgement of individual professors and academic departments rather than to a system-wide edict (Maassen and Olsen, 2007). Academic units also reflect a balance between internal institutional norms and those of the discipline. Most of the recent efforts in the United States to improve undergraduate teaching in the sciences, engineering and mathematics run into conflicting messages from the institution and the discipline both about the nature of good teaching and about the importance of teaching in decisions about faculty performance (Fairweather, 2008; PCAST, 2012; Singer, 2012). Here the dynamic is best captured by faculty identities: Is the faculty member primarily, for example, a physicist whose primary responsibility is to the discipline or is he/she first and foremost a member of a particular university whose primary responsibilities are local (Fairweather and Paulson, 2008; Powell and DiMaggio, 1999)? This dynamic plays out between the value of research and scholarship, which has a national or even global reach, and teaching and public service where the focus is on the local institution and perhaps its geographic region (Fairweather, 1996).

What has changed in the past decade or two is the emergence of a dominant vision, or at least shared desired goals, for higher education policy across nations and continents. Despite the deep differences about the perceived relative importance of the public and private benefits of higher education (e.g. Bowen, 1977), most nations and even individual institutions increasingly view higher education as crucial to providing the human capital to allow (or continue to allow) countries to compete in the global economy (Fairweather, 2006; Jongbloed, 2010). The emphasis here focuses on both quality *and* access. The race is on to educate as many people as possible and to do so competently. Most countries, even those with a history of elite higher education such as the United Kingdom, now provide (or aspire to provide) mass higher education.

One consequence of the simultaneous pursuit of access and quality is the considerable diversification both across and within academic institutions to meet these distinct goals (Huisman, Meek and Wood, 2007). Within institutions, on the academic side of the house, diversification is based on academic discipline. Academic departments (and related structural forms such as centres and institutes) provide a means to respond both to institutional goals and to those of the discipline (Clark, 1972). Diversification between institutions is typically based on mission. The Netherlands and Finland, for example, have distinct systems for universities and polytechnics. The US state California has a three-part system with research universities (University of California), teaching-oriented colleges (California State University) and community colleges. In practice, the line between the first two is blurred because the demand for graduate-level education exceeds the ability of the University of California to provide enough of it. In the United States, the Carnegie Foundation for the Advancement of Teaching developed the most widely used classification scheme for academic institutions. Based on mission, it ranges from doctoral/research-intensive universities to teaching-oriented institutions (master's and bachelor's institutions), community colleges and specialized institutions (Carnegie Foundation for the Advancement of Teaching, 2010).

In addition, today we have an emerging consensus about the 'best' form of higher education – the highest quality – and it is based on the prestige of the faculty members primarily through their research and scholarship (and sometimes the selectivity of students) (Altbach and Balan, 2007). Although this vision is not uniformly held – selective liberal arts colleges in the United States are quite prestigious despite focusing mainly on teaching (Clark, 1992) and Brazilian higher education places very high value on professional preparation and certification (Schwartzman, 2007) – it is prevalent. The various international and national rankings of institutional (and sometimes programmes) quality reflect the dominance of this view of quality as well as the triumph of prestige as the coin of the higher education realm (e.g. Times Higher Education, 2014). This comparison also indicates the increasing importance of internationalization in higher education (Stensaker et al., 2008) and the global basis on which institutions are compared. Although the pursuit of prestige in higher education is not new (Fairweather, 1996), the widespread emphasis on prestige across national systems today is quite pronounced. Even though most countries have found ways to provide non-elite higher education – polytechnics, community colleges and other teaching-oriented institutions – the national goal is often to raise the prestige and visibility of higher education as a whole.

The pursuit of greater access and quality has challenged most countries and institutions to find ways to fund higher education. The debate about whether or not tuition is a legitimate cost category – challenged in the Nordic countries and accepted in the United States, among others (Jongbloed, 2010) – cannot disguise the fundamental challenge of finding ways to fund such a labour-intensive activity where the cost of adapting to a rapidly changing world of ideas and technology is going up (Fairweather, 2006). Indeed, in the United States the cost of attending a four-year public university is the fastest growing cost category in the national inflation index (College Board, 2014).

Another consequence of the pursuit of access and quality is the growth of quality assurance, accreditation and other mechanisms to attempt to preserve (or attain) quality in mass higher education systems (Westerheijden, 2010). Accreditation is meant to ensure that an institution (and, in some cases, an academic programme) meets the minimum fiscal and academic standards to offer degrees. Philosophically, quality assurance differs from accreditation in its focus on distinguishing levels of quality between institutions and academic programmes. In practice, the large-scale application of quality assurance requires reliance in part on the same rather generic measures used in accreditation (Westerheijden, 2010).

Cost control and the pursuit of prestige combine in interesting ways. In Finland, for example, the University Act of 2009 decentralized the ministry-based system to legally autonomous institutions. The goals of this act were (1) to increase the quality (and prestige) of academic institutions by increasing their ability to adapt to change more quickly and (2) to reduce the percentage of operating costs paid directly by the national government (Finnish Ministry of Education and Culture, 2014).

As a 'case study' of these various policy influences and the response by academic institutions, consider the Bologna Process and Lisbon Strategy in Europe. In the 1998 and 1999 Bologna declarations, the European Ministers of Education indicated their intention to create greater access to and mobility within higher education based upon international cooperation and academic exchange (i.e. increase access). The subsequent Lisbon Strategy in 2000, initiated by the European Union (EU), officially declared the crucial role of higher education through research and graduate education in the economic future of Europe. To promote student mobility, key components of the Bologna Process were a common credit system for student work and a common structure for bachelor's and master's degrees. Many European universities increased their course offerings in English to encourage greater student mobility. There is little doubt that the Bologna Process has increased student mobility across national boundaries (Amaral et al., 2010).

Among the motivations for the Bologna Process and especially the Lisbon Strategy was increased effectiveness of European higher education in preparing graduates for the global economy and enhanced prestige of European universities internationally (Jongbloed, 2010). The continued lacklustre economic recovery in Europe in recent years makes it difficult at this point to assess changes in the effectiveness of higher education in this regard. In addition to the structural adaptations by many European universities and the designation by many national systems to link higher education to economic development more directly, a (perhaps) unanticipated consequence was an increased reliance on the EU as a source for research funds to help offset the increased costs in the pursuit of greater quality and access envisioned in the Bologna Process (Jongbloed, 2010). Most important for our discussion, as is true for most top-down policy reform efforts in higher education, it is easier to trace the structural changes in academic institutions and systems in response to the Bologna Process and Lisbon Strategy than it is to identify changes in the cultures inside academic institutions, that is, instructional approaches, student–faculty relationships and leadership (Kezar, 2014). Ultimately, these cultural reforms hold the keys to long-term improvements in student learning outcomes, quality and links with economic development (Birnbaum, 1988).

The uniqueness of higher education

The nature and evolution of higher education systems and individual institutions are unique in relation to other policy and government agencies. Institutions of higher education are peculiar, each to one another and to other public policy agencies. Whether governed by ministries, state and local government or independently (privately), their perceived and actual market-responsiveness, or their participation in processes like Bologna, institutions of higher education make adjustments or reforms to many of these environmental influences.

The peculiarity of higher education to other public policy agencies is probably most evident in terms of the 'purpose' of higher education. Higher education, regardless of governance, typically has multiple objectives: the production of knowledge (education), the attentiveness to community (service) and the advancement of research (Duderstadt, 2007; Kerr, 1982). Maassen and Stensaker (2011) characterized the main functions of the university as 'the diffusion and formation of a dominant belief system, selection of elites, generation of new knowledge, and the training of the bureaucracy' (p. 758).

Most agree that the mission of higher education is multifaceted. One could also argue that all institutions of higher education (as well as the systems in which they operate) share the same challenges: providing quality instruction and (for many) quality research, maintaining or increasing access and managing budgets while controlling cost and price. Hence, how do governing systems and policy influence the behaviour of higher education towards its pursuit of increased prestige; of the production of knowledge; and of training a new workforce for service or bureaucracy? Further, does the system by which an institution of higher education is governed create clearer directives? What kinds of allowances do institutes of higher education have depending on their system of national or state government or educational governance? These questions, crucial to understanding the function of academic institutions, are examined in later chapters of this book.

Here we focus on the broader question of how institutions of higher education differ from other government agencies in how they operate and in their relationships to national and state governments. Almost all academic institutions face the threefold challenge of quality, access and cost, and their response to these challenges may look the same or different regardless of their governing structure. Nearly all academic institutions provide instruction. Many also conduct research. Some provide public service and technology transfer. And many – even those primarily focused on teaching – aspire to achieve greater prestige by adding doctoral programmes and seeking designation as a 'university' (Trow, 1984). The pursuit of quality and access and even prestige is partly imbedded in government and institutional policies, but these pursuits cannot be achieved solely by edict. They rely on cultural norms deeply imbedded in the academic disciplines and in the graduate training of future faculty members (Wulff and Austin, 2004). For example, in an effort to enhance prestige a US university may invest heavily in the academic disciplines it believes will increase the stature of the institution. Similarly, an increased focus on prestige in European nations may shift the attention of academic quality to a rankings race (Maassen and Stensaker, 2011). Whether either effort *results in* enhanced prestige is a different matter. It depends on what the faculty members accomplish and how it is perceived by their peers elsewhere (Fairweather, 2002, 2005).

Edicts are not limited to governments and system offices. An academic institution can seek to improve the quality of undergraduate teaching by promoting policies to reward effective teaching and to alter the ways that faculty work is documented. Whether or not teaching becomes more valued, however, rests more on what the faculty believe and how they act, which is at least influenced by their graduate training and by what their peers (within and outside the institution) believe about the importance of teaching (Fairweather, 2002, 2005; Kezar, 2014). What makes academic institutions distinct is that these cultural norms transcend the institution and affect the ability of policy makers – inside and outside the institution – to affect faculty behaviour (Clark, 1972).

As institutions of knowledge production, colleges and universities also differ from other government agencies in the relationship between investment and outcomes. Adding funds to welfare agencies will increase the funds made available to each individual assuming a constant number of people being supported by that agency. In this sense, increased investment has a demonstrable outcome, namely greater average welfare income per individual and the concomitant increase in economic activity resulting from that investment. Some increased investments in higher education also have demonstrable benefits. Adding money for facilities allows academic institutions to modernize laboratories, improve classroom space, teach more students and the like. Yet other investments are not so easily judged on a return-on-investment basis. Adding funds for new faculty positions can reduce class size, but the improvement of instruction often requires changes in the ways that faculty members approach teaching. Additional funds can add to an institution's personnel capacity, but it does not guarantee higher individual faculty scholarly output or changes in perceived institutional status. These latter outcomes rest on faculty accomplishments, which again is subject to disciplinary norms and faculty socialization as much as it is to investment (Clark, 1972). They are also subject to the vagaries of knowledge production; often we do not know which ideas will lead to major societal improvements in advance.

For example, China's multi-year experiment with dramatic increases in funding for higher education shows the limitations of such an approach to improving institutional quality. Investment provided dramatic increases in the number of academic institutions and in overall enrolment capacity but the hoped for large-scale increase in quality, prestige and status across the system largely has not yet taken place (Li, 2010; Ma, 2007). Recent government policies have targeted fewer and fewer institutions for more and more of the total higher education resources, the latest being Project 985 which provides targeted funding for only 39 out of the 5,000 or so academic institutions in China. The most prestigious academic institutions in China, so acknowledged by their international peers, remain the ones with longer histories and with deeply imbedded academic cultures that place a high value on scholarly productivity and the search for new knowledge. Such cultures take time to develop and require intentional personnel decisions and leadership, not simply resources (Ma, 2007).

Competing origins, philosophies and challenges

In this section, we examine the origins, philosophies and ongoing challenges that shaped and continue to influence higher education nationally and internationally. Our task is to describe how distinct origins and philosophies contributed to the substantial variation between and within higher education systems and institutions and to show that despite these differences a more-or-less shared view of the challenges that lie ahead has emerged. In this section, we discuss the maturation of higher education in an era of massification. Next, we describe the benefits of higher education, and how the philosophical emphasis on public versus private benefits helped shape higher education systems. In addition, we describe the continuum from ministry-based to market-based systems, current trends along this continuum and the implications for the restructuring of higher education. We conclude this section with two of the most prominent forces affecting higher education: (1) access to higher education and (2) the cost of attending higher education and who pays for it.

The maturation of higher education post-massification

Art Levine (2001), former President of Teacher's College, Columbia University, drew a distinction between two types of macro-economic environments for higher education: (1) an era of growth and expansion on the way towards massification (Trow, 1974) and (2) a mature industry post-massification. In the first policy environment, the focus is on expansion and growth. In the latter, the policy focus shifts to efficiency, return on investment, effectiveness and 'value added'. This distinction is crucial because it affects how leaders in government and higher education must manage their institutions. Economists have characterized higher education as both labour-intensive (Baumol and Bowen, 1966) and governed by the ethic of spending all the money that can be raised (Bowen, 1977). In this ethos, academic leaders typically are more comfortable with adding programmes, hiring additional faculty members and adding students – all part of an era of growth. Operating in a mature industry means different policy choices: not adding new programmes but substituting a new one for an old one, phasing out programs that no longer enrol many students even if the faculty members teaching in them have permanent positions and so on. Academic (and governmental) leadership in a 'mature era' requires answering questions about cost-benefits and productivity rather than just benefits (Levine, 2001). In this context, the likelihood is that government contributions to higher education after attaining mass higher education will experience very slow growth, stabilization or even decline over time, putting pressure on academic leaders to find new sources of revenue. Regardless of philosophical and structural traditions, the macro-economic ethos – either growth or maturity – affects the range of policy and programmatic choices available to governments and academic leaders alike.

Benefits of higher education

Among the key 'philosophical divides' in the world of higher education is whether the primary beneficiary is seen as the populace at large (a public good) or whether it is the individual (a private good). This distinction lies at the heart of many, perhaps most, systems of higher education. Most systems with low or no tuition, many of them with strong ministries of education, often ascribe to the public benefit argument. Here the view is that the public benefits more than individuals, which justifies the outsized contribution of the government to subsidize institutions of higher education.

In contrast, the rationale for charging tuition in more market-oriented systems (even when combined with some form of government subsidy) is justified in part by the individual being perceived as the primary beneficiary of higher education. Even within market-based systems, though, we find differences between the amount of government financial support by region, state or type of institution. In the United States, states where private institutions are the most prominent – the Northeast and Mid-Atlantic – tend to provide lower government subsidies for their public institutions than those in the Midwest and West (Fairweather, 2006). Community colleges in the United States receive a higher portion of their operating costs from the state and local governments in part because of their perceived public benefit, including responding to local and regional economic needs, and in part because the contribution of lifelong earnings is considerably less than for a bachelor's or higher degree (Zumeta, 2006).

These distinctions, though deeply held, are in many ways polemical rather than real. The distinction ignores the ways that higher education benefits *both* the public and individuals irrespective of the system in which they matriculate. Decades ago, Feldman and Newcomb (1969) showed that college and university students invariably benefited in their personal (psychological, social, emotional) development, a 'private' benefit. Howard Bowen's (1977) seminal work on the economics of higher education found both public and private benefits of all forms of higher education. His work was extended by the Institute for Higher Education Policy (2005) which categorized both public and private benefits into social and economic categories. Public social benefits range from reduced crime rates to increased quality of civic life, and public economic benefits range from greater tax revenues to greater productivity and to increased workforce flexibility. Private social benefits range from improved health and life expectancy to the improved quality of life for offspring, and private economic benefits range from higher lifelong incomes to greater career options and to personal and professional mobility (IHEP, 2005). Although these results vary somewhat, the patterns are strikingly similar across nations (OECD, 2012).

In addition, as discussed below, many countries with high levels of government subsidies for higher education gradually are decreasing their contribution as a percentage of operating expenses because their ability to keep up with the costs of simultaneously maintaining quality while improving access is limited. The same pattern is true in the United States where for the past 20 years or more the individual state contributions to public higher education have decreased in absolute terms (Zumeta, 2006).

The ministry-to-market-based continuum

The relationship between the nation and its institutions of higher education can be characterized by ideal types: on the one hand, governance by a strong ministry of education that controls budgets and gives direction to academic decisions and, on the other, markets where the role of government is less direct and visible. In reality, most systems combine the two. In the United States, the state governments, not the national government, are constitutionally responsible for education. Many institutions are private, not subject to state control. Yet the federal government has substantial indirect influence on both public and private academic institutions through student financial aid and research funding (Gladieux and King, 1999). In ministry-based systems, despite the emphasis on strong central steering, many academic decisions remain the responsibility of local faculty and departments (Maassen, 2012).

Internationally, the trend in national higher education policy is to move away from strong central control by a ministry towards a combination of ministry and institutional (market) control. Gornitzka and Maassen (2007) and Huisman (2009) describe trends in Europe towards this hybrid model where the ministerial control is reduced by the autonomy of individual institutions still constrained by the persistence of some form of ministry control. In Europe, this movement coincides in part with the Bologna Process, which has encouraged competition between European institutions for students and research funding (Maassen, 2012). This movement is justified by purportedly promoting institutional adaptability and by controlling government subsidies for higher education (Hearn and McLendon, 2011).

As mentioned previously, philosophic roots and traditions play key roles in this 'ministry versus market' debate about which vision of higher education should prevail. 'Market' in higher education has been interpreted in some countries to mean 'for profit' (Slaughter and Rhoades, 2004) and hence in conflict with the public good. Although for-profit education has grown in the past decade, especially in the United States, for the most part academic institutions are non-profit. More importantly, 'market' need not imply profit; at heart, it means responding to demands and needs not currently met by the institution or academic system in question. In this context, market-based means adaptability to meet the changing needs of society (Hearn and McLendon, 2011).

Markets certainly do imply competition. In the increasingly global higher education marketplace, institutions (and nations) compete for students, resources and prestige. This competitive environment is offset somewhat by academic norms that promote collaborations within the disciplines and among colleagues. For example, in the Association of American Universities (AAU), which includes the top 60 US research universities and two from Canada, member institutions compete for research grants and students but cooperate to lobby for increased federal contributions to research and student financial aid. Many of them also collaborate in networks to improve, for example, undergraduate instruction such as in the AAU Initiative to Improve Undergraduate STEM Education (AAU) and in the Center for the Integration of Research, Teaching, and Learning (CIRTL). These examples are further evidence of the unique, symbiotic relationship in institutions of higher education between market competition and collegiality.

Resolution of the tension between ministry and market views of higher education with their concomitant historical and philosophical origins is one key to the future direction of the enterprise. Although not a new concern (see Ashby, 1974), how to ensure a voice for government (and societal) interests while allowing institutions to respond to changes in academic disciplines, student demand and the like remains a central challenge for all of higher education.

Access

Among the most important developments in higher education policy internationally in the past 20 years or so is the recognition that secondary education is no longer sufficient to prepare most people for the global economy. In developing countries, after decades of emphasizing literacy and primary/secondary education, the World Bank now acknowledges that higher education, not lower levels of education, is the key to long-term economic prosperity (World Bank, 2002). In the United States, the gap in career earnings between any type of secondary (high school diploma) and post-secondary education (community college, bachelor's, master's, PhD) continues to grow because of the continuing *decline* in the value of a secondary credential (Fairweather, 2006). In developed countries, this shift coincides with the evolution of traditional manufacturing industries towards higher use of technology with manual labour jobs shipped to less expensive locales. For example, in the United States, high school graduates no longer can expect lifelong, well-paying careers working on an assembly line. These factors underlie the Lisbon strategy and its emphasis on the importance of higher education in the future European economy (European Commission, 2005). Many developing countries see the handwriting on the wall too: China, for example, is no longer the centre for manufacturing based on inexpensive labour. Its major investment in higher education is based in part on the recognition that future economic development requires preparing Chinese youth through higher education for more complex and often changing roles in a modern economy (Li, 2010; Ma, 2007).

In addition to access writ large, participation in higher education for specific groups remains problematic. In many countries, fewer women major in the sciences, engineering and mathematics than men (PCAST, 2012). Worldwide fewer women hold faculty positions than men (Enders and de Weert, 2009). In countries such as the United States, racial and ethnic minorities remain under-represented in higher education, especially at the university level (e.g. Coles, 2013).

Countries that currently do not have sufficient capacity to meet existing demand, while at the same time demand is increasing, are in an especially challenging environment. As one example, the public universities in Brazil, which include the oldest and most prestigious institutions, do not have the capacity to meet current demand. Even with substantial additional public investments to preserve quality and status, it seems unlikely that these institutions will expand enrolments greatly. Here, as in some other countries, less prestigious private institutions have developed to meet some of the as-yet-unmet demands (Altbach, Reisberg and Rumbley, 2009). Many of these privates are non-profit, but some are for-profit.

Another approach to increase access and better meet demand is the development of online education both in traditional institutions and as stand-alone entities. Online education seems especially well suited for people located some distance from academic institutions or who are working and cannot take the time away from their jobs. Online education is leading the way in competency-based degree programmes (Paulsen, 2002) where students earn degrees by passing competency examinations rather than by accumulating credits. Whether or not online institutions attain the credibility of traditional forms of higher education remains to be seen. In the United States, the University of Phoenix is one example of a for-profit university that has attained traditional accredited status.

Access to higher education is and always will be justified because it enhances the public good. Better educated populations live happier, more productive lives, contribute to community development, support the fine arts, develop fewer health problems and the like (Bowen, 1977; IHEP, 2005). In the modern global economy, however, access to some form of higher education has become a *necessity*. Access is no longer solely relevant to the philosophical debate about higher education as a public or private good. Access to higher education has become a requirement to prepare a nation's youth individually and in aggregate for the global economy, an economy that changes rapidly and is not limited by national boundaries.

Paying for higher education

In this section, we focus on the dynamics of funding higher education in a world moving towards trying simultaneously to achieve greater access, higher quality, positioning for the global economy and prestige. These issues are covered in more detail in the chapters by Jongbloed and Lepori (Chapter 24, this volume) and Zumeta and Li (Chapter 25, this volume). We require common terminology to examine costs and revenues. 'Appropriations' refers to revenue contributed by a state or national government (through a ministry or other means) to support the operation of public institutions of higher education. In the United States, except for special institutions (e.g. the military academies), appropriations do *not* include federal support for student financial aid and research because these mechanisms are not meant to support basic operations. In ministry-based systems, direct contributions towards operating costs are considered appropriations. 'Other sources of revenue' are resources other than those provided by direct government subsidy. These include tuition, research funds received from various sources and alumni gift giving. In higher education systems with both public and private institutions appropriations rarely go to the private institutions. Hence for operating costs they rely on majority of their revenues from non-governmental sources such as tuition. "Expenditures" are the funds spent by academic institutions to carry out their missions – teaching, research and, in some cases, service. Appropriations come in many forms – a block grant based on performance factors or alternatively on projected enrolment, targeted funding by category of operation and so on. Expenditures by institutions cover many categories, including *educational and general expenditures* (the costs of teaching, research and public service as well as the administrative costs to support those functions) and *all other expenditures* (from athletics, to hospitals, to technology transfer) (Fairweather, 2006).

A key to understanding the past and likely future evolution of higher education is the shifting percentages within revenue categories. For public institutions, the basic categories include some form of government subsidy (national, state, regional or local), tuition and fees, research and service contracts and grants, and private gifts. For private institutions, the categories are similar minus the government subsidy (Fairweather, 2006). Keep in mind that cost control in traditional forms of higher education is constrained by the labour intensity of the enterprise so that in the course of time costs tend to increase regardless of cost-cutting measures. In the United States, as costs increased over time the percentage of revenue contributed from governmental sources to (public) institution operating expenses has declined compared to other forms of revenue. In both public and private institutions, the fastest growing revenue category is student tuition and fees. For larger institutions, the dependency on external governmental and private sources for research and service has also increased. American research universities now treat revenues from research overhead as part of basic operating revenue rather than as income designated to support research. As one consequence of this evolution, some public universities in the United States receive less than 5% of their operating costs from state governments (Zumeta, 2006). In addition, today student financial aid debt in the United States exceeds total credit card debt. The political fallout is not surprising – policies meant to constrain the increase in tuition costs as well as to tie efficiency in time-to-degree to government subsidies abound.

The pattern in Europe with a much longer tradition of tuition-free education and high levels of government subsidy has shown similar though less drastic shifts. Today several European countries allow their institutions to charge for tuition (Jongbloed, 2010). Even in Finland, which retains tuition-free education for domestic and foreign students, universities are now allowed to charge tuition and fees to international students whose governments pay for their education. Oxford and Cambridge universities, among the oldest and most prestigious institutions in the world, now have active gifting programmes to raise additional revenue from alumni. As European nations attempt to rein in their contributions to research as part of an overall cost-control process, their institutions have turned to the EU as an important source of research fund support.

As Altbach and Balan (2007) show, the 'losers' in this process are nations without the national or institutional resources to expand their traditional sources of revenue. Other 'losers' are nations currently unable to meet the demand for higher education, requiring them to spend additional revenues on finding ways to provide space for students rather than on increasing quality.

These financial trends can run into political resistance for both economic and philosophical reasons. In developed countries, funds for higher education compete with other 'public goods', especially social welfare and health care. In deciding to allow academic institutions to charge tuition, even when justified on a financial basis, government agencies or their designated decision-makers (e.g. boards of trustees) run the political risk of appearing to violate the commitment to higher education as a public good. For many community colleges in the United States, the historical commitment to a tuition-free or very low-cost policy environment is in jeopardy as these institutions struggle to find ways to educate as many as one-half of all American students in higher education.

Dissimilar histories and structures, similar challenges

The challenges facing higher education are profound: simultaneously trying to educate more students while preserving quality, finding ways to increase quality while controlling government subsidies and tuition rates, enhancing prestige while expanding access. These choices can (and will) conflict even though there is every reason for higher education systems and their institutions to pursue them. Further, despite very different histories, cultures and structures, these pressures apply in one form or another to almost all national systems of higher education.

In the chapters that follow, readers will find detailed descriptions and analyses of the policy and administrative challenges facing higher education and the ways that academic institutions and their governing systems have adapted to attempt to fulfil these varied (and sometimes conflicting) missions. Keep in mind that in the past dramatic changes in higher education accompanied periods with the magnitude of changes in policy environments that we find today. We may well look back on this era as a line of demarcation between what higher education has been and what it will become. What might we expect to find? Among many possibilities, there are

- increased use of online instruction, especially for professional fields requiring regular updated training;
- an increased split among the faculty between the 'haves' and 'have-nots' where the former have permanent positions but the latter do not, and where the latter carry out more of the teaching and service functions than the permanent faculty;
- greater separation between institutions based less on espoused mission and more on resources; and

- the capitulation of the philosophy of education for personal development in favour of education as human capital where the professional development of students and their potential success in the global marketplace take precedence over academic policy.

References

Altbach, P., and J. Balan (2007) *World Class Worldwide: Transforming Research Universities in Asia and Latin America* (Baltimore: Johns Hopkins University Press).

Altbach, P., Reisberg, L., and L. Rumbley (2009) *Trends in Global Higher Education: Tracking an Academic Revolution* (Paris: UNESCO).

Amaral, A., Neave, G., Musselin, C., and P. Maassen (2010) *European Integration and the Governance of Higher Education and Research* (Dordrecht: Springer).

Ashby, E. (1974) *Adapting Universities to a Technological Society* (San Francisco: Jossey-Bass).

Association of American Universities. http://stemhub.org/groups.aau.

Baumol, W., and G. Bowen (1966) *Performing Arts: The Economic Dilemma* (New York: Twentieth Century Fund).

Birnbaum, R. (1988) *How Colleges Work: The Cybernetics of Academic Organization and Leadership* (San Francisco: Jossey-Bass).

Bowen, H. (1977) *Investment in Learning: The Individual and Social Value of American Higher Education*, 1st edn (San Francisco: Jossey-Bass Publishers).

Carnegie Foundation for the Advancement of Teaching (2010) *A Classification of Institutions of Higher Education* (Palo Alto, CA: Carnegie Foundation for the Advancement of Teaching).

Center for the Integration of Research, Teaching, and Learning. http://www.cirtl.net.

Clark, R. (1972) 'The organizational saga in higher education', *Administrative Science Quarterly*, 17(2), 178–184.

Clark, R. (1992) *Distinctive Colleges: Antioch, Reed, and Swarthmore* (Chicago: Aldine).

Coles, A. (2013) *Investment Payoff: Reassessing and Supporting Efforts to Maximize the Benefits of Higher Education for Underserved Populations* (Washington, DC: Institute for Higher Education Policy).

College Board (2014) *Trends in College Pricing 2014* (New York: College Board).

Duderstadt, J. (2007) *The View from the Helm: Leading the American Research University during an Era of Change* (Ann Arbor, MI: University of Michigan Press).

Enders, J., and E. de Weert (eds) (2009) *The Changing Face of Academic Life* (New York: Palgrave MacMillan).

European Commission (2005) *Mobilising the Brainpower of Europe: Enabling Universities to Make Their Full Contribution to the Lisbon Strategy* (Brussels: European Commission).

Fairweather, J. (1996) *Faculty Work and Public Trust: Restoring the Value of Teaching and Public Service in American Academic Life* (Boston: Allyn & Bacon).

Fairweather, J. (2002) 'The ultimate faculty evaluation: promotion and tenure decisions', in C. Colbeck (ed) *Evaluating Faculty Performance* (pp. 97–108) New Directions for Institutional Research (San Francisco: Jossey-Bass).

Fairweather, J. (2005) 'Beyond the rhetoric: trends in the relative value of teaching and research in faculty salaries', *Journal of Higher Education*, 76(4), 401–422.

Fairweather, J. (2006) *Higher Education and the New Economy: Who Pays, Who Benefits?* (East Lansing, MI: Educational Policy Center, Michigan State University).

Fairweather, J. (2008) 'Linking evidence and promising practices in STEM undergraduate education', *National Academy of Sciences White Paper* (Washington, DC: National Academy of Sciences).

Fairweather, J., and K. Paulson (2008) 'The evolution of scientific fields in American universities: disciplinary differences, institutional isomorphism', in J. Valimaa and O. Ylijoki (eds) *Cultural Perspectives in Higher Education* (pp. 197–212) (Dordrecht: Springer, 2008).

Feldman, K., and T. Newcomb (1969) *The Impact of College on Students* (San Francisco: Jossey-Bass).

Finnish Ministry of Education and Culture (2014). http://www.minedu.fi/OPM/Koulutus/ koulutuspolitiikka/Hankkeet/Yliopistolaitoksen_uudistaminen/?lang=en.

Geiger, R. (2015) *The History of American Higher Education: Learning and Culture from the Founding to WWII* (Princeton, NJ: Princeton University Press) e-book version.

Gladieux, L., and J. King (1999) 'The federal government and higher education', in P. Altbach, P. Gumport and R. Berdahl (eds) *American Higher Education in the 21st Century: Social, Political, and Economic Challenges* (pp. 152–182) (Baltimore: Johns Hopkins University Press).

Gornitzka, Å. and P. Maassen (2007) 'An instrument for national political agendas: the hierarchical vision', in J. Olsen and P. Maassen (eds) *University Dynamics and European Integration* (pp. 81–98) (Dordrecht: Springer).

Hearn, J. and M. McLendon (2011) 'Governance research: from adolescence toward maturity', in M. Bastedo (ed) *The Organization of Higher Education: Managing Colleges for a New Era* (pp. 45–85) (Baltimore: The Johns Hopkins University Press).

Huisman, J. (ed) (2009) *International Perspectives on the Governance of Higher Education: Alternative Frameworks for Coordination* (New York: Routledge).

Huisman, J., Meek, L. and F. Wood (2007) 'Institutional diversity in higher education: a cross-national and longitudinal analysis', *Higher Education Quarterly*, 61(4), 564–577.

Institute for Higher Education Policy (2005) *The Investment Payoff: A 50-State Analysis of the Public and Private Benefits of Higher Education* (Washington, DC: IHEP).

Jongbloed, B. (2010) *Funding Higher Education: A View across Europe* (Brussels: ESMU).

Kezar, A. (2014) *How Change Works in Higher Education* (New York: Routledge).

Kerr, C. (1982) *The Uses of the University* (Cambridge, MA: Harvard University Press).

Knorr-Cetina, K. (1999) *Epistemic Cultures: How the Sciences Make Knowledge* (Cambridge, MA: Harvard University Press).

Levine. A. (2001) 'Higher education as a mature industry', in P. Altbach, P. Gumport and D. Johnstone (eds) *In Defense of American Higher Education* (pp. 38–58) (Baltimore: Johns Hopkins University Press).

Li, H. (2010) 'Higher Education in China', in C. Clotfelter (ed) *American Universities in a Global Market* (pp. 269–304) (Chicago: University of Chicago Press).

Ma, W. (2007) 'The flagship university and China's economic reform', in P. Altbach and J. Balan (eds) *World Class Worldwide: Transforming Research Universities in Asia and Latin America* (pp. 31–53) (Baltimore: Johns Hopkins University Press).

Maassen, P. A. M. (2012) 'Change dynamics and higher education reforms', in Vukasović, M. (ed) *Effects of Higher Education Reforms Change Dynamics* (pp. 1–18) (Rotterdam; Boston: Sense Publishers).

Maassen, P. A. M., and J. P. Olsen (eds) (2007) *University Dynamics and European Integration* (Dordrecht: Springer).

Maassen, P., and B. Stensaker (2011) 'The knowledge triangle, European higher education policy logics and policy implications', *Higher Education*, 61(6), 757–769. doi:10.1007/s10734-010-9360-4.

Organisation for Economic Co-operation and Development (OECD) (2012) *Education Indicators in Focus 2012*. http://www.oecd-ilibrary.org/docserver/download/

5k961169d8tg.pdf?expires=1418061752&id=id&accname=guest&checksum=368FA8C
C8D91A08DE0A24FD741E1A21E.

Orton, J., and K. Weick (1990) 'Loosely coupled systems: a reconceptualization', *Academy of Management Review*, 15(2), 203–223.

Paulsen, K. (2002) 'Reconfiguring faculty roles in virtual settings', *Journal of Higher Education*, 73(1), 123–148.

Powell, W., and P. DiMaggio (eds) (1999) *The New Institutionalism in Organizational Analysis* (Chicago: University of Chicago Press).

President's Council of Advisors on Science and Technology (PCAST) (2012) *Engage to Excel* (Washington, DC: PCAST).

Singer, S. (ed) (2012) *Discipline-Based Education Research: Understanding and Improving Learning in Undergraduate Science and Engineering* (Washington, DC: National Research Council).

Schwartzman, S. (2007) 'Brazil's leading university: original ideals and contemporary goals', in P. Altbach and J. Balan (eds) *World Class Worldwide: Transforming Research Universities in Asia and Latin America* (pp. 143–172) (Baltimore: Johns Hopkins University Press).

Slaughter, S., and G. Rhoades (2004) *Academic Capitalism and the New Economy: Markets, States, and Higher Education* (Baltimore: Johns Hopkins University Press).

Stensaker, B., Frølich, N., Gornitzka, Å. and P. Maassen (2008) 'Internationalisation of higher education: the gap between national policy-making and institutional needs', *Globalisation, Societies and Education*, 6(1), 1–11. doi:10.1080/14767720701855550

Times Higher Education Rankings (2014) http://www.timeshighereducation.co.uk/world-university-rankings.

Trow, M. (1974) 'Problems in the transition from elite to mass higher education', *Conference on the Future Structure of Post-Secondary Education* (Paris: OECD).

Trow, M. (1984) 'The analysis of status', in R. Clark (ed) *Perspectives in Higher Education: Eight Disciplinary and Comparative Views* (pp. 132–164) (Berkeley: University of California Press).

Westerheijden, D. (2010) *Quality Assurance in Higher Education: Trends in Regulation, Translation, and Transformation* (Dordrecht: Springer).

World Bank (2002) *Constructing Knowledge Societies: New Challenges for Tertiary Education* (Washington, DC: World Bank).

Wulff, D., and Austin, A. (2004) *Paths to the Professoriate: Strategies for Enriching the Preparation of Future Faculty* (San Francisco: Jossey-Bass).

Zumeta, W. (2006) 'The new finance of public higher education', in H. Wechsler (ed) *The NEA 2006 Almanac of Higher Education* (pp. 37–48) (Washington, DC: National Education Association).

2
Approaches to Policy and Governance in Higher Education

Emanuela Reale and Emilia Primeri

This chapter deals with the general approaches to policy and governance as presented in the literature and as applied to the field of higher education (HE). We examine issues related to both politics and polity. By 'politics' we mean the focus on the resolution of conflict and development of consent, resulting in decision-making processes (the procedural dimension). By 'polity' we mean the focus on state organization and the management of the system to obtain political order and stability, through laws, regulations and institutions in different types of politically organized communities (March and Olsen, 1984; North, 1990).

The aim is to guide the readers systematically through key concepts used in the general policy and governance literature and in the HE literature as 'steering', 'government' and 'governance', highlighting the differences between them when appropriate. By 'steering' we refer to the instruments and arrangements externally developed and aimed at controlling academic institutions and behaviours. With the term 'government' we consider the actions of governing taken by institutional actors in charge of decision-making process while the concept of 'governance' underlines a change in the meaning of government and a new process of governing (Rhodes, 1997). In the HE context, the term 'governance' refers to modes of social coordination undertaken by actors, that is, academic institutions, in the making and implementation of rules to provide a collective good.

The chapter also outlines the shift from the traditional government model in the HE sector to different and new forms of governance. In the recent years, in fact, the role of the state in HE has undergone important changes, mainly moving from a control-based model towards a state-steering model relationship, more market-based and aimed at granting universities greater autonomy and promoting academic institutions' self-regulatory capacity (Ferlie, Musselin and Andresani, 2008; Krücken and Meier, 2006; Neave and van Vught, 1991; Paradeise et al., 2009a; van Vught, 2008).

In particular after 1980, the regulating power of national states generally weakened (i.e. the 'hollowing out' of the nation state). This, in the HE sector, implied a new steering system: the state pulled back from the universities and moved in the direction of a 'steering from a distance' model based on ex ante incentives and ex post performance measures (Paradeise et al., 2009a, p. 229). Higher education institutions (HEIs) started to borrow business instruments from the private sector so that concepts like strategic planning and strategic management are increasingly being used in HE (Maassen and van Vught, 1992). In this respect, the chapter provides a discussion of changed HE governance and steering patterns according to main narratives of public management reforms, namely New Public Management (NPM) and the Network Governance narrative (Ferlie et al., 2008). Key sources and the major differences between schools of thought are explained. We present and examine disciplinary perspectives, including public administration and public policy, political science and sociology, in order to capture the specificities of universities and of the HE sector as a whole.

The first section of the chapter introduces the concepts of HEIs as complete organizations, in order to identify any specific characteristics. HEIs being the primary actors in the HE field, it is important to present a description of particularities of HEIs as organizations before moving to the discussion about policy and governance concepts in the HE. The second section deals with main narratives of the public sector focusing on reforms, which have modified the nature of public administration. In the third section, we look at the changing relationships between the state and the society. Stakeholders, organizations and individuals involved in the relationships are analysed, outlying the changes currently under way and the division of responsibilities and power between the state and other actors in the field of HE and the emergence of market. The fourth section introduces the shift from 'government' to 'governance', and the differences between the two concepts, dealing with the specific features of governance in the HE. New structures and processes are introduced referring to the concept of networks. The section with conclusions draws lessons learned and offers suggestions for future research.

Higher education institutions as organizations

Organizational theories generally refer to organizations as heavily tied structures, constructed and managed according to rational assumptions and observable through rational instruments (Scott, 2008). Part of the literature suggests organizations are conceptually distinct from institutions: 'If institutions are the rules of the game, organizations and their entrepreneurs are the players. Organizations are made up of groups of individuals bound together by some common purpose to achieve certain objectives' (North, 1990, p. 3).

Other authors criticized the distinction between institutions and organizations, claiming the latter include their own system rules; hence, as HEIs, they are themselves a special type of institution. What appears to be 'special' about universities (and other educational organizations) is that they function through less rationalized, looser connections, they use unclear technologies and are characterized by weak authority. Given this, they have at times been described as 'loosely coupled' (Weick, 1976), or labelled as 'organized anarchies'. According to Weick (1976), loosely coupled organizations are made up of several events with different degrees of tightness or looseness: they are soft structures, but still with characteristics of persistence, order, efficiency and coordination. The primary coupling mechanisms within most organizations are the 'logic of tasks' (the technical core of organization, including technology, tasks, subtasks, role, territory and individuals) and the 'authority of office' (positions, offices, responsibilities, opportunities, rewards and sanctions).

Educational organizations are also defined as 'organized anarchies' (Cohen, March and Olsen, 1972) characterized by fluid participation, unclear technologies and 'problematic' preferences. Fluid participation means that participants and decision makers' involvement in HE decisions vary over time both for the amount of time and effort they devote to them. Unclear technologies mean that since members and participants of organizations often do not know HEIs processes, they proceed in decision-making through trial and error procedures. Finally, problematic preferences indicate that HEIs decisions and choices are mostly based on a loose collection of preferences rather than on consistent and shared goals among HE members and decision-makers (Cohen et al., 1972; March and Olsen, 1984).

A 'garbage can' model of decision-making applies in such contexts, meaning a mix of choices, problems and solutions, from which participants are partially uncoupled. Educational organizations, so far, are less governed by authority and hierarchy (Peters, 2002), decisions are mostly taken by 'flight or oversight' (Cohen et al., 1972, p. 9) or are likely to result from actions of bounded rationality (Simon, 2000), meaning they are based on uncertainty about goals and expected outcomes. This assumption raises troubling questions of how universities are governed.

In line with the above conceptual considerations, Musselin (2007) considers universities as 'specific organizations' with basic units (departments, faculties, institutes) mostly loosely coupled, whose core functions of teaching and research are unclear, weakly standardized processes. Hierarchical relationships exist but they are weaker than in other organizations, since universities are mostly organizations of experts, benefiting from high degrees of autonomy and subject to limited control. These features make universities 'incomplete organizations' (Brunsson and Sahlin-Andersson, 2000) and different from most other public sector organizations. Attempts at constructing universities as 'complete organizations' would need change in three main components: (i) identity, by strengthening organizational autonomy, controlling resources, building boundaries and defining elements to make the organization 'special' compared to other competing organizations; (ii) hierarchy, through devices to control and coordinate activities, personnel and practices; and (iii) rationality, through devices aimed at establishing strategies, setting objectives, dividing responsibilities and measuring performance.

The concepts presented here provide insights into the limits of authority-based mechanisms, uncertainties in technology and the difficulties in establishing coherent preference when participation is fluid (in the actors that shape outcomes, the means of exercising power and decisions on arrangements). This allows to better understand governance issues in HE (Krücken and Meier, 2006; Peters and Pierre, 2001). Before going through governance and steering concepts in the HE sector, it is useful to introduce some narratives of the public sector and their evolution from the 1970s since these are relevant to understand changes in the HE sector.

Narratives about changes in the public sector and in HE

This section focuses on the emergence of New Public Management and governance narratives[1] (NPM, Network Governance and New Public Governance (NPG)) which are used to analyse change in public sectors.

The narratives are related to modifications in the nature of public administration, particularly to the emergence of public management (Osborne, 2006; Ostrom and Ostrom, 1971). Salamon (2000) describes how governments are modifying not only the scope and scale of their works but also the forms of their actions, meaning the basic tools and instruments used to address public problems, changing the very nature of public administration (Osborne, 2006; Peters, 2003). In fact, traditional public administration theories distinguish politics and administration as separate spheres, which are to be hierarchically organized and aim at accomplishing state purposes. Ostrom and Ostrom (1971, p. 211) instead indicate public management as a 'different approach to the study of public administration', with a shift towards an 'efficiency-based' concept of public administration. The primary goal of such public sector reform is to permit use and choice among alternative instruments for public action. The new tools of public management permit tailoring of public action to the nature of the problems to be addressed, above all by bringing in an array of additional actors from outside of the typical sphere of public administration.

Reform in public management is conceived as 'a means to an end, not an end in itself' or rather a 'means to potentially multiple ends' (Pollitt and Bouckaert, 2004, p. 6). Pollitt and Bouckaert (2004) identify at least five definitions of public management, most of these blending the traditional concept of public administration with more generic management principles. Such definitions serve to unite the concepts of the state with those of civil society, in an input–output type of model (Pierre, 2000) which apply both at the level of specific programmes and of individual organizations. Osborne (2006) points out that both Public Administration and Management have passed through three main modes: until late 1980s a public administration mode characterized by a state and bureaucratic view, then a NPM mode, and from the beginning of 21st century the move towards a NPG mode. Since the 1990s, then, three core narratives have emerged in public sector reforms: NPM, Network Governance and NPG (Ferlie et al., 2008; Osborne, 2006; Paradeise et al., 2009a, 2009b).

New Public Management (NPM) is often associated with the public sector reforms from the 1980s on, under the Thatcher governments of the United Kingdom. Such reform draws on organizational economics and aims at transforming the public sector into a more efficient and results-oriented sector. The main features are (i) focus on markets instead of government planning; (ii) strong emphasis on performance, achieved by management for systems improvement and constant monitoring and measurement of results (see Chapter 4); and (iii) finally, pressure to apply entrepreneurial rather than collegial management (Ferlie et al., 2008; Osborne, 2006). In the HE sector, this type of reform has resulted in the introduction of managerial types of government oversight and of stated criteria for management within the HEIs and the sector as a whole (Paradeise et al., 2009a); consequently, the reforms tend to make the HE sector more efficient and more market-oriented.

Network Governance reforms are primarily based on the implementation of the concept that the state, once it has abandoned traditional models based on hierarchical relationships and social controls, must steer 'through contracts, alliances and partnerships building and persuasion rather than hierarchy' (Ferlie et al., 2008, p. 336). This model advocates network-based models of governing, with expanding participation from greater numbers of diverse social and economic actors. In this context, the Neo-Weberian reforms proposed by Pollitt and Bouckaert (2004) as alternative to NPM in continental Europe are worth mentioning, which 'assumes a positive role of the state, a distinctive public service and a particular legal order' (Paradeise et al., 2009a, p. 244).

Finally, NPG is in turn closely related to the rise of public management (Osborne, 2006) and changes it has introduced. The NPG combines into a new paradigm main features and strengths of the NPM narrative and that of Public Administration and Public Administration Management. It relies on the existence of a plural state, which refers to multiple actors contributing to deliver public services, and a pluralist state, that refers to multiple processes informing the policy-making system.

The narratives introduced here highlight changes in the scope, the ways and tools of governing which have characterized the public sector (including HE). Such changes also enhance a different role of the state in the policy domain and in the HE system. Hence, we move now to look at the relationship between the state and the society (sectors, organizations and individuals) and the way HEIs are governed in the following section.

The state role in HE: Changes in the modes of steering

In studying HE, scholarly attention is heavily weighted towards conceptualizing the state's role in the policy domain and the ways that it can govern the HE system. The redefinition of the state role in relation to HE can be observed in almost all the European systems, although with more or less intensity and different combinations of features from one system to another (Paradeise et al., 2009b). A key issue in studying the politics of HE is also to understand how the changing relationships between the HEIs, the state and the various sectors, organizations and actors of society impact power distribution and coordination among actors as a response to different socio-economic and organizational arrangements. The peculiarities of HEIs as organizations largely affect the evolution of the role the state played and the way of steering.

The post-war role of the state in the HE sector

The post-war period was one of great stability in the relationship between governments and the HE sector. Until the 1980s, most Western European governments took an important role in steering HE, in order to support rapid economic expansion and respond to increasing social demand for education. HEIs were seen as responsible for training and education, while government would provide the necessary funding. This type of relationship was accompanied by declining institutional autonomy, strengthened autonomy for the individual academics and ultimately by budgetary compression and increasing demands for efficiency in HEIs (Neave and van Vught, 1991).[2]

The traditional model of steering universities was shaped by the varying combinations and distributions of authority at three main levels (Becher and Kogan, 1992; Clark, 1983): (i) the level of the basic units, meaning the individual professors and their collective peer groups (departments, faculties); (ii) the level of the university bureaucratic apparatus and trustees; and (iii) the level of the governing political and administrative authorities. Regarding the coordination of the HE system, Clark (1983) proposed a triangular model, with the vertices of the state, as the primary coordinating actor, the academics and the market. In the case where the state plays a strongly dominant role, the result is a centralized system, in some instances with the universities being treated as homogeneous bodies with very limited autonomy. The state can alternatively continue to play a dominant role, but limited to more supervisory tasks, fixing the general principles for the functioning of the system and leaving the institutions free to regulate themselves (van Vught, 1995). In the second case, where the market is the dominant force for coordinating the system, universities will tend towards quasi-market behaviours.[3] In this situation the HEIs develop highly flexible internal structures, readily capable of adapting to the needs of their external clients. In the final case, it is the professors and their disciplinary networks that carry out coordination of the organizational system (Clark, 1983). In the so-called continental model of HE (Clark, 1983), coordination of the system takes place through a combination of the professorial bodies and government bureaucracy, with only weak influence from the university institutional level. The institutional role is lessened due to the absence of university trustees, and instead a strong role is assigned to the academic corporations.

Elaborating on Clark's triangle, van Vught (1995) proposed a reduction to two models of coordination: 'state-controlled' (as seen in continental Europe) and 'state-supervising' (as seen in the English-speaking nations). In the former model, authority is exercised by the state and academic oligarchy. In the latter, power is shared between academics and university managers, while the state supervises the system in the style of steering from a distance. Other authors (Braun and Merrien, 1999) have proposed a conceptualization that instead adds two dimensions to Clark's triangle: the type of autonomy (procedural or substantial, as per Berdahl, 1990) and the government's 'belief system concerning universities as cultural or service institutions' and its resulting 'accentuation of the dynamics of governance'. These authors thus designed a 'three dimensional cube of governance, which integrates Clark's former governance model and the new managerialism model' (Braun and Merrien, 1999, p. 3).

The turn of the 2000s

From the 1990s, the state's role in HE underwent significant changes. The previous 'implicit agreement' with HEIs was replaced by sets of 'conditional contracts' (Neave and van Vught, 1991, p. 244) aimed at improving awareness of HE towards market and society and increasing the HEIs' strategic management capacities. Governments start driving a shift from a political model of institutional management to an entrepreneurial model and implementing new systems of control and planning for greater rationality (Neave and van Vught, 1991). Planning emerged as a strategic tool for the rational and orderly management of the entire academic enterprise. The question was then raised as to whether strategic planning in HE is now driven more by management for greater rationality (Dooris, Kelley and Trainer, 2004; Kotler and Murphy, 1981) rather than by the types of learning and creativity aims that should be typical of the academic sphere.

The three main features of the shift towards an entrepreneurial management model for HEIs are

i) readjustment of the HEIs' constituent elements and interests towards stronger staff, student and local stakeholder involvement, for increased democratization and to raise challenges to assumed missions and goals;

ii) emergence of HEI strategic management, planning and objective-setting, for more efficient use of resources, thus reinforcing HEIs as organizations; and

iii) introduction of values and techniques borrowed from the business sphere.

Neave and van Vught (1991, p. 11) describe the new relation between state and the HE system as 'interlarding self-regulation strategies with rational planning and control'. Thus the autonomy of the HEIs is now increasingly bounded, continuously steered by government-imposed policies and negotiated on the basis of available resources.

The introduction of the market economy in the public sector has involved significant modifications in the action of national governments, including the application of incentives and performance indicators in place of the former tools of central planning and detailed regulation. Neave (1998) describes this as 'the rise of the evaluative state'. For universities, the new steering system means that the state draws back from control over their strategic functions and that universities adopt their own micro-management concepts. Steering moves from a top-down guidance model with indirect steering and 'substantial itemized rules and ex-ante control', to a model with 'ex-ante incentives and ex-post performance measures' (Neave, 1998, p. 229). Saying differently, steering become a set of 'externally derived instruments and institutional arrangements aimed at governing organizational and academic behaviours' (Ferlie et al., 2008, p. 326), through which the state seeks to shape the HE system.

In the last decade, the changes affecting the public sector and the HE anticipated then the shift from traditional state-organizations arrangements to new governance configurations.

Clark's triangle is criticized as inadequately representing the interdependencies between the three spheres of the academics, universities and the national system, appearing at once too hierarchical and narrow, or relative to the reality of the complex of relationships. The triangle does not represent the complexity of macro-level impacts on the micro level, and in viewing all three vertices, does not 'grasp the impact that coordination modalities may have in each of them' (Musselin, 2004, p. 11). Musselin (2004) proposes the concept of 'university configurations' as an analytical framework for 'how the three types of collective action – those of universities, the overseeing authorities and the academic professor – fit and function together'. The assumptions of this approach allow for high levels of heterogeneity and variation in the purposes, roles and functions of the academics, the universities and the state. The university configuration occurring in any particular context must be detected by empirical research, using evidence that discloses the structure, nature and content of the interdependencies in that particular configuration (Musselin, 2004).

Other approaches emerge as useful to analyse the HE sector. Streeck and Schmitter (1985) identify four 'social orders' or 'logics', each defined according to a core guiding principle and serving as a basis for institutional development: (i) the community, operating through spontaneous solidarity; (ii) the market, operating through dispersed competition; (iii) the state or bureaucracy, featuring hierarchical control and coordination of the state actors; and (iv) the association, guided by principles of organizational consultation. Central to the description of all these orders is the motivation of the various actors to engage in collective and social actions and how they can then become involved.

A further consideration is that modern societies are increasingly characterized by the rise of new systems of multi-level and multi-actor governance. The actors are differentiated in both vertical and horizontal senses; they are supranational organizations, nation states and local governments, which come from the public arena, society and the market economy (Van Heffen, Kickert and Thomassen, 2001). This means that universities, like other modern organizations, see multiple actors entering their affairs, acting as stakeholders and influencing their governance (Texeira et al., 2004). Whitley (2007) observes that over the past two decades, the implementation of evaluation systems produces broad effects in the state–science relationship and follows a path-dependent character according to the nature of the public research systems in different countries.

Finally, transformations in the models of steering and coordination of universities highlight changes occurring to the concept of hierarchy in HE. The shift from hierarchical state–society relationships to a distributed power, shared by the state with market and other network actors (Huisman, 2009; Thompson et al., 1991) in fact, let emerge a conceptualization of hierarchy as the capability of coordinating actors and establishing devices for control and management in order to create 'a collective entity that is engaged in a common project and aiming at shared priorities' (De Boer, Enders and Leisyte, 2007, p. 33). The organizational literature (Ferlie et al., 2008) assimilates HEIs to professional organizations, built for the purpose of specific groups of professionals, and devoted to assure the dominance of some groups on others, through a well-developed vertical differentiation among groups. Diefenbach and Sillince (2011) stated that professional organizations also work according to the principle of professional autonomy, focusing on the content of the work, intrinsically based on self-regulation, which contribute to shaping the hierarchical order, clashing to some extent with the principle of seniority because it is against the idea of dominance, subordination and obedience. In this respect, informal hierarchies emerged in HEIs as ways for convergence, and the informal principle of hierarchical order became the domination among semi-autonomous professionals organizations.

Summing up, the new modes of steering the HE sector underline state and HE relationships deeply modified, moving from a control-based model with the state playing a central and dominant role over HEIs to a steering model where the state role becomes more and more nuanced. Also, new actors intervene in the state and HEIs relationships, figuring an increasing role of the society, academics and markets in the HE sector.

From government to governance

For a long period of time, the terms 'governance' and 'governing' were roughly synonymous, simply indicating the process of government (Mayntz, 1998, 2003). Governance now refers to a new mode of governing that differs from the hierarchical model of state control over the civil sector. The shift in the meaning of governance took place beginning in the 1970s, with the onset of changes from the interventionist-hierarchical control model to that of more cooperative state–society relationships. Governance then became a form of political steering where hierarchical authority is no longer exerted and is instead replaced by non-hierarchical political controls. Klijn (2005) asserts that as government, business and civil society continue developing new forms of network relationships, the mode of governance also continues to change. Börzel and Risse (2010) define governance as 'the various institutionalized modes of social coordination to produce and implement collectively binding rules, or to provide collective goods' (p. 114). In sum, the concept of government refers to actions taken by institutional actors in charge of decision-making process, while the concept of governance indicates the processes and structures by which decisions are formulated and implemented as a results of interactions and coordination of all the actors involved: governmental, non-governmental, national and transnational (Braun and Merrien, 1999; Djelic and Sahlin-Andersson, 2006; Magalhães and Amaral, 2009; Musselin, 2004).

Governance consists of both structure and process (Börzel and Risse, 2010). As structure it refers to constellations of state and non-state institutions and individual actors, operating in competition and negotiation systems. The competition systems are composed of firms, interest groups, non-governmental organizations and others, mostly relying on market-based forms of coordination. In the negotiation systems, networks are the main actors.[4] Governance as process refers to the modes of social coordination by which these various actors engage in rule-making, for implementation of their actions and provision of the collective good. Coordination of governance can be hierarchical, where decisions are taken through authoritative processes, or non-hierarchical, with coordination based primarily on bargaining, voluntary commitment and voluntary compliance (Amaral, Jones and Karseth, 2002; Peters and Pierre, 2001).

Conceptual developments of governance in the public administration literature

Authors that try to conceptualize different types of governance further enriched the speculation on this topic, with arguments impacting the HE sector as well. Newman (2001) designs a framework to represent models of governance based on (a) the degree to which power is centralized or decentralized and (b) the orientation towards change – continuity and stability versus innovation. Four models with specific dynamics of change resulted, namely the self-governance and the open systems models (both decentralized) and the hierarchy and the rational goal models (both centralized). Kooiman (2003) proposes an approach focused on actors. 'Self-governance' refers to the capacity of social entities to govern themselves autonomously for the management of their interactions. 'Co-governance' refers to situations where a dominant, central actor is missing and the actors themselves are the main protagonists in decisions and interplay, using organized forms of interactions for governing purposes. 'Hierarchical governance' refers to interactions that mostly based on top-down relationships. Finally, 'governance' can be labelled as good governance, meaning the distribution of internal and external political and economic power, thus a political use of governance, or as a socio-cybernetic system, meaning that governance is a patterned structure that emerges in a socio-political system as a result of the efforts of several actors (Kooiman, 2003).

Rhodes (1997) considers governance as a new mode of government. Governance is viewed as the minimal state, so that the role of public intervention is reduced, or as corporate governance, meaning the 'system by which organizations are directed and controlled' (Rhodes, 1997). Rosenau and Czempiel (1992) describe the concept of 'governance without government', and Peters and Pierre (2001) suggest partnerships and markets as alternatives to the state in the governing process, particularly in action through networks. Peters and Pierre (1998) and Peters (2012) so far consider governance as a special form of political steering, where public and private actors provide directions and control to society and economy. Börzel and Risse (2010) instead question the possibility of governance without state control and suggest that a 'shadow of hierarchy' (Scharpf, 1997) still exists.

Despite the different perspectives, the governance modes show that the state no more directly controls HEIs but starts influencing their decisions. The state withdraws from control models of governance then, but it still uses binding rules and laws to 'threaten' national and local actors and steer their decisions. In this respect, Hood and colleagues (2004) distinguishes four forms of control:

(i) mutuality, through formal or informal group processes; (ii) competition, denoting control over individuals by processes of rivalry; (iii) contrived randomness, for example, the use of elections or selections with unpredictable results; and (iv) oversight, meaning scrutiny and steering from above or outside the individual or organization. The authors observed that in universities, different from other sectors of the public administration, control is most likely to take place through forms of oversight and mutuality, each employing different dynamics.

How these conceptualizations in the governance modes couple with the HE sector is discussed in the following section.

Governance developments in the higher education sector

The literature on the shift from government to governance in HE considers the literature quoted above, but assumes specific features, which are presented here. Ferlie et al. (2008) identify three main modes of governing which HE has gone through. The first relies on the concept of *academic freedom* and on academic power over key decision in HE, so that the role of the state is limited to ensure autonomy to HEIs. According to this view governance of the HE sector is to be considered mostly separated from other public policy sectors and any governance reform is likely to have limited impact on HE governance. The second mode considers HE sector similar to other *publicly funded services* over which the State has a control and steering power to counterbalance academic power. The third mode focuses on the role of the market in the governance of HE (Dill, 1997) where the state is expected to stimulate *HE to borrow market features* and to intervene to limit them when needed.

Paradeise et al. (2009a) underline as main governance developments in the HE sector in the last 30 years encompassed the shift from a bureaucratic model of governing to a managerial approach, following to some extent 'the same routes and trends of other public sector' such as health, security, justice (Paradeise et al., 2009a, p. 246). The authors observe as the development of managerial tools, the most evident being that of promotion of strategic planning, definitely reinforced the micro-management of universities and the role of senior management weakening the control model of governance and reinforcing instead the 'symmetrical governance relationships between central administration and individual universities' (Paradeise et al., 2009b, p. 217). This evolution goes with the implementation of steering at-the-distance instruments as ex ante incentives and ex-post performance assessments (Reale and Seeber, 2013; Whitley, 2007), and other forms of accountability. Moreover, these shifts also implied the reinforcement of the leadership and the managerial mode of governance within HEIs (Shattock, 2014).

Thus, university governance over the past few decades moves from the classical notion of the university as a republic of scholars, based on professorial self-regulation mode of governing, towards the notion of university as a 'stakeholder organization' (Bleiklie and Kogan, 2007, p. 477), passing through a business model based of governance, where university leaders are likely to adopt strategic decisions to meet stakeholders needs. The move towards a professional self-regulation model of university governance to a more business likely model based on stakeholders means that academic freedom is more and more circumscribed by the interests of several stakeholders, that governance is less representative of academics and that decisions are more and more spread along different levels. This concept introduces the idea of a hierarchical structure with multiple levels designed to take decisions. Multilevel governance (Bache and Flinders, 2004) and the process of European integration (Hooghe and Marks, 2001), which became increasingly relevant with the emergence for instance of the European Union, are an example (for multi-level governance, see other chapters in this volume).

Universities' governance, management and leadership structures are challenged by changes taking place in the internal and external environments HEIs operate in HEIs are likely to adapt to such changes modifying the relationships with the environment (i.e. fundraising and technology transfer), creating or modifying authority relationships and defining new ways for resources allocation (Sporn, 1999). This suggests that changes in HE governance can assume highly diversified forms and modes. Capano (2011) investigating governance modes, classified on the basis of governmental decision on objectives to be achieved and means universities can adopt, shows that, even if government continues to govern, governance mixes play a key role to policy effectiveness.

So far, the governance modes appear complex and often unclear, with multifaceted aspects. On the one hand, the literature observes an increase in the autonomy of academic institutions, through greater decentralization of steering activities (Kooiman, 2003). On the other hand, some (Gornitzka and Maassen, 2000; Gornitzka, Kogan and Amaral, 2005) refer to the rise of new governance assets in HE, characterized by hybrid steering approaches. This means that there is a change in government steering away from setting conditions as a means of control and towards awarding control over performance to the institutions. Moreover, the governance reforms in different countries affect the distribution of authority and allow for the emergence of new kinds of authoritative agencies beyond the state, increasing the complexity of the system (Whitley, 2012). In this respect, Gläser (2010) argues that, instead of focusing on institutional or process aspects, investigating governance with a focus on the authority relationships between independent actors owning a legitimate power allows to understand how coordination between them occur in HE systems.

In sum, changes in governance in HE highlight the move from a 'command and control' mode of governing to the emergence of an evaluative mode of governance where non-state actors are more and more involved in the decisional processes concerning public policy and policies of the HE sector.

Conclusions

The chapter introduces a discussion of HEIs as organizations highlighting its particularities and main characteristics, which make them different from most public sector organizations. HEIs are characterized by less rationalized and less tightly connections, unclear technologies and weak authority relationships which allow for labelling them as loosely coupled systems or organized anarchies. Peculiarities of HEIs raise the question about the way they are governed. To answer this question, the chapter has gone through some key concepts and narratives of the public administration and public sector policies focusing on the governance theme as key issue. Differences and similarities between these notions in the public sector and in the HE field have been addressed. The debate and conceptualization of government and governance, as well as its developments in the HE sector, led to drawing some key lessons briefly summarized below.

In recent decades, there has been a shift from traditional state-centred governing arrangements to alternative modes of governance in almost all public sectors, including HE (Ferlie et al., 2008). The approaches to policy and governance in HE underwent a deep transformation, and scholars attempt to come to terms with the evolution of public sector composition, the new configuration of the state role and the changes in the university actorhood (Gläser, 2010; Whitley, 2012).

The current trends in governance remain challenging: the emergence of new governance modes does not entail that processes of transformations within HE sectors have been linear or completed, rather they highlight the HE sector is more and more complex, for different steering levels and modes are increasingly intertwined. The chapter also points out that although HE indeed shows specific features, borrowing concepts from other disciplines clearly offers very useful insights. It improves the opportunities for learning and provides new instruments to analyse and understand the changes taking place in the sector. The idea of HE as a 'stand-alone' research field has been challenged by studies that illustrate similarities with other professionalized public sectors. HE in fact shares a list of characteristics with other sectors: aspects of structuring and institutionalization, of public funding and state regulation of the institutions and a mix of professional and bureaucratic elements (Ferlie et al., 2008; Paradeise et al., 2009a).

Building bridges between the HE, policy and governance disciplines is a way to confirm, adjust or discard certain expectations, particularly concerning the steering, funding and regulatory relationships between the state and universities (Huisman, 2009). To this aim, a key issue in research is to continue to explore and apply the available concepts and notions, strengthening 'the relationships between higher education and the main disciplines represented among higher education specialists' (Musselin, 2014, p. 9).

Notes

1. Narratives mix technical, political and normative elements from different sources in new policy and management arrangements, rather than providing purely analytical frameworks (Ferlie, Musselin and Andresani, 2008; Paradeise et al., 2009a).
2. Concerning institutional autonomy, Berdahl (1990) distinguishes between substantive and procedural autonomy, the former allowing determining activities and their contents (e.g. institutional aims, research programmes, curricula), the latter being limited to define the instruments to pursue them.
3. Market may be referred to as a 'coordination device that involves voluntary exchange of goods and services between two parties at a known price' (Thompson et al., 1991, p. 21), and it is generally associated with price-setting mechanisms of supply and demand. The relevance of the market for HEIs is not always clear. However, concepts such as 'quasi-market' or 'market-like' have gained increasing importance, since they boost some private sector' rhetoric for improved efficiency, and also permit the continued inclusion of the public sphere for purposes of equity (Dill, 1997; Marginson, 1997).
4. 'Network' is a generic label for the various states to interest-group relationships that enter into the new distributed policy-making process (Huisman, 2009; Kogan and Hanney, 2000). Networks can operate through features such as membership (often limited), integration (frequently based on basic values), resources (generally available to all networks participants) and power (usually equally distributed). 'Issue networks' typically affect a wide range of interests, with fluctuations in contracts, level and forms of agreement, inequalities in access to resources and power distribution.

References

Amaral, A., Jones, G. A. and B. Karseth (2002) *Governing Higher Education: National Perspectives on Institutional Governance* (Dordrecht: Kluwer).

Bache, I. and M. Flinders (2004) *Multi-level Governance* (Oxford: Oxford University).

Becher, T. and M. Kogan (1992) *Process and Structure in Higher Education* (Milton Keynes: Open University).

Berdahl, R. (1990) 'Academic freedom, autonomy and accountability in British universities', *Studies in Higher Education*, 15(2), 169–180.

Bleiklie, I. and M. Kogan (2007) 'Organization and governance of universities', *Higher Education Policy*, 20, 477–493.

Börzel, T. and T. Risse (2010) 'Governance without a state: can it work?' *Regulation and Governance*, 4, 113–134.

Braun, D. and F. X. Merrien (1999) *Towards a Model of Governance for Universities. A Comparative View* (London: Jessica Kingsley).

Brusson, N. and K. Sahlin-Andersson (2000) 'Constructing organizations: the example of public sector reform', *Organization Studies*, 21, 721–746.

Capano, G. (2011) 'Government continues to do its job: a comparative study on governance shift in the higher education sector', *Public Administration*, 89(4), 1622–1642.

Clark, B. R. (ed) (1983) *Perspectives on Higher Education: Eight Disciplinary and Comparative Views* (Berkeley: University of California Press).

Cohen, M. D., March, G. J. and P. J. Olsen (1972) 'A garbage can model of organizational choice', *Administrative Science Quarterly*, 17(1), 1–25.

De Boer, H., Enders, J. and L. Leisyte (2007) 'Public sector reform in Dutch higher educa-tion: the organizational transformation of the university', *Public Administration*, 85(1), 27–46.

Diefenbach, T. and J. A. A. Sillince (2011) 'Formal and informal hierarchy in different types of organizations', *Organization Studies*, 32(11), 1515–1537.

Dill, D. (1997) 'Higher education markets and public policy', *Higher Education Policy*, 10(3–4), 167–185.

Djelic, M. L. and K. Sahlin-Andersson (2006) *Transnational Governance: Institutional Dynamics of Regulation* (Cambridge: Cambridge University).

Dooris, M. J., Kelley, J. M. and J. M. Trainer (2004) 'Strategic planning in higher education', *New Directions for Institutional Research*, 5–11.

Ferlie, E., Musselin, C. and L. Andresani (2008) 'The "Steering" of higher education systems: a public management perspective', *Higher Education*, 56(3), 325–348.

Gläser, J. (2010) 'From governance to authority relations', in R. Whitley, J. Gläser and L. Engwall (eds) *Reconfiguring Knowledge Production* (pp. 357–369) (Oxford: Oxford University Press).

Gornitzka, A. and P. Maassen (2000) 'Hybrid steering approaches with respect to European higher education', *Higher Education Policy*, 13(3), 267–268.

Gornitzka, A., Kogan M. and A. Amaral (2005) *Reform and Change in Higher Education* (Dordrecht: Springer).

Hood, C., James, O., Peters, B. G. and C. Scott (eds) (2004) *Controlling Modern Government: Variety, Commonality and Change* (Cheltenham: Edward Elgar).

Hooghe, L. and G. Marks (2001) *Multi-level Governance and European Integration* (Lanham: Rowman and Littlefiel).

Huisman, J. (2009) 'Coming to terms with governance in higher education', in J. Huisman (ed) *International Perspectives on the Governance of Higher education. Alternative Frameworks for Coordination* (pp. 1–9) (New York: Routledge).

Klijn, E. H. (2005) 'Networks and interorganizational coordination', in E. Ferlie, L. Lynn and C. Pollit (eds) *The Oxford Handbook of Public Management* (Oxford: Oxford University).

Kogan, M. and S. Hanney (2000) *Reforming Higher Education* (Philadelphia: Jessica Kingsley).

Kooiman, J. (2003) *Governing as Governance* (London: Sage).

Kotler, P. and P. E. Murphy (1981) 'Strategic planning for higher education', *Journal of Education*, 52(5), 470–489.

Krucken, G. and F. Meier (2006) 'Turning the university into an organizational actor', in G. Drori, J. Meyer and H. Hwang (eds) *Globalization and Organization* (pp. 241–257) (Oxford: Oxford University).

Maassen, P. and F. A. van Vught (1992) 'Strategic planning', in B. R. Clark and G. Neave (eds) *The Encyclopedia of Higher Education*, Volume 2 (pp. 1483–1494) (Oxford: Pergamon).

Magalhães, A. and A. Amaral (2009) 'Mapping out discourses on higher education gover-nance', in J. Huisman (ed) *International Perspectives on the Governance of Higher Education: Alternative Frameworks for Coordination* (pp. 182–198) (New York: Routledge).

March, G. J. and P. J. Olsen (1984) 'The new institutionalism: organizational factors in political life', *American Political Science Review*, 78(3), 734–749.

Marginson, S. (1997) *Markets in Education* (New South Wales: Allen and Unwin).

Mayntz, R. (1998) *New Challenges to Governance Theory*, Jean Monet Chair Papers, No. 50, European University Institute.

Mayntz, R. (2003) 'From government to governance: political steering in modern societies', *Summer Academy on IPP*, Wuerzburg, September 7–11, 2003.

Musselin, C. (2014) 'Research issues and institutional prospects for higher education studies', *Studies in Higher Education*, 39(8).

Musselin, C. (2007) 'Are universities specific organizations?' in G. Krucken, A. Kosmutzky and M. Torka (eds) *Towards a Multiversity? Universities between Global Trends and National Traditions* (pp. 63–84) (Bielefeld: Transcript Verlag).

Musselin, C. (2004) *The Long March of French Universities* (New York: Routledge).

Neave, G. (1998) 'The evaluative state revisited. 20th Anniversary Issue of Review of Trends in Higher Education', *European Journal of Education*, 33(3), 265–284.

Neave, G. and F. A. van Vught (1991) *Prometheus Bound: The Changing Relationship between Government and Higher Education in Western Europe* (Oxford: Pergamon).

Newman, J. (2001) *Modernizing Governance* (London: Sage).

North, D. (1990) *Institutions, Institutional Change, and Economic Performance* (Cambridge: Cambridge University).

Osborne, S. P. (2006) 'The new public governance', *Public Management Review*, 8(3), 377–387.

Ostrom, V. and E. Ostrom (1971) 'Public choice: a different approach to the study of public administration', *Public Administration Review*, 31(2), 203–216.

Paradeise, C., Reale, E., Goestellac, G. and I. Bleiklie (2009a) 'University steering: between stories and history', in C. Paradeise, E. Reale, I. Bleiklie and E. Ferlie (eds) *University Governance: Western European Comparative Perspectives* (pp. 227–246) (Dordrecht: Springer).

Paradeise, C., Reale, E., Bleiklie, I. and E. Ferlie (2009b) 'A comparative approach to higher education reforms in Western European countries', in C. Paradeise, E. Reale, I. Bleiklie and E. Ferlie (eds) *University Governance: Western European Comparative Perspectives* (pp. 197–225) (Dordrecht: Springer).

Peters, B. G. (2012) 'Governance as political theory', in D. Levy-Faur (ed) *Oxford Handbook on Governance* (pp. 19–32) (Oxford: Oxford University Press).

Peters, B. G. (2003) 'Changing nature of public administration: from easy answers to hard questions', *Viesoji Politika Ir Administravimas*, 5, 7–20.

Peters, B. G. (2002) 'Governance: a garbage can perspective', *Political Science Series*, 84, Institute for Advanced Studies, Vienna.

Peters, B. G. and J. Pierre (2001) 'Developments in intergovernmental relations: towards multi-level governance', *Policy and Politics*, 29(2), 131–135.

Peters, B. G. and J. Pierre (1998) 'Governance without government? rethinking public administration', *Journal of Public Administration, Research and Theory*, 8, 223–243.

Pierre, J. (2000) *Debating Governance* (Oxford: Oxford University).

Pollitt, C. and G. Bouckeart (2004) *Public Management Reform: A Comparative Analysis* (Oxford: Oxford University).

Reale, E. and M. Seeber (2013) 'Instruments as empirical evidence for the analysis of higher education policies', *Higher Education*, 65, 135–151.

Rhodes, R. A. W. (1997) *Understanding Governance: Policy Networks, Governance, Reflexivity and Accountability* (London: Open University).

Rosenau, J. N. and E. O. Czempiel (1992) *Governance without Government: Order and Change in World Politics* (Cambridge: Cambridge University).

Salamon, L. M. (2000) 'The new governance and the tools of public action: an introduction', in L. M. Salamon (ed) *The Tools of Government: A Guide to New Governance* (pp. 1–47) (New York: Oxford University).

Scharpf, F. W. (1997) *Games Real Actors Play. Actor-Centered Institutionalism in Policy Research* (Boulder: Westview).

Scott, W. R. (2008) *Institutions and Organizations: Ideas and Interests*, 3rd edn (Los Angeles: Sage Publications).

Shattock, M. (ed) (2014) *International Trends in University Governance. Autonomy, Self-government and the Distribution of Authority* (pp. 34–48) (London: Routledge).

Simon, H. A. (2000) 'Bounded rationality in social science: today and tomorrow', *Mind & Society*, 1, 25–39.

Sporn, B. (1999) *Adaptive University Structures: An Analysis of Adaptation to Socioeconomic Environments of US and European Universities* (London: Jessica Kingsley Publishers).

Streeck, W. and P. C. Schmitter (1985) *Private Interest Government: Beyond Market and State* (London: Sage).

Texeira, P., Jongbloed, B., Dill, D. and A. Amaral (2004) *Markets in Higher Education: Rhetoric or Reality?* (Dordrecht: Kluwer).

Thompson, G., Frances, J., Levacic, R. and J. Mitchell (1991) *Markets, Hierarchies and Networks: The Coordination of Social Life* (London: Sage).

van Heffen, O., Kickert, W. J. M., and J. Thomassen (2001) 'Governance in modern society: effects, change and formation of government institutions', *Library of Public Policy and Public Administration*, 4.

van Vught, F. A. (2008) 'Mission diversity and reputation in higher education', *Higher Education Policy*, 21, 151–174. doi:10.1057/hep.2008.5.

van Vught, F. A. (1995) 'Policy models and policy instruments in higher education: the effects of governmental policy-making on the innovative behaviour of higher education institutions', *Institute for Higher Studies*, Series No. 26, Vienna.

Weick, K. F. (1976) 'Educational organizations as loosely coupled systems', *Administrative Science Quarterly*, 21(1), 1–19.

Whitley, R. (2007) 'Introduction', in R. Whitley and J. Gläser (eds) *The Changing Governance of the Sciences* (pp. 3–30) (Dordrecht: Springer).

Whitley, R. (2012) 'Transforming universities: national conditions of their varied organisational actorhood', *Minerva*, 50(4), 493–510.

3
Governance Models and Policy Instruments

Frans van Vught and Harry de Boer

Introduction

Appropriate governance is seen as a precondition for achieving the goals of maintaining or creating effective, competitive and attractive higher education systems (De Boer et al., 2012; van Vught, 1989a). In response to the challenges stemming from developments such as the emergence of mass higher education, globalization, privatization and fiscal crises, and inspired by neoliberal ideologies (such as New Public Management), contemporary governments continuously are in pursuit of approaches to governance that 'fit' (see also Clark, 1983b). The topic of governance finds itself in the centre of higher education politics and policies.

In this chapter, we will describe and analyse two classic governance models by asking ourselves which governance model suits contemporary higher education well and what policy instruments may be expected to be successful? While doing so we will also present a broad overview of these policy instruments. We define a governance model as a set of general postures, assumptions and guidelines that appear to be followed when a government, without necessarily excluding other stakeholders from the equation, steers the decisions and actions of specific societal actors according to the objectives the government has set and by using instruments the government has at its disposal.[1] This definition implies that we take a state-centric view, meaning that the state plays a pivotal role in establishing frameworks, objectives and priorities (see Pierre and Peters, 2000; Bell and Hindmoor, 2009).

The two classic governance models that will be explored are the *model of rational planning and control* and the *model of self-regulation*. In higher education, these governance models have been referred to as the *state control model* and the *state supervising model* (van Vught, 1988, 1992). Our analysis of the governance models is based on a two-dimensional framework. The first dimension concerns the basic features of the steering object, in our case higher education institutions. The second dimension regards the attributes of the products or services to be delivered, in our case 'knowledge' (i.e. teaching and research). Based on this analytical framework, we will discuss the fit of governance models and policy instruments in the concluding section. We will start to present the two classic governance models in the next section.

Two classic governance models

From the huge number of governance models and concepts that have been developed after the Second World War,[2] we distinguish two clearly conceptually different governance models: the model of rational planning and control and the model of self-regulation (for an elaborate description see van Vught, 1995). For the purpose of our analysis, we use these two classic models as ideal types.

The *model of rational planning and control* rests on the fundamental normative ideal of the rationalist perspective on decision-making. As an ideal type, the model assumes that there is firm knowledge of the object of regulation, complete control over the object of regulation and a holistic self-image of the regulating subject. The government's steering capacities are 'limitless': it is able to acquire comprehensive and 'true' knowledge to rightfully steer society according to its own objectives. As an ideal type, the model of rational planning and control implies the centralization of decision-making and a large amount of control over both actual choices to be made and the implementation of the chosen policy. The hard core version of this model's rationalistic perspective has attracted severe criticism (e.g. Simon, 1957; Lindblom, 1959, 1965). The limited intellectual capacities, the inadequacy of information gathering and costliness of analysis prevent that choices can ever be perfectly rational. Confronted with the limitations of this ideal in actual practice, it takes refuge in confidence in centralization and control.

The *model of self-regulation* is basically the opposite of the model of rational planning and control. The basic assumptions are that knowledge is highly uncertain, control over the object should to a large extent be avoided and an atomistic self-image instead of a holistic one has important advantages. The idea of self-regulation is grounded in the cybernetic perspective on decision-making, which assumes that a cybernetic decision-making unit is able to regulate itself (Ashby, 1956; Beer, 1975). The model of self-regulation emphasizes the self-regulatory capacities of decentralized decision-making units. The complex interrelations between these units are respected. Government activities are limited to monitoring the performance of the overall system of the interrelated self-regulating decision-making units and to evaluating the rules which to a large extent define this performance. The government's role in this model is one of being an arbiter and 'game designer'. The government watches the rules of a game played by relatively autonomous players and changes these rules when the game is no longer able to lead to satisfactory results.

The model of rational planning and control and the model of self-regulation are also clearly visible in governance models applied to higher education systems and, respectively, have been referred to as the *state control model* and *the state supervising model* (van Vught, 1988, 1992). The state control model, largely based on the model of rational planning and control, is traditionally found in the continental European higher education systems. For a long time, continental European governments, with all the existing variations, have been the (prime) funders and the overarching and powerful regulators of *their* higher education systems. According to the state control model of governance, the government controls, at least formally, nearly all aspects of the dynamics of the higher education system. It regulates, for example, institutional missions (mandates), access, curricula, degrees, (academic) staff appointments, employment conditions; owns physical assets; and prescribes in detail how public funds are to be spent (line item budgeting).

Simultaneously, in these continental European systems the strong and centralized powers of the government typically go together with a strong authority at the level of the senior chaired professors. These chair-holders are able to exercise strong collegial control within the faculties and the institutions. We will discuss this institutional feature in more detail later (as part of our analytical framework). In terms of the different decision-making levels in the systems, the traditional continental model is characterized by a strong top (the state), a weak middle level (the institutional administration) and a strong bottom (the senior chair-holders) (Clark, 1983a, p. 127; Glenny, 1979).

The general governance model of self-regulation is linked to the state supervisory model that has its roots both in the United States and the traditional British higher education system. The American and British models show far less governmental influence on higher education than the continental model (Clark, 1983a). The government sees itself as a supervisor, steering from a distance and using 'broad terms' of regulation. It stimulates the self-regulating capabilities of the higher education institutions. In this traditional model, British universities are chartered corporations, responsible for their own management. Each individual university and college is allowed to decide upon its admission, its curricula and the hiring of its faculty. The American institutions also are established as chartered corporations, but the boards of trustees and the institutional administrators (presidents) play a more important role than their British colleagues traditionally did.

During the last decades, several governance reforms have taken place in higher education systems (for governance reforms in Europe, see De Boer et al., 2010). The transformations worked out differently for the traditional modes of governance (Kehm and Lanzendorf, 2006; De Boer, Enders and Schimank, 2008). In general, one can observe that the traditional British state supervising model has moved towards a 'non-British' state control model, whereas in many continental systems a shift from state control to state supervision has become visible (De Boer et al., 2008, 2012; Neave and van Vught, 1991). In continental Europe, the government's role has become evaluative rather than directive (Neave, 1988). In the United States, the government's authority in general has been growing, but this increase of government authority is moving towards 'adaptations of market control mechanisms' such as outcomes assessment legislation and performance-based funding (Dill, 1992, pp. 53–54).

The government's tool kit

A widely used definition of a public policy instrument is a means, tool or technique by which a government wields its power in attempting to ensure support or effect, or prevent, social change (Vedung, 1998, p. 21). Governing means using policy instruments; without them public policies would be no more than abstract ideals or fantasies (Hood and Margetts, 2007). Hence, studying policy instruments is one of the core businesses of public policy analysis, which has resulted in an extended body of literature (for an overview, see Schram (2005)). In the 1950s and 1960s, important theoretical concepts have been developed in the classical publications of Dahl and Lindblom (1976) and Etzioni (1968). During the last three decades, new (political) ideologies (stressing neoliberal values), new modes of governance ('reinventing government') and new technologies have contributed to the continuous (scholarly) interest in the study of policy instruments (Hood, 2007).

Over the last three decades, many different views on and definitions of policy instruments have been developed (see Table 3.1). Three general approaches on classifying policy instruments can be distinguished (Craft, 2011; Hood, 2007; Hood and Margetts, 2007).[3] The first one, *the institutions-as-tools approach*, identifies different specific forms of organization through which public policy is conducted (Lascoumes and le Galès, 2007; Salamon, 2000). The second one, *the politics-of-instrument-choice approach* is focused on the politics that lie behind the selection of whatever tools governments use (Howlett, 2009; Linder and Peters, 1998). It deals with the ideologies, politics and cognitive frames that, in pursuing policy objectives, lead to one kind of instrument rather than another; in this sense it explores the linkages between instrument choice and societal problems. The third approach, *the generic institution-free approach* focuses on cataloguing the government's toolkit, asking what government does. This latter contains the work of Elmore (1987) who sees government instruments as variants of four intervention strategies, namely comprising mandates, inducements, capacity-building and system-changing. Also Schneider and Ingram's classification (1990, 1997) belong to this third approach. They distinguish authority tools, incentive tools, capacity tools, symbolic and hortatory tools, and learning tools. A third widely used classification within the generic approach is

Table 3.1   Selective overview of 'policy instrument classification studies'

Dahl and Linblom (1953)	Price system (control of and by leaders), hierarchy (control by leaders), polyarchy (control of leaders) and bargaining (control among leaders)
Etzioni (1968)	Coercive, utilitarian and normative relationships
Lindblom (1977)	Coercion, persuasion and transactions (exchange)
Bardach (1979)	Prescription, enabling, positive incentives and deterrence
Mitnick (1980)	Regulation by directives and regulation by incentives
Hood (1983); Hood and Margetts (2007)	Nodality, authority, treasure and organization
Elmore (1987); McDonnell (1988)	Mandates (providing constraining rules), inducements (providing financial resources to encourage certain activities), capacity (providing financial resources to enable actors to take certain actions) and instruments of system change (that alter the arrangement of agencies in a policy network)
Schneider and Ingram (1990, 1997)	Authority tools, incentive tools, capacity tools, symbolic and hortatory tools and learning tools
Van der Doelen and Klok (1989); Bemelmans-Videc, Rist and Vedung (1998); Vedung and Van der Doelen (1998)	The legal family, the economic family and the communications family: Carrots, sticks and sermons; further refined by distinguishing stimulating and repressive instruments
Salamon (2000)	Grouping instruments by degree of coerciveness, directedness, automaticity and visibility
Persson (2006)	Command and control, economic instruments, liability and damage compensation, education and information, voluntary approaches, and management and planning

Vedung's distinction between carrots, sticks and sermons (Bemelmans-Videc et al., 1998). Following Hood and Margetts' reasoning (2007), we argue that the three approaches are answers to different questions and largely complement each other. The choice between them depends on the research purpose. The third approach – the generic institution-free catalogue approach – fits the purposes of our chapter best and for the remainder of this section we have picked the most well-known classification, expounded in Hood's 1983 classic *The Tools of Government* and its successor *The Tools of Government in the Digital Age* (Hood and Margetts, 2007).

Hood's classification has received many words of praise as well as criticism. One strand of criticism argues that the world, including the world of governance, has drastically changed since 1983, calling for and enabling new policy tools. Following Hood and Margetts (2007, pp. 136–138), we would, however, argue that in essence there is nothing new under the sun, although there is a vast scope for novelty in the use of tools that the government has at its disposal. 'Novelty may mean a combination or mix of instruments different from what existed before. The ingredients are the same but the recipe is different' (Hood and Margetts, 2007, p. 138). New technologies most definitely have affected, and changed, the potential and use of traditional tools of government, particularly the information-gathering tools (the detectors – see below), but the (adapted) generic tools are still in place.

Starting point of Hood's categorization stems from cybernetics stating that any system of control needs detecting and effecting tools. Defecting tools are geared towards information gathering. Effecting tools concern action to shape or change behaviour to pursue the set policy objectives. Next, a government has resources, 'by virtue of being governments, and upon which they can draw for detecting and effecting tools' (Hood and Margetts, 2007, p. 5). These resources are 'nodality', 'authority', 'treasure' and 'organization' – the NATO classification. Each resource can be used as the basis for detecting as well as effecting tools, leading to eight basic kind of tools that a government can employ (see Table 3.2).[4]

The first category of instruments concerns the provision of *information*. From its specific position in society, government has the advantage of being 'a store of information'. Compared with other institutions, governmental agencies often have extra possibilities to develop rather broad, panoramic overviews of societal conditions. Hence, government can use the information it has at its disposal to try to reach its policy objectives.

The second category of policy instruments is formed by the *instruments of authority*. They are intended to command and to forbid, to commend and to permit. Instruments of authority vary depending on the degree of restriction they seek to introduce into the behaviour of the targeted subjects. Least constraining in this sense are certificates and approvals. Certificates are authoritative declarations by government about the properties of a specific individual or object. Approvals are authoritative declarations in a general sense; approvals apply to the world at large or to whomever it may concern. A subcategory of authority instruments are conditionals and enablements. Conditionals are the promises by government to act in a certain way when certain conditions arise. Enablements are the tokens which permit certain activities. Modern governments use a large variety of enablements. Licences, quotas, warrants, coupons, vouchers and permits are all types of enablements. They all allow (but do not compel) the undertaking of certain activities. The instrument of authority which asks for compulsive action is the instrument called constraint. Constraints demand or prohibit certain activities. Constraints can be positive (commanding) and negative (forbidding). In both cases, they imply a compulsory restriction by government of societal behaviour.

Table 3.2 Instruments of government: an overview

Resource	Detecting (Gathering Information)	Effecting (Action to Change or Shape Behaviour)
Nodality	• Unsolicited tenders (spontaneous information-gathering) • Info as by-product • Ear trumpet • Scrutiny of free media • Direct enquiry	• Direct information propagation and asking others to provide information • Bespoke messages (direct notification, unprompted query responses, prompted query responses) • Group-target messages • Broadcast messages (privished messages, packaged self-serve messages, propaganda)
Authority	• Obligation to notify • Returns • Interrogation and inspection	• Directed tokens: certificates • Conditional tokens: bonds, guarantees, contracts • Enablements: licences, warrants, quotas, coupons, vouchers, permits, exemption certificates • Constraints • Group-targeted tokens • Blanketed tokens: standard approval, code of conduct, open compact, open permits, standard constraints
Treasure	• Unsolicited propositions • Advertised rewards and application • Information exchange and propositions	• Customized payments: contracts, grants, loans, transfers • Conduits • Open payments: bounties • 'Bearer-directed' payments
Organization	• Turnstiles and fixed scanners • Mobile and hidden scanners	• Individual treatment: marking, storage and custody, transportation and distribution, processing • Group treatment • At-large treatment (operational activities)

Source: Modified from Hood (1983) and Hood and Margetts (2007).

The third category of policy instruments concerns *the power of treasure*. Treasure is what enables government to buy favours, to court popularity, to hire mercenaries and so on. Government can use its treasure in two main ways. It can exchange it for some good or service or it can give it away (transfer payments without requiring any *quid pro quo*). According to Hood, the two main instruments of the exchange of treasure are contracts and bounties. Contracts are governmental payments made to specific individuals or organizations, under the condition that the recipient supplies a specified product or service. Contracts are payments 'with strings attached'. Like contracts, bounties also are payments made in exchange for some *quid pro quo*, but in this case the individual, group or organization is not specified. A bounty is awarded to anyone who produces the product or service asked for. The two main governmental instruments of the other method of using the power of treasure (the 'give it away' option) are transfers and bearer-directed payments. Transfers are gifts, made to specific individuals or organizations for specific purposes or reasons. Bearer-directed payments also do not involve a clear *quid pro quo*. But, unlike transfers, bearer-directed payments are made to all those who, by some token, are eligible for them.

Hood's fourth category is *organization* (sometimes referred to as 'architecture'). Within this category fall all kinds of operational government activity directly influencing citizens, their property, or their environment. Government can use its own individuals, buildings, equipment and stocks of lands to directly produce certain outcomes or to perform certain tasks. The instruments of organization to a large extent are related to the traditional monopoly on the use of violence and the enforcement of law. As such these instruments tend to be restricted to some specific areas of governmental control. Next to these areas, the instruments of organization are often used for providing collective goods (like defence and dikes).

Hood's classification offers a good overview of the tool kit a government has at its disposal in controlling society. The various instruments differ according to their specific characteristics and may be assumed to show different levels of fit across policy sectors, across time as well as across governance models.

Framework for analysing governance models and policy instruments

Features of higher education institutions

After having presented governance models as well as the government's toolkit, we turn to our key question: Which of the two higher education governance models and which type of tools are best suited for higher education systems? We argue that the governance fit rests on two dimensions: the characteristics of the objects the government wishes to steer (the higher education institutions) and the attributes of the goods delivered in higher education (teaching and research – see the next subsection).

Kerr (1982, p. 152) has pointed out that in a comparative perspective, higher education institutions have hardly changed during the past centuries. This striking permanence has to do with some of the most fundamental characteristics of higher education institutions. As in the past, these institutions can still be seen as a social system in which the handling of knowledge is the most crucial activity. If there is anything fundamental to systems of higher education, it is this handling of knowledge (Clark, 1983a, p. 12). The primacy of the handling of knowledge is related to some other fundamental characteristics of higher education institutions (see also van Vught, 1989b; Gornitzka, 1999; Enders, 2002).

A primary characteristic concerns the authority of the academic professionals. In higher education institutions, many decisions can only be taken by academics because of their expertise regarding the knowledge-based goods and services produced. Highly specialized knowledge on what and how to investigate, and on what and how to teach, come, to a large extent, under the direct supervision of the academics (Clark, 1983b, p. 20). Of course, not all decisions in higher education institutions are taken by professionals. Other stakeholders, both internal (managers, support staff, students) and external (government, funding agencies, evaluating committees, research contractors), take, or influence, decisions as well. Nevertheless, the influence of academics on the decision-making processes in higher education institutions is extensive.

A second important characteristic is that knowledge areas form the basic foci of attention. They are the organizational building blocks of a higher education institution and without some institutionalization of these knowledge areas a higher education institution cannot exist. As the result of that fragmentation is abundant in these organizations. Throughout the organization specialized cells exist which are only loosely coupled (Weick, 1976). The crucial activities take place within these rather autonomous cells. Largely insulated from the rest of the organization, academics use their autonomy and expertise to perform the basic activities of the higher education institution: 'specialized professionals have little need to relate to one another within the local shop ... They can produce on their own ... Producing separately for the most part, the many groups become an extreme case of loosely-linked production' (Clark, 1983b, p. 21). This organizational fragmentation largely explains the substantial adaptability of higher education institutions.

A further fundamental characteristic of higher education institutions is the extreme diffusion of the decision-making power. When the production processes are knowledge-intensive, there is a need to decentralize. When such an organization is also heavily fragmented, decision-making powers will be spread over many units and actors. It is like a federal system, in which 'semi-autonomous departments and schools, chairs and faculties act like small sovereign states as they pursue distinctive self-interests and stand over against the authority of the whole' (Clark, 1983a, pp. 266–267). Typical for many continental and traditional British higher education institutions is that authority has been located at the lower levels of the organization ('bottom heavy'). At the level of the institutional apex authority is rather weak. Institutional managers only have a limited capacity to steer 'their' organization.

Reforms in higher education over the last decades are believed to have changed some of these characteristics. Generally speaking, institutional management has been empowered, among other things, as the result of devolving authorities from the state, with the aim to establish more tightly coupling (e.g. De Boer, Enders and Leisyte, 2007). To what extent this has eroded other characteristics such as the professional autonomy remains unclear, although many voice strongly this being the case (e.g. Rhoades and Slaughter, 1997; Lapworth, 2004; Pechar, 2012; Hyde, Clarke and Drennan, 2013).

Reviewing the fundamental characteristics of higher education institutions, it is clear that these characteristics of the objects the government wants to control, confronts government with some specific challenges. The professional autonomy, the organizational fragmentation and the diffusion of decision-making powers make it difficult to completely control these institutions externally. Higher education institutions remain to be complex associations of largely autonomous cells. They effectively cherish the traditional norms and values of the 'republic of science' (Polanyi, 1962), which enable them to perform their highly professional tasks, although it does not make them immune from attempts to change their behaviour.

The fundamental characteristics of higher education institutions suggest that these institutions can only be externally controlled if the organizational variety is greatly reduced and if the professional autonomy is largely restrained. However, when such an external control is imposed, the professional tasks these institutions perform may be severely damaged. Confronted with detailed regulation and with an extreme restriction of their behaviour, academics may feel the disillusionment of not being able to explore the paths their professional consciousness stimulates them to pursue.

Attributes of teaching and research

The specific attributes of goods and services in higher education form the second dimension in our analytical framework to assess the fit of governance models and policy instruments. Attributes of goods affect the position and interaction among actors, and hence affect the ways of governing. In the economics of information three types of goods are distinguished: search, experience and credence goods (Darby and Karni, 1973; Nelson, 1970, 1974). Goods can be categorized according to their search attributes and the costs connected to these searches. Goods range on a continuum from easy to difficult to evaluate (Howden and Pressey, 2008). Search goods have attributes that allow for full information prior to purchase (e.g. buying a new computer), implying that ex ante assessment is possible. Experience goods have qualities that cannot be determined prior to use (Nelson, 1970) or for which information search is too costly. The value of experience goods can only be judged after consumption (e.g. restaurants, travel) or be based on peers' reviews (second-hand experience).

Experience often still provides ambiguous information, and thus consumers may remain uncertain about product quality even after gaining experience. A third type of good, credence goods, has attributes that cannot be verified even after purchase (Darby and Karni, 1973). They are the most difficult to evaluate, because specialized knowledge is required: even after consumption it is hard to know the quality (e.g. professional services such as accounting). Credence goods are bought at high risk and are sold on a promise. Emons (1997, p. 107) further states that as regards credence goods suppliers not just provide the services but also act as the experts who determine how much service is needed, since the customer is unfamiliar with the intricacies and peculiarities of the service in question.

The distinction in type of good determines, among other things, the position of the client/customer vis-à-vis the provider: 'the impact of the market power of consumers... will operate quite differently for search and experience qualities' (Nelson, 194, p. 730). In the case of experience goods, and even more with credence goods, consumer power is much less potent than with search qualities. Experience and credence goods cause an information asymmetry between provider and customer.[5] For customers the provision of these goods is wrapped in mystery (Darby and Karni, 1973, p. 67). The service provider determines the client's requirements, which implies that its role is essential to customer value creation (e.g. Darby and Karni, 1973; Howden and Pressey, 2008, p. 789). An important condition concerns the frequency of purchase – the distinction between durables and non-durables. Repeated purchases increase customer power. Once-only services shut the door on 'punishing' the supplier for inadequate service delivery directly (of course, in the case of once-only purchases customer complaints may somewhat affect the provider, for instance in its reputation). There is no incentive whatsoever to discipline provider behaviour in such a way that customer instead of provider interests are being served.

Customer 'ignorance', in the sense of not being fully informed ex ante, makes the customer dependent of the service provider. It creates favourable conditions for opportunistic provider behaviour. The service provider has no incentive to provide the correct information about the quality of the product. He may want to tout for customers to have as many customers as possible. The information provided is then primarily meant to serve his interests. Providers may recommend goods that are not (really) necessary (but are beyond costumer's judgement) or may decide not to perform an urgently needed service if other activities are more profitable (e.g. doing more research while teaching is needed).

In the case of experience and credence goods, the chances of clients/customers finding out about such opportunistic behaviour are limited. Obviously there is a need for mechanisms to discipline opportunistic provider behaviour. One option is to separate diagnosis from actual provision (Emons,

1997). Another option is governmental intervention or selecting certain policy tools. Because professional services are often subject to licensing, funding and regulation, the government is theoretically in the position to force suppliers to inform the customer correctly. Thus, intervention is geared towards information asymmetry reduction.

Governance and policy tools fit

The model of rational planning and control is founded on the basic assumption of the rationalistic perspective on decision-making. The model of self-regulation is based on the cybernetic decision-making perspective, aiming to make use of the self-regulatory capacities of decentralized decision-making units. The role of the government clearly varies in the two models.

According to the model of rational planning and control government micromanages public sectors, as sitting on top of a hierarchy. A government judges it to be its prerogative to restrain the behavioural options of other actors to reach national goals. Highly restrictive instruments such as authority (constraints) or rather restrictive instruments of treasure are assumed to be the most effective, expressing the confidence in centralized control.

The model of state control is based on assumptions that are at odds with some of the fundamental characteristics of higher education institutions such as the high level of professional autonomy, the large organizational fragmentation and the large diffusion of the decision-making power. These characteristics contrast with the core features of the state control model. Firm knowledge of, complete control over, and a holistic self-image of higher education institutions are given the institution's fundamental characteristics completely unreal. Moreover, by introducing rigid and detailed procedures of hierarchical control, the government cuts itself off from the possible knowledge advantages of the lower level decision-making units and thereby loses a large potential. As Sowell (1980, pp. 13–14) argues:

> [T]he effectiveness of hierarchical subordination varies with the extent to which the subordinate unit has knowledge advantages over the higher unit. In those cases where the subordinate unit has better information, then in terms of the whole decision-making process the knowledge is one place and the power is another; the quality of decisions suffers as a result. Moreover, subordination itself becomes illusory to the extent that the lower level unit can use its knowledge to evade, counteract, or redirect the thrust of orders from its nominal superiors.

In the governance model of self-regulation, government puts its confidence in the self-regulatory capacities of decentralized units. Governmental activities are mainly limited to gathering information to watch overall system activities and to providing and changing the broad frameworks that enable and stimulate such a system to work effectively. The theoretically relevant instruments are the instruments of information (responses and messages) and the mildly restrictive instruments of authority (certificates and approvals). A special set of instruments may be formed by the indirect instruments of treasure to install mechanisms influencing actors to change their behaviour without reducing their self-regulatory capacities.

Compared to the model of state control, the state supervising model offers a better fit. It addresses these systems by taking the fundamental characteristics of higher education institutions more serious. It leaves sufficient room for the (semi) autonomous professionals and basic units, and it does not try to coordinate the large variety in a higher education system by (a limited set of) strict rules. To stimulate system effectiveness, the state supervising model instead tries to make use of some of these characteristics. By limiting itself to only global forms of steering and by putting its confidence in the self-regulatory capacities of academics and basic units of the higher education institutions, this model has the potential to be an effective paradigm for successful operational policies with respect to higher education (Neave and van Vught, 1991).

Our preliminary conclusion of preferring the state supervision model over the state control model, however, needs reconsideration when we take the second dimension of our framework into account. Well-informed client/customer choice will not easily be realized in higher education and research, because teaching and research are experience or credence goods.[6] Students' and third-party funders' views on quality and price during or after consumption of teaching or research is 'imprecise at best' but usually largely unknown. Higher education institutions by and large determine their client/customer requirements. A substantial information asymmetry exits. In the pure state supervisory model, hardly any incentive exists for higher education institutions to discipline their behaviour according to the client/customer's preferences, because usually teaching and research are once-only services of which quality and price are largely unknown prior to consumption.

Therefore, mechanisms are needed in higher education to discipline potential institutional opportunistic behaviour. As a market engineer, upholder of justice or game designer, the government is positioned to reduce the information asymmetry by selecting tools that increase the customer's ability to judge the services offered. This implies a more active government role than assumed in the purest form of the state supervision model. We see customer protection aiming to repair the information imbalance between provider and client/customer as a government responsibility. Choosing tools to enforce or incentivize higher education institutions to be trustworthy and transparent about their services should be no means imply a return to the state control model (based on our first analytical dimension). We should be careful not to throw the baby out with the bathwater. The state supervision model must be left intact but with a government protecting the client/customer against opportunistic provider behaviour.

We conclude this chapter by shortly addressing two types of instruments that fit the adapted state supervision model. These are mixes of types of Hood's information, authority and treasure instruments, which seem to (slowly) attract more attention in contemporary higher education. The first tool is the use of performance-based contracts, which is a promising medium of interaction: 'The public sector will operate better if contracts are made explicitly, stating what is expected in terms of outputs and how accountability for outcomes can be exercised' (Lane, 2000, p. 193). In an exchange process between government and (individual) higher education institutions, a government attaches conditions to institutional provisions in return to public funding or other facilities (certificates and conditionals in Hood's terminology). Setting minimal quality standards or accountability requirements can be part of such contracts. It provides opportunities to better secure the client/customers position. Next, contracting implies bargaining, reciprocity and mutual consent, which does justice to both the government's responsibility and the characteristics of higher education institutions.

Another set of tools to lessen the information asymmetry between providers and clients/customers are transparency tools such as mapping, scoreboards, league tables, multidimensional ranking, profiling and benchmarking (Burquel and van Vught, 2010; van Vught, 2009; van Vught and Huisman, 2013; van Vught and Westerheijden, 2012; van Vught and Ziegele, 2012). Systematically portraying, presenting and analysing the specific activity profiles of higher education institutions, and their performance can serve as powerful reference points, providing valuable information on teaching, learning and research activities and performance, which further inform clients/customers and thereby strengthen their position. Such transparency tools need government-induced rules, otherwise higher education institutions will exploit their information advantage even further by solely presenting information at their, and not the client/customer's, benefit. New technologies increase the potential of Hood's traditional 'detecting' tools. The digital age offers great chances for government's organizational capacity (Hood and Margetts, 2007). It calls for an active government in a state supervision mode.

Notes

1. There are many definitions of governance. See, for instance, Sowell (1980, p. 145), Rhodes (1997), Pierre and Peters (2000, p. 1), Mayntz (2004, p. 6) or, more specific in higher education, Gallagher (2001, p. 49) or Middlehurst and Teixeira (2012).

2. References of early-day and more recent models are bounded rationality (Simon, 1957); incremental model (Braybrooke and Lindblom, 1963); mixed scanning (Etzioni, 1968); normative optimum model (Dror, 1968); systems model (Jantsch, 1972); transactive model (Friedmann, 1973); communicative model (Van Gunsteren, 1976); hierarchies, markets and networks (Powell, 1990); participatory state model; flexible government model; deregulated government model (Peters, 1996); network governance (Sørensen, 2002); and market-based governance (De Boer and Jongbloed, 2012).
3. In this section, we only present approaches from the general public administration literature (a higher education application can be found in the final section). Such general classifications and approaches also have been widely used in higher education: for example, Maassen and van Vught (1994), van Vught (1995), Dill (1997), Gornitzka (1999), Salmi and Saroyan (2007), Huisman and Pausits (2010), Huisman and Pausits (2010), Capano (2011), Reale and Seeber (2013), Borrás and Edquist (2013), Dill and Beerkens (2013) and Li and Gerstl-Pepin (2014).
4. For reasons of having limited space, we leave aside the interesting discussion about the criteria that underlie Hood's as well as other classifications.
5. An interesting development is the Internet that has great potential to affect the provider-customer relationship (also in higher education) as it in principle lowers the cost of gathering and sharing information and offering new ways to learn about products (Huang, Lurie and Mitra, 2009, p. 55). For reasons of limited space, we leave this development and its potential consequences aside in this chapter.
6. 'The line between experience and credence qualities of a good may not be always sharp' (Darby and Karni, 1973, p. 69), which also is the case in higher education (Franck and Schönfelder, 2000; Howden and Pressey, 2008). Some teaching and research goods are closer to experience goods, others to credence goods.

References

Ashby, W. R. (1956) *An Introduction to Cybernetics* (London: Chapman and Hall).
Bardach, E. (1979) *The Implementation Game* (Cambridge, MA: MIT Press).
Beer, S. (1975) *Platform for Change* (New York: John Wiley).
Bell, S. and A. Hindmoor (2009) *Rethinking Governance. The Centrality of the State in Modern Society* (Cambridge: Cambridge University Press).
Bemelmans-Videc, M. L., Rist, R.C. and E. Vedung (eds) (1998) *Carrots, Sticks and Sermons: Policy Instruments and Their Evaluation* (New Brunswick, NJ: Transaction Publishers).
Borrás, S. and Ch. Edquist (2013) 'The choice of innovation policy instruments', *Technological Forecasting and Social Change*, 80(8), 1513–1522.
Braybrooke, D. and Ch. E. Lindblom (1963) *A Strategy of Decision, Policy Evaluation as a Social Process* (New York: Free Press).
Burquel, N. and F. A. van Vught (2010) 'Benchmarking in European higher education: a step beyond current quality models', *Tertiary Education and Management*, 16(3), 243–255.
Capano, G. (2011) 'Government continues to do its job: a comparative study of governance shifts in the higher education sector', *Public Administration*, 89(4), 1622–1642.
Clark, B. R. (1983a) *The Higher Education System* (Berkeley: University of California Press).
Clark, B. R. (1983b) 'Governing the higher education system', in M. Shattock (ed) *The Structure and Governance of Higher Education* (Guildford: Society for Research into Higher Education).

Craft, J. M. (2011) 'Exploring the use of nodality based information policy tolls by Canadian electoral agencies', *Revue Gouvernance*, winter, 1–18.

Dahl, R. A. and Ch. E. Lindblom (1976) *Politics, Economics and Welfare* (orig. 1953) (Chicago: University of Chicago Press).

Darby, M. R. and E. Karni (1973) 'Free competition and the optimal amount of fraud', *Journal of Law and Economics*, 16, 67–88.

De Boer, H. and B. Jongbloed (2012) 'A cross-national comparison of higher education markets in Western Europe', in A. Curaj, P. Scott, L. Vlasceanu and L. Wilson (eds) *European Higher Education at the Crossroads: Between the Bologna Process and National Reforms* (pp. 553–572) (Dordrecht: Springer).

De Boer, H. F., Enders, J. and U. Schimank (2008) 'Comparing higher education governance systems in four European countries', in N. C. Soguel and P. Jaccard (eds) *Governance and Performance of Education Systems* (pp. 35–54) (Dordrecht: Springer).

De Boer, H., Enders, J., File, J. and B. Jongbloed (2010) *Governance Reform. Progress in Higher Education Reform across Europe. Volume 1: Executive Summary Main Report* (Brussels: European Commission).

De Boer, H., Jongbloed, B., Benneworth, P., Westerheijden, D. and J. File (2012) *Engaging in the Modernisation Agenda for European Higher Education* (Brussels: ESMU).

De Boer, H. F., Enders, J. and L. Leisyte (2007) 'Public sector reform in Dutch higher education: the organizational transformation of the university', *Public Administration*, 85 (1), 27–46.

Dill, D. D. (1992) 'Quality by design: toward a framework for academic quality management', in J. Smart (ed) *Higher Education: Handbook of Theory and Research*, Vol. VIII (New York: Agathon Press).

Dill, D. D. (1997) 'Higher education markets and public policy', *Higher Education Policy*, 10(3–4), 167–185.

Dill, D. D. and M. Beerkens (2013) 'Designing the framework conditions for assuring academic standards: lessons learned about professional, market, and government regulation of academic quality', *Higher Education*, 65(3), 341–357.

Dror, Y. (1968) *Public Policymaking Re-Examined* (San Francisco: Chandler).

Elmore, R. F. (1987) 'Instruments and strategy in public policy', *Policy Studies Review*, 7(1), 174–186.

Emons, W. (1997) 'Credence goods and fraudulent experts', *The RAND Journal of Economics*, 28(1), 107–119.

Enders, J. (2002) *Governing the Academic Commons: About Blurring Boundaries, Blistering Organisations, and Growing Demands* (Inaugural lecture), in CHEPS Inaugurals 2002, (pp. 69–105) (Enschede: University of Twente).

Etzioni, A. (1968) *The Active Society* (New York: Free Press).

Franck, E. P. and B. Schönfelder (2000) 'On the role of competition in higher education – uses and abuses of the economic metaphor', *Schmalenbach Business Review*, 52, 214–237.

Friedmann, J. (1973) *Retracking America, A Theory of Transactive Planning* (New York: Garden City).

Gallagher, M. (2001) 'Modern university governance: a national perspective', in The Australia Institute *The idea of a university*, 49, conference proceedings.

Glenny, L. A. (ed) (1979) *Funding Higher Education: A Six-Nation Analysis* (New York: Praeger).

Gornitzka, Å. (1999) 'Governmental policies and organisational change in higher education', *Higher Education*, 38(1), 5–31.

Hood, Ch. C. and H. Z. Margetts (2007) *The Tools of Government in the Digital Age* (Houndmills: Palgrave Macmillan).

Hood, Ch. (2007) 'Intellectual obsolescence and intellectual makeovers: reflections on the tools of government after two decades', *Governance*, 20(1), 127–144.

Hood, Ch. C. (1983) *The Tools of Government* (London: MacMillan).

Howden, C. and A. D. Pressey (2008) 'Customer value creation in professional service relationships: the case of credence goods', *The Service Industries Journal*, 28(6), 789–812.

Howlett, M. (2009) 'Governance modes, policy regimes and operational plans: A multi-level nested model of policy instrument choice and policy design', *Policy Science*, 42, 73–89.

Huang, P., Lurie, N. H. and S. Mitra (2009) 'Searching for experience on the web: an empirical examination of consumer behaviour for search and experience goods', *Journal for Marketing*, 73, 55–69.

Huisman, J. and A. Pausits (eds) (2010) *Higher Education Management and Development. Compendium for Managers* (Munster: Waxmann Verlag).

Hyde, A., Clarke, M. and J. Drennan (2013) 'The changing role of academics and the rise of managerialism', in B. M. Kehm and U. Teichler (eds) *The Academic Profession in Europe: New Tasks and New Challenges* (The Changing Academy – The Changing Academic Profession in International Comparative Perspective 5) (Dordrecht: Springer Science+Business Media).

Jantsch, E. (1972) *Technological Planning and Social Futures* (London: Cassel/Associated Business Programmes).

Kehm, B. M. and U. Lanzendorf (eds) (2006) *Reforming University Governance. Changing Conditions for Research in Four European Countries* (Bonn: Lemmens).

Kerr, C. (1982) *The Uses of the University*, 3rd edn (Cambridge: Harvard University Press).

Lane, J. E. (2000) *New Public Management* (London/New York: Routledge).

Lapworth, S. (2004) 'Arresting decline in shared governance: towards a flexible model for academic participation', *Higher Education Quarterly*, 58(4), 299–314.

Lascoumes, P. and P. Le Galès (2007) 'Introduction: understanding public policy through its instruments – from the nature of instruments to the sociology of public policy instrumentation', *Governance*, 20(1), 1–21.

Li, Q. and C. Gerstl-Pepin (eds) (2014) *Survival of the Fittest. The Shifting Contours of Higher Education in China and the United States* (Heidelberg/New York/Dordrecht/London: Springer).

Lindblom, Ch. (1977) *Politics and Markets* (New York: Basic Books).

Lindblom, Ch. E. (1959) 'The Science of muddling through', *Public Administration Review*, 19 (2), 79–99.

Lindblom, Ch. E. (1965) *Intelligence of Democracy* (New York: Free Press).

Linder, S. H. and B. G. Peters (1998) 'The study of policy instruments: four schools of thought', in B. G. Peters and F. K. M. Nispen (eds) *Public Policy Instruments. Evaluating the Tools of Public Administration* (pp. 33–45) (Cheltenham: Edward Elgar).

Maassen, P. and F. van Vught (1994) 'Alternative models of governmental steering in higher education: an analysis of steering models and policy-instruments in five countries', *Comparative Policy Studies in Higher Education*, 35–65.

Mayntz, R. (2004) 'Governance im modernen Staat', in A. Benz (ed) *Governance – Regieren in komplexen Regelsystemen. Eine Einführung* (pp. 65–76) (Wiesbaden: Verlag für Sozialwissenschaften).

Mcdonnell, L. (1988) *Policy Design as Instrument Design*, paper presented at the 1988 annual meeting of the American Political Science Association. Washington DC.

Middlehurst, R. and P. N. Teixeira (2012) 'Governance within the EHEA: dynamic trends, common challenges, and national particularities', in A. Curaj, P. Scott, L. Vlasceanu and

L. Wilson (eds) *European Higher Education at the Crossroads: Between the Bologna Process and National Reforms* (pp. 527–552) (Dordrecht: Springer).

Mitnick, B. M. (1980) *The Political Economy of Regulation; Creating, Designing and Removing Regulatory Reforms* (New York: Columbia University Press).

Neave, G. (1988) 'On the cultivation of quality, efficiency and enterprise: an overview of recent trends in higher education in Western Europe, 1986-1988', *European Journal of Education*, 7–23.

Neave, G. and F. A. van Vught (eds) (1991) *Prometheus Bound, the Changing Relationship Between Government and Higher Education in Western Europe* (London: Pergamon).

Nelson, P. (1970) 'Information and consumer behaviour', *Journal of Political Economy*, 78(2), 311–329.

Nelson, P. (1974) 'Advertising as information', *Journal of Political Economy*, 82(4), 729–754.

Pechar, H. (2012) 'The decline of an academic oligarchy. The Bologna process and "Humboldt's last warriors" ', in A. Curaj, P. Scott, L. Vlasceanu and L. Wilson (eds) *European Higher Education at the Crossroads: Between the Bologna Process and National Reforms* (pp. 613–629) (Dordrecht: Springer).

Persson, A. (2006) 'Characterizing the policy instrument mixes for municipal waste in Sweden and England', *European Environment*, 16, 213–231.

Peters, B. G. (1996) *The Future of Governing: Four Emerging Models* (Lawrence: University Press of Kansas).

Pierre, J. and B. G. Peters (2000) *Governance, Politics and the State* (Houndmills Basingstoke: Macmillan Press).

Polanyi, M. (1962) 'The Republic of Science: its political and economic theory', *Minerva*, 1(summer/autumn), 54–73.

Powell, W. W. (1990) 'Neither market nor hierarchy: network forms of organization', *Research in Organizational Behavior*, 12, 295–336.

Reale, E. and M. Seeber (2013) 'Instruments as empirical evidence for the analysis of higher education policies', *Higher Education*, 65(1), 135–151.

Rhoades, G. and S. Slaughter (1997) 'Academic capitalism, managed professionals, and supply-side higher education', *Social Text*, 9–38.

Rhodes, R. A. W. (1997) *Understanding Governance. Policy Networks, Governance, Reflexivity and Accountability* (Buckingham: Open University Press).

Salamon, L. M. (2000) 'The new governance and the tools of public action: an introduction', *Fordham Urban Law Journal*, 28(5), 1611–1674.

Salmi, J. and A. Saroyan (2007) 'League tables as policy instruments: uses and misuses', *Higher Education Management and Policy*, 19(2), 31–67.

Schneider, A. and H. Ingram (1990) 'Behavioral assumptions of policy tools', *Journal of Politics*, 52 (2), 510–530.

Schneider, A. L. and H. M. Ingram (1997) *Policy Design for Democracy* (Lawrence, KS: University Press of Kansas).

Schram, F. (2005) *Het sturen van de samenleving. Mogelijkheden van een beleidsinstrumenten-benadering* (Spoor veranderingsmanagement. B. O. Vlaanderen) (Leuven: Bestuurlijke Organisatie Vlaanderen, 210).

Simon, H. A. (1957) *Administrative Behavior*, 2nd edn (New York: Macmillan).

Sørensen, E. (2002) 'Democratic theory and network governance', *Administrative Theory & Praxis*, 24(4), 693–720.

Sowell, Th. (1980) *Knowledge and Decisions* (New York: Basic Books).

Van der Doelen, F. C. J. and P. J. Klok (1989) 'Beleidsinstrumenten', in A. Hoogerwerf (ed) *Overheidsbeleid* (pp. 73–91) (Alphen aan den Rijn).

Van Gunsteren, H. R. (1976) *The Quest for Control, A Critique of the Rational-Central Rule Approach in Public Affairs* (New York: Wiley).

van Vught, F. A. (1988) 'A new autonomy in European higher education? an exploration and analysis of the strategy of self-regulation in higher education governance', *International Journal of Institutional Management in Higher Education*, 12(1), 16–27.

van Vught, F. A. (ed) (1989a) *Governmental Strategies and Innovation in Higher Education* (Higher education policy series) (London: Jessica Kingsley).

van Vught, F. A. (1989b) 'Creating innovations in higher education', *European Journal of Education*, 24(3), 249–270.

van Vught, F. A. (1992) *Autonomy and Accountability in Government-University Relationships*, paper presented at the World Bank Worldwide Senior Policy Seminar on Improvement and Innovation of Higher Education in Developing Countries. Kuala Lumpur, June 30–July 4.

van Vught, F. A. (1995) Policy models and policy instruments in higher education. The effects of governmental policy-making on the innovative behaviour of higher education institutions. *Vienna, IHS Political Science Series 26*, October 1995.

van Vught, F. A. (ed) (2009) *Mapping the Higher Education Landscape* (Dordrecht: Springer Science + Business Media BV).

van Vught, F. A. and D. F. Westerheijden (2012) 'Transparency, quality and accountability', in F. A. van Vught and F. Ziegele (eds) *Multidimensional Ranking: The Design and Development of U-Multirank* (Dordrecht: Springer Science + Business Media BV).

van Vught, F. A. and F. Ziegele (eds) (2012) *Multidimensional Ranking: The Design and Development of U-Multirank* (Dordrecht: Springer Science + Business Media BV).

van Vught, F. and J. Huisman (2013) 'Institutional profiles: some strategic tools', *Tuning Journal for Higher Education*, 1, 21–36.

Vedung, E. (1998) 'Policy instruments: typologies and theories', in M. Bemelmans-Videc, R. C. Rist and E. Vedung (eds) *Carrots, Sticks, and Sermons: Policy Instruments and Their Evaluation* (pp. 21–58) (New Brunswick, NJ: Transaction Publishers).

Vedung, E. and F. van der Doelen (1998) 'The sermon: information programs in the public policy process – choice, effects, and evaluation', in M. Bemelmans-Videc, R. C. Rist and E. Vedung (eds) *Carrots, Sticks & Sermons: Policy Instruments and Their Evaluation* (pp. 103–128) (New Brunswick, NJ: Transaction Publishers).

Weick, K. F. (1976) 'Educational organizations as loosely Coupled systems', *Administrative Science Quarterly*, 21(1), 1–19.

4
New Public Management in Higher Education

Bruno Broucker and Kurt De Wit

Introduction

During the last decades, all OECD countries have implemented public sector reforms to increase the efficiency and to enhance the effectiveness and performance of public organizations (Pollitt and Bouckaert, 2000). These reforms have also taken place in higher education (HE), more or less to achieve the same objectives (Dobbins, Knill and Vögtle, 2011). The reforms, which OECD countries have been confronted with, have to a large extent been theoretically classified under the concept of New Public Management (NPM), emphasizing the accountability of the public sector and the focus on results (Hood, 1995).

This chapter discusses NPM and investigates its characteristics in HE. It is divided into three sections. First, the concept of NPM and its characteristics are discussed. In the second stage, the implications of NPM in HE are illustrated. Finally, policy developments in HE in a select number of countries will be discussed within the NPM framework. We conclude with a brief overview and evaluation of NPM in HE.

New Public Management: Diversity under the same umbrella

In the late 1970s, financial crises, bureaucracy, the heaviness of administrative procedures and a decreasing level of public trust increased the discontent with the public sector (Pollitt, Van Thiel and Homburg, 2007). Since then, public sector organizations and administrations worldwide have been modernized in order to increase their efficiency and effectiveness, to enhance their performance and to orient their services more to the expectations of their citizens (customers). This discontent has led to the introduction of new, managerialist ideas in the public sector and has been called the New Public Management (Pollitt et al., 2007). The term 'NPM' encompassed various new management styles (Hood, 1995). During the last decades, researchers worldwide have highlighted this trend and have investigated public sector reforms that have been carried out under the impulse of NPM principles. However, NPM is not a straightforward concept.

First, NPM stands for the general idea that private practices, business concepts, techniques and values can improve public sector performance (Hood, 1995). This perspective actually states the superiority of private sector techniques assuming that its implementation in the public sector automatically leads to an improved performance. From the literature, the following list of basic principles of NPM can be derived (Ferlie, Musselin and Andresani, 2008; Gruening, 2001; Osborne, 2006; Pollitt and Bouckaert, 2000): (1) an attention to lesson-drawing from private sector management; (2) the presence of hands-on management and the organizational distance between policy implementation and policy making; (3) entrepreneurial leadership; (4) input and output controls, evaluation and performance management and audit; (5) the disaggregation of public services to their most basic units and a focus on their cost management; (6) the growth of the use of markets, competition and contracts for resource allocation and service delivery within public services; (7) the will to treat service users as customers; and (8) the will to produce smaller, more efficient and result-oriented public sector organizations. During the last decades, many public sector organizations and administrations have been reforming according to (some of) those principles. As such, the basic idea of the reforms was highly comparable, which stresses some kind of uniformity.

Second, NPM stands for not only a 'general belief' and a 'basic idea', but also for the various ways this general belief has been implemented in the concrete. In this sense, NPM is principally an umbrella concept, given the fact that the implementation has taken many forms and has been implemented with various levels of intensity and at different periods (Pollitt and Bouckaert, 2000). This has also been argued by Pollitt et al. (2007, p. 4) who state that within Europe, the implementation of NPM can be likened to a 'chameleon, constantly changing its appearance to blend with the local context'. Even in 1995 it was already assumed that NPM would take numerous shapes within the OECD (Hood, 1995).

Since its emergence, NPM has had its opponents and advocates (Osborne, 2006). Hood (1991) posits that the advocates saw NPM as an answer to the old bureaucracy and as such as the best route to success to modernize the public sector (see also Pollitt and Dan, 2011). The pro-NPM literature assumes that the application of business methods will result in a public sector that is cheaper, more efficient and more responsive to its 'customers' (Pollitt and Dan, 2011). The opponents, states Hood (1991), argue that NPM has been an assault on a valuable public service and is only a vague packet without real content. It has an intra-governmental focus in an increasingly pluralist world (Osborne, 2006) and leads to side-effects such as fragmentation, diminished coordination, lower social cohesion and negative consequences on personnel (Hammerschmid et al., 2013). NPM is suggested to have a limited geographical reach, focusing on Anglo-American, Australasian and (some) Scandinavian arenas (Osborne, 2006). Regarding the impact of NPM, some scholars argue that NPM was a disappointment to governments who implemented NPM reforms: they were confronted with negative experiences with management consultancy, with performance measurement that were reduced to 'happy sheets' or 'tick box exercises' and with private ideas that were misfit to the peculiarities of the public sector (Curry, 2014).

Pitching a side is difficult as empirical evidence regarding the outcomes and effects of NPM are scarce. As Pollitt and Dan (2011, pp. 51–52) state: 'there have been endless publications concerned with NPM-like programmes and techniques. Yet, our solid, scientific knowledge of the general *outcomes* of all this thinking and activity is very limited'. In other words, NPM has to a large extent been investigated in terms of implementation and processes, but not in terms of outcomes. Little is known about whether NPM 'works' and whether it actually results in increased efficiency and lower costs.

This overall scepticism has led to a period of post-NPM paradigms. For instance, the concept of 'whole-of-government' was introduced, emphasizing integration and coordination instead of the economic perspective and the perceived disaggregated effect of NPM reforms (Christensen and Laegreid, 2007). Another example is 'digital era governance', a concept emphasizing the role of IT-centred changes and focusing on reintegration, needs-based holism and digitization, striving to reintegrate functions into the government thereby closely connecting technological, organizational, cultural and social effects (Dunleavy et al., 2005). Another perspective is that of New Public Governance (NPG), wherein public management reforms are perceived as a variety of interactive forms of governing that are less 'centred' and are more based on interactivity, transparency, collaboration and participation between stakeholders and networks. NPG is often used as a new umbrella concept to define the difference between the new and older modes of governing (Osborne, 2006). As an umbrella concept, NPG encompasses a cluster of principles, such as process focus, coordination, participation and co-production (Torfing and Triantafillou, 2014). The three highlighted post-NPM concepts to a high degree emphasize the same elements: more integration, inter-connectedness, and inter-organizational networks. In this way, these newer concepts are a reaction to the economic principles and ideas underlying NPM.

Now that we have defined NPM as a general concept, we can specify in the next paragraph what the characteristics of NPM are when applied to HE.

New Public Management in higher education

Reforming HE

Higher education institutions (HEIs) have during the last decades been subjected to many reforms, encouraged by the emergence of the knowledge society, economic crises, increased competition and demographic evolutions (Dobbins et al., 2011). Within that context, European and other countries have been seeking new ways to steer the HE sector (de Boer and File, 2009). In the context of budgetary restrictions, governments have been reducing their expenditure on HE and have increasingly introduced the market as a new coordination mechanism (Middlehurst and Teixeira, 2012). Other management principles such as liberalization and privatization have also become part of HE governance in many countries (Broucker and De Wit, 2013; de Boer, Enders and Jongbloed, 2009). Generally speaking, one could state that those reform tendencies aimed to increase the efficiency and the effectiveness of the HE sector in the same way governments have tried to do in other public sector organizations and policy domains. As a result, the principles of NPM have to a large extent been introduced in HE in Europe and beyond, be it quite often partially.

As a concept with clear roots in neoliberalism, NPM became a general approach to governance and management in the public sector (Goedegebuure and Hayden, 2007). Through isomorphic processes, NPM also evolved into becoming a transnational myth about what constitutes a rational management structure for HEIs (Kretek, Dragsic and Kehm, 2013). HEIs were from then on considered as organizations, rather than as sui generis collegial structures, with the company as an ideal type leading the direction of governance reforms (Kretek et al., 2013; Tahar and Boutellier, 2013). In other words, reforms based on NPM were introduced to transform a state-dependent organization into a complete organization wherein aspects as identity, hierarchy and rationality were introduced (Brunsson and Sahlin-Andersson, 2000). In this context new university models emerged, such as the entrepreneurial university (Clark, 1998) and the adaptive university (Sporn, 1999). The governance reforms have mostly followed the route laid out by the NPM concept (Bleiklie and Michelsen, 2013; de Boer, Enders and Schimank, 2008).

However, the principles of NPM are not implemented in every HE sector in the same way or to the same degree (Broucker and De Wit, 2013), which is comparable with other sectors that have been subjected to NPM: '[t]here is no predominant model for higher education governance in Europe: diversity remains the hallmark of European higher education' (Eurydice, 2008, p. 104). In other words, the national context is important to understand HE governance in a given system, because 'the same reform repertoire gives birth to interpretations that vary from one country and from one university to the other' (Paradeise, 2012, p. 596). As a result of the path dependency of the implementation of NPM (Dill, 2011), it seems that NPM, also in HE, is an umbrella or chameleon-like concept that can be used for various guises of governance reform. The question then is what characteristics can be identified when NPM is applied in HE?

New Public Management: Characteristics

Several authors have summarized the characteristics NPM would have within HE. Marginson (2009) emphasizes corporatization reform, growth in student fee-charging, an expansion of the role of private institutions, encouragement of commercial business activity in research, the creation of competition for parcels of government-provided resources, and output modelling. The OECD accentuates leadership principles, incentives, and competition between public sector agencies and private entities to enhance the outcomes and cost efficiency of public services (Hénard and Mitterle, 2006). Bleiklie and Michelsen (2013) stress hierarchization (leadership and management), budgetary constraints, the formalization of evaluation, and the increased autonomy for institutions. Ferlie et al. (2008) arrive at a list of ten characteristics, including market-based reforms such as the stimulation of competition for students and funding and the encouragement of private sector providers; the development of real prices for student fees and research contracts; the development of audit and checking systems; and vertical steering with stronger and more overt managerialism.

In sum, NPM in HE contains a wide range of characteristics, which can be classified under four broad areas (see Table 4.1). Although the delineation of these four areas is not clear-cut, they do offer a solid approach to analyse reforms in HE in different contexts.

It is clear that NPM contains a diversity of elements, but in the actual implementation of reforms not every element needs to be implemented to the same extent to be able to call it an NPM reform (de Boer et al., 2008). In the next sections we discuss to what extent the four elements are present in some countries and what this means for HE, since, as Bleiklie already stated in 1998:

> [I]ntroducing these ideas in a public university system should make an apt case for the exploration of the potential and limitations of NPM as a universal approach to management reform. In Higher Education, where institutional autonomy and academic freedom are fundamental values, the compatibility between the rationale of the reform policies and the substantive field in which they are supposed to operate is posed more acutely than in most other policy fields. (p. 299)

An international comparison

In this section we use the fourfold classification to briefly discuss the core NPM elements in five countries representing the different administrative traditions discerned by Bleiklie and Michelsen (2013): England and New Zealand for the Anglo-American tradition, the Netherlands for the Germanic tradition, Portugal for the Napoleonic tradition, and Finland for the Scandinavian tradition. With this selection, we include both early NPM adopters (the Netherlands

Table 4.1 NPM areas in higher education

	Marginson (2009)	Hénard and Mitterle (2006)	Bleiklie and Michelsen (2013)	Ferlie et al. (2008)
Market-based reforms	Role expansion of private institutions; encouragement of commercial activity; competition creation	Competition between public agencies and private entities		Competition for students and funding; market entrance encouragement and failure acceptability
Budgetary reforms	Growth in student fee-charging	Financial incentives	Budgetary constraints	Value for money; real prices development and introduction of higher student fees; hardening of soft budgetary constraints
Autonomy, accountability and performance	Output modelling	Incentives	Formalization of evaluation; more autonomy	Performance measurement and monitoring; audit and checking systems; vertical steering
New management style and new management techniques	Corporatization reform	Leadership principles	Hierarchization	Development of strong executive and managerial roles; reduction in faculty representation; local government influence reduction

and especially England and New Zealand) and latecomers (Portugal, Finland). Where beneficial, we included some information on the United States.

Market-based reforms

Many OECD governments have moved towards increased marketization of the HE sector, in a bid for the enhancement of efficiency and accountability, while reducing the financial burden for the government (Meek and Davies, 2009).

In **Portugal**, throughout the 2000s changes have been framed within NPM (Kauko and Diogo, 2011; Magalhães et al., 2013). Based on OECD recommendations that HEIs should still be supported financially by the government, but should operate within the private sector, the government accorded in 2007 a new legal status to universities, together with a state budget drop urging them to generate more income (Kauko and Diogo, 2011). At the same time, the role of the provision of HE changed: the development of the private sector has been encouraged to cover the capacity lack in HE (Ferlie et al., 2008). This has increased competition between institutions for attracting students (Cardoso, Carvalho and Santiago, 2011). The question remains whether Portugal will evolve towards full liberalization, with, among other things a deregulation of employment conditions for professors and researchers (Kauko and Diogo, 2011). In **England** increasing competitive pressure has been the key change (de Boer, Enders and Schimank, 2008), in the first place between existing HEIs, but also by allowing private providers to become degree-granting institutions. These private activities – sometimes established in partnership with public HEIs – 'blur existing boundaries around the sector with the result that it is both more diverse, more flexible, and in a number of cases, less accountable' (Robertson, 2010, p. 31). The implementation of NPM principles has involved cutting budgets and tightening controls, creating internal competition, and introducing monitoring mechanisms (Shattock, 2008). This scenario was implemented at the system level but had an equivalent impact on the institutional level, leading to an emphasis on the primacy of management over bureaucratic procedures, towards monitoring of performance and auditing quality, and to the establishment of (financial) targets (Shattock, 2008). This is comparable to the **United States** where HE is basically characterized by strong competition to enter the field and between and within universities for students and funding (Ramirez and Christensen, 2013; Slaughter and Cantwell, 2011).

In the **Netherlands**, the concept of 'steering at a distance' was introduced in 1985, meaning that the government only defines the general framework for HE (de Boer, Enders and Schimank, 2008). Incentives-based funding has led to market-type behaviour and a more distinct profiling by the HEIs (ibid.). In other words, HEIs were re-defined as strategic actors that have to take responsibility for 'maintaining quality, providing an adequate range of teaching and research programmes, and ensuring access to higher education' (Maassen, Moen and

Stensaker, 2011, p. 487). In **Finland** universities have traditionally been under strict legal control as they were in fact part of the national administration. However, a new law was drawn up over 2008–2009 introducing an entrepreneurial culture. The main aim was to increase autonomy for universities, 'which will be afforded legal status in their own right, and will have much increased financial freedom' (Aarrevaara, Dobson and Elander, 2009, p. 5).

New Zealand adopted already in the 1980s neoliberalism into its HE. It was argued that differences in the social status of different kinds of institutions was outdated and 'buttressed by funding regimes that awarded universities higher levels of government support' (Strathdee, 2011, p. 28). The guaranteed funding for HEIs was abolished, government funding was made more equal across different kinds of institutions offering similar kinds of training, and a system of tuition fees was introduced (Strathdee, 2011). This led to a quasi-market in HE, but had unintended effects (Strathdee, 2011): many new providers opted to offer degrees in competition with universities, and the cost of provision to the state grew enormously. In reaction, new policies were introduced in 1999. From then on, the government could determine what kind of training and how much of this training can be offered by HE providers; and research funding was concentrated in research intensive institutions (Strathdee, 2011).

Budgetary reforms

Budgetary reforms to steer on performance while granting more autonomy is perceived as a typical NPM tool. In most countries the state remains the main funder, albeit that funding is allocated on both input and output indicators and in competitive ways (Jongbloed, 2008).

Although the recent **Finnish** reforms have turned universities into independent legal entities with more possibilities to seek private funding, the state remains the principal source of income (Aarrevaara et al., 2009; Kauko and Diogo, 2011). Also in **Portugal**, public HE has traditionally relied on state funding, whereas private institutions only can rely on state scholarships for their students (File, 2008). From the mid-1990s onwards, government policies have increased the focus on competition for research funds and have promoted public-private partnerships (Magalhães and Santiago, 2011). Since 2005, the allocation mechanism became progressively based on performance and quality indicators, but due to frequent changes in the criteria, little has changed in terms of the budget each HEI receives (Teixeira, 2010). The competition for funding is, as already highlighted above, very strong in **England**, especially through the Research Assessment Exercise or Research Excellence Framework as it is now called. Introduced in 1986, this research assessment clearly installed competition between institutions (Robertson, 2010). The overall funding system changed even further in 1992 when the polytechnics were relabelled as universities, a decision followed by budget cuts and the increase in tuition fees for students up to 25% of the cost of an average study programme (Robertson, 2010). Finally, in 2012, student fees were increased, capped at GBP 9,000 per year (Eurydice, 2014).

This competitive context for funding can also be seen in the **United States**: while in the 1990s performance funding was popular, it was dropped by several states during the mid-2000s. However, these policies have re-emerged now: Since 2013, 33 governors have committed to pursuing performance funding and results-oriented efforts for HE (Rutherford and Rabovski, 2014). Next to state-funding, colleges and universities have funds from different sources, such as tuition and fee payments, grants, contracts from governments, private gifts and so on (Eckel and King, 2004).

In the **Netherlands**, according to de Boer, Enders and Schimank (2008, p. 44), 'the tools of government increasingly changed from directives to financial incentives', with performance funding and contractual relations between state and HEIs on the rise. Government funding consists of a closed envelope distributed on the basis of performance indicators such as the number of degrees and PhD's awarded, the establishment of research schools, and strategic research funding (de Weert and Boezerooy, 2007).

Given the criticism on neoliberalism in **New Zealand**, in 2002 it was decided that the government only funds providers to deliver HE according to individual 'investment plans' (designed to increase differences between different types of providers and to increase the labour market relevance of the training provided). Investment plans are developed by all providers and set out the areas wherein providers are to offer training and detail the number of state-funded places that can be offered to students in each institution. Besides, to limit the cost of tuition to students, a fee-maxima policy was introduced (Strathdee, 2011). At this point, every university is part-funded (around 50% of total income) by the government (Ministry of Education, 2015).

Autonomy, accountability and performance

HE has, in many countries, shifted from a state control model to a state supervisory model (Meek and Davies, 2009; Neave and van Vught, 1991). This has enlarged the freedom of HEIs, increasing significantly their autonomy, but moderated by accountability (Meek and Davies, 2009).

The **Netherlands** introduced this idea in 1985, when the government declared its 'steering at a distance' policy. This strategy was adopted by law in 1993 implementing a transition from ex ante standards and rules to ex post evaluation, implying accountability and performance. This increased autonomy and accountability, while the government retained strong correctional powers. Both internal and external evaluations of teaching and research are obligatory, and as of 2007 a supervisory board of external stakeholders, appointed by the minister, was installed for each institution (de Boer et al.,

2010). The relationship between HEIs and the government has increasingly become a contractual relationship: HEIs develop strategic plans but within parameters negotiated with the government (de Boer, Enders and Schimank, 2008). This kind of reform is not straightforward for all countries: for instance, in **Finland**, management by results has been implemented to increase the performance of HEIs. According to Kauko and Diogo (2011), this system is opposed, as it has been implemented as in other public sector domains, forced by the Ministry of Finance, and without taking the peculiarities of universities into account. In **England** governmental pressure on HEIs has been intensified, albeit starting from a point where government intervention was very low. The 'British exception' of independence from the state has gradually been over-ruled by state intervention and even implied 'state micro-management on a scale comparable to other European systems' (Shattock, 2008). In the process research funding has become heavily reliant on indicators. Also in teaching and education evaluation indicators have become part and parcel of HE poli-cies, through quality assessment of subjects and institutional audits. The results of these assessments are published and can, as such, lead to reputational conse-quences influencing the level of income (Capano, 2011). In **Portugal** HEIs 'are able to determine their own mission and strategy but within a policy frame-work and set of regulations that constrain their choices, mainly because the public funding has been reduced progressively' (de Boer and File 2009, p. 30). There is state interference in that an accreditation system was put in place for both study programmes and institutions, a minimal number of students for study programmes was introduced, and in the allocation system quality indicators were included (Magalhães and Santiago, 2011). HEIs have also been made more accountable to external stakeholders (see also above): an executive council has been established with almost a third of members being external stakeholders, on top of the verticalization of internal decision-making (Teixeira, 2010).

The changes introduced in **New Zealand** created a new approach to funding and monitoring. As already stated, the government invests in areas of educa-tion that meet its strategic objectives (Freeman, 2014). Institutions must have charters that outline a provider's contribution to HE and to its stakeholders, and that reflect regional variations in the demand for skills. In turn, this feeds into the policies and practices of the universities, which invest in areas that match the priorities established by the government. An important new method which increased HE performance is the publishing since 2008 of the external evalua-tion and review of providers, and which contributed to the government's future funding decisions. As a result this is truly a performance-based funding system (Ministry of Education, 2015). In addition, other performance information (e.g. retention and completion rates) about HE providers was made more widely available to allow students and employers to make informed decisions about education, and to create an incentive for providers to improve performance (Strathdee, 2011).

Some of the above described elements can also be seen in the **United States**: the last few decades policy makers have demanded the universities to account for their performance, and public universities are required to collect, report, and analyse data across a wide range of performance indicators (Rutherford and Rabovsky, 2014).

New management style

The last broad area of NPM relates to the introduction of a new management style, typified by corporatization, verticalization, hierarchization, leadership and the demise of representative governance structures.

Portugal implemented several changes regarding their governmental bodies in HEIs. First, HEIs should be governed by a government-appointed board of trustees (Kauko and Diogo, 2011). Rectors used to be elected by the university assembly but would now be elected by secret ballot by the general council. Second, university senates, formerly the governing body in Portuguese HEIs, lost power and sometimes even disappeared (Kauko and Diogo, 2011). Third, in addition to academic and student representatives, 30% of members of the general council should consist of individuals who do not belong to the institution. Finally, administrative councils have been replaced by management boards with identical responsibilities: administrative, financial and human resources management of the institution (Kauko and Diogo, 2011). In **Finland**, public universities have a board, a rector and a university collegiate body. The highest executive body, the board, would consist of seven to 14 members, of whom at least 40% are external stakeholders. The rector is elected by the board and holds the main executive power. In private institutions, the main organs are the board, the rector and an 'overall multi-member administrative body'. The latter can be compared to the collegiate body of a public university. The rector is elected by the board and has approximately the same executive power as rectors in public universities. One of the most significant changes was the reformulation of the rector's position: while this person used to be elected by the university community, he has now become more or less a CEO responsible to the board (Kauko and Diogo, 2011). Countries like the **Netherlands** also passed new laws and created similar university boards, who would consist, partly or exclusively of non-university members, and were expected 'to play the role of an American board of trustees, while setting priorities, approving budget and validating strategies' (Ferlie et al., 2008, p. 334). In the Netherlands, this had led to centralization of decision-making at the top of HEIs, increased executive leadership and a declining role for collegial bodies (de Boer, Enders and Schimank, 2008; de Boer and File, 2009). In **England**, corporate management was strengthened; at the post-1992 universities' (former polytechnics) managerialism was at the heart of governance reforms, but also later in the pre-1992 universities this seemed to comply best with the exigencies of funding councils (Shattock, 2008). The allocation of resources and the drawing up of quality rankings has increased pressures on academic staff to do more with less (Deem, 2011). There are also internal pressures in the form of 'explicit and overt management of academic staff and their work by academic managers and career administrators' (Deem, 2011, p. 48). In sum, this has resulted in a verticalization of internal decision-making and a weakening of the collegial power of the academic bodies, and externally in more competition and institutional differentiation. Nevertheless, although collegial governance is under threat, it seems that top and middle management have acted in favour of traditional academic values and practices. Managers often are manager-academics pursuing policies in response to external pressures, but with respect for academic traditions (de Boer, Enders and Schimank, 2008) while asserting their 'right to manage' (Deem and Brehony, 2008).

In **New Zealand**, universities are autonomous, meaning that they are independently managed and governed by a council drawn from the community, business, staff and the student body, together with local and central government representatives (Ministry of Education, 2015). As a result, the councils are constituted to represent various interests and to be properly *representative* of the wider community (Edwards, 2000).

In the **United States**, the situation is quite diverse since states are responsible for governing public colleges and universities (Eckel and King, 2004): some institutions have constitutional autonomy, others have elected boards of trustees. In some states, a governing board is appointed by the governor, while in others the state board only plays an advisory function (Eckel and King, 2004). Interesting is that 'the trustees or regents are largely comprised of corporate CEOs and professionals external to academe' (Slaughter and Cantwell, 2011, p. 593).

Overview

Table 4.2 shows a comparative overview of the most important NPM characteristics. The United States is not included, since it has only been introduced in the text as comparative illustration.

Discussion and conclusion

Under the influence of NPM many changes have been introduced in the HE sector in various countries. It was termed 'new' because of this very reason (Gunter and Fitzgerald, 2013). Never before had 'management' so clearly been positioned as an alternative to collegial governance that now was perceived as slow and inefficient. Traditional universities were 'invaded' by managerialism,

Table 4.2 Overview of international comparison

	Market	Budget	Autonomy	Management
England	Increase in internal competition; growth of private initiatives	State budget drop; strong competition for funding	More government interference; use of indicators and quality assessment	Strengthened executive leadership ('managerialism')
Portugal	Increase in internal competition; promotion of private sector	State budget drop; increase in performance- and competition-based funding	Autonomy for HEIs but within a clear set of rules including quality indicators	Strengthened executive leadership (board with external members)
Netherlands	Market-type behaviour by HEIs; institutional profiling	Increase in performance-based funding; contractual relations	'Steering at a distance'; increase in ex post-evaluation and quality assessment	Strengthened executive leadership (decentralization of decision-making)
Finland	HEIs under strict legal control	State as main funder; some private funding possible	Increased autonomy; management by results	Strengthened executive leadership (position of rector, board with external members)
New Zealand	Diminishing marketization; increasing competition	State as main funder; investments plans; fee-maxima policy; performance-based funding	Use of performance information; autonomy but within governments' vision	Independent council representative for the wider community

and NPM was an inspiration to steer the sector differently (Amaral, 2008). We identified four main reform areas in HE: marketization, budgetary reforms, autonomy complemented by accountability and a new management style. When we look at the described developments, a pattern is visible: when reforms are made, they go in the direction that NPM would suggest. This leads to the conclusion that NPM has penetrated HE policy of many Western countries. On this basis, policy makers have looked to the same instruments to implement reforms. In this way, the general thrust of reforms shows similarity across countries: elements of marketization have been introduced; state budgets have been reduced and made competitive; autonomy has been granted but has also been complemented with ex post control; and management structures have been verticalized.

But although an 'NPM pattern' can be discerned in the rationale underlying the 'modernization' of HE, we can at the same time identify substantial differences between the countries with regard to the actual implementation of NPM-based reforms, that is, the timing, their intensity and their content. Governments have implemented a different mix of instruments and have put a different focus on each of the instruments (for instance, giving priority to budgetary reform). In sum, NPM in HE has been and still is a concept underlying HE reforms in many countries, notwithstanding different national contexts and administrative traditions. Even in late-adopting countries such as Portugal and Finland, NPM has a foot in the door. This does not mean, however, that all HE sectors have evolved towards a full NPM model in the actual implementation of reforms, quite on the contrary. Like in other policy domains, NPM has found its way in HE and HEIs, but at a different speed and with varied intensity, and always filtered by the national context. Governments use the 'toolbox' of NPM as they see fit, in the light of policy goals which in many cases include tightening of the governmental budget.

Next to the implementation differences, our country overview resonates with the findings from Pollitt and Dan (2011) that it is not clear what the effects of the reforms have been. Research does not seem to focus a lot on the actual outcomes and effects of NPM implementation. This makes it hard to assess whether NPM reforms have actually led to cost reduction, more efficiency and more responsiveness to society. In contrast, some of the general critiques on NPM clearly hold true for HE: (1) the economic, neoliberal background of NPM is often found unfit for HE; (2) elements of the collegial system still exist in HE; (3) there is resistance both from the HEIs towards the government and within HEIs from academics who do not feel that they have more autonomy and who perceive quality and performance measurement primarily as an administrative burden of tickbox exercises (cf. Fumasoli, Gornitzka and Maassen, 2014); (4) increased autonomy has not led to a retreat of the government; and (5) quality assurance systems were set up as a means of regulating the sector (Jarvis, 2014).

In this way, those NPM developments have not led to less but to a different kind of governmental steering which could be classified under the concept of 'the evaluative state', as referred to by Neave (1998). In other words, government continues to govern (Capano, 2011), albeit in other ways such as digital era governance (Peters, 2013) or network governance (Bleiklie et al., 2011; De Wit, 2010; Ferlie et al., 2008). As a result, we do not have evidence that NPM-inspired reforms have made universities more efficient and effective. For a part, this is due to the fact that research has not focused on the actual outcomes of NPM. But for another part, the reason is that NPM is not a 'package deal' but rather a set of instruments or tools from which policy makers can pick and choose depending on the circumstances (policy goals, political resistance, unintended consequences in the implementation phase, etc.). Because NPM is an umbrella concept, it is useful as a way to describe changes in HE, as we have done in this chapter, but it lacks the conceptual clarity needed to be able to link observed effects directly to the concept and its use in HE policy.

Moreover, the scepticism of post-NPM narratives can also be applied to HE. Although NPM favours hierarchization, it has also led to more horizontal relations within and between markets (Amaral, 2008). Post-NPM narratives point to degrees of integration, inter-connectedness, and inter-organizational networking that cannot be captured by the NPM concept. Some have therefore proclaimed NPM to be dead (Dunleavy et al., 2005, cited in Gunter and Fitzgerald, 2013). This, however, seems to be a claim that comes too early (Gunter and Fitzgerald, 2013): as a concept NPM is still pervasive. It can be seen as an ideal type that is for the moment here to stay, just as collegial governance has not been completely uprooted by NPM but has to an extent kept its place alongside NPM (Goedegebuure and Hayden, 2007). This is also seen in the public sector where traditional bureaucratic culture persists (Wynen and Verhoest, 2013). However, it is no wonder that post-NPM concepts such as New Public Governance are starting to emerge (compare Paradeise et al., 2009). New Zealand, for instance, as a trendsetter outside Europe, is shifting its policy from a neoliberal discourse towards a more controlled market where negotiations and participative decision-making with involvement from societal actors gain more prominence. Another example of counter-developments is the case of tuition fees in Germany: they were introduced in most *Länder* (provinces in Germany) in 2007, but were abolished again in 2014 (Woelert, 2014). It is highly possible that similar 'waves' will be identified in other countries in the near future. As our analysis showed that governments often use instruments, try them and change policies afterwards.

To conclude, for HE research, the challenge will be to grasp these and similar contemporary developments in HE that are focused on connectedness, integration and networking. This will very likely lead to the construction of a new ideal-type steering model, that will exist next to NPM or gradually replace the

NPM model. The essence will be, first, to unpack the narrative behind the new concept when it is used in HE as a management ideal, and second, to find consensus on a clear definition of the management tools and instruments that are an inherent part of the new concept, in order to turn the ideal type into a research concept that can be used to not only describe, but to critically analyse and evaluate reforms in HE. Moreover, an important task for HE researchers is not only to focus on the analysis of the developments, but also to pay considerable attention to the effects (positive and negative) of future reforms.

References

Aarrevaara, T., Dobson, I. R. and C. Elander (2009) 'Brave new world: higher education reform in Finland', *Higher Education Management and Policy*, 21(2), 1–18.

Amaral, A. (2008) 'Transforming higher education', in A. Amaral, I. Bleiklie and C. Musselin (eds) *From Governance to Identity. Festschrift for Mary Henkel* (pp. 81–94) (Dordrecht: Springer).

Bleiklie, I. (1998) 'Justifying the evaluative state: new public management ideals in higher education', *European Journal of Education*, 33(3), 299–316.

Bleiklie, I. and S. Michelsen (2013) 'Comparing HE policies in Europe: structures and reform outputs in eight countries', *Higher Education*, 65, 113–133.

Bleiklie, I., Enders, J., Lepori, B. and C. Musselin (2011) 'New public management, network governance and the university as a changing professional organization', in T. Christensen and P. Laegreid (eds) *The Ashgate Research Companion to New Public Management* (pp. 161–176) (Farnham: Ashgate).

Broucker, B. and K. De Wit (2013) 'Liberalisation and privatisation of higher education in Flanders: passing the point of no return? A case study', *European Educational Research Journal*, 12(4), 514–525.

Brunsson, N. and K. Sahlin-Andersson (2000) 'Constructing organisations: the example of public sector reform', *Organization Studies*, 21(4), 721–746.

Capano, G. (2011) 'Government continues to do its job: a comparative study of governance shifts in the higher education sector', *Public Administration*, 89(4), 1622–1642.

Cardoso, S., Carvalho, T. and R. Santiago (2011) 'From students to consumers: reflections on the marketisation of Portuguese higher education', *European Journal of Education*, 46(2), 271–284.

Christensen, T. and P. Laegreid (2007) 'The whole-of-government approach to public sector reform', *Public Administration Review*, 67(6), 1059–1066.

Clark, B. (1998) *Creating Entrepreneurial Universities* (London: Pergamon).

Curry, D. (2014) *Trends for the Future of Public Sector Reform: A Critical Review of Future-Looking Research in Public Administration* (Brussels: European Commission, COCOPS).

de Boer, H. F., Enders, J. and U. Schimank (2008) 'Comparing higher education governance systems in four European countries', in N. C. Soguel and P. Jaccard (eds) *Governance and Performance of Education Systems* (pp. 35–54) (Dordrecht: Springer).

de Boer, H., Enders, J. and B. Jongbloed (2009) 'Market governance in higher education', in B. M. Kehm, J. Huisman and B. Stensaker (eds) *The European Higher Education Area: Perspectives on a Moving Target* (pp. 61–78) (Rotterdam and Taipei: Sense Publishers).

de Boer, H. and J. File (2009) *Higher Education Governance Reforms across Europe* (Brussels: ESMU).

de Boer, H., Jongbloed, B., Enders, J. and J. File (2010) *Progress in Higher Education Reform across Europe. Governance Reform*, Volume 3 (Brussels: European Commission).

de Weert, E. and P. Boezerooy (2007) *Higher Education in the Netherlands. Country Report CHEPS. International Higher Education Monitor* (Enschede: University of Twente, CHEPS).

De Wit, K. (2010) 'The networked university. The structure, culture, and policy of universities in a changing environment', *Tertiary Education and Management*, 16(1), 1–14.

Deem, R. (2011) ' "New managerialism" and higher education: the management of performances and cultures in universities in the United Kingdom', *International Studies in Sociology of Education*, 8(1), 47–70.

Deem, R. and K. J. Brehony (2008) 'Management as ideology: the case of "new managerialism" in higher education', *Oxford Review of Education*, 31(2), 217–235.

Dill, D. D. (2011) *Public Policy Design and University Reform: Insights into Academic Change*. Revised version of a plenary paper presented at the Third International Conference of Réseau d'Etude sur l'Enseignement Supérieur (RESUP), Reforming Higher Education and Research, at Sciences Po, Paris, France, on 27 January 2011, www.unc .edu/~ddill/Paris.pdf, date accessed 27 January 2015.

Dobbins, M., Knill, C. and E. Vögtle (2011) 'An analytical framework for the cross-country comparison of higher education governance', *Higher Education*, 62, 665–683.

Dunleavy, P., Margetts, H., Bastow, S. and J. Tinkler (2005) 'New public management is dead – long live digital-era governance', *Journal of Public Administration, Research and Theory*, 16, 467–494.

Eckel, P. and J. King (2004) *An Overview of Higher Education in the United States: Diversity, Access and Role of the Marketplace* (Washington: American Council on Education).

Edwards, M. (2000) *University Governance: A Mapping and Some Issues*. Paper presented at the Life Long Learning National Conference, https://www.atem.org.au/uploads/ publications/-Governance.pdf, date accessed 27 January 2015.

Eurydice (2008) *Higher Education Governance in Europe: Policies, Structures, Funding and Academic Staff* (Brussels: European Commission, Eurydice).

Eurydice (2014) *National Student Fee and Support Systems in European Higher Education* (Brussels: European Commission, Eurydice).

Ferlie, E., Musselin, C. and G. Andresani (2008) 'The steering of higher education systems – a public management perspective', *Higher Education*, 56(3), 325–348.

File, J. (2008) *Higher Education in Portugal. Country Report CHEPS International Higher Education Monitor* (Enschede: University of Twente, CHEPS).

Freeman, B. (2014) 'Benchmarking Australian and New Zealand university meta-policy in an increasingly regulated tertiary environment', *Journal of Higher Education Policy and Management*, 36(1), 74–87.

Fumasoli, T., Gornitzka, A. and P. Maassen (2014) *University Autonomy and Organizational Change Dynamics. ARENA Working Paper 8* (Oslo: University of Oslo, Arena).

Goedegebuure, L. and M. Hayden (2007) 'Overview: governance in higher education – concepts and issues', *Higher Education Research and Development*, 26(1), 1–11.

Gruening, G. (2001) 'Origin and theoretical basis of new public management', *International Public Management Journal*, 4, 1–25.

Gunter, H. M. and T. Fitzgerald (2013) 'New public management and the modernisation of education systems 1', *Journal of Educational Administration and History*, 45(3), 213–219.

Hammerschmid, G., Van de Walle, S., Oprisor, A. and V. Stimac (2013) *Trends and Impact of Public Administration Reforms in Europe: Views and Experiences from Senior Public Sector Executives. European Policy Brief* (Brussels: European Commission, COCOPS).

Hénard, F. and A. Mitterle (2006) *Governance and Quality Guidelines in Higher Education. A Review on Governance Arrangements and Quality Assurance Guidelines* (Paris: OECD).

Hood, C. (1991) 'A public management for all seasons?', *Public Administration*, 69, 3–19.

Hood, C. (1995) 'The "New Public Management" in the 1980s: variations on a theme', *Acounting and Organisations and Society*, 20(2/3), 93–109.

Jarvis, D. S. L. (2014) 'Regulating higher education: quality assurance and neo-liberal managerailism in higher education', *Policy and Society*, 33(3), 155–166.

Jongbloed, B. (2008) *'Funding Higher Education: A View from Europe'*, paper prepared for the seminar Funding Higher Education: A Comparative Overview organised by the National Trade Confederation of Goods, Services and Tourism (CNC), Brasilia. Retrieved October 13, 2008, from http://www.utwente.nl/bms/cheps/summer_school/Literature/Brazil%20funding%20vs2.pdf, date accessed 27 January 2015.

Kauko, J. and S. Diogo (2011) 'Comparing higher education reforms in Finland and Portugal: different contexts, same solutions?', *Higher Education Management and Policy*, 23(3), 1–20.

Kretek, P. M., Dragsic, Z. and B. M. Kehm (2013) 'Transformation of university governance: on the role of university board members', *Higher Education*, 65, 39–58.

Maassen, P., Moen, E. and B. Stensaker (2011) 'Reforming higher education in the Netherlands and Norway: the role of the state and national modes of governance', *Policy Studies*, 32(5), 479–495.

Magalhães, A. M., Veiga, A., Amaral, A., Sousa, S. and F. Ribeiro (2013) 'Governance of governance in higher education: practices and lessons drawn from the Portuguese case', *Higher Education Quarterly*, 67(3), 295–311.

Magalhães, A. M. and R. Santiago (2011) 'Public management, new governance models and changing environments in Portuguese higher education', in P. N. Teixeira and D. D. Dill (eds) *Public Vices, Private Virtues? Assessing the Effects of Marketization in Higher Education* (pp. 177–192) (Rotterdam and Taipei: Sense).

Marginson, S. (2009) *The Limits of Market Reform in Higher Education,* paper presented at Research Institute for Higher Education (RIHE), Hiroshima University, Japan. Retrieved 17 August 2009, from http://www.cshe.unimelb.edu.au/people/marginson_docs/RIHE_17Aug09_paper.pdf, date accessed 27 January 2015.

Meek, V. and D. Davies (2009) 'Policy dynamics in higher education and research: concepts and observations', in V. Meek, U. Teichler and M. Kaerney (eds) *Higher Education, Research and Innovation: Changing Dynamics* (Kassel: INCHER).

Middlehurst, R. and P. N. Teixeira (2012) 'Governance within the EHEA: dynamic trends, common challenges, and national particularities', in A. Curaj, P. Scott, L. Vlasceanu and L. Wilson (eds) *European Higher Education at the Crossroads. Between the Bologna Process and National Reforms* (pp. 527–551) (Dordrecht: Springer).

Ministry of Education (2015) *New Zealand Education System Overview. University Education,* http://www.minedu.govt.nz/NZEducation/EducationPolicies/InternationalEducation/ForInternationalStudentsAndParents/NZEdOverview/University_Education.aspx, date accessed 8 January 2015.

Neave, G. (1998) 'The evaluative state reconsidered', *European Journal of Education*, 33(3), 265–284.

Neave, G. and F. van Vught (eds) (1991) *Prometheus Bound: The Changing Relationship Between Government and Higher Education in Western Europe* (Oxford: Pergamon Press).

Osborne, S. (2006) 'The new public governance?', *Public Management Review*, 8(3), 377–387.

Paradeise, C. (2012) 'Tools and implementation for a new governance of universities: understanding variability between and within countries', in A. Curaj, P. Scott, L. Vlasceanu and L. Wilson (eds) *European Higher Education at the Crossroads. Between the Bologna Process and National Reforms* (Dordrecht: Springer).

Paradeise, C., Bleiklie, I., Enders, J., Goastellec, G., Michelsen, S., Reale, E. and D. Westerheijden (2009) 'Reform policies and change processes in Europe', in J. Huisman (ed) *International Perspectives on the Governance of Higher Education. Alternative Frameworks for Coordination* (New York and London: Routledge).

Peters, M. A. (2013) 'Managerialism and the neoliberal university: prospects for new forms of "open management"', *Higher Education, Contemporary Readings in Law and Social Justice*, 1, 11–26.

Pollitt, C. and G. Bouckaert (2000) *Public Management Reform: A Comparative Analysis* (Oxford: Oxford University Press).

Pollitt, C. and S. Dan (2011) *The Impact of the New Public Management in Europe: A Meta-Analysis* (Brussels: European Commission, COCOPS).

Pollitt, C., Van Thiel, S. and V. Homburg (2007) 'New public management in Europe', *Management Online Review*, http://www.morexpertise.com/view.php?id=78, date accessed 27 January 2015.

Ramirez, F. and T. Christensen (2013) 'The formalization of the university: rules, roots, and routes', *Higher Education*, 65, 695–708.

Robertson, S. L. (2010) *Globalising UK Higher Education. LLAKES Research Paper 16* (London: Centre for Learning and Life Chances in Knowledge Economies and Societies), http://www.llakes.org/wp-content/uploads/2010/10/Online-Robertson.pdf, date accessed 27 January 2015.

Rutherford, A. and T. Rabovsky (2014) 'Evaluating impacts of performance funding policies on student outcomes in higher education', *The ANNALS of the American Academy of Political and Social Science*, 655(1), 185–208.

Shattock, M. (2008) 'The change from private to public governance of British higher education: its consequences for higher education policy making 1980–2006', *Higher Education Quarterly*, 62(3), 181–203.

Slaughter, S. and B. Cantwell (2011) 'Transatlantic moves to the market: the United States and the European Union', *Higher Education*, 63, 583–606.

Sporn, B. (1999) *Adaptive University Structures: An Analysis of Adaptation to Socioeconomic Environments of US and European Universities* (London: Jessica Kingsley).

Strathdee, R. (2011) 'Educational reform, inequality and the structure of higher education in New Zealand', *Journal of Education and Work*, 24(1–2), 27–48.

Tahar, S. and R. Boutellier (2013) 'Resource allocation in higher education in the context of NPM', *Public Management Review*, 15(5), 687–711.

Teixeira, P. (2010) 'Governance and funding reform in the European higher education area. National system analysis: Portugal', in European Commission (2010) *Progress in Higher Education Reform across Europe. Governance and Funding Reform. Volume 2: Methodology, Performance Data, Literature Survey, National System Analyses and Case Studies* (pp. 487–498) (Brussels: European Commission).

Torfing, J. and P. Triantafillou (2014) 'What's in a name? Grasping new public governance as a political-administrative system', *International Review of Public Administration*, 18(2), 9–25.

Woelert, P. (2014) *'Between "Autonomy and Control": A Comparative Perspective on University governance reforms'*, paper presented at the EAIR 36th Annual Forum in Essen, Germany, 27–30 August 2014. Retrieved January 2015, from http://eairaww.websites.xs4all.nl/forum/essen/PDF/1458.pdf.

Wynen, J. and K. Verhoest (2013) 'Do NPM-type reforms lead to a cultural revolution within public sector organizations?', *Public Management Review*, 8, 1–26.

5
Multi-level Governance in Higher Education Research

Tatiana Fumasoli

Introduction

It is a common understanding that the historical steering function of the nation state has been challenged by other coordination modes. Scholarly debate has highlighted the blurring boundaries of the sovereign state along three dimensions relating to society, sub-national units and international arenas. Such shifts in the tasks of the state have been primarily explained by the retreat of the welfare state, by the increasing relevance of supranational entities such as the European Union (EU) and by globalization forces engendering growing interdependencies out of the control of sovereign states (Hooghe and Marks, 2003; Piattoni, 2010; Scharpf, 1997). Additionally, in order to legitimize policies in democratic settings, states have increasingly involved a growing number of disparate stakeholders in policy processes. This can also be seen in higher education: reforms have granted institutional autonomy to universities, signalling changes in the division of competencies and distribution of responsibilities between governments and higher education institutions; public–private partnerships have been enhanced to increase societal relevance and socio-economic development at both national and regional levels. And the increasing role of Europe – in particular, the construction of the European Research Area and the European Higher Education Area – has added an additional governance level to higher education.

Against this backdrop the concept of multi-level governance (MLG) has been proposed to better understand the complexity of actors and linkages that underlie contemporary polities (Hooghe and Marks, 2001; Piattoni, 2009). The MLG perspective, as initially formulated by Marks (1992, 1993), aims to capture how changes in the political structure in Europe undermine state control over sub-national units as well as over international and supranational institutions – that is, a dispersion of authority away from central government along a vertical dimension. Equally, authority has been diffused along the horizontal dimension between state and society – for example, through public–private cooperation.

Nonetheless the MLG perspective has also several critics (Bache, 2008; Peters and Pierre, 2009). First, for its lack of explanatory power – what hypotheses can be formulated and tested?; second, for its normative stance – MLG is presented as more efficient and democratic than command and control; and third, for assuming that shared participation on decision-making amounts to equal power among actors, particularly in policy implementation. To address some of these criticisms, this chapter proposes an organizational approach to MLG, arguing that the institutional and organized settings in which social and political actors are located constitute an important factor in analysing – and explaining – policy processes (Egeberg, 2004, 2006, 2012; March and Olsen, 1989, 1995). Additionally, when it comes to higher education, contiguous policy sectors like research and innovation have to be taken into consideration to examine broader dynamics of change and stability in the political and social order.

In higher education studies, a multi-level perspective is not new: Clark (1983) distinguishes system (national), enterprise (organizational), professional (academic) and discipline levels and elaborates on integration and disintegration forces at systemic level. However, MLG challenges Clark's vision of higher education as significantly coordinated by national public administration and agencies (Clark, 1983, pp. 119–123). On the one hand, it is clear that, especially in Europe, global and supranational levels have affected national higher education systems significantly (see also Chapter 6 by Van Wageningen). On the other hand, stagnating or shrinking state funding and the assumed link between innovation and regional development have brought to the fore actors such as local public authorities, business and industry, as well as other stakeholders: for example, students. While Clark discusses these developments, he advocates 'entrepreneurial' universities (1998), focusing more on university strategy and management and less on systemic and policy integration. Furthermore, MLG challenges traditional comparative analysis research, based primarily on national systems and higher education institutions (Kosmützky, 2015). An MLG approach calls not only for a broader scope for scrutiny but also for a substantially more fine-grained analysis and research design.

The chapter is organized as follows: the next section discusses MLG according to its main concepts and dimensions. The following section reviews the main applications of MLG in higher education, research and innovation studies. The subsequent section illustrates how an organizational approach contributes to the MLG perspective in higher education studies. The final section presents some avenues for further research.

Concepts and uses of multi-level governance

The term 'multi-level governance' has been coined by Marks (1993, 1996) and subsequently developed by Hooghe and Marks (2001) as a theoretical approach to explain the increasing complexity and interdependency in EU governance. It was deemed to provide new insights into European integration and the innovative characteristics of the European polity beyond supranationalism, that is, integration through a supranational authority, and the so-called 'liberal intergovernmentalist' perspective, which sees the EU as the aggregate of bargaining among states (Wiener and Diez, 2009).

MLG distinctively focuses on actors and disentangles the state in the multitude of subunits, ministries and other agencies participating in policy-making. Hence political actors – and not 'the state' – are the real players in contemporary policy processes (Marks, 1996). Such actors behave according to institutional rules, which define opportunities for action. While this approach goes a step further in disentangling the state and understanding its complexities, it still holds a rationalist premise and considers political actors as interest-oriented, constantly acting according to their agendas, although admittedly constrained by bounded rationality. If political leaders shift responsibilities downwards, upwards or sideways, it is because they decide to focus on other priorities, or they are unable to control dispersal of authority.

In an effort to strengthen the explanatory power of MLG, Hooghe and Marks (2003) have distinguished between Type I and Type II. Type I refers to traditional federalist structures, where multiple layers of authority are nested and membership of the different jurisdictions does not overlap. Type I is generally the outcome of a system-wide architecture and includes only a limited number of levels. In other words, decision-making processes and actors' prerogatives are designed to last. Thus such structures are only subject to (intended) incremental change. Type II, on the other hand, is organized around task-specific jurisdictions, whose number varies over time according to contingent necessities. Membership intersects several jurisdictions, and the overall structure is the outcome of a flexible design. Hence, change in Type II is constant and evolutionary. While Type I is founded around the primacy of the nation state, Type II assumes that the sovereign state constitutes one actor among others.

Scholars hold diverse views on the drivers of Type II. For some, the necessity for flexible governance arrangements and several jurisdictions – instead of one – is both an evolution of modern liberal democracies and a model aimed at efficiency and legitimacy (Scharpf, 1997). For others, Type II is a 'negotiated order' (Peters and Pierre, 2004), signalling the ongoing institutionalization of new decision-making and policy structures. In this respect, the central question relates to the sustainability of MLG and the characteristics of the emerging political system.

While it is recognized the state has lost its monopoly, it is an empirical question how authority has spread among actors across territorial and jurisdictional levels. Building on the concepts of Types I and II, Bache (2008) analyses to what extent participation in the EU drives MLG in contemporary states. He distinguishes further between a rationalist and a sociological understanding: the first perspective focuses on strategic behaviour and power of actors, the second perspective favours learning and socialization processes. Bache also argues that characteristics, positions and resources of the various actors frame their concrete capability to affect policies and proposes a distinction between 'participation' and 'governance'. Many stakeholders might participate in policy processes, but not all are able to exert control on the outputs of such processes and, even more importantly, on policy implementation.

Another contribution to the conceptualization of MLG has been provided by Piattoni (2010), who argues that MLG takes place along three dimensions of state unbundling. First, the centre-periphery dimension: the state shifts authority to subnational state actors, either according to Type I (e.g. granting institutional autonomy to public universities) or to Type II (e.g. incentivising local authorities to participate in university funding). Second, the domestic–international dimension: the sovereign state shifts authority to an international or supranational level (e.g. the role of the Bologna Process in curriculum design and of the European commission in research funding). Third, the state–society dimension: the state shifts authority to societal actors such as economic sectors (e.g. public–private partnerships in research), and professions (e.g. the academic profession decides on career structures, experts participate in committees). While MLG has been studied mainly with respect to public policy, its scope is broader and covers politics and polity (Piattoni, 2010). Hence, analyses should address how actors mobilize across levels and jurisdictions (politics), as well as how institution-building takes place (polity). When it comes to higher education, politics involve the increasingly active participation of interest groups and their lobbying at regional, national and supranational level (e.g. students unions), polity relates to the creation of different agencies and organizations, which deal with specific policy dimensions (e.g. intermediary agencies such as research councils and evaluation agencies).

The MLG model has been debated with respect to efficiency and democracy. In a functionalist perspective, Scharpf (1997) sees the effectiveness of MLG related to its problem-solving capacity under conditions of global economic integration. The latter conflicts with international, national, European politics and policy making, and since global economic forces are stronger, nation states are not able anymore to oversee their boundaries. Hence a less state-centric, more flexible governance system can better grapple with existing (economic) interdependencies and provide a less fragmented framework for policy and politics. In the same vein, also Hooghe and Marks (2001) contend that MLG diffuses authority to the extent that policy coordination costs are reduced to the lowest level. This optimistic view has been criticized for ignoring that policy networks can be either inclusive or exclusive, depending on the social and political structures in which linkages and nodes are embedded (Börzel and Heard-Lauréote, 2009). Peters and Pierre (2009, p. 96; see also Peters, 2002) point to how MLG empowers and shapes regions in the EU differently, and claim that a garbage can logic underpins MLG, where the best organized and resourceful actors dominate the policy process.

Finally, the MLG perspective poses empirical challenges when it comes to research design and operationalization. A key question in this respect is what is meant by 'level'. Type I assumes few embedded territorial jurisdictions, like in the case of the Swiss federal system – municipality, canton, federal level. However, in Type II this definition seems to overlap with the concept of jurisdiction (Piattoni, 2011). In Type II MLG, levels, jurisdictions, policy networks and actors are not only changing according to tasks at hand, but are also framed across territorial levels and, as mentioned previously, have intersecting memberships. Additionally, in an MLG framework informal dimensions might be more relevant than ever in analysing the dynamics in place (Börzel and Heard-Lauréote, 2009).

Multi-level governance in higher education research

In order to illustrate and assess the use of the MLG approach in higher education research, we have conducted a literature review based on a Google Scholar search. Our main objective was to identify publications addressing explicitly MLG theory, that is beyond the simple description of the higher education policy sector as 'multi-level'. We searched for 'multi-level governance' and 'education'. We thought that education was more representative as a policy sector in political science and public administration journals. It also provided us with a broader sample of articles and papers, book chapters and books, from which we could select in a second stage the most relevant works. In this respect, we looked at titles and abstracts of 250 publications listed by Google Scholar according to their relevance. These publications appeared between 1995 and 2014. We then selected those articles that address the concept of MLG in higher education (policy) as a core part of the overall paper. Tables 5.1, 5.2, 5.3 and 5.4 list the selected 25 articles, book chapters and books, which address MLG in higher education (as well as one paper on education), and related fields such as research policy and innovation.

Our literature review shows that most papers address the domestic-international dimension of MLG, while the centre-periphery and state-society dimensions are targeted mostly in political science journals. Also, only a few papers engage with more than one dimension of MLG. Finally, our analysis of extant literature indicates that traditional federal states like for instance Belgium, Canada, Germany, Switzerland and the United States (Type I MLG) represent only a small part of sample. The publications focusing on the centre-periphery dimension appear to account more for recent devolution processes, like in the United Kingdom, and address whether and how the state's central capacity for policy formulation has been affected. We have organized our literature review following the three dimensions of MLG elaborated by Piattoni (2010).

Table 5.1 Domestic–international

Author(s), year of publication	Source	Topic/research questions	Type of paper
de Wit, 2003	*Higher Education Policy*	Influence of European policies on national higher education and research	Conceptual
Gornitzka, 2009	Book chapter in Amaral et al.	How the growing European administrative capacity affects national higher education	Empirical (Europe/EU)
Maassen and Musselin, 2009	Book chapter in Amaral et al.	How intergovernmental and supranational dynamics trigger European integration, horizontal and vertical convergence	Conceptual
Pabian, 2009	Book chapter in Amaral et al.	How the Bologna Process has affected the governance of higher education	Empirical (Czech Republic)
Gornitzka, 2010	*European Journal of Education*	How the Bologna Process affects the coordination of policy sectors	Conceptual
Amaral and Veiga, 2012	*Educacao, Sociedade & Culturas*	How the implementation of the Bologna Process and the Lisbon strategy enhance the role of the European Commission	Conceptual
Magalhães et al., 2013	*Higher Education*	The influence of European governance in evaluation and funding policies	Empirical (comparative eight European countries)
Vukasovic and Elken, 2014	Book chapter in Zgaga et al.	The influence of the Bologna Process in the horizontal and vertical convergence of policy processes	Empirical (comparative four European countries)

Table 5.2 Centre–periphery

Author(s), year of publication	Source	Topic	Type of paper
Bache, 2003	*Political Studies*	How central government controls education in a MLG system	Empirical (England)
Crespy, Heraud and Perry, 2007	*Regional Studies*	How competitive science policy enhance local actors in a centralized state	Empirical (France)
Kotschatzky and Henning Kroll, 2007	*Regional Studies*	Division of labour between regional and national authorities in science and innovation	Empirical (Germany)
Lyall, 2007	*Science and Public Policy*	How the prominence of the nation state in regional science and innovation affects policy integration	Empirical (Scotland)
Perry, 2007	*Regional Studies*	How power relations shape MLG systems in science policy	Empirical (England)
Sotarauta and Kautonen, 2007	*Regional Studies*	Co-evolution dynamics of national and local policies of innovation and science in a centralized state	Empirical (Finland)
Jones and Oleksiyenko, 2011	*Higher Education*	The interrelation between national, regional and institutional policy levels in internationalization of research	Empirical (Canada)

Table 5.3 State–society

Author(s), year of publication	Source	Topic	Type of paper
Kickert, 1995	*Governance*	Networked governance discussed in terms of systems and cybernetics approach	Empirical (the Netherlands)
Kuhlmann, 2001	*Research Policy*	Elaboration of scenarios on how European, national, transnational and regional political systems affect the governance of innovation systems	Conceptual
Harloe and Perry, 2004	*International Journal of Urban and Regional Research*	How societal expectations enhance the local and regional role of universities	Conceptual
Ferlie et al., 2008	*Higher Education*	Discussion of networked governance	Conceptual

Table 5.4 More than one MLG dimension

Author(s), year of publication	Source	Topic	Type of paper
Larédo, 2003	*Science and Public Policy*	Discussion of public intervention in national science and technology from a regional and supranational perspective	Conceptual
Kitagawa, 2004	*European Planning Studies*	How networking among institutional, regional and national levels should be strategically designed	Empirical (England)
Enders, 2004	*Higher Education*	Changing relevance of nation state in globalization, internationalization and regionalization	Conceptual
Kaiser and Prange, 2004, 2005	*Journal of European Public Policy; Journal of Public Policy*	How heterogeneity of national research and innovation systems hampers European integration	Empirical (European/EU)
Hedmo and Wedlin, 2008	Book chapter in Mazza et al.	The evolution and integration of governance models in higher education and research at European, national and societal level	Conceptual
Piattoni, 2010	Book chapter in Piattoni	How higher education has changed according to European policies, regional developments and emerging societal actors	Empirical (Europe/EU)

Domestic–international

Some higher education research focuses on supranational governance at European level and accounts for the Bologna Process and Lisbon Strategy as key drivers for change in traditional national steering. Equally globalization, internationalization, regionalization, as well as Europeanization, have been conceptualized and integrated in higher education research, adding a supplementary level of analysis above nation states (de Wit, 2003; Enders, 2004; Ferlie, Musselin and Andresani, 2008; Gornitzka, 2009; Pabian, 2009). Vukasovic and Elken (2014) discuss how the Bologna Process (1999) and the Lisbon Agenda (2000) have challenged the principle of subsidiarity of higher education and examine how the Open Method of Coordination has constituted a new governance mechanism to deal with increasing complexity. The authors explain how an 'additional governance layer has been added' by the Bologna

Process (Vukasovic and Elken, 2014, pp. 6–7). Similarly Amaral and Veiga (2012) illustrate the policy instruments introduced with the Lisbon Agenda and Bologna Process supporting processes of integration and policy making in European higher education. Magalhães and his colleagues (2013) take a critical stance towards MLG and propose a 'European governance' approach to understand how European political processes shape discourses and practices at national level. The authors analyse quality reforms and changes in funding schemes arguing that the EU main objective is policy coordination. To achieve this, the EU legitimizes distinctive policies, which are then (re)formulated and implemented at national and institutional levels. Gornitzka (2009) explains how networking administration represents an alternative to market and hierarchical coordinating models; she draws attention to the fact that networks are shaped by organized arrangements and inhabited by different types of actors. Of these actors, the state remains still preponderant, even with a diminished role. The Open Method of Coordination is characterized as a typical instrument of MLG (Kaiser and Prange, 2004, 2005 for the European Research Area).

Centre–periphery

Scholars of research policy and innovation studies have addressed also the centre-periphery dimension of MLG, focusing on the role of sub-national actors. Crespy, Heraud and Perry (2007) illustrate how the empowerment of regional actors in research policy has questioned the principle of equality of territories in traditionally unitary and highly centralized France. Sotarauta and Kautonen (2007) account for how the Finnish centralized system of research and innovation has developed MLG features: city-regions have increasingly shaped regional innovation policies along with the state. In their opinion, the co-evolution of local and national dynamics of innovation policies has eventually boosted performance of the Finnish system. In a similar vein, Kitagawa (2004) contends that policy makers and institutional leaders have to take into consideration the interactions between public policy and institutional behaviour in the new MLG landscape. The author argues that networking between universities and regional authorities should be organized strategically, reflecting both policy and organizational objectives. Such learning processes are important not only for regional development and resource acquisition by universities, but more in general for innovation policy and the socioeconomic development of society.

Lyall (2007) highlights how science and innovation in Scotland remains fragmented due to the predominance and gate-keeping role of the public sector in the United Kingdom. In spite of devolution reforms (i.e. Type I MLG), the capacity of the central state persists and remains pervasive. Similarly, Perry (2007) focuses on the path-dependency ensuing from previous policy paradigms, which, in spite of an emerging MLG framework, constrains the development of science policy in Scotland, in particular when it comes to partnerships between science and industry. Jones and Oleksiyenko (2011) combine Clark's levels of authority (1983) with global, national and local levels (referring to Marginson and Rhoades, 2002) and show their complex interconnections in a non-European setting (for education policy in the United States, see also Hirschland and Steinmo, 2003). In their view, on the one hand, decentralization of policy-making induces strategic ambitions not followed by implementation, on the other hand a more trial and error/evolutionary approach triggers incremental change.

State–society

While publications on MLG started to appear at the beginning of the 2000s, Kickert already in 1995 reflects on the changes in state steering of higher education in the Netherlands and points to the increasing number of state and non-state actors in the national context. In the same vein, besides the challenges posed by enhanced institutional autonomy of higher education institutions, other issues are highlighted such as the divide between public and private missions of universities, the role of transnational academic elites, the internationalization of financial and human resources, and integration dynamics both across levels and across national and organizational boundaries (Bache, 2003).

Piattoni (2010) illustrates how the MLG framework can explain recent changes in higher education and particularly how European governance has become stratified across policy levels, but also has blurred the divide between politics and society, centre and periphery, and domestic and international. The increasing autonomy of universities, granted across European countries in the last decades, has made them prone to play a more active role in the higher education sector. On the one hand, universities connect with regional authorities, who have themselves acquired a more active role in national and international contexts, on the other hand, universities link directly to the European level by participating in research programmes (e.g. Framework programmes and Horizon, 2020). Similarly, the convergence of academic curricula through the Bologna Process has somewhat decoupled universities from their national higher education system and recoupled them supranationally. At the same time, universities and academics, organized around their status and disciplines, promote interest groups at local, national and European level depending on their objectives (Fligstein, 2008; Piattoni, 2010, p. 173). Finally and importantly, the boundary between the state and society is shifting also when looking at the growing importance of students. This is related not only to the so-called notion of 'student-consumers', who have a say in curricula and teaching, but also to students' organized activities regionally, nationally and internationally. The restructuring of European student associations is an example of the organized capacity of students to advocate their interests in several arenas (Elken and Vukasovic, 2014).

Enders (2004) discusses globalization, internationalization and regionalization in higher education as three distinctive processes. The first leads to increasing economic interdependence and convergence, the second to more intensive cooperation among states and the third – which includes Europeanization – leads to shifts upwards (supranationally), downward (sub-nationally) and to the side (private sector, and de-regulation). As such, Enders discusses, although in different terms than MLG scholars, the blurring boundaries of the sovereign state.

All in all, the theory of MLG is limitedly used in higher education studies: the number of publications is not large and few address all dimensions of MLG. Even more, the MLG explanatory model appears not to be extensively employed. It serves rather as a holistic device to describe sector steering, policies and actors. Implicitly though, scholars tackling Europeanization and globalization processes seem to relate to MLG in order to explain ongoing transformations in higher education, research and innovation, when they refer to growing complexity and the need for coordination. Finally, it appears that the innovative characteristics of MLG, the ambiguous division of labour among overlapping jurisdictions and the shifting policy networks among heterogeneous actors, have not been picked up by higher education scholars.

Elaborating an organizational approach to multi-level governance in higher education

The organizational approach attempts to integrate the theoretical framework provided by MLG with the analysis of relevant actors embedded in institutional and organized settings. Such settings – their structure, identity and centrality – concur in explaining, on the one hand, how MLG comes about and, on the other hand, the implications of MLG for higher education. This means that organizational factors affect how MLG plays out in terms of actors' capacity, actors' linkages, distribution of resources and opportunities, and policy integration.

The organizational approach assumes that actors' behaviour is (partly) affected by their position in organizations. Organizations and organizational sub-units connect with other organizations and organizational sub-units at multiple levels according to their autonomy, their resources, their strategy and environmental conditions (Brunsson and Olsen, 1998; Egeberg, 2012). In some ways, organizations themselves can be understood as networks whose nodes interlink both inside and outside the organizational boundaries (Brunsson and Olsen; 1998; March, 1999). Drawing and expanding on this literature, we elaborate three main indicators to analyse actors' capacity in such configurations.

These indicators are specifically developed for higher education, accordingly they relate to state actors – for example, ministry of education and research councils; public organizations – higher education institutions and public research organizations; other organizations – for example, private universities and firms. Besides collective 'organizational' actors, individual actors and interest groups should be taken into account. Higher education research classically distinguishes between public authorities, higher education institutions, institutional and academic leadership, academics, administrators and students. In the following we present our conceptualization of actors and the notions of organizational structure, membership and centrality.

We assume bounded rationality of actors, who are unable to consider all possible alternatives and their consequences (March and Simon, 1993; Simon, 1965). Second, actors partly pursue a logic of instrumentality, by defining their own interests and trying to achieve them. Third, actors partly follow a logic of appropriateness, whereby they perceive their role as appropriate on moral grounds (March and Olsen, 1989; March and Olsen, 2006). Accordingly, organized settings empower and shape actors' behaviour when they provide them with a framework for simplifying decision-making, when they balance control and reward systems to align their members' interests with organizational strategic objectives (Aldrich and Ruef, 2006). Finally, organizations provide a formal framework in which actors fulfil their own role according to normative frameworks as well as established routines and practices that are taken for granted (March and Olsen, 2006; Scott, 2008).

Organizational structure

A first analytical concept of the organizational approach is the organizational structure in which actors are embedded. The organizational structure is conceived of as a social structure of 'patterns and regularised aspects of the relationships existing among participants in an organisation' (Scott, 2003, p. 18). Depending on the position in the organizational structure actors are endowed with material and symbolic resources, hold formal and informal power (to decide, take action), influence policy formulation and implementation. From their position, actors connect to other actors within and in other organizational structures enacting those configurations captured by MLG. Overall, an organizational structure reflects how hierarchy and authority are designed and dispersed, thus revealing the arrangements shaping possibilities, opportunities and constraints of actors.

Organizational structures can be observed in terms of centralization, formalization and standardization, which indicate the degree of institutional integration. Recent reforms in higher education represent an attempt to strengthen central organizational leadership roles, formalize and standardize procedures and processes within universities (Seeber et al., 2014; Fumasoli, Gornitzka and

Maassen, 2014). This means that professional norms and identities have come under strain: new roles and new configurations of actors have emerged, actors are able to operate at different levels and connect to policy making processes. This concerns, on one side, the rebalancing of autonomy and control between the state and higher education institutions, on the other side, the shifting level of centralization within universities themselves.

In an MLG framework, the influence of different organizational affiliations should be considered. This is particularly relevant in higher education, where actors are located in several settings, for instance an academic is affiliated to his/her higher education institution, other institutes, professional and discipline-based associations and may be member of national and international committees. Depending on the context, these organized settings play a major or minor role in shaping action, from an instrumental, normative and cognitive perspective.

Finally, an organizational structure may be more or less loosely coupled. Loose coupling leads to more idiosyncratic decision processes and thus unexpected results (March and Olsen, 1976). By design, an organized anarchy offers a framework enhancing discovery, in other words, it provides the necessary flexibility for innovation to take place in academia (Whitley, 2012). Key characteristics of such governance processes come close to improvisation and adhocracies (Mintzberg, 1979) where ambiguity and unclear goals lead to learning processes, shifting attention and fluid participation (Cohen and March, 1974).

Membership and identity

The composition of staff within an organization is characterized by entrance requirements and socialization processes, that is, membership criteria. These can be described by type of employment contracts and conditions, career structures and professional training. In other words, organizational boundaries have to be observed in terms of their tightness or looseness (e.g. permanent vs. non-permanent contracts, stricter or broader entrance criteria) to understand how actors are positioned and endowed with resources to pursue their own as well as organizational objectives.

Organizational identity is another indicator of behaviour of organizational, group and individual actors. While leadership quite often designs an organizational identity in line with organizational strategy, members belonging to the academic profession, with their multiple affiliations and loyalties, will comply with organizational identity only to a certain extent (Fumasoli, Pinheiro and Stensaker, 2015). This is the case especially in higher education institutions, where senior academic staff has traditionally governed recruitment and promotion processes, thus affecting substantially the characteristics of the workforce.

Centrality

While often neglected, we contend that a measure of organizational centrality should always be part of the analysis. Where is the organization located along the continuum between centre and periphery? Centre-periphery should be understood in geographical, political, economic and cultural terms. Whether a university is located in a major city, in the capital, in the financial, economic or industrial centre of the country or in a large and historical metropolitan area constitutes an important factor affecting its possibilities to gather material and symbolic resources. Similarly, some have observed that, depending on the level of the MLG structure where they are located, actors have different capacities to operate. This means that not only there are several types of resources, but also that diverse learning processes can be triggered. For these reasons, assuming that MLG provides equal opportunities to all actors to participate and influence policy processes in higher education, is not realistic and differences should be examined carefully (Kaiser and Prange, 2004; Piattoni, 2012; Schout, 2009).

Avenues for further research in higher education using MLG

This chapter has contended that MLG framework is not only relevant for studies of higher education governance and policy, but also offers a conceptual framework that has still to be exploited. The governance of higher education can be analysed distinguishing vertical (supranational and sub-national) and horizontal (societal) coordination. By presenting an organizational approach to MLG, the chapter advocates an emphasis on actors and their organizational embedding. The increasingly complex governance of higher education can be better understood once we analyse more systematically how and why different actors participate and affect policy processes. This seems to be a relevant question, if the number and type of actors is growing along vertical and horizontal lines of policy coordination.

MLG theory has been used to scrutinize the increasing impact of the European level in higher education and research, for instance in relation with converging policies addressing curricula, quality and research funding. However MLG indicates other relevant aspects to investigate: Europe has become also an arena for competition and cooperation, triggering strategic behaviour of an increasing number of actors, such as universities (Fumasoli and Huisman, 2013), but also academics, and students. These actors can now link up to European institutions getting involved in policy formulation and lobbying, participating in research programmes, as well as in various committees, potentially 'bypassing' their national authorities. Empirical research on the implications of such increasingly dense linkages and interdependencies could shed light on the changing dynamics of higher education governance and policy.

Another relevant avenue for future research is a reappraisal of the relationship between the form of the state, its steering mode, and higher education policy and governance (Gornitzka and Maassen, 2000; Jungblut and Vukasovic, 2013). One would expect that centralized states move more slowly towards MLG, for such systems allow for less autonomy of subnational actors, and tend to coordinate higher education policy more tightly in order to foster alignment of national objectives. However, the organizational approach argues that the planning capacity of higher education systems play an important role in the ability to make changes. In the end, size matters and well-integrated national systems could achieve their objectives more homogeneously than relatively fragmented (federal) systems. This research question further relates to the impact on system performance of the different governance modes.

Similarly, societal involvement in higher education policy and governance could be analysed according to the MLG framework and organizational approach. The interconnections between policy makers, higher education institutions and academics, the private sector as well as civil society can be expected to increase, as more and more actors identify opportunities to engage at different levels. This is detectable in the attempts of coordinating higher education, research and innovation, which can be observed both at EU and national level (Maassen and Stensaker, 2011).

An organizational approach to MLG theory in higher education provides the instruments for a fine-grained analysis of complex configurations and networks where the division of labour is unclear or shifting, actors possess different resources and leeway and pursue different objectives, and where idiosyncratic characteristics have to be singled out from relevant features.

References

Aldrich, H. E. and M. Ruef (2006) *Organizations Evolving*, 2nd ed. (London: Sage).

Amaral, A. and A. Veiga (2012) 'The European higher education area. Various perspectives on the complexities of a multi-level governance system', *Educacao, Sociedade & Culturas*, 36, 25–48.

Bache, I. (2003) 'Governing through governance: education policy control under new labour', *Political Studies*, 51(2), 300–314.

Bache, I. (2008) *Europeanization and Multi-Level Governance: Empirical Findings and Conceptual Challenges*, Arena Working Paper 16/08 (Oslo: University of Oslo, ARENA Centre for European Studies).

Börzel, T. A. and K. Heard-Lauréote (2009) 'Networks in EU multi-level governance: concepts and contributions', *Journal of Public Policy*, 29, 135–151.

Brunsson, N. and J. P. Olsen (1998) 'Organization theory: thirty years of dismantling, and then...?' in N. Brunsson and J. P. Olsen (eds) *Organizing Organizations* (pp. 13–43) (Norway: Fagbokforlaget).

Clark, B. (1983) *The Higher Education System: Academic Organization in Cross-National Perspective* (Berkeley, CA: University of California Press).

Clark, B. (1998) *Entrepreneurial Universities: Organizational Pathways of Transformation* (Bingley: Emerald).

Cohen, M. and J. G. March (1974) *Leadership and Ambiguity* (Boston: Harvard Business School Press).

Crespy, C., Heraud, J. A. and B. Perry (2007) 'Multi-level governance, regions and science in France: between competition and equality', *Regional Studies*, 41(8), 1069–1084.

de Wit, K. (2003) 'The consequences of European integration for higher education', *Higher Education Policy*, 16, 161–178.

Egeberg, M. (2004) 'An organizational approach to European integration: outline of a complementary perspective', *European Journal of Political Research*, 43, 199–219.

Egeberg, M. (ed) (2006) *Multilevel Union Administration. The Transformation of Executive Politics in Europe* (Basingstoke: Palgrave MacMillan).

Egeberg, M. (2012) 'How bureaucratic structure matters: an organizational perspective', in G. B. Peters and J. Pierre (eds) *The SAGE Handbook of Public Administration*, 2nd ed. (pp. 157–168) (London: SAGE).

Elken, M. and M. Vukasovic (2014) 'Dynamics of voluntary coordination: actors and networks in the Bologna Process', in M. H. Chou and Å. Gornitzka (eds) *Building the Knowledge Economy in Europe. New Constellations in European Research and Higher Education Governance* (pp. 131–159) (Cheltenham: Edward Elgar).

Enders, J. (2004) 'Higher education, internationalization, and the nation-state: recent developments and challenges to governance theory', *Higher Education*, 47, 361–382.

Ferlie, E., Musselin, C. and G. Andresani (2008) 'The steering of higher education systems: a public management perspective', *Higher Education*, 56, 325–348.

Fligstein, N. (2008) *Euroclash. The EU, European Identity, and the Future of Europe* (Oxford: Oxford University Press).

Fumasoli, T. and J. Huisman (2013) 'Strategic agency and system diversity: conceptualizing institutional positioning in higher education', *Minerva*, 51(2), 155–169.

Fumasoli, T., Pinheiro, R. and B. Stensaker (2015) 'Handling uncertainty of strategic ambitions. The use of organizational identity as a risk-reducing device', *International Journal of Public Administration*, published online 30 July 2015, DOI: 10.1080/01900692.2014.988868.

Fumasoli, T., Gornitzka, A. and P. Maassen (2014). *Institutional Autonomy and Organizational Change*. ARENA Working Paper 08/14 (Oslo: University of Oslo, ARENA Centre for European Studies).

Gornitzka, Å. (2009) 'Networking administration in areas of national sensitivity: the commission and European higher education', in A. Amaral, G. Neave, C. Musselin and P. Maassen (eds) *European Integration and the Governance of Higher Education and Research* (pp. 109–131) (Dordrecht: Springer).

Gornitzka, Å. (2010) 'Bologna in context: a horizontal perspective on the dynamics of governance sites for a Europe of knowledge', *European Journal of Education*, 45(4), 535–548.

Gornitzka, Å. and P. Maassen (2000) 'Hybrid steering approaches with respect to European higher education', *Higher Education Policy*, 13(3), 267–286.

Harloe, M. and B. Perry (2004) 'Universities, localities and regional development: the emergence of the "Mode2" university?', *International Journal of Urban and Regional Research*, 28(1), 212–223.

Hedmo, T. and L. Wedlin (2008) 'New modes of governance: the re-regulation of European higher education and research', in C. Mazza, P. Quattrone and A. Riccaboni (eds) *European Universities in Transition: Issues Models and Cases* (pp. 113–132) (Cheltenham: Edward Elgar).

Hirschland, M. J. and S. Steinmo (2003) 'Correcting the record: understanding the history of federal intervention and failure in securing U.S. educational reform', *Educational Policy*, 17(3), 343–364.

Hooghe, L. and G. Marks (2001) *Multi-level Governance and European Integration* (New York: Rowman and Littlefield).

Hooghe, L. and G. Marks (2003) 'Unraveling the central state, but how? Types of multi-level governance', *American Political Science Review*, 97, 222–243.

Jones, G. A. and A. Oleksiyenko (2011) 'The internationalization of Canadian university research: a global higher education matrix analysis of multi-level governance', *Higher Education*, 61, 41–57.

Jungblut, J. P. W. and M. Vukasovic (2013) 'And now for something completely different? re-examining hybrid steering approaches in higher education', *Higher Education Policy*, 26(4), 447–461.

Larédo, P. (2003) 'Six major challenges facing public intervention in higher education, science, technology and innovation', *Science and Public Policy*, 30(1), 4–12.

Lyall, C. (2007) 'Changing boundaries: the role of policy networks in the multi-level governance of science and innovation in Scotland', *Science and Public Policy*, 34(1), 3–14.

Kaiser, R. and H. Prange (2004) 'Managing diversity in a system of multi-level governance: the open method of co-ordination in innovation policy', *Journal of European Public Policy*, 11(2), 249–266.

Kaiser, R. and H. Prange (2005) 'Missing the Lisbon target? Multi-level innovation and EU policy coordination', *Journal of Public Policy*, 25(2), 241–263.

Kickert, W. (1995) 'Steering at a distance: a new paradigm of public governance in Dutch higher education', *Governance*, 8(1), 135–157.

Kitagawa, F. (2004) 'Universities and regional advantage: higher education and innovation policies in English regions', *European Planning Studies*, 12(6), 835–852.

Kotschatzky, K. and H. Kroll (2007) 'Which side of the coin? The regional governance of science and innovation', *Regional Studies*, 41(8), 1115–1127.

Kosmützky, A. (2015) 'In defense of international comparative studies. On the analytical and explanatory power of the nation-state in international comparative higher education research', *European Journal of Higher Education*, published online 16 March, DOI: 10.1080/21568235.2015.1015107.

Kuhlmann, S. (2001) 'Future governance of innovation policy in Europe – three scenarios', *Research Policy*, 30, 953–976.

Maassen, P. and C. Musselin (2009) 'European integration and the Europeanization of higher education', in A. Amaral, G. Neave, C. Musselin and P. Maassen (eds) *European Integration and the Governance of Higher Education and Research* (pp. 3–14) (Dordrecht: Springer).

Maassen, P. and B. Stensaker (2011) 'The knowledge triangle, European higher education policy logics and policy implications', *Higher Education*, 61(6), 757–769.

Magalhães, A., Veiga, A., Ribeiro, F. M., Sousa, S. and R. Santiago (2013) 'Creating a common grammar for European higher education governance', *Higher Education*, 65, 95–112.

March, J. G. (1999) 'A learning perspective on the network dynamics of institutional integration', in M. Egeberg and P. Lægreid (eds) *Organizing Political Institutions. Essays for Johan P. Olsen* (pp. 129–155) (Oslo: Scandinavian University Press).

March, J. G. and J. P. Olsen (1976) *Ambiguity and Choice in Organizations* (Bergen: Universitetsforlaget).

March, J. G. and J. P. Olsen (1989) *Rediscovering Institutions. The Organizational Basis of Politics* (New York: Collier Macmillan).

March, J. G. and J. P. Olsen (1995) *Democratic Governance* (New York: The Free Press).
March J. G. and Olsen, J. P. (2006) 'The logic of appropriateness', in M. Moran, M. Rein and R. E. Goodin (eds) *The Oxford Handbook of Public Policy* (pp. 689–708) (Oxford: Oxford University Press).
March, J. G. and H. Simon (1993) *Organizations*, 2nd ed. (Oxford: Blackwell Publishers).
Marginson, S. and G. Rhoades (2002) 'Beyond national states, markets and systems of higher education: a glonacal agency heuristics', *Higher Education*, 43(3), 282–309.
Marks, G. (1992) 'Structural policy in the European community', in A. Sbragia (ed) *Euro-Politics. Institutions and Policy Making in the 'New' European Community* (pp. 191–224) (Washington: The Brookings Institution).
Marks, G. (1993) 'Structural policy and multi-level governance in the EC', in A. Cafruny and G. Rosenthal (eds) *The State of the European Community. Vol. 2: The Maastricht Debate and Beyond* (pp. 391–410) (Harlow, Essex: Longman and Boulder: Lynne Rienner).
Marks, G. (1996) 'An actor-centred approach to multi-level governance', *Regional & Federal Studies*, 6(2), 20–38.
Mintzberg, H. (1979) *The Structuring of Organizations* (Englewood Cliffs, NJ: Prentice-Hall).
Pabian, P. (2009) 'Europeanization of higher education governance in the post-communist context: the case of the Czech republic', in A. Amaral, G. Neave, C. Musselin and P. Maassen (eds) *European Integration and the Governance of Higher Education and Research* (pp. 257–278) (Dordrecht: Springer).
Peters, B. G. (2002) *Governance: A Garbage Can Perspective*, Political Science Series 84 (Vienna: Institute for Advanced Studies).
Peters, B. G. and J. Pierre (2004) 'Multi-level governance and democracy: a Faustian bargain?' in I. Bache and M. Flinders (eds) *Multi-level Governance* (pp. 75–89) (Oxford: Oxford University Press).
Peters, B. G. and J. Pierre (2009) 'Governance approaches', in A. Wiener and T. Diez (eds) *European Integration Theory*, 2nd ed. (pp. 91–104) (Oxford: Oxford University Press).
Perry, B. (2007) 'The multi-level governance of science policy in England', *Regional Studies*, 41(8), 1051–1067.
Piattoni, S. (2009) 'Multi-level governance: a historical and conceptual analysis', *European integration*, 31(2), 163–180.
Piattoni, S. (2010) *The Theory of Multi-level Governance. Conceptual, Empirical, and Normative Challenges* (Oxford: Oxford University Press).
Piattoni, S. (2011) 'The problematic coexistence of functional and territorial representation in the EU', *European Integration*, 33(4), 369–384.
Piattoni, S. (2012) 'Multi-level governance and public administration', in G. B. Peters and J. Pierre (eds) *The SAGE Handbook of Public Administration*, 2nd ed. (pp. 764–775) (London: SAGE).
Scharpf, F. W. (1997) 'Introduction: the problem solving capacity of multi-level governance', *Journal of European Public Policy*, 4(4), 520–538.
Scott, W. R. (2008) *Institutions and Organizations. Ideas and Interests* (Thousand Oaks, CA: Sage).
Scott, W. R. (2003) *Organizations: Rational, Natural, and Open Systems,* 5th edn (Pearson Education International).
Schout, A. (2009) 'Organizational learning in the EU's multi-level governance system', *Journal of European Public Policy*, 16(8), 1124–1144.
Seeber, M., Lepori, B., Montauti, M., Enders, J., de Boer, H., Weyer, E., Bleiklie, I., Hope, K., Michelsen, M., Mathisen, G., Frølich, N., Scordato, L., Stensaker, B., Waagene, E., Dragsic, Z., Kretek, P., Krücken, G., Magalhães, A., Ribeiro, F. M., Sousa, S., Veiga, A., Santiago, R., Marini, G. and E. Reale (2014) 'European universities

as complete organizations? Understanding identity, hierarchy and rationality in public organizations', *Public Management Review,* published online 28 July 2014, DOI:10.1080/14719037.2014.943268.

Simon, H. (1965) *Administrative Behavior, A Study of Decision-Making Processes in Administrative Organization,* 2nd ed. (New York: Free Press, London: Collier MacMillan).

Sotarauta, M. and M. Kautonen (2007) 'Co-evolution of the Finnish national and local innovation and science arenas: towards a dynamic understanding of multi-level governance', *Regional Studies*, 41(8), 1085–1098.

Vukasovic, M. and M. Elken (2014) 'Higher education policy dynamics in a multi-level governance context: comparative study of four post-communist countries', in P. Zgaga, U. Teichler and J. Brennan (eds) *The Globalization Challenge for European Higher Education. Convergence and Diversities, Centres and Peripheries* (pp. 261–286) (Frankfurt am Main: Peter Lang).

Whitley, R. (2012) *Institutional Change and Scientific Innovations: The Roles of Protected Space and Flexibility,* paper presented in the 28th EGOS Colloquium (Subtheme 17: Organizing Science: The Increasingly Formal Structuring of Academic Research, Helsinki, Finland, 5–7 July).

Wiener, A. and T. Diez (2009) *European Integration Theory,* 2nd ed. (Oxford: Oxford University Press).

6

The Legal Constitution of Higher Education Policy and Governance of the European Union

Anne C. van Wageningen

Introduction to EU higher education law[1]

Whereas nation states (and possibly regional governments) used to be key in setting the directions for their higher education systems, institutions and sometimes individuals within these institutions, recently – in Europe – a supranational layer of governance has gained prominence. This supranational layer is constituted, first of all, by the Bologna Process, to which 47 states (totalling more than 800 million inhabitants) adhere as members (Garben, 2011), and second, by the European Union (EU) with 28 Member States (totalling more than 500 million inhabitants). Both seem to function independently but interact through the membership of Member States of the EU in the Bologna Process as well. Moreover, the EU itself is a member of the Bologna Process, being represented by the European Commission (henceforth: Commission). Therefore, a complex patchwork of a European-level higher education policy and governance structure seems to emerge. Although both systems have been commented upon thoroughly (see e.g. Amaral et al., 2009; Maassen and Olsen, 2007; Corbett, 2005; De Witte, 1988; Lenaerts, 1994; Shaw, 1992, 1999; Neave, 2001, 2003, 2009), these structures have mainly been commented upon separately. Garben, however, has discussed both systems in an important legal study on harmonising European higher education (Garben, 2011). The aim of this contribution is to expand on the work that has been done so far and to create a deeper understanding of the complexity of supranational governance in Europe. Therefore, this contribution will present a description and analysis of the constitutional and administrative legal framework of the EU higher education system.

For most states in Europe, one of the main public tasks of a state is to guarantee the provision of higher education (Amaral et al., 2009; Council of Europe, declarations on education). Neave (2001, p. 26) describes this connection between universities and the state in a historical perspective, giving a clear idea of the issues at stake for the state:

> The concomitant of the rise of the Nation-State in Europe was the incorporation of the university into the coordinating ambit of the state, both as a symbol and as a repository of national identity, as an instrument for the preservation of the nation's culture and trough the unification of that culture as a manifestation of a country's claim to a place amongst the nations – the cultural equivalent of today's more restricted concern with economic competitiveness.

This 'contract' has changed considerably over the past decades (e.g. Neave, 2009). Severe cutbacks have been forced through, and many argue that students are turning into customers and higher education is changing from a public service to a consumer commodity. However, universities are still strongly embedded in the public domain. For instance, universities in the Netherlands are still established by public law and mainly funded by the public purse (Van Wageningen, 2003). Consequentially, higher education can still be considered an important part of the state's realm. Important parts of higher education are regulated not only by special branches of administrative law, but also by general administrative and constitutional law.

Nevertheless, the European states are not the sole governance actors anymore. To assess the European-level influences, I aim to give an overview of important legal aspects of European higher education law. More specifically, I aim to contribute to the understanding of the supranational constitutional and administrative legal frameworks for higher education in the EU.

Following Van der Hoeven (1989), public law fulfils three functions. First, it sets norms; second, it creates a tool kit for government to steer policy choices; and third, it safeguards against arbitrary ruling. To make sound decisions, public administration needs to have room to manoeuvre to steer and implement political choices. Therefore, useful laws include margins of appreciation or discretion for public administration to be able to fulfil its mandate. Nevertheless, judges will evaluate if these margins have not been trespassed. Especially within a legal framework with a hierarchy of norms, such as the EU–Member State legal nexus, the higher level norm defines part of the subordinate margins. Consequently, I assume that (higher education) law determines the 'margins of appreciation' that are available to develop national higher education policies and governance. It is therefore crucial to comprehend the rules and limits of higher education law to be able to create national higher education policies and to govern higher education.

The EU started in 1958 as an integration project focusing on the internal market. Initially, there was no provision in the Treaty establishing the European

Economic Community (EEC Treaty) for education, except for a single provision for vocational training policy. With the Maastricht Treaty, however, the Member States altered the vocational policy provision and included the current Articles 165 and 166 of the Treaty on the Functioning of the European Union (TFEU). According to these provisions the EU has the possibility to support and to supplement Member States' action in education, while fully respecting their responsibility for the content of teaching and the organisation of education systems and their cultural and linguistic diversity.

For example, the Council mentions the regulation of the mutual recognition of diplomas and the proactive role of the EU in policy-making, for example the Europe 2020 strategy (Council, 2015). However, diploma recognition – at face value a supportive and supplementary action – can have pervasive impacts on national higher education; it can, in the long run, affect quality assurance and requirements for study programme recognition. Also, the Europe 2020 strategy as the direct follow-up of the 2000 Lisbon Strategy can be seen as the Council's attempt to evade the limits of power conferral of the Treaties. The Treaties did not create policy options at the European level for education, research, labour markets and social security. But creating such policy options is exactly what both the Lisbon Strategy (Gornitzka, 2007) and the Europe 2020 strategy (Armstrong, 2010) aim to do, especially for education. For example, the Council concluded on a strategic framework for European cooperation in education and training (Council, ET 2020).

Furthermore, due to the case law of the Court of Justice of the European Union (CJEU), education and the internal market have become intertwined within the Treaty framework. This intertwinement is the result of the CJEU's need to further European integration in establishing a connection between enforceable treaty provisions and education (see section the constitutional dimension). By connecting the internal market to education, the CJEU created possibilities for itself to pass judgement on (higher) education.

Taking all this into account, it can safely be stated that the EU offers more than just a framework of cooperation or exchange of information between Member States. How this has been done is relevant to assess the possibilities and margins of appreciation left to European States to make their own higher education policy and governance choices.

Member States founded the EU. As members they are still considered the masters of the Treaties (Barnard, 2014). Via the representatives at ministerial level, Member States have assured that they jointly (co-)decide over all decisions of the EU. As such the Council is crucial in the Union's decision-making process. However, due to power conferral there are limits to what the EU can do in the field of higher education. Some Member States considered coordinated action in the area of higher education in 1998. This was the start of the Bologna Process, which even if desired, could not be accommodated within the

EU framework. Nevertheless, this process has influenced EU higher education policies in several ways.

In this contribution the Bologna Process is considered as the second strand of Member States' higher education policies within and without the EU framework. The aim of the Bologna Process was to reform national education systems (Corbett, 2005; Neave, 2003). Nowadays, 'Bologna' states are following a convergence strategy, which for EU Member States neatly corresponds to the Lisbon Strategy of 2000, and the current 2020 strategy concerning knowledge, research and development. However, the Bologna Process has no legal status and does not bind its members. It is a process of volunteers within a system lacking the possibilities of law enforcement. The Bologna Process works with ministerial conferences and the Bologna Follow-up Group (BFUG) to safeguard continuity between ministerial meetings. Due to the voluntary character of the process, policy changes that have been agreed on in these meetings are only implemented if states decide to do so. Nevertheless, the Bologna Process has importantly inspired to change national systems of higher education. Furthermore, it has welcomed the Commission as a member. Lacking a legal framework with enforceable rules, this contribution will not expand further on the Bologna Process.

The remainder of the chapter aims to unpack the different roles the European level has played in policy and governance by focusing on the EU constitutional dimension, the institutional legal dimension and some general outcomes for higher education decided by the CJEU. Firstly, the discussion of the constitutional dimension addresses the underpinning for the power conferral of any legal framework. Then, the discussion of the institutional legal dimension zooms in on the key institutional actors in EU law and EU governance, such as the Council, the Commission and the European Parliament (EP). The discussion of the CJEU focuses on the problem that this institution is referee and player at the same time.

The constitutional dimension

Legal boundaries are the result of constitutional arrangements. Constitutions attribute powers and confer these powers to institutions to act accordingly (Kapteyn, 2005). For the EU this is not different. Member States instituted the EU and conferred (a limited set of) powers to it.

Weiler (1991) substantiated the constitutional dimension of EU law.[2] He develops the argument that the CJEU enabled the EU to absorb Member State competences without having the necessary legal powers. He argues:

> [T]he Community's 'operating system' is [...] governed by [...] a specified interstate governmental structure defined by a constitutional charter and

constitutional principles...Legal and constitutional structural change have been crucial, but only in their interaction with the Community political process.

(Weiler, p. 2407)

And he pursues to state the focus of his article:

I shall try to analyze the Community constitutional order with particular regard to its living political matrix; the interactions between norms and norm-making, constitution and institutions, principles and practice, and the Court of Justice and the political organs will lie at the core of this Article.

(Weiler, p. 2409)

Weiler points to the relationship between EU law and policy. Furthermore, he underscores the constitutional dimension of education cases. He does this by commenting on the Casagrande case (1974). The claim in that case had nothing to do with higher education, but with the consequences of the freedom of workers (a key element of the EU law) and the accessory rules on social advantages. In this case in Bavaria, a child of an Italian worker had to pay more for secondary education than his German classmates. This case offered the first opportunity for the CJEU to express itself on educational matters. In paragraph 12 of its ruling the CJEU stated the following:

Although educational and training policy is not as such included in the spheres which the treaty has entrusted to the community institutions, it does not follow that the exercise of powers transferred to the community is in some way limited if it is of such a nature as to affect the measures taken in the execution of a policy such as that of education and training.

For our purpose, the Casagrande case raises the issue of its constitutional impact on Member States. Member States made a case of not giving decision-making power to the European Union institutions (Shaw, 1999). Consequently they deprived the EU from explicit policy and governance tools. The CJEU has circumvented this policy blockade by using other Treaty provisions. In order to circumvent this blockade the CJEU connected education to the four freedoms of the internal market, specifically the freedoms of workers and services, and secondary rights derived from the status of workers. Whenever a limitation of the internal market could possibly occur, the other rule, action or government decision had to give way (Barnard, 2014).

Whereas the CJEU ruling suggests a logical and firm decision, De Witte (1989, p. 72) notes the CJEU itself 'wondered whether the Council by including educational provisions in a regulation implementing the free movement of workers had not overstepped the substantive limits of Community competence'. In addition, Lenaerts observes that the words 'as such' in paragraph 12 forecast more EU influence on higher education. He notes that the concept of 'educational and training policy as such' is not defined. Therefore, '[a]ny reasonable exercise of that power must be tolerated by the Member States, even if it affects aspects of the national educational policy' (Lenaerts, 1994, p. 12).

Key to the Casagrande ruling was Regulation 1612/68. This regulation about the free movement of workers would lay the foundation for EU higher education law. Thereupon, the Member States became fully aware of the possible impact of EU rules on their higher education systems. However, they never stopped the development of further integration of higher education. Thirty years later, they even gave the Commission an important role in the Bologna Process (Corbett, 2005). Moreover, the Council has taken numerous decisions (in)directly concerning higher education.

CJEU jurisprudence inspired Member States to include two articles in the Maastricht Treaty, the wording being actually the same as in Articles 165 and 166 TFEU. Lenaerts noted it was the first time the term 'education' was mentioned in the EC Treaty (1994, p. 7). And Shaw follows up (1999, p. 572):

> The Member States could hardly have written a more trenchant defence of their national sovereignty in this field without an explicit refutation of any Community competence to act at all.

Internal market provisions would inspire the CJEU to rule the majority of cases concerning higher education until the European citizenship provisions of the Maastricht Treaty came into force (Garben, 2011; Van Nuffelen and Cambien, 2009). Henceforth, the internal market connection were loosened and the social welfare aspects of education were strengthened. By then, the EU had a firm influence on higher education in the Member States.

Since the Maastricht Treaty, and the subsequent treaty changes concluded in Amsterdam in 1997, in Nice in 2000, in Lisbon in 2009, and several accession treaties, EU higher education law has developed tremendously. Member States could have decided to stop the development of an EU education policy by changing the Treaty provisions, but they chose not to do so. On the contrary, with most treaty changes or enlargements treaties, they have added possibilities. Furthermore, they have used these possibilities to add or change secondary rules, like directive 2004/38 which absorbed different directives including student directive 93/96. Its goal was to regulate access and residence rights in other Member States than one's state of origin.

Not having legal competences, Member States showed real political and governmental ingenuity. The outstanding example is the Lisbon Strategy of 2000, combining four policy areas in which the EU had no legal competencies. In one phrase the EC stated it wanted Europe to be the most competitive knowledge economy of the world in the year 2010. This strategy connected education, research, labour policies and social policies. Well aware they had no competencies on EU level, Member States developed the open method of coordination (OMC) (Armstrong, 2010). The European Council described the OMC in the Lisbon declaration of 2000 as

> the means of spreading best practice and achieving greater convergence towards the main EU goals.

This method resembles the method used for the Bologna Process (Garben, 2011). According to the European Council, the OMC is designed to help Member States to progressively develop their own policies. It does so by fixing European guidelines, monitored, evaluated and peer reviewed on the basis of quantitative and qualitative indicators and benchmarks, translated into national and regional policies by setting specific targets and adopting measures, taking into account national and regional differences. It was observed that the OMC partly transfers the capacity to govern from the national to the European level (Armstrong, 2010).

In summary, judging by their words, Member States are not keen at all to be affected by EU influence. However, judging by their deeds, Member States actively support the EU to exercise influence. First and foremost, Member States conclude the Treaties and subsequently they enact secondary legislation within the Council. Conversely, Member States have also actively participated in the Bologna Process and Lisbon Strategy and have so given an active role to the Commission (Corbett, 2005). Contrary to explicit Treaty provisions on education, the EU plays an important role in higher education. Therefore, in the following section a description of the institutional framework and of the EU institutional action further clarifies this apparent paradox.

The institutional legal dimension

The EU's operating system is complex (Barnard, 2014). The first subsection therefore presents the EU institutional actors. The second section describes the Treaty framework and some important subsequent rules for higher education.

Presenting the EU institutional actors

Member States have a double role. First, as states they make the treaties. They decide on which policies they want the EU to execute, and they decide upon the precise attached conferral of powers and the limits of powers. Member States entrust the EU with decision-making powers and there is an independent court to enforce that. Furthermore, they have created institutions which need to act within their given prerogatives according to the principle of the conferral of power. Depending on which kind of power needs to be exercised, the EU uses different institutions.

The second role of Member States is within the EU. Their ministers act as members of the Council. Not entirely entrusting the Commission as a key decider in the EU, Member States designed a system in which they have to enact the Commission's legislative propositions. Thus, without the Council's consent no acts are passed. Within that system, the Commission always has the right of initiative. Therefore, the Commission and the Council have to cooperate. The EP was included in that cooperation in the area of education. Since the Amsterdam Treaty, the EP even has the right to veto propositions, and has thus become increasingly important.

The Commission not only proposes new rules, but also ensures the application thereof. It can ask Member States to comply with EU law. If Member States do not comply, the Commission can take action before the CJEU. If the claim is well founded, the CJEU can pass judgement which all parties have to obey. The Commission did so several times against Member States, thus further shaping EU higher education law (Kwikkers and van Wageningen, 2012).

The role of the CJEU is to ensure that 'in the interpretation and application of the Treaties the law is observed' (Article 19 TEU). Due to the CJEU role in legal disputes concerning education, legal scholars have commented extensively on CJEU case law (for instance Dougan, 2005; van der Mei, 2003; Kwikkers and van Wageningen, 2012). It is important to stress that the Court never hesitates to apply a wide interpretation if that is useful for stimulating European integration, thus causing commentaries about its political role (Alter, 1998; Weiler, 1991).

Following Weiler's lead to describe the living political matrix, the legal dynamics of higher education policy and governance will next be addressed, focusing on Member States of the EU, the EU itself, institutional actors such as higher education institutions (HEIs), students, parents, European citizens, who all have to reckon with the constitutional dimensions of EU higher education law. These dimensions give the legal framework, the legal functioning, the legal leeway and limitations, and the legal safeguards of higher education policies and governance.

The Treaty framework and subsequent rules

The direct legal framework consists of the following Treaty articles and their subsequent secondary legislation. This framework depicts the European higher education policy which the Member States wanted the EU to execute.

The initial Article 128 EEC Treaty limited itself to evoking education in terms of vocational training to help contribute to the harmonious development of national economies and of the common market. Currently, the Lisbon Treaty has six treaty provisions explicitly mentioning education or elements thereof

(Articles 6(e), 9, 53, 165, 166 TFEU; Article 14 Charter of Fundamental Rights of the EU), while six other treaty provisions and subsequent secondary legislation indirectly contribute to education, regulating the freedom of movement for workers within the Union, and the right of citizens of the Union and their family members to move and reside freely within the territory of the Member States (Articles 18, 20, 21, 45, 57 TFEU; Regulation 492/2011; Directive 2004/38). Furthermore, diploma recognition is and has been covered by a range of directives.

According to the treaties, for all of its policies and activities the EU strives for a high level of education, training and protection of human health (Article 9 TFEU) and the Member States are determined 'to promote the development of the highest possible level of knowledge for their peoples through a wide access to education' (Preamble TFEU). Article 165 TFEU is clear about the Union's ambitions and methods for education and Article 166 TFEU is equally clear about vocational training. The EU shall aim at developing the European dimension in education, teaching and dissemination of the languages of the Member States, encouraging mobility of students and teachers, encouraging inter alia, the academic recognition of diplomas and periods of study, promoting cooperation between educational establishments, developing exchanges of information and experience on issues common to the education systems of the Member States, encouraging the development of distance education. Moreover the EU shall aim at facilitating adaptation to industrial changes, in particular through vocational training and retraining, improve initial and continuing vocational training in order to facilitate vocational integration and reintegration into the labour market, facilitate access to vocational training and encourage mobility of instructors and trainees and particularly young people, stimulate cooperation on training between educational or training establishments and firms, develop exchanges of information and experience on issues common to the training systems of the Member States. Garben (2011, pp. 143–145) argues that these points of actions all correspond to the Bologna objectives.

However, there are limits, due to the enumeration of competences. According to Article 6(e) TFEU, the 'Union shall have competence to carry out actions to support, coordinate or supplement the actions of the Member States. The areas of such action shall, at European level, be: [...] (e) education, vocational training, youth and sport'. And the first and the fourth paragraphs of Article 165 TFEU impose that trenchant limit:

1. The Union shall contribute to the development of quality education by encouraging cooperation between Member States and, if necessary, by supporting and supplementing their action, while fully respecting the responsibility of the Member States for the content of teaching and the organisation of education systems and their cultural and linguistic diversity.

Furthermore, the EP and the Council 'shall adopt incentive measures, excluding any harmonisation of the laws and regulations of the Member States' (Article 165 TFEU). Incentive measures and recommendations are far from the conferral of powers to change education. These limits are repeated in Article 166 TFEU for the content and the organisation of vocational training.

Conversely, the institutions of the EU used the Treaty provisions concerning the internal market to affect education as well. Article 53 TFEU made it possible to 'issue directives for the mutual recognition of diplomas, certificates and other evidence of formal qualifications and for the coordination of the provisions laid down by law, regulation or administrative action in Member States concerning the taking-up and pursuit of activities as self-employed persons.' More specifically, for the medical and allied and pharmaceutical professions, it could make rules for the progressive abolition of restrictions on the freedom of establishment. However, these rules shall be dependent upon coordination of the conditions for their exercise in the various Member States. Moreover, provisions prohibiting any discrimination on grounds of nationality of other EU nationals (Article 18), European citizenship provisions (Articles 20 and 21 TFEU) and provisions for the freedom of workers (Articles 45 and 46 TFEU) made it possible to enact secondary legislation with due to its impact on higher education.

Secondary legislation is not necessarily solely addressed to aspects of education, but the CJEU derives aspects relevant for education from it. First, Regulation 492/2011 on freedom of movement for workers within the Union – the new codification of regulation 1612/68/EEC – has contributed to developing European higher education law. This Regulation was one of the measures based on Article 46 TFEU. The statement of reasons as well as its title makes it very clear that the objective of this regulation is to ensure the freedom of workers. More specifically, Article 7 regulates the rights of workers being nationals of Member States in the host Member State and Article 10 (formerly Article 12, Regulation 1612/68) regulates the rights of children of workers within the EU. Considering these articles, the CJEU clarified that a worker and his family are entitled to the same educational rights as nationals. Secondly, Directive 2004/38 codified amongst other directives the student directive 93/96 and sets the rules for maintenance and other study grants. It makes it possible to set time constrains before being eligible for maintenance grants (Article 24), as was confirmed in the Förster case. States may impose a maximum period of five years of legal residence for students to be eligible for maintenance grants. Five years of legal residence corresponds with the maximum period a citizen has to reside in the host Member State, before becoming eligible for all social security measures of that state. Third, diploma recognition is regulated in Directive 2005/36 EC on the recognition of professional qualifications.

The CJEU contribution to EU higher education law

In a truly constitutional court system such as the EU, the court ultimately decides. Therefore, the idea of treating the CJEU as a political body makes sense. It is a fact that the CJEU shaped modes of interaction of the Union's political process, using a broad interpretation of the Treaties. The remainder of this section will deal with the CJEU's contribution to the development of higher education law. However, the legal framework depicted in the previous section also limits the CJEU's room to manoeuvre.

To start, the CJEU needed and constructed a connection with the free movement of workers and the free movement of services as part of the internal market. Subsequent legal conflicts would concentrate on the explanation and application of these aspects. In 15 years and six cases, the CJEU handed over to the Member States a rough copy of European Community higher education law, evolving to a more and more precise draft of EU higher education law (in chronological order: Casagrande, 1974; Forcheri, 1983; Gravier, 1985; Blaizot, 1988; Commission v. Belgium, 1988; Erasmus, 1989).

Although it may have looked as if the CJEU had a master plan towards the development of a 'constitution' of EU (higher) education law, this is hardly likely, since two serious constrains are imposed on the CJEU. Firstly, the CJEU is absolutely dependent on the litigant filing complaint as regards to which case to judge. Secondly and consequently, the coherence of the system is not a chronological construction, but bears all elements of a coincidental approach. Nevertheless, after more than 40 years of jurisprudence it is possible to show the CJEU used a focus on citizens' rights and discrimination. To start, Casagrande and the subsequent rulings built on the connection with the four main freedoms of the European Economic Community, which are the freedom of goods, of capital, of services and of labour and secondary rights derived from the status of workers (Regulation 492/2011). Then, since the European citizenship assertion in the Grzelczyk case, the CJEU rested many of its cases on the prohibition of discrimination, the freedom to move and reside freely in another Member State, and the subsequent Directive 2004/38.

Higher education as an accessory right

Accessory rights stem from the idea of the free movement of workers and services, and from the prohibition to discriminate. The CJEU already assessed that in the Casagrande and Forcheri cases. In both cases, the discriminatory treatment affected family members joining the worker in his or her new country of residence. This was different in the Gravier case. Françoise Gravier is a French national who came independently to Belgium to study art. The Belgian authorities charged her an additional fee on top of the fee Belgian nationals have to pay. Refusing to pay this, she was not allowed to continue her studies.

The Belgian court referred the case to the CJEU which dismissed the possibility to charge additional tuition fees for foreigners to enter universities on the grounds that higher education prepared for a profession. So, it used an enforceable internal market provision (freedom of workers) to judge a case of higher education.

This legal dispute was fought chiefly over the assessment of the conferral of power, which in substance meant the CJEU had to let prevail a provision for education or a provision for the internal market. The CJEU concluded that studying strip cartoon art prepares a student for a professional career, and therefore falls within the scope of Article 7 of Regulation 1612/68. The Belgian state and the *Communauté Française* put forward the argument that such a decision would create an imbalance to financing education, which has serious consequences for the national education budget. Therefore, foreign students could not be considered to be discriminated by the obligation of paying an extra fee. In support of the Belgian state, the Danish state and the UK advocated that each Member State may favour its own nationals in the area of education.[3] To the contrary, the Commission argued that a differentiation of student fees does not concern the educational system, but the free movement of persons, especially the free movement of workers, the right of establishment and the freedom to provide services, if a student attends a programme for vocational training. The differentiation of student fees on grounds of nationality therefore amounts to discrimination contrary to the Treaty provisions (Article 18 TFEU).

The CJEU ruled in favour of Gravier. The Member States may have legitimate concerns about the macro effects of access to educational systems, but for the CJEU the macro effects are not the issue; it is about one person seeking to be admitted under the same conditions as all others. It is not about the organisation of a cultural and educational service, but about the possibility of one person to obtain a degree in order to get a job in the future. This case has given the CJEU the possibility to define the term vocational training, to determine its range, and to clarify the limits of European law (van Wageningen, 2005).

With the Blaizot case – again against Belgium – the CJEU extended the definition of 'vocational education' to include university training. It reiterated its Gravier judgement, that vocational training may include an element of general education. It then analysed if university studies by their nature can constitute vocational training or that it is a sheer side effect of university studies to prepare for a qualification for a particular profession. It observed that the Treaty provisions did not exclude the possibility that university education could also be interpreted as vocational training. Furthermore, it observed that in all Member States some university studies provided students, at the academic level, with certain knowledge, training and skills as preparation for specific occupations. Finally, it observed that most Member States signed the European Social Charter, which treats university education as a type of vocational training.[4] It concluded that the exclusion of university training from the definition of the term 'vocational training' would thus result in unequal application of the Treaty in different Member States. It concluded, therefore, that the Treaty provisions are also applicable to university education.

After having anchored higher education to the internal market, the CJEU further defined the terms 'student', of 'teaching staff' and of 'university'. If someone is duly enrolled as a student according to the Member State laws, the CJEU assumes s/he is a student. Moreover, in the Erasmus case the CJEU observed that some students studying for a doctorate are doing research. No student, however, is a child of migrant workers following primary or secondary education (Humbel and Edel, 1988).

The CJEU has also ruled that 'a proportion of university staff devote its time exclusively to research but research constitutes in principle an essential element in the work of most university teachers' (Erasmus, 1989, para. 34). The CJEU has given no further clues to what in a European context should be considered teaching staff. This corresponds with the impediment of Article 165 TFEU which stipulates that the EU cannot rule over the organisation of education systems. However, ruling that university teachers do research, is ruling about a crucial aspect of organising an university.

In general, universities can offer vocational training programmes, but they are no vocational school (Blaizot; Brown, 1988). The CJEU states that vocational schools are exclusively:

establishments which provide only instruction interposed between periods of employment or else closely connected with employment, particularly during apprenticeship.

(Brown, 1988, para. 12).

And the same day in Lair, the CJEU ruled that vocational schools:

provide only instruction either alternating with or closely linked to an occupational activity, particularly during apprenticeship.

(Lair, 1988, para. 26)

Yet, with one negative (no vocational school) and one positive (research) element, it still is not sharply defined what universities are. Although in some Member States there is a difference between universities and HEIs that offer profession-oriented programmes, the CJEU apparently follows a one-tier system. All HEIs are universities within the framework of the Treaties.

Requirements and conditions for education
The responsibility of a Member State for the content of teaching and the organisation of education systems boils down to quality control and budget control. Even though they are not presented as such, the real problems of the Belgian

authorities in the Gravier and the Blaizot cases are financial in nature. They argued that a supplementary enrolment fee was justified to prevent an influx of foreign students to the point of endangering the educational system because of to heavy financial burdens for universities. The CJEU noted that European law does not block the possibilities of Member States to limit access to university education to a certain maximum. However, it stated that such measures cannot have the effect of discrimination on grounds of nationality, which is prohibited by the same European law.

In some cases the CJEU even suggested to adopt specific non-discriminatory measures such as the establishment of an entry examination or the requirement of a minimum grade (Bressol, 2010, para. 29; Commission v. Austria, 2005; Commission v. Belgium, 2004):

> The Member States are thus free to opt for an education system based on free access – without restriction on the number of students who may register – or for a system based on controlled access in which the students are selected. However, where they opt for one of those systems or for a combination of them, the rules of the chosen system must comply with European Union law and, in particular, the principle of non-discrimination on grounds of nationality.

Diploma recognition is laid down in Directive 2005/36/EC on the recognition of professional qualifications. In principle, Member States determine their own requirements, but accept those of other Member States as equally valid on the basis of mutual recognition of diplomas. They may assess the equivalence of a foreign diploma, but exclusively in the light of the level of knowledge and qualifications (Vlassopoulou, 1991). However, it may be justified for Member States to assure the high standard of university education. These measures have to satisfy the requirements of proportionality and may not prevent, for instance, the freedom of establishment of private HEIs (Neri, 2003).

Paying for education

The position of Member States is ambiguous regarding student mobility. Some Member States welcome foreign students, other Member States are happy to see their nationals go abroad, and some Member States are not happy to see other nationals come to use their allocated higher education capacity. The only resemblance between them is that, considering Member States' arguments in court, their policy choices are primarily informed by a financial rationale. However, when applied to by students and the EC, the CJEU has ruled over and over again that the sole argument of a financial burden to the public purse is not acceptable (Gravier; Blaizot; Commission v. Austria; Commission v. Belgium; Bidar, 2005; Giersch, 2013).

Student loans or grants can be divided in maintenance grants and all other grants concerning admission to universities (Kwikkers and van Wageningen, 2012). Dependent on which secondary legislation applies, students can be seen as workers, children of workers or just European citizens. If Regulation 492/2011 (on workers) applies, students are eligible for full maintenance grants. If Directive 2004/38 (on citizens) applies, then students are only eligible for assistance intended to cover the costs of access to the course given to nationals has to be given to other Member States nationals as well (Raulin, 1992). Therefore, it is important to define which rules apply to a student's situation.

Arguments to treat other Member States' students differently from a Member State's own nationals can never be accepted if they are inspired only by purely financial reasons (Bidar, 2005; Commission v. Netherlands, 2012). It is, however, acceptable to argue that to promote the development of the economy, students need to pay back their grant or loan, or that students need to work in the Member State where they received the support for a certain amount of time (Giersch, 2013). It follows from Directive 2004/38 that the right to receive maintenance aid is acquired only after a five year period of legal residence (Förster, 2008; Giersch, 2013). However, measures need to be proportionate to attain this legitimate objective (Bressol, 2010; Giersch, 2013). So, if parents already worked in the Member state for a minimum of 23 years without living there, this is considered more than enough to be eligible for maintenance grants (Giersch, 2013).

The case of Schwarz and Gootjes-Schwarz (2007) and the joined cases Morgan and Bucher (2007) clarify some important financial aspects of European education and Member State solidarity. The conclusions of these rulings in conjunction with the Bidar and Förster cases, are, that the Member States of which the student has the nationality is charged as much as possible and the host Member State is exonerated as much as possible from the financial burden.

From these cases four main strands can be derived. Students who study in another Member State in which they or their parents lawfully work have exactly the same rights as Member State nationals under Regulation 492/2011. This means they can apply for study and maintenance grants or loans, depending on the system in use (Raulin, 1992). Students who study in another Member State, thus using their right to move and reside in this state can benefit from coverage of the enrolment and tuition fees by that Member State. Students who study in another Member State, having left the State of which they retain the nationality, can benefit from maintenance grants or loans, but this depends on the degree of integration in the Member State of origin (Morgan and Bucher, 2007). Students who study in their own state, but prior to that have been using their right to use the internal market freedoms, cannot be deprived of their own

Member State's social security after finishing their studies if they have used their internal market freedoms (D'Hoop, 2002). However, for each of these strands, Member States are allowed limitations in accordance with European law.

Conclusion

Education does matter to the EU and its Member States. This chapter addressed the constitutional and institutional dimensions of European higher education law. It was discussed how EU higher education law developed, with the CJEU as the driving force behind this development. Nevertheless, as Shaw (1992, p. 442) observed, one should not 'overstate the case for the Community'. Member States have no obligation to take joint action, merely to cooperate.

However, many decisions have been taken by the Council (being the Member State representatives with ministerial powers), either by itself or in cooperation with the EP. This has been made possible by the Treaties, which all have been negotiated and unanimously ratified by the Member States. The direct legal rules for education were drafted to make sure the Member States kept control and the EU could take no decisive action. Then the CJEU connected education to internal market rights, making education an accessory right. This phase ended with the Maastricht Treaty, which marked the introduction of European citizenship. European citizenship provisions created new possibilities for Member State citizens to export grants of receive grants depending on national or host Member State regulations. Nevertheless, the role of the politically responsible institutions such as the Council, seconded by the Commission and the EP, cannot be neglected.

EU higher education law consists of a mixture of enforceable and less enforceable legal rules. The EU has its methods to influence education and so does the Bologna Process. Both processes have an enormous driving force towards harmonisation or convergence. Although it falls outside the scope of this contribution, it would be interesting to investigate the mutual state of synchronisation of both. This analysis could start at the double role the EU, and all EU Member States play within the Bologna Process.

Both integration processes have changed the Member States' responsibility towards students. How many students are and were involved is not part of this contribution, but nevertheless an important issue for higher education policies. Although, on the one hand, the CJEU does not accept financial arguments because it judges over single cases of one or a few students, on the other hand, Member States' governments sometimes fear budgetary problems after their assessment of the potential numbers of students that might benefit from the first judgement. Therefore, at first glance it seems the CJEU and the Member States are in two different realities. However, in actual fact they are two sides of the same coin. A decision of the CJEU can actually change national (by)laws.

This means a single case can be the snowflake, starting the avalanche which reforms national higher education systems.

Notes

1. I copy this terminology from Garben's book: *EU Higher Education Law: The Bologna Process and Harmonization by Stealth* (2011).
2. Since 1958, EU law has developed and so did its terminology and treaties numbering. In this contribution, we adhere to the terminology in use since the Lisbon Treaty (since 2009), except for quotations and for references formulated before 2009.
3. In accordance with rules concerning the procedures in court, all Member States and European institutions are allowed to give their opinion before the CJEU.
4. Article 10 European Social Charter.

References

Amaral, A., Neave G., Musselin C. and, Maassen P. (eds) (2009) *European Integration and the Governance of Higher Education and Research* (Dordrecht: Springer).

Alter, K. J. (1998) 'Who are the "Masters of the Treaty"?: European governments and the European Court of Justice', *International Organizations*, 52, 121–147.

Armstrong, K. A. (2010) *Governing Social Inclusion: Europeanization through Policy Coordination* (Oxford: Oxford University Press).

Barnard, C. and Steve P. (eds) (2014) *European Union Law* (Oxford: Oxford University Press).

Corbett, A. (2005) *Universities and the Europe of Knowledge: Ideas, Institutions and Policy Entrepreneurship in European Union Higher Education Policy 1955–2005* (Houndsmill: Palgrave MacMillan).

Council (2015) http://www.consilium.europa.eu/en/council-eu/configurations/eycs/, date accessed 27 February 2015.

Council (ET 2020) Council conclusions of 12 May 2009 on a strategic framework for European cooperation in education and training ('ET 2020'), 2009/C 119/02.

Craig, P. and G. de Búrca (eds) (1999) *The Evolution of EU Law* (Oxford: Oxford University Press).

De Witte, B. (ed) (1988) *European Community Law of Education* (Baden-Baden: Nomos Verlagsgeschellschaft).

Dougan, M. (2005) 'Fees, grants, loans and dole cheques: who covers the costs of migrant education within the EU?' *Common Market Law Review*, 42(4), 943–986.

European Council (ECcil 2000), presidency conclusions Lisbon 23 and 24 march 2000, http://www.consilium.europa.eu/en/uedocs/cms_data/docs/pressdata/en/ec/00100-r1.en0.htm.

Garben, S. (2011) *EU Higher Education Law: The Bologna Process and Harmonization by Stealth* (Alphen aan den Rijn: Kluwer Law International).

Gornitzka, Å. (2007) 'The Lisbon process: a supranational policy perspective in', P. Maassen and Johan P. Olsen (eds) *University Dynamics and European Integration* (pp. 155–178) (Dordrecht: Springer).

Huisman, J., Maassen, P. and G. Neave (eds) (2001) *Higher Education and the Nation State, the International Dimension of Higher Education* (Oxford: Pergamon).

Kapteyn, P. J. G (2005) 'Over het Hoe en Waarom van een Europese "Grondwet"', in Working Papers European Studies, Amsterdam.

Kwikkers, P. and A. van Wageningen (2012) 'A space for the European higher education area', *Higher Education Policy*, 25, 39–63.

Lenaerts, K. (1994) 'Education in European community law after Maastricht', *Common Market Law Review*, 31, 7–41.

Maassen, P. and J. P. Olsen (eds) (2007) *University Dynamics and European Integration* (Dordrecht: Springer).

Neave, G. (2001) 'The European dimension in higher education: an excursion into the modern use of historical analogues', in J. Huisman, P. Maassen and G. Neave (eds) *Higher Education and the Nation State, the International Dimension of Higher Education* (pp. 13–73) (Oxford: Pergamon).

Neave, G. (2003) 'The Bologna declaration: some of the historic dilemmas posed by the reconstruction of the community in Europe's systems of higher education', *Educational Policy*, 17(1), 141–164.

Neave, G. (2009) 'The Bologna process as Alpha or Omega, or, on interpreting history and context as inputs to Bologna, Prague, Berlin and Beyond', in A. Amaral, G. Neave, C. Musselin and P. Maassen (eds) *European Integration and the Governance of Higher Education and Research* (pp. 17–58) (Dordrecht: Springer).

Shaw, J. (1992) 'Education and the law in the European community', *Journal of Law & Education*, 21(3), 415–442.

Shaw, J. (1999) 'From the margins to the centre: education and training law and policy', in P. Craig and G. de Búrca (eds) *The Evolution of EU Law* (pp. 555–595) (Oxford: Oxford University Press).

Van der Hoeven, J. (1989) *De drie dimensies van het bestuursrecht: ontstaan en vorming van het Nederlandse algemene bestuursrecht* (Alphen aan den Rijn: Samsom H.D. Tjeenk Willink).

Van der Mei, A. P. (2003) *Free Movement of Persons within the European Community: Cross-Border Access to Public Benefits* (Oxford: Hart).

Van Nuffelen, P. and Cambien, N. (2009) 'De vrijheid van economisch niet-actieve EU-burgers om binnen de EU te reizen, te verblijven en te studeren', *Sociaal Economische Wetgeving*, 57(4), 144–154.

van Wageningen, A. C. (2003) *De staat van de universiteit; een rechtsvergelijkende studie naar de institutionalisering van de universiteit in Nederland, Frankrijk en Nordrhein-Westfalen* (Enschede: Universiteit Twente/CHEPS).

van Wageningen, A. C. (2005) 'Het Hof, hoger onderwijs en financiering; universiteiten binnen de contouren van één Europees hoger onderwijs stelsel', in L. Versteegh, A. van Wageningen en J. J. Wirken (eds) *De veelzijdige burger, opstellen voor prof. mr. P.J.G Kapteyn* (pp. 143–158) (Amsterdam: Pallas Publications).

Versteegh, L., van Wageningen, A. and J. J. Wirken (eds) (2005) *De veelzijdige burger, opstellen voor prof. mr. P.J.G Kapteyn* (Amsterdam: Pallas Publications).

Weiler, J. H. H. (1991) 'The Transformation of Europe', *The Yale Law Journal*, 100(8), 2403–2483.

Jurisprudence and legislation

Bidar (2005) Case C-209/03 [2005] ECR p. I-2119.

Blaizot (1988) Case 24/86 [1988] ECR p. 379.

Bressol (2010) Case C-73/08 [2010] ECR p. I-2735.

Brown (1988) Case 197/86 [1988] ECR p. 3205.

Casagrande v. Landeshauptstadt München (1974) Case 9/74 [1974] ECR p. 773.

Commission v. Belgium (1988) Case C-42/87 [1988] ECR p. I-5445.
Commission v. Belgium (2004) Case C-65/03 [2004] ECR p. I-6427.
Commission v. Netherlands (2012) Case C- 542/09 ECLI:EU:C:2012:346.
Commission v. Republic of Austria (2005) Case C-147/03 [2005] ECR p. I-5969.
D'Hoop (2002) Case 224/98 [2002] ECR p. I-6191.
Erasmus (1989) Case 242/87 [1989] ECR p. 1425.
Forcheri (1983) Case 152/82 [1983] ECR p. 2323.
Förster (2008) Case C-158/07 [2008] ECR p. I-8507.
Giersch (2013) Case C-20/12 ECLI:EU:C:2013:411.
Gravier v. City of Liège (1985) Case 293/85 [1985] ECR p. 593.
Grzelczyk (2001) Case C-184/99 [2001] ECR p. I-6193.
Humbel and Edel (1988) Case C-263/86 [1988] ECR p. 5365.
Lair (1988) Case 39/86 [1988] ECR p. I-3161.
Morgan & Bucher (2007) Joined Cases C-11/06 and C-12/06 [2007] ECR p. I-9161.
Neri (2003) Case C-153/02 [2003] ECR p. I-13555.
Raulin (1992) Case C-357/89 [1992] ECR p. I-1027.
Schwarz & Gootjes-Schwarz (2007) Case C-76/05 [2007] ECR p. I-6849.
Vlassopoulou (1991) Case C-340/89 [1991] ECR p. I-2357.
Consolidated versions of the Treaty on European Union and the Treaty on the Functioning of the European Union and the Charter of Fundamental Rights of the European Union (2010) doi:10.2860/58644 (Luxembourg: Publications Office of the European Union).
Directive 2004/38/EC of the European Parliament and of the Council of 29 April 2004 on the right of citizens of the Union and their family members to move and reside freely within the territory of the Member States amending Regulation (EEC) No 1612/68 and repealing Directives 64/221/EEC, 68/360/EEC, 72/194/EEC, 73/148/EEC, 75/34/EEC, 75/35/EEC, 90/364/EEC, 90/365/EEC and 93/96/EEC, (OJ L 158, 30 April 2004, p. 77).
Regulation (EEC) No 1612/68 (Regulation 1612/68) of the Council of 15 October 1968 on freedom of movement for workers within the Community, OJ L 257, 19 October 1968, pp. 2–12 (DE, FR, IT, NL), English special edition: Series I Volume 1968(II) pp. 475–484.
Regulation (EU) No 492/2011 (Regulation 492/2011) of the European Parliament and of the Council of 5 April 2011 on freedom of movement for workers within the Union, OJ L 141, 27 May 2011, pp. 1–12.

7
Institutionalism and Organizational Change

Sara Diogo, Teresa Carvalho and Alberto Amaral

Introduction

Institutional theory usually refers to a broad group of perspectives that interpret the relationship between institutions and human behaviour, assuming that not only human actions (i.e. behaviour, perceptions, power, policy preferences, decision-making processes) shape institutions, but these are also influenced by them. More specifically, institutionalism focuses on the need of organizations to adapt to their institutional environment, such as norms, rules and under-standings about what is an acceptable or normal behaviour and that cannot be changed easily and/or instantaneously (March and Olsen, 1984; Meyer and Rowan, 1977). It argues that organizations take rules and norms for granted because they seem obvious or natural. Failure to act in accordance with norms and expectations may lead to conflict and illegitimacy. Changes occurring at the institutional field of higher education (HE) are said to increasingly constrain higher education institutions (HEIs). Given this, it is increasingly relevant to analyse the development of institutionalist theories and the way they have been adapted to the HE field.

The works of Selznick (1948, 1957) and Parsons (1956) are usually considered pioneers in the study of organizations. These scholars theorized on the richness and importance of the institutional environment for organizational structures and processes: for example, how institutions function to integrate organizations in society through universalistic rules, contracts and authority (Thornton and Ocasio, 2008, pp. 99–100). Throughout the 1970s and 1980s, a new approach to institutional analysis emerged with Meyer and Rowan (1977), Zucker (1977), DiMaggio and Powell (1983) and Meyer and Scott (1983) who stressed the role of culture and cognition in institutional analysis (Thornton and Ocasio, 2008). In addition to the technical elements and resources, these institutionalists argued that organizations must consider their 'institutional' (internal) environment: regulative, normative and cultural-cognitive features that define 'social fitness', that is, rational myths, knowledge legitimated by education, professions and legislation as *shapers and influencers* of organizational practices and structures (Powell, 2007).

Modern governance largely occurs in and through institutions, under the influence of the actors who exert power and mobilize institutional resources, political relationships and *struggles* (Bell, 2002). In fact, governance theories (and narratives) draw on institutional theory to better grasp power-dependent relationships and organizations in the processes of policy design and implementation and in decision-making dynamics. Institutions can also play an important role not only in reducing transaction and information costs and various associated forms of market uncertainty, but also in helping to monitor and enforce contracts and/or agreements (Bell, 2002, pp. 3–5). Nevertheless, because *influencing and shaping* institutional dynamics does not explain *all* institutional phenomena and actors' preferences, institutionalism is considered a 'middle-range' theory as change can be derived from other sources. For example, Thoenig (2012) points to structural forces influencing institutions' life, such as globalization, international economic and political agendas and pressures on national structures. For example, governance structures look at the environment in terms of the internal strategies to adapt to or to minimize the influence of surroundings upon organizations, for example, much recent change within HE can be seen as an organizational response to market dynamics (Ordorika, 2014). Also cultural factors, institutional capacities and relationships among actors are factors that *shape behaviour.*

Among the strands of institutional theory, this chapter focuses mostly on the new institutionalism[1] approach to institutional analysis of HE. This approach is elected because it allows us to better understand the interaction between institutional contexts (also known as the organizational field) and actors in HE policy at the organizational and national levels (Witte, 2006). New institutionalism rejects the causal primacy of efficiency, in contrast to such perspectives as resource dependence (Pfeffer and Salancik, 1978), transaction cost analysis (Williamson, 1981) and organizational demography/ecology (Hannan and Freeman, 1977), which focus on concrete exchange processes within and between organizations (Lounsbury and Ventresca, 2003).

Research on the influence of organization studies in HE policy research started with Burton Clark's (1970, 1972) case studies on selected HEIs in the United States (Fumasoli and Stensaker, 2013), with Cohen, March and Olsen's (1972) famous 'garbage can model' on universities' decision-making processes and with Cohen and March's (1974) description of universities as 'organised anarchies'. As we will see later on, institutionalism has been useful in several domains in the HE field. Changes in institutional governance; in decision-making practices and patterns of leadership; in the roles of academic leadership;

in the funding models of the sector; and in the challenges facing the academic profession, the rise of managerialism, the institutionalization of policy design and implementation processes, and the (different) effects on the functioning of HEIs and institutional autonomy have been major research topics analysed through institutional lenses (Carvalho, 2014; Carvalho and Santiago, 2010a; Fumasoli and Stensaker, 2013; Veiga, 2010; Witte, 2006).

It should be mentioned that the concept of *institution* is not synonymous with *organization* (Amaral and Magalhães, 2003; Scott, 2001, p. 48), although it is common to see in the literature the words 'organization' and 'institution' being used interchangeably. However, under new institutionalism, institutions are seen as different from organizations in the sense that the set of norms and culture that constitute an institution are not only associated with the organizational processes of an organization (Scott, 2001) but include influencing institutional actors' actions and vice versa in a way that organizations cannot (March and Olsen, 2005). Considering that the use of institutional theory in HE allows to better interpret HEIs' behaviour, their actors and interactions between these, universities and/or polytechnics are viewed as institutions rather than as organizations, and therefore not focusing so much on issues related to management, control and success. Furthermore, as clarified by Marilena Chaui (1999), 'The University as a social practice is "based upon the public recognition of its legitimacy and of its attributions which grant its autonomy in relation to other social institutions, being structured by its own internal ordinances, rules, norms and values of recognition and legitimacy"' (in Amaral and Magalhães, 2003, p. 247). As social institutions, modern universities conquered their legitimacy not only from the idea that knowledge is autonomous from religion and the state and therefore inseparable from the ideas of education, reflection, creation and critique (Amaral and Magalhães, 2003), but also on the institutional 'taken for granted' rules and behaviours. One can say that HEIs evolved and persist as a way for society to preserve and disseminate knowledge, especially nowadays when they have an unquestionable role in the creation of the so-called knowledge economies and societies. It is this instrumentality that positions the university as a social institution. Also Meyer and Rowan (1977) argued that education is both a central feature for society as an institution per se and simultaneously an instrument to the needs of society and labour.

In this chapter, a brief overview of the origins and developments of institutionalism as well as some basic concepts and ideas in order to better understand how this theory has been applied in HE policy and governance is provided. The following sections draws upon the three approaches to new institutionalism as traditionally classified by Hall and Taylor (1996) and how some studies in HE field have used these perspectives. A similar *process* is used in the section devoted to explain institutional change and isomorphism. The chapter follows then with a discussion of the use of institutional theory in

HE research. We conclude with some final remarks (and criticisms), as well as pointing some questions/topics for future research.

The three approaches to new institutionalism

For Hall and Taylor (1996, p. 936) there is considerable confusion about to what sort of questions the new institutionalism answers to. They argue this confusion can be minimized by recognizing that institutionalism does not constitute a unified body of thought, but rather three different but complementary analytical approaches, 'each of which calls itself "new institutionalism" '. These three schools of thought are the historical (comparative) institutionalism, the rational choice institutionalism (also associated with the economic institutionalism due to the similarities of both approaches) and the sociological (organizational) institutionalism. All of them devoted attention to the understanding of the role institutions play in the determination of individuals' behaviour, although they explain social, political and organizational world relationships and outcomes in different ways. As such, the concept of *institution* assumes different meanings in these different types of theoretical approaches.

According to Mahoney and Thelen (2010, p. 7), these three institutionalisms explain what sustains institutions over time while simultaneously account for cases in which exogenous shocks or shifts prompt institutional change. Extrapolating authors' analysis, we can combine these three strands of thought to better understand why the specific nature of HEIs allows them to endure over time and how external events affect institutional change. Roughly speaking, these three complementary views share the conception of institutions as *relatively enduring* features of political and social life (Mahoney and Thelen, 2010, p. 4). This is why it makes sense to look at HE as an institution and to consider the consequences of its extensive and intensive institutionalization processes (Meyer et al., 2008). In institutional thinking, environments constitute local situations – establishing and defining their core entities, purposes and relations – and therefore local HE arrangements are heavily dependent on broader institutions (Meyer et al., 2008), such as quality assurance agencies, central government institutions, international organizations and so on. Thus, looking at HE as an institution allows us to see the cultural scripts and organizational rules built into the global, international and national environments that establish the main features of local situations: 'together with their disciplinary fields and academic roles, HEIs are defined, measured, and instantiated in essentially every country in explicitly global terms' (Meyer et al., 2008, p. 188).

According to historical institutionalists, the long life of universities as institutions is not justified by specific economic and political functions or shaped by particular historical legacies or power struggles, but by their association with the development of social progress and knowledge societies (Hall and

Taylor, 1996). Historical institutionalism seeks to explain institutions by reference to the past, focusing on their unique features and conventions (Bevir, 2009, p. 110). Institutions are part of a chain of causes and effects that take into account factors like the dissemination of ideas and socio-economic development. For most of historical institutionalists, institutions are likely to be path-dependent or even 'sticky' (Fligstein, 2008). Institutions tend to *resist* change because they embed actors' interests and also because institutions are implicated in actors' cognitive frames and habits. *Path dependency* elucidates on the nature and speed of changes and whether these are on the same continuum as previous developments or whether they cause discontinuities. According to historical institutionalism, actual and future actions are the reflection of experience and radical changes in public administration hardly occur. In fact, one of the criticisms to historical institutionalism is its focus on developmental continuity, hampering its capacity to explain institutional innovation and rapid change (Hodgson, 2008, pp. 4–5). Also interesting is the point of Aspinwall and Schneider (2000, p. 30) who argue that the label of historical institutionalism is 'misnomer' because every social phenomenon can be attributed to the influence of history. It is thus duty of the researcher to be able to differentiate between important and 'unimportant' historical influences.

Johanna Witte's (2006) study on the implementation of the Bologna degree structure in four different national and institutional settings uses mostly historical institutionalism to analyse policy responses to similar challenges. In this scenario, she concludes that cultural and historical arguments seemed to feature particularly stronger in Germany and Italy when compared to the Netherlands, and that the success or smooth implementation of change in HEIs depends on the conformity and/or dependences of institutions' path.

Rational choice institutionalism relies on rational choice theory. Rational choice institutionalism assumes that all actors are rational, and therefore each person ponders his/her decisions in terms of utility for him/herself. Actors behave in a purely utilitarian way to maximize the satisfaction of their preferences, being efficiency the factor that conditions choice. Institutions and actors are clearly separable (Hall and Taylor, 1996). The maximization of individual preferences might lead to suboptimal outcomes for the community that, by behaving rationally, assumes a quality-related perspective. Thus, according to this perspective, both governmental institutions and the market are important factors in explaining why some countries develop efficient economies and others not (Koelble, 1995, p. 232). In turn, economic developments or the opposite scenario – for example, economic crises – determine governments and institutions strategies towards these external *pressures*. Institutions are thus capable of affecting individuals' choices and actions but not of determining them (Koelble, 1995). Institutions change because people's preferences also change (Bell, 2002). This view differs significantly from historical institutionalism, which sees actors *embedded* in social, economic and political relationships beyond their control (Koelble, 1995, p. 235).

Sociological institutionalism defines not only institutions broadly, including the rules, procedures and norms, but also the symbols. In turn, economic developments or the opposite scenario, for example, economic crisis, determine governments and institutions strategies towards these external *pressures*. March and Olsen (1984) see institutions from a Weberian view, as constructs designed to assign rewards and sanctions and to establish guidelines for acceptable behaviour – giving birth to the value of meritocracy and promoting the idea of social mobility (Koelble, 1995). March and Olsen (1984, 1989) argued that human behaviour is guided and shaped by a *logic of appropriateness* which shapes behaviour and choices besides the maximization of utility. They explained that individuals perceive the need to follow rules, which associate particular identities to particular situations in order to acquire personal self-knowledge skills, which in turn will help in decision-making processes. In this case, *appropriateness* refers to cognitive and ethical dimensions, targets and aspirations, and it guides individuals to *fit* within an institution.

Important differences between the sociological and the rational choice schools lay in the way decision-making processes are made. When making decisions, sociological institutionalists do not ask, '[H]ow do I maximize my interests in this situation?' They rather ask, '[W]hat is the appropriate response to this situation given my position and responsibilities?' (Koelble, 1995, p. 233). Thus, more than the utility maximizing thought, institutions and their set of rules of conduct and behaviour provide legitimacy and appropriateness to institutional actors (Koelble, 1995, p. 232). Within HEIs there are legal, administrative and professional procedures, which facilitate and direct both institutions and actors to gain meaning, authority and legitimacy. Nevertheless, power relations lead to situations where often it is more important to embody exogenously legitimated properties than it is to adapt to local possibilities and demands (Meyer et al., 2008, p. 192). For example, in the case of profiling research, the interests of the university leaders may not be in line with the interests of the policy-makers (Pietilä, 2014). If the values and aims of the actors are in disagreement, the leaders might respond to external demand symbolically in order to defend the organization's inside core. It is vital for the organization to achieve a normative match between the values and beliefs of the proposed policy reform and the identity and traditions of the organization (Pietilä, 2014).

Also with respect to differences between both the sociological and rational choice institutionalisms, Kaplan (2006) points out that institutional effects upon the decision-making processes of HEIs can be expressed in various ways.[2] For example, (political) struggles over institutional resources and strategy as well as the allocation of benefits and/or sanctions 'will be shaped by structural features of the organization, the organization's relationship to its environment, and the social environment in which its participants are embedded' (2006, p. 216).

Institutional change and isomorphism

For institutionalists change happens through institutionalization of a certain organizational field and/or sector, that is, a set of organizations that, in aggregate, constitute a recognized area of institutional life. In fact, it is this theorization on organizational fields (DiMaggio and Powell, 1983), sectors or strategic action fields (Meyer and Scott, 1983) that makes new institutionalism to stand out among other perspectives of organizational behaviour. Structure and context are primary factors to consider when studying collective behaviour. By conceiving institutions as entities that structure fields and help to guide actors through the muddle around them, institutions define who was in what position in the field, give people rules and cognitive structures to interpret others' actions, and scripts to follow under conditions of uncertainty (DiMaggio and Powell, 1983; Meyer and Scott, 1983). Institutionalisation happens when '(...) social processes, obligations, or actualities come to take on a rule-like status in social thought and action' (Meyer and Rowan, 1977). In turn, coercive institutionalisation is likely to result in actors' frustration, loss of identification with the institution and even alienation (cf. Amaral, Jones and Karseth, 2002; Välimaa, 2005; Diogo, 2014a).

According to Meyer and Rowan (1985, pp. 94–95) the formal structure of an organisation is a social myth. Institutions avoid social censure, minimize demands for external accountability, improve their chances of securing necessary resources and try to raise their probability of survival (Greenwood et al., 2008, p. 4). The formal, symbolic structure may be window dressing and not aimed at changing the organizational *status quo*. Therefore, what institutional actors do in practice (the reality) is different from what they appear to do (the facade) (Meyer and Rowan, 1985, p. 96). The institutional forms and practices used are not chosen because they are more effective, as implied by the notion of rationality. Institutional forms function as cultural practices compared to the myths and ceremonies that happen in societies and that organizations incorporate, gaining legitimacy, resources, stability, and enhanced survival prospects (Meyer and Rowan, 1977, p. 340). Thus, variations in the organizational structure also affect the cultural content carried and transmitted by HEIs: while some HE systems are adverse to change and to establish links with societies, others are more prone to engage in a wider array of activities (Meyer et al., 2008).

DiMaggio and Powell (1983) identified a paradox in organizational behaviour: since the moment a group of organizations emerge as a field, actors make their organizations increasingly similar while trying to change them. 'Why is there such startling homogeneity of organizational forms and practices?' (DiMaggio and Powell, 1983, p. 147). What can lead organizations, after becoming an institutional field, to adopt a common set of patterns, characteristics and specific behaviour, leading them to be increasingly homogenous? Under what conditions public organizations imitate each other and avoid innovation (Thoenig, 2012)? Even when organizations try to change and seek new ways to improve their performance, after some time these efforts are not balanced with the level of diversity that exists within a field (DiMaggio and Powell, 1983). This happens due to the structuration of *organizational fields*. In the short term, pressures towards isomorphism are strong (Thoenig, 2012). For DiMaggio and Powell (1983), the process that most clearly translates the cognitive dimension of isomorphic behaviour is imitation, that is, mimetic processes, as explained bellow. As fields mature, there is an inexorable push towards homogenization as powerful forces emerge, leading institutions to become more similar (Greenwood et al., 2008, p. 6). Institutions and their actors deal with uncertainty by imitating others they consider models or successful ones in the same field (Scott, 2001).

Institutionalization occurs through three forms of institutional isomorphism, or 'mechanisms of diffusion': *coercive*, *mimetic* and *normative* isomorphism (DiMaggio and Powell, 1983, p. 150). These mechanisms decrease systematic diversity, since all of them lead to increasing similarity in institutions' behaviour. 'Coercive factors involved political pressures and the force of the state, providing regulatory oversight and control; normative factors stemmed from the potent influence of the professions and the role of education; and mimetic forces drew on habitual, taken-for-granted responses to circumstances of uncertainty' (Powell, 2007, p. 2). A strong factor that causes homogeneity of structures and behaviour within the HE sector is the tendency to emphasize research excellence when research intensive universities are the role models that other HEIs mimic. Emphasis on research excellence is accelerated by national and institutional evaluations, benchmarking and funding schemes (Pietilä, 2014). This happens mostly through coercive and mimetic factors.

Ramirez (2012) also addresses the question of what makes persons, organizations, and nation-states to pursue some routes and not others. In HE, it can be asked why some educational trends and reforms diffuse and others not. How do they travel, assuming that they do? 'The local indeed matters, but how much it matters varies over time and space' (Ramirez, 2012, p. 434). Indeed, understanding time and space is one of the keys to avoid the most common pitfalls in comparative (educational) research: assuming that all HE systems are experiencing the same changes and at the same pace (Nóvoa and Yariv-Mashal, 2003). Institutionalism has been a useful framework for the study of the international diffusion of governance structures of HE (Whitley and Gläser, 2014).

Scott (2001) further argued that institutions are based in three distinct pillars – regulative, normative and cultural-cognitive, which provide stability and meaning to social behaviour. Additionally, each of Scott's pillars offered a different rationale for institutional legitimacy, either by being legally sanctioned, morally authorized, or culturally supported (Powell, 2007). According to Scott (2001) each pillar provides a basis for legitimacy. 'Legitimacy is not a commodity to be possessed or exchange but a condition reflecting cultural alignment, normative support, or consonance with relevant rules or laws' (2001, p. 45).

The regulative element stands for institutions' rules and constraints that condition actors' behaviour: for example, regulatory processes, monitoring and sanctioning activities (Scott, 2001, p. 35). Economists and economic historians see institutions mainly based on the regulative pillar which operates through coercive isomorphism. The existence of a common legal environment affects many aspects of HEIs, such as behaviour, structure and responses to external pressures/impositions. Coercive isomorphism may also emerge from soft regulation mechanisms (e.g. European Commission *modus operandi* in the area of educational policy-making[3]). The Bologna Process reflects an example of *imposing* and spreading a common educational model to different countries, promoting convergence of national HE systems (Veiga and Amaral, 2012).

The normative pillar includes values, norms, roles and normative rules that introduce a prescriptive, evaluative and obligatory dimension into social life (Scott, 2001, p. 37). Normative schemes push compliance for social obligations. Normative isomorphism stems from professionalization as it is subjected to the same process of socialization, and behavioural norms to become similar (DiMaggio and Powell, 1983). For example, HEIs need to cope with innovation, which might challenge the *traditional* model of knowledge transmission. Situations like these can lead to more diverse forms of delivering knowledge, or, innovation might lead to common responses from institutions of the same sector by seeing how successful organizations operate (Meyer et al., 2008).

The cultural-cognitive pillar corresponds to the shared conceptions of the rules that constitute the nature of social reality and the frames through which meaning is made. At the inter-organizational level, social scientists recognized the presence of *scripts* and shared beliefs as indicators of cultural-cognitive schemes.[4] The most important cognitive elements are the constitutive rules (Scott, 2001), involving the creation of categories and typifications, which in turn contribute to the social construction of actors and interests (Scott, 2001, p. 41). The cognitive pillar relates to mimetic isomorphism as organizations are motivated by their interpretation of others' successful behaviour (Greenwood et al., 2008, p. 7). As such, it results from competitive market forces contrary to normative conformity, which happens through strong social and cultural expectations for certain organizational behaviour (Bess and Dee, 2008, pp. 142–143). Mimetic isomorphism happens when institutions 'copy' each other behaviours in order to find solutions which do not demand a high investment and it is driven by uncertainty. These three pillars balance institutional dynamics and help us to understand how institutional theory works in practice.

Institutional theory in higher education research

This section analyses why organizational institutionalism is a good theoretical ground for the study of HE, especially HE reforms (Ferlie, Musselin and Andresani, 2008, p. 273). *Inter alia*, by shedding light on the structures and processes of HE, institutionalism helps us to understand political transformations in organizations and the relationships between institutions and the government, and their internal dynamics (Gornitzka, 1999). More specifically, key contributions of (new) institutionalism are found in interpretations of HEIs' behaviour, HEIs actors, and interactions between these both *settings* and their internal and external environments.

The environment where HEIs operate is frequently associated with the idea of *open systems* (Scott, 2001), which emphasizes 'the importance of the wider context or environment as it constrains, shapes, and penetrates the organisation' (Scott, 2001, p. xiv). From this perspective, HEIs are viewed as complex organizations, embedded in multiple environments, receiving inputs from and producing outputs for their environments, to which institutions must respond. Within each institution there are independent units, which are separated and/or tied from its environments according to their level of loose or tight coupling (Scott, 2001). The idea of the university as a loosely coupled organization attempts to provide an image of a more fluid and decentralized institution (Weick, 1976). Open and social systems produce social norms and cognitive references (Thoenig, 2012). Thus, change in HE, can be explained by the interaction process between institutions and their environment. As dynamic tensions and pressures for change are built into institutions, there are different types of institutional change (Mahoney and Thelen, 2010, p. 15).

After his pioneer work on HE research from the organizational studies perspective, Clark developed a framework for *identifying* and studying entrepreneurial universities (1998, 2004). He advocated that universities are constructed through a combination of structural and cultural factors which provided them with a distinctive identity and, simultaneously, to maintain a steady and adequate state of change in a shifting environment (Fumasoli and Stensaker, 2013). The institutional context is defined as the widespread social understandings that define what it means to be rational – *rationalized myths*, as 'the rules, norms and ideologies of the wider society' (Meyer and Rowan, 1985, p. 84). It both regularizes behaviour and provides opportunity for agency and change (Thornton and Ocasio, 2008, p. 102). Institutional contexts are often pluralistic and inconsistent, and they do not react similarly to the same *institutional pressures*, but they work in a twofold way: both enabling and limiting institutions and actors' possibilities and opportunities. This is why institutionalism is a powerful theoretical ground to analyse HE in concrete terms, as a set of specific and local organizations, roles, interactions and economic transactions (Meyer et al., 2008, p. 187). Furthermore, over the past decade, institutionalism has become one of the dominant approaches to the study of European integration (Pollack, 2009; Souto-Otero, Fleckenstein and Dacombe, 2008).

Changes in HE should be understood in the light of the emergence of a context of public sector reforms, framed by neoliberalism, where governance is conceptualized as a minimal state. Instead of hollowing out the state, the neoliberal movement 'created new patterns of service delivery based on complex sets of organisations drawn from all of the public, private, and voluntary sectors' (Bevir, 2009, p. 6). The greater emphasis on informal institutions led institutionalists to gain increasing interest in the study not only of formal bureaucracies but also of policy networks, concluding that under the new governance, the state had to rely less on rules and more on indirect management, based on negotiation and trust (2009, p. 112). In this scenario and according to rational choice theory, in the absence of/or less government, one expects that the stability of organizational norms, agreements and patterns of rules (*loose norms*) dictate individuals' behaviour. In other words, in the absence of any *higher authority* or any *enforcing agent*, networks and logics of appropriateness also help to guide institutional actors beyond what is *legally/officially* stipulated.

Public sector organizations, like HEIs, can be *responsible* for symbolic and normative changes because they pass (with success or not) images and references to other institutions (i.e. a kind of institutional facade). Not only HEIs create pressures, but also they are highly vulnerable to the same pressures. In any HEI, different actors assume distinct roles and are expected to show different behaviours. Nevertheless, once clearly established, rules and procedures (e.g. old habits, practices and traditions) still prevail. Individuals then tend to follow (old) routines, either because it is easier and more comfortable to them and/or because this is what they think is expected from them.

(New) institutionalism gained particular attention in the field of HE research as a tool to analyse the institutional restructuring that happened with the public policy reforms of the 1970s that affected public administration in general and consequently HEIs. Prior to this, with the consolidation of the nation-state system around the turn of the 19th century, the globally institutionalized model of HE expanded and changed. Therefore, institutionalism has gained supporters as a useful theory to analyse the role of the state in public sector reform when confronted with such changes (Gornitzka, 1999; Kaplan, 2006). Institutional theory tries to put forward explanations on why HE around the world reflects common models and why HE systems, although at different paths, achieved almost universal expansion (Meyer et al., 2008, p. 197).

Another account explaining convergence towards a common model or processes of 'catching-up' of countries regarding educational performance lays in the combination of path dependency and historical institutionalism with sociological institutionalism. Whereas legislation passed by governments compels 'laggard' national HE systems to 'catch-up' with more developed ones (Nagel, Martens and Windzio, 2010), both at the national and institutional level, it is possible to observe increasing similarities in terms of policies, structures and modes of functioning (e.g. the Bologna Process, changes in governance and management structures). These diffusion processes happen due to, among other reasons, normative pressures passed to and by professionals, definition of common goals and adoption of similar practices and routines. As we have seen, new institutionalism provides a kind of mental map to explain persistence/continuity and convergence upon common behaviours.

At the macro level, new institutionalism provides a fruitful framework for analysing institutional restructuring and destructuring/de-*institutionalizing* processes, as well as reproduction and production mechanisms in HE systems and institutions. Explaining the processes of institutionalization and de-institutionalization, Carvalho and Santiago (2010b) point out that new institutionalism allows us to better understand the outcomes that follow from these processes. However, they also draw attention to the fact that a theoretical approach that restricts itself to environmental relations may neglect the analysis of both processes of institutionalization and de-institutionalization imposed on HEIs, as well as to limit the analysis of how academics interpret and respond to managerialist pressures at the micro-organizational level (2010b, p. 166). As the authors note, 'If strategic responses to external pressures differ for each institution, internal responses may also be expected to differ' (Carvalho and Santiago, 2010b, p. 166). This is so because institutional restructuring emerges at two levels. It originates first in the political initiatives to reshape the structures, roles and routines of HEIs and its academic cultures. Second, it emerges in the procedures to legitimate a new cultural-cognitive 'milieu' or 'order', closely bonded to market ideologies (Carvalho and Santiago, 2010b, p. 165).

Following NPM reforms, Brückmann and Carvalho (2014) draw on institutionalism to analyse the 2007 Portuguese HE reform process, and more specifically the reorganization of governance and management structures in order to assess whether it resulted in greater diversity of organizational models. They concluded that although coercive factors are similar due to imposed legislation, it is possible to find some diversity in institutional responses. Namely, HEIs could chose the total number of the General Council members, the number of external members who belong to the General Council, the existence or not of an academic senate, etc.

Fumasoli and Stensaker (2013) provide several examples of HE studies that describe the emergence of diverse forms of university. Bleiklie and Kogan (2007) outline the stakeholder model, which reflects how a shift in societal values has implications for the university. In parallel, the role of an emerging university leadership has been highlighted by looking at how rectorates and boards take action in the new governance frameworks (Fumasoli and Stensaker, 2013, p. 481).

In sum, new institutionalism has been a conceptual and theoretical framework used by HE research to better understand how *external* and *internal* tensions affect HEIs actors' behaviour and what we may (or not) expect from them giving their role; how do they design, implement and develop national and institutional *reforms* and strategies targeting HE, and how institutional governance and management practices are *redefined* in order to meet increasing demands and possibilities as well.

Final remarks

To understand how HE systems and institutions adapt, how this is perceived by the public, by the representatives or administrative authorities and how HE should meet external change are (still) relevant issues in HE research (Neave, 2012). The previous sections shed some light on why institutional theory is a tool to better understand institutional dynamics and to extrapolate lessons of institutional behaviour and institutional relationships. However, due to its importance in social sciences and political life, it is challenging to approach the vast span of topics, definitions, research and methodology of institutional theory. In turn, this varies according to the specific strand of thought used to depict institutional phenomena.

Particularly, rational choice institutionalism has had very significant impacts on recent major reforms in public sector management and institutional design, namely governance reforms since the 1970s and 1980s. According to Hall and Taylor (1996, p. 952), rational choice institutionalism has produced the 'most elegant accounts' of institutional origins and explanations on the reasons why existing institutions continue to exist by analysing their functions and the benefits they provide. Nevertheless, the authors also note that this strand of thought has been criticized because it lacks convincing explanations for institutional inefficiencies and overemphasizes the efficiency that some institutions show (Hall and Taylor, 1996). When making decisions, people tend to act in a balanced calculated way, pondering their main motivations (which might not be rational), and then attempt to fulfil their needs the best they can. In this sense, individuals act based upon limited information. At the highest institutional hierarchy level – that is, HEIs' top management – behaviours and circumstances change. In other words, it might be argued that, although HEIs' decision-makers are engaged in the 'Herculean task' of calculating every possible aspect of utility involved in taking a decision, they might lack the ability and/or the resources to achieve an optimal solution (Koelble, 1995, p. 233). As such, they need to narrow their best available choices by using their rationality and chose the best satisfying strategy instead of the optimal one (Simon, 1947). Students do not behave as perfect informed clients either.

Simultaneously, HEIs have varied considerably in the extent to which they construct separate organizational identities and have been able to exert some independence from the state (Whitley and Gläser, 2014). Complementary theoretical grounds then need to be formulated to frame these developments. We believe that it would be erroneous to focus only in one new institutionalism chapter and isolate it from its siblings when focusing on HE research.

Kaplan (2006) reminds us of the importance of both institutions and *key* actors and/or *strategic* groups. Institutions represent the context within which polities come to decisions about policy. They make certain outcomes possible and stable and make other outcomes unlikely. However, if institutions retain such power in society, if they control and shape outcomes, they possibly award some advantages to some groups over others: How is this then translated in institutional life? Which groups are these and how do these dynamics vary in HEIs with different governance structures and management practices? And, at the system level, how can different government types and rules affect decision-making processes and change policies when governments change? These questions led us to the conceptualization and formulations on institutionalization processes. We know from institutionalism that full institutionalization of a structure is likely to depend on the conjoint effects of relatively low resistance by opposing groups. The reversal of this process, de-institutionalization, is likely to require a major shift in the environment which may lead to conflict between actors whose interests are in opposition to others with different cognitive frameworks (Pietilä, 2014).

We believe that more research should be developed in order to resolve the gap of studies on institutionalization processes (Tolbert and Zucker, 1996, p. 175). As process-based approach, institutionalization is almost always treated as a qualitative state: structures are institutionalized, or they are not (Tolbert and Zucker, 1996). As such, we lack knowledge on questions related to the determinants of variations in levels of institutionalization, as well as of how such variation might affect the degree of similarity among sets of organizations. A clearer understanding of institutionalization processes would also enlarge more understanding not only on aspects related to decision-making practices, levels of reform acceptance and cooperation according to different institutional groups (i.e. top management, middle management, faculty, non-teaching staff and students), but also on the relationship between the government and HEIs. Developing research on this could make institutionalism even more useful in the study of HE dynamics, particularly on governance and policy implementation frameworks. Furthermore, in an era of increasing internationalization of HE, institutionalism may shed light on possible rationales for the tensions and/or contradictions between environmental pressures to conform and the need to maintain elements of national diversity. Ultimately, institutional theory has helped to frame and create some order and give meaning to the different metamorphosis of HE systems and their institutions.

Notes

1. The term 'new institutionalism' was coined by March and Olsen in 1984 to distinguish it from both the approaches to public administration theory in the United States and administrative science in Europe. The label 'new' accounts mostly to note that there was an 'old institutionalism' which was *updated* regarding the way institutions are seen and studied in political science (March and Olsen, 1984, p. 738).
2. An interesting point is that Kaplan (2006, p. 216) refers to universities as 'soft institutions' in opposition to the hard institutions focused on by economists and political scientists whose governance is based on written and implied rules for governing interaction.
3. Cf. Souto-Otero, Fleckenstein and Dacombe (2008) on this topic.
4. Cf. Greenwood and Hinings (1993) for the concept of archetype.

References

Amaral, A., Jones, G. and B. Karseth (eds) (2002) *Governing Higher Education: National Perspectives on Institutional Governance* (Dordrecht: Springer).
Amaral, A. and A. Magalhães (2003) 'The triple crisis of the university and its reinvention', *Higher Education Policy*, 16(2), 239–253.
Aspinwall, M. D. and G. Schneider (2000) 'Same menu, separate tables: the institutionalist turn in political science and the study of European integration', *European Journal of Political Research*, 38(1), 1–36.
Bell, S. (2002) 'Institutionalism', in J. Summers (ed) *Government, Politics, Power and Policy in Australia* (pp. 363–380) (Melbourne: Pearson Education Australia).
Bess, J. and J. Dee (2008) 'The application of organizational theory to colleges and universities', in *Understanding College and University Organization: Theories of Effective Policy and Practice VI* (pp. 1–17) (Sterling, VA: Stylus Publishing).
Bevir, M. (2009) *Key Concepts in Governance* (Los Angeles: SAGE).
Bleiklie, I. and M. Kogan (2007) 'Organization and governance of universities', *Higher Education Policy*, 20, 477–493.
Bruckmann, S. and T. Carvalho (2014) 'The reform process of Portuguese higher education institutions: from collegial to managerial governance', *Tertiary Education and Management*, 30(3), 193–206.
Carvalho, T. and R. Santiago (2010a) 'Still academics after all', *Higher Education Policy*, 23, 397–411.
Carvalho, T. and R. Santiago (2010b) 'New public management and "middle management": how do deans influence institutional policies?', in L. Meek, L. Goedegebuure, R. Santiago and T. Carvalho (eds) *The Changing Dynamics of Higher Education Middle Management* (pp. 165–196) (Dordrecht: Springer).
Carvalho, T. (2014) 'Changing connections between professionalism and managerialism: a case study of nursing in Portugal', *Professions and Organization*, 1(2), 1–15.

Chaui, M. (1999) 'A universidade em ruínas', in H. Trindade (ed) *Universidade em ruínas na república dos professors* (pp. 211–222) (Petrópolis: Editora Vozes).

Clark, B. (ed) (1970) *The Distinctive College* (Chicago: Aldine).

Clark, B. (1972) 'The organizational saga in higher education', *Administrative Science Quarterly*, 17(2), 178–184.

Clark, B. (ed) (1998) *Creating Entrepreneurial Universities: Organizational Pathways of Transformation* (New York: International Association of Universities Press/Pergamon: Elsevier Science).

Clark, B. (2004) 'Delineating the character of the entrepreneurial university', *Higher Education Policy*, 17(4), 355–370.

Cohen, M., March, J. and J. Olsen (1972) 'A garbage can model of organizational choice', *Administrative Science Quarterly*, 17, 1–25.

Cohen, M. and J. March (1974) *Leadership and Ambiguity: The American College President* (New York: McGraw-Hill).

DiMaggio, P. and W. Powell (1983) (eds) *The New Institutionalism in Organizational Analysis* (Chicago: University of Chicago Press).

Diogo, S. (2014a) 'Implementing the Bologna Process in Portugal and in Finland: national and institutional realities in perspective', *Journal of the European Higher Education Area*, 1(1), 35–54.

Ferlie, E., Musselin, C. and G. Andresani (2008) 'The steering of higher education systems: a public management perspective', *Higher Education*, 56(3), 325–348.

Fligstein, N. (2008) 'Fields, Power and Social Skill: A Critical Analysis of the New Institutionalisms', *Center for Culture, Organizations and Politics*. UC Berkeley: Center for Culture, Organizations and Politics. Retrieved from: https://escholarship.org/uc/item/89m770dv.

Fumasoli, T. and B. Stensaker (2013) 'Organizational studies in higher education: a reflection on historical themes and prospective trends', *Higher Education Policy*, 26, 479–496.

Gornitzka, Å. (1999) 'Governmental policies and organisational change', *Higher Education*, 38(1), 5–29.

Greenwood, R. and C. Hinings (1993) 'Understanding strategic change: the contribution of archetypes', *The Academy of Management Journal*, 36(5), 1052–1081.

Greenwood, R., Oliver, C., Sahlin, K. and R. Suddaby (eds) (2008) 'Introduction', *The SAGE Handbook of Organizational Institutionalism* (pp. 1–46) (London: SAGE Publications Ltd).

Hall, P. and R. Taylor (1996) 'Political science and the three new institutionalisms', *Political Studies*, 44(5), 936–957.

Hannan, T. and J. Freeman (1977) 'The population ecology of organizations', *The American Journal of Sociology*, 82(5), 929–964.

Hodgson, G. (2008) 'The emergence of the idea of institutions as repositories of knowledge', in A. Ebner and N. Beck (eds) *The Institutions of the Market: Organizations, Social Systems, and Governance* (pp. 23–40) (Oxford: Oxford University Press).

Kaplan, G. (2006) 'Institutions of academic governance and institutional theory: a framework for further research', in J. C. Smart (ed) *Higher Education: Handbook of Theory and Research*, Volume XXI (pp. 213–281) (Dordrecht: Springer).

Koelble, T. (1995) 'The new institutionalism in political science and sociology', *Comparative Politics*, 27(2), 231–243.

Lounsbury, M. and M. Ventresca (2003) 'The new structuralism in organizational theory', *Organization*, 10(3), 457–480.

Mahoney, J. and K. Thelen (eds) (2010) *Explaining Institutional Change – Ambiguity, Agency, and Power* (Cambridge: Cambridge University Press).

March, J. and J. Olsen (eds) (1989) *Rediscovering Institutions: The Organizational Basis of Politics* (New York, NY: Free Press).

March, J. and J. Olsen (1984) 'The new institutionalism: organizational factors in political life', *The American Political Science Review*, 78(3), 734–749.

March, J. and J. Olsen (2005) 'Elaborating the new institutionalism', *Working Paper*, 11, http://www.arena.uio.no retrieved November 2014.

Meyer, J. and B. Rowan (1977) 'Institutionalized organizations: formal structure as myth and ceremony', *American Journal of Sociology*, 83(2), 340–363.

Meyer, J. and B. Rowan (1985) 'The structure of educational organizations', in J. Meyer, and R. Scott (eds) *Organizational Environments: Rituals and Rationality* (pp. 71–97) (Beverly Hills, CA: Sage).

Meyer, J. and R. Scott (1983) *Organizational Environments* (Beverly Hills, CA: Sage).

Meyer, J., Ramirez, F., Frank, D. and E. Schofer (2008) 'Higher education as an institution', in P. Gumport (ed) *Sociology of Higher Education: Contributions and Their Contexts* (pp. 187–221) (Baltimore: Johns Hopkins University Press).

Nagel, A., Martens, K. and M. Windzio (2010) 'Introduction – education policy in transformation', in K. Martens, K. Nagel, M. Windzio and A. Weymann (eds) *Transformation of Education Policy* (pp. 3–27) (Houndmills: Palgrave Macmillan).

Neave, G. (ed) (2012) *The Evaluative State, Institutional Autonomy and Re-engineering Higher Education in Western Europe. The Prince and His Pleasure* (Basingstoke and New York: Palgrave Macmillan).

Nóvoa, A. and T. Yariv-Mashal (2003) 'Comparative research in education: a mode of governance or a historical journey?', *Comparative Education*, 39(4), 423–439.

Ordorika, I. (2014) 'Governance and change in higher education: the debate between classical political sociology, new institutionalism and critical theories', *Bordon*, 66(1), 107–121.

Souto-Otero, M., Fleckenstein, T. and R. Dacombe (2008) 'Filling in the gaps: European governance, the open method of coordination and the European commission', *Journal of Education Policy*, 23(3), 231–249.

Pietilä, M. (2014) 'The many faces of research profiling: academic leaders' conceptions of research steering', *Higher Education*, 67, 303–316.

Parsons, T. (1956) 'Suggestions for a sociological approach to the theory of organizations', *Administrative Science Quarterly*, 1, 63–85.

Pfeffer, J. and G. Salancik (eds) (1978) *The External Control of Organizations: A Resource Dependence Perspective* (New York: Harper & Row).

Pollack, M. (2009) 'The new institutionalisms and European integration', in A. Wiener and T. Diez (eds) *European Integration Theory* (pp. 125–144) (Oxford: Oxford University Press).

Powell, W. (2007) 'The new institutionalism', *The International Encyclopedia of Organization Studies* (Thousand Oaks, CA: SAGE Publications).

Ramirez, F. (2012) 'The world society perspective: concepts, assumptions and strategies', *Comparative Education*, 48(4), 423–439.

Scott, R. (2001) *Institutions and Organizations* (Thousand Oaks, CA: Sage).

Selznick, P. (1948) 'Foundations of the theory of organizations', *American Sociological Review*, 13(1), 25–35.

Selznick, P. (1957) *Leadership in Administration: A Sociological Interpretation* (Berkeley: University of California Press).

Simon, R. A. (1947) *Administrative Behavior: A Study of Decision-Making Processes in Administrative Organization* (New York: The Macmillan Co).

Thoenig, J. C. (2012) 'Institutional theories and public institutions: traditions and appropriateness', in G. Peters and J. Pierre (eds) *Handbook of Public Administration* (pp. 127–138) (Thousand Oaks, CA: SAGE Knowledge).

Thornton, P. and W. Ocasio (2008) 'Institutional logics', in R. Greenwood, C. Oliver, K. Sahlin and R. Suddaby (eds) *The SAGE Handbook of Organizational Institutionalism* (pp. 99–129) (Thousand Oaks, CA: SAGE Publications Ltd).

Tolbert, P. and L. Zucker (1996) 'The institutionalization of institutional theory', in S. Clegg, C. Hardy and W. Nord (eds) *Handbook of Organization Studies* (pp. 175–190) (London: SAGE).

Veiga, A. (2010) *Bologna and the Institutionalisation of the European Higher Education Area*, Doctoral Dissertation (Porto: University of Porto).

Veiga, A. and A. Amaral (2012) 'Soft law and implementation problems of the Bologna process', *Educação, Sociedade e Culturas*, 36, 121–140.

Välimaa, J. (2005) 'Social dynamics of higher education reforms: the case of Finland', in Å. Gornitzka, M. Kogan and A. Amaral (eds) *Reform and Change in Higher Education. Analysing Policy Implementation* (pp. 245–269) (Dordrecht: Springer).

Weick, K. (1976) 'Educational organizations as loosely coupled systems', *Administrative Science Quarterly*, 21(1), 1–19.

Whitley, R. and J. Gläser (eds) (2014) *Organizational Transformation and Scientific Change: The Impact of Institutional Restructuring on Universities and Intellectual Innovation* (Bingley: Emerald Group Publishing Limited).

Williamson, O. (1981) 'The economics of organization: the transaction cost approach', *American Journal of Sociology*, 87(3), 548–577.

Witte, J. (2006) *Change of Degrees and Degrees of Change: Comparing Adaptations of European Higher Education Systems in the Context of the Bologna Process*, Doctoral Dissertation (Twente: Center for Higher Education Policy Studies, University of Twente).

Zucker, L. (1977) 'The role of institutionalization in cultural persistence', *American Sociological Review*, 42, 726–743.

8
Agency Theory as a Framework for Higher Education Governance

Jussi Kivistö and Inga Zalyevska

Introduction

Agency theory (also known as the principal-agent or principal agency theory/model) describes the relationship between two or more parties, in which one party, designated as the principal, engages another party, designated as the agent, to perform some task on behalf of the principal (Jensen and Meckling, 1976; Moe, 1984; Ross, 1973). The theory assumes that once principals delegate authority to agents, they often have problems controlling them, because agents' goals often differ from their own and because agents often have better information about their capacity and activities than do principals. The key question of the principal–agent framework is, 'How does one empower an agent to fulfil the needs of the principal, while at the same time constraining the agent from shirking on their responsibilities?'

Although strongly influenced by its original background in economics (Alchian and Demsetz, 1972; Jensen and Meckling, 1976; Ross, 1973) and political science (Mitnick, 1975; Moe, 1984; Rose-Ackerman, 1978), agency theory has never been the exclusive property of any particular paradigm, discipline or field of study.[1] Rather, due to its generic nature, it has proven to be a widely applied theoretical and empirical framework in many different disciplines and approaches. To this date, the theory has been utilized widely in fields as diverse as accounting, finance, marketing, law, sociology, public administration, organization and management studies and applied psychology, to name a few. Its growing popularity lies in its ability in providing insights for bilateral relations between self-interested parties, where each party is faced with information asymmetry about the other party's effort and interests (cf. Cuevas-Rodríguez, Gomez-Mejia and Wiseman, 2012).

In the field of higher education research, agency theory remained largely unknown throughout 1980s and 1990s. Several scholars (e.g. Ferris, 1991; Hölttä, 1995; Williams, 1995; Massy, 1996; Geuna, 1999) did acknowledge the principal–agent settings in higher education, but deeper and more systematic examination of this relationship as an agency relationship was left aside. It wasn't until 2000s that a number of researchers started applying the theory in a more thorough manner to examination of government–higher education institution relationships (Kivistö, 2005, 2007; Lane, 2005, 2007; Lane and Kivistö, 2008; Liefner, 2003). More recently, the context of application of the theory has been extended to cover a broader range of topics such as leadership and strategic planning in higher education institutions (Auld, 2010), regulation and monitoring of cross-border higher education (Borgos, 2013; Lane, Kinser and Knox, 2013) and university autonomy (Enders, de Boer and Weyer, 2013).

In this chapter, we provide an overview of basic concepts of agency theory and analyse how it can be framed in the context of higher education governance. We then review existing work that incorporates agency theory in higher education research and identify strengths and weaknesses of agency theory in this context. Finally, we draw conclusions and briefly suggest a few directions for future research. Although our discussion throughout the chapter relates mostly to the general relationship between governments and universities, we also provide examples of other types of agency relationships whenever appropriate.

Principals, agents and agency relationships

Agency relationships are a ubiquitous phenomenon. In the broadest sense, whenever one party (the principal) depends on the action of another party (the agent), agency relationship arises (Pratt and Zeckhauser, 1985). The basic reason for establishing an agency relationship – whether it be contractual or hierarchical – is that the principal, for whatever reason, needs a certain task to be performed and is ready to compensate the agent for performing this task. Although the traditional forms of agency theory have focused on relations between individuals, the applicability of the theory has been proven relevant at the group and organizational level as well.

The foundation to application of agency theory in higher education studies is defining principals and agents, as well as different levels of agency relationship. The first systematic attempt to provide such an account was made by Liefner (2003) in the context of examining forms of resource allocation and their effect on performance in higher education institutions. According to his analysis, the principal can be a ministry of science and education, the university board, the president, a dean or a department chair. The agents are those actors who receive salaries and assignments from principals. By this token, most of the institutional managers and management bodies of universities may act as both principals and agents, whereas some groups and individuals, such as academic staff members, will be primarily in the agent role (chain of agency relationships).

When agency theory first emerged in the higher education field in the early 2000s, the focus was primarily on the government–university relationship. This relationship was the subject of both theoretical (Kivistö, 2005, 2007, 2008; Lane and Kivistö, 2008) and applied studies in a number of policy and geographical contexts (Gornitzka et al., 2004; Lane, 2005, 2007; Liefner, 2003). According to Kivistö (2007), the government–university relationship can be considered as an agency relationship if the following three conditions in this relationship are present: (1) tasks that the government delegates to a university; (2) resources that the government allocates to a university for accomplishing the tasks; and (3) government interest in monitoring the accomplishment of the tasks. The form of the agency relationship between the government and a university can be hierarchical, contractual or some combination of these two. In the case of a purely hierarchical relationship (traditional governance by law and regulations), universities are viewed more as public agencies implementing government policies, whereas in relationships containing contractual elements (e.g. performance agreements between the government and universities), stronger sense of reciprocity and negotiation is included in the relationship (Gornitzka et al., 2004).

The government, as a principal, can be defined differently depending on the context and perspective. When understood in a narrower sense, the government can be viewed as a public bureau or agency, such as a ministry or department of education. Also intermediary agencies, such as funding councils, operating under auspices of ministries/departments, can be considered as principals as far as they play a role in setting the tasks, allocating the resources and monitoring the institutions. A university, as an agent, is considered to be a higher education institution which has identifiable legal and economical boundaries separating it from the body of government. Both the government and universities are viewed as aggregations of individual human members forming one unitary actor.

In addition to the government–university relationship, more recently a diversity of possible perspectives has been explored more widely. For example, Lane's analysis (2005), based on the perspective of political science, further distinguished between three types of principals: single, multiple and collective. In Lane's framework, the single principal situation is the least complex but also the least common, generally corresponding to the individual level of the agency relationship. On the other hand, collective principals are differentiated from these by being single entities, where 'multiple individuals must agree on the nature of the contract with the agent' (p. 22). It is also common for multiple principals to coexist (e.g. in the US context – governor, legislator, higher education commissioner, coordinating board).

Looking at effects of performance-based pay on academic teaching, Wilkesman and Schmid (2012) considered the social and cultural variations of the principal–agent roles. The authors claim that, traditionally, in German universities, the professor was an independent principal. Academic staff are acquiring agentic status with the advent of managerial governance, but, coming from such deep roots of professional independence, there is room for personal interpretation of one's role. The authors then posit a hypothesis that professors' behaviour depends less on the objective resource dependency and formal relationships and more on personal identification as agents or principals.

Assumptions: Informational asymmetries and goal conflicts

There are two important assumptions that are very important to agency theory – the existence of informational asymmetries and goal conflicts (e.g. Moe, 1984; Eisenhardt, 1989). Informational asymmetries refer to the claim that the agent possesses more or better information about his or her capacity to perform the task and the progress of individual tasks assigned to him than the principal. Goal conflicts, in their turn, are understood as differences or conflicts in a principal's and an agent's desires and interests. Goal conflicts arise due to the assumed self-interest[2] of principals and agents, which consequently leads agents to pursue different courses of action than expected by their principals.

Informational asymmetries are prevalent in the sphere of higher education in general, and in government–university relationships in particular. Kivistö (2007) identified three main sources of informational asymmetries in the government–university relationship: the nature of academic work, organizational complexity of universities and complex production technology. In relation to academic work, the high potential for information asymmetries stems from the intangible nature of its core substance – knowledge. Academic work is also specialized, making it difficult to understand its deliverables for outsiders, and complex with a multiplicity of specific tasks, making it difficult to measure the time spent on one or another. In fact, many specific tasks that constitute academic work tend to blend and are not tied to specific time and place.

Organizational complexities also increase the level of informational asymmetries. Despite the recent management trends promoting stronger and tighter management systems, universities are still to a large extent 'loosely coupled' organizations (Birnbaum, 1988; Weick, 1976) with their character, structure and purpose supporting diversity and non-uniformity (Patterson, 2001). An important element adding to complexity is the matrix structure where units belong simultaneously to both the institution and the discipline (Alpert, 1985; Clark, 1983). This characteristic is important from the perspective of information asymmetries – even though the universities are relatively flat structures hierarchically. Information asymmetries originate both on the side of the academic staff (due to, for example, information having to pass through at least two or three disciplinary and administrative levels) and on the side of the administration (due to the increasingly more specialized nature of its operations) (Kivistö, 2007).

The assumption about goal conflicts can be considered as valid and relevant in higher education context as in any other societal contexts. Governments throughout the world are increasingly using legislation and various accountability measures in order to link the goals of universities to policy priorities. At the same time, universities are more prone to motivate their staff with performance-linked salary systems and promotion schemes, which also include incentives in line with governments' policy priorities. If there was an assumption of perfect goal congruence throughout the chains of principal–agent dyads between the government, university management and academic staff, it is likely that these measures would not be as universally accepted and applied as they are in the contemporary higher education sector landscape. As in other contexts, goal conflicts arise because of a self-interest; universities and individual academics sometime prioritize issues (e.g. influence, prestige, revenue, leisure) which may be at odds with the policy goals of their principals (e.g. higher quality and efficiency, more value for money). The depth and intensity of goal conflicts may naturally vary at different points in time, by different goals and by different tasks (Kivistö, 2007).

Agency problem, contracts and governance mechanisms

Informational asymmetries and goal conflicts are considered to be the two 'spark plugs' of the agency theory (Waterman and Meier, 1998, p. 177), and, taken together, they constitute the agency problem, that is, the possibility of opportunistic behaviour on the agent's part that goes against the principal's interest. Agency problem manifests itself at two stages of the agency relationship, pre- and post-contractual. The question that guides pre-contractual process is, 'How can the principal choose the right type of agent for accomplishing the task?', resulting in what is called the problem of 'adverse selection'.[3] After the agent is chosen and a contract is formed, another question emerges, 'How can the principal make the agent behave according to the principal's goals?', resulting in the second aspect of the agency problem, the 'moral hazard'. Concrete aspects of the moral hazard problem may include shirking or any other form of self-serving behaviour, which is not in the best interests of the principal. Self-interest can also make the agent reluctant to share performance information with the principal, or even worse, motivate the agent to send wrong information to the principal (Milgrom and Roberts, 1992). The principal has two basic options to control opportunistic behaviour in terms of contracts to be agreed upon: 'behaviour-based contracts' and 'outcome-based contracts' (Eisenhardt, 1989). As the name implies, in behaviour-based contracts, the principal invests in monitoring the agent's actions and then rewards them to the extent that they correspond to principal's goals. On the other hand, outcome-based contracts, rewarding the produced outcomes, are more rational when monitoring is too impractical or expensive. The rationale is that such contracts reduce goal conflict and incentivize the agent to pursue directly those outcomes compatible with the principal's goals.

As an assumption, the possibility of opportunism is universal in the sense that it is not limited to any profession, sector or field of activity. Therefore, every action of a university and an individual academic could turn into a form of opportunistic behaviour whenever this behaviour is being motivated by self-interest going against the best interests of the principal. At the universities, possible manifestations of opportunistic behaviour can include, but are not limited to, shirking, opportunistic pursuit of prestige or revenue revenues, opportunistic cross-subsidization and the distortion of monitoring information (see Kivistö, 2007). Opportunistic activities are often completed in hiding, and, therefore, their occurrence can be detected mainly on the basis of their negative effects on individual or institutional performance.

At the level of government–university relationships, many governance procedures employed by the government have a logical analogy with behaviour-based contracts. These include, but are not limited to, reporting requests, site visits, reviews, evaluations, assessments and audits that focus on monitoring productive activities, with the primary purpose of informing the government about how universities are 'behaving' in economic and operational terms. For instance, Gornitzka et al. (2004) used the concept of informational asymmetries to evaluate the strengths and weaknesses of established contract arrangements in Finland, Sweden and Denmark. After their analysis, the authors concluded that closer integration of external quality evaluation systems with other instruments of behaviour-based governance serves to minimize informational asymmetries, even if it remains impossible to reduce them to zero. According to Kivistö (2005), different forms of input-based funding arrangements (line-item budgeting or input-based formula funding), in which the amount of funding allocated is based on the resources used or the activities carried out by the universities, represent another type of 'behaviour-based governance' procedures.

The other option for the government to prevent the moral hazard problem from occurring is to offer output-related incentives to universities. Similarly, with outcome-based contracts, the general objective of output-based governance is to reduce goal conflicts by aligning the goals of universities with the ones of the government by specifying targeted outputs to be measured and rewarded. Output-based governance is usually organized through performance-based funding practices that are constructed on some output-based funding formula, such as credits obtained, the number of degrees granted, graduate employability, weighted number of research publications, research income, the number of patents and the number of doctoral degrees granted and so forth.

Agency costs and agency variables

Governance mechanisms designed to limit agency problems can be considered second-best solutions. A first-best solution would occur if alignment of goals between principals and agents were assured without the added costs of governance. Unfortunately, first-best solution is an unfeasible option for the principals, because agents might hold separate goals at some point during the relationship without principals acknowledging it (Gomez-Meijia and Wiseman, 2006). Therefore, the central challenge for principals is to structure their relationships with their agents in a way which maximizes the control effects under the limited budget constraint (McLendon, 2003). For this challenge, agency theory presents the two interrelated concepts known as 'agency variables' and 'agency costs', which can offer either general or case-specific ex-ante, as well as ex-post insights concerning the costs, efficiency and effectiveness of particular governance methods.

Agency variables depict the benefits and shortcomings of different control procedures in a certain context, and therefore, they can be used as predictors in search for most efficient contracting choice in a given situation.[4] Although the exact number of agency variables has varied within different research settings, at least four variables, namely, 'outcome measurability', 'outcome uncertainty', 'task programmability' and 'goal conflict' have been used in several applications of the theory. When outcomes of the delegated task are not easily measurable (outcome measurability) and when success in their production is uncertain due to some factors outside of the agent's control (outcome uncertainty), it is assumed that the principal will prefer behaviour-based contracts instead of outcome-based contracts, as the latter become more risky. However, if the delegated task is highly complex, making direct monitoring of the agent impossible or very expensive (task programmability), the principal is expected to prefer outcome-based contracts to behaviour-based contracts. Similarly, if divergences of interests between the principal and agent are expected to be high (goal conflicts), principal is more likely to choose outcome-based contracts over the behaviour-based contracts in order to align his or hers and the agent's incentives more strongly (Kivistö, 2008).

When we examine agency variables in government–university relationship at a general and broad level, it seems that governments are likely to face challenges with both types of governance procedures, albeit for different reasons. For instance, teaching and research outputs are both, to a large extent, immeasurable (definitional problems of what are the 'right' outputs) and uncertain (uncontrollable aspects in student behaviour, unpredictable nature of research work), indicating that the government should make use of behaviour-based governance procedures. However, the low task programmability of teaching and research activities (non-repeatable tasks requiring high levels of expertise) suggests that the government should turn to output-based governance mechanisms in order to bypass the informational asymmetries related to low task programmability. Furthermore, high or even moderate goal conflicts between the government and university can create incentive problems which increase the possibility of opportunistic behaviour. This again would lead to the suggestion of the use of output-based governance (Kivistö, 2008). It is a matter of concrete context, opinion and political debate which side of problems pointed by the agency variables are to be given higher emphasis. For instance, the increasing use and importance of output-based funding measures over the past decade in European higher education systems (see e.g. Jongbloed et al., 2010, pp. 49–51) could imply that the challenges related to output/outcome measurability and uncertainty have been considered as a 'lesser-evil' than relying on alternative funding schemes (e.g. input-based funding arrangements coupled with monitoring and reporting responsibilities).

The other concept, agency costs, can be understood as the total costs of different contracting choices, that is, costs resulting from neutralizing information asymmetries and goal conflicts plus the costs resulting from remaining agent opportunism (cf. Jensen and Meckling, 1976). Even though the monetary costs of governance in a given concrete situation are impossible to calculate in precision, they can be estimated. For instance, the cost of governance procedures could be evaluated indirectly as the amount of planning they require to be established and to operate, the number of new employment positions required or new hierarchies their application creates and the observable or estimated dysfunctions (including administrative burdens) they inflict on the production behaviour of the universities. Due to the invisible and unperceivable nature of opportunistic behaviour, the costs of detected and undetected opportunism are even more difficult to calculate. Nevertheless, as a theoretical concept, they can offer interesting perspectives on the meaningfulness and effects of the university governance (Kivistö, 2007).

The government faces a trade-off between two costly options: either it attempts to decrease informational asymmetries and pays the costs related to behaviour-based governance or it reduces goal conflict by choosing the output-based form of governing and pays the agency costs related to output-based governance. Naturally, the government can do both by simultaneously introducing a funding formula which contains elements of behaviour- and output-based governance. In such a situation, however, all the benefits and shortcomings of both behaviour- and output-based governance will occur at a magnitude related to the weight they have in the funding formula and other governance arrangements. Nevertheless, on the basis of predictions indicated by the agency variables, it can be argued that the government will inevitably suffer relatively high agency costs. The only difference is how large these costs can become and the ways in which they are accumulated. Hypothetically speaking, if the costs resulting from ungoverned opportunism are expected to remain lower than the governing costs of opportunism, the cost-efficient solution would be to reduce governance efforts (Kivistö, 2007).

The role of agency theory in recent higher education studies

In recent years, agency theory has been applied in higher education studies to explore new manifestations of the principal–agent relationship and a wider range of practical contexts in higher education administration. However, owing to the divergent development of agency theory in different disciplines – mainly economics (including New Institutional Economics and Organizational Economics) and political science – application of the theory to higher education governance and policy has developed in a somewhat disjointed and non-unitary manner. As in other disciplinary settings, agency theory has been used and interpreted in many ways depending on the author's disciplinary tradition and the problem at hand. Despite this diversity, in this section we provide an overview of some of the most important recent studies utilizing agency theory in higher education setting. We will proceed by examining how agency theory concepts have been theoretically conceptualized and applied in these studies at three different levels of the principal–agent relationship: university–government, government–university president and university–faculty.

In his doctoral dissertation, Kivistö (2007) examined thoroughly the key perceptions and insights that agency theory offers for investigating government–university relationship. Although the main focus in Kivistö's study was in theoretical conceptualization, an empirical case (implementation of the government 'Programme for Increasing Education in Information Industry Fields' in 1998–2005) was utilized as an illustrative device to refine and illuminate the theory. Based on his analysis, Kivistö concluded that agency theory can provide an applicable framework for analysing government–university interaction, since it is able to offer explanatory insights for government governance behaviour. For instance, by highlighting the importance of information asymmetries, goal conflicts and the possibility of opportunistic behaviour, agency theory offers, within its limitations, structured and coherent explanations for the use of quality assurance mechanisms and performance-based funding. Especially accepting opportunism as a possible explanation for implementation and governance failures has a potential to generate useful views about the productive and economic behaviour of universities. By offering theoretical understandings and solutions for the phenomena of inefficiency and cost growth, agency theory is able to underline many of the most topical issues in the higher education community: performance-based funding, incentives and compensation for management and faculty, university-business partnerships, management of overseas branches and so on. Granted, agency theory is subject to shortcomings of its own, which we address in the next section.

Lane and Kivistö (2008) explored further the theoretical and conceptual issues related to importing agency theory into the study of higher education governance. The main emphasis of Lane and Kivistö's study was to investigate differences in assumptions in economics-oriented version of agency theory (more prevalent in European higher education studies, and also the model outlined in preceding sections of this chapter) and political science-oriented version (more prevalent in higher education studies in the United States) when applying agency theory in the context of higher education. By focusing on seven key dimensions (contract, unit of analysis, actor motivation, principal–agent relationships, principal's primary mode of control, outputs of the agency relationship and the source of agent opportunistic shirking), Lane and Kivistö highlighted several differences between the two orientations. For instance, from the vantage of political science, 'government' actually comprises multiple principals (in the United States, legislature, governor, boards) and it cannot automatically be viewed as a single entity. When these separate principals act harmoniously, then the government may be assumed to be acting as a single principal. However, when these principals act in contradictory ways, it is important to recognize the existence of these multiple entities as it has a significant impact on how the university operates. At times, it is assumed that the university may have to select between competing goals, and therefore, from the perspective of determining the level of culpability, it becomes important to know why the university acted in the opportunistic way it did. Moreover, political science orientation has identified an issue called 'slippage' – the concept indicating that university miscompliance may be due to information lost in communication, particularly when there are extended principal–agent chains, rather than intended agent opportunism.

On the other hand, the economics version of the agency theory gives conceptual priority to economic aspects of the principal–agent relationship by investigating and analysing the agent's opportunism and the principal's means to overcome it. In this sense, the economics-oriented version is more 'principal's theory', since it takes more strongly the perspective of securing the principal's welfare against agent opportunism. In the sphere of higher education, this approach manifests itself in the focus on economic issues like costs, productivity and the efficiency and effectiveness of government's control and governance procedures. Moreover, economics-oriented agency theory understands and examines agency relationships mainly as bilateral relationships between one principal and one or more agents. Despite these and other differences in conceptualization, Lane and Kivistö (2008) conclude that agency theory holds great benefit for scholars of tertiary education governance systems. Both perspectives are useful in attempting to understand and explain the government–university relationship. However, acknowledging some of the conditional requirements and differing basic assumptions is critical for further applications and development of the theory.

An example of how exactly the agency problem between universities and the government plays out around a specific goal is provided by Blalark (2012). He shows how the university and the state diverge on a seemingly common goal of raising the education level in the population with the university prioritizing graduation rates and the state – overall baccalaureate degree attainment. While the state focuses on raising attainment levels among the traditionally underserved populations, these groups may be perceived as an enrolment risk for the university as they are also more likely to drop out. Informational asymmetries that activate the agency problem persist due to both technological challenges – developing data collection and reporting methods fit for the task and the conceptual challenge of performance comparison across a set of non-homogenous institutions (p. 8).

Agency theory is also being applied to understand university–government relationships in relatively new areas, such as cross-border education. It has proven useful in studies that aim to disentangle the various vectors of influence involved in regulating and assuring quality of cross-border education. Lane, Kinser and Knox (2013) used it in their study of regulations pertaining to U.S. public universities exporting their educational services to another state. They noted that an alteration to the basic agency relationship occurs in this case, as all states (with only three exceptions) retain their role in regulating the university's activity outside state borders, while a new agent–principal relationship also emerges between the university and the importing state. Looking at the content of regulations, the study found that the governments developed much heavier regulations for importing educational services than for export. This led the authors to suggest that there is value in investigating further the differences in the principal–agent relationship with the regulating government between importing and indigenous higher education institutions. In a separate study, Borgos (2013) examined the establishment of international medical branch campuses and also demonstrated how in cross-border education goal conflicts and informational asymmetries become more complex. The added complexities were found with regard to the increased number of principals who had a stake in quality assurance and educational outcomes in the two cases of overseas medical campuses chosen for the study. For example, the accrediting institutions for the home and overseas campuses of a U.S.-based medical school were different, opening up the potential for goal conflicts, and the level of expertise between the local government, local sponsors and the importing institutions were also different, leading to greater potential for informational asymmetries.

Although agency theory studies of higher education have predominantly focused on the government–university relationship at the level of legislation, in more recent years we have seen a shift down in the level of analysis that McLendon (2003) called for. In a recent extensive study, Macias (2012) uses agency theory to provide an analysis of the funding allocations and budgeting processes between a public university and the system office to which it reports (the author also frames this in more universal terms as a board–university relationship). In her focus on expectations that the principal has of the agent, Macias' study provides evidence of both explicit and implicit arrangements that exist between them and how the risks associated with the agency problem are often mitigated through collaborative negotiation of goals and expectations.

Auld (2010) applied agency theory framework to the level of government–university president relationship in order to explain the difficulties associated with the development and execution of strategic plans by universities. In the context of institutional strategic planning, he views the president as the primary agent and the government as the principal. In articulating and executing a mission and vision for the university, it is the president's complex role to interpret and reconcile the governmental goals with the often diverse goals of the university board members and with the culture and aspirations of the institution at large. Auld then suggests that paying attention to four contractual principles ('Informative Principle', 'Incentive Intensity Principle', 'Monitoring Principle' and 'Equal Compensation Principle'[5]) in the principal–agent framework will bring the process of strategic planning and negotiation closer to an optimal outcome. Together, contractual principles help ensure the optimal amount of information available to the government about the effort dedicated to its goals, the optimal balance of incentives and monitoring that does not divert too much energy away into micro-management or excessive bureaucracy, and optimal alignment between the university's and governmental goals.

A set of studies have also analysed the university–faculty relationship in principal–agent terms (Wilkesmann, 2013; Wilkesmann and Schmid, 2012). Examining the impact of new managerialism on academic teaching, the studies compared the influence of a set of factors drawn from within and outside the principal–agent framework. Even though governments, along with university boards and rectors, have been recasting their relationship with the faculty in principal–agent terms, the authors point out that classroom teaching in German universities remains a domain where administration has relatively limited means of influence or performance control. Measures such as merit pay, performance-based budgeting, management by objectives and teaching awards are all designed to create incentives for the faculty to continually improve the quality of their teaching. The authors studied the influence of these incentives in comparison with factors such as a professor's own perception of one's status as an agent or principal and socialization of teaching behaviour. As the result of their analysis based on a survey of over 1,000 German professors, the authors have found no effects of managerial instruments on the significance that professors attached to academic teaching, but found strong positive influence of social or cultural factors.

Strengths and weaknesses of agency theory

Like other theories, agency theory has several strengths and weaknesses in general, and in the context of higher education governance in particular. In the following sections, we provide a short and concise summary about the main merits and demerits of the theory.[6]

Strong theories are often simple and generic. The universality of agency relationships has made agency theory sufficiently simple and generic to allow for its application to different contexts and research settings. The fact that agency theory has been used in a variety settings, suggests to us that it has broad applicability and can be moulded to incorporate many different contextual factors (Gomez-Meijia and Wiseman, 2006). As it has been shown in preceding sections of this chapter, the field of higher education governance and policy has offered a range of research settings where agency theory has been able to contribute. Apparently, this is due to the fact that agency framework with its basic concepts and assumptions (principal and agent, agency relationship, goal conflicts and informational asymmetries, agency problems, agency variables and agency costs) have been relatively easy to adapt to different levels of relationships (system, inter-organizational, intra-organizational, interpersonal) and phenomena.

Good theories are also useful. A theory can be considered useful in terms of its explanatory potential and predictive adequacy and also in terms of its capability to increase understanding by describing a phenomenon. Indeed, a good theory can illuminate options for action that would not otherwise be apparent, stimulate greater understanding and evoke new and unexpected insights (Harmon and Mayer, 1986; Kezar, 2006). Even though the validation of explanatory and predictive capabilities of agency theory is still far from being fully tested in higher education setting, it has proven to focus attention on several higher education governance issues which other theories or frameworks do not pay sufficient attention. Firstly, in terms of the usefulness, one of the greatest overall strengths of agency theory is that it offers insights on the economic behaviour of universities. For instance, describing and identifying different forms of opportunistic behaviour is theoretically investigated in higher education research. Agency theory, however, is able to provide a platform for conceptualizing different forms of institutional and individual opportunism and analysing the expected effects of opportunistic behaviour on individual and institutional productivity. If opportunistic behaviour is recognized as a possible explanation for performance failures, this would need to be acknowledged in the context of developing governance mechanisms, such as performance measurement, funding models and quality assessment by taking into account the concrete forms of opportunistic behaviour. This could provide new and valuable insights especially in assessing the impact of various governance mechanisms on university behaviour and performance, thereby making more effective and accurate use of these mechanisms.

Secondly, agency theory provides unique insights by examining the economic characteristics of universities with respect to the behavioural implications for governance mechanisms. As such, agency theory seems to be able to offer a broad but logically consistent framework related to governance of universities, in which other concepts, frameworks and even theories could be integrated in a meaningful way. And, thirdly, as an important part of discerning the governance of agency problem, agency theory introduces the concepts of agency cost and agency variables that are able to offer insights concerning the costs, efficiency and effectiveness of particular governance methods. When choosing between different governance procedures, the government or some other higher education principal can analyse and make predictions about the applicability and cost of each procedure in light of the agency variables. In addition to their predictive capabilities, the use of these variables offers help both for conceptualizing and analysing many of the strengths and weaknesses that are inherent in using particular behaviour- and output-based governance procedures.

In addition to the reported strengths, agency theory has also faced heavy criticism (see e.g. Perrow, 1986; Donaldson, 1990; Shapiro, 2005), and some of it is relevant in the context of higher education. Paradoxically, most of this criticism is related to one of the perceived strengths of the theory – simplicity of the basic assumptions and the general framework of the theory. Especially the behavioural assumptions concerning human motivation and behaviour have been contested. The critics argue that the theory presents a far too narrow and negative model of human motives and behaviour. As the theory is focusing only on self-interested motives leading to opportunistic behaviour, it fails to recognize a wider range of human motives, including altruism, trust, respect and intrinsic motivation of an inherently satisfying task. If the principal was more trusting and cooperative towards the agent, the theory's normative focus on agency problems becomes meaningless or at least less relevant. This criticism also has validity when agency theory is utilized for analysing higher education governance; if universities and their academic staff are considered only as self-interested opportunists, a high level of realism and objectivity will be lost. Even though agency theory does not suggest that opportunistic self-interest is the only motivator of human beings, the theory mostly fails to distinguish an agent's non-opportunistic performance failures from the opportunistic ones.

Assumptions related to the nature of agency relationship have likewise been criticized. Some scholars have considered relationships modelled by agency theory as acontextual, ahistorical and static. In reality, interpersonal relationships are more dynamic and organic, taking into account aspects related to broader social context, learning and reciprocity (Shapiro, 2005). Moreover, the fact that agency theory is not able to include third parties, stakeholders or competing principals holistically in its analysis is clearly a great weakness. This can be a problem especially in the sphere of higher education, where universities and individual academics have several stakeholder groups acting as their principals (e.g. research councils, fee-paying students, business and employers, alumni, local communities and governments, supranational financier organizations). The existence of numerous resource providers often leads universities into a situation, where the task fulfilment of one stakeholder group can be considered as opportunistic behaviour going against the interests of others.

Finally, the fact that agency theory examines agency relationships without questioning the legitimacy or sensibility of the principal's goals can also be considered as a limitation of the theory, although not from the logical but from the ethical perspective. Sometimes the principal's goals and tasks submitted to agents can be unclear, pernicious or even contradictory. If agency theory is considered as a normative and prescriptive theory – as some of its critics do – the relationships between a government and universities can become particularly problematic and raise many difficult questions: should universities accept and comply with all goals and tasks as they are given? What if the government assigns universities insensible or illegitimate tasks impossible for universities to complete? Should deviations from government objectives always be considered as an agency problem that needs to be resolved? Indeed, one of the most cited critics of agency theory, sociologist Charles Perrow, once warned that agency theory may be dangerous, particularly because 'theories shape our world; they encourage us to see it in a certain way, and then we exclude other visions that direct our actions' (Perrow, 1986, p. 235).

Conclusions and some future directions of research

'Why do universities need to be held accountable for the resources they receive?' Unlike many other theories and frameworks, agency theory suggests it has an answer to this simple, but one of the most crucial, questions related to higher education governance. From the vantage of agency theory, governments do not – and in fact they should not – trust universities, as they may act opportunistically, if not held accountable, with appropriate means, for the resources they receive. This answer is rather straightforward, but logical. Whether we like it or not, part of organizational life, including in the field of higher education, is also based on people's self-interest, goal conflict and opportunism.

The greatest strengths of agency theory are related to its capability to provide alternative insights by examining the economic characteristics of universities with respect to the behavioural implications for governance and resource allocation mechanisms. Particularly, the insights from informational asymmetries, goal conflicts and available governance methods can offer guidance in the design and selection of efficient and effective governance procedures in a given context. This can be achieved in practice by applying agency theory to generate a set of questions about the principal–agent relationship in order to elucidate its constituent roles and dynamics. As the result, outcomes of the different possible contracts between the university and the ministry, the president and the board and so on can be simulated. Nevertheless, the value of the insightfulness is constrained by the fact that agency suffers narrowness in many respects. The theory is built on rather narrow views of human motivation and behaviour, and it pays attention to mainly formal and economic aspects of relationships without the intention to grasp the complexity and diversity of the empirical reality. For this reason, application of the theory to a specific relationship must be imbued by context: the length and history of the relationship, reputation of the agent, characteristics of the industries, organizations and employees and so on. In other words, whereas agency theory provides the bare walls to a model of the relationship, predicting possible goal conflicts and informational asymmetries, it is the remit of the involved participants to decide what additional personal and social factors to account for in their case. We have seen how self-perception and cultural characteristics are capable of overpowering the expected dynamics of the principal–agent relationship (Wilkesmann, 2013).

In higher education studies, agency theory has been utilized primarily as a conceptual framework aimed to offer insights related to university governance. As it has been suggested earlier (Lane and Kivistö, 2008), the number of empirical studies applying agency theory, especially, studies utilizing quantitative methods, have remained relatively low. We have seen, however, a diversification in application of agency theory to new levels of principal–agent relationship and new areas of activity in higher education. Even though the goal of these studies has not been primarily to test agency theory per se, it is through these applications that the usefulness and limitations of the theory are being more fully defined and placed into social context. As we build up a richer stock of empirical applications, comprehensive testing of the explanatory and predictive potential of agency theory in the context of higher education becomes more feasible.

Finally, due to its focus, agency theory shares the same broad area of interest with several approaches in higher education governance and policy, such as studies on funding mechanisms and performance measurement, studies on policy instruments and steering, policy implementation studies and programme evaluation studies. However, these approaches often lack a broader theoretical structure or framework which would unite the relationships between theoretical concepts and observed empirical phenomena in a coherent, structured and logical manner. Future studies could explore the possibilities of merging agency theoretical perspectives with these and other approaches. This should make the agency theory even more useful in the study of higher education governance and policy.

Notes

1. For more comprehensive overviews on disciplinary origins and development of agency theory in, please refer, for example, to Shapiro (2005).
2. The content and meaning of 'self-interest' assumption varies across different versions of agency theory. Some of the agency theorists postulate principals and agents as economic utility maximizers, whereas others do not make such an assumption. Prominent agency theorist Michael Jensen (1994) has suggested that the self-interest assumption does not mean that people do not behave altruistically, but that 'because people pursue their own best interests, conflicts of interests inevitably arise over at least some issues when they engage in cooperative endeavours' (p. 41). Regardless of the precise definition of the self-interest assumption, the key issue is that it may lead the agents to pursue courses of actions that are against the interests of their principals.
3. Due to the word limit of this article, the discussion related to adverse selection is left aside here. For more comprehensive introduction of adverse selection in the context of higher education, please refer to Kivistö (2007).
4. Outcome-based contracts can be considered to be the first choice of the principal. However, the problem with an outcome-based contract is the risk premium which more risk-averse agents may demand for bearing the risk of outcome uncertainty. From an agent's perspective, the outcome-based compensation is more insecure than the compensation based on his behaviour. Thus, an outcome-based contract is efficient only when the cost of transferring the risk to agent (risk premium) is less than the costs of monitoring the agent (Kivistö, 2007).
5. The Informative Principle states that a measure of performance that reveals how much effort an agent puts into a problem should be foreseen in the compensation relationship between the principal and agent. Incentive Intensity Principle states that setting the most intense incentives is not always optimal and defines several factors that should determine the level of incentives' intensity. The Monitoring Intensity Principle states that if there are high levels of incentive intensity, the level of monitoring must also be on high level. And the fourth Equal Compensation Principle relates the value of activities from both agent and principal perspective in the sense that activities of high value to the principal should be equally valued by the agent (Auld, 2010).
6. This section builds to a large extent on the earlier analysis conducted in Kivistö (2007, pp. 178–193).

References

Alchian, A. A. and H. Demsetz (1972) 'Production, information costs, and economic organization', *The American Economic Review*, 62(5), 777–795.

Alpert, D. (1985) 'Performance and Paralysis: The Organizational Context of the American Research University', *The Journal of Higher Education*, 56(3), 241–281.

Auld, D. (2010) 'Strategic planning and the principal-agent issue in higher education leadership', *Academic Leadership*, 8(3), 31–35.

Birnbaum, R. (1988) *How Colleges Work. The Cybernetics of Academic Organization and Leadership* (San Francisco: Jossey-Bass).

Blalark, F. J. (2012) *Utilizing Principal-Agent Theory and Data Envelopment Analysis to Examine Efficiency of Resource Utilization in Undergraduate Education for Public and Private Non-Profit Four-Year Research Universities* (Doctoral dissertation) (The University of Minnesota Digital Conservancy, http://purl.umn.edu/136257).

Borgos, J. (2013) 'Using principal-agent theory as a framework for analysis in evaluating the multiple stakeholders involved in the accreditation and quality assurance of international medical branch campuses', *Quality in Higher Education*, 19(2), 173–190.

Clark, B. R. (1983) *The Higher Education System. Academic Organization in Cross-National Perspective* (Berkeley: University of California Press).

Cuevas-Rodríguez, G., Gomez-Mejia, L. R. and R. M. Wiseman (2012) 'Has agency theory run its course?: Making the theory more flexible to inform the management of reward systems', *Corporate Governance: An International Review*, 20, 526–546.

Donaldson, L. (1990) 'The ethereal hand: Organizational economics and management theory', *Academy of Management Review*, 15(3), 369–381.

Enders, J., de Boer, H. and E. Weyer (2013) 'Regulatory autonomy and performance: The reform of higher education re-visited', *Higher Education*, 65, 5–23.

Eisenhardt, K. (1989) 'Agency theory: An assessment and review', *Academy of Management Review*, 14(1), 57–74.

Ferris, J. M. (1991) 'Contracting and higher education', *The Journal of Higher Education*, 62(1), 1–24.

Geuna, A. (1999) *The Economics of Knowledge Production: Funding and Structure of University research* (Cheltenham: Edward Elgar).

Gomez-Meijia, L. R. and R. M. Wiseman (2006) 'Commentary: Does agency theory have universal relevance? A reply to Lubatkin, Lane, Collin, and Very', *Journal of Organizational Behaviour*, 28, 81–88.

Gornitzka, Å., Stensaker, B., Smeby, J-C. and H. de Boer (2004) 'Contract arrangements in the Nordic countries: Solving the efficiency/effectiveness dilemma?' *Higher Education in Europe*, 29(1), 87–101.

Harmon, M. M. and R. T. Mayer (1986) *Organization Theory for Public Administration* (Glenview: Scott, Foresman and Company).

Hölttä, S. (1995) *Towards the Self-Regulative University* (Doctoral dissertation) (Joensuu: University of Joensuu).

Jensen, M. C. and W. H. Meckling (1976) 'Theory of the Firm: Managerial behaviour, agency costs and ownership structure', *Journal of Financial Economics*, 3(4), 305–360.

Jensen, M. C. (1994) 'Self-interest, altruism, incentives, and agency theory', *Journal of Applied Corporate Finance*, 7(2), 40–45.

Jongbloed, B., de Boer, H., Enders, J. and J. File (2010) *Progress in Higher Education Reform across Europe: Funding Reform. Volume 1, Executive Summary and main report* (Enschede: CHEPS).

Kezar, A. (2006) 'To use or not to use theory: Is that the question?' in J. C. Smart (ed) *Higher Education: Handbook of Theory and Research* (pp. 283–344) (Dordrecht: Springer).

Kivistö, J. (2005) 'Government-higher education institution relationship: Theoretical considerations from the perspective of agency theory', *Tertiary Education and Management*, 11(1), 1–17.

Kivistö, J. (2007) *Agency Theory as a Framework for the Government-University Relationship* (Doctoral dissertation) (Tampere: Tampere University Press).

Kivistö, J. (2008) 'Agency theory as a framework for government-university relationship: Assessment of the theory', *Journal of Higher Education Policy and Management*, 30(4), 339–350.

Lane, J. E. (2005, November) *Agency Problems with Complex Principals: State Oversight of Higher Education: A Theoretical Review of Agency Problems with Complex Principals*, Paper presented at the annual conference of the Association for the Study of Higher Education (Philadelphia, United States).

Lane, J. E. (2007) 'Spider web of oversight: Latent and manifest regulatory controls in higher education', *Journal of Higher Education*, 78(6), 1–30.

Lane, J. E., Kinser, K. and D. Knox (2013) 'Regulating cross-border higher education: A case study of the United States', *Higher Education Policy*, 26, 147–172.

Lane, J. E. and J. Kivistö (2008) 'Interests, information, and incentives in higher education: Principal-agent theory and its potential applications to the study of higher education governance', in J. C. Smart (ed) *Higher education: Handbook of Theory and Research* (pp. 141–179) (Dordrecht: Springer).

Liefner, I. (2003) 'Funding, resource allocation, and performance in higher education systems', *Higher Education*, 46, 469–489.

Macias, A. (2012) *A Case Study Using Principal-Agent Theory to Explore How a Public, Four-Year University Interacts with a System Office*, Doctoral dissertation (Las Vegas: Digital Scholarship at University of Nevada, available from: http://digitalscholarship.unlv.edu/).

Massy, W. F. (1996) 'Reengineering resource allocation systems', in W. F. Massy (ed) *Resource Allocation in Higher Education* (pp. 15–47) (Ann Arbor: The University of Michigan Press).

McLendon, M. K. (2003) 'The politics of higher education: Toward an expanded research agenda', *Educational Policy*, 17(1), 165–191.

Milgrom, P. and J. Roberts (1992) *Economics, Organization and Management* (New Jersey: Prentice Hall).

Mitnick, B. M. (1975) 'The Theory of Agency: The Policing "Paradox" and Regulatory Behaviour', *Public Choice*, 24, 27–42.

Moe, T. M. (1984) 'The new economics of organization', *American Journal of Political Science*, 28(4), 739–777.

Patterson, G. (2001) 'The applicability of institutional goals to the university organisation', *Journal of Higher Education Policy and Management*, 23(2), 159–169.

Perrow, C. (1986) *Complex Organizations: A Critical Essay* (New York: Random House).

Pratt, J. W. and R. J. Zeckhauser (1985) 'Principals and agents: An overview', in J. W. Pratt and R. J. Zeckhauser (eds) *Principals and Agents: The Structure of Business* (pp. 1–35) (Boston: Harvard Business School Press).

Rose-Ackerman, S. (1978) *Corruption. A Study in Political Economy* (New York: Academic Press).

Ross, S. A. (1973) 'The economic theory of agency: The principal's problem', *American Economic Review*, 63(2), 134–139.

Shapiro, S. P. (2005) 'Agency theory', *Annual Review of Sociology*, 31(3), 263–284.

Waterman, R. W. and K. J. Meier (1998) 'Principal-agent models: An expansion', *Journal of Public Administration Research and Theory*, 8(2), 173–202.

Weick, K. E. (1976) 'Educational organizations as loosely coupled systems', *Administrative Science Quarterly*, 21(1), 1–19.

Wilkesmann, U. (2013) 'Effects of transactional and transformational governance on academic teaching: Empirical evidence from two types of higher education institutions', *Tertiary Education and Management*, 19(4), 281–300.

Wilkesmann, U. and C. Schmid (2012) 'The impacts of new governance on teaching at German universities: Findings from a national survey', *Higher Education*, 63, 33–52.

Williams, G. (1995) 'The "marketization" of higher education: Reforms and potential reforms in higher education finance', in D. D. Dill and B. Sporn (eds) *Emerging Patterns of Social Demand and University Reform: Through a Glass Darkly* (pp. 170–193) (Oxford: IAU Press/Pergamon).

9
Systems Theoretical Perspectives on Higher Education Policy and Governance

Thomas Pfeffer and Rudolf Stichweh

Since the days of Talcott Parsons (1973), Joseph Ben-David (1977) and Burton Clark (1983), higher education research has been deeply rooted in the analysis of individual national higher education systems and in their comparison. For a long time this has been an appropriate and fruitful approach, since in many countries of the world higher education has predominantly been organized as a service of the public sector, and universities and other higher education institutions have been mainly regarded as national institutions. But this approach becomes inadequate in our days. This is one of the arguments which will be made in this chapter.

To suggest a more convincing approach and to establish systems theoretical perspectives on higher education policy and governance, the following sections will (1) explain the need to avoid methodological nationalism and (2) sketch some core concepts of sociological systems theory, (3) which are applied to define universities and nation states. These definitions will be used to further (4) elaborate on the relationships of universities to education, science and nation state and (5) reflect upon the ways in which these relationships are changing due to the emergence of a world system of universities. (6) A conclusion will summarize the main claim of this chapter – that sociological systems theory is the most adequate theoretical approach to analyse new relations of reciprocal observation in the global university system.

The authors are grateful to Manuel Souto-Otero for valuable comments and suggestions on earlier drafts of this chapter.

The problem of methodological nationalism

Methodological nationalism

Depending on the theoretical framework applied, the focus on national higher education systems can also come with the risk of methodological nationalism, if one assumes that the nation state is the natural social and political form of the modern world and the terminal unit for the demarcation of phenomena for social science. First coined by Martins (1974), the term 'methodological nationalism' indicates the conceptual equation between society and the modern nation state in scholarly debates and – as a consequence – the tendency to explain social phenomena and change as predominantly endogenous, internally driven by the nation state. In such an understanding, individual nation states would be regarded as self-contained entities and the main source, dominant actor and sole end of changes in higher education. But such an approach does not sufficiently take into account that science and education, the two function systems which mainly define the university as an organization, are global function systems – and from this, sharp limits arise regarding the capability of the nation states to shape their university systems. Additionally, methodological nationalism tends to regard universities as instruments to fulfil national interests. It therefore tends to presuppose similarity of perspective and goals between the nation state and its universities and to underestimate the self-reproducing requirements and the self-steering capacities of individual universities as organizations.

Concepts of world society

Probably the most prominent among contemporary sociologists, who take world society as the social reference space for their theorizing, are John W. Meyer and Niklas Luhmann. Their respective theoretical concepts, neo-institutionalism and systems theory, show many similarities, for example the social constructivist background and the rejection of methodological individualism. However, there also exist some principal differences between the two theories.

Meyer's version of neo-institutionalism is strongly interested in standardization as the major trend in globalization. It therefore deals with the emergence of convergence and isomorphism on a global scale by analysing the diffusion of models, norms and rule-like assumptions. However, neo-institutionalism observes this process of standardization mainly from the perspective of the nation state as an actor of standardization, which again creates the problem of methodological nationalism. This is due to the fact that neo-institutionalism looks at all the other functional domains from the perspective of the nation state and its cognitive constructions, which imports a kind of political action view into the explication of very diverse social realities (Stichweh, 2015, pp. 24–26). The basic classification of analytical levels in neo-institutionalism is the threefold classification of individuals, organizations and nation states which points to the near identification of the concept of society with the plurality of nation states.

In contrast to this relative neglect of functional differentiation, the hypothesis of functional differentiation of world society into societal subsystems is perhaps the most important characteristic of Luhmann's approach to systems theory, which positions the hypothesis of a global communicative space in the core of the concept of function system. Systems theory does not assume the dominance of one thematically specialized domain (e.g. the economy or politics) over all the other domains (e.g. education or science), but rather emphasizes their distinctness and autonomy. Systems theory proposes interaction, organization and society as its classification of system levels (Stichweh, 2011). Since systems theory takes communication rather than action as the elementary unit of society, the individual is regarded as a structural prerequisite, but not as a structural part of society. The substitution of interaction for individuals as the most elementary level substitutes a social system of its own for the individual which in systems theory is seen as somehow extra-societal. And the nation state, the privileged macro unit of the neo-institutionalist, in systems theory, is seen as a subsystem of a subsystem of society.

Even if neo-institutionalism offers interesting insights for the analysis of world society, this brief comparison explains our preference for systems theory as the instrument of choice for overcoming methodological nationalism and for doing research on higher education.

Core concepts of sociological systems theory

Given the range of Luhmann's oeuvre (according to Seidl and Becker (2005, p. 11), it comprises more than 70 books and several hundred articles), the non-linearity of his approach and the multitude of concepts he developed, it is impossible to summarize his theory in a few paragraphs.

For the purpose of this chapter, we will sketch only a few of his core concepts such as autopoiesis, observation and distinction, communication and action, social systems and actors. They are key concepts in Luhmann's theory, which focuses on the dynamics of distinct events (operations) and their recursive connections to self-reproducing systems – a theory that rejects substantialist ontologies of stable entities (e.g. structures).

Not all of these concepts will explicitly be used in this chapter, but one needs them for the explanation of other key concepts, especially for understanding the differentiation of social systems and for the definition of the terms 'societal function system' and 'organization'. In later sections, these core concepts of sociological systems theory will be linked to the central topic of this chapter: higher education policy and governance.

Autopoietic (self-reproducing) systems

One of the cornerstones of Luhmann's theory is the concept of autopoietic (self-reproducing) systems, which originates from Humberto Maturana and Francisco Varela. In tackling the question 'What is life?' the answer of the two Chilean biologists was that living systems reproduce themselves from their own operations. A living cell, for example, reproduces itself from the network of its own bio-physical reactions, which are recursively connected to realize the unity of the cell (Seidl, 2005, p. 22).

Luhmann abstracted from this originally biological concept and developed a general theory of autopoiesis, which then could be re-specified to a variety of disciplines, for example biology, psychology and sociology. Following his suggestion, the self-reproduction of systems from their own operations can be found not only in living systems, but also in psychic systems and in social systems (Seidl, 2005, p. 25).

Different types of systems require different types of operations. While living systems reproduce themselves from their own bio-physical operations, psychic systems (the consciousness of individual human beings) reproduce themselves from thoughts and social systems from communications.

The concept of self-reproduction has several implications. On the one hand, it requires continuous activity, because each individual system only exists as long as the reproduction of internal operations is continued. This explains why the continuation of its own operations is of existential relevance for every autopoietic system.

On the other hand, self-reproduction requires operative closure. Autopoietic systems separate themselves from their environment by connecting only to their own operations; no operation can enter or leave the system. Nevertheless, autopoietic systems have contacts to and depend on their respective environments, without which they could not exist. For example, living systems require matter and energy, and psychic and social systems require stimulations from their environments. However, the way in which external influences are processed is determined by the internal operations of the system. Operative closure is the mechanism for creating individuation and (operative) autonomy of every autopoietic system, while interactional openness is the prerequisite for the contacts with the environment.

Observations and distinctions

Following the calculus of distinction presented by George Spencer Brown's *The Laws of Form* (1971), Luhmann focuses on the process of observing rather than on the object of observation (e.g. Luhmann, 2002). In keeping with Spencer Brown, observations have to be described as operations of an observer. To be able to make an observation, one has to draw a distinction, which distinguishes between two sides of the distinction (e.g. 'left' and 'right'; 'big' and 'small') and which indicates only one (and not the other) side of the distinction. In making use of a distinction, one cannot observe this distinction at the same time. To be able to do this, one needs to make use of another distinction to observe with its help the first distinction. Doing this kind of work with distinctions creates a sequence or dynamic chain of operations, which allows for more and more complex observations, but will never bring about a final picture or stable state.

At least two consequences can be derived from these considerations. On the one hand, it becomes clear that observations are time bound and very limited in scope. Any observer can observe only on the basis of his/her own distinctions and only during the process of observing. On the other hand, the distinctions used for making observations become important topics for (meta-)observation and analysis.

Additionally, observations are system specific. The most important distinction for any autopoietic system is the distinction of system and environment. Then many other and increasingly specific distinctions can be added (Seidl, 2005, pp. 50ff.).

Communication and action

Another important innovation in Luhmann's theory is the shift from action to communication as the elementary unit of social systems and, therefore, as the basic unit of analysis for sociological theory. Many sociologists (e.g. Weber, Parsons, Habermas, Münch) based their theories on the concept of action: Actions have to be attributed to individual actors or to collective actors as stable reference points. In contrast to that, Luhmann proposed the operation of communication as the basic element of social systems which always needs the participation of at least two processors (participants) for an individual communicative act to come about (Luhmann, 2005, p. 70). Regarding communication, there is no possibility of going back to only one originator.

Luhmann defined the individual unit of communication as a threefold selection of information, utterance and understanding. Information is the selection of a difference which seems relevant, and utterance means the decision by a system to risk the communication of this difference and the attributions of responsibility coming with it. While information and utterance are concentrated around one system, the third selection of understanding requires a second system (an alter Ego) to complete the unity of communication. According to Luhmann's definition, understanding takes place, when Alter is able to reconstruct the difference of information and utterance in connecting to the communication. This concept of understanding includes cases of misunderstanding since the concept is completely formal, only demanding to make use of the distinction (not a correct use). Misunderstanding and understanding are ways of connecting to ongoing communicative processes (Luhmann, 2005, pp. 66ff.).

This preference for communication as the elementary unit of social systems makes it necessary to redefine the relevance of action. Social systems require the attribution of actions to Alter and Ego for the continuation of the communication process (Luhmann, 2005, pp. 69f.). Action is not given before communication takes place. Rather, it is a product of communication, the attribution of information and utterance to Ego and of understanding to Alter (and vice versa), attributions that trigger further communication. Since communication cannot be observed directly and has to be deduced, social systems need the attribution of actions for their self-observation and self-description (Luhmann, 1984, pp. 226ff.)

Social systems and actors

The clear distinction between living systems, psychic systems and social systems is another consequence of the theory of autopoietic systems. Therefore, human beings cannot be part of social systems, neither as bodies, nor as minds.

However, communication presupposes the involvement of a multitude of actors (either psychic systems or organizations). The concept of autopoiesis just makes it necessary to distinguish between different systems of reference, for example between the internal operations of systems to which actor status can be attributed and the communication taking place between them. This difference does not reduce the importance of human beings or individual actors; rather, it grants them more autonomy from society.

This particular form of distinguishing actors and communication has highly practical consequences, as can be shown in the cases of systemic family therapy and systemic approaches to consultancy and organization research, two fields that heavily drew from Luhmann's theory. Systemic family therapy, for example, shifts the attention from in-depth analysis of individual patients to the analysis and treatment of the communication between family members. Similarly, systemic consultancy distinguishes not only between the internal communications of organizations and their communication with their environment but also between the operations of the client system and those of the consultants, which limits and specifies the opportunities for intervention.

Types of social systems: Interactions, organizations, society

In a first approximation, Luhmann (1975) identified three basic types of social systems: interactions, organizations and society. Interaction systems form themselves on the basis of communications between individuals, which are present in a space of mutual perception, and organizations from communications between their members and/or subunits, communications which in the case of organizations at the end always result in decisions. Organizations need to know decisions (their own and those of other organizations) to be able to go on.

Society comprises all communications and nothing but communications. This is how society distinguishes itself from its environment, for example from all non-communicative circumstances and events. While in former times, different regional societies existed, which did not know about each other, the current situation is characterized by the existence of only one comprehensive world society (Luhmann, 1984, p. 557).

Society constitutes a global communicative space, which has been made possible by communication technologies, like rhetoric, script, print, audiovisual technologies and the computer. These technologies hugely enhance the temporal and spatial reach of communicative accessibility by putting a distance between the selection of understanding (e.g. reading, watching television, retrieving) and the selection of information and utterance (e.g. writing, recording, posting).

Based on worldwide communicative accessibility, society is segmented in different societal function systems, for example economy, politics, the legal system, education and science. The reach of these thematic domains cannot be limited by national borders, even if their unfolding can follow regional peculiarities.

Societal function systems

From the perspective of systems theory, functional differentiation is not the only, but currently by far the dominant, structural principle of world society (Stichweh, 2013). By maintaining one social hierarchy including all individuals into one rank order that dominated all social spheres, most earlier societies were organized as orders of stratification. In contrast to that, modern world society differentiates itself into a plurality of function systems, which exist in parallel to each other. Function systems, such as religion, the economy, politics, law, science and education, are thematic specifications of communication. A societal function system emerges when it distinguishes itself from its environment by connecting actions and communications of the same kind. Linking communications of the same kind is the prerequisite for operational closure and the self-reproduction (autopoiesis) of a function system. Examples for this mechanism can be found in the education system, which specializes on communication that circles around the intentional change of individuals (e.g. teaching, learning, testing), or in the science system that focuses on communication about the understanding of the world (e.g. solving problems of ignorance, searching for explanations, claiming truth). Similarly, communication in the political system specializes on power, authority and enforcement, in the economic system on ownership, money and the capacity to pay, in the legal system on law, rights and liability (Table 9.1).

Two consequences follow from this theoretical proposition. First, each function system has its unique operations and respective rationales. Function

Table 9.1 Some function systems and their respective binary distinctions

Function system	Binary distinction
Politics	Powerful/subject of power
Economics	Having/not having Paying/not paying
Law	Legal/illegal, to be at fault
Education	Knowing/not knowing Passed/not passed
Science	True/not true Published/not published
Religion	Transcendent/immanent
Health care system	Ill/healthy
Art system	Beautiful/ugly Improbable/expected

systems may rely on or limit each other, but their respective mode of operation cannot be substituted by or substituted for the rationale of any other function system. The differentiation of world society into various function systems is a segmental structure, not a hierarchical one. Second, the specific rationale of each function system has the tendency to go beyond local, regional or national contexts. Each function system claims universal relevance for its unique rationale, and thereby drives globalization in its own thematic domain. This expansive mechanism goes beyond world policy and world economy. It also can be found in other function systems, like law (e.g. universal human rights), science (e.g. universal claims of truth) and education (e.g. global expansion of mass education).

Organizations

Organizations emerged in co-evolution with function systems (Stichweh, 2007, p. 137), since the existence of specialized roles is a prerequisite for organizations. On the other hand, organizations contribute to the development of the internal complexity of function systems. Without commercial companies, economic activities would still rely on barter, without diversified legal institutions, jurisprudence would still be the task of the monarch, without universities and their commitment to principles of rationality and secular knowledge, our perception of the world would still follow tradition-based beliefs (Simon, 2009, p. 44).

Organizations are characterized by the fact that they emerge from the communication among their members and from limitations of and conditions for membership they postulate. They reproduce themselves by distinguishing their own communications from the noise that goes on in their environment. More specifically, decisions, which are attributed to the organization, are the core operations of any organization. Only their own decisions are recursively connected, which leads to the operational closure of organizations. This has to be seen as an ongoing 'process of organizing' (Weick, 1979), which implies volatility and the need for permanent reproduction. If communication among members, or better decision-making, stops, the organization vanishes as well.

Reproduction from its own decisions, which constitutes operational closure, is the prerequisite for openness to external information (Luhmann, 1997, pp. 835f.). Only based on their own, internal structures, organizations are able to observe their environment and to generate information from these observations. There is no direct or linear causality between external stimuli and the reaction of the individual organization. For example, changes in the legal framework conditions or in the market situation can put organizations under pressure. Responses to questions as to which of these changes in its environment an organization observes, which information it generates from these changes and how it reacts to this information are determined by the internal structures and decisions of the organization, and not by its environment.

Organizations can also be described as autonomous 'actors', which means that they are the only type of social systems which are able to communicate and interact with other actors in their environments, namely with individuals or other organizations. The collective ability to act goes beyond joint activities; it requires the ability to communicate in the name of the collective (Luhmann, 1997, p. 834). It is possible to attribute actions and communications to organizations, similar to the way actions are attributed to individuals. The prerequisite for this characteristic are internal decisions, and the fact that organizations are highly formalized, which makes them independent from their concrete members. In difference to associations of persons (e.g. families), organizations can stabilize their internal structures, regulations and processes, even if they continuously change their personnel. This makes it possible to distinguish between organizations and their members. Members only contribute their actions to the process called organization. Their physical or psychical totality is not operational part of the organization itself but a necessary prerequisite in its environment (Simon, 2009, p. 43).

The principle of formal organization exists orthogonal to functional differentiation (Stichweh, 2015, p. 29). Since societal function systems cannot communicate with other social systems, organizations are an important mechanism of structural coupling with other function systems (Luhmann, 1997, p. 843). Organizations have the capacity to participate in different societal function systems and to contribute actions to different thematic domains. However, many of them tend to focus their activities on selected function systems. Therefore, specialized types of organizations emerge, for example banks and enterprises in the economic system, governments and public administration in the political system and courts and prisons in the legal system.

Defining universities and nation states

Before analysing the relation between universities and the nation state, both phenomena have to be redefined in the terminology of systems theory, especially along the distinction between function system and organization. Both universities and nation states are organizations or consist from organizations, but both are clearly related to one or more function systems.

Universities

Universities are among the oldest existing organizations. In mediaeval times, they emerged as associations either of students (1088 in Bologna) or of teachers (1160 in Paris), while later both groups were regarded members of the university (*universitas magistrorum et scolarium*, loosely translated as the community of teachers and students).

At the beginning, universities were set up mainly as organizations of formal learning. Their education focused on knowledge domains of particular societal relevance, namely theology, medicine and law, complemented by various types of arts (e.g. grammar, rhetoric, arithmetic), which served as general education and preparation for the core subjects (Stichweh, 2006, pp. 33f.).

Later, in the period of enlightenment, the amount of available knowledge hugely expanded, which led to the differentiation of academic disciplines. Research as a distinct professional activity emerged, testing claims of truth, raising questions of ignorance and systematically searching for new knowledge and insights. Even if alternative settings (e.g. academies) for doing research came into existence as well, at least in quantitative terms universities became the most important research organizations. The combination of research with higher learning in one type of organization has proven to be a successful model, since it proliferated all over the world.

Universities reproduce themselves on the basis of three types of communication: educational communication, dealing with the intentional change of individuals; research communication, dealing with questions and claims of truth; and organizational communication, dealing with decisions on the organization of education and research (Baecker, 2010, p. 358). This threefold distinction is crucial, since it allows distinguishing questions of management, policy and governance from the core activities of education and research.

If educating and doing research are the main communication processes, and thereby the main production processes of the organization called university, it is fair to ask, what are the typical, generalizable products resulting from these processes?

In the case of education, one can regard certificates (degrees, grades) as one of the generalizable products of universities. Educational communication deals with the knowledge, skills and competencies of individuals, aiming at changing (improving) them. To communicate these results beyond the context of the classroom, degrees and certificates, which document the individual's achievements, are necessary requirements. Issued by the university, certificates are highly generalized products, which allow the communication with other institutional complexes, not only within the education system (the next teacher, another education institution) but also beyond (potential employers). Certificates are also a prerequisite for more complex educational arrangements, such as larger degree programmes composed from individual courses, which lead to diplomas composed from smaller credentials.

In the case of science, publications are the generalizable products of universities. The constant communication in the medium of truth aims at creating new insights and discoveries. Scholarly publications are the dominant form of communicating insights and claims of truth to a wider audience. References, which are part of every scholarly publication, place the publication in the research discourse and couple it to distinct threads of communication and to respective schools of thought. Universities were among the first institutional publishers after the invention of print and still play an important role for the scholarly publication system (Nentwich, 2001, pp. 22ff.) as producers, publishers, buyers and preservers of publications.

Summing up, the main function of both certificates and publications from within their respective function systems is to allow for the continuation of system-specific communication, for educational communication in the case of certificates and, for scientific communication in the case of publications. Both certificates and publications may be structurally coupled with other purposes, for example the employability of graduates and or the applicability of scientific knowledge, but analysing these purposes requires switching to other systems, for example to the labour market and to markets for goods and services.

Nation states

Nation states are a comparatively younger phenomenon than universities, and their genesis is in most cases not linked to the genesis of universities. The Peace of Westphalia, which ended the Thirty Year's War in 1648, built an early basis for national self-determination in Europe as it linked the concept of nations (collectives which share joint cultural characteristics) with the concept of politically sovereign states. It is an even more recent development that the nation state became the dominant form of political control over territories on a global scale. Only since 1945, the formerly stratified structures of large empires or colonial states, which controlled remote provinces or colonies, have been largely substituted by a segmental structure of formally equal nation states (Stichweh, 2010a, p. 299). This led to the establishment of more than 130 new nation states since the Second World War (Meyer et al., 1997, p. 158), a development still going on as new nation states regularly are formed from the decomposition of existent states.

This historical account demonstrates that nation states are internal differentiations of the political system of the world. As political entities, the main function of nation states is to generate collectively binding decisions, a mechanism based on the inclusion of its members into the global political system. However, most modern states can also be seen as welfare states, since they tend to mediate the inclusion of their members into other societal function systems as well, without being able to control the operations of function systems. One form of this mediation is the management of access opportunities for their members to different function systems (Stichweh, 2010a, p. 305).

It is an important claim of systems theory that nation states do not constitute separate societies, but rather subunits of world society. Nation states are neither interaction systems nor function systems (but subsystems of the political system of world society). To a certain extent, they have characteristics of organizations, for example when they distinguish between members (citizens) and non-members (foreigners) and when they communicate on behalf of the collective. On the other hand, only totalitarian regimes try to establish states as one central, rigidly integrated bureaucracy and to treat their members as fully controllable in every aspect of their lives. The more common pattern of organizational form for nation states is that of a wide variety of organizations, which mutually observe one another and occasionally interact. These different organizations are also more or less subject to political influence and enjoy more or less proximity to public administration. Some activities are organized as part of the state bureaucracies, while in other cases the state only sets framework conditions. These varieties also apply to higher education policy and governance and to the relationship between public administration and individual universities.

In the late medieval situation in which the European university arose, there were no nation states and therefore no interrelations between universities and nation states. Early European universities until the 16th century mostly were related to the papacy and to the Holy Roman Empire as the two political and clerical authorities who had to give privileges to enable the foundation of a new university anywhere in Europe. Only after the reformation was there a shift from these two universal powers to more regional, territorial political authorities, who now understood the universities they acquired or established as knowledge institutions to be used for the build-up of territorially limited political units in early modern Europe. Late in the 18th century, the concept of the nation entered the scene, and from the 1760s there is an extensive literature which interprets universities as institutions of 'national education' (Stichweh, 1991). At the end of the 18th century, national education was at many places postulated as the primary task of universities.

Universities in the context of education, research and the nation state

After having established distinctions between universities and the nation state and also between the function systems education and science in prior sections, we will use the following section to elaborate on the relationship of universities not only to the education system and to the system of science but also to the national university policy (nation state's interest in and goals for its universities) and to the national governance of universities (mechanisms and instruments used by a nation state to influence its universities).

Universities and (higher) education

The socio-spatial embedding of universities strongly depends on their educational function. The first European universities emerged with the claim that they instituted education processes of European (which at that time meant global) relevance and reach. Globality was the distinguishing characteristic of the university compared to local and regional educational organizations. Later centuries brought the territorial closure of nation states and the simultaneous development of national education systems, which were reactions against transnational structures, like the Jesuit Order. Subsequently, universities also had to develop links to their regional environments and to the cities they were located in. From a historical perspective, the European university in its developed form is characterized by the equal relevance of interrelations with its global, national, regional and local environments (Stichweh, 2010b, pp. 15–17).

Surprisingly, American universities experienced an inverse development of their socio-spatial embedding. Following Karabel (2006), one can take three of the oldest American universities (Harvard, Yale and Princeton) as typical examples for this development, claiming that they have been institutions of rather regional reach for more than 200 years. Not before the 1930s they started to recruit nationwide, and only in the last few decades the international composition of their student body became part of their institutional self-description. About 15 years ago, they expanded the principle of 'need blind admission' to foreign students as well, which is a strong symbol of their transformation into 'world universities' (Stichweh, 2010b, p. 16).

The demarcation of universities against other institutions of the education system is not a given, but rather volatile. For a long time, universities had to substitute for deficits of non-existing or weak secondary schools, a task frequently fulfilled by the arts or by philosophical faculties of the medieval university, which provided preparatory training in fields like grammar, rhetoric, logic or algebra, before students entered education in the professional faculties. In principle, this distinction between different levels of education at the same institution can today be found in the sequence of undergraduate and graduate studies, and in the American case we still have the liberal arts college, which in some respects is near to the premodern curriculum (although it has internalized disciplinary differentiation). At least since the emergence of national education systems, universities took the highest ranks in these hierarchical, sequentially structured national systems of formal education (Pfeffer and Skrivanek, 2013, p. 65). Subsequently, not only the status of primary and secondary education institutions but also their content was defined in relation to universities. In other words, the modern education system (with its consecutive steps of primary, secondary, tertiary education) differentiated itself from and in relation to higher education at universities.

Education at medieval universities was focusing on professional training in three disciplines: theology, law and medicine. Each of these knowledge systems embodied crucial aspects of social control, either the control of souls and beliefs (theology) of the living together in society (law) or of physical bodies (medicine). Universities trained the learned professions as practitioners of social control in their respective fields. This focus was pushed back by the emergence of academic disciplines in the late enlightenment and romanticism, which led to an internal differentiation of universities and to a variety of discipline-specific degrees. The academic discipline and its body of knowledge drove the majority of degrees, and not an occupational field or profession. However, recent decades brought a return of professionalism, a new emphasis on the education and training of practitioners in a vast variety of new knowledge-based fields, which are not necessarily rooted in academic disciplines (Stichweh, 2006, p. 47). This new professionalism in university education is clearly related to the worldwide growth of universities, which include ever-bigger percentages of the relevant age groups into their educational processes.

Universities and research

The reform of universities in early 19th-century society, especially the ascendancy of the German university as a consequence of these reform processes brought about a coupling of universities to the idea of research. Research meant that dealing with knowledge was no longer about the affirmation and stabilization of those aspects of learned knowledge, which had been known for long times already but was always a search process intent on changing knowledge, incessantly adding new particles of knowledge and changing structures of knowledge as a consequence of these ongoing processes of adding novelties.

It is in this development for the first time in history that we have a clear structural coupling of the university as an organization with the knowledge processes in the system of science which is now well to be identified as a function system in its own right with an ongoing dynamics of its own not necessarily related to what is going on in universities.

In the German universities in the early 19th century arose the 'research imperative', that is, the normative expectation addressed to all professorial university members to be actively involved in research and even to teach in the spirit of research, that is, to teach as if they were just going to find out for the first time ever the knowledge they transmitted. This resulted in the maxim, very earnestly followed by many professors to realize a 'unity of teaching and research'. For the students this implied that in listening to a lecture they were supposed to participate in the emergence of research knowledge and not in the transmission of a load of long-established traditions. And after they had spent a few semesters in the universities, capable students were allowed to become active members of seminars in which they were thought to work on problems which were research problems.

In the German university, there never was a clear separation of normal university teaching and the education of advanced students. Instead, there existed a continuity of transitions from basic learning in the disciplines to research participation. Only after 1870, when some American universities, first among them Johns Hopkins in Baltimore, institutionalized advanced scientific education for those having finished college, they invented what today is called graduate education (Veblen, 1918). In the present day, this split of undergraduate and graduate education is institutionalized worldwide and defines the character of the respective university, that is, to what extent it is seen as a research university.

Universities and national university policy

Since the rise of the territorial state, which 200–300 years later became the nation state, each university was to be identified as part of a national university system. For much of the 19th and 20th centuries, universities could be largely characterized by their membership in their respective national system (Stichweh, 2009, p. 2). However, it would be wrong to equate individual universities with their respective national system. Because of this transformation of universities into national institutions, political authorities replaced religious authorities as primary form of external control and tried to instrumentalize universities for the purposes of the nation state. Taking a systems theoretical perspective, what could these aims of national policy have been?

Probably one of the top priorities for each new nation state is to take over existing institutions and to re-establish them as national ones, which demonstrates political power and creates legitimacy for the nation state. In the case of universities, the nation state could easily execute its political influence by assigning (or withdrawing) degree-awarding power to universities as the power to award national qualifications (degrees, certificates), qualifications, which often imply the right of access to regulated professions. Through the control of universities, the nation state could also gain political control over nationally acknowledged qualifications and professional associations.

To a certain extent, this nationalization of universities undermined the former claim of universal (global) validity of university degrees. Now, transnational mobility of qualifications has become the exception, which requires recognition by national universities, professional associations or other public authorities.

For a long time, nation states used their universities for the formation and the recruitment of their national elites, especially in the learned professions. Universities always have been inclusive institutions insofar as social or regional origin did not play an important role for recruitment. As a criterion for recruitment purposes, meritocratic achievement in university education became an alternative to social origin. However, during the 20th century, universities became inclusive institutions in quantitative terms as well. While in 1900 less than 1% of the global age cohort participated in higher education, until 2000 the share rose to about 20% (based on Schofer and Meyer, 2005). Prior waves of expansion in primary and secondary education in the 20th century (Baker, 2014, p. 24) created huge pools of candidates for inclusion into tertiary education, which forced nation states to increase access opportunities as a means to foster the inclusion of larger percentages of the respective age groups into higher education. This growth in enrolment ratios has been accompanied by the rapid proliferation of universities and the diversification in types of higher education institutions (Riddle, 1989). The new idea seems to be that nearly everybody in all occupations and professions can profit from some higher education – and in 2014, in the OECD countries, we observe that at least 30%, in some cases (South Korea, New Zealand, Taiwan) nearly 90%, of the population study at higher educational institutions at some point in their lives. The societal and political relevance of university and higher education changes from being based in the future elite status of its students to a nearly universal relevance of higher education for everybody.

In 'economic theory and research' arises an interesting term for this near universal relevance of higher education in the concept of human capital. What happens in higher education is recorded as addition to the human capital of individual persons. Even minor additions to the length of time somebody spends in higher educational institutions can be observed from the perspective of differences and accumulations in human capital. Human capital then is something which has been inculcated into somebody on the basis of participation in higher education. The inculcated human capital can be used for activities in society and can be measured by the remuneration somebody will get for the activities chosen. The concept of 'human capital' is tautological inso-far as it can only be measured in money terms and not in terms of knowledge inculcated. It does not function as an evaluative standard which allows to dis-criminate between useful and useless activities. But it is exactly this extreme simplification (years and months of life invested into education) that explains the enormous success of the concept.

The growth of social inclusion into higher education and the accumulation of human capital are two indicators of what happens internal to a national system of higher education. They are system-defining features. They define the social relevance and economic weight of a system of higher education in a national frame of reference. In some respects, the two features balance one another: human capital being a proof that higher education is not a waste of precious life time without social effects – social inclusion demonstrating that in the end it is not only about money.

Related to the birth of research as a separate activity at universities and at some other institutions which only had to do research and did not partici-pate in education (the first research institutes such as the *Physikalisch-technische Reichsanstalt*, est. 1887) is the perception of 'science policy' as a policy domain of its own. This concept of 'science policy' was formulated around 1900 and it is clearly related to these two structures: the institutionalization of the first research institutes independent from universities and the emergence of the same structures of instrument-based experimental research independent from educational functions in universities, too. The structure behind both devel-opments is the research laboratory as an organizational structure which can be realized in universities, as well as in institutions (business firms, research institutes) outside of universities.

Universities and national governance of universities

Taking a system theoretical perspective, universities are self-reproducing organi-zations. External interventions can only be regarded as stimuli (e.g. incentives or limitations), which have to be observed and processed by the internal operations of the system to take effect.

From this point of view, it is easy to distinguish between Continental European and Anglo-Saxon approaches to the national governance of universi-ties. The traditional Continental European approach has been to reduce the self-steering capacity of universities by making them subordinated units of the state administration (typically the national ministry of education and/or science) and by defining detailed legal regulations. In contrast to that, the Anglo-Saxon tradition has been more familiar with self-steered public institu-tions, which are governed only by brief framework regulations and via assign-ing/withdrawing entitlements (e.g. degree awarding powers). While European states tried to govern their universities via command and control of the organization (although simultaneously providing substantial freedoms for the individual scholar or student), Anglo-Saxon countries traditionally preferred an approach of checks and balances between different types of institutions (e.g. between universities, ministries and accreditation agencies).

Another form of governance is the control over funding streams for universities. Traditionally, Continental European countries tended to treat their universities as subunits of the state bureaucracy and to apply ear-marked funding mechanisms for infrastructure, buildings and salaries, while Anglo-Saxon countries tended to pay lump sums for services (e.g. study places or research contracts).

Structural changes in the global university system

The global university system can be described as an inter-organizational system, based on relationships of observation, interaction, cooperation and competition (Stichweh, 2010b, p. 14) among the more than 20,000 universities in the world. While the visibility of the emergence of this global university system had been limited by a primacy of national university systems until the second half of the 20th century, this is changing rapidly.

Organizational autonomy for the managerial university

One of the reasons for this development is the strengthening of the organizational autonomy of the individual university in the last two to three decades. Previously, the disciplinary peculiarities of academic communities and the bureaucratic mechanisms of public administration left little space for the local self-determination of a university (especially in continental Europe). Organizational communication and decision-making mainly dealt with the coordination of internal groups and interests, with interpreting detailed legal requirements, with a regional–historical specificity and identity of the university, but not with a global self-defined role and strategy of the individual university. Policy reforms are changing this situation, by introducing more institutional autonomy in combination with increased institutional accountability, which once more needs autonomy to institutionalize accountability in an autonomous organization (Power 1997 on 'Audit Society'). Following the analysis of Krücken and Meier (2006) on how universities are turned into organizational actors, universities increasingly have to define distinct institutional goals and to justify themselves in external quality assurance processes; both are mechanisms which increase strategy development and the external communication on behalf of the collective. These new requirements lead to an expansion of formal administrative structures and to the professionalization of university management.

Transnational comparisons and rankings

One important circumstance is the rise of global comparisons and global rankings of universities. This is a very recent development with college rankings being available in the United States since 1983 (published by the magazine *U.S. News & World Report*) and the first world ranking (the '*Academic Ranking of World Universities*') only having been published in 2003 (then by the Shanghai Jiao Tong University, since 2009 by the Shanghai Ranking Consultancy (Shanghai Ranking Consultancy 2014). There exists no consensus on the epistemic validity and orientation value of university rankings. But this does not limit the enormous influence of rankings on university development. At the outset, they stabilize the tendency to look at a university as one coherent organization with a level of quality and excellence consistent over a significant number of departments. Even if this is not true at the moment, it will probably strengthen administrative tendencies to somehow achieve such a consistent quality over the departments of a given university. Rankings will further contribute to the hierarchization of national university systems, but more important is the tendency of rankings to favour comparisons which transcend national boundaries. In this way, rankings will contribute to the worldwide transmission of educational and scientific ideas and ideals. If something is relevant for success in rankings (and there are more of these relevancies if there is a plurality of rankings), it is probable that it will diffuse through the world system of universities.

Internationalization of individual universities

Coupled with, but historically independent from, rankings is the tendency towards the internationalization of individual universities. In several of the rankings, internationalization functions as an indicator that contributes to the measurement of the quality of the university. And internationalization is a widely shared ideology with a tradition going back to the 12th-century origins of universities. Therefore, today, universities are supposed to have an internationalization strategy, and they compare themselves with other universities from the point of view of having the best-defined internationalization strategy. This preference for internationalization even includes the individual student who is supposed to get some international experience and therefore to integrate a stay in a foreign university into his/her study plan.

Unilocality even in the context of branch campuses

An interesting aspect of the globalization and internationalization of the university always was that the individual university remained located at only one place and one city in the world (often at a closely concentrated campus). This distinguishes the university from other organizations which equally claim global relevance (e.g. multinational enterprises or churches). There are some alternative structures to this strongly localized university: federal universities with campuses in several cities, such as the Eidgenössische Technische Hochschule (Zürich, Lausanne) or the 'University of California' (ten campuses from Berkeley 1868 to Merced 2005). But in most of these cases, once more there is a tendency towards an organizational autonomy of the individual campus and a weakening of the federal level. More recent is the trend towards 'International Branch Campuses', which have been established especially by American and English universities, primarily in the Middle East and sometimes in East Asia. Mostly, these International Branch Campuses have been financed by the countries where they were opened. This seems to point not to an expansion strategy of the most successful universities of the world (most of whom do not participate in this movement anyway) but more to an opportunistic strategy of universities making use of chances to get additional financing. And a number of these branch campuses have already been closed again after only few years, which lets us doubt regarding the permanence of this recent trend. Therefore, there are good reasons to hold fast to the hypothesis of the unilocality of the university as organization.

Globalization of degrees

Whereas universities still do not migrate (mostly), there exists a different trend regarding university curricula. Among the many institutions which will be imitated and transferred in a global university system are some curricular structures which are less localized than the universities where they are realized. There is, as the most well-known case, the MBA, which somehow inverts the hierarchy of organization and curriculum, as the curriculum has a higher visibility than the university offering the respective curriculum. In this case, universities are founded to enter the competition among organizations in offering MBA degrees. Another prominent case is 'Philosophy, Politics and Economics' (PPE), a curriculum which was invented in Oxford in the 1920s and in recent years is introduced in ever more universities in the world. Another aspect of this globalization of curricula is what has been called 'the rise of the practical arts'. Both curricula mentioned here are part of this trend which means the loss of relevance of many of the classical academic disciplines as primary subjects of study and instead the emergence of interdisciplinary fields such as Communication, Health and Public Administration, which are mainly conceived from the point of view of practical usages ascribed to them (Brint, 2002).

Transnational degree architectures and qualification frameworks

Besides this trend towards the globalization of some curricular structures, there arise more general frameworks for qualifications and degrees. Since the 1950s, there exist European conventions on the equivalence of certificates of eligibility for university entrance, for the duration of studies at universities and for the recognition of academic degrees and certificates (Kasparovsky, 2003, p. 3). One can read these conventions as attempts to transcend the limited reach of national degrees, thereby improving the accessibility and permeability of transnational education. Again, higher education was a pioneer for other parts of the education and qualification system, in particular for the regulated professions, where similar conventions emerged. Many of these conventions deal with legally binding regulations, which lead to concrete entitlements, for example the right to apply for studying at a university and the right to access regulated segments of the labour market. However, conventions that are more recent use legally non-binding forms of coordination, which put stronger emphasis on simplified and improved communication about the knowledge, skills and competencies of individuals. Not only the development of a transnational degree architecture in the Bologna Process but also the respective development of national and transnational qualification frameworks are examples of this emphasis on the standardisation of categories (Biffl and Pfeffer, 2013; Pfeffer and Skrivanek, 2013). Transnational qualification frameworks, which focus on specific world regions, also emerged in other regions, for example in the Caribbean, in South Africa and in Southeast Asia (Keevy, Chakroun and Deij, 2010).

Conclusions

Throughout this chapter, we have argued for the rise of a world system of universities in which national states and 'their' universities are subsystems that observe one another and compete with one another. And the links from national states to the universities, which are part of the respective national system, become weaker over time – some universities which perceive global imperatives trying to loosen their bonds to the national system. In this respect, we even have to do with an individualization of universities, individual universities opting for strategies of their own and trying to find their individual place in a world system.

The most important factor behind the tendency to global structural changes in the system of world universities is the intensity of mutual observation possible under contemporary conditions of communication. Ever new comparisons are invented for looking at universities from a comparative point of view and for motivating imitations and innovations and structural changes resulting from them. This is the major factor in the dynamics which characterizes a world system which includes all the universities in the world into one system of potential linkages and cooperations and at the same time the competitive search for innovative identities. In contrast to what DiMaggio and Powell (1983) regarded as the main consequence of an organizational field, namely the pressure towards standardization and isomorphism, the perspective of systems theory on the global university system allows to observe at least as many signs for organizational differentiation and variation.

Quite probably different types of universities (and different subject areas within universities) will be affected by these developments to very different degrees. While some subject areas (e.g. training of lawyers, teacher training for primary and secondary education) need to follow national regulations or regional cultures, others (e.g. MBAs) can and have to address international audiences. International comparisons can also lead to the discovery of new niches in education and research and, subsequently, to new educational and research activities. For many universities, internationalization is welcomed as a means to escape at least some national restrictions and dependencies.

A systems theoretical perspective on national university systems also allows to observe and predict differentiation and variation between national policies. It is already obvious that some countries encourage their universities to use internationalization as a means to generate new funding streams, which might reduce their dependence on national funding and relieve national budgets. A complementary form of national higher education policy is paying for access opportunities of their own citizens in the global higher education system, for example via international scholarships. Leaving behind the idea of self-contained national university systems, which produce all the skills and research needed by a nation state, one can think of a division of labour between different nation states and their national university systems.

Rather than having to assume an objectively given reality, systems theory describes the distinctiveness of different autopoietic systems and their respective ways to observe and to operate. This allows for paying tribute to the internal rationale of every system, while simultaneously acknowledging external influences as stimulations and irritations. The main challenge for systems theoretical research is to specify the system one refers to and to make visible as clear as possible, when a switch of the reference system takes place.

In practical terms, systems theory helps to understand that and why the nation state is only one among other relevant contexts (e.g. global function systems like education and research) for universities, and that national institutions (ministries, agencies) are only a few among other relevant organizations in the environment of universities. This does not exclude the nation state from analysis, but it limits and specifies its role, while opening up the opportunities for understanding the worldwide university system of our days and its structural coupling to education and science as two of the global function systems of world society.

References

Baecker, D. (2010) 'A systems primer on universities', *Soziale Systeme: Zeitschrift für soziologische Theorie*, 16(2), 356–367.

Baker, D. P. (2014). *The Schooled Society. The Educational Transformation of Global Culture* (Stanford: Stanford University Press).

Ben-David, J. (1977) *Centers of Learning. Britain, France, Germany, United States* (New York: Mc Graw Hill).

Biffl, G. and T. Pfeffer (2013) Recognition of qualifications of citizens of another EU Member State. Background paper for the Europe on the move conference – Participation and Integration of EU-citizens, Vienna: Bundesministerium für Inneres (bm.i).

Brint, S. (2002). 'The rise of the "practical arts" ', in S. Brint (ed) *The Future of the City of Intellect: The Changing American University* (pp. 231–259) (Stanford: Stanford University Press).

Clark, B. R. (1983) *The Higher Education System: Academic Organization in Cross-National Perspective* (Berkeley: University of California Press).

DiMaggio, P. J. and W. W. Powell (1983) 'The iron cage revisited: institutional isomorphism and collective rationality in organizational fields', *American Sociological Review*, 48(2), 147–160.

Karabel, J. (2006) *The Chosen. The Hidden History of Admission and Exclusion at Harvard, Yale and Princeton* (Boston, NY: Mariner Books).

Kasparovsky, H. (2003) *Lissabon-Empfehlung allgemein 2004. Übereinkommen über die Anerkennung von Qualifikationen im Hochschulbereich in der europäischen Region. Erläuternde Bemerkungen und Empfehlungen zur Durchführung* (Vienna: bm:bwk).

Keevy, J., Chakroun, B. and A. Deij (2010) *Transnational Qualifications Frameworks* (Report commissioned by the European Training Foundation) (Luxembourg: Publications Office of the European Union).

Krücken, G. and F. Meier (2006) 'Turning the university into an organizational actor', in G. S. Drori, J. W. Meyer and K. Hwang (eds) *Globalization and Organization. World Society and Organizational Change* (pp. 241–257) (Oxford: Oxford University Press).

Luhmann, N. (1975) 'Interaktion, Organisation, Gesellschaft. Anwendungen der Systemtheorie', in *Soziologische Aufklärung 2. Aufsätze zur Theorie der Gesellschaft* (Opladen: Westdeutscher Verlag).

Luhmann, N. (1984) *Soziale Systeme: Grundriß einer allgemeinen Theorie* (Frankfurt am Main: Suhrkamp).

Luhmann, N. (1997) *Die Gesellschaft der Gesellschaft* (Bde. 1–2) (Frankfurt am Main: Suhrkamp).

Luhmann, N. (2002). 'I see something you don't see', in W. Rasch (ed) *Theories of Distinction. Redescribing the Description of Modernity* (pp. 187–193) (Stanford: Stanford University Press).

Luhmann, N. (2005) 'The autopoiesis of social systems', in D. Seidl and K. H. Becker (eds) *Niklas Luhmann and Organization Studies* (S. 64–70) (Malmö: Liber & Copenhagen Business School Press).

Martins, H. (1974) 'Time and theory in sociology', in J. Rex (ed) *Approaches to Sociology* (S. 246–294) (London: Routledge and Kegan Paul).

Meyer, J. W., Boli, J., Thomas, G. M. and F. O. Ramirez (1997) 'World society and the nation state', *American Journal of Sociology*, 103, 144–181.

Nentwich, M. (2001) '(Re-)De-commodification in academic knowledge distribution?' *Science Studies*, 14(2), 21–42.

Parsons, T. and G. M. Platt (1973) *The American University*, 2nd Print edn (Cambridge: Harvard University Press).

Pfeffer, T. and I. Skrivanek (2013) 'Institutionelle Verfahren zur Anerkennung ausländischer Qualifikationen und zur Validierung nicht formal oder informell erworbener Kompetenzen in Österreich // Institutionalized procedures for the recognition of foreign qualifications and for the validation of non-formal or informal competencies in Austria', *Zeitschrift für Bildungsforschung*, 3(1), doi: 10.1007/s35834-013-0058-4.

Power, M. (1997) *The Audit Society: Rituals of Verification* (Oxford: Oxford University Press)

Riddle, P. (1989) *University and the State: Political Competition and the Rise of the Universities, 1200–1985* (Stanford: Stanford University).

Schofer, E. and J. W. Meyer (2005) 'The worldwide expansion of higher education in the twentieth century', *American Sociological Review*, 70, 898–920.

Seidl, D. (2005). 'The basic concepts of Luhmann's theory of social systems', in D. Seidl and K. H. Becker (eds) *Niklas Luhmann and Organization Studies* (Malmö: Liber & Copenhagen Business School Press).

Seidl, D. and K. H. Becker (2005) 'Introduction: Luhmann's organization theory', in D. Seidl and K. H. Becker (eds) *Niklas Luhmann and Organization Studies* (pp. S8–18) (Malmö: Liber & Copenhagen Business School Press).

Shanghai Ranking Consultancy (2014) 'About Academic Ranking of World Universities', http://www.shanghairanking.com/aboutarwu.html (retrieved 4 June 2015).

Simon, F. B. (2009) 'Wurzeln der systemtheoretischen Organisationstheorie', in R. Wimmer, J. O. Meissner and P. Wolf (eds) *Praktische Organisationswissenschaft. Lehrbuch für Studium und Beruf* (Heidelberg: Carl-Auer-Systeme).

Spencer Brown, G. (1971) *Laws of Form* (London: George Allen and Unwin Ltd).

Stichweh, R. (1991) *Der frühmoderne Staat und die europäische Universität. Zur Interaktion von Politik und Erziehungssystem im Prozess ihrer Ausdifferenzierung (16–18 Jahrhundert)* (Frankfurt a.M.: Suhrkamp).

Stichweh, R. (2006) 'Die Universität in der Wissensgesellschaft: Wissensbegriffe und Umweltbeziehungen der modernen Universität', *Soziale Systeme*, 12, 33–53.

Stichweh, R. (2007) 'The eigenstructures of world society and the regional cultures of the world', in I. Rossi (ed) *Frontiers of Globalization Research. Theoretical and Methodological Approaches* (pp. 133–150) (New York: Springer).

Stichweh, R. (2009) *Center and Periphery in a Global University System* (Luzern: University of Lucerne).

Stichweh, R. (2010a) 'Funktionale Differenzierung der Weltgesellschaft', in G. Albert and S. Sigmund (eds) *Soziologische Theorie kontrovers. Sonderheft 50/2010 der Kölner Zeitschrift für Soziologie und Sozialpsychologie*, 50, pp. 299–306.

Stichweh, R. (2010b) *Die Universität in der Weltgesellschaft* (Luzerner Universitätsreden Nr. 19).

Stichweh, R. (2011) 'Niklas Luhmann', in G. Ritzer and J. Stepnisky (eds) *Major Social Theorists. Vol. II. Contemporary Social Theorists* (pp. 287–309) (Malden, MA: Wiley-Blackwell).

Stichweh, R. (2013) 'The history and systematics of functional differentiation in sociology', in M. Albert, B. Buzan and M. Zürn (eds) *Bringing Sociology to International Relations. World Politics as Differentiation Theory* (pp. 50–70) (Cambridge: Cambridge University Press).

Stichweh, R. (2015) 'Comparing systems theory and sociological neo-institutionalism: explaining functional differentiation', in B. Holzer, F. Kastner and T. Werron (eds) *From Globalization to World Society. Neo-Institutional and Systems-Theoretical Perspectives* (pp. 23–36) (New York and London: Routledge).

Veblen, Th. B. (1918) *The Higher Learning in America. A Memorandum on the Conduct of Universities by Business Men.* (New York: Augustus M. Kelley).

Weick, K. E. (1979) *Der Prozess des Organisierens* (Frankfurt am Main: Suhrkamp).

10
Research on Higher Education Policy and Institutional Management

Malcolm Tight

Introduction

This chapter reviews the state of research into higher education policy and institutional management. It does so by reanalysing in more detail data collected for previous analyses of the state of higher education research overall (Tight, 2003, 2012a), which focused in particular on the articles published in specialist higher education journals in 2000 and 2010.

The chapter starts by presenting an overall assessment of the contemporary state of higher education research, and of the importance of research into higher education policy and institutional management as an element of this. The role of specialist and generic higher education journals is considered. Succeeding sections then focus on the characteristics of the published articles: the methods and methodologies used, the theoretical frameworks applied, the levels at which analyses are pitched and the characteristics of the researchers involved. The kinds of topics being researched are then explored in more detail, before some conclusions are drawn.

The analysis shows that research on these topics

- primarily employs documentary and multivariate analysis, at varying levels of sophistication;
- emphasizes larger scales of analysis (institutions or nations) than in other areas of higher education research;
- remains dominated by men, including significant numbers of senior higher education managers;
- appears stronger in the United States and continental Europe than in the United Kingdom and Australasia; and
- continues to focus on changing policy, funding arrangements, leadership and governance, and their consequences.

Higher education research: The overall picture

Fifteen specialist higher education journals were selected for analysis – *Assessment and Evaluation in Higher Education* (AEHE), *Higher Education* (HE), *Higher Education Management and Policy* (HEMP), *Higher Education Policy* (HEP), *Higher Education Quarterly* (HEQ), *Higher Education Research and Development* (HERD), *Innovative Higher Education* (IHE), *Journal of College Student Development* (JCSD), *Journal of Higher Education* (JHE), *Journal of Higher Education Policy and Management* (JHEPM), *Research in Higher Education* (ResHE), *Review of Higher Education* (RevHE), *Studies in Higher Education* (SHE), *Teaching in Higher Education* (THE) and *Tertiary Education and Management* (TEAM) – and all of the articles they published in the years 2000 and 2010 were obtained, read and analysed.

The journals were selected for analysis on the basis that they only published articles on higher education and in the English language and that they represented the higher-quality end of the publishing spectrum. They are spread internationally, based in the United Kingdom (AEHE, HEQ, SHE, THE), the rest of Europe (HE, HEMP, HEP, TEAM), the United States (IHE, JCSD, JHE, ResHE, RevHE) or Australia (HERD, JHEPM). In all, the 15 journals published 567 articles in 2010, an increase of 46% on the 388 articles published ten years earlier. This expansion was most notable in the journals published outside of the United States (Tight, 2012b).

In terms of the themes or issues they addressed, the articles were classified into eight categories: teaching and learning, course design, the student experience, quality, system policy, institutional management, academic work, knowledge and research. Of these, two, system policy and institutional management – which contain writing on higher education policy and governance, the subject of this Handbook – form the focus of this chapter. These two subject groups accounted for 54 and 53 respectively, or just under 10% each, of the total of 567 articles published in the 15 journals in 2010. In the year 2000, they accounted for similar numbers of articles, 59 and 49 respectively, but a rather larger proportion of the smaller total of 388 (15% and 13%, respectively).

While system policy and institutional management are clearly not the most popular topics overall in terms of numbers of articles published (two other topics, course design and the student experience, accounted for 55% of the articles published in 2010, and 45% of those published in 2000), they do, therefore, comprise an important subset of higher education research and publishing.

Of course, as some of their titles suggest, many higher education journals specialize in particular aspects of the field, while others are more generic in what they publish. Thus, of the journals examined here, HEP shows a strong focus on policy issues (10 of 27 articles (37%) published in 2010 and 10 of 21 (48%) published in 2000), while TEAM has a similar focus on management (10 of 20 articles (50%) published in 2010 and 8 of 20 (40%) published in 2000).

Of the other obvious candidates, HEMP (which has recently discontinued publication) published 8 (of 20: 40%) articles focusing on either system policy or institutional management in 2010 (and 20 of 24 (83%) in 2000), while JHEPM published 14 (of 40: 35%) articles on these themes in 2010 and 7 (of 14: 50%) in 2000.

But most of the journals appear open to publishing some articles focusing on policy or management issues, perhaps more targeted to their specialist interests. Thus, of the 15 journals, only 3 (AEHE, JCSD and THE) published no articles on either of these themes in 2010, and only 1 (THE) did not do so in 2000.

Characteristics of the published articles

Methods and methodologies used

The methods and/or methodologies (I will use the compound term method/ologies because these terms are, in practice, used in overlapping ways) employed in the articles analysed were classified in six categories: the dominant social science method/ologies of surveys and multivariate analyses (or multivariate analysis for short), documentary analyses and interview-based analyses, and the more niche approaches of conceptual analysis, critical analysis and phenomenography (for more detail on these approaches, see, for example, Jackson (2000), Marshall (1997) or Bowden and Walsh (2000), respectively). Overall, multivariate analyses accounted for 44% of the articles published in 2010 (and 39% of those published in 2000), with documentary analyses making up 26% (30%) and interview-based analyses 21% (20%).

The patterns for articles focusing on system policy and institutional management were rather different. Thus, in 2010 the majority (70%; 66% in 2000) of the articles on system policy used a documentary analysis approach, with a further 22% (29%) employing multivariate analysis. For institutional management, 47% of the articles published in 2010 (59% in 2000) used documentary analysis, with 32% (27%) employing multivariate analysis.

Method/ological engagement and complexity varied a great deal. Thus, the majority of the articles using documentary analysis relied on a fairly straightforward reading of the documents of interest (whether their focus was on system policy or institutional management), and many did not even engage in method/ological discussion; while a minority skilfully employed specialist techniques such as discourse analysis. Similarly, many of the articles employing multivariate analysis relied on relatively simple surveys (though here some, albeit often brief, method/ological discussion – of sample sizes, response rates and so forth – was normal); but others – and particularly those stemming from and published in North America (Tight, 2007, 2014d) – utilized sophisticated multivariate analysis techniques, such as factor analysis and structural equation modelling, to interrogate large data sets.

Theory applied

Both subject areas – as with higher education research in general – were characterized by the development of new theory and the application of existing theories from other disciplines (often, of course, the disciplines from which the researchers themselves had come or were still based in: see Tight, 2014a). Thus, for example, in system policy, academic drift (or institutional isomorphism: Tight, 2014c) and massification had each been the focus of developing theoretical frameworks for at least a few decades; while human capital theory and stakeholder theory had been appropriated and applied from other social sciences.

Similarly, in the area of institutional management, institutional missions and diversity, for example, have been the subject of some theorization; while theories on economies of scale, leadership and managerialism (Tight, 2014b) and, more generally, institutional theory, have been imported and applied from elsewhere.

Levels of analysis

Eight levels of analysis were recognized, ranging from articles pitched at the level of the individual (student or academic), through the course, department, institution, region and nation (with 'system' used where the nation being examined was not made explicit) to the international. Overall, the most common levels focused on were national (37% of articles published in 2010, 36% in 2000) and institutional (26% and 30%).

Not surprisingly, the levels at which analyses were pitched varied somewhat in terms of the topic being studied. Thus, in 2010, the majority, 74% (68% in 2000) of the articles published on system policy focused on the national level, with a further 22% (19%) at the international level. That is, the policies being analysed were those applying within a single nation, or a group of nations such as the European Union, or two or more nations' policies were being compared.

The patterns were more varied for articles dealing with institutional management. In 2010, 45% of these focused at the national level, 26% at the institutional level and 21% at the international level. The proportions were rather different in 2000, however – 33% at national level, the majority, 51%, at institutional level and only 4% at international level – illustrating a degree of variation over the years. In other words, articles examining the experiences of particular higher education institutions were also popular, alongside those exploring institutional management issues in particular nations or internationally.

Compared to other areas of higher education research, therefore, those researching policy or management are much more likely to focus on larger-scale trends or issues.

Researcher characteristics

The 567 articles published in 2010 had a total of 1187 authors, or an average of 2.1 authors per article. The analysis in this section will focus on the 567 first-named authors, and in particular on the 107 who contributed articles on system policy or institutional management.

Interestingly, while women made up more of the first authors than men (55% to 45%, having excluded 10% whose sex I was unable to determine) in 2010 overall, men dominated as first authors for both system policy and institutional management. Thus, men made up 73% of the first authors of articles on system policy, and 67% of those on institutional management.

Overall, in terms of their broad disciplinary background, the most common locations for the authors published in 2010 were in education (32%), social science (14%) or business (10%), though for 19% of authors no such information was given. For authors of articles on system policy and institutional management, the patterns were broadly similar, with 37% and 28%, respectively, in education departments, 15% and 11% in social science and 11% and 17% in business. These research topics also, however, attract the attention and interest of those working in the university administration, with 7% of system policy and 17% of institutional management articles stemming from this source.

Overall, the greatest proportion of authors came from North America (33%), followed by Australasia (24%), the United Kingdom (17%) the rest of Europe (16%), Asia (5%), Africa (4%) and Latin America (less than 1%). These patterns are, of course, not that surprising, given the focus on English language journals.

North America also led the way for authoring articles on system policy (37% of first authors) and institutional management (34%), though this is partly a function of American-based journals tending to publish primarily or solely North American-based authors (Tight, 2007, 2014d). However, Australasian authors were less represented in these fields (only 7% and 15% of first authors, respectively), with authors from the rest of Europe (24% and 21%) and Asia (13% and 9%) providing above-average proportions of authors and the United Kingdom (15% and 13%) also below par.

Topics researched

Let us now examine in a little more detail what was being researched and published that was labelled as system policy or institutional management. In doing so, it must be stressed, as already indicated, that the articles published in these 15 journals in 2000 and 2010 may not be entirely typical or representative of the contemporary research field; but they should, at least, be indicative or suggestive. We will start with the 2010 data, before looking at 2000, comparing the two data sets and then looking at more recent publications.

System policy

In 2010, the 54 articles published on system policy in the 15 journals included two or more focused on each of the following issues:

- funding issues and arrangements (e.g. Filippakou, Salter and Tapper, 2010; Toutkoushian and Shafiq, 2010)
- institutional diversity (e.g. Kitigawa and Oba, 2010; Rossi, 2010)
- internationalization (e.g. Horta, 2010; Rivers, 2010)
- politics (as they effected higher education: e.g. Doyle, 2010; Tandberg, 2010)
- regional policy (e.g. Kirwan, 2010; Saarivirta, 2010)
- research policy and funding (e.g. Lepori and Kyvik, 2010; Olayiwola, 2010)
- social inclusion (e.g. Gidley et al., 2010; Harrison and Hatt, 2010)
- student funding (e.g. Miller, 2010; Ness, 2010)
- the Bologna reform process (e.g. Kehm, Michelsen and Vabo, 2010; Reichert, 2010)
- the knowledge society (e.g. Bastalich, 2010; Varela-Petito, 2010)
- transforming universities (e.g. Bruininks, Keeney and Thorp, 2010; Spanier, 2010)

Other articles focused on policy relating to issues as diverse as, for example, accountability (Bogue and Johnson, 2010), immigration (Dougherty, Nienhusser and Vega, 2010), international development (Collins and Rhoads, 2010) and outcomes assessment (Kushimoto, 2010).

Looking at the outputs in the same publications in the year 2000, we find two or more articles focusing on each of the following topics:

- changing national policies (e.g. Mora and Vidal, 2000; Williams, 2000)
- changing study patterns (e.g. Moore, 2000; Slantcheva, 2000)
- expansion or massification and its effects (e.g. Doughney, 2000; Hodgson and Spours, 2000)
- funding issues and arrangements (e.g. Sav, 2000; Thomas, 2000)
- institutional diversity (e.g. Lang, 2000; Neave, 2000; this topic was actually the subject of special issues of both HEP and JHE)
- institutional relationships (e.g. Crespo, 2000; Harman, 2000b)
- internationalization (e.g. Mok and Lee, 2000; Yang, 2000)
- lifelong learning (e.g. Brennan et al., 2000; Candy, 2000)
- particular types of university (e.g. Pham, 2000; Polster, 2000)
- research policy and funding (e.g. Caraca, Conceicao and Heitor, 2000; Harman, 2000a)
- the United Kingdom's research assessment exercise (e.g. Elton, 2000; Talib and Steele, 2000)

Once again, as well as addressing these themes, there were examples of individual articles on a varied range of topics, including performance funding (Burke and Modarresi, 2000), the role of the private sector (Amaral and Teixeira, 2000), sports policy (Shehu, 2000) and student loans (Monteverde, 2000).

There are clearly similarities between the subjects of the articles published in 2000 and 2010, as 4 (funding issues and arrangements, institutional diversity, internationalization and research policy and funding) of the 12 themes identified for the two years are common (as, of course, were some of the authors). Some of the other themes are closely related, and some are indicative of the transitory popularity of particular issues at different times: for example, the UK research assessment exercise, now replaced, in 2000 publications, and the impact of the Bologna reform process, as it reached its fruition, in 2010 publications.

Institutional management

In 2010, the articles published on institutional management had a particular focus on the following themes:

- alumni (e.g. Meer and Rosen, 2010; Weerts, Cabrera and Sandford, 2010)
- community engagement (e.g. Boehm, 2010; Weerts and Sandmann, 2010)
- funding (e.g. Essack, Naidoo and Barnes, 2010; Rollwagen, 2010)
- governance (e.g. de Boer, Huisman and Meister-Scheytt, 2010; Mok, 2010)
- institutional efficiency (e.g. Eckles, 2010; Sellers-Rubio, Mas-Ruiz and Casado-Diaz, 2010)
- leadership (e.g. Breakwell and Tytherleigh, 2010; Middlehurst, 2010)
- networking (e.g. De Wit, 2010; Flora and Hirt, 2010)
- offshoring (e.g. Craig and Gunn, 2010; Poole and Ewan, 2010)
- particular leadership roles (e.g. Bray, 2010; Scott et al., 2010)
- performance (e.g. Sarrico, 2010; Shin, 2010)
- research management (e.g. Scobie et al., 2010; Shelley, 2010)

In addition, there were single articles published which tackled topics such as entrepreneurial architecture (Nelles and Vorley, 2010), fundraising (Caboni, 2010), mergers (Ursin et al., 2010) and plagiarism management (Sutherland-Smith, 2010).

Articles on institutional management published in the 15 journals examined in the year 2000 demonstrated a particular focus on the following issues:

- administrative effectiveness (e.g. Heck, Johnsrud and Rosser, 2000; Pounder, 2000)
- diversity (e.g. Chang, 2000; Connolly, 2000)
- financial management (e.g. Gill and Gill, 2000; Shuen, 2000)

- governance (e.g. Eckel, 2000; Kulati, 2000)
- institutional forms (e.g. Askling and Kristensen, 2000; Mouwen, 2000)
- leadership (e.g. van den Bosch and Teelken, 2000; Kezar, 2000)
- organizational change (e.g. El Khawas, 2000; Gumport, 2000)
- sexual harassment (e.g. Kelley and Parsons, 2000; Shultz, Scherman and Marshall, 2000)
- strategic planning (e.g. Morphew, 2000; Morrill, 2000)

Individual articles published in that year covered issues as diverse as drinking policies (Colby, Raymond and Colby, 2000), learning and teaching strategies (Gibbs, Habeshaw and Yorke, 2000), sports policies (Thelin, 2000) and wicked issues (Watson, 2000).

As in the case of system policy, some of the themes of the articles published were common to both 2000 and 2010 – most notably governance and leadership – while others addressed similar or related topics.

Writing on system policy and institutional management compared

In addition to noting the continuing and developing focus on particular topics for research and publication within the system policy and institutional management themes, we may also observe a certain degree of overlap between the themes. This should not be surprising, of course, because system policy and institutional management are cognate fields, and many articles address elements of both (though they have here been classified under their dominant focus).

Thus, a strong and continuing interest in funding issues is apparent. In some cases, this may be directed at the system level (e.g. changing national policies for funding higher education) or particular aspects of it (e.g. funding for research or students). In other cases, the focus is at the institutional level: on how institutions raise funds, manage the funds they have or use them strategically and efficiently.

The other topic that stands out as being of interest across the two themes is diversity. As it expresses itself in studies of institutional management, the focus is on different types of higher education institution, or on diversity within academic and, particularly, student groups, and how this may be fostered and developed further. In terms of system policy, the interest is in overall patterns of diversity (of higher education institutions or students usually) within particular national systems.

More recent writing

To check whether the sample years 2000 and 2010 were unusual, and whether the topics on which articles focused then were still being researched currently, the articles published in four of the journals sampled in 2014 (at the time of writing) were examined. This analysis suggests that the years 2000 and 2010 were by no means unusual, and that interest was being maintained and developed in most of the topics identified.

Looking first at HEQ, a UK-based journal, we can see that research on system policy continues to examine internationalization (Haigh, 2014, part of a special issue on globalization) and changing national policies (Callender, 2014, part of another special issue on the impact of the Robbins report). There were no articles in the issues published at the time of writing that focused on institutional management.

In the case of JHEPM, an Australian-based journal, articles on system policy addressed issues such as changing national policies (Freeman, 2014) and research policy and funding (Warshaw and Hearn, 2014). Similarly, research on institutional management maintained its interest in governance (Vilkinas and Peters, 2014) and leadership (Odhiambo, 2014).

In the case of ResHE, a US-based journal, research into system policy still demonstrates a keen interest in funding issues and arrangements (Delaney and Doyle, 2014), and in student funding in particular (Hillman, Tandberg and Gross, 2014). Research into institutional management published in this journal has continued to take an interest in alumni behaviour (Borden, Shaker and Kienker, 2014) and financial management (Fowles, 2014).

Finally, looking at TEAM, a European journal, interest in researching system policy has maintained its focus on, for example, internationalization (de Haan, 2014) and research policy (Jung, 2014). Studies of institutional management have continued to focus on governance (Bruckmann and Carvalho, 2014) and particular leadership roles (Ngo, de Boer and Enders, 2014).

Conclusions

This examination of the contemporary state of research into system policy and institutional management in higher education has revealed some interesting patterns. While we must emphasize the limitations of the analysis, in that it is based primarily on the articles published in 15 English language journals in 2000 and 2010, the evidence seems strong and indicative.

Thus, research into system policy and institutional management shows a heavy reliance on documentary and/or multivariate forms of analysis. Interview-based, conceptual and other forms of method/ology are relatively rare. Research tends to focus at the institutional (for studies of institutional management), national (for studies of both system policy and institutional management) or international levels (for both). While the widespread attention paid to international and comparative studies is commendable, the relative ignorance of what happens below the level of the institution – in terms, for example, of policy implementation and management strategies – is regrettable.

Unlike research into other aspects of higher education, male authors still appear to dominate research into system policy and institutional management. This seems likely to be related to the tendency for men to continue to dominate actual higher education policy and management. Researchers into these themes tend, like most other higher education researchers, to be based mainly in education, social science or business departments, but a significant minority are based in the university administration, including numbers of institutional leaders. Most of the researchers who publish in the English language journals studied are located in North America, the United Kingdom, the rest of Europe and Australasia, with more limited numbers spread throughout the rest of the world.

The two themes – system policy and institutional management – that have been focused on are not wholly distinct; rather they are closely related. Contemporary research on system policy takes a keen interest in changing national and international policies, in funding arrangements (both general and more specific), and in how higher education systems look (e.g. in terms of institutional forms and diversity) and behave (e.g. in terms of student recruitment and support). Research into institutional management shows a particular focus on leadership and governance issues, on how institutions raise and manage their finances, and on how they deliver their various roles.

Alongside these shared and continuing concerns, research into other, more specialized, aspects of system policy and institutional management is also carried out. Emphases vary between different parts of the world, with US-based researchers, for example, more interested in the role of religion and sport in higher education, as well as being ahead in studying alumni relations; while those in Europe have been much more engaged in international collaboration and standards as a result of European Union policy. The research base also continues to develop, particularly as new theoretical frameworks are applied from other disciplines or created within higher education research itself.

To conclude, research into system policy and institutional management in higher education appears to be healthy and developing, though it attracts relatively less attention from higher education researchers than does course design or the student experience.

References

Amaral, A. and P. Teixeira (2000) 'The rise and fall of the private sector in Portuguese higher education', *Higher Education Policy*, 13(3), 245–266.

Askling, B. and B. Kristensen (2000) 'Towards the "learning organisation": implications for institutional governance and leadership', *Higher Education Management*, 12(2), 17–41.

Bastalich, W. (2010) 'Knowledge economy and research innovation', *Studies in Higher Education*, 35(7), 845–857.

Boehm, A. (2010) 'University involvement in social planning: perspectives of community institutions and universities', *Journal of Higher Education Policy and Management*, 32(1), 97–109.

de Boer, H., Huisman, J. and C. Meister-Scheytt (2010) 'Supervision in "modern" university governance: boards under scrutiny', *Studies in Higher Education*, 35(3), 317–333.

Bogue, G. and B. Johnson (2010) 'Performance incentives and public college accountability in the United States: a quarter century policy audit', *Higher Education Management and Policy*, 22(2), 9–30.

Borden, C., Shaker, G. and B. Kienker (2014) 'The impact of alumni status on institutional giving by faculty and staff', *Research in Higher Education*, 55(2), 196–217.

Bosch, H. van den and C. Teelken (2000) 'Organisation and leadership in higher Education: learning from experiences in the Netherlands', *Higher Education Policy*, 13(4), 379–397.

Bowden, J. and E. Walsh (eds) (2000) *Phenomenography* (Melbourne: RMIT Press).

Bray, N. (2010) 'The deanship and its faculty interpreters: do Mertonian norms of science translate into norms for administration?' *Journal of Higher Education*, 81(3), 284–316.

Breakwell, G. and M. Tytherleigh (2010) 'University leaders and university performance in the United Kingdom: is it "who" leads or "where" they lead that matter most', *Higher Education*, 60(5), 491–506.

Brennan, J., Mills, J., Shah, T. and A. Woodley (2000) 'Lifelong learning for employment and equity: the role of part-time degrees', *Higher Education Quarterly*, 54(4), 411–418.

Bruckmann, S. and T. Carvalho (2014) 'The reform process of Portuguese higher education institutions: from collegial to managerial governance', *Tertiary Education and Management*, 20(3), 193–206.

Bruininks, R., Keeney, B. and J. Thorp (2010) 'Transforming America's universities to compete in the "new normal" ', *Innovative Higher Education*, 35, 113–125.

Burke, J. and S. Modarresi (2000) 'To keep or not to keep performance funding: signals from stakeholders', *Journal of Higher Education*, 71(4), 432–453.

Caboni, T. (2010) 'The normative structure of college and university fundraising behaviors', *Journal of Higher Education*, 81(3), 339–365.

Callender, C. (2014) 'Student numbers and funding: does Robbins add up?' *Higher Education Quarterly*, 68(2), 164–186.

Candy, P. (2000) 'Knowledge navigators and lifelong learners: producing graduates for the information society', *Higher Education Research and Development*, 19(3), 261–277.

Caraca, J., Conceicao, P. and M. Heitor (2000) 'Towards a public policy for the research university in Portugal', *Higher Education Policy*, 13(2), 181–201.

Chang, M. (2000) 'Improving campus racial dynamics: a balancing act among competing interests', *Review of Higher Education*, 23(2), 153–175.

Colby, J., Raymond, G. and S. Colby (2000) 'Evaluation of a college policy mandating treatment for students with substantiated drinking problems', *Journal of College Student Development*, 41(4), 395–404.

Collins, C. and R. Rhoads (2010) 'The World Bank, support for universities and asymmetrical power relations in international development', *Higher Education*, 59(2), 181–205.

Connolly, M. (2000) 'What's in a name? a historical look at native American-related nicknames and symbols at three US universities', *Journal of Higher Education*, 71(5), 515–547.

Craig, J. and Gunn, A. (2010) 'Higher skills and the knowledge economy: the challenge of offshoring', *Higher Education Management and Policy*, 22(3), 107–123.

Crespo, M. (2000) 'Managing regional collaboration in higher education: the case of the North American free trade agreement (NAFTA)', *Higher Education Management*, 11(3), 23–39.

Delaney, J. and W. Doyle (2014) 'State spending on higher education capital outlays', *Research in Higher Education*, 55(5), 433–466.

Dougherty, K., Nienhusser, K. and B. Vega (2010) 'Undocumented immigrants and state higher education policy: the politics of in-state tuition eligibility in Texas and Arizona', *Review of Higher Education*, 34(1), 123–173.

Doughney, L. (2000) 'Universal tertiary education: how dual-sector universities can challenge the binary divide between TAFE and higher education – the case of Victoria university of technology', *Journal of Higher Education Policy and Management*, 22(1), 59–72.

Doyle, W. (2010) 'Does merit-based aid "crowd out" need-based aid?' *Research in Higher Education*, 51, 397–415.

Eckel, P. (2000) 'The role of shared governance in institutional hard decisions: enabler or antagonist?' *Review of Higher Education*, 24(1), 15–39.

Eckles, J. (2010) 'Evaluating the efficiency of top liberal arts colleges', *Research in Higher Education*, 51, 266–293.

El-Khawas, E. (2000) 'The impetus for organisational change: an exploration', *Tertiary Education and Management*, 6(1), 37–46.

Elton, L. (2000) 'The UK research assessment exercise: unintended consequences', *Higher Education Quarterly*, 54(3), 274–283.

Essack, S. Naidoo, I. and G. Barnes (2010) 'Government funding as leverage for quality teaching and learning: a South African perspective', *Higher Education Management and Policy*, 22(3), 93–105.

Filippakou, O., Salter, B. and T. Tapper (2010) 'Compliance, resistance and seduction: reflections on 20 years of the funding council model of governance', *Higher Education*, 60(5), 543–557.

Flora, B. and J. Hirt (2010) 'Educational consortia in a knowledge economy: collaboration, competition and organizational equilibrium', *Review of Higher Education*, 33(4), 569–592.

Fowles, J. (2014) 'Funding and focus: resource dependence in public higher education', *Research in Higher Education*, 55(3), 272–287.

Freeman, B. (2014) 'Benchmarking Australian and New Zealand university meta-policy in an increasingly regulated tertiary environment', *Journal of Higher Education Policy and Management*, 36(1), 74–87.

Gibbs, G., Habeshaw, T. and M. Yorke (2000) 'Institutional learning and teaching strategies in English higher education', *Higher Education*, 40(3), 351–372.

Gidley, J., Hampson, G., Wheeler, L. and E. Bereded-Samuel (2010) 'From access to success: an integrated approach to quality higher education informed by social inclusion theory and practice', *Higher Education Policy*, 23(1), 123–147.

Gill, T. and S. Gill (2000) 'Financial management of universities in developing countries', *Higher Education Policy*, 13(2), 125–130.

Gumport, P. (2000) 'Academic restructuring: organizational change and institutional imperatives', *Higher Education*, 39(1), 67–91.

de Haan, H. (2014) 'Where is the gap between internationalization strategic planning and its implementation? a study of 16 Dutch universities' internationalization plans', *Tertiary Education and Management*, 20(2), 135–150.

Haigh, M. (2014) 'From internationalisation to education for global citizenship: a multi-layered history', *Higher Education Quarterly*, 68(1), 6–27.

Harman, G. (2000a) 'Allocating research infrastructure grants in post-binary higher education systems: British and Australian approaches', *Journal of Higher Education Policy and Management*, 22(2), 111–126.

Harman, G. (2000b) 'Institutional mergers in Australian higher education since 1960', *Higher Education Quarterly*, 54(4), 343–366.

Harrison, N. and S. Hatt (2010) ' "Disadvantaged learners": who are we targeting? understanding the targeting of widening participation activity in the United Kingdom using geo-demographic data from southwest England', *Higher Education Quarterly*, 64(1), 65–88.

Heck, R., Johnsrud, L. and V. Rosser (2000) 'Administrative effectiveness in higher education: improving assessment procedures', *Research in Higher Education*, 41(6), 663–684.

Hillman, N., Tandberg, D. and J. Gross (2014) 'Market-based higher education: does Colorado's voucher model improve higher education access and efficiency?' *Research in Higher Education*, 55(6), 601–625.

Hodgson, A. and K. Spours (2000) 'Expanding higher education in the UK: from "system slowdown" to "system acceleration" ', *Higher Education Quarterly*, 54(4), 295–322.

Horta, H. (2010) 'The role of the state in the internationalization of universities in catching-up countries: an analysis of the Portuguese higher education system', *Higher Education Policy*, 23(1), 63–81.

Jackson, F. (2000) *From Metaphysics to Ethics: A Defence of Conceptual Analysis* (Oxford: Oxford University Press).

Jung, J. (2014) 'Research productivity by career stage among Korean academics', *Tertiary Education and Management*, 20(2), 85–105.

Kehm, B., Michelsen, S. and A. Vabo (2010) 'Towards the two-cycle degree structure: Bologna, reform and path dependency in German and Norwegian universities', *Higher Education Policy*, 23(2), 227–245.

Kelley, M. and B. Parsons (2000) 'Sexual harassment in the 1990s: a university-wide survey of female faculty, administrators, staff and students', *Journal of Higher Education*, 71(5), 548–568.

Kezar, A. (2000) 'Pluralistic leadership: incorporating diverse voices', *Journal of Higher Education*, 71(6), 722–743.

Kirwan, W. (2010) 'The 21st century: the century of the American research university', *Innovative Higher Education*, 35, 101–111.

Kitagawa, F. and J. Oba (2010) 'Managing differentation of higher education system in Japan: connecting excellence and diversity', *Higher Education*, 59(4), 507–524.

Kulati, T. (2000) 'Governance, leadership and institutional change in South African higher education: grappling with instability', *Tertiary Education and Management*, 6(3), 177–192.

Kushimoto, T. (2010) 'Outcomes assessment and its role in self-reviews of undergraduate education: in the context of Japanese higher education reforms since the 1990s', *Higher Education*, 59, 589–598.

Lang, D. (2000) 'Similarities and differences: measuring diversity and selecting peers in higher education', *Higher Education*, 39(1), 93–129.

Lepori, B. and S. Kyvik (2010) 'The research mission of universities of applied sciences and the future configuration of higher education systems in Europe', *Higher Education Policy*, 23(3), 295–316.

Marshall, C. (ed) (1997) *Feminist Critical Policy Analysis* (London: Falmer).

Meer, J. and S. Rosen (2010) 'Family bonding with universities', *Research in Higher Education*, 51, 641–658.

Middlehurst, R. (2010) 'Sustaining leadership in challenging times', *Higher Education Management and Policy*, 22(3), 73–91.

Miller, B. (2010) 'The price of higher education: how rational is British tuition fee policy?' *Journal of Higher Education Policy and Management*, 32(1), 85–95.

Mok, K. H. (2010) 'When state centralism meets neo-liberalism: managing university governance change in Singapore and Malaysia', *Higher Education*, 60(4), 419–440.

Mok, K. H. and H. H. Lee (2000) 'Globalization or re-colonization? higher education reforms in Hong Kong', *Higher Education Policy*, 13(4), 361–377.

Monteverde, K. (2000) 'Managing student loan default risk: evidence from a privately guaranteed portfolio', *Research in Higher Education*, 41(3), 331–352.

Moore, E. (2000) 'The changing patterns of university studies: towards lifelong learning in Finnish universities', *Higher Education Management*, 12(3), 113–127.

Mora, J. G. and J. Vidal (2000) 'Adequate policies and unintended effects in Spanish higher education', *Tertiary Education and Management*, 6(4), 247–258.

Morphew, C. (2000) 'The realities of strategic planning: program termination at East central university', *Review of Higher Education*, 23(3), 257–280.

Morrill, R. (2000) 'The use of indicators in the strategic management of universities', *Higher Education Management*, 12(1), 105–112.

Mouwen, K. (2000) 'Strategy, structure and culture of the hybrid university: towards the university of the 21st century', *Tertiary Education and Management*, 6(1), 47–56.

Neave, G. (2000) 'Diversity, differentiation and the market: the debate we never had but which we ought to have done', *Higher Education Policy*, 13(1), 7–21.

Nelles, J. and T. Vorley (2010) 'Constructing an entrepreneurial architecture: an emergent framework for studying the contemporary university beyond the entrepreneurial turn', *Innovative Higher Education*, 35, 161–176.

Ness, E. (2010) 'The politics of determining merit aid eligibility criteria: an analysis of the policy process', *Journal of Higher Education*, 81(1), 34–60.

Ngo, J., de Boer, H. and J. Enders (2014) 'The way deans run their faculties in Indonesian universities', *Tertiary Education and Management*, 20(1), 1–13.

Odhiambo, G. (2014) 'The challenges and future of public higher education leadership in Kenya', *Journal of Higher Education Policy and Management*, 36(2), 183–195.

Olayiwola, S. (2010) 'Alternative model of funding for academic research in Nigerian universities', *Higher Education Quarterly*, 64(2), 149–160.

Pham, B. (2000) 'Research at regional universities in Australia: vision and realization', *Higher Education Management*, 12(2), 117–130.

Polster, C. (2000) 'The future of the liberal university in the era of the global knowledge grab', *Higher Education*, 39(1), 19–41.

Poole, D. and C. Ewan (2010) 'Academics as part-time marketeers in university offshore programs: an exploratory study', *Journal of Higher Education Policy and Management*, 32(2), 149–158.

Pounder, J. (2000) 'Towards a model of institutional effectiveness in higher education: implications of a Hong Kong study', *Higher Education Management*, 12(2), 81–96.

Reichert, S. (2010) 'The intended and unintended effects of the Bologna reforms', *Higher Education Management and Policy*, 22(1), 99–118.

Rivers, D. (2010) 'Ideologies of internationalisation and the treatment of diversity within Japanese higher education', *Journal of Higher Education Policy and Management*, 32(5), 441–454.

Rollwagen, I. (2010) 'Project economy approaches for higher education: diversifying the revenue base of German universities', *Higher Education Management and Policy*, 22(3), 9–29.

Rossi, F. (2010) 'Massification, competition and organizational diversity in higher education: evidence from Italy', *Studies in Higher Education*, 35(3), 277–300.

Saarivirta, T. (2010) 'Finnish higher education expansion and regional policy', *Higher Education Quarterly*, 64(4), 353–372.

Sarrico, C. (2010) 'On performance in higher education: towards performance governance', *Tertiary Education and Management*, 16(2), 145–158.

Sav, G. (2000) 'Institutional funding and managerial differences in racially dual higher education systems', *Higher Education Management*, 11(3), 41–54.

Scobie, R., Dickson, K., Hanney, S. and G. Rodgers (2010) 'Institutional strategies for capturing socio-economic impact of higher education research', *Journal of Higher Education Policy and Management*, 32(5), 499–510.

Scott, G., Bell, S., Coates, H. and L. Grebennikov (2010) 'Australian higher education leaders in times of change: the role of pro vice-chancellor and deputy vice-chancellor', *Journal of Higher Education Policy and Management*, 32(4), 401–418.

Shelley, L. (2010) 'Research managers uncovered: changing roles and "shifting arenas" in the academy', *Higher Education Quarterly*, 64(1), 41–64.

Shultz, S., Scherman, A. and L. Marshall (2000) 'Evaluation of a university-based date rape prevention program: effect on attitudes and behaviour related to rape', *Journal of College Student Development*, 41(2), 193–201.

Sellers-Rubio, R., Mas-Ruiz, F. and A. Casado-Diaz (2010) 'University efficiency: complementariness versus trade-off between teaching, research and administrative activities', *Higher Education Quarterly*, 64(4), 373–391.

Shin, J. (2010) 'Impacts of performance-based accountability on institutional performance in the US', *Higher Education*, 60(1), 47–68.

Shehu, J. (2000) 'Sport in higher education: an assessment of the implementation of the national sports development policy in Nigerian universities', *Assessment and Evaluation in Higher Education*, 25(1), 39–50.

Shuen, A. (2000) 'University financial management under a contraction of government funding: the case of Hong Kong, China', *Higher Education Management*, 12(3), 61–74.

Slantcheva, S. (2000) 'The challenges to vertical degree differentiation within Bulgarian universities: the problematic introduction of the three-level system of higher education', *Tertiary Education and Management*, 6(3), 209–225.

Spanier, G. (2010) 'Creating adaptable universities', *Innovative Higher Education*, 35, 91–99.

Sutherland-Smith, W. (2010) 'Retribution, deterrence and reform: the dilemmas of plagiarism management in universities', *Journal of Higher Education Policy and Management*, 32(1), 5–16.

Talib, A. and A. Steele (2000) 'The research assessment exercise: strategies and trade-offs', *Higher Education Quarterly*, 54(1), 68–87.

Tandberg, D. (2010) 'Politics, interest groups and state funding of public higher education', *Research in Higher Education*, 51, 416–450.

Thelin, J. (2000) 'Good sports? historical perspective on the political economy of intercollegiate athletics in the era of Title IX: 1972–1997', *Journal of Higher Education*, 71(4), 391–410.

Thomas, H. (2000) 'Power in the resource allocation process: the impact of "rational" systems', *Journal of Higher Education Policy and Management*, 22(2), 127–137.

Tight, M. (2003) *Researching Higher Education* (Maidenhead: Open University Press).

Tight, M. (2007) 'Bridging the divide: a comparative analysis of articles in higher education journals published inside and outside North America', *Higher Education*, 53(2), 235–253.

Tight, M. (2012a) *Researching Higher Education*, 2nd edn (Maidenhead: Open University Press).

Tight, M. (2012b) 'Higher education research 2000–2010: changing journal publication patterns', *Higher Education Research and Development*, 31(5), 723–740.

Tight, M. (2014a) 'Discipline and theory in higher education research', *Research Papers in Education*, 29(1), 93–110.

Tight, M. (2014b) 'Collegiality and managerialism: a false dichotomy? Evidence from the higher education research literature', *Tertiary Education and Management*, 20(4), 294–306.

Tight, M. (2014c) 'Theory development and application in higher education research: the case of academic drift', *Journal of Educational Administration and History*, forthcoming.

Tight, M. (2014d) 'Working in separate silos? What citation patterns reveal about higher education research internationally', *Higher Education*, 68(3), 379–395.

Toutkoushian, R. and M. Shafiq (2010) 'A conceptual analysis of state support for higher education: appropriations versus need-based financial aid', *Research in Higher Education*, 51, 40–64.

Ursin, J., Aittola, H., Henderson, C. and J. Valimaa (2010) 'Is education getting lost in university mergers?' *Tertiary Education and Management*, 16(4), 327–340.

Varela-Petito, G. (2010) 'Facing the knowledge society: Mexico's public universities', *Higher Education Policy*, 23(3), 436–449.

Vilkinas, T. and M. Peters (2014) 'Academic governance provided by academic boards within the Australian higher education sector', *Journal of Higher Education Policy and Management*, 36(1), 15–28.

Warshaw, J. and J. Hearn (2014) 'Leveraging university research to serve economic development: an analysis of policy dynamics in and across three US states', *Journal of Higher Education Policy and Management*, 36(2), 196–211.

Watson, D. (2000) 'Managing in higher education: the "wicked issues" ', *Higher Education Quarterly*, 54(1), 5–21.

Weerts, D., Cabrera, A. and T. Sandford (2010) 'Beyond giving: political advocacy and volunteer behaviors of public university alumni', *Research in Higher Education*, 51, 346–365.

Weerts, D. and L. Sandmann (2010) 'Community engagement and boundary-spanning roles at research universities', *Journal of Higher Education*, 81(6), 632–657.

Williams, B. (2000) 'Australian universities 1939–1999: how different now?' *Higher Education Quarterly*, 54(2), 147–165.

de Wit, K. (2010) 'The networked university: the structure, culture and policy of universities in a changing environment', *Tertiary Education and Management*, 16(1), 1–14.

Yang, R. (2000) 'Tensions between the global and the local: a comparative illustration of the re-organization of China's higher education in the 1950s and 1990s', *Higher Education*, 39(3), 319–337.

11
Institutional Research and Planning: Its Role in Higher Education Decision Support and Policy Development

Karen L. Webber and Angel J. Calderon

Introduction

Contemporary higher education institutions (HEIs) are faced with new challenges, including economic reductions, debates on the public versus private good of higher education, changing governance and academic structures, rapidly changing technologies, increasing requirements for quality assurance and institutional rankings and how to balance the missions of teaching, research and service. Although higher education in one region or country may have some traditions that are different from other geographic areas, there are many common goals and organizational elements that are shared. Within this context, institutional research (IR) practitioners have the knowledge and skills to adeptly assist in providing decision support for many of the issues that challenge our increasingly globalized world of higher education.

Although the term 'IR' has only been in vogue since the late 1950s (Reichard, 2012), tasks related to IR have existed as long as there have been institutions of higher learning. The roots of IR reside in the United States, where its practice is clearly identified in terms of its roles, functions and professional endeavours (Calderon and Mathies, 2013; Saupe, 1990). The term 'IR' has greater salience in the United States, Australia, the United Kingdom and in other European countries; but it is increasingly recognized in other regions of the world.

Across regions and national systems of education, there are vast differences in the composition, governance structure and funding arrangements of HEIs and that makes a single IR typology difficult, if not impossible. There are some prominent functions that resonate across many IR units; however, there are also different areas of emphasis, and it is fitting to ponder what is meant by institutional research. This chapter will provide a brief discussion of the decision support function known as institutional research (IR), how it varies in

HEIs across the world and how it relates to scholarly research on higher education. This chapter will also discuss IR's extended reach and how it is used for effective institutional decision-making that support government priorities, civil society and addresses market forces that affect higher education. In this chapter, the term 'policy development' is used broadly to indicate activities related to higher education organizational planning and strategy, as well as the implementation and evaluation of organizational plans.

What is institutional research?

Perhaps the most widely used definition of IR is that by Saupe (1990), which describes it 'as the sum of all activities directed at empirically describing the full spectrum of functions (educational, administrative, and support) at HEIs which are used for the purposes of institutional planning, policy development, and decision making' (p. 1). Similarly, Neave (2003) says that IR provides intelligence to the institution's leaders to enable them to shape the policy, posture and institutional development. In essence, IR is viewed as a set of functions, activities and roles that practitioners perform to assist decision-makers in making well-versed or evidence-based decisions. Institutional research (IR) is the sum of activities that aim to explore the intricacies of an institution – including its origins, where it is and where it is going, and understanding its sets of relations within the wider social, economic and geographical context in which it operates and has a reach. From an IR perspective, the study of and research on higher education is channelled through the various lenses of actors, activities, purposes and other elements that characterize institutions. Along with internal stakeholders, the role and breadth of the country's or region's government will affect the work tasks and level of engagement expected by the IR unit. Compared to other systems of higher education around the world, and noting the recent changes that are occurring across the globe related to decentralization, the United States has, overall, experienced less control and coordination (McLendon and Hearn, 2009). The balance of centralized versus decentralized control affects IR in the types of data reported, and perhaps even how the data will be utilized by government and institution officials.

Fincher (1985) described IR as a specialized administrative function and fittingly styled its practitioners as organizational intelligence specialists. In considering the existing literature on the foundations and practice of IR, IR offices are seen as the engine rooms of the university; developers of policy-related research and research-led policy and catalysts for institutional change. Fincher's work prompted Pat Terenzini to consider the forms of personal and professional competence, institutional understanding and knowledge needed for effective IR practice. The Three Tiers of Institutional Intelligence (Terenzini, 1999, 2013) describe the skills and broad knowledge that are required for effective IR practice. According to Terenzini, Tier 1's *technical and analytical intelligence* is the foundational building block. It includes technical knowledge of basic higher education definitions and categories, and analytical knowledge of social science research. The acquisition of basic definitions and categories provides Tier 1 practitioners with an understanding of higher education people and organizational structures. Analytic knowledge includes a basic understanding of how to measure, collect and analyse data, along with principles of research design, statistical methods and use of statistical software. While many of these research and technical skills are often learned in one's graduate programme, some of the knowledge can be acquired or further enhanced through on the job training. In particular, definitions and systems that are unique to an institution must be learned on the job (Terenzini, 2013).

IR officials who have a solid understanding of the institution's organizational structure, leadership and organizational practices may be engaging in Tier 2, *issues intelligence*. At this tier, the researcher is aware of issues that contribute to senior leader decisions and constraints that may affect those decisions. Tier 2, similar to Tier 1, is most often learned through a mixture of on-the-job training and formal coursework. This knowledge comes from practical experience, as well as being informed through regular review of scholarly writings in the field.

Terenzini's (2013) third tier, *contextual intelligence*, is the 'pinnacle of the pyramid' (p. 143) and occurs for the seasoned professional who understands how to blend the intelligences of the first two tiers. It includes an understanding of the institution's evolution, formal and informal political structures, how business is accomplished, and who are the key players. It also includes knowledge of the local, state, national and international environments and how they impact the organization. Terenzini purports that this highest tier can only be acquired through 'on-the-job' work experience and is the form of intelligence that earns IR professionals legitimacy, trust and respect (1999).

Some of what is known about institutional research comes from several multistate and national surveys conducted in the 1980s and 1990s, gathering information from members of the international and regional groups for the Association of Institutional Research (Knight, Moore and Coperthwaite, 1997; Lindquist, 1999; Muffo, 1999). A recent survey of over 3,300 professional staff members in the United States and Canada (reported in Volkwein, 2011) found that 38% of these units in HEIs have office names including traditional terminology like 'institutional research', 'analysis', 'information', 'reporting' or 'studies'. A second large group (35%) has office names including words like 'assessment', 'accountability', 'evaluation', 'effectiveness' and 'performance'. There is a wide array among these units of other names and combinations of names with 'planning' and 'IR'. Institutional researchers and IR functions are also embedded in offices of strategic planning, enrolment management, budget, policy analysis, information technology and the student registration.

In this chapter, the terms 'institutional research' or 'IR' encompass all of these variations.

Another survey in 2013 examined work tasks assumed by IR practitioners in the United States and Canada. Initial results found a broad range of tasks being completed, and professionals in larger IR offices completed a wider range of work tasks (Lillibridge, Jones and Ross, 2013). Further analysis of the 2013 data by Webber, Dawson and Rogers (2015) mapped the 769 work tasks to Terenzini's Tiers of Intelligence and found that the vast majority of reported tasks are situated in Tier 1 and Tier 2. The preliminary sort of all tasks showed approximately 500 reported items falling into Tier 1, 225 in Tier 2 and 50 in Tier 3. This imbalance to lower tiers shows the need for additional discussion and education of issues related to contextual intelligence for IR professionals in the United States. (Webber et al., 2015).

As a professional field, IR is over 50 years old in the United States. IR units and practitioners have engaged in data analysis and reporting for over 25 years in other countries, including Australia and South Africa. With European origins in Sweden and Britain in the late 1950s and 1960s, the trajectory of IR has taken more a path of combining research, policy and practice, given the variety of national systems and purposes higher education serve (Huisman, Hoekstra and York, 2015; Neave, 2003). In the 1980s, as some EU national governments granted HEIs more autonomy in exchange for forms of accountability (Neave and van Vught, 1991), institutions were prompted to use their internal capacity to generate information and data in order to satisfy governmental demands to oversee institutions. This encouraged a greater need for IR practitioners.

In the new millennium, greater accountability needs and changes in government policy promoting higher education have led institutions to recognize the need to expand their IR capacity to compete effectively for students and resources. Although IR does not have an established identity in some regions of the world, institutional leaders increasingly identify the potential for IR to help institutions navigate through times of turbulence and rapid change and to operate in a more resource-constrained and competitive context (Whitchurch, 2008; Woodfield, 2015). IR practitioners' knowledge of higher education culture, organizational operations, future directions and impact of external stakeholder needs can position them well to contribute strongly to quality assurance and short- and long-range planning.

Similarities and differences between IR and educational research

While there are common issues, activities and strategic directions for institutional research (IR) and higher education research (HER), there are some differences as well. Some differences are subtle and others are more substantial.

Awareness of the differences can assist in IR effectiveness and academic planning across all HEIs.

Typically, institutional research serves key decision-makers (primarily executive and senior academic staff) at a college or university, providing competitive advantage in attracting students or academic staff, or in obtaining funding from competitive sources (mainly research grants). Institutional research also assists in providing information to senior leaders who may assist in allocating financial and human resources as part of budgeting and management processes. Higher education researchers, on the other hand, are a community of peer scholars who pursue scholarly study of higher education. Particularly in Europe and Australia, higher education research (HER) may also serve decision-making and resource allocation purposes, often including regional and national governments because basic research may lead to policy suggestions. For example, government officials who serve on education committees may request the study of topics such as assessment of student outcomes, or diversity of students or the effectiveness of funding allocations. Findings from such studies may contribute to new or revised policy. Typically, both IR and HER seek improvement, although HER may be in pursuit of broad strategic policy development and/or knowledge for its own sake. In institutional research, the target of improvement is typically a specific institution's programme(s) and overall efficiency and effectiveness, while HER examines problems and potential avenues for improvement in a sector or region broadly. Most scholars agree with the applied versus broad, academic-based distinction for IR versus HER. Dressel and Associates (1971) report that successful IR should focus on effectiveness of the institution. Discussing the relationships between research and practice, El-Khawas (2000) identifies three spheres of activity: research, policy and practice. With a strong theoretical base, HER occurs through scholarly knowledge production and through instruction (research evidence shared with students in the classroom). Policy research provides information to address or achieve improvements in high-level strategy and policy development, typically not focused at single institution improvement, but aimed at state-, region- or country-level issues.

With its base in practice, IR is that which is often linked to management of the institution, thus providing practical and focused information. Somewhat similarly, Teichler (2000) sees research on higher education classified according to disciplines, themes and institutional settings. Although the boundaries between policy and practice-oriented researchers blur, Teichler (1996, 2000) suggests that experts be divided into six groups according to their links to academic theory, field knowledge and policy and practice. However, there is overlap; Teichler (2000) sees interrelationships between the academically based HER and those involved in policy and management.

Because the target audience and major purpose for IR versus HER may differ, the format and content of studies often diverge. Institutional research studies are more likely be infused in a local context and include information regarding the history of the issue within the institution and the implications for decisions related to the results. Moreover, IR would likely be cast in relatively functional or simple terms, with a spotlight on practical implications and complex technical aspects of research methodology or statistical analysis downplayed. HER, in contrast, would likely be cast in terms of the lines of theoretical frameworks that guide the inquiry and relevant research previously pursued. The full complexities of research methodology and analysis would be well developed for scrutiny by experts in these techniques and as the ultimate criteria for credibility and judgment of academic value (and publication prospects). There are times when the lines between IR and HER blur, such as when the IR analyst serves as the scholar in Volkwein's (1999) faces of IR or as a key informant in Neave's *The Evaluative State Reconsidered* (1998). However, in more typical cases, IR analyses are more applied and focus on improvement of a specific institution.

In considering the challenges that face higher education in the future, Teichler (2014) discusses differences between educational research and institutional research, reminding readers that higher education research examines the views, activities and work context of those who study current activities and policies. While anticipating the future of higher education and the role of future actions, higher education researchers can focus on theoretical concepts and relationships. Although policy makers are increasingly looking for useful information that can be directly applied to an issue at hand, to some degree, HER may not necessarily address practical solutions. However, the analytical work undertaken by institutional researchers is more often linked to near-term decision-making and may emphasize the immediate practical value of HER.

With some differences as well as similarities between IR and HER, an overlap represents research that serves both the local institution and broader purposes. It is in the overlap where IR and HER may find opportunities for great cooperation and collaboration. Teichler's (2003) wise assertion of the need to be forward looking recognizes that both IR practitioners and HER scholars must anticipate future activities, trends, potential problems and considerations for resolution.

The dimensions of decision support for effective institutional decision-making related to government priorities, civil society and market forces

There have been numerous drivers of change in higher education, and the configuration of the actions by government, civil society and market forces have shaped the directions for higher education's future (Dill, 2014; Pusser, 2014). The breadth and depth of IR depends on the environment within the

HEI and within the boundaries where institutions operate. Generally, there is more institutional autonomy today (Neave and van Vught, 1991); governments set the policy environment and the broad parameters that institutions are expected to fulfil in pursuit of the state agenda. Relatedly, the increased emphasis on accountability and quality assurance has elevated the role for IR. National and local accreditation and accountability systems enable IR officials to play an important role in data collection, analysis and reporting. Changes over the last half-century have been shaped by market forces and have influenced on the nature and pace of change in higher education. These market forces have also affected the conduct of HEIs through their influence as funders. HEI's role in society is important to social, cultural and economic development, but these roles speak to a variety of interest groups (and sometimes these can be in conflict with one another). Jongbloed, Enders and Salerno (2008) astutely describe the need for universities to carefully consider the relationships with various stakeholder groups. Mindful of incentive schemes and government requirements that may exist (McLendon and Hearn, 2003), institution officials must balance stakeholder needs and desires while also considering implications for governance and accountability.

Moving beyond institutional reporting

Historically, IR and planning offices have been charged with responsibility for extracting, validating and reporting institutional data. Having access to information, tools and methods for analysis has underpinned the foundation for IR to undertake a range of studies to better understand institutional performance, as well as provide foundation for institutional repositioning and setting strategic directions.

Indeed, decisions made by HEI leaders are influenced by funding needs and sources. While there are different levels of each by type of institution, there are four main sources of institutional funds: government, student tuition and fees, enterprise and philanthropy. Each of these entities prompts HEIs to respond to a variety of objectives. All of these drivers and developments are adding a layer of complexity to the nature of work in general. The extent to which institutions are accountable to a variety of actors has increased significantly. Two recent examples include the US Obama administration's plan to implement a ratings system for colleges and universities that will provide measures of institutional success and subsequent federal funding (http://www.ed.gov/college-affordability/college-ratings-and-paying-performance) and the Australian government's launch of a 'MyUniversity' website in 2012 designed to provide information to students about institutional performance on a variety of measures and to guide students' choices where and what to study (http://myuniversity.gov.au/). In both cases, individuals in the HE community are in support of the information that can be gleaned from the data, but they are unsure, about the proposed measures and their ability to authenticate institutional goal completion. This is an example, where IR practitioners have the opportunity to actively consider the state of higher education in general (regionally and globally), identify unique facets of the institution and how those facets fit in the larger higher education issues.

Awareness of broad processes and policies

In many countries, governments have enacted legislation for institutions to provide information about how institutions spend public funds and how HEIs are transforming the lives of those people who benefit from education. In addition, other actors that are supporting the HE enterprise (i.e. funding agencies) also require evidence on how their funds and support are being used. All of this is evidenced by the variety of metrics and reporting regimes that universities utilize in order to demonstrate how resources are being spent, transform and improve the lives of the people who benefit.

These developments elevate the role for institutional research, planning and decision support in institutions. While the pivotal role assumed by IR practitioners has been cemented through the requirements for statistical and other types of institutional information, the increase of accountabilities beyond government are shaping the nature and practice of IR across institutions. This prompts IR practitioners to be not only adept at providing data for general institutional management and accountability but also aware of political climates, relationships across and needs for all levels and sectors of education, and how organizations address these challenges. Equipped with this knowledge, IR practitioners can become engaged in data analysis and information distribution, both elements of highly valued decision support.

The wave of reforms that have shaped HE since the 1990s have resulted in an expansion of administrative staff and have spurred leaders to adopt or refine managerial practices that meet the challenges of expanding staffs and students. This is evidenced in HEIs by the adoption of management tools (such as strategic planning, performance-based funding and benchmarking). HEIs are now competing one against another, behave like business enterprises, are expected to have annual productivity increases and demonstrate profits year after year (see, for example, Stromquist, 2012; Marginson and Considine, 2000; Vaira, 2004).

All of these reforms have led to changes in the nature of institutional organization, as evidenced by how decisions are made. In the past, institutions were focused on the collegial nature of academia, the collective good and the use of educational outcomes. Although debate (has always) existed, decisions were generally made along collegial lines. Now institutions have largely adopted managerial practices in how decisions are made (Olssen and Peters, 2005). Numerous discussions about faculty governance in academic journals show that the decision-making role for the academic senate has diminished (Amaral, Jones, and Karseth, 2000; Tierney, 2004).

There is significant transformation in the way institutions are governed (Maassen and Olsen, 2007; McLendon and Hearn, 2009), which can be attributed, in part, to not only the convergence of competing forces driving change in HE but also a consequence of the fact that institutions are operating beyond their traditional or originally established boundaries. HEI constituents and strategic actors are drawn not only from their local community but also across jurisdictions, and many are operating across multiple national borders. HEIs are drawing students from a variety of geographies and satisfying skills, training and research needs from a range of industry and other stakeholders. In this regard, globalization has added a layer of complexity to the way institutions are governed and the depth and breadth of information needed for decision-making.

The extended reach of IR

This chapter's discussion thus far has focused on the forces of change that are shaping HEIs and how these have had an impact in the way institutions are managed and governed. In this regard, institutional leaders rely on the services that are fulfilled by professional staff, including those who perform institutional research, planning, and related functions. As argued by Calderon and Mathies (2013), increasingly important functions performed by IR professionals include monitoring and responding to the external environment and devising responses that address the impact that external forces have on institutions. This is less true in the United States (Gagliardi and Wellman, 2014) where IR workers are more focused on Tier 1 tasks and less so involved in policy-level decisions and theory-based research. More so in Europe and Australia than some other parts of the world, IR practitioners have become an instrument of support for decision-makers to navigate change and to position institutions strategically in a competitive environment.

Involvement in strategic planning and policy development

While fulfilling reporting requirements is a central to the practice of IR, it is important that IR be an active participant in the development of strategies and policy setting. While IR professionals are needed to provide information for internal and external accountability demands, IR professionals can be utilized more effectively to inform and leverage strategic change and organizational learning. IR practitioners can assist well in developing as well as providing information for strategic planning, annual benchmarks, scenario planning, forecasting and long-range planning. With deep knowledge of higher education trends and needs, IR practitioners can contribute to discussions on the roles and value of higher education locally, regionally and globally.

Although the practice of IR gets fully involved in planning and strategy formulation in certain regions such as Australia, this is currently happening to a lesser extent in the United States. With a deep focus on data collection and manipulation and responsibility reporting and accountability, IR practitioners are less often engaged in policy-level discussions. Except in a few instances where IR is staffed with multiple members and who are senior in their higher education experiences, US college leaders often have other senior advisors who are called on for strategy decisions. With more intentional focus on Tier 3 tasks, IR practitioners may be able to assume a more active role in institutional strategy and policy formation.

Huisman (2013) adroitly questions if current IR practitioners are too inward looking. His review of mission statements for some IR units in the United States reveals a strong focus on reactive data gathering and monitoring. He postulates that IR practitioners are strong in technical intelligence, but less so in contextual intelligence. In the language of Volkwein's (1999) four faces, IR practitioners perform well as information authorities, but become less involved as policy analysts and scholar/researchers.

Broadening decision support practice

In some parts of the world, IR practitioners are undertaking studies within and across industry sectors that require specialized knowledge residing outside IR and planning offices. For example, some Australian practitioners are working with industry partners to do scenario planning and forecasting. In addition, they are collaborating to examine influences on the nature of work, the drivers of change and the implications of further tertiary education for this sector. In these broader collaborations, the decision-making process at the institutional level is not only multilayered across various entities (some which may also respond to different legislative, accreditation and reporting requirements, among many other things), but it is also dispersed across stakeholders within and outside the institution. In turn, this requires that IR practitioners be aware of the wider spectrum of institutional activities, strategic intent and policy within the education industry and across industries over multiple jurisdictions. Further, traditional models of university governance are progressively being transformed so that universities are becoming not only strategic actors competing in decentralized markets in a comparable manner to private companies but are also knowledge production actors supporting public policy goals of government, with an ever-increased public accountability, but with shrinking government financial support. These reforms in HE are changing the nature and characteristics of institutional management and the way activities are planned, developed and assessed and, subsequently, have an impact on the roles, functions and purpose of IR. Dedicated IR practitioners not only are required to adapt and embrace new forms of day-to-day operations also but need to respond by broadening and deepening their skills so they can be effective in understanding and responding to trends and issues that affect higher education broadly. Institutional management is likely to be further transformed as HEIs are required to respond more to market forces and compete with other institutions for scarce resources, including students (Olssen and Peters, 2005; Pusser, 2014).

The future of institutional research and planning

Much has been said about the forces of change that are rapidly transforming higher education: globalization, demographic shifts, rapid technological changes and innovation are among the drivers. These key drivers are having an impact on every facet of human activity. Technology has increased the accessibility to larger amounts and more timely data, along with the capacity for analysis to support decision-making. Globalization has exponentially increased the mobility of people and skills, capital, trade flow between countries and borderless diffusion of knowledge and production chains. Demographic shifts have widened diversity in the student mix. All these changes are influencing the way HEIs are perceived to benefit society.

The alignment of competing demands from the state, the civil society and market forces are determining the future of higher education (Dill, 2014; Pusser, 2014). Governments expect that HEIs will contribute to their public policy objectives, and governments ensure completion of these objectives through the funding arrangements and other instruments (e.g. mission-based compacts between government and HEIs and reports on institutional performance made available on websites) to ensure compliance with the array of demands placed on HEIs. The space that HEIs occupy in society is considered important to economic development, but the alliances between HEIs and a variety of associations and interest groups are dispersed (and these can conflict with the stated mission of HEIs). Further, the adoption of market-driven mechanisms to support and develop higher education is shifting the dynamics in how institutions operate, behave and interact with its various stakeholders and strategic actors.

In many regions of the world, IR is a recognized and established part of higher education. Armed with knowledge and experience, IR professionals can continue to provide information for organizational planning and required accountability reporting, but when positioned well, they can be contributors in the shaping of national and perhaps international policy. At the US national level, higher education scholars are often part of US Department of Education discussions on topics such as student financial aid, the growth of science and engineering fields and post-degree employability. Such contributions require deep knowledge and appreciation of local and domestic imperatives, all of which are fundamental to the institutional strength and future viability. As IR practitioners continue their focus on the individual institution, awareness of the broader region, including possible scenarios and implications for change is in order. The development of strategic plans in HEIs is no longer optional, and the input of IR practitioners in this process is pivotal. This is happening to a greater extent in certain regions of the world, and can become more intentional in other regions such as the United States.

Historically, the focus of IR has been on self-studies for institutional planning and some specialized research on relevant issues that impact a particular institution (Gagliardi and Wellman, 2014; Volkwein, Liu, and Woodell, 2012). However, due to global and market forces that are ubiquitous, the scope of effective IR work requires expansion, knowledge about the state of higher education in local and global economies, and a shift to decision support that is infused with deep knowledge of higher education challenges and potential actions that support resolution. While a focus remains specific to providing information for institutional planning, institutional leaders must think broadly. HEIs are part of regional or national systems of education that must respond to varying national policy imperatives.

Balancing IR expectations and tensions

Given the variety of roles and functions performed by IR practitioners, it is not surprising that tensions exist as a result of the varying expectations about what IR does within the institution, and what it does for the education sector overall. Volkwein (1999, 2008) describes the contradictory 'faces' by which IR practitioners can be characterized in terms of their organizational role and culture and the purposes and audiences of IR. These tensions apart from remaining unresolved, given the nature of IR and the evolution of HE across the globe, are also the challenges that are likely to define the IR profession in years to come, regardless of the type of institutions in which IR is practised or exercised. Other researchers have also discussed the tensions confronting IR (Calderon, 2011; Huisman, 2013).

With actors or forces of change occurring rapidly, higher education institutions need to respond to a variety of expectations and requirements. This offers a role for IR practitioners as interpreters, adaptors and catalyst for change. Not only do they need to interpret, decode and translate into meaningful context what the expectations of these actors, but, in addition, they need to ensure that our institutions respond and adapt as required (Calderon and Webber, 2015).

Models of governance in higher education are changing, and there are increasingly more external agents that are forcing consideration on how to accomplish institutional goals. This reflects the new public management agenda that has permeated throughout higher education (Estermann, Nokkala, and Steinel, 2011). Some models of institutional governance need to embed actors from multiple jurisdictions (either within the state or interstate and even overseas). Academics are no longer the obvious successors to steer the course of institutions; in a growing number of instances, external agents are introducing new forms of institutional management. Through legislative and institutional policy changes, the roles for institutional leaders have expanded and the expectations for performance have increased. In a decision support capacity, IR practitioners need to adapt and combine external and internal practices for the long-term sustainability of the profession and HEIs.

As shifts continue to occur in the nature of institutional funding, away from state reliance to a variety of funding sources (government, students, enterprise and philanthropy), the governance boundaries of institutions are likely to be further altered and traditional academic structures modified. For example, where there is an increase in the number of interdisciplinary faculty members who are jointly funded by two or more academic departments, institution practitioners must rethink how to counts faculty member effort, research and instruction outcomes, and which unit will receive credit for each activity. Changes in institutional structures like this offer the opportunity for IR to navigate through the transformation, steering a course that supports sound decision-making and clearly articulated strategic directions. Changes in institutional governance together with globalization and technological transformation add complexity to the nature and practice of IR. These shifts are likely to demand greater discernment from IR practitioners in the way advice is given to senior management. The more information that is collected, the greater are the complexities in managing it; and yet it exponentially widens the scope for analysis, and it provides an opportunity for exploring new possibilities and for fostering institutional innovation. Innovation requires IR practitioners to have a very good understanding of the data, as well as the ability to interpret and draw inferences about a variety of internal and external data sources (Webber and Calderon, 2015).

As demand for decision support grows, IR will be advantaged by its position in the organization's hierarchy and its adeptness to collaborate. Along with accounting for external stakeholder interests, decision making occurs across a range of units within the institution that respond to different legislative, accreditation and reporting requirements. In some world regions, traditional models of university governance are progressively being transformed so that universities are becoming not only strategic actors competing in decentralized markets with private companies but are also knowledge production actors supporting public policy goals of government with an ever-increased public accountability and scrutiny, but with shrinking government financial support (Whitley and Gläser, 2014). Significant reforms in higher education are indeed changing the nature and characteristics of institutional management and the way activities are planned and assessed.

Looking forward

Higher education institutions need knowledgeable and engaged IR and planning practitioners. To maximize IR's effectiveness in decision support, IR units need decision-makers who provide support, vision and commitment in resources for the objectives institutions seek to achieve. While there is a distinction between IR and HER, there are some important questions that fill the overlapping area. In concert with colleagues who study the future of higher education, it is important for IR practitioners to identify current challenges and considerations for higher education reform. Teichler (2003) delineates a number of important issues that require current attention and prompt strategies for future planning. At the organizational level, IR can monitor numeric trends in enrolments for expansion and diversity, but it can also be an agent of decision support that asks forward-looking questions such as the following:

- Will the institution or regional system move further towards mass higher education and, if so, what are the implications for students and staff?
- For societal needs, what is a reasonable balance of technical versus higher education degree production?
- How does the increase in higher education degrees contribute to employability? Will the current emphasis on degrees production result in substantial underemployment?
- With government financing of higher education declining, how much can students be expected to pay, and without resulting in heightened loan default? and
- How is globalized education and collaborative scholarship affecting student and staff mobility, communications and multi-location study?

Answers to these and other similar questions enable the IR practitioner to blend one's technical and analytic knowledge with a deep knowledge of the institutional and general structures, functions and dynamics of higher education. This blend of proactive knowledge and decision support positions IR to contribute to strong institutional leadership that can be a valued asset to organizational managers.

References

Amaral, A., Jones, G. A. and B. Karseth (2002) 'Governing higher education: Comparing national perspectives', in A. Amaral, G. A. Jones and B. Karseth (eds) *Governing Higher Education: National Perspectives on Institutional Governance* (pp. 279–298) (Dordrecht: Kluwer).

Calderon, A. (2011, June) 'Challenges and paradigms for institutional research in a globalised higher education system'. Keynote address, *Fourth Conference of U.K. and Ireland Institutional Research* (London, England).

Calderon, A. and C. Mathies (2013) 'Institutional research in the future: Challenges within higher education and the need for excellence in professional practice', in A. Calderon and K. Webber (eds) *Global Issues in Institutional Research, New Directions for Institutional Research*, No. 157 (pp. 77–90) (San Francisco, CA: Jossey Bass).

Calderon, A. and K. L. Webber (2015) 'Institutional research, planning, and decision support in higher education today', in K. Webber and A. Calderon (eds) *Institutional Research and Planning: Global Themes and Contexts* (New York: Routledge/Taylor & Francis).

Dressel, P. L. and Associates (1971) *Institutional Research in the University: A Handbook* (San Francisco: Jossey-Bass).

Dill, D. (2014) 'Public policy design and university reform: Insights into academic change', in C. Musselin and P. N. Teixeira (eds) *Reforming Higher Education: Public Policy Design and Implementation* (pp. 21–57) (Dordrecht, Netherlands: Springer).

El-Khawas, E. (2000) 'Research, policy and practice: Assessing their actual and potential linkages', in U. Teichler and J. Sadlak (eds) *Higher Education Research: Its Relationship to Policy and Practice* (Oxford, England: Pergamon/IAU Press).

Estermann, T., Nokkala, T. and M. Steinel (2011) *University Autonomy in Europe II: The Scorecard* (Brussels, Belgium: European University Association).

Fincher, C. (1985) 'The art and science of institutional research', in M. W. Peterson and M. Corcoran (eds) *Institutional Research in Transition. New Directions for Institutional Research*, No. 46 (pp. 17–37) (San Francisco, CA: Jossey-Bass).

Gagliardi, J. and J. Wellman (2014) *Meeting Demands for Improvements in Public System Institutional Research*. Progress Report on the NASH Project in IR, Washington, DC: National Association of System Heads.

Huisman, J. (2013, July) 'Institutional Research in Higher Education: Speaking truth to power ... and whether it would be wise to do that on your own'. Keynote address, *Sixth Conference U.K. and Ireland Institutional Research* (Birmingham, England).

Huisman, J., Hoekstra, P. and M. Yorke (2015) 'Institutional Research in Europe: A View from the European Association for Institutional Research', in *Institutional Research and Planning: Global Themes and Contexts* (New York: Routledge/Taylor & Francis).

Jongbloed, B., Enders, J. and C. Salerno (2008) 'Higher education and its communities: Interconnections, interdependencies and a research agenda', *Higher Education*, 56(3), 303–324.

Knight, W. E., Moore, M. E. and C. A. Coperthwaite (1997) 'Institutional research: Knowledge, skills, and perceptions of effectiveness', *Research in Higher Education*, 38(4), 419–433.

Lillibridge, F., Jones, D. and L. Ross (2014) Defining IR: Findings from a National study of IR Work Tasks. Presentation at the 2014 AIR Forum. Orlando, FL.

Lindquist, S. B. (1999) 'A profile of institutional researchers from AIR national membership surveys', in J. F. Volkwein (ed) *What Is Institutional Research All about? A Critical and Comprehensive Assessment of the Profession: New Directions for Institutional Research*, Vol. 104 (pp. 41–50) (San Francisco, CA: Jossey-Bass).

Maassen, P. and J. Olsen (2007) *University Dynamics and European Integration* (Dordrecht, the Netherlands: Springer).

Marginson S. and M. Considine (2000) *The Enterprise University: Governance and Reinvention in Australian Higher Education* (Melbourne, AU: Cambridge University Press).

McLendon, M. K. and J. C. Hearn (2003) 'Introduction: The politics of higher education', in M. K. McLendon and J. C. Hearn (ed) The politics of education yearbook special issue: The politics of higher education. *Educational Policy*, 17(1), 3–11.

McLendon, M. K. and J. C. Hearn (2009) 'Viewing recent US governance reforms whole: "Decentralization"' in distinctive context', in J. Huisman (ed) *International Perspectives on the Governance of Higher Education Alternative Frameworks for Coordination* (pp. 161–181) (New York, NY: Routledge).

Muffo, J. A. (1999) 'A comparison of findings from regional studies of institutional research offices', in J. F. Volkwein (ed) *What is Institutional Research all about? A Critical and Comprehensive Assessment of the Profession: New Directions for Institutional Research*, Vol. 104 (pp. 51–60) (San Francisco, CA: Jossey-Bass).

Neave, G. (1998) 'The evaluative state reconsidered', *European Journal of Education*, 33(3), 265–284.

Neave, G. (2003) 'Institutional research: From case study to strategic instrument', in *The Dialogue between Higher Education Research and Practice* (pp. 3–14) (Dordrecht, Netherlands: Kluwer).

Neave, G. and F. A. van Vught (eds) (1991) *Prometheus Bound: The Changing Relationship between Government and Higher Education in Western Europe* (Oxford: Pergamon).

Olssen, M. and M. A. Peters (2005) 'Neoliberalism, higher education and the knowledge economy: From the free market to knowledge capitalism', *Journal of Education Policy*, 20(3), 313–345.

Pusser, B. (2014) 'Forces in tension: The state, civil society and market in the future of the university', in P. Gibbs and R. Barnett (eds) *Thinking about Higher Education* (pp. 71–89) (Switzerland: Springer International Publishing).

Reichard, D. J. (2012) 'The history of institutional research', in R. D. Howard, G. W. McLaughlin and W. E. Knight (eds) *The Handbook of Institutional Research* (pp. 3–21) (San Francisco, CA: Jossey-Bass).

Saupe, J. L. (1990) *The Functions of Institutional Research*, 2nd ed (Tallahassee, FL: Association for Institutional Research). Retrieved from http://www.airweb.org/page.asp?page=85.

Stromquist, N. P. (2012) 'The provost office as key decision-maker in the contemporary US University', in *University Governance and Reform* (pp. 25–46), Retrieved from http://www.palgraveconnect.com/pc/doifinder/10.1057/9781137040107.0009.

Teichler, U. (1996) 'Comparative higher education: Potentials and limits', *Higher Education*, 32, 431–465.

Teichler, U. (2000) 'Higher education research and its institutional basis', in S. Schwarz and U. Teichler (eds) *The Institutional Basis of Higher Educational Research* (pp. 13–24) (Dordrecht, Netherlands: Kluwer Academic Publishers).

Teichler, U. (2003) 'The future of higher education and the future of higher education research', *Tertiary Education and Management*, 9, 171–185.

Teichler, U. (2014) 'Possible futures for higher education: Challenges for higher education research', in J. C. Shin and U. Teichler (eds) *The Future of the Post-Massified University at the Crossroads: Restructuring Systems and Functions* (Switzerland: Springer International Publishing).

Terenzini, P. T. (1999) 'On the nature of institutional research and the knowledge and skills it requires', in J. F. Volkwein (ed) *What is Institutional Research all about? A Critical and Comprehensive Assessment of the Profession: New Directions for Institutional Research*, No. 104 (pp. 21–29) (San Francisco, CA: Jossey Bass).

Terenzini, P. T. (2013) '"On the nature of institutional research" revisited: Plus ça change...?' *Research in Higher Education*, 54(2), 137–148.

Tierney, W. (2004) *Competing Conceptions of Academic Governance: Negotiating the Perfect Storm* (Baltimore, MD: Johns Hopkins University Press).

Vaira, M. (2004) 'Globalization and higher education organizational change: A framework for analysis', *Higher Education*, 48(4), 483–510.

Volkwein, F. (1999) 'Four faces of IR', in F. Volkwein (ed) *What Is Institutional Research All About? A Critical and Comprehensive Assessment of the Profession: New Directions for Institutional Research* (Vol. 104, pp. 9–19) (San Francisco, CA: Jossey Bass).

Volkwein, J. F. (2008) 'The foundations and evolution of institutional research', in D. G. Terkla (ed) *Institutional Research: More Than Just Data: New Directions for Higher Education*, (Vol. 141, pp. 5–20) (San Francisco, CA: Jossey Bass).

Volkwein, J. F. (2011) *Gaining Ground: The Role of Institutional Research in Assessing Student Outcomes and Demonstrating Institutional Effectiveness*. National Institute for Learning Outcomes Assessment, Occasional Paper #11, Champaign, IL.

Volkwein, J. F., Liu, Y. and J. Woodell (2012) 'The structure and functions of institutional research offices', in R. Howard, G. McLaughlin and W. Knight (eds) *The Handbook of Institutional Research* (pp. 22–39) (San Francisco, CA: Jossey Bass).

Webber, K. L. and Calderon, A. J. (2015) *Institutional Research and Planning in Higher Education: Global Themes and Contexts* (New York: Routledge/Taylor & Francis).

Webber, K. L., Dawson, L. J. and S. Rogers (2015, May) Additional findings from the 2013 AIR Work Tasks Survey. Session to be presented at the AIR Forum, Denver, CO.

Whitchurch, C. (2008) 'Shifting identities and blurring boundaries: The emergence of third space professionals in UK higher education', *Higher Education Quarterly*, 62(4), 377–396.

Whitley, R. and J. Gläser (2014) 'The impact of institutional reforms on the nature of universities as organisations', *Research in the Sociology of Organizations*, 42, 19–39.

Woodfield, S. (2015) 'Institutional research in the UK and Ireland', in K. Webber and A. Calderon (eds) *Institutional Research and Planning: Global Themes and Contexts* (New York, NY: Routledge/Taylor & Francis).

12
Operationalizing Network Analysis for Higher Education Research

Robin Shields

Over the past decade, research on higher education has increasingly utilized networks as a conceptual approach for understanding contemporary policy and practice. This perspective shifts the focus of analysis from atomic units of study (whether individuals, institutions or governments) to the links that connect them, adding a new layer of complexity and emphasizing patterns of connectivity over the intrinsic characteristics and qualities of these atomic units. While networks have been employed in the literature as a conceptual approach, the empirical application of network analysis has been much more limited: studies employing social network analysis methods to investigate higher education empirically are relatively scarce. This chapter provides a foundation for future empirical research on higher education networks by operationalizing the empirical application of network analysis (or social network analysis) for higher education research, with a particular focus on quantitative methods. It reviews potential sources of network data and identifies how the network perspective can offer unique insights that are unavailable through more traditional methods.

The network approach

In recent years, much literature has used the concept of networks to approach the study of higher education. This literature includes both academic research and policy documents, reports from funding agencies and institutional strategies. For example, a 2011 report from the British Royal Society entitled *Knowledge, Networks and Nations* describes how contemporary scientific research is driven by 'self-organizing networks' of researchers that are 'motivated by the bottom-up exchange of scientific insight, knowledge and skills, span the globe, and are changing the focus of science from the national to the global level' (p. 62). The report argues that governments must 'tap into' these networks in order to ensure future academic and economic competitiveness.

Others have independently used the term 'network university' to describe contemporary higher education institutions (Grant, 2013; Lewis, Marginson, and Snyder, 2005). This terminology implicitly references and extends a body of literature relating to the 'network society' – a term popularized by Manuel Castells (1996) to refer to societies characterized by the pervasive of influence of global electronic media networks (e.g. the Internet and social media) on nearly all aspects of social life. According to Castells (1996), these networks connect different aspects of social life (e.g. business, religion and academia) and transmit information and ideas rapidly around the globe, leading to increased integration across time and space.

However, despite the advent of 'network speak' in higher education literature, there remains a scarcity of empirical research on higher education networks. This chapter operationalizes social network analysis for higher education research, introducing key concepts, indicating possible sources of network data and demonstrating the types of research questions that can a network perspective might best address. The perspectives and methodologies discussed are rooted in the field of social network analysis, which first emerged in the mid-20th century and remains an active area of methodological research, with new techniques and software under ongoing development (Wasserman and Faust, 1994). However, in this chapter the term 'social' is often omitted from 'social network analysis' in recognition that higher education networks are often formed between institutions (e.g. universities and nation states) rather than individuals. Throughout the chapter, the focus is primarily on quantitative network analysis, although this emphasis does not negate the importance of qualitative approaches to network analysis, for example Ball and Junemann's (2012) work on network ethnography.

The network perspective entails several fundamental departures from actor-based research. First, network datasets are necessarily larger and more complex than an equivalent actor-based dataset, as the number of potential ties between individuals grows exponentially with network size. For example, if we were to consider a network of research collaboration in a department of 20 individuals, there are 190 possible different links (i.e. unique bilateral collaborations).[1] Second, network studies generally focus on explaining global structure (i.e. the totality of ties in the network) by studying local selection processes – tendencies for actors to form ties with one another. In this sense, the overall structure of the network is said to be 'self-organizing', as it is often driven by the decisions of individual actors rather than a central authority.

In contrast, most quantitative actor-based studies focus on establishing relationships between variables, testing whether a set of predictor variables (independent variables) relate to an outcome of interest (the dependent variable). For example, much research has looked at factors related to research productivity, analysing whether academic mobility, job satisfaction, time in job and other personal factors relate to an individual's publication record

(Dundar and Lewis, 1998; Fairweather, 2002; Sheehan and Welch, 1996). In contrast, a network perspective would seek to study relationships between actors: possibly asking whether more productive researchers are more likely to form research collaborations, work with researchers in other disciplines and so on. This example does not claim that actor-based approaches are 'wrong' or that the network approach is necessarily better, but rather it illustrates how the fundamental unit of analysis differs between the two approaches.

The distinctiveness and unique affordances of an empirical network study are best understood through an illustrative example. Thus, for the purposes of this chapter, we will consider the example of a network of 18 universities that are engaged in an international cooperation consortium. Specifically, we will look at the social media network that exists between these institutions, examining which university Twitter accounts follow other accounts. These are real data that have been obtained from the Twitter API, although they have been edited to improve the clarity of the discussion.

The chapter begins by introducing key concepts and terms in social network analysis, providing a vocabulary with which to discuss research and laying a foundation for applying research in higher education. It then continues to discuss sources of network data in higher education and looks at how they have been used in published research. Finally, the chapter discusses Exponential Random Graph Models (ERGMs) – a new method of analysing networks that simultaneously accounts for external variables and internal structural relationships.

Concepts and terms

As mentioned above, network analyses seek to explain macroscopic network structure as an outcome of local selection forces – tendencies for actors in the network to form ties. Before examining higher education networks in detail, it is worth introducing a few key concepts in network analysis to inform the discussion.

Terminology

A network consists of a set of connected individuals or institutions, which we generally call 'nodes' or 'actors'. The connections between these actors are referred to as 'ties' or 'links', although it is worth noting that more mathematical literature on networks will often refer to 'actors' as 'vertices' and 'ties' as 'edges'. Networks' ties come in several different forms, with distinctions between 'directed' and 'non-directed' ties as well as valued and binary ties. Directed ties are those in which there is a clear flow or direction, for example when one author cites another, the 'direction' of the citation works in only one way (i.e. A cites B, but B does not necessarily cite A). Other ties have no clear directionality, for example data representing co-authorship (see example below) are non-directed; if A has co-authored with B, then it is necessarily true that B has co-authored with B.

In many networks, ties are 'binary', meaning that they are either entirely absent or present. However, in some cases the ties may be 'valued', meaning that they are a numerical value indicating the strength of a connection between two actors. Often these two types of ties are interchangeable: for example, a network of co-authorship (see example below) could contain a tie between every pair of academics who have been involved in at least one co-authored publication, or it could contain a count of the number of co-authored publications. Although ties can be valued or binary, the latter is more common in social network analysis and is generally assumed to be the case in examples presented below.

In our exemplar network of 18 universities, ties are directed and binary. Although institution A follows institution B, B may or may not reciprocate the tie. Thus, there is clear directionality. Similarly, Twitter following is either entirely present or absent, there is no other possible value and hence the ties are binary. Often a first step in social network analysis is visualization of the data to inspect any prominent trends or features of the network. A visualization is provided in Figure 12.1 below. The position of points is determined using

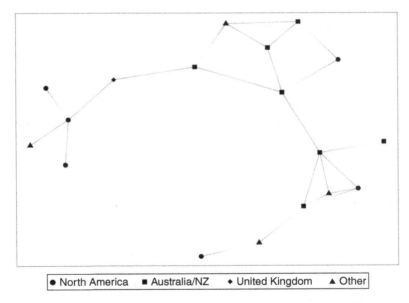

Figure 12.1 A visualization of the exemplar dataset, which is useful for providing an overview of patterns and clusters in the data. Point makers use different shapes to illustrate the geographic distribution of network members

a Fruchterman-Reingold algorithm (Fruchterman and Reingold, 1991), which places highly connected actors close to one another and minimizes crossing lines for clarity. The directionality of ties is represented using a gradient line, fading from light grey (follower) to dark grey (followed). Reciprocal lines are the same colour throughout. The diagram indicates that there is connectivity through Twitter across the consortium. However, the field of connections is not uniform: some actors have many connections to others, while others have only one.

Density

One of the most basic and important features of any network is proportion of possible ties that are present, a measure of the network's density. Density is bounded between 0 and 1; in a network with a density of 0, there are no ties whatsoever, and with a density of 1 all actors are connected to one another. In our exemplar network, there are 18 actors, yielding a possible 306 of ties (18 × 17 every actor could be connected to every other, except itself). However, there are only 37 realized ties, meaning the density is 0.121 (i.e. 12.1% of the possible ties are present).

Reciprocity

A fundamental property of directed networks is its actors' tendencies to reciprocate ties: if A is connected to B, is it often the case that B is also connected to A? This tendency is measured through reciprocity (occasionally called mutuality), the proportion of all ties within a network that are reciprocated. Reciprocity can often be an indicator of status and hierarchies in network data. For example, celebrities on Twitter will often have thousands of followers, but likely follow relatively few people themselves. In our exemplar network, 28 of the 37 ties are reciprocal in nature, meaning the *edgewise reciprocity* is 0.757 (i.e. 75.7% of all present ties are reciprocal). If we include absent ties (i.e. reciprocal non-ties as well as ties), then 288 of the 306 ties are reciprocal in nature. This measurement is referred to as the 'dyadic reciprocity' and is 0.941 in our network (Wasserman and Faust, 1994). Thus, there appears to be a strong tendency towards reciprocity in the network.

Transitivity

The tendency to form ties with mutual acquaintances is common in many social networks. In other words, if A is connected to B, and B is connected to C, then the tendency for A to also connect with C increases. This pattern of connectivity is called transitivity or clustering in social networks, and it is measured as the number of realized transitive connections as proportion of all possible transitive connections.

For our exemplar network, the transitivity is 0.303 (i.e. 30% of possible mutual connections are present). In order to assess whether a value is high or low, social network analysis often compares the properties of the observed data to random networks (i.e. pseudo data generated without any intentionality behind ties), a method known as conditional uniform testing (Wasserman and Faust, 1994, p. 535). A random set of 100 networks with the same density as the exemplar network had an average transitivity of 0.126, indicating that this level of transitivity in our exemplar is quite high. Therefore, the observed value is likely indicative of actors forming ties on the basis of a mutual connection.

Centrality and centralization

It is usually apparent that that some actors within a network are more integrated than others; in social network analysis, this level of integration is referred to as 'centrality'. While the concept and term seem straightforward, the measurement of centrality is quite complicated because there are many different ways in which one could systematically operationalize what it means for an actor to be 'central' or 'integrated'.

The simplest measure of centrality is known as degree centrality, which is simply a count of the number of ties to a given actor. For directed networks, it is possible to distinguish between indegree centrality (the number of incoming ties) and outdegree centrality (the number of outgoing ties). However, Burris (2004, p. 251) aptly notes, 'not all social connections are of equal value' – and ties from well-connected actors are more valuable in many social networks. This perspective underpins the notion of eigenvector centrality, in which an actor's centrality is not only based upon the number of connections but also weighted by the connections' own centrality. Although this definition may seem somewhat circular (i.e. one actor's centrality is dependent on knowing all others' centrality), the problem is solved through elegant yet complex applications of linear algebra. There are many other ways to define and calculate centrality: how often an actor acts as a bridge between others ('betweenness centrality') or the number of connections needed to reach other actors in the network ('closeness centrality'). Looking at the network diagram (Figure 12.1), it is clear that some actors are not very 'close' in the sense that information would have to travel through many intermediaries (up to eight) to reach the full extent of the network.

While centrality is a measure of *each actor's* integration into the network, centralization refers to the distribution of centrality *across the network as a whole*. In some networks, all actors may have more or less the same level of centrality, while other networks might exhibit a stronger core–periphery structure, with a small number of highly central actors and a larger periphery with minimal connections. Centralization is inequality in centrality, and most measures of centrality (e.g. degree, eigenvector) can be used to compute a centralization value for the network as a whole, using methods described by Freeman (1978). Looking at the plot of our exemplar network (Figure 12.1), some nodes clearly have more connections than others, and there are areas of the network that could clearly be considered a 'periphery'. The level of degree centralization (0.161) is higher than that of a sample of random networks (0.113), indicating a tendency towards centralization.

Cliques and neighbourhoods

A final key concept in social network analysis is that of the 'clique' or 'neighbourhood'. Many social networks can be broken down into smaller groups of actors that have relatively high levels of interconnectivity within them, while connections between these cliques may be much less dense. Research in social network analysis has developed several ways to define and identify cliques. Some of these methods work from the top-down, by subdividing the entire network into the two most interconnected groups, then subdividing each of those groups again, and continuing this process to greater levels of subdivision. The researcher can then specify a level of group subdivision and interpret the groupings. Other clique-detection algorithms work from the bottom up, looking for 'maximal sub-groups' – those groupings in which all actors are interconnected – with techniques to find the largest possible subgroup. From Figure 12.1, it is clear that the largest clique – that is, a group with all actors connected to one another – is only three nodes in size.

The relevance of network structures

The terms and measures discussed above provide a foundation with which to consider patterns and relationships in higher education networks. However, the information provided is by no means exhaustive, and readers wishing to apply social network analysis in their own research should consult with a comprehensive text (e.g. Wasserman and Faust, 1994).

However, more important than the actual application of each concept and measurement is understanding how the structure of networks – that is, the total of relationships among actors – encodes important information. Network structures determine how communication and information flows: actors with minimal connections are less able to access information, and networks with highly centralized structures will have different patterns of communication from more decentralized and interconnected structures. Similarly, network structure relates to status: depending upon the type of network under investigation, an actor's level of centrality or the level of reciprocity in the network can be used to understand which actors hold higher levels of status or prestige. These issues are both important to research in higher education, but in addition to methods and a conceptual vocabulary any social network analysis also requires empirical data.

Higher education network data and their use in higher education research

Now that basic concepts and measures of social network analysis have been introduced, the next concern is how these methods might be applied to research in higher education. When applying network analysis methods in higher education research, a fundamental concern is the type of network, as higher education institutions are often embedded in multiple networks which may have very different structures. This section provides an overview of different types of network data relevant to higher education and discusses how they have been used in previous publications.

Research networks and bibliometric data

Much interest in higher education networks relates to research. If the claims of the Royal Society cited above are true, then integration and positionality in networks is key to understanding contemporary research. Bibliometric databases (e.g. 'Web of Science' and 'Scopus' provide a wealth of information that can be used in social network analysis. These data have several key benefits: they are often readily accessible (particularly to researchers in institutions with many database subscriptions), data collection takes minimal time, and they contain a fairly complete coverage of all relevant actors. A corresponding downside is that these databases are owned by commercial organizations (e.g. Thompson Reuters, Elsevier) and access can be expensive for individual researchers outside subscribing institutions.

Co-authorship networks are those in which authors in an academic discipline are connected to all others with whom they have co-authored a publication. For example, Moody (2004) analyses the structure of co-authorship networks in sociological journals over a 36-year period. Looking at degree centrality, he finds that the network is relatively decentralized and not dependent upon a small number of 'star' researchers to hold it together (p. 228). Similarly, his analysis of transitivity and clustering reveals that boundaries between theoretical approaches and specializations are permeable – in other words the network is not composed of distinct and separate cliques (Moody, 2004).

In contrast to co-authorship, other studies of research networks focus upon works that an author cites. There are several variations in how citation networks can be constructed, depending upon the focus of the research. One of the most straightforward approaches to citational network analysis is through a dataset in which each actor is connected to other authors whom he or she has cited at least once. Such a network is binary and directed; however, it is also possible to create a valued network based upon the actual number of citations. Similarly, it is also possible to create a dataset in which the 'actors' are the individual publications, or the publication journal, both of which would be connected to other similar 'actors' on the basis of citations.

All three approaches are used by Brandes and Pich (2011) in their social network analysis of publications in the field of social network analysis (the circular and nature of their research topic is admittedly challenging on first reading), which develops new ways of visualizing networks across multiple domains (i.e. authors, works/papers and journals). Their contribution is primarily methodological, suggesting that their approach to visualization and analysis might be used fruitfully in other research. Otte and Rousseau (2002) also analyse social network analysis publications, calculating centrality values and visualizing citational networks. They use this analysis to identify particularly influential authors in the field of social network analysis.

International networks

There are many types of networks in which the actors are not individuals or institutions, but nation states. An example of such data is the flow of international students between countries. Each year, over three million students undertake degree study outside their home country, a dramatic increase from a figure of 1.4 million in 1999 (UNESCO Institute for Statistics, 2011). These flows of international students create a complex network between nation states, in which connections are valued (according to the number of students) and directional. Detailed data on international student mobility data are collected through a joint initiative between the UNESCO Institute for Statistics (UIS), the OECD and Eurostat (2011), which collect data from national governments on the numbers of incoming international students by country of origin (2011). These data are distributed by the respective organization, with the UIS offering convenient access through its online data centre (UNESCO Institute for Statistics, 2011).

International student networks are highly centralized; a small number of countries (mainly English-speaking) account for a disproportionate share of international student enrolment. However, countries such as South Africa, Japan, South Korea and India are attracting rapidly growing numbers of international students, providing some competition to established hubs (Shields and Edwards, 2010). In other work, the author has analysed the changes in the structure of international student mobility over a ten-year period (Shields, 2013), finding that rather than becoming a 'flat world' the network has actually become increasingly centralized. This analysis also shows that the network of international students is closely related to the networks of world trade and international organizations (e.g. the United Nations, European Union), but that the latter relationship is the stronger of the two.

Institutional networks

Data are also available on networks between higher education institutions. Such networks can take on many forms, for instance it would be possible create a network dataset of institutions that are connected through membership in consortia and alliances (e.g. Universitas 21, the World University Network, Association of Commonwealth Universities). Data on membership are easily obtainable through the websites of the respective associations. Similarly, it would be possible to examine bilateral relationships – for example, bilateral exchange agreements signed through the Erasmus programme – although data are harder to obtain as there is no central registration of the information. However, compiling and analysing networks of Erasmus student mobility would be a promising area for future research.

Val Burris (2004) analyses networks between US higher education institutions by looking at patterns of academic hiring – that is, the network of institutions that hire graduates from other institutions. Using eigenvector centrality, he shows that the structure of interdepartmental hiring is a better predictor of institutions' prestige and reputation ratings than other (actor-based) measurements such as research output and citations.

Social media networks

One of the most remarkable developments of the 21st century has been the growth in social media networks. Websites like Facebook, Twitter and LinkedIn have led to new levels of connectivity between individuals and new patterns of communication. These technologies have also made an impact in higher education, with many academics and managers tweeting about their work, and have led to the development of specialized networks such as Academia.edu and ResearchGate.

Social media can provide a rich source of data on higher education networks: it is possible for researchers to look at not only connectivity in networks (e.g. who follows who on Twitter or Academia.edu) but also the content of the connections (what people are saying in certain networks). Furthermore, automated data collection methods have become increasingly available, as many websites expose access to their data through an Application Programming Interface (API). Open source software like NodeXL leverages this feature to allow users to collect data on social networks, while data analysis software such as R and NVivo contain packages for automated social media data collection.

Collecting network data

In addition to the data sources discussed here, it is always possible to collect new network data. In this sense, the number of networks available is almost inexhaustible: one might gather data on how students in a particular class seek advice from one another (and perhaps relate this class performance), transitions between institutions for undergraduate and post-graduate study and so on.

However, collecting network data is not easy and differs from typical questionnaires in many respects. First, anonymization of data sources is challenging: if one were to look at networks of advice and support between students in a class, it would be necessary to list all students in the class on a survey, and also collect the name of the student providing data. While this information can be subsequently anonymized, it is more personal and sensitive than other forms of survey data. For this reason, it is always important to follow relevant research ethics guidelines (e.g. the American Educational Research Association's 'Code of Ethics') and gain necessary approvals and informed consent before collecting network data.

New horizons: Exponential Random Graph Models

A key question for much research on social networks is to determine the probability of a tie: who is more likely to be connected to whom? More specifically, much research seeks to test hypotheses about network data: is it true that actors are more likely to connect to others of a higher status, or who are similar to them in some way? ERGMS allow researchers to answer such question, expressing the probability of a tie between two actors in relation to the following:

Endogenous Factors: Other ties in the network, or structural factors. For instance, is a tie more likely to be formed if it is reciprocal, or if actors have another mutual connection? In our exemplar data, we might test the hypothesis that universities are more likely to connect to those that are already following them (i.e. to form reciprocal connections) or to follow institutions that are already central in the network. (i.e. a tendency to centralization)

Exogenous Factors: Relationships that are external to the network structure, for instance the location of actors, their gender, nationality and so on. In our exemplar data, we might test the idea that universities are more likely to connect to those that are located in the same country, or that have a similar research focus, or are of a similar size.

In recent years, the development of a new approach to statistical modelling of network data, the ERGM has allowed researchers to answer these questions. Much like a logistic regression, an ERGM expresses the probability of a tie between two individuals as dependent variable that is the outcome of a set of covariates (i.e. predictors or independent variables) with associated weights. Additionally, an ERGM estimates the standard error (variability) in each coefficient, so that we specify the statistical significance of each parameter in our analysis.

The key innovation in ERGMs is the ability to account for the highly dependent structure of network data: to model the probability of a tie from A to B, we would likely need to know the corresponding tie from A to B (to measure the

Table 12.1 Output from an ERGM of tie formation in the exemplar network. Results show that reciprocity and transitivity are both significantly related to tie formation, but that location in the same country is not

Term	Estimate	Std. Err.
Edges	−3.640**	0.372
Reciprocity	4.365**	0.737
Transitivity	0.266*	0.132
Country-Match	0.322	0.225

effect of reciprocity) and all other actors in the network (to measure transitivity, i.e. mutual connections). The mathematics and statistical reasoning behind ERGMs is complex and beyond the scope of this article; however, excellent introductions are available from Robins et al. (2007), Robins and Lusher (2013) and Snijders (2011).

Table 12.1 shows the results of an ERGM of the exemplar data. Similar to a logistic regression, the 'estimates' column represents the relationship between the predictor term and the probability of a tie formation. The first term, 'edges', represents the baseline probability of a tie, its role is similar to that of an intercept in regression analysis. All model terms are expressed in log-odds, but can be converted to a probability with the equation 12.1. Thus, the baseline probability for a tie in our network is 0.026.

$$P = \frac{e^x}{1+e^x} = \frac{e^{-3.640}}{1+e^{-3.640}} = 0.26 = 2.6\%$$ (12.1)

Equation 12.1 Converting network terms to estimated probabilities. The baseline probability of tie formation is 2.6%.

The model includes two endogenous terms: reciprocity and transitivity. Each of these is significantly related to tie formation, meaning that there is a 95% confidence interval that the estimated value differs from zero. Furthermore, the relationship between reciprocity and tie formation appears to be much larger than that of transitivity. Substituting the estimate for reciprocity into Equation 12.1 (above), the probability of a tie increases to 0.674 if it would result in a reciprocal connection (Equation 12.2).

$$P = \frac{e^{-3.640+4.365}}{1+e^{-3.640+4.365}} = 0.674 = 67.4\%$$ (12.2)

Equation 12.2 Calculation of estimated probability for a reciprocal tie. The probability is notably higher than the baseline.

The exogenous term – 'country-match' – tests the hypothesis that institutions in the same country tend to form ties with one another. This is not significant, meaning that a researcher could not be confident in saying that a relationship between these variables exists. Overall, the results of the ERGM analysis show that for the exemplar data, endogenous factors (reciprocity in particular), are most likely to predict the formation of ties in our network.

Discussion: Networks and possibilities

This chapter has introduced key concepts in social network analysis and operationalized their use in higher education. It has introduced key concepts associated with social network analysis (e.g. actors and ties), discussed measurements of structure (e.g. reciprocity, transitivity and centralization), presented several forms of network data and illustrated the analysis of an exemplar dataset. Thus, the chapter should lay a valuable foundation for researchers seeking to use social network analysis to better understand higher education or those reading and interpreting the results of research that uses social network analysis.

The case for applying network methods in higher education research has never been stronger: the chapter began by showing how 'network speak' – that is, the use of networks as a conceptual approach – has been on the rise in higher education literature. However, the application of empirical social network methodologies has been prominently absent. These methods allow researchers to investigate complex social situations from a new perspective and to address issues that feature prominently in higher education research (e.g. the importance of status, communities of individuals and institutions), and often to provide insights that are not available through actor-centric analyses. Thus, the preceding discussion should serve a springboard for the application of these methods and the development of new understandings of contemporary higher education networks.

Note

1. There are 20 individuals who could each be connected with 19 others (individuals can't collaborate with themselves). However, ties are reciprocal, so the total must be divided by 2 ($20 \times 19/2 = 190$).

References

Ball, S. J. and C. Junemann (2012) *Networks, New Governance, and Education* (Bristol: Policy Press).

Brandes, U. and C. Pich (2011) 'Explorative visualization of citation patterns in social network research', *Journal of Social Structure*, 12(8), 1–19.

Burris, V. (2004). 'The academic caste system: prestige hierarchies in PhD exchange networks', *American Sociological Review*, 69(2), 239–264.

Castells, M. (1996) *The Rise of the Network Society* (Oxford: Blackwell Publishers Limited).

Dundar, H. and D. R. Lewis (1998) 'Determinant of research productivity in higher education', *Research in Higher Education*, 39(6), 607–631.

Fairweather, J. S. (2002). 'The mythologies of faculty productivity: implications for institutional policy and decision-making', *The Journal of Higher Education*, 73(1), 27–48.

Freeman, Linton C. (1978) 'Centrality in social networks: conceptual clarification', *Social Networks*, 1(3), 215–239.

Fruchterman, T. M. J. and E. M. Reingold (1991) 'Graph drawing by force-directed placement', *Software: Practice and Experience*, 21(11), 1129–1164. Doi: 10.1002/spe.4380211102

Grant, C. B. (2013) Losing our chains? Contexts and ethics of university internationalisation. Leadership Foundation for Higher Education Stimulus Paper. ISBN: 978-1-906627-42-3.

Lewis, T., Marginson, S. and I. Synder (2005) 'The network university? Technology, culture and organisational complexity in contemporary higher education', *Higher Education Quarterly*, 59(1), 56–75.

Moody, J. (2004) 'The structure of a social science collaboration network: disciplinary cohesion from 1963 to 1999', *American Sociological Review*, 69(2), 213–238.

Otte, E. and R. Rousseau (2002) 'Social network analysis: a powerful strategy, also for the information sciences', *Journal of Information Science*, 28(6), 441–453.

Robins, G., Pattison, P., Kalish, Y. and D. Lusher (2007) 'An introduction to exponential random graph models(p*) for social networks', *Social Networks*, 29(2), 173–191.

Robins, G. and D. Lusher (2013) 'What are exponential random graph models?' in D. Lusher, J. Kokinen and G. Robins (eds) *Exponential Random Graph Models for Social Networks: Theory, Methods and Applications* (pp. 9–15) (Cambridge: Cambridge University Press).

Royal Society (2011) *Knowledge, Networks and Nations: Global Scientific Collaboration in the 21st century*. ISBN: 978-0-85403-890-9.

Sheehan, B. S. and A. R. Welch (1996) 'The Australian academic profession', in P. G. Altbach (ed) *The International Academic Profession: Portraits of Fourteen Countries* (pp. 51–96) (San Francisco, CA: Jossey-Bass Publishers).

Shields, R. (2013) 'Globalization and international student mobility: a network analysis', *Comparative Education Review*, 57(4), 609–636.

Shields, R. and R. Edwards (2010) 'Student mobility and emerging hubs in global higher education', in V. D. Rust, L. M. Portnoi and S. S. Bagley (eds) *Higher Education, Policy, and the Global Competition Phenomenon* (New York: Palgrave Macmillan).

Snijders, T. (2011) 'Statistical models for social networks', *Annual Review of Sociology*, 37, 131–153.

UNESCO Institute for Statistics, OECD, and Eurostat (2011) UOE Data Collection on Education Systems. Vol 1. Montreal, Paris, and Luxembourg: UNESCO-UIS, OECD, and Eurostat.

UNESCO Institute for Statistics (2011) *Global Education Digest 2011: Comparing Education Statistics across the World*. Montreal: UNESCO Institute for Statistics.

UNESCO Institute for Statistics (2014) Data Center. Accessed at http://data.uis.unesco.org/ on 10 December 2014.

Wasserman, S. and K. Faust (1994) *Social Network Analysis: Methods and Applications* (Cambridge: Cambridge University Press).

Part II Themes

A. Higher Education, Society and the Economy

13
The Role of Higher Education in Society and the Changing Institutionalized Features in Higher Education

Rómulo Pinheiro, Gerald Wangenge-Ouma, Elizabeth Balbachevsky and Yuzhuo Cai

Introduction

Higher education institutions (HEIs) are under increasing pressure to show their societal relevance (Perry, 2012; Temple, 2011). This is partly a function of the impetus brought about by the rise of the knowledge-based economy and, concurrently, the premium put on the manipulation and transfer of knowledge assets (Varga, 2009), in addition to high-level skills embodied in the human capital of nations and regions (OECD, 2007). External pressures manifest themselves in a variety of forms, among them, shifts in the economy and the nature of the labour market, demographic trends and the demands and expectations of interest groups, and are, to a large degree, associated with the notion of higher education (HE) as an instrument for reaching certain societal agendas (Maassen and Olsen, 2007) like democratization, social mobility, economic development and innovation. As a result of these (and other) external pressures, governments across the world have enacted several bold reforms aimed at modernizing HE with the aim of responding better to the aforementioned pressures and to increase efficiency, quality and accountability (Amaral, Bleiklie and Musselin, 2008; Stensaker and Harvey, 2011; Vukasovic et al., 2012). These efforts, in turn, have generated a series of strategic responses by HEIs and their primary actors, academics and professional administrators (Kwiek and Maassen, 2012; Pinheiro and Stensaker, 2014a). What is more, the changes have led to a shift in the nature of the traditional relationship or 'social pact' between HE and society, brokered via the state (Maassen, 2014; Schwartzman, Pinheiro and Pillay, 2015).

This chapter takes stock of the external pressures facing HEIs across four world regions: *Europe*, focusing on the Nordic countries; *Southern Africa*, anchored around its most matured system, South Africa; *South East Asia*, with a special emphasis on its fastest growing economy, China; and *South America*, with a look at developments within its strongest economy, Brazil. In so doing, we investigate the *external pressures* facing HE systems in these countries, followed by a look at how *governments* across the case regions have responded to these pressures. Finally, we illuminate on the *types of responses* by HEIs to the changes in their external environment.

External pressures

The types of pressures facing national systems and HEIs can be split into two relatively distinct groups. Firstly, there are generic global pressures, both socio-cultural and economic, that affect various societal domains. These pressures are to a large degree universal. Secondly, there is a set of more 'localized' pressures that are linked to national specificities and the endogenous characteristics of their HE systems. Local pressures can also be distinguished between those that are socio-cultural in nature and those that are linked to instrumentalist, economic imperatives. These global and local pressures are closely intertwined (see Figure 13.1).

Global pressures

Since the late 1980s, the most prevalent global pressures facing societies the world over pertain to the phenomenon commonly known as *globalization*; a multifaceted phenomenon characterized by increasing variety and diversity (Ervin and Smith, 2008; Lechner, 2009). Globalization has a *socio-cultural* component associated with the worldwide spread of ideas, belief systems, fashions,

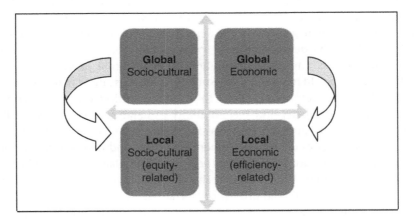

Figure 13.1   Global vs. local pressures
Source: Authors.

lifestyles, what some term 'world-society' (Drori, Meyer and Hwang, 2006), aided by the increasing mobility of people and information across the globe. Equally, it has a *political* dimension associated with the changing (not necessarily declining) role of the state. Globalization also has a strong *economic* dimension, linked to the notion of the world as a 'single-market place' and a set of universalistic rules embodied in the World Trade Organization (WTO) and its various sub-components. One of the many socio-cultural, and also political, effects associated with globalization, pertains to a decline in traditional notions of national identity and sovereignty. On the economic front, the rise of a 'global market place' has resulted in aggressive competition among firms and other service providers (HEIs included) for not only customers but also talented knowledge workers, who are expected to enhance the market reputation and/or social prestige enjoyed by their respective organizations.

Globalization was and remains aided by another global trend, namely, the so-called ICT-revolution initiated in the 1980s, resulting *inter alia* in increasing connectivity and the rise of the network society (Castells, 2010). The increasing importance attributed to *knowledge*, as a critical factor of production, has relegated capital and land as the most important sources of sustainable competitive advantage (Porter, 1998), giving rise to the so-called knowledge economy (Rooney, Hearn and Ninan, 2008). This, in turn, has altered traditional public and academic conceptions of, for example, the role and production of knowledge (Gibbons et al., 1994; Nowotny, Scott and Gibbons, 2002), and the importance attributed to new, high-tech research areas around STEM-related fields such as nano- and bio-technology, and the link between science, innovation and economic growth more generally (Colombo, Grilli and Piscitello, 2011). The aforementioned external developments have disrupted the traditional functioning of all economic sectors, including the provision of HE services and the production and transfer of academic-generated knowledge (Douglass, King and Feller, 2009; Drori, 2003; Marginson and Rhoades, 2002). Finally, it is worth acknowledging the fact that globalization (its effects) manifests itself primarily at the local level (Coleman and Sajed, 2013). Thus, some of the local pressures (discussed below) either result from or are intertwined with the more universalistic trends identified above.

Local pressures

In this section, we discuss local pressures facing HE in our four case regions. As already indicated, we see these local pressures as local manifestations of pressures that are otherwise global in nature.

There are three major local pressures facing Chinese HE, namely, demand for high quality HE, demand for HE-industry collaborations and rising urbanization. Demand for high-quality education has been increasing partly because of improved economic conditions in the country. While more students are able to sit the HE entrance examination, and have a better chance to pass the exam, the competition for entering good universities has become fiercer. Of the more than 2000 HEIs in China, only about 100 universities (mostly 'Project 211' universities[1]) are considered to be of high quality or prestigious. As a result, there are increasingly many Chinese who seek high-quality HE overseas. The rising demand for HE-industry collaborations, in the context of economic development and innovation, requires universities to enhance quality, and to link their core activities, both teaching and research, more strongly to the country's (and its various regions) economic needs. Urbanization and its associated social disparity problems have aggravated equity-related challenges in two ways. Firstly, partly due to inequitable economic development, HEIs are not distributed equitably among the country's municipal cities and provinces, and secondly, students from poorer families and regions have unequal access to good quality secondary education, thus leading to lesser chances of gaining access to the most prestigious HEIs and careers (Feng, 2011; Ma, 2011).

Regarding Brazil, one of the key local pressures facing HE is access. Since the mid-1990s when the Government succeeded in stabilizing the economy, the Brazilian society has experienced a strong upward social mobility, which, in turn, has resulted into an expanded demand for access to HE (Neves, 2015). Demand for HE is not only by families with teenagers but also by adults interested in upgrading their labour market credentials. More than half of the domestic HE student population is composed of young adults (25–35-year-olds) already employed and searching for evening programmes that can be conciliated with the demands of a full-time work schedule. Access to exclusive institutions (public universities) is restricted by a *numerus clausus* policy, which limits the number of positions open to freshmen in each career track. Candidates at undergraduate level are selected through a highly competitive public examination. Until the last decade, this meritocratic perspective was dominant and highly accepted across Brazilian society. However, the last 12 years have witnessed a strong change in society's values with the rise of a new social agenda centred on issues of minority rights and democratic access to public universities (Balbachevsky, 2015).

As in the case of Brazil, one of the key pressures facing South African higher education is the demand for increased access. In addition, South African HE also faces pressures related to declining state financial support and demands for enhanced research productivity. Access to higher education in South Africa is linked to (1) the realization of social justice in terms of improving the participation of previously marginalized communities, given the country's apartheid history and (2) advancing socio-economic development in terms of producing the skills required by the South African economy. In 2013, South Africa had a higher education participation rate of 17.3% and aspires to realize a participation rate of 25% by 2030, which translates into a growth of about 937,000 students in 2011 to about 1.6 million enrolments in 2030 (DHET, 2013a). Regarding funding, South African universities are not immune to funding-related pressures that are experienced in other higher education systems globally. A recent analysis by a ministerial committee shows: 'Between 2000 and 2010, state funding per full-time equivalent (FTE) enrolled student fell by 1.1% annually, in real terms' (DHET, 2013b, p. 7). Finally, when it comes to research, the country's National Development Plan (NPC, 2012) and White Paper for Post-school Education and Training (DHET, 2013a) foreground the critical role of universities in the economic competitiveness of South Africa in the context of a knowledge-driven economic paradigm. HEIs are therefore called upon to enhance their research and innovation capacities and enhance their outputs in the realms of graduate and postgraduate education.

One of the key challenges facing Nordic higher education is increasing pressures to respond to the needs and demands of various stakeholder groups. The traditional social pact, based on trust between HE and society has gradually been replaced by a strong emphasis on accountability and performance, illustrated in the rise of contractual arrangements between the state and domestic providers (Gornitzka et al., 2004). There are increasing concerns as regards the role of HE in society (impact), which, to a degree, is resulting into the need for HEIs (which still command rather large public budgets) to constantly legitimize their functions and strategic priorities to a wide variety of stakeholder groups (Pinheiro, Geschwind and Aarrevaara, 2014; Pinheiro, 2015). Finland and Denmark have both been affected by the recent financial crisis which, in turn, has exacerbated fiscal pressures and the need 'to do more with less' resources. Finally, the need to be globally competitive in science is resulting in the increasing concentration of resources (people and funding) and social prestige around a selected group of providers, exacerbating the differences between the 'haves' and 'have nots', and resulting in a new meritocratic ethos that has come to substitute the old egalitarian orientation so characteristic of Nordic HE (Pinheiro and Geschwind, 2014).

Governmental responses and effects

The sections that follow describe the various ways in which governments in the respective countries and regions have responded to global and local pressures.

China

The Chinese government has launched a series of policy reforms as a means of responding to the global and domestic pressures identified earlier (Cai, 2011; Cai and Yan, 2015; Yang et al., 2015). For instance, in 1998 it announced a national plan for massification of higher education, which included a rapid growth of private HEIs. Following the promulgation of this initiative, the gross enrolment rate rose from 9.1% to 26.5% in 2010. Meanwhile, the number of HEIs increased from 1,022 in 1998 to 2358 (including 647 private institutions) in 2010. The rapid growth in enrolments has generated a number of challenges, namely a decline in quality, inequality of access and high levels of graduate unemployment.

To increase China's competitiveness in the global marketplace, and also to address some of the challenges resulting from rapid enrolment growth, the government successively launched 'Project 211' in 1995 and 'Project 985' in 1998, with the main aim of raising the research profiles of selected top HEIs. These HEIs received significant funding support, and are tasked with training high-level human resources mainly doctoral graduates, and generating research and innovations required to drive the knowledge economy in China. Related, while the reforms of the late 1990s and the early 2000s emphasized mainly research rather than teaching quality, the 'Action Plan for Invigorating Education 2003–2007', promulgated by the Ministry of Education, with the approval of the State Council, shifted the focus towards teaching and teaching quality, by establishing quality assurance systems. Quality assurance is overseen by two governmental agencies (under the Ministry of Education), responsible for graduate and undergraduate education. In addition, many provincial and municipal educational departments have established regional higher education quality assurance agencies and most HEIs have also set up their own quality assurance departments for internal evaluation. In November 2010, the National Association for Higher Education Quality Assurance and Evaluation Agencies were established with the key aims of coordinating quality evaluation across the country, promoting experience sharing and enhancing self-discipline with regard to quality assurance practices.

About 100 vocational colleges have been established to address the human resources needs arising from the growth of technological industries. In addition, in 2014, the government announced that about 600 regional universities would become vocational or offer professionally oriented programmes. To further strengthen the role of universities in economic development, the government launched the '2011 project', aimed at promoting innovation through collaboration among universities, research institutes, industries and governments.

Brazil

As aforementioned, the most important challenge facing Brazilian HE is access. Massification of HE was aided by the rise of a rather unregulated private (for-profit) sector, responsible for providing close to 70% of undergraduate enrolments. Since the mid-1960s, the private sector has acted as an escape valve for the access pressures in Brazilian HE. Since 2003, the federal government has maintained a programme (University for All) directed to the for-profit sector, exchanging fiscal benefits for tuition exemption for about 1 million of low-income and minority students. In 2010, the government reformed and expanded a programme for financial assistance for lower-income students in the private sector. From the point of view of the Ministry of Education, the focus is on strengthening the instruments for regulating the private sector, while simultaneously supporting access for students coming from poor families. The rather sophisticated monitoring apparatus of the government (targeting the entire sector) encompasses inter alia: (1) a system of accreditation, designed as an instrument for monitoring and ensuring that HEIs are producing the expected outcomes, (2) a nationwide evaluation for all students in their last year of their undergraduate studies and (3) national rankings for all undergraduate programs.

In response to the access pressures the public sector faces, the government has introduced two policy instruments. Firstly, the government has since 2003 been encouraging quota programmes in public universities targeting minorities and students that come from poor socio-economic backgrounds. Special programmes, designed to support these students, have also been devised. In 2012, these initiatives were consolidated in a law, meaning that half of the entrance positions at the undergraduate level at federal universities are reserved for candidates from the public basic education system and minorities. Secondly, a new programme, REUNI (Program for Restructuration and Expansion of Federal Universities), was established in 2008 to support the expansion of the federal HE sector by enlarging existing and creating new (evening) programmes, by building new campuses and by creating new federal universities. The REUNI programme adopted what Braun (2003, p. 312) has termed 'delegation by incentives', that is, setting incentives in the form of price signals over some performance indicators, while allowing universities' to decide on how to reach them. In other words, the strategy adopted by government was one of restricting universities' level of *substantive* autonomy ('the what') while enlarging the room for manoeuvre for *procedural* matters ('the how') (see Schmidtlein and Berdahl, 2005).

South Africa

The South African government has implemented several initiatives to address the key challenges facing its HE system. It should be understood that the pressure to increase access, especially to communities marginalized by apartheid, is a deliberate government policy, requiring universities to reform in accord with the transformation imperative of the post-apartheid state. Accordingly, the government has deliberately foregrounded access and equity of access in all its HE-related policies. Specific state-driven responses to the access challenge include the establishment of the National Student Financial Aid Scheme

(NSFAS) to support talented but financially challenged students, funding for foundation programmes to support academically weak students (Wangenge-Ouma, 2013), expansion of the HE sector through the establishment of new universities and the call upon contact institutions with the necessary capacity to consider offering distance education programmes (DHET, 2013a).

South African HEIs have responded to resource dependence difficulties resulting from declining state funding mainly by increasing tuition fees. Between 2000 and 2010, tuition fees per FTE student increased by 2.5% annually, in real terms (DHET, 2013b). This situation is a concern for the South African government because of its potential negative implications for equitable access. While the state has not enhanced its capitation for HE to meet the costs related mainly to increasing enrolments, it has invested in NSFAS significantly in an attempt to cushion poor students from the rising costs of HE. Unfortunately, the demand for financial aid outstrips by far the available supply, meaning that not all deserving students receive financial support (Wangenge-Ouma, 2012). It can be argued, therefore, that the government's responses to financial pressures facing HEIs have not been successful in mitigating them fully – both universities and students remain underfunded.

Regarding research, a recent analysis by Cloete (2014) indicates that globally South Africa is a medium knowledge-producing system. However, the country is the leading knowledge producer in Africa, accounting for about 37% of all publications. This leading role in research in Africa is not only a result of the country's strong HEIs (compared to others on the continent) but also the strong role of the state in steering research productivity, mainly through funding mechanisms. The funding framework for HEIs rewards universities for publications and master's and doctoral student outputs. Competitive funding for research is also available through the Department of Science and Technology and agencies such as the Medical Research Council.

The Nordics

Governments across the Nordic countries have, in the last decade or so, enacted a series of reforms as a means of responding to the external and domestic challenges mentioned earlier. Both Denmark and Finland have embarked on major reform efforts aimed at reducing the number of HEIs through voluntary mergers, with the aim of enhancing quality (teaching) on the one hand and global excellence (research) on the other. Norway and Sweden have followed suit, with the result being the erosion of the traditional binary divide (case of Norway) and the concentration of resources in fewer, but much larger, HEIs (Pinheiro, Geschwind and Aarrevaara, in press). Excellence, but also relevance, was catapulted to the forefront of the policy agenda, in the form of newly devised instruments such as Centers for Research Excellence and for Applied Innovation (Aksnes et al., 2012), focusing on mode-1 and mode-2 knowledge production, respectively. Triple helix arrangements aimed at strengthening the links between academic groups and industry (local and national levels), as well as the public sector at large (hospitals, local municipalities, etc.), were forged (Lester and Sotarauta, 2007; Pinheiro, 2012). External stakeholders (as members of HEIs boards), as well as Technology Transfer Offices (TTOs) and research liaison offices, became distinctive features of Nordic HEIs. Increasingly, leaders at various levels across Nordic HEIs are appointed by the Board instead of being elected (Engwall, 2014). Partly as a result of new public management-inspired reforms, rationalization and professionalization have been intensified, with the aim of making Nordic HEIs more accountable, responsive and predictable (Pinheiro and Stensaker, 2014b). Efficiency and quality-related concerns have also been addressed, in the form of changes in the public allocation of funding to HEIs (now with a performance element alongside a basic component) and through contractual arrangements specifying intended outcomes per core activity (Gornitzka et al., 2004).

Institutional responses

China

Chinese HEIs are susceptible to both the global/local pressures and an environment resulting from governmental policy initiatives. Although the Chinese 1988 Higher Education Law stipulates a rather high level of autonomy for HEIs in formulating their own institutional strategies and plans, in practice their autonomy is regulated (Yang, Vidovich and Currie, 2007). This means that they cannot independently determine their strategic thrusts, institutional trajectories and education programmes, but they can, to a large extent, determine the means by which their goals and programmes will be pursued (see also Schmidtlein and Berdahl, 2005). In this context, Chinese HEIs mainly address the demands emanating from the central government. This situation has two key potential consequences. Firstly, it hampers long-term planning since institutional actions are dependent on signals from the state, and secondly, the extent to which HEIs are able to respond successfully to external pressures is largely dependent on the appropriateness of state policy.

Regardless, universities' individual approach to follow policy guidelines, the reforms planned by government often resulted in conflicting logics in the field of HE, which in turn may confuse HEIs and complicate their strategic actions (Cai, 2004). As the result of the conflicting logics tensions arise, such as tensions between (1) China's socialist ideology and Western values, (2) the traditional steering model and the active participation of society (more active role of stakeholders), (3) inadequate conditions at the level of HEIs and resource stringencies in the public purse, (4) short-term market demands and long-term national development priorities or public interests, (5) weak legal consciousness and requirements for a regulated market system and (6) the historical tradition of the absence of domestic competition, weak creativity and the need to become globally competitive. In addition, some new tensions have emerged as a result of recent reforms. The most profound ones pertain to HE as an ivory tower and the pursuit of scientific (global) excellence against the logic of HE for market needs, that is knowledge production for business use and education for skills enhancement.

Brazil

REUNI was successful in mobilizing new resources for Federal universities and produced a substantial expansion in enrolments at the undergraduate level. Between 2007 and 2013, enrolments at federal universities almost doubled to just over 1 million. It also resulted in innovative designs for courses and the establishment of new universities, such as the new Federal University of ABC (founded in 2005), which adopted an integrated (interdisciplinary) perspective for undergraduate studies. Yet, REUNI also nurtured some idiosyncratic responses from public universities. Many of its associated programmes have little attraction to students and society at large, and new campuses lack the most basic infrastructure. There is a new cohort of academics emerging, better qualified than their senior peers, yet working in worse conditions and burdened with large teaching loads. What is more, the federal system as a whole shows a decline in the efficiency at the undergraduate level.

A similar picture emerges from the way universities responded to the challenges posed by the new design adopted by the science policy, which has evolved to adopt a special focus on innovation. The new focus stresses social and economic relevance instead of the old linear mode focused exclusively on disciplinary relevance. Inside public universities, research activities tend to be concentrated on graduate programmes and around centres and laboratories. Traditionally, these research-oriented micro-environments developed from the initiative of more entrepreneurial academics, counting with direct support from the S&T agencies and small interference (or support) from universities' central administration (Balbachevsky, 2013). However, in the last decade, the Science and Technology agencies launched ambitious programmes focused on long-term goals, such as providing alternatives for the country's environmental challenges, developing technologies for industry and agriculture and searching for policy alternatives for the country's main social problems. These programmes demand support from the university, in terms of infrastructure, buildings and human resources. This, however, is something most public universities are not willing to do. The politicized internal environment poses resistance to a stronger institutional involvement with teams viewed as already 'privileged' by their access to external funds.

Turning to the private sector, the operational environment established by the strict regulatory framework in tandem with the competitive drive for growth profoundly changed private HE, leading to processes of concentration and differentiation. Private HEIs changed from being small, family-owned businesses towards a corporate model characterized by a hierarchical (business-like) internal governance system. Two distinct dynamics are present in this sector. Firstly, the growth of huge for-profit corporate institutions fiercely competing for students in a commodity-like market, where the lower price charged for education is the main differential, leaving little room for considerations regarding improving quality. Within this market, the extra financial burden created by compliance with the strict governmental regulations accelerated the process of concentration. Only with scale can these institutions be able to cope with the costs, centred in producing figures that attest to the presence of basic research activities (Castro, 2015). This subsector also diversified their portfolio of programmes and expanded their geographic reach by opening new campuses in inner cities and by intensively exploring distance education opportunities. Secondly, the rise of a small set of highly reputed private elite-oriented HEIs, providing mainly undergraduate education targeting the upper niches of the labour market, has helped to blur the boundaries between public and private HEIs.

South Africa

South African universities have responded to the three identified challenges in various ways, driven mainly by policy and state steering. Regarding the pressure for expanded access by especially black students, several HEIs, especially historically white institutions, have set targets for enrolment of black students. To realize these enrolment targets, these institutions have implemented strategies such as the setting of quotas for black students in university residences, changing institutional cultures to accommodate a diverse student population and, more importantly, allocating internally generated funds for bursaries and student loans. According to Daca (2014), HEIs allocated about R200 million (approximately US$ 17.8 million) towards student loans and bursaries in 2013.

As mentioned earlier, the primary response to declining state capitation by South African public universities is by increasing tuition fees. Many of these institutions have made adjustments in the manner in which tuition fees are levied to ensure both cost recovery and optimal revenue generation. Other than implementing regular increases in tuition fees, differential pricing of various instructional services has also ensured high earnings from tuition fees (Wangenge-Ouma and Cloete, 2008). In 2010, tuition fees accounted for 30% of the income of public universities compared to 24% in 2000 (DHET, 2013b).

A wide range of practices has been observed in terms of responses to the research challenge. These practices include support for doctoral and post-doctoral education (HESA, 2014); incentivization of successful supervision of research master's and PhD students, and publication in accredited journals (Mouton, 2012); appointment of adjunct and honorary professors; and development of international research networks (Wangenge-Ouma, 2014). It should be pointed out that the pressure to improve research productivity has elicited some responses that are inimical to the engendering of a robust research culture, such as the appointment of honorary professors for the sole purpose of claiming state subsidy for their publications (Wangenge-Ouma, 2014).

The Nordics

Nordic HEIs have responded to the challenges posed by the new regulative framework and operational environment in five distinct yet interrelated ways. Internally, they have strengthened the size and scope of their steering core (Clark, 1998), both central and subunit levels, including support functions aimed at leveraging teaching quality, strengthen research capacity (global excellence) and links with society (relevance impact). Secondly, and associated with the first element, they have centralized decision-making activities (strategic planning) and concentrated resources (people and funds) across selected teaching and research areas per their existing capacity, emerging (market) opportunities and direct contribution to addressing key challenges facing society (local, national and global levels). Thirdly, they have embraced excellence as their modus operandi and have initiated a gradual process of de-institutionalizing traditional notions of egalitarianism (e.g. manifested in the cross subsidization of weaker study or research fields) by replacing it (re-institutionalization) with a new meritocratic ethos or institutional logic which puts an emphasis on competition and the survival of the fittest a la Salerno (2007).[2] Directly related to this is the fourth response type, materialized around changes in organizational models or templates either in the form of mergers or amalgamations among regional HEIs – with the aim of increasing both the size and scope of their operations – or in the adoption of new structural features in the form of stand-alone (relatively autonomous) units such as centres of excellence or of innovation and/or business schools, as well as matrix-type organizational structures (Pinheiro and Stensaker, 2014a, 2014b), and other types of structural arrangements such as multi-campus systems (Pinheiro, Charles and Jones, forthcoming) and membership in international consortia. Finally, and intrinsically linked to the search for talented students and staff in the context of world-class aspirations, many HEIs have started revamping their human resources practices and procedures as well as contractual arrangements as a means of enhancing their national and global competitiveness.

As for the observed effects, the centralization of decision-making has resulted in new tensions both within HEIs (between academics and administrators) and between academics and external stakeholders, around the valorization and commodification of knowledge and perceived threats to academic autonomy (Pinheiro, Geschwind and Aarrevaara, 2014). Finally, vertical differentiation (stratification) has become more pronounced, with a smaller number of players – the flagship universities and technological institutes – commanding the bulk of research publications and competitive (national and EU) funding (Pinheiro and Geschwind, 2014).

Discussion and conclusion

While adapting their societal roles and functions to accommodate the emerging external demands and expectations, HEIs in China, South Africa, Brazil and the Nordic countries are confronted with a set of *institutional logics* (Thornton, Ocasio and Lounsbury, 2012) which are often at odds with one another (for earlier assessments, see Castells, 2001; Trow, 1970). Recent government-led reform initiatives aimed at steering their respective national systems to the new set of global and local trends and pressures are laden with a series of embedded tensions and interwoven dilemmas for HEIs to resolve (Pinheiro, Geschwind and Aarrevaara, 2014). These include trying to find an adequate balance between the following:

- *Global* and *local* imperatives (Marginson, 2004; Pinheiro, 2012), and the quest for simultaneously achieving societal relevance and scientific excellence (see Perry, 2012);
- *Equity* and *efficiency* imperatives, including enhanced scrutiny on the types of students to be admitted and the associated short- and long-term costs and benefits (Cai, 2004; Gornitzka et al., 2004);
- *Autonomy* and *accountability* (Stensaker and Harvey, 2011), where the general trend is to provide HEIs with enhanced procedural autonomy (means) while restricting their substantive autonomy (ends) (see Schmidtlein and Berdahl, 2005); and
- Change or adaptation and stability or inertia (Clark, 1983), for example, around the notions of HE as social institution ('knowledge as a public good') in contrast to that of an extension of industry and the idea of 'knowledge as a private commodity' (Slaughter and Cantwell, 2012).

Together, the aforementioned aspects are placing new demands on both the steering core (leadership structures) of HEIs and their academic communities, for example, achieving equity and efficiency in a context of declining state funding. That said, the type and nature of responses by HEIs differ, both across and within countries, taking into account *path-dependencies* (Krücken, 2003), *institutional missions* (Enders and Boer, 2009), *strategic aspirations* (Pinheiro and

Stensaker, 2014b) and *decision-making procedures* (Frølich et al., 2014), in addition to social positioning or *status hierarchies* (Hazelkorn, 2009). This means that despite universalistic trends and global recipes or scripts (Gornitzka and Maassen, 2011; Ramirez, Byrkjeflot, and Pinheiro, forthcoming), context still matters as far as HE system dynamics and institutional affairs are concerned.

In the majority of our cases, the responses to external pressures by HEIs are shaped generally by changing regulative and operational environments. These environments thus constitute a 'local translation' of the global and local pressures facing the HE systems (Marginson and Rhoades, 2002; Sahlin and Wedlin, 2008). This translation, in turn, is embodied in the various reform packages pursued so far, with both mixed results and (some) unintended or (so far) unforeseen consequences (Gornitzka, Kogan, and Amaral, 2005; Pinheiro and Kyvik, 2009).

Finally, while most HEIs tend to narrow their strategic focus by pursuing and maximizing their short- and long-term benefits in the light of the opportunities brought about by existing governmental policies and instruments, the *real* operational challenge lies in how to reconcile the conflicting logics inherent to 'old' and 'new' features at a variety of critical domains and levels (Berg and Pinheiro, forthcoming; Pache and Santos, 2013). Going forward, future research inquiries could help cast light on the ways in which the newly infused policy and institutional logics either support or hinder (or do both) the strategic aspirations of both governments and HEIs in the light of the multiple and often contradictory demands of various stakeholders.

Notes

1. The project is the Chinese government's attempt to strengthen about 100 HEIs and key disciplinary areas in light of key national – social and economic – policy priorities, for example enhance international competitiveness in science, technology and innovation.
2. For a discussion on *institutionalization, de-institutionalization* and *re-institutionalization* in the context of (European) HE one may consult Pinheiro (2012) and Kwiek (2012).

References

Aksnes, D., Benner, M., Brorstad Borlaug, S., Hansen, H., Kallerud, E., Kristiansen, E., Langfeldt, L., Pelkonen, A. and G. Sivertsen (2012) *Centres of Excellence in the Nordic Countries: A Comparative Study of Research Excellence Policy and Excellence Centre Schemes in Denmark, Finland, Norway and Sweden* (Oslo: NIFU).

Amaral, A., Bleiklie, I. and C. Musselin (2008) *From Governance to Identity: A Festschrift for Mary Henkel* (Dordrecht: Springer).

Balbachevsky, E. (2013) 'Academic research and advanced training: building up research universities in Brazil', in J. Balán (ed) *Latin's America's New Knowledge Economy: Higher Education, Government and International Collaboration* (pp. 113–133) (Washington: Institute of International Education).

Balbachevsky, E. (2015) 'The role of internal and external stakeholders in Brazilian higher education', in S. Schwartzman, R. Pinheiro and P. Pillay (eds) *Higher Education in the BRICS Countries: Investigating the Pact between Higher Education and Society* (pp. 193–214) (Dordrecht: Springer).

Berg, L. and R. Pinheiro (forthcoming) 'Handling different institutional logics in the public sector: comparing management in Norwegian universities and hospitals, in R. Pinheiro, F. Ramirez, K. Vrabæk and H. Byrkjeflot (eds) *Towards a Comparative Institutionalism?: Forms, Dynamics and Logics across Health and Higher Education Fields* (Bingley: Emerald).

Braun, D. (2003) 'Lasting tensions in research policy making: a delegation problem', *Science and Public Policy*, 30(5), 309–321.

Cai, Y. (2004) 'Confronting the global and the local – A case study of Chinese higher education', *Tertiary Education and Management*, 10(2), 157–169.

Cai, Y. (2011) *Chinese Higher Education Reforms and Tendencies: Implications for Norwegian Higher Education in Cooperating with China* (Bergen: Norwegian Centre for International Cooperation in Education, SIU). *SIU Report Series* [Internet]. Available at: http://www .siu.no/nor/content/download/7700/79536/file/Chinese%20higher%20education%20 reforms%20and%20tendencies%20-%20til%20publisering.pdf (Accessed: 18 December 2011).

Cai, Y. and F. Yan (2015) 'Supply and demand in Chinese higher education', in S. Schwartzman, R. Pinheiro and P. Pillay (eds) *Higher Education in the BRICS Countries: Investigating the Pact between Higher Education and Society* (pp. 149–170) (Drodrecht: Springer).

Castells, M. (2001) 'Universities as dynamic systems of contradictory functions', in J. Muller, N. Cloete and S. Badat (eds) *Challenges of Globalisation: South African Debates with Manuel Castells* (pp. 206–233) (Cape Town: Maskew Miller Longman).

Castells, M. (2010) *The Rise of the Network Society* (West Sussex: Wiley-Blackwell).

Castro, M. H. (2015) 'Higher education policies in Brazil: A case of failure in market regulation', in S. Schwartzman, R. Pinheiro and P. Pillay (eds) *Higher Education in the BRICS Countries: Investigating the Pact between Higher Education and Society* (pp. 271–290) (Drodrecht: Springer).

Clark, B. R. (1983) *The Higher Education System: Academic Organization in Cross-National Perspective* (Los Angeles, CA: University of California Press).

Clark, B. R. (1998) *Creating Entrepreneurial Universities: Organizational Pathways of Transformation* (New York: Pergamon).

Cloete, N. (2014) 'The South African higher education system: performance and policy', *Studies in Higher Education*, 39(8), 1355–1368.

Coleman, W. and A. Sajed (2013) *Fifty Key Thinkers on Globalization* (Milton Park: Taylor & Francis).

Colombo, M. G., Grilli, L. and L. Piscitello, L. (2011) *Science and Innovation Policy for the New Knowledge Economy* (Cheltenham: Edward Elgar Publishing, Incorporated).

Daca, M. (2014) 'NSFAS's perspectives on the nature and scale of the funding challenges' Presentation prepared for the *HESA-DHET-NSFAS Colloquium in Johannesburg, 2014* (28–29 July, Johannesburg: HESA-DHET-NSFAS).

DHET (2013a) *White Paper for Post-School Education and Training. Building an Expanded, Effective and Integrated Post-School System* (Pretoria: DHET).

DHET (2013b) *Report of the Ministerial Committee for the Review of the Funding of Universities* (Pretoria: DHET).

Douglass, J. A., King, C. J. I. and Feller (2009) *Globalization's Muse: Universities and Higher Education Systems in a Changing World* (Berkeley: Berkeley Public Policy Press).

Drori, G. S. (2003) *Science in the Modern World Polity: Institutionalization and Globalization* (Standford, CA: Stanford University Press).

Drori, G. S., Meyer, J. W. and H. Hwang (2006) *Globalization and Organization: World Society and Organizational Change* (Oxford: Oxford University Press).

Enders, J. and H. Boer (2009) 'The mission impossible of the European university: Institutional confusion and institutional diversity', in A. Amaral, G. Neave, C. Musselin and P. Maassen (eds) *European Integration and the Governance of Higher Education and Research* (pp. 159–178) (Dordrecht: Springer).

Engwall, L. (2014) 'The recruitment of university top leaders: Politics, communities and markets in interaction', *Scandinavian Journal of Management*, 30(3), 332–343.

Ervin, J. and Z. A. Smith (2008) *Globalization: A Reference Handbook* (Santa Barbara, CA: ABC-CLIO).

Feng, Y. (2011) 'Challenges and strategies in the stage of post-massification higher education in China: an analysis of stratification mobility rates in Yunnan and Guangdong provinces', in Y. Cai and J. Kivistö (eds) *Higher Education Reforms in Finland and China: Experiences and Challenges in Post-Massification era* (pp. 71–89) (Tampere: Tampere University Press).

Frølich, N., Stensaker, B., Scordato, L. and P. Botas (2014) 'The strategically manageable university: Perceptions of strategic choice and strategic change among key decision makers', *Higher Education Studies*, 4(5), 80.

Gibbons, M., Nowotny, H., Schwartzman, S., Scott, P. and M. Trow (1994) *The New Production of Knowledge: The Dynamics of Science and Research in Contemporary Societies* (Thousand Oaks, CA: Sage).

Gornitzka, Å., Kogan, M. and A. Amaral (2005) *Reform and Change in Higher Education: Analysing Policy Implementation* (Dordrecht: Springer).

Gornitzka, Å. and P. Maassen (2011) 'University governance reforms, global scripts and the "Nordic Model"'. Accounting for policy change?' in J. Schmid, K. Amos and A. T. J. Schrader (eds) *Welten der Bildung? Vergleichende Analysen von Bildungspolitik und Bildungssystemen* (pp. 149–177) (Baden-Baden: Nomos Verlagsgesellschaft).

Gornitzka, Å., Stensaker, B., Smeby, J.-C. and H. De Boer (2004) 'Contract arrangements in the Nordic countries: solving the efficiency-effectiveness dilemma?' *Higher Education in Europe*, 29(1), 87–101.

Hazelkorn, H. (2009) 'Rankings and the battle for world-class excellence: Institutional strategies and policy choice', *Higher Education Management and Policy*, 21(1), 1–22.

HESA (2014) *HESA Presentation to the Portfolio Committee on Higher Education and Training* (Cape Town: HESA).

Krücken, G. (2003) 'Learning the "New, New Thing": On the role of path dependency in university structures', *Higher Education*, 46(3), 315–339.

Kwiek, M. (2012) 'Changing higher education policies: From the deinstitutionalization to the reinstitutionalization of the research mission in Polish universities', *Science and Public Policy*, 39(5), 641–654.

Kwiek, M. and P. Maassen (2012) *National Higher Education Reforms in a European Context: Comparative Reflections on Poland and Norway* (Berlin: Peter Lang).

Lechner, F. J. (2009) *Globalization: The Making of World Society* (Chicester: Wiley).

Lester, R. and M. Sotarauta (2007) *Innovation, Universities and the Competitiveness of Regions* (Helsinki: Tekes).

Ma, W. (2011) 'Post mass higher education: the role of public research universities in equity and access', in Y. Cai and J. Kivistö (eds) *Higher Education Reforms in Finland and China: Experiences and Challenges in Post-Massification Era* (pp. 55–70) (Tampere: Tampere University Press).

Maassen, P. (2014) 'A new social contract for higher education?' in G. Goastellec and F. Picard (eds) *Higher Education in Societies* (pp. 33–50) (Rotterdam: SensePublishers).

Maassen, P. and J. P. Olsen (2007) *University Dynamics and European Integration* (Dordrecht: Springer).

Marginson, S. (2004) 'Competition and Markets in Higher Education: A "glonacal" analysis', *Policy Futures in Education*, 2(2), 175–244.

Marginson, S. and G. Rhoades (2002) 'Beyond national states, markets, and systems of higher education: A glonacal agency heuristic', *Higher Education*, 43(3), 281–309.

Mouton, J. (2012) 'Measuring differentiation in research production at South African universities' Presentation prepared for *HESA (Higher Education South Africa) Conference* (4 April, Cape Town: HESA).

Neves, C. (2015) 'Demand and supply for higher education in Brazil', in S. Schwartzman, R. Pinheiro and P. Pillay (eds) *Higher Education in the BRICS Countries: Investigating the Pact between Higher Education and Society* (pp. 73–96) (Drodrecht: Springer).

Nowotny, H., Scott, P. and M. Gibbons (2002) *Re-Thinking Science: Knowledge and the Public in an Age of Uncertainty* (Cambridge: Polity Press).

NPC (2012). *National Development Plan: Vision 2030* (Pretoria: National Planning Commission).

OECD (2007) *Higher Education and Regions: Globally Competitive, Locally Engaged* (Paris: Organisation for Economic Co-operation and Development).

Pache, A.-C. and F. Santos (2013) 'Inside the hybrid organization: Selective coupling as a response to competing institutional logics', *Academy of Management Journal*, 56(4), 972–1001.

Perry, B. (2012) 'Excellence, relevance and the construction of regional science policy: Science frictions and fictions in the north west of England', in R. Pinheiro, P. Benneworth and G. A. Jones (eds) *Universities and Regional Development: A Critical Assessment of Tensions and Contradictions* (pp. 105–123) (London Milton Park & New York: Routledge).

Pinheiro, R. (2012) *In the Region, for the Region? A Comparative Study of the Institutionalisation of the Regional Mission of Universities* (Oslo: University of Oslo Press).

Pinheiro, R. (2015) 'The role of internal and external stakeholders', in S. Schwartzman, R. Pinheiro and P. Pillay (eds) *Higher Education in the BRICS Countries: Investigating the Pact between Higher Education and Society* (pp. 43–58) (Drodrecht: Springer).

Pinheiro, R. and S. Kyvik (2009) 'Norway: Separate but connected', in N. Garrod and B. Macfarlane (eds) *Challenging Boundaries: Managing the Integration of Post-Secondary Education* (pp. 47–58) (New York: Routledge).

Pinheiro, R. and Geschwind, L. (2014) 'Rising the summit or flatenning the agora? The Elitist Turn in science and higher education policy in Northern Europe', *ECPR Conference* (3–6 September, Glasgow: ECPR).

Pinheiro, R. and B. Stensaker (2014a) 'Designing the entrepreneurial university: The interpretation of a global idea', *Public Organization Review*, 14(4), 497–516.

Pinheiro, R. and B. Stensaker (2014b) 'Strategic actor-hood and internal transformation: The rise of the quadruple-helix university?' in J. Brankovik, M. Klemencik, P. Lazetic and P. Zgaga (eds) *Global Challenges, Local Responses in Higher Education: The Contemporary Issues in National and Comparative Perspective* (pp. 171–189) (Rotterdam: Sense Publishers).

Pinheiro, R., Charles, D. G. A. and Jones, G. A. (forthcoming) 'Special Iissue on multi-campus systems', *Tertiary Education & Management*.

Pinheiro, R., Geschwind, L. and T. Aarrevaara (2014) 'Nested tensions and interwoven dilemmas in higher education: The view from the Nordic countries', *Cambridge Journal of Regions, Economy and Society*, 7(2), 233–250.

Pinheiro, R., Geschwind, L. and T. Aarrevaara (in press) *Mergers in Higher Education: The Experiences from Northern Europe* (Dordrecht: Springer).

Porter, M. E. (1998) *Competitive Advantage: Creating and Sustaining Superior Performance* (New York: Free Press).

Ramirez, F., Byrkjeflot, H., and R. Pinheiro (forthcoming) 'Higher education and health organizational fields in the age of "world class" and "best practices"', in R. Pinheiro, L. Geschwind, F. Ramirez and K. Vrabæk (eds), *Towards a Comparative Institutionalism? Forms, Dynamics and Logics Across Health and Higher Education Fields* (Bingley Emerald).

Rooney, D., Hearn, G. and A. Ninan (2008) *Handbook on the Knowledge Economy* (Cheltenham: Edward Elgar).

Sahlin, K. and L. Wedlin (2008) 'Circulating ideas: Imitation, translation and editing', in R. Greenwood, K. Sahlin-Andersson and R. Suddaby (eds) *The Sage Handbook of Organizational Institutionalism* (pp. 218–242) (London: Sage).

Salerno, C. (2007) 'A service enterprise: The market vision', in P. Maassen and J. P. Olsen (eds) *University Dynamics and European Integration* (pp. 119–132) (Dordrecht: Springer).

Schmidtlein, F. and R. Berdahl (2005) 'Autonomy and accountability: Who controls academe?' in P. Altbach, R. Berdahl and P. Gumport (eds) *American Higher Education in the Twenty-First Century: Social, Political, and Economic Challenges* (pp. 71–90) (Baltimore: John Hopkins University Press).

Schwartzman, S., Pinheiro, R. and P. Pillay (2015) *Higher Education in the BRICS Countries: Investigating the Pact between Higher Education and Society* (Drodrecht: Springer).

Slaughter, S. and B. Cantwell (2012) 'Transatlantic moves to the market: The United States and the European Union', *Higher Education*, 63(5), 583–606.

Stensaker, B. and L. Harvey (2011) *Accountability in Higher Education: Global Perspectives on Trust and Power* (New york: Taylor & Francis).

Temple, P. (2011) *Universities in the Knowledge Economy: Higher Education Organisation and Global Change* (London and New York: Taylor & Francis).

Thornton, P. H., Ocasio, W. and M. Lounsbury (2012) *The Institutional Logics Perspective: A New Approach to Culture, Structure, and Process* (Oxford: Oxford University Press).

Trow, M. (1970) 'Reflections on the transition from mass to universal higher education', *Daedalus*, 99(1), 1–42.

Varga, A. (2009) *Universities, Knowledge Transfer and Regional Development: Geography, Entrepreneurship and Policy* (Northampton, MA: Edward Elgar Pub).

Vukasovic, M., Maassen, P., Nerland, M., Pinheiro, R., Stensaker, B. and A. Vabø (2012) *Effects of Higher Education Reforms: Change Dynamics* (Rotterdam: Sense Publishers).

Wangenge-Ouma, G. (2012) 'Tuition fees and the challenge of making higher education a popular commodity in South Africa', *Higher Education*, 64(6), 831–844.

Wangenge-Ouma, G. (2013) *Widening Participation in South Africa*. Retrieved November 11, 2014, from http://www.hefce.ac.uk/media/hefce/content/pubs/indirreports/2013/wpinternationalresearch/2013_WPeffectivenessSAfrica.pdf.

Wangenge-Ouma, G. (2014) 'Diaspora linkages and the challenge of strengthening the academic core in African universities', in M. Stiasny and T. Gore (eds) *Global Education: Knowledge-Based Economies for 21st Century Nations* (pp. 19–28) (Bangley: Emerald).

Wangenge-Ouma, G. and N. Cloete (2008) 'Financing higher education in South Africa: Public funding, non-government revenue and tuition fees', *South African Journal of Higher Education*, 22(4), 906–919.

Yang, P., Jing, M., Cai, Y., Lyytinen, A. and S. Hölttä (2015) 'Transformation of local universities and international experiences (In Chinese)', *Journal of National Academy of Education Administration*, 2015(2), 83–90.

Yang, R., Vidovich, L. and J. Currie (2007) ' "Dancing in a cage": Changing autonomy in Chinese higher education', *Higher Education*, 54(4), 575–592.

14
Research, Development and Innovation: International, National and Regional Perspectives

Fumi Kitagawa

Introduction

University research has undergone profound transformation over the past three decades. Some of the well-known theses and models about the transformation in the academic system and the changing nature of science – such as the 'Mode 2' of knowledge production (Gibbons et al., 1994; Nowotny, Scott and Gibbons, 2001) and the 'triple helix' (Etzkowitz and Leydesdorff, 1997) model of interactions between government, university and industry – present broad pictures of the transformation of academic and research organization. In addition, in many parts of the world, universities are acknowledged to be important contributors to economic growth and crucial elements of 'national innovation systems' (Edquist, 2005; Mowery and Sampat, 2005; Nelson and Rosenberg, 1993) via the different mechanisms of academic knowledge transfers and exchanges at local, national and international level.

There are three interrelated external and internal forces that have fundamentally changed the nature of the university and the differentiated use of publicly funded research. First, there is a growing role of business and industry in university life and research activities (Williams, 2003), which has transformed the nature of science-based research – the process that Slaughter and Leslie (1997) called 'academic capitalism' (Slaughter and Leslie, 1997). Second, national higher education policy and reforms are part of wider changes in the public services management ideology and mechanisms. Thus the 'new managerialism' or New Public Management (NPM) approach which has been introduced in many industrialized countries has transformed the contexts and framework conditions for universities and their research (see Deem, 1998; Deem, Hullyard and Reed, 2007; Hood, 2004; Meek and Davies, 2009). Third, combined with the reduced public resources available to universities, the concept of 'entrepreneurial university' (Clark, 1998) presents universities' strategic attempts to respond to reductions in public funding and to actively engage with industry and businesses (Shattock, 2005). The global spread of the concepts such as 'the entrepreneurial university', 'the enterprise university' (Marginson and Considine, 2000) and 'the triple helix' of government-industry-university relationships (Etzkowitz and Leydesdorff, 1997) seem to have triggered a shift in the function of the university and accordingly a 'new social contract in university-industry-government relations' (Leydesdorff and Meyer, 2010).

In the so called knowledge-based economy, the need to connect knowledge from universities to wealth creation and well-being of society has become an increasingly important policy agenda (Dill and van Vught, 2010). Broadly speaking, universities provide institutional structures to organize scientific enquiry (research) and to augment human capital (teaching). Universities are now being encouraged by various policy and funding instruments to actively engage in 'knowledge exchange' through multiple channels with wider engagement with knowledge users (Hughes, 2011). In conjunction with traditional Science and Technology (S&T) policies, governmental concerns on how best to support innovation in order to maintain and enhance global economic competitiveness, university research has been primarily seen as a driver of economic growth (Geiger and Sa, 2008). Consequently, university–industry collaboration, the commercialization of research results and the protection and exploitation of intellectual property emanating from universities have become major policy and research drivers towards the promotion of innovation and economic development (e.g. Geuna, 1999; Mowery and Sampat, 2005; Bercovitz and Feldman, 2006).

This chapter critically examines changing nature and roles of university research and the governance issues of universities' interactions with different knowledge users within both national and regional 'innovation systems'. It highlights the tensions surrounding the recent evolution of national science and higher education policies. On the one hand, many countries are trying to make the university a place of *research excellence* and *world-class* status (Hazelkorn, 2011) and trying to raise national scientific reputation and advance national economic competitiveness agenda. There is also a new expectation for universities to meet the needs of their region and relevance to a variety of local conditions (Lester, 2005). University research can be important ingredients for local/regional development policy, aiming to enhance the *relevance* of the university through local/regional engagement (see Pinheiro, Geschwind and Aarrevaara, 2014).

The chapter is structured in the following way. Following this introduction, the second section discusses policy dynamics and rationales for public support of science from the national innovation system perspectives. The third section analyses knowledge flows and exchange between academic research and various users from the higher education policy and governance perspective. The fourth section discusses the research, development and innovation from a perspective of regional and local institutional environments, as well as pointing out the rapidly developing internationalization of university–industry relations for research collaboration and mobility. This raises further issues concerning governance structures and management processes of knowledge and innovation. The chapter concludes by summarizing key issues with future research and policy agendas.

Universities in national systems of research and innovation

Hicks (2012, p. 251) points out the 'dual identity' of university research, which is important in light of national policy and governance of higher education.

> On the one hand, university research is part of the larger enterprise of the university and is shaped by university governance and university related policy making. On the other hand, university research is a substantial element of every national innovation system, and so is of concern to scholars of innovation and to governments seeking to enhance the innovativeness of their economies.

At the national level, recognized 'variance' (Nedeva, 2013, p. 222) exists in terms of division of labour between universities and other research organizations (see Martin, 2003), national career structures and individual career paths. These are grounded in national resources for science, innovation and the rules for their exchange between public and private organizations as national or federal governments have funding instruments and incentive mechanisms that shape characteristics of national research and innovation systems of which higher education is part.[1]

As Salter and Martin (2001) point out, in general, publicly funded basic research includes much of the basic research conducted in universities, government research institutes and hospitals, whereas applied research tends to have stronger links with private sponsors from industry. However, there is no straightforward relationship between basic and applied research and public and private sponsors (see Cohen, Nelson and Walsh, 2002). For example, increasingly, publicly funded research includes both university and industry researchers working collaboratively. There are other different types of research activities and associated forms of funding mechanisms reflecting the nature of diversifying forms of knowledge creation and uses of research such as 'basic frontier', 'strategic basic', 'experimental and applied' and 'societal grand challenge' research. Across various OECD countries, different nations have had various research-funding patterns (see OECD, 2014) as part of their national innovation systems, combined with various funding instruments targeting different types of activities (e.g. 'competitive grant-based' projects, 'thematic programmes', 'institutional mission-based' and 'institutional block research' funding).

In recent years, governments in Europe, Australia, New Zealand and many other parts of the world have developed the 'performance-based research funding systems' (PRFSs) trying to develop evaluation methods to assess and rank universities' research performance (Hicks, 2012; see also Geuna and Martin, 2003; Jongbloed and Vossensteyn, 2001, for international overviews). For example, in the United Kingdom, where the funding framework is based on a 'dual support system' (Hughes et al., 2013), the Higher Education Funding Councils allocate institutional block grant funding based on the Research Assessment Exercise (RAE) which has been recently renamed as the Research Excellence Framework (REF) while specific research projects and programmes are funded primarily by the research councils based on the peer reviews of research proposals (see McNay, 1999; Henkel, 1999; Lucas, 2009; Smith, Ward and House, 2011 for the influence of the RAE and REF at individuals, research group and university levels).

The research-funding environments are getting more competitive in general, with a varying degree of 'state steering model' (Gornitzka and Massen, 2000) adopted in each national context. As a consequence, funding and evaluation agencies at various levels are seen as important actors as they contribute to 'constructing, reproducing and changing the institutional order of academic research' (Benner and Sandstrom, 2000, p. 293). For the university system, the 'criteria for resource allocation' both to universities and particular research groups, and 'public regulation of the performance of research' (Benner and Sandstrom, 2000) condition the forms of research and innovation. There are competitive research-funding mechanisms at different levels including researchers, projects, programmes, departments and institutions. For example, Australia, Canada, Finland, Germany, Japan and the Netherlands have adopted a competitive approach to strengthening research doctoral training, either through 'competitive national fellowships' to support PhD students or through 'competitive grants' for the development of selected graduate or research schools, or both (Dill and van Vught, 2010). International comparative studies suggest that the relationship between the competitiveness of research funding and research performance is a complex one affected by a number of factors (e.g. Himanen et al., 2009).

Since the 1980s, many governments have utilized the higher education sector for further national economic growth through building 'centers of research excellence and relevance' (Rip, 2004; OECD, 2014).[2] In different national policy contexts, research centres as 'policy tools' (Rogers, Youtie and Kay, 2012) have been adopted and developed differently (see Sa and Oleksiyenko). In recent years, a growing number of governments use the concept of 'centre of excellence' (Hellstrom, 2011) as a policy tool to create 'world-class' universities by concentrating research resources to a fewer number of institutions and/or research centres (see OECD, 2014). The extent to which these initiatives to create 'world-class universities' are successful has to be measured against the specific objectives of each initiative and taking into consideration the strategic direction of the 'ecosystems' of higher education, research and innovation in each national context (see Wigren-Kristoferson, Gabrielsson and Kitagawa, 2011). Concentration of resources and talents has to be matched with national and institutional leadership and the regulatory frameworks such as governance structures and management processes at both national and institutional levels (Salmi, 2011). It is also argued that international research networks and scientific mobility of researchers may provide a prerequisite to build capacity and 'world-class excellence' for both developed and emerging economies (Jacob and Meek, 2013).

Governance and strategies of knowledge exchange between university and businesses

Knowledge produced in the universities is disseminated and exchanged through a variety of channels. There are several commercial channels, for example, through licensing patents, consulting, or forming spin-off companies, which are broadly known as 'academic entrepreneurship' (Henderson, Jaffe and Trajtenberg, 1998; Rothaermel, Agung and Jiang, 2007). The Bayh–Dole Act of 1980 in the United States is often considered as a 'landmark' in patenting legislation. This law granted permission for federally funded researchers to file for patents and to issue licenses for these patents to other parties (Leydesdorff and Meyer, 2010). Following the Bayh–Dole Act in the United States, similar legislative reforms have been introduced in many countries concerning universities' use of intellectual property (IP) (Mowery and Sampat, 2005). By the end of the 1990s, several OECD countries had in place either new legislation or were employing existing law to pursue objectives that were at least similar in spirit to the Bayh–Dole Act (OECD, 2003). In addition to the legal framework, technology transfer offices (TTOs) have become the mechanism of choice for facilitating the widespread transfer of academic research results into practice in developed and developing countries. However, authors have pointed out that the cost of running TTOs may outweigh the returns to the university. A number of studies in the United States and elsewhere have begun to debate the suitability and sustainability of the new system against the old informal system (Harrison and Leitch, 2010; Leydesdorff and Meyer, 2010; Walsh et al., 2008).

It has been acknowledged that economic return from patent application and university spin-off companies is small and rather skewed, and that the probability that any given university will derive 'significant financial benefits' from its technology transfer activities (spin-offs, patents and licensing) is fairly low (Harrison and Leitch, 2010; Mowery and Sampat, 2005). D'Este and Patel (2007) argue that undue policy and research interest has been placed on the commercialization of research results, and the protection of IP emanating from universities, neglecting other types of entrepreneurial and engagement activities which can be less visible, but equally or even more important. Most published studies focus on university technology transfer and IP activity, perhaps because of the availability of data compiled by the Association of University Technology Managers (AUTM) in the United States and Canada, and similar organizations elsewhere (Rossi and Rosli, 2014). A too much focus on IP protection may even hinder collaborative arrangements by imposing additional transaction costs on firms (Nelson, 2001) and may come at the expense of other, more valuable, types of engagement and may hinder 'open-ended' collaboration with risky nature. A concern has been also raised that emphasizing technology transfer may undermine scientific norms of autonomy (Etzkowitz, 1998; Merton, 1942).

Recent works have pointed to the much wider channels of communication between academia and industry (Howells, Ramlogan and Cheng, 2012; Perkmann and Walsh, 2007). There are 'relationship-based' activities between university and industry (Perkmann and Walsh, 2007), also known as 'academic engagement' activities (Perkmann et al., 2013); for example, collaborative research, commissioned research, consultancy, equipment sharing, advisory roles, joint supervision, joint publication and student placements. Other scholars have demonstrated that transfer mainly occurs through other means; for instance, through softer or open channels such as publications and consultancy activities (Cohen, Nelson and Walsh, 2002; Perkmann and Walsh, 2007), student placements and generally the production of graduates. Close relationship fostered by staff and student mobility between academic and industrial contexts (Perkmann and Walsh, 2007) is believed to reduce the 'inherently high levels of uncertainty in knowledge transfer' (Gertner, Roberts and Charles, 2011) between university and industry.

Overtime, in parallel with a recognition that flows of knowledge are inherently two-way processes, the term 'knowledge exchange' (KE) has become used in preference to 'knowledge transfer' (KT) (Abreu et al., 2009). The growing economic and social importance attributed to universities' engagement in KT/KE activities has led to policy instruments for incentivizing, monitoring and evaluating universities' KT/KE performances. In the United Kingdom, for example, higher education funding councils have been attempting to further diversify the funding base of universities by offering competitive 'third-stream' funding to promote greater KT/KE activities between universities, and industry and communities (Molas-Gallart and Castro-Martinnez, 2007). Consequently, universities are placing a higher priority on being relevant and responsive to national, regional and local needs, and these efforts have resulted in a progressive 'institutionalisation' of such knowledge exchange activities. Some universities have always been more tightly integrated as part of their locality throughout their history, encompassing a broad range of activities; interacting with local schools, firms, local authorities and communities; and providing consultancy and Continuing Professional Development (CPD) training provisions to local industry. Other universities, often the more traditional and prestigious institutions, tend to emphasize their national and international orientations of research, teaching and other scholarly activities, rather than local and regional connections. Nevertheless, recent years have witnessed that even those less locally oriented institutions are increasingly looking to their regions and localities for support, and they also claim 'credit' for adding to the area's economic and social strength (Charles, Kitagawa and Uyarra, 2014).

The choice of indicators for knowledge exchange and innovation processes carries important implications for universities (Leydesdorff and Meyer, 2010; Molas-Gallart and Castro-Martinnez, 2007; Rossi and Rosli, 2014). The development of indicators may influence institutional behaviours in an unintended way and negatively affect research impact and innovation capabilities. Indicators related to technology transfer and commercialization activities (such as patenting, licensing and sale of IP and the formation of university spin-off companies) are relatively well captured, but these represent only a limited range of activities. For example, if the choice of indicators rewards universities that transfer knowledge through the sale of patents and licences, this would incentivize universities to apply for more patents even when this is not beneficial or desirable. The impact of publicly funded programmes on KE/KT and innovation has been mainly measured on a narrow set of indicators, neglecting other outputs (e.g. joint workshops and meetings) and 'open' interactions – those informal and tacit in nature, which show significance in terms of influencing firms' innovation outcomes (Howells, Ramlogan and Cheng, 2012). The value of KT/KE activities cannot easily be captured in economic terms (Rossi and Rosli, 2014), while there are varieties of objectives and outcomes, going beyond commercialization.

Multi-level governance of research, innovation and higher education policies

The role that higher education institutions (HEIs) play in the regional and national innovation systems is conditioned by knowledge infrastructure, industry environments and knowledge transfer systems, as well as policies at transnational, national and local levels and strategies adopted by individual institutions, such as firms, innovation support organizations, universities and research laboratories (see also Chapter 5 by Fumasoli). While varying degrees of powers and responsibilities related to science and innovation policy are devolved to regional governments, national and transnational governments still tend to retain significant influence, especially with regard to the social shaping of the 'national science base' (Pavitt, 1998).

National research and innovation policies may induce 'one size fits all' form of S&T policy and technology transfer, providing incentives for basic research on one hand, and promoting tangible commercial outcomes from research on the other. Studies in the United Kingdom and United States, where performance-based competitive research policies are well developed, show that basic research has tended to be concentrated in research-intensive institutions (Dill and van Vught, 2010; Hughes et al., 2013). Furthermore, leading research universities seem to benefit from economic impact from commercialization of publicly funded research. While some 'world-class' universities may produce technology artefacts that are transferable globally, for most universities effective knowledge transfer is a more 'local process, contingent upon the nature of industrial development in the regional economy' (Dill, 2014). This would have implications for local and regional economic development policies, especially in consideration of policy support for the roles of universities to meet the specific local and societal needs, particularly, in less favoured regions (Harrison and Leitch, 2010; Lester, 2005).

In terms of a national and local/regional economic development agenda, recently the convergence between science and technology (S&T) and higher education policies, and innovation and industrial policies has occurred in many industrialized countries, especially at the local/regional level, for example, through cluster policies that promote the links between university research and local industry. National and regional debates on the role of regional science, and the role of universities and other higher education institutions, are intrinsically linked to wider issues over governance, which constitute a multi-level governance structure of science and innovation policy (Perry and May, 2007; Sanz-Menendz and Cruz-Castro, 2005). In some countries, higher education is funded nationally, while in others it is funded by, or through, regional governments. Countries such as the United States, Canada, Australia, Brazil, Germany, Spain, among many others, have a federal system of government. In more centralized countries such as Japan, South Korea and England, for instance, the regional role of universities is mostly promoted by the national government. As Dill and van Vught (2010) argue, while the identification, support and dissemination of regionally relevant university research remain an appropriate and necessary role for sub-national governments, an increasingly important policy role for national governments is to coordinate an R&D agenda to provide public goods at the national level, as well as to develop the capacity of the sub-national governments to perform their role effectively while avoiding wasteful duplications.

University research can be important ingredients for local/regional development policy aiming to enhance the *relevance* of the university through local/regional engagement (see Pinheiro, Geschwind and Aarrevaara, 2014). The contribution of HEIs to regional development has been emphasized by both international and national policy communities (OECD, 2007). The important role that universities play for their regions in mobilizing research and innovation efforts has been emphasized in policy documents published by the European Commission (e.g. CEC, 2003; EC, 2011). In European literature, academic concepts such as regional and local entrepreneurship and innovation systems (see Cooke, Uranga and Etxebarria, 1997) have stood out over the last decades (e.g. Klofsten and Jones-Evans, 2000; Kitagawa, 2005; Lawton Smith et al., 2014). The scope of policy expectation and academic studies has gradually broadened, too, in recognizing the broad and interactive nature of innovation, and there is also an increased understanding about the different roles that universities can play as well as the different relationships that universities establish with other actors (Uyarra, 2010).

Universities also play a crucial role by providing a 'public space' in which, through meetings, research conferences, and industrial liaison programmes, local business practitioners can discuss the future direction of technologies, markets and regional industrial development (Lester, 2005). As studies in the United States point out, individual universities have developed various relationships and networks with their own locality, constituting regional innovation systems and sometimes acting as 'knowledge hubs' (Youtie and Shapira, 2008). They may fulfil a useful role in blurring the line between these different levels by 'regionalizing' world-class and small high-tech firm relationships and by making knowledge available to actors whose innovative locus is much more regional in character. In other words, universities as knowledge infrastructures affect the knowledge flows between themselves and connect other institutions and actors to different geographical scales (Huggins, Johnston and Stride, 2012). Etzkowitz (2002) argues 'the triple helix' interaction between university–industry–government includes a move towards a new global model for the management of knowledge and technology where an internationalization strategy emerges within domestic policy structures and perceived market constraints to meet challenges as well as opportunities within the globalized knowledge economies. Universities also act as local 'anchor institutions' embedded in their local cities and regions to a varying degree, and as such, some institutions may face more 'vulnerabilities' than others at the time of economic turbulence (Goddard et al., 2014).

Recent work has also begun to question the high level of policy expectations of the roles played by universities, which can be seen as 'overstated ingredients' (Lawton Smith, 2007) in territorial development. This is associated with little understanding of the actual processes of knowledge flows, the extent to which regional economic development can be actually achieved through the utilization of university knowledge, and the appropriateness of the support mechanisms and policies at national, sub-national and institutional levels (Harrison and Leitch, 2010; Laursen, Reichtein and Salter, 2011; Power and Malmberg, 2008).

Concluding and reflective remarks

Higher education policy and governance relates to research, development and innovation, encompassing different governments from international, national to sub-national levels, accompanied by specific sets of institutional missions, implementation strategies and practices. Thus definitions of higher education policy, governance and management depend on the level of analysis – national, local, institutional, sub-unit or discipline levels (Meek and Davies, 2009). The international trends of research policy have been enhancing *research excellence* by concentrating public resources to a small number of institutions. However, over the longer term, the 'one size fit all' national policy approach to research excellence may negatively affect innovation capacity of the nations and regions (Dill and van Vught, 2010; Lester, 2005; Sánchez-Barrioluengo, 2014). On the one hand, with fewer public resources available for higher education, many universities increasingly find the need to access additional funding sources. On the other hand, for over a decade now, governments at different levels have increasingly promoted the collaboration between universities and external actors through a range of initiatives and infrastructure, aiming to meet diverse local needs, societal benefits and *relevance*.

It is against such broad international policy contexts and tensions between *excellence* and *relevance*, and within complex sets of missions, functions, activities and relationships that universities in many parts of the world are encouraged to move beyond the 'ivory tower' to reach out to the industry, business and community to develop new synergy between research, development and innovation. The need to connect knowledge from universities to the process of wealth creation and well-being of society has been considered as an increasingly important policy agenda in many parts of the world. This chapter focused on a 'variance' of national policy, funding and governance of higher education as part of the 'national innovation systems', drawing on literature on higher education policy, S&T policy studies and innovation studies. Attention has been drawn to the diversity and dynamics of higher education systems and institutional governance mechanisms across countries as well as institutional diversity within each of the national systems.

In a current policy framework, universities have been pushed towards internal change to meet environmental demand through a variety of institutional governance mechanisms, which include an increased internal peer control (Clark, 1998; Dill, 2014; Hood, 2004). Within the national higher education system, different 'types' of universities have historically different functions, resources, networks and spatial aspirations within diversifying national higher education and innovation systems (see Teichler, 1988; Laredo, 2007). This is influenced by a number of factors such as their history, the national system of higher education, culture, geographical location, resource base, status, leadership, stakeholders and ambitions (see Feldman and Desrochers, 2003; Vorley and Nells, 2008). This leads to weakening of centralized 'one-size-fits-all' model of higher education policy and university management (see Chapter 15 for further discussion of institutional strategies on research and innovation).

Recent conceptual developments of 'academic engagement' (Perkmann et al., 2013), 'valorisation' (Jongbloed and Zomer, 2011) as well as policy discussion on the economic and societal 'impact' of academic research (Smith, Ward and House, 2011) have also enhanced the understanding of a number of institutional, organizational and individual factors influencing forms of university–industry relationships and outputs. There are recognized barriers to effective collaboration between university and industry, including the 'different institutional norms between universities and firms' (Bruneel, D'Este and Salter, 2010). Therefore, different types of policy instruments and incentive mechanisms that connect the two sides of communities have been promoted by many of the industrialized governments with an expectation that such interactions will lead to economic development (Geuna and Muscio, 2009). Studies note the significance of 'inter-organisational collaborations' with 'person to person interactions' (e.g. student placements) (Perkmann et al., 2013), as well as informal and tacit interactions that influence innovation activities in industry (Howells, Ramlogan and Cheng, 2012).

A question remains how to design higher education funding, incentives and innovation support mechanisms, where a variety of actors for research, development and innovation coexist. Understanding the role of the university's organizational factors and that of multiple micro-level units (e.g. university departments, research groups) as well as individuals in multi-level innovation processes is deemed to be important. This chapter concludes by suggesting a few additional areas for future investigation.

First, further investigation would be required to better understand the institutional conditions for a particular balance between national research excellence and local relevance, set within a multi-level innovation system. For example, challenges for universities are found when they work with local small and medium enterprises (SMEs) where open innovative interactions may happen with customer, end-users and suppliers rather than through formal R&D contexts (Von Hippel, 2009). Appropriate roles played by the national and sub-national governments need to be identified, enabling diverse higher education and innovation ecosystems where different types of institutions with different strengths coexist in a complementary way.

Second, questions remain regarding the educational role of the university, as well as the effects of education on research, innovation and knowledge exchanges (Healey et al., 2014). Somewhat understudied areas in higher education policy and innovation processes are found in relation to the transition of research skills and training within the university system, demands of scientific and innovation skills and competences within the broader R&D systems. Such knowledge would provide an important insight for policy and institutional practices as well as guide individuals to select and build new 'competencies in a scientific career' (Rip, 2004, p. 157) in a specific system of 'competence building and innovation' (Lam and Lundvall, 2006).

Third, there is a needed research on policies and practices regarding university research and innovation performance indicators, benchmarking mechanisms and ranking systems (see e.g. Montesinos et al., 2008). There is inherent challenge in identifying appropriate indicators and measuring the contribution of universities in innovation processes (Molas-Gallart and Castro-Martinnez, 2007). Knowledge flows and relationships between universities and different knowledge users, including different types of businesses, public and third sectors, need to be acknowledged, captured and developed.

Notes

1. In France, there is a division of labour between advanced teaching delivered by the universities and *grandes écoles* and an academic research enterprise largely based around 'national research institutions', most notably through the various institutes of the Centre National de la Recherche Scientifique (CNRS). Other European nations have a broadly similar research and higher education system where traditionally largely teaching-focused universities and essentially basic research-oriented major national academic research institutions coexist (e.g. Consejo Superior de Investigaciones Científicas (CSIC) in Spain and Consiglio Nazionale delle Ricerche (CNR) in Italy). Other national systems developed complex research institutes and networks, which connect through basic research to applied research. In the early to mid-20th century, Germany established a large and complex national research system with a wide range of non-university public research institutes (PRIs), both in applied or mission-oriented research and in basic research, including the Max Planck Institutes with an orientation towards basic research, the Fraunhofer institutes, oriented towards more applied research, and other networks of research institutes and facilities. In East Asia, there is a national variation – in many countries, in addition to the university sector, a strong role has been played by PRIs or government research institutes (GRIs). These PRIs or other forms of public agencies seem to work as 'intermediary organizations' linking research and industry, sometimes between universities and local industry. For example, a variety of public research institutes (PRIs) in Taiwan, Singapore, South Korea and Japan have historically played important roles in promoting research, development and innovation.

2. In Germany, for example, the federal and state governments initiated the 'Excellence Initiative' in 2005, which aims to strengthen Germany's cutting-edge research activities by concentrating resources to certain institutions. National governments in East Asia have also launched programmes to invest in higher education to create 'world-class' universities. In Japan, the government started the academically oriented Centre of Excellence (COE) programmes in 2002 as part of higher education structural reform, trying to attract foreign students and building research centres of excellence at the global level (Kitagawa and Oba, 2010). In South Korea, the national government initiated programmes in the late 1990s to create research excellence centres through the Brain Korea 21 project (see Lee, 2000). In China, the government provided funding to create prestigious universities (e.g. Project 985, 211). The nine universities that received the most supplemental government funding (Project 985) to enhance their global competitiveness recently self-identified as the C9 – China's Ivy League (Levin, 2010). This parallels the rapid growth in number of institutions and enrolment of students at Chinese universities since 1998.

References

Abreu, M., Grinevich, V., Hughes, A. and M. Kitson (2009) *Knowledge Exchange between Academics and the Business, Public and Third Sectors* (UK Innovation Research Centre: University of Cambridge and Imperial College London).

Benner, M. and U. Sandstrom (2000) 'Institutionalization of triple helix: research funding and norms in academic system', *Research Policy*, 29(2), 291–301.

Bercovitz, J. and M. P. Feldman (2006) 'Entrepreneurial universities and technology transfer: a conceptual framework for understanding knowledge-based economic development', *Journal of Technology Transfer*, 31(1), 175–188.

Bruneel, J., D'Este, P. and A. Salter (2010) 'Investigating the factors that diminish the barriers to university-industry collaboration', *Research Policy*, 39(7), 858–868.

Charles, D., Kitagawa, F. and E. Uyarra (2014) 'Universities in crisis?: new challenges and strategies in two english city-regions', *Cambridge Journal of Regions, Economy and Society*, 7(2), 327–348.

Clark, B. R. (1998) *Creating the Entrepreneurial University* (Oxford: IAU Press/Pergammon).

Cohen, W. M., Nelson, R. and J. Walsh (2002) 'Links and impacts: the influence of public research on industrial R & D', *Management Science*, 48(1), 1–23.

Commission of the European Communities (CEC) (2003) *The Role of the Universities in the Europe of Knowledge*, COM (2003) 58 final (Brussels: CEC).

Cooke, P., Uranga, M. and G. Etxebarria (1997) 'Regional innovation systems: Institutional and organisational dimensions', *Research Policy*, 26(4–5).

Deem, R. (1998) 'New managerialism in higher education – the management of performances and cultures in universities', *International Studies in the Sociology of Education*, 8(1), 47–70.

Deem, R., Hullyard, S. and Reed, M. (2007) *Knowledge, Higher Education and the New Managerialism: The Changing Management of UK Universities* (Oxford: Oxford University Press).

D'Este, P. and Patel, P. (2007) University – industry linkages in the UK: What are the factors underlying the variety of interactions with industry? Research Policy 36: 1295–1313.

Dill, D. (2014) 'Public policy design and university reform: insights into academic change', in C. Musselin and P. N. Teixeira (eds) *Reforming Higher Education: Public Policy Design and Implementation* (pp. 21–37) (Dordrecht, The Netherlands: Springer).

Dill, D. and F. van Vught (2010) *National Innovation and the Academic Research Enterprise: Public Policy in Global Perspective* (Baltimore: Johns Hopkins University Press).

Edquist, C (2005) 'Systems of innovation: perspectives and challenges', in J. Fagerberg, D. Mowery and R. R. Nelson (eds) *The Oxford Handbook of Innovation* (pp. 181–208) (Oxford: Oxford University Press).

Etzkowitz, H. (2002) *MIT and the Rise of Entrepreneurial Science*. (London and New York: Routledge).

Etzkowitz, H. (1998) 'The norms of entrepreneurial science: cognitive effects of the new university–industry linkages', *Research Policy*, 27(8), 823–833.

Etzkowitz, H. and L. Leydesdorff (eds) (1997) *Universities and the Global Knowledge Economy: A Triple Helix of University-Industry-Government Relations* (London: Pinter).

European Commission (EC) (2011) *Connecting Universities to Regional Growth* (CEC, Brussels: European Commission).

Feldman, M. and P. Desrochers (2003) 'Research universities and local economic development: lessons from the history of the Johns Hopkins university', *Industry & Innovation*, 10(1), 5–24.

Geiger, R. L. and C. M. Sá (2008) *Tapping the Riches of Science: Universities and the Promise of Economic Growth* (Cambridge, MA: Harvard University Press).

Gertner, D., Roberts, J. and D. Charles (2011) 'University-industry collaboration: a CoP approach to KTP', *Journal of Knowledge Management*, 15(4), 625–647.

Geuna, A (1999) *The Economics of knowledge production: Funding and the structure of university research*. (Cheltenham: Edward Elgar).

Geuna, A. and B. Martin (2003) 'University research evaluation and funding: an international comparison', *Minerva*, 41(4), 277–304.

Geuna, A. and A. Muscio (2009) 'The governance of university knowledge transfer: a critical review of the literature', *Minerva*, 47(1), 93–114.

Gibbons, M., Limoges, C., Nowotny, H., Schwartzman, S., Scott, P. and M. Trow (1994) *The New Production of Knowledge: The Dynamics of Science and Research in Contemporary Societies* (London: Sage).

Goddard, J., Coombes, M., Kempton, L. and P. Vallance (2014) 'Universities as anchor institutions in cities in a turbulent funding environment: vulnerable institutions and vulnerable places in England', *Cambridge Journal of Regions, Economy and Society*, 7(2), 307–325.

Gornitzka, A. and M. Massen (2000) 'Hybrid steering approaches with respect to European higher education', *Higher Educaiton Policy*, 13(3), 267–285.

Harrison, R. and C. Leitch (2010) 'Voodoo institution or entrepreneurial university? spin-off companies, the entrepreneurial system and regional development in the UK', *Regional Studies*, 44(9), 1241–1262.

Hazelkorn, E. (2011) *Rankings and the Reshaping of Higher Education: The Battle for World-Class Excellence* (London: Palgrave MacMillan).

Healy A., Perkman M., Goddard J. and L. Kempton (2014) HYPERLINK *"http://www.ncl.ac.uk/curds/publications/publication/210569" "view complete information on this publication" Measuring the Impact of University-Business Cooperation: Final Report*. Brussels: Directorate General for Education and Culture, European Commission.

Hellstrom, T. (2011) 'Homing in on excellence: dimensions of appraisal in Center of Excellence program evaluations', *Evaluation*, 17(2), 117–131.

Henderson, R., Jaffe, A. and M. Trajtenberg (1998) 'Universities as a source of commercial technology: a detailed analysis of university patenting, 1965–1988', *Review of Economics and Statistics*, 80(1), 119–127.

Henkel, M. (1999) 'The modernisation of research evaluation: the case of the UK', *Higher Education*, 38(1), 105–122.

Hicks, D. (2012) 'Performance based university research funding systems', *Research Policy*, 41(2), 251–261.

Himanen, L., Auranen, O., Puuska, H-M. and M. Mieminen (2009) 'Influence of research funding and science policy on university research performance: a comparison of five countries', *Science and Public Policy*, 36(6), 419–430.

Hood, C. (2004) 'Conclusion: making sense of controls over government', in C. Hood, O. James, B. G. Peters and C. Scott (eds) *Controlling Modern Government: Variety, Commonality, and Change* (pp. 185–205) (Cheltenham: Edward Elgar).

Howells, J., Ramlogan, R. and S-L. Cheng (2012) 'Innovation and university collaboration: paradox and complexity within the knowledge economy', *Cambridge Journal of Economics*, 36(3), 703–721.

Huggins, R., Johnston, A. and C. Stride (2012) 'Knowledge networks and universities: locational and organisational aspects of knowledge transfer interactions', *Entrepreneurship & Regional Development: An International Journal*, 24(7–8), 475–502.

Hughes, A. (2011) 'Open innovation, the Haldane principle and the new production of knowledge: science policy and university–industry links in the UK after the financial crisis', *Prometheus*, 29(4), 411–442.

Hughes, A., Kitson, M., Bullock, A. and I. Millner (2013) *The Dual Funding Structure for Research in the UK: Research Council and Funding Council Allocation Methods and the Pathways to Impact of UK Academics*, A report from CBR/UK~IRC to BIS.

Jacob, M. and L. Meek (2013) 'Scientific mobility and international research networks: trends and policy tools for promoting research excellence and capacity building', *Studies in Higher Education*, 38(3), 331–344(14), Special issue: Research Universities: Networking the Knowledge Economy.

Jongbloed, B. and H. Vossensteyn (2001) 'Keeping up performances: an international survey of performance-based funding in higher education', *Journal of Higher Education Policy and Management*, 23(2), 127–145.

Jongbloed, B. and A. Zomer (2011) 'Valorisation, knowledge transfer and IP: creating value from academic knowledge', in P. Temple (ed) *Universities in the Knowledge Economy: Higher Education Organisation and Global Change* (pp. 82–102) (New York: Routledge).

Kitagawa, F. (2005) 'Entrepreneurial universities and the development of regional societies: a spatial view of the Europe of knowledge', *Higher Education Management and Policy*, 17(3), 65–90, Special Issue on *Entrepreneurship* Paris: OECD.

Kitagawa, F. and J. Oba (2010) 'Managing differentiation of higher education system in Japan: connecting excellence and diversity', *Higher Education*, 59(4), 507–24.

Klofsten, M. and D. Jones-Evans (2000) 'Comparing academic entrepreneurship in Europe – the case of Sweden and Ireland', *Small Business Economics*, 14(4), 299–309.

Lam, A. and B-A. Lundvall (2006) 'The learning organisation and national systems of competence building and innovation', in E. Lorenz and B. Lundvall (eds) *How European Economies Learn: Coordinating Competing Models* (pp. 109–139) (Oxford: Oxford University Press).

Laredo, P. (2007) 'Revisiting the third mission of universities: towards a renewed categorisation of university activities?' *Higher Education Policy*, 20(4), 441–456.

Laursen, K., Reichstein, T. and A. Salter (2011) 'Exploring the effect of geographical proximity and university quality on university–industry collaboration in the United Kingdom', *Regional Studies*, 45(4), 507–523.

Lawton Smith, H. (2007) 'Universities, innovation and territorial development: a review of the evidence', *Environment and Planning C: Government and Policy*, 25(1), 98–114.

Lawton Smith, H., Chapman, D., Wood, P., Barnes, T. and R. Saverio (2014) 'Entrepreneurial academics and regional innovation systems: the case of spin-offs from London's universities', *Environment and Planning C: Government and Policy*, 32(2), 341–359.

Lester, R. (2005) Universities, Innovation and the Competitiveness of Local Economies: A Summary Report from the Local Innovation Systems Project – Phase I. Retrieved December 23, 2014, from http://web.mit.edu/lis/papers/LIS05-010.pdf.

Lee, G. E-J. (2000) 'Brain Korea 21: a development-oriented national policy in Korean higher education', *International Higher Education*, 19(Spring).

Levin, R. (2010) The Rise of Asia's Universities, HEPI Lecturer 2010. Retrieved December 23, 2014, from http://www.hepi.ac.uk/wp-content/uploads/2014/03/1.Seventh-Annual-HEPI-Lecture-Richard-Levin.pdf.

Leydesdorff, L. and M. Meyer (2010) 'The decline of university patenting and the end of the Bayh-Dole effect', *Scientometric*, 83(2), 355–362.

Lucas, L. (2009) 'Research management and research cultures: power and productivity', in A. Brew and L. Lucas (eds) *Academic Research and Researchers* (pp. 66–79) (Maidenhead: SRHE/Open University Press).

Marginson, S. and M. Considine (2000) *The Enterprise University: Power, Governance and Re-invention in Australia* (Cambridge University Press).

Martin, B. (2003) 'The changing social contract for science and the evolution of the university', in A. Geuna, A. Salter and W. E. Steinmueller (eds) *Science and Innovation: Rethinking the Rationale for Funding and Governance* (pp. 7–29) (London, UK: Edward Elgar).

McNay, I (1999) 'The paradoxes of research assessment and funding', in M. Henkel and B. Little (eds) *Changing Relationships between Higher Education and the State* (pp. 191–203) (London: Jessica Kingsley Publishers).

Meek, L. and D. Davies (2009) 'Policy dynamics in higher education and research: concepts and observations', *Higher Education, Research and Innovation: Changing Dynamics*, Report on the UNESCO Forum on Higher Education, Research and Knowledge 2001–2009. Retrieved November 20, 2014, from http://unesdoc.unesco.org/images/0018/001830/183071E.pdf.

Merton, R. (1942) 'The normative structures of science', in R. K. Merton (ed) *The Sociology of Science: Theoretical and Empirical Investigations*, 1973 (pp. 267–78) (Chicago: University of Chicago Press).

Molas-Gallart, J. and E. Castro-Martinnez (2007) 'Ambiguity and conflict in the development of "Third Mission" indicators', *Research Evaluation*, 16(4), 321–330.

Montesinos, P., Carot, J. M., Martinez, J-M. and M. Francisco (2008) 'Third mission ranking for world class universities: beyond teaching and research', *Higher Education in Europe*, 33(2/3), 259–271.

Mowery, D. and B. N. Sampat (2005) 'Universities in national innovation systems', in J. Fagerberg, D. Mowery and R. R. Nelson (eds) *The Oxford Handbook of Innovation* (pp. 209–239) (Oxford: Oxford University Press).

Nedeva, M. (2013) 'Between the global and the national: organising European science', *Research Policy*, 42(1), 220–230.

Nelson, R. and N. Rosenberg (1993) 'Technical innovation and national systems', in R. Nelson (ed) *National Innovation Systems: A Comparative Analysis* (pp. 3–22) (New York: Oxford University Press).

Nelson, R. R. (2001) 'Observations on the post-Bayh-Dole rise of patenting at American universities', *The journal of Technology Transfer*, 26(1), 13–19.

Nowotny, H., Scott, P. and M. Gibbons (2001) *Re-Thinking Science: Knowledge and the Public in an Age of Uncertainty* (Cambridge: Polity).

Organisation for Economic Cooperation and Development (OECD) (2003) *Turning Science into Business: Patenting and Licensing at Public Research* (Paris: OECD).

Organisation for Economic Cooperation and Development (OECD) (2007) *Higher Education and Regions, Globally Competitive, Locally Engaged* (Paris: OECD).

Organisation for Economic Cooperation and Development (OECD) (2014) *Promoting Research Excellence: New Approaches to Funding* (Paris: OECD).

Pavitt, K. (1998) 'The Social Shaping of the National Science Base', *Research Policy*, 27(8): 793–805.

Perkmann, M., Tartari, V., McKelvey, M., Autio, E., Broström, A., D'Este, P., Fini, R., Geuna, A., Grimaldi, R., Hughes, A., Krabel, S., Kitson, M., Llerena, P., Lissoni, F., Salter, A. and M. Sobrero (2013) 'Academic engagement and commercialisation: a review of the literature on university–industry relations', *Research Policy*, 42(2), 423–442.

Perkmann, M. and K. Walsh (2007) 'University-industry relationships and open innovation: towards a research agenda', *International Journal of Management Reviews*, 9(4), 259–280.

Perry, B. and T. May (2007) 'Governance, science policy and regions: an introduction', *Regional Studies*, 41(8), 1039–1050.

Pinheiro, R., Geschwind, L. and T. Aarrevaara (2014) 'Nested tensions and interwoven dilemmas in higher education: the view from the Nordic countries', *Cambridge Journal of Regions, Economy and Society*, 7(2), 271–288.

Power, D. and A. Malmberg (2008) 'The contribution of universities to innovation and economic development: in what sense a regional problem?' *Cambridge Journal of Regions, Economy and Society*, 1(2), 233–245.

Rip, A. (2004) 'Strategic research, post-modern universities and research training', *Higher Education Policy*, 17(2), 153–166.

Rogers, J., Youtie, J. and L. Kay (2012) 'Program level assessment of research centers: contribution of Nano-Science and Engineering Centers (NSEC) to US Nanotechnology National Initiative (NNI) goals', *Research Evaluation*, 21(5), 368–380.

Rossi, F. and A. Rosli (2014) 'Indicators of university-industry knowledge transfer performance and their implications for universities: Evidence from the United Kingdom', *Studies in Higher Education*, ahead-of-print, 1–22.

Rothaermel, F. T., Agung, S. D. and L. Jiang (2007) 'University entrepreneurship: a taxonomy of the literature', *Industrial and Corporate Change*, 16(4), 691–791.

Sa, C. and A. Oleksiyenko (2010) 'Between the local and the global: organized research units and international collaborations in the health sciences', *Higher Education*, 62(3).

Salmi, J. (2011) 'Nine common errors in building a new world class university', *International Higher Education*, 62(Winter).

Salter, A. J. and B. R. Martin (2001) 'The economic benefits of publicly funded basic research: a critical review', *Research Policy*, 30(3), 509–532.

Sánchez-Barrioluengo, M. (2014) 'Articulating three missions in Spanish universities', *Research Policy*, 43(10), 1760–1773.

Sanz-Menendz, L. and L. Cruz-Castro (2005) 'Explaining the science and technology policies of regional governments', *Regional Studies*, 39(7), 939–954.

Shattock, M. (2005) 'European universities for entrepreneurship: their Role in the Europe of Knowledge – the theoretical context', *Higher Education Management and Policy*, 17(3), 13–25.

Slaughter, S. and R. Leslie (1997) *Academic Capitalism: Policies and the Entrepreneurial University* (Baltimore: Johns Hopkins University Press).

Smith, S. O., Ward, V. and A. House (2011) ' "Impact" in the proposals for the UK's research excellence framework: shifting the boundaries of academic autonomy', *Research Policy*, 40(10), 1369–1379.

Teichler, U. (1988) *Changing Patterns of the Higher Education System: The Experience of Three Decades* (London: Jessica Kingsley).

Uyarra, E. (2010) 'Conceptualizing the regional roles of universities, implications and contradictions', *European Planning Studies*, 18(8), 1227–1246.

Von Hippel, E. (2009) 'Democratising innovation: the evolving phenomenon of user innovation', *International Journal of Innovation Science*, 1(1), 29–40.

Vorley, T. and J. Nells (2008) '(Re)conceptualising the third mission: entrepreneurial architecture of higher education institutions', *Policy Futures in Education*, 7(3), 284–296.

Walsh, J. P., Baba, Y., Goto, A. and Y. Yasaki (2008) 'Promoting university-industry linkage in Japan', *Prometheus*, 26(1), 39–54.

Wigren-Kristoferson, C., Gabrielsson, J. and F. Kitagawa (2011) 'Mind the gap and bridge the gap: research excellence and diffusion of academic knowledge in Sweden', *Science and Public Policy*, 38(6), 481–492.

Williams, G. (2003) *The Enterprising University* (Maidenhead: Open University Press).

Youtie, J. and P. Shapira (2008) 'Building an innovation hub: a case study of the transformation of university roles in regional technological and economic development', *Research Policy*, 37(8), 1188–1204.

15

Institutional Governance, Leadership and Management of Research for Innovation and Development

Fabiana Barros de Barros, Leo Goedegebuure, V. Lynn Meek and Alan Pettigrew

Introduction

Higher education institutions undertake a significant portion of a country's research effort. Basic and applied research, the development of human capital, in particular through doctoral education, and knowledge transfer processes are key university contributions within national innovation policies and strategies. In particular, basic research, which over the long term provides the foundation for innovation, takes place predominantly in publicly funded universities and research laboratories. Also, these institutions have primary responsibility for public good research that often does not attract direct economic interest but nonetheless is fundamental to the health and well-being of society, such as many forms of public health research. Yet how policy-making affects academic research and how higher education institutions are responding and adapting to new national innovation policies and priorities remain complex, not well understood and at times contested issues. The social contract governing the effective steering of systems and their research-intensive institutions is challenged by new demands posed by broader rationales concerning global economic competitiveness, scientific mobility and national security in both developed and developing nations.

There probably has always been some degree of management of research, both within the university and the broader society. Examples come readily to mind, such as the control exercised by the 'god professor' in the 19th-century German university, or the control of Britain's Royal Society over the direction of scientific development dating back to the 15th century. But realistically it was not until after the Second World War that governments became concerned about the funding and development of science and research in a big way, with the landmark 1945 report to the US president by Vannevar Bush – *Science, the Endless Frontier* – which led to the establishment of the National Science Foundation in that country. Governments recognized the potential benefits of scientific research as evidenced by such efforts as the Manhattan Project during the Second World War, and for reasons both military and economic wished to bend scientific research to national purposes.

This chapter examines research management, development and innovation at the institutional level, drawing examples and arguments from a variety of countries and a range of authors interested in various aspects of research governance, leadership and management. It should be read in conjunction with Chapter 14 in this volume which focuses on research, development and innovation at the national/macro level.

The discussion is limited to those themes having the most direct relevance to how institutional governance and management practices impact the ways in which research contributes to innovation and development. The chapter first examines the competitive funding environment shaping leadership and management of research within institutions, including some examples of how these issues have been approached in different countries. The next section looks at approaches to strengthening research management capacity. Knowledge transfer and community engagement are discussed in the penultimate section. The conclusion suggests what appear to be important areas for future research.

Research management and the competitive funding environment

Increasingly, research universities are faced with a highly competitive funding environment (Meek and Davies, 2009). The way in which public funds are administered in higher education systems has particularly affected how universities perform and support their research activities. Many developed countries have moved from a funding system of relatively stable reliance on core-institutional funding to a situation where the bulk of funding is competitively allocated. As a consequence, research management has become an area of strategic focus for academic leaders, requiring of managers the ability to maximize existing resources and diversify the funding base while maintaining excellence and institutional cohesion.

University research management capacity is advancing, although at a different pace, around the world. The nations that are members of the Organisation for Economic Cooperation and Development (OECD) have been undergoing substantial change and development (Connell, 2004), and emerging economies are devising ways to catch up in terms of research productivity and relevance to national development (Cloete, Bailey and Maassen, 2011). Universities in the United States have led the way in developing more sophisticated research management capabilities, given their historical reliance on competitively allocated federal funds (Geiger, 1993). University research centres have developed as a major coping mechanism allowing universities to survive and thrive in the American system and internationally (Bushaway, 2003; Geiger, 1990).

The spread of policies based upon the national innovation system's perspective coupled with changes in funding models have significantly impacted academic research (Dill and van Vught, 2010; Henkel and Kogan, 2010). Policies aimed at steering and increasing competition in the academic research sector have facilitated the introduction of new funding instruments available to academic research (Orr, Jaeger and Wespel, 2011), influencing behaviour and strategies at the institutional level. Such policies are justified on the grounds of increasing academic research performance and optimizing the return on investment of public funds. Relevance is commonly associated with socio-economic priorities, specially contributing to technological innovation. Decreasing fragmentation at the national level by increasing the links between public research organizations and connecting research producers with research users (particularly firms) is another recurring theme impacting management at the institutional level. In terms of research performance, promoting research excellence is considered key to enhancing the international standing of national research capabilities, which in turn is a critical factor for participating in international scientific networks responsible for scientific breakthroughs. In this regard, policies aimed at promoting collaboration and excellence through partnerships are particularly favoured (Hellstrom, 2011).

Steering research through funding is generally implemented through a wide range of funding sources and thematic streams which adopt mechanisms such as performance-based institutional funding (Hicks, 2012) and competitive project-based funding, including the creation of Centres of Excellence (CoEs) and cooperative research centres driven by end-user needs. Programmes to create collaborative research centres or CoEs have been widely adopted in developed nations. Some of the main goals of CoE programmes are to tackle more complex research topics and problems by concentrating resources and facilitating the creation of a critical mass and by building synergies amongst key stakeholders during longer funding timelines (in comparison to traditional project-based funding). Some of the benefits derived from CoEs include the strengthening of system coordination and the exploitation of synergies by requiring inter-institutional and inter-sector collaboration, the creation of research groups with the required scale to tackle more significant research problems, the concentration of resources in order to attract high-quality staff nationally and internationally, increased participation in research networks at the cutting edge of science, the provision of comprehensive and rich research training environments for PhD students and early-career researchers and the provision of critical research support services by specialized management personnel.

Linking funding to performance has led to a greater concentration and selectivity in terms of research priorities and in the allocation of funds to fewer research performers, allegedly contributing to positive effects such as increased quality, greater impact by achieving a critical mass, reducing fragmentation and promoting greater accountability in the use of public funds (Hicks and Katz, 2011). However, negative side effects are also attributed to concentration and selectivity and include system stratification by reinforcing the dominance of top institutions (Beerkens, 2013a) at the expense of institutional diversity (van Vught, 2007); a focus on publication counts rather than quality (Butler, 2003); and adverse impacts on academic work and knowledge production through increased risk aversion and predictability of outcomes (Braun, 1998; Harley, 2002).

Related to concentration and selectivity in research funding is the desire by many governments to set national research priorities. This influences strategic directions in research at the institutional level, perhaps negatively in some instances. For example, Öquist and Benner (2012, p. 10), in their comparative research on why Swedish research with an international impact has fallen behind that of Denmark, the Netherlands and Switzerland, identify three primary factors: 'priority setting at the national level; direction and funding of research; and governance of universities'. The Swedish research system 'contains a substantial element of "sectoral research", where relevance often takes precedence over academic quality' (Öquist and Benner, 2012). Most research in Sweden is funded through external agencies setting the research priorities, whereas in Denmark, the Netherlands and Switzerland, the universities have more control over both funding and priority setting.

Öquist and Benner argue that Sweden's dependence on external research funding and priority setting has turned the country's universities into 'research hotels' where their own priorities are 'overshadowed and emphasis is laid on how to obtain funding rather than which research to select' (p. 11). This appears to have weakened academic research leadership within Swedish universities, whereas 'by contrast, the more successful universities in the reference countries emphasize academic leadership, whose principal function is to strengthen quality in education and research through recruitment', and emphasizing 'creating environments for ground-breaking research' (p. 12). This argument will be revisited in the conclusion to the chapter.

National examples

The following initiatives illustrate how different countries have implemented policies to promote scientific excellence, innovation and competitiveness, as well as build capacity to tackle national and global challenges.

The Nordic countries have been particularly active in promoting excellence initiatives as a way to cope with the socio-economic challenges posed by globalization. Recent comparative studies mapped excellence initiatives and investigated the effects of different instruments (Aksnes et al., 2012; Langfeldt et al., 2013). Some of the advantages of CoEs are that recruitment of academic staff is easier and less bureaucratic; they provide excellent opportunities for young researchers; and they provide opportunities for strategic initiatives and linkages within and among universities. One of the management challenges in CoEs is to maintain an appropriate balance between more fundamental research and commercialization of research results.

In Australia, where the majority of R&D is performed in the public sector, public investment outweighs private investment. Both the federal and state governments exert a great deal of influence on the academic sector through performance-based funding schemes and priority setting, leading to a significant level of selectivity and concentration of resources (Australian Government, 2011). In response to a particularly dynamic policy and funding environment, universities have come to devote increasing attention and resources to research management at the institutional and centre levels (Beerkens, 2013b; Meek, Goedegebuure and Van der Lee, 2010), though it should also be noted that over the last 15 years this has not changed the proportion of competitive grant funding received by individual institutions (Bentley, Goedegebuure and Pettigrew, 2014). Moreover, in Australia, the internal allocation of research funds provided to individual institutions as a block grant is generally based on the same factors and categories upon which it is received, rather than institutions being proactive in setting and supporting their own research priorities, an issue commented on in more detail below and in the conclusion (Meek and Hayden, 2005).

In Germany, the Excellence Initiative was introduced as a national reaction to the perception that some universities could be lagging behind in international rankings (which are primarily based on research metrics), a threat also perceived in many other European countries (Lambert and Butler, 2006). The Excellence Initiative is based on the rationale of fostering a diversified higher education system containing a limited number of 'world-class' research-intensive institutions (Kehm and Pasternack, 2008).

Canada was one of the first countries to introduce national programmes for the creation of CoEs in the mid-1980s. The iconic NCE programme (Networks of Centres of Excellence) served as an inspiration for other programmes worldwide focused on academic–industry partnerships and the commercialization of research results (Atkinson-Grosjean, 2006). As the programmes evolved and matured in pursuing a dual agenda of research excellence and economic relevance, specialized research management became a critical factor for reconciling expectations and the overall success of these networks (Fisher, Atkinson-Grosjean and House, 2001).

In all cases, the shift from direct state regulation to 'steering at a distance' has given greater autonomy and discretion to institutions to create internal capacities and mechanisms that allow them to cope and respond more dynamically to external opportunities. There is evidence to suggest, however, that institutions can go too far in strengthening their management capacity, stifling academic creativity and promoting alienation. Australia and the United Kingdom have probably gone further down the road of entrenching professional higher education management practices then is the case in many other countries. A recent comparative analysis of academic satisfaction among 25 countries demonstrated that the rift between academics and management was by far the greatest in Australian and British universities (Bentley et al., 2013).

Strengthening of research management capacity of universities

Universities respond to external demands and opportunities by developing institutional capacity in professional research management (Connell, 2004). It is a fact of life that research, as with any highly intellectual and creative activity, might be perceived as an activity unsuited to be 'managed' (Taylor, 2006). In practice, however, particularly in collaborative, inter-institutional projects, it becomes clear that the success of large-scale, complex research endeavours depends as much on research management as it does on research excellence (Schuetzenmeister, 2010). Research management is regarded as the element that 'makes or breaks the networks' in the words of a programme officer (Fisher et al., 2001, p. 317) and is increasingly associated with research productivity at universities (Beerkens, 2013b). There is no ideal way of organizing research management and each institutional approach will depend on context and vision (Rhoades, 2000). Nonetheless, research suggests that there are some underlying principles and approaches to research management that are more or less generic. A recent large-scale empirical study of research management and leadership, drawing on the experience of universities in both developed and developing countries, delineates in five thematic areas what appear to be the most essential management and leadership skills and characteristics (Olsson and Meek, 2013, pp. 12–14):

1. Leadership of research in institutions

   - *Institutional governance*, including developing a vision and a timeframe, designing feasible and achievable strategies, designing a performance framework for the institution and establishing a process for reviewing the plan over time. Other areas include the development of a critical mass of researchers, research infrastructure, delegation to senior members of the management team and risk management.
   - *Awareness of the research and innovation setting*, including analysing the external environment and the role of the institution; taking account of key matters such as global research trends, policy settings and funding sources; the institution's comparative advantage; and communication with staff and governments.

- *Establishing a research culture and ethos*, including the development of a strong research culture, hosting leading researchers from other countries, providing support staff and developing and implementing incentives and rewards for positive performance consistent with the goals of the institution.

2. Management to support leadership of research in institutions

- *Organizational structure*, including creating a critical mass of researchers, interdisciplinary support, practical issues such as space, infrastructure and other academic obligations, provision of effective management and administrative support to the research groups, and support for colleagues in positions of responsibility.
- *Executive and management operations*, including ensuring roles are clearly defined and without duplication, and ensuring coordination in support for the implementation of the institutional plan.
- *Committee operations*, including the balance between purpose, frequency and effectiveness of the group.
- *Research management and administration*, including research support, research translation/commercialization, financial management, asset management and performance data recording and analysis.

3. Leadership of researchers in institutions

- *Research students, postdoctoral and newly independent researchers*, including staff appointments, staff development, conditions of employment and performance management, assurance of the relevance and the quality of the research training and the research environment, and understanding the attitudes of younger generations.
- *Development of research leadership*, including coordination of activities, selection of people, assembling teams, motivating workers, resolving problems, creating a supportive environment, communication and providing focus and leadership reward systems that are both fair and capable of motivating excellence and also capable of attracting and retaining the best people, resource management and identification and support for emerging areas of strength and advantages.

4. Management to support leadership of researchers

- *Research student management*, including ensuring the relevance of their contribution to external policy settings, establishment of enrolment requirements, student induction, supervision arrangements and training, research methods and intellectual property management, training programmes for research methods, support for travel and conference attendance, support for secondments to industry, monitoring progress and support, examination process and graduation confirmation.

- *Staff management*, including position descriptions, setting performance expectations, responsibilities and accountabilities, process for recruitment, selection and appointment of staff, contract arrangements, advising on research integrity, staff development, assisting and management conflict resolution, data analysis for trends in personnel profiles, supporting and managing staff surveys and feedback options, strategy and management support for workplace change.

5. Personal behaviour and qualities of research leaders and managers

- *Behaviour of leaders*, including clear performance expectations, transparent and rigorous incentive systems, recognition and reward, provision of feedback, transparent and consistent decision-making, dealing effectively with misconduct, provision of development opportunities, rewarding and celebrating individual and team successes, delegation, communication and being available to provide advice and assistance.
- *Personal qualities of leaders*, including acceptance of the responsibility and accountability that comes with the role of being a leader, recognition and appreciation of teamwork in leadership and management, soliciting and accepting personal feedback on personal performance and the performance of the senior team, communicating with empathy, adapting to changing circumstances, advocating with passion and demonstrating honesty and integrity.

The following are some more specific developments which reflect institutional initiatives to improve the management of research.

Enhancing international competitiveness

Governing and managing research is at once a global activity and one that is constrained by the history, culture, politics and regulatory frameworks of specific nations and institutions. Dubbed 'the fourth age of research' (Adams, 2013), research has increasingly become a collaborative activity, with a global emphasis, requiring new and more sophisticated governance and management approaches and understandings. It is through international knowledge networks that research is having its greatest impact. The evidence clearly indicates that 'researchers are increasingly networked across national and organisational borders' (OECD, 2011, p. 47) and that scientific papers with multiple international authors have the highest citation impact (Mitchum, 2014; Jacob and Meek, 2013; Smith et al., 2014).

The increase in the importance of international scientific networks has enhanced the significance of national research-intensive universities. These institutions serve as international hubs linking the 'best and brightest' from around the globe. International scientific networks are fundamental to the production of knowledge and enhancing institutional and research group competitive advantage (Beerkens and Derwende, 2007; Huisman and Van der Wende, 2005). This may exacerbate tensions between research-intensive institutions and the rest, for 'institutions that do not form international collaborations risk progressive disenfranchisement' (Adams, 2013, p. 557).

The internationalization of research networks raises a number of new challenges for leaders and managers of research. Research managers need to be aware of the variety of research-funding opportunities available internationally. Many of the funding requirements of international programmes are arduous and complicated, the European Union's Horizon 2020 being a case in point. Researchers are increasingly mobile and, if institutions are going to participate fully, they are going to need to work out how best to facilitate this mobility. Cultural sensitivity and understanding are becoming part of the repertoire of many if not most managers of research. Researchers will need resources to participate in international research networks, and leaders of research teams will need to have the personal diplomatic skills to deal with colleagues from a variety of cultural backgrounds. Recruitment of the best international research students and postdoctoral researchers is becoming increasing competitive globally and effective participation in this realm of activity will require well-formulated strategies.

The Executive Summary of the UK Royal Society's report (2011) on global scientific collaboration documents the spectacular growth in international research collaboration. The Society strongly supports international research collaborations and recommends among other things that 'international activities and collaboration should be embedded in national science and innovation strategies' (p. 8). To be successfully accomplished, this should be done at both the sector and institutional levels.

Jacob and Meek (2013) argue that one of the ways in which globalization is manifesting itself in higher education and research is through the increasing importance and emphasis on scientific mobility. They provide an overview and analysis of current trends and policy tools for promoting mobility. They indicate that the mobility of scientific labour is an indispensable prerequisite for capacity-building and building world-class excellence. Mobility is still a mixed blessing since scientific labour like other scarce resources has a tendency to cluster towards the centre. However, given advances in communication technology and the presence of good research infrastructure, a core group of networked researchers can go a long way towards helping nations achieve world-class excellence.

International research networks require careful leadership across both institutions and disciplines. Cummings and Kiesler (2005) conclude that it is somewhat easier to manage and coordinate projects that involve multiple disciplines than multiple institutions. This may be due to a greater understanding of project goals among the researchers compared to institutional leaders.

Once existing strengths and areas for potential growth are identified, universities concentrate on developing their existing strengths by exploiting niche areas through prestigious research excellence initiatives such as CoEs and creating research alliances with other world-class institutions. The pursuit of excellence and the establishment of flagship campuses particularly for young universities are a challenging process but achievable if addressed in a strategic way (Salmi, 2013). Some of these strategies include the reorganization of academic departments into larger research units with better prospects of performing high-quality research and attracting research income (Jongbloed, 2011). Various universities are creating internal financial incentives to foster institutional interdisciplinary research collaborations and the establishment of interdisciplinary centres (Henkel et al., 2000; Sá, 2008). Interdisciplinary research centres are often the focus of international research collaborations dealing with some of the most pressing problems globally – such as climate change.

Professionalization of research leaders and managers

Research management has become a professionalized area with its own journals, professional societies and in some jurisdictions external processes of accreditation. Research has emerged as a specialized area of management in response to demands that did not exist 10 to 20 years ago. It involves attracting funding, managing funds, liaising with funding bodies, project planning, implementation, monitoring and evaluation, as well as recording publications, facilitating research dissemination and, in some cases, promoting commercialization. An example of the professionalization of research management is the Global Research Management Network that connects members from over 40 countries. Its journal *Research Global* addresses research management issues, including structures for research management, risk management, research evaluation, research management tools and research collaboration. Most developed countries have their own individual research management societies and in some cases journals. These societies usually have chapters on individual campuses and are active in assisting institutional managers and human resource units in the staff development of their research communities. Another example is the UK Vitae Research Development Framework which has global appeal and is available online (https://www.vitae.ac.uk).

Sustaining the academic profession

In addition to routine human resource administrative tasks, leaders and managers of research need to think strategically about both the present and future research staff profiles of their institutions. This will in part involve arriving at an appropriate balance between research and teaching staff and, in part, possibly questioning the presumed research–teaching nexus. But, even more fundamentally, various external pressures may force the reinvention of what is considered as a normal academic research career.

The demographics of the academic professional in many nations will have a broad impact across the globe. As 'the bulge' of academic baby boomers passes through higher education systems and institutions, there will be significant gaps in the ranks of senior academics in the richer countries. This will result in competition for the best and the brightest around the world and the temptation to poach academic staff from developing countries.

Evidence suggests that there is a need to rethink the nature of academic work, particularly given the shift from elite to mass higher education. In many countries, a reduction in public funding for universities has resulted in declining employment conditions and an increasing reliance on casual academic staff, academic salaries declining in relation to average weekly earnings and fewer opportunities to engage in research. The structure of academic work deters the participation of women who take employment breaks to care for children (Bell, 2010). In the United States, there is declining interest in studying doctorates among American students, who are opting for professional programmes offering better employment prospects (Ehrenberg and Kuh, 2009).

Developed countries need to reinvigorate the academic profession whereas in many developing countries the task is to build it up. However, many of the issues are the same. Global competition for the 'best and the brightest' will invariably escalate, whether the intention is to replace existing faculty members in a mature system or to recruit new ones to a younger system. In either case, it appears that the present very lengthy process of producing senior academics, involving a significant number of years in research training and then academics having to prove themselves through advancement up the academic ranks, is no longer feasible or desirable. Moreover, competition for faculty will be fuelled not only by demographics but also by the apparent disinterest in an academic career by many young people, including recent PhD graduates (Edwards and Smith, 2010).

The systems of rewards for academics are extremely important. For example, promotions and funding based on publication in top-ranked international journals may create disincentives to research issues in small, developing countries. In many developing countries pay rates for academics are poor, resulting in moonlighting. Another important question concerns whether all academics in universities actually need to be research active.

According to Coates and Goedegebuure (2012, p. 23), 'with a bit of imagination one can envisage an almost endless variety of career options that moves us far away from the simplistic assistant–lecturer–senior–associate–professor ladder'. An important question raised in their article is: In what way can mobility in and out of the academic profession be encouraged? This is likely to be a particularly important consideration in many countries where there is a small pool of highly skilled workers. Another specific national characteristic that may impact the internal researcher career structure and mobility is that it appears that the transition from PhD to a postdoc position to an early career research appointment is smoother in countries that rely more on block grants compared to competitive funding of research (Öquist and Benner, 2012).

Managing the engaged university in the innovation era: balancing complexities

Engagement, knowledge transfer and community development have taken an increasingly central role in the university mission with the transition from the industrial to the knowledge-based economy. As Shattock (2010, p. 252) succinctly puts it:

> [R]ecognition of the dependence of the knowledge economy on university outputs, both nationally and regionally, has led to creation of a third mission in most countries which requires universities to maximize their community and regional contributions.

While many would argue that this third mission has been part and parcel of the modern university for a long time, it is equally true that much of this engagement was an add-on to the 'real' functions of teaching and research (Goedegebuure, Van der Lee and Meek, 2006). It originally started to gain somewhat more prominence in the heyday of the technology transfer offices (TTO) which sprang up in universities across the globe in the wake of their apparent success following the introduction in the United States of the Bayh–Dole Act in 1980. Intended to be a facilitator and go-between in the university–industry interface, the rise of the TTOs can be seen as a classic university management response to the key issue of, on the one hand, translating basic research outcomes into (technological) innovation and, on the other hand, reaping the economic benefits of this through licensing and other commercial arrangements. While TTOs indeed started generating a new income stream for universities and appeared to assist with the pace of technological diffusion, their overall effectiveness more recently has been questioned (Mowery et al., 2001; Siegel, Waldman and Link, 2003), with particular reference to their narrow remit (Dodgson, 2015). Alternatively, this view of managing technology transfer has been coined 'science push innovation' with universities the driver of developing and commercializing technologies as the product of their academic research (Meyer, 2000).

In the wake of the rise of the knowledge economy and the fundamental challenges posed by a series of global economic storms in the first part of the 21st century, universities increasingly have been looked upon by national governments as active partners in stimulating and further enhancing national innovation systems by simultaneously being intimately linked to global knowledge networks. As elaborated in Chapter 14, across many jurisdictions universities are asked to contribute to national research and innovation priorities *interacting* with other key stakeholders, industry being key in this. While national research priorities for a long time have been part of the (competitive) research scene, the explicit focus on industry and stakeholder interaction is a new addition that raises a number of key issues for the leadership and management of the research enterprise. Managing complexity is central in this.

As has been summarized by Coates Ulrichsen (2015, p. 2), the contribution of today's universities to the innovation system are many and diverse (see Table 15.1).

Even with all its complexities, Table 15.1 provides the ultimate overview of why managing research in an engaged university in the innovation era is such a daunting challenge. It moves way beyond the original concept of the entrepreneurial university as introduced by Clark (1998). Although Clark introduced the strengthened steering core (institutional management) and the developmental periphery (external engagement), the categories and functions incorporated in Table 15.1 are much more far reaching, placing universities squarely as a key actor – but not the sole actor – in the innovation ecosystem. The categories and functions link back to the five thematic areas identified in the previous section. While not mapping one-on-one on the diverse array of functions contained in Table 15.1, there is sufficient convergence to substantiate the claim that the importance and complexity of research management in an engaged university are difficult to overstate.

This claim appears to be confirmed in a number of recent studies in which universities are depicted as 'innovation hubs'. Youtie and Shapira (2008) in their study on Georgia Tech's transformation into a knowledge hub emphasize the importance of new approaches to leadership, programme development, organizational structures and boundary-spanning roles that mediate between 'academic, educational, entrepreneurial, venture capital, industrial and public spheres' (Youtie and Shapira, 2008, p. 1188). In a similar vein, Lim (2014) outlines the broad range of activities initiated by the Singapore Institute of Technology to strengthen its ties with industry, resulting in the creation of an Enterprise and Innovation Hub.

The concept of the innovation hub as such is not new, despite the fact that they appear to have sprung up all around us. Its original form probably is best traced back to the foundation of the Massachusetts Institute of Technology in Cambridge in the United States some 150 years ago (MIT, 2014). More

Table 15.1 Diversity of functions performed by universities in the innovation system

Category	Function
Developing talent and human capital	Developing skilled labour (both generic- and domain-specific skills)
	Developing entrepreneurial/enterprise skills
	Workforce development and training (generic, advanced)
Developing and deploying knowledge/technologies for innovation and problem solving	Knowledge generation through user-funded research/co-produced research
	Adding to the stock of codified knowledge, for example through publications, patents, prototypes
	Transferring existing knowledge/know-how, for example through consultancy, informal linkages
	Investing and enabling access to specialized infrastructure, instrumentation and equipment
	Providing technical assistance
	Commercializing new technologies through new venture creation and licensing
Strengthening (spatial) conditions for innovation	Providing policy leadership and expertise to inform local policies and strategies
	Strengthening local capabilities and capacity for entrepreneurship and innovation
	Supporting internationalization activities of local firms and attracting talent, investment, resources
	Developing infrastructure supporting local innovation and economic growth
	Developing business assistance
	Strengthening other regional competitiveness conditions (e.g. quality of life)
Accessing finance	Facilitating access to finance for R&D and innovation
Providing spaces for open-ended conversations and entrepreneurial experimentation	Convening academics/industry/researchers/innovators networks
	Supporting creation of industry identity
	Developing industry-responsive curricula
	Bridging disconnected actors in system
	Hosting and participating in standards setting forums
	Providing forums for potential investors
	Understanding industrial development pathways and market opportunities
	Providing spaces with necessary support encouraging entrepreneurial experimentation (e.g. incubators/innovation centres)

Source: Coates Ulrichsen, 2015, p. 2.

recently, it can be traced to the creation of the Warwick Manufacturing Group in 1980. The purpose here was to revitalize the ailing manufacturing industry in mid-England, and the Group subsequently evolved into an engine for innovation with collaborative centres around the globe, with the university centre stage. Leading universities now are embracing the concept, heralding the onset of a new ecosystem for innovation, often focused on tackling the Global Grand Challenges. A recent example of such an initiative is the creation of 'Imperial West' by London's Imperial College. But equally illustrative examples can be found across Continental Europe in cities such as Eindhoven (the Netherlands), Malmo and Stockholm (Sweden), Grenoble (France) and Stuttgart (Germany) and in the United States, for example, San Diego, San Francisco and Boston. All of these places have universities that have opened out to local and regional economies, with strong industry engagement – incubators for research-intensive start-ups – and can be considered hotbeds of creativity and innovation bringing together the best, brightest and youngest minds.

Yet, one should not forget that the university–industry interface is different across the globe in terms of intensity. Both the World Economic Forum (WEF) and the OECD in their respective Global Competitiveness and Science and Technology Reports highlight the significant differences not only between developed and developing countries, but also between developed countries. While, for example, Australia takes 21st place in the WEF university–industry index out of 144 countries, it comes last on the same indicator in the most recent OECD university–industry indicator. Thus, care needs to be taken in terms of both generalizations and extrapolations of what may appear to be successful initiatives. There is no single best management model for enhancing university–industry relationships. The types of successful linkages, transfer channels and partnerships appear to depend greatly on the context in which they occur, and no doubt on the skills, vision and persuasive attributes of the 'champions' who drive these initiatives. The national context is important, but so are the regional and the global.

While much more remains to be learned, a few generalizations about university–industry partnerships are possible. First, it seems that the quality of the relationships and the free flow of information, particularly based upon tacit knowledge, is as important if not more so than the actual commercialization of a research product. Second, interactive partnerships are becoming more the norm rather than simple contractual arrangements designed to develop a specific product. Third, university and other forms of publicly funded research provide the core support for knowledge transfer and innovation. Fourth, while in many jurisdictions universities and industry are coming closer together, the distinctive qualities of each must nonetheless be preserved. Fifth, university–industry partnerships are beginning to be regarded as an important policy instrument for regional development and are seen in the overall context of community engagement that extends from the local to the global, rather than a simple university department/industrial firm arrangement. Finally, and related to the last point, a more multidisciplinary approach to university–industry relationships is starting to emerge where it is being recognized that social and cultural factors and the involvement of social scientists are as important in bringing about successful innovation as the more scientific- and technology-oriented aspects of such ventures.

Conclusion

This chapter has stressed that there are various ways to manage research within universities, reflecting system-wide and institutional-specific circumstances. Although there is no single best model, critical factors include the ability to respond quickly to opportunities, appropriate devolution of authority and responsibility, flexible human and financial resource allocation, interdisciplinary research support, visionary leadership and professional and accountable managers. Universities require a framework to deal with the legal and ethical issues involved in research, as well as mechanisms for quality assurance and resource allocation.

But academia has been slow to embrace either the need for or the principles of professional management and leadership of either the academy generally or the research specifically. Under the rhetoric of scientific freedom, until fairly recently, for some, the idea of management of any kind in the university was an anathema, if not an oxymoron. While time has changed, it was not so long ago that ideas such as those of Michael Polanyi in *The Republic of Science* held sway over both the study and setting of science policy and research management:

> Any attempt to organize the [scientific] group...under a single authority would eliminate their independent initiatives and thus reduce their joint effectiveness to that of the single person directing them from the centre....[A]ny authority which would undertake to direct the work of the scientist centrally would bring the progress of science virtually to a standstill.
>
> (1962, p. 56)

Although influential at the time, Polanyi's *Republic of Science* today sounds at best quaint. But the underlying theme that academic creativity and innovation require autonomy and freedom to pursue ideas wherever they may lead retains a degree of enduring 'gospel' if not truth. As indicated above, there is evidence to suggest that too much emphasis on management imperatives can be counterproductive to the effective running of universities and the furthering of the research agenda (Coates et al., 2009; Taylor, 2006). Yet there also is little denying that a certain degree of management is needed in terms of structuring a complex enterprise, setting priorities under conditions of resource constraints, and facilitating effective collaborations, internally and externally. What is required is much more systematic research into how best to promote effective research management practices while supporting and enhancing academic research creativity and innovation.

Competition and selectivity have become the underlying principles of research management at both the institutional and systems levels. But too much emphasis on competition may be counterproductive, driving institutions and their academics towards competition for competition's sake, rather than a rational pursuit of achievable and worthwhile research objectives. More research on how individual universities may better manage their individual research profiles and set priorities that reflect specific institutional missions and regional locations is required. The current obsession with university rankings encourages a degree of global competition where there are few winners, but nonetheless a heavy commitment of resources to the competitive game.

Related to the above point is the need for more research and analysis into how to create 'world-class' higher education systems as well as individual world-class research-intensive universities. This involves questions of how to manage diversity at both the institutional and systems levels. The evidence suggests that what is required is a rational division of labour among a range of institutions with different missions and orientations, rather than a blind pursuit by all institutions to be research intensive. But how to achieve this end is extremely complex and fraught with several political difficulties at both the institutional and systems levels.

The task of the institutional leader and manager of research is how to nurture the creative energy of academic staff while simultaneously challenging that energy in directions that benefit not only the institution but also the society generally. Given the complexity of research governance and management as outlined in this chapter, this is no simple task. But what seems certain is that, in all jurisdictions, the need to achieve professional and effective research management and leadership will continue to increase significantly.

References

Adams, J. (2013) 'The fourth age of research', *Nature*, 497, 557–560.

Aksnes, D., Benner, M., Borlaug, S. B., Hansen, H. F., Kallerud, E., Kristiansen, E. and G. Sivertsen (2012) *Centres of Excellence in the Nordic Countries: A Comparative Study of Research Excellence Policy and Excellence Centre Schemes in Denmark, Finland, Norway and Sweden*, Working Paper 4/2012 (Oslo: NIFU).

Atkinson-Grosjean, J. (2006) *Public Science, Private Interests: Culture and Commerce in Canada's Networks of Centres of Excellence* (Toronto: University of Toronto Press).

Australian Government (2011) *Focusing Australia's Publicly Funded Research Review: Maximising the Innovation Dividend*, Review consultation paper (Canberra: Department of Innovation, Industry, Science and Research).

Beerkens, M. (2013a) 'Competition and concentration in the academic research industry: an empirical analysis of the sector dynamics in Australia 1990–2008', *Science and Public Policy*, 40(2), 157–170, Doi: 10.1093/scipol/scs076.

Beerkens, M. (2013b) 'Facts and fads in academic research management: the effect of management practices on research productivity in Australia', *Research Policy*, 42(9), 1679–1693, Doi: http://dx.doi.org/10.1016/j.respol.2013.07.014.

Beerkens, E. and M. Derwende (2007) 'The paradox in international cooperation: Institutionally embedded universities in a global environment', *Higher Education*, 53, 61–79.

Bell, S. (2010) 'Women in science: the persistence of gender in Australia', *Higher Education Management and Policy*, 22(1), 21–40.

Bentley, P., Coates, H., Dobson, I., Goedegebuure, L. and V. L. Meek (eds) (2013) *Job Satisfaction Around the Academic World* (Dordrecht: Springer).

Bentley, P., Goedegebuure, L. and A. Pettigrew (2014) *An Analysis of the Australian Research Block Grant System*, Internal research memorandum (Melbourne: LH Martin Institute).

Braun, D. (1998) 'The role of funding agencies in the cognitive development of science', *Research Policy*, 27, 807–821.

Bushaway, R. W. (2003) *Managing Research* (Philadelphia: Open University).

Butler, L. (2003) 'Explaining Australia's increased share of ISI publications: the effects of a funding formula based on publication counts', *Research Policy*, 32, 143–155.

Clark, B. R. (1998) *Creating Entrepreneurial Universities: Pathways to Transformation* (Paris/Oxford: IAU/Elsevier Science).

Cloete, N., Bailey, T. and P. Maassen (2011) *Universities and Economic Development in Africa. Pact, Academic Core and Coordination* (Cape Town: CHET).

Coates, H., Dobson, I., Friedman, T., Goedegebuure, L. and V. L. Meek (2009) *The Attractiveness of the Australian Academic Profession: A Comparative Analysis*, Research briefing (Melbourne: LH Martin Institute and ACER).

Coates, H. and L. Goedegebuure (2012) 'Recasting the academic workforce: why the attractiveness of the academic profession needs to be increased and eight possible strategies for how to go about this from an Australian perspective', *Higher Education*, 64(6), 875–889.

Coates Ulrichsen, T. (2015) *Commercialising University Research: Building Multi-focus Knowledge Hubs and the Rise of Strategic Partnerships* (London: British Council).

Connell, H. (2004) *University Research Management: Meeting the Institutional Challenge* (Paris: OECD).

Cummings, J. and S. Kiesler (2005) *Collaborative Research across Disciplinary and Organizational Boundaries*. School of Computer Science, Carnegie Mellon University, Research Showcase @CMU, http://repository.cmu.edu/cgi/viewcontent.cgi?article=1092&context=hcii.

Dill, D. and F. A. van Vught (2010) 'Introduction', in D. Dill and F. A. van Vught (eds) *National Innovation and the Academic Research Entreprise: Public Policy in Global Perspective* (Baltimore, MD: Johns Hopkins University Press).

Dodgson, M. (2015) *Towards the Fully Engaged University: The Particular Australian Challenge* (London: British Council).

Edwards, D. and F. Smith (2010) 'Supply issues for science academics in Australia: now and in the future', *Higher Education*, 60(1), 19–32.

Ehrenberg, R. and C. Kuh (2009) *Doctoral Education and the Faculty of the Future* (London: Cornell University Press, Ithaca).

Fisher, D., Atkinson-Grosjean, J. and D. House (2001) 'Changes in academy/industry/state relations in Canada: the creation and development of the networks of excellence', *Minerva*, 39(3), 299–325.

Geiger, R. L. (1990) 'Organized research units: their role in the development of university research', *Journal of Higher Education*, 61(1), 1–19, doi: 10.2307/1982031.

Geiger, R. L. (1993) *Research and Relevant Knowledge: American Research Universities since World War II* (New York: Oxford University Press).

Goedegebuure, L., Van der Lee, J. J. and V. L. Meek (2006) *In Search of Evidence: Measuring Community Engagement: A Pilot Study* (Brisbane: EIDOS).

Harley, S. (2002) 'The impact of research selectivity on academic work and identity in UK universities', *Studies in Higher Education*, 27(2), 187–205.

Hellstrom, T. (2011) 'Homing in on excellence: dimensions of appraisal in Center of Excellence program evaluations', *Evaluation*, 2(17), 117–131.

Henkel, M., Hanney, S., Kogan, M., Vaux, J. and D. Von Walden Laing (2000) *Academic Responses to the UK Foresight Programme* (Uxbridge: Brunel University).

Henkel, M. and M. Kogan (2010) 'National science policy and universities', in P. Peterson, E. Baker and B. McGaw (eds) *International Encyclopedia of Education*, 3rd edn (pp. 294–299) (Oxford: Elsevier).

Hicks, D. (2012) 'Performance-based university research funding systems', *Research Policy*, 41, 251–261.

Hicks, D. and S. Katz (2011) 'Equity and excellence in research funding', *Minerva*, 49, 137–151.

Huisman, J. and M. C. Van der Wende (eds) (2005) *On Cooperation and Competition. Institutional Responses to Internationalisation, Europeanisation and Globalisation* (Bonn: Lemmens).

Jacob, M. and V. L. Meek (2013) 'Scientific mobility and international research networks: trends and policy tools for promoting research excellence and capacity building', *Studies in Higher Education*, 38(3), 331–344.

Jongbloed, B. (2011) 'The Netherlands', in D. Dill and F. A. van Vught (eds) *National Innovation and the Academic Research Entreprise: Public Policy in Global Perspective* (Baltimore: The Johns Hopkins University Press).

Kehm, B. M. and P. Pasternack (2008) 'The German "Excellence Initiative" and its role in restructuring the national higher education landscape', in D. Palfreyman and T. Tapper (eds) *Structuring Mass Higher Education: The Role of Elite Institutions* (pp. 113–127) (New York: Routledge).

Lambert, R. and N. Butler (2006) *The Future of European Universities: Renaissance or Decay?* (London: Centre for European Reform).

Langfeldt, L., Borlaug, S., Aksnes, D., Benner, M., Hansen, H. F., Kallerud, E. and G. Sivertsen (2013) *Excellence Initiatives in Nordic Research Policies: Policy Issues – Tensions and Options*, Working Paper 10/2013 (Oslo: PEAC Project, NIFU).

Lim, K. M. (2014) *Linkage and Collaboration between Universities and Industries in Singapore*, paper presented at SEAMEO RIHED Regional Seminar on Linkage and Collaboration between the Higher Education Institutions and Industries. Da Nang, Vietnam.

Meek, V. L. and D. Davies (2009) 'Policy dynamics in higher education and research: concepts and observations', in V. L. Meek, U. Teichler and M. Kearney (eds) *Higher Education, Research and Innovation: Changing Dynamics* (pp. 41–84) (Kassel: UNESCO).

Meek, V. L., Goedegebuure, L. and J. Van der Lee (2010) 'Australia', in D. D. Dill and V. L. Meek (eds) *National Innovation and the Academic Research Enterprise: Public Policy in Global Perspective* (Baltimore: The Johns Hopkins University Press).

Meek, V. L. and M. Hayden (2005) 'The governance of public universities in Australia: trends and contemporary issues', in F. Iacobucci and C. Tuohy (eds) *Taking Public Universities Seriously* (pp. 379–401) (Toronto: University of Toronto Press).

Meyer, M. (2000) 'Does science push technology? Patents citing scientific literature', *Research Policy*, 29, 409–434.

MIT (Massachusetts Institute of Technology) (2014) *The MIT Innovation Initiative: Sustaining and Extending a Legacy of Innovation – Preliminary Report*, http://innovation.mit.edu/sites/default/files/images/MIT_Innovation_Initiative_PreliminaryReport_12-03-14.pdf.

Mitchum, R. (2014) *International Collaborations Produce More Influential Science* (Computation Institute: University of Chicago).

Mowery, D. C., Nelson, R. R., Sampat, B. and A. A. Ziedonis (2001) 'The growth of patenting and licensing by US universities: an assessment of the effects of the Bayh–Dole Act of 1980', *Research Policy*, 30, 99–119.

OECD (2011) 'International mobility', *OECD Science, Technology and Industry Scoreboard 2011* (pp. 98–99) (Paris: OECD Publishing).

Olsson, A. and V. L. Meek (eds) (2013) *Effectiveness of Research and Innovation Management at Policy and Institutional Levels* (Paris: OECD).

Öquist, G. and M. Benner (2012) *Akademirapport – Fostering Breakthrough Research: A Comparative Study* (Stockholm: The Royal Swedish Academy of Sciences).

Orr, D., Jaeger, M. and J. Wespel (2011) *New Forms of Incentive Funding for Public Research: A Concept Paper on Research Excellence Initiatives* (Paris: OECD).

Polanyi, M. (1962) 'The republic of science: its political and economic theory', *Minerva*, 1(1), 54–73.

Rhoades, G. (2000) 'Who's doing it right? Strategic activity in public research universities', *Review of Higher Education*, 24(1), 41–66.

The Royal Society (2011) *Knowledge, Networks and Nations: Global Scientific Collaboration in the 21st century* (London: The Royal Society).

Sá, C. M. (2008) ' "Interdisciplinary strategies" in US research universities', *Higher Education*, 55(5), 537–552.

Salmi, J. (2013) 'The vintage handicap: can a young university achieve world-class status?' *International Higher Education*, 70(Winter), 2–3.

Schuetzenmeister, F. (2010) *University Research Management: An Exploratory Literature Review* (Berkeley, CA: Institute of European Studies, University of California at Berkeley), http://escholarship.org/uc/item/77p3j2hr.

Shattock, M. (2010) 'Managerialism and collegialism in higher education institutions', in *International Encyclopedia of Higher Education* (pp. 251–55) (Amsterdam: Elsevier).

Siegel, D. S., Waldman, D. and A. Link (2003) 'Assessing the impact of organizational practices on the relative productivity of university technology transfer offices: an exploratory study', *Research Policy*, 32, 27–48.

Smith, M. J., Weinberger, C., Bruna, E. M. and S. Allesina (2014) 'The scientific impact of nations: journal placement and citation performance', *PLoS ONE*, 9(10), e109195, Doi: 10.1371/journal.pone.0109195.

Taylor, J. (2006) 'Managing the unmanageable: the management of research in research-intensive universities', *Higher Education Management and Policy*, 18(2), 1–25.

van Vught, F. A. (2007) *Diversity and Differentiation in Higher Education Systems*, paper presented at the CHET Anniversary Conference, Cape Town.

Youtie, J. and P. Shapira (2008) 'Building an innovation hub: a case study on the transformation of university roles in regional technological and economic development', *Research Policy*, 37, 1188–1204.

16
Higher Education and the Employability Agenda

Cheryl A. Matherly and Martin J. Tillman

The term 'employability' is part of mainstream discourse about expected outcomes for higher education. The increased stress on the employability of their graduates has challenged colleges and universities to evaluate and prioritize the fit between education and training and the workplace. In this chapter, we explore how employability has influenced higher education policies and practices globally. We first review the definition for employability and discuss the related theoretical framework of human capital. We next examine employability of college graduates as an objective of the economic strategies of supranational, regional and national organizations. We then consider the knowledge, skills and attitudes that make a graduate in the 21st century employable and conclude with a review of how higher education institutions have responded to what is commonly referred to as the 'employability agenda'.

While the term 'employability' is most widely used in developed economies, we have endeavoured to make a broadly descriptive review of how national higher education systems are influenced by or are influencing the employability of their graduates, including those in transitioning economies. We are aware there are many regions that have grappled with the education-work transition in ways that cannot be fully examined in the context of a single chapter.

Employability and human capital

The definitions for employability fall into two categories: employment-centred and competence-centred (European Commission/EACEA/Eurydice, 2014). Hillage and Pollard's (1998, p. 1) widely cited employment-centred definition describes employability as the 'capability to gain initial employment, maintain employment and obtain new employment if required. It is also, ideally, about the quality of such work or employment'. Bologna's Working Group on Employability defines employability as 'the ability [of graduates] to gain initial meaningful employment or to become self-employed to maintain employment and to be able to move around within the labour market' (Working Group on Employability, 2009, p. 1).

An alternative and complementary approach defines employability in terms of the skills and competencies students develop while enrolled at university, specifically those needed and demanded by employers (European Commission/EACEA/Eurydice, 2014). The European Centre for the Development of Vocational Training assumes that employability refers to factors that enable individuals to obtain and retain employment as well as to progress during their careers. It is also dependent upon an individual's attributes, or knowledge, skills and attitude, how these personal attributes are presented on the labour market, environmental and social contexts, including opportunities to update and validate their knowledge and skills, and the economic context. Employability, distinct from employment rates, addresses the graduates' capability for finding and performing work commensurate with a university degree (CEDEFOP, 2014; Knight and Yorke, 2006; Yorke, 2004).

Employability is widely understood to be consistent with Becker's theory of human capital, which assumes that investment in an individual's education and training is similar to that which businesses make in equipment. The education, experience and abilities of an employee have an economic value for employers and for the economy as a whole (Becker, 1993).

> Economic growth depends on a number of factors among which a principal and essential factor is education. Human resource development is variously defined as a process by which knowledge, skills, and capacities of every individual are increased. Human capital arguments presume schooling provides not only skills or knowledge, but also a way of resolving problems.
>
> (Becker, 1993, in Wiseman and Alromi, 2007, p. 39)

In short, the human capital theory argues that education increases individuals' productivity, which consequently enhances job performance. Education provides marketable skills and abilities relevant to job performance so that the more highly educated people are, the more successful they will be in labour markets in terms of both incomes and work opportunities (Cai, 2013). The process of obtaining a degree should enable students to acquire skills and knowledge that is valued by the workforce, and when graduates experience problems finding work, it may indicate that their skills are poor, inadequate or otherwise not aligned with the labour market (see Mason, Williams and Cranmer, 2009, for a discussion of matching theory).

Employability, the knowledge economy and the skills agenda

Higher education systems have adopted an 'employability agenda', both influencing and influenced by the expansion of higher education in the last half of the 20th century. In the United Kingdom, the Robbins Report, issued in 1963, called for the expansion of higher education, declaring that university seats 'should be available to all who are qualified by ability and attainment to pursue them and who wish to do so' (Gibney, 2013, p. 1). At the same time, Clark Kerr, President of the University of California system, created the model for public universities in the United States, what he called the 'multiversity', that accommodated explosive growth in higher education enrolment, as well as new demands that universities provide research, graduate education and professional training (Kerr, 1963). This new era of massification of higher education drew more attention to the ways in which a degree benefited graduates, specifically with regard to their ability to attain employment. Wiseman and Alromi (2007) describe that faith in this education-work connection was particularly strong in newly developed or transitioning economies, which also experienced the rapid expansion and development of their systems of education throughout the 20th century.

These twin influences – massification of higher education and needs of the labour market – are reasons that employability has become a desirable outcome for higher education. Under human capital theory, the task of government is to foster conditions that encourage growth in the stock of human capital, since this is seen as vital to the performance of knowledge-based economies in a globalized society (Yorke, 2006). In fact, a major driver in national policies to promote employability as an outcome of higher education is instrumental: employment rates are highest among higher education graduates, and graduates tend to earn relatively high salaries and enjoy stable employment conditions (OECD, 2013). This is largely influenced by the continued expansion of occupations requiring higher level skills at the same time that occupations associated with lower education levels are shrinking (OECD, 2013). This 'knowledge-based economy' in which economic success is based upon the utilization of intangible assets, such as knowledge, skills and innovative potential, is understood as a key component affecting national economic competitive advantage. The assumption is that innovation will result in a successful economy, measured by an increased wealth, employment generation and social equality and that the knowledge gap impedes national economic advantage (Kok Report, 2004; OECD, 1996).

The OECD (1996, p. 387) advised that the shift towards a knowledge-based economy requires a long-term set of policies in member countries to increase investment in the 'knowledge infrastructure, knowledge distribution system, and the human knowledge component (human resources, education, training, and organizational change)'. It assumes that higher education can advance economic growth in several ways: through university research that creates new technologies, products, concepts and social practices, through the preparation of students with particular career expertise and through professional development and opportunities for life-long learning (Yorke and Knight, 2006a).

Employability agendas at various policy levels

In this fluid environment, international, regional and national bodies have adopted their own employability agendas. Beginning in the mid-1990s, the OECD advocated for labour market policies that targeted 'low-paid and unskilled job seekers [and enhanced] the effectiveness of active labour market policies and lifelong learning to maintain employability' (OECD, 1998, p. 4). The knowledge-based economy, argued OECD labour ministers, demanded a particular investment in young people who risked high and persistent unemployment and low pay. Human capital was considered an 'intangible asset with the capacity to enhance or support productivity, innovation, and employability' that demanded particular attention to education and training (OECD, 1998, p. 9). Recent OECD reports on the state of global higher education note that graduates have been less affected by the rise of unemployment since the 2008 global financial crisis due to the expansion of occupations requiring higher level skills, while the share of employment for occupations associated with lower education levels has shrunk on average across OECD countries (e.g. OECD, 2013).

The United Nations (UN) made employability one of its four priorities for national policy action on youth employment, along with entrepreneurship, equal opportunities between young men and women and employment creation. The UN's Youth Employment Network is challenging countries to review, rethink and reorient their education, vocational training and labour market policies to facilitate the school to work transition and has supported innovative pilot projects to accomplish this. In several African nations, for example, youth entrepreneurship facilities have been set up to build capacity, promote expansion of the private sector to create jobs and support opportunities for youths to explore entrepreneurship as a career option (UN Youth Employment Network, 2014).

At a regional level, employability formed one of the four original pillars of the European Employment Strategy and remains an important component of Europe 2020 and the Education and Training 2020 strategies (McQuaid and Lindsay, 2005; European Commission/EACEA/Eurydice, 2014). The Council of the European Union adopted the benchmark that by 2020, 82% of college graduates, 20–34-years-old, should be employed within three years of finishing their degree or training. European Commission policy stresses the particular importance for higher education institutions to equip graduates with the knowledge and transferrable skills required to successfully compete in high-skill occupations (European Commission/EACEA/Eurydice, 2014). The European Commission places responsibility on employers to provide apprentice or internship opportunities for young people in order to facilitate their school-to-work transition and on higher education institutions to monitor the career paths of their alumni in order evaluate and improve the relevance of their degree programmes for the labour market (European Commission/EACEA/Eurydice, 2014).

Organizations representing developing economies are similarly concerned with a lack of alignment between higher education and the needs of the workforce. The Asian Development Bank (ADB) addressed employability at a regional level in its report, 'Improving Transitions from School to University to Workplace':

> Higher education systems in developing economies in Asia face the daunting tasks of making the best use of limited resources to prepare more of their citizens for an increasingly knowledge-based economy. The ability of Asian countries to compete in a globalized world depends upon the readiness of students entering university, the availability of qualified graduates for the labor market, and the application of science and technology for creating new products.
>
> (Asian Development Bank, 2012, p. 4)

In China, Indonesia and Thailand, for example, the percentage of university graduates in the workforce is now about 20%, double what it was 15–20 years ago (ADB, 2012). Thailand now graduates about 250,000 students from higher education annually, yet 80% of Thai firms report difficulties in filling job vacancies due to graduates lacking basic and technical skills (World Bank, 2011).

The Association of African Universities (AAU) outlined the future employability agenda of selected African nations in relation to the continent's targets for post-2015 UN Millennium Development Goals. The agenda for reforming the higher education sector prioritized the goal of graduating students prepared to address the issues of poverty reduction, infrastructure improvement, medical research and related development problems, citing a 'lack of a clear-cut relationship between the university and the job market that has created a mismatch in African economies, in terms of the type of training universities provided and the demand of the job market' (AAU, 2013, p. 22). The AAU identified factors that lead to the unemployability of African graduates, including:

- a lack of innovation in higher education;
- the lack of involvement by the private sector;
- an absence of regular feedback from students, especially about of the performance of their professors;
- a lack of funding for higher education;
- a lack of government strategies to encourage job growth in key economic sectors;
- labour market saturation and poor working conditions; and

- over-enrolment in universities without consideration of employment opportunities of graduates.

A British Council report examined the challenge of designing higher education policy to solve employment problems in Sub-Saharan Africa, in particular, noting that '...unemployment is a "privilege" of the wealthy, with their greater financial security enabling them to wait for an ideal job, while the less well-off have to engage in a range of provisional income generating activities' (British Council, 2014, p. 7).

Since the global recession began in 2008, national policies have particularly considered how to strengthen the alignment of education with the needs of industry. In the United Kingdom, for example, improving the employability of young people was a key theme in the government's National Employment Action Plans, specifically outlining an agenda to prepare students, the long-term unemployed, the disabled and other disadvantaged job seekers with skills in demand by the labour market (Department of Work and Pensions, 2004). Policy makers recognize that the United Kingdom has, in the past ten years, seen significant growth in knowledge-intensive industries and occupations, a change further reinforced by the recession. Fewer jobs were lost in knowledge-intensive industries as compared with other sectors: between April and June 2008 and 2009, 84% of all jobs lost were in manual, unskilled and administrative occupations (Wright, 2010). The Scottish Government's report 'Putting Learners at the Centre' (2011) specifically names as a national imperative that education at all levels align with the needs of the knowledge economy as a key recovery measure from the deep recession. The report recommends that funding for universities should be accountable to their performance with regard to the government's priorities for post-16 learning, specifically jobs and growth, life chances and sustainability.

While the term 'employability' is not widely used in North America, the concept has influenced the direction of national higher education policies. The US government has long sought to tie employability to issues of access to higher education and economic competitiveness. The Obama administration's 'Building Skills Through Community Colleges' (2014) defines a particular role for two year colleges in its two national goals: by 2020, America will have the highest proportion of college graduates in the world, and community colleges will graduate an additional 5 million students. The initiative calls on community colleges to develop, among other things, better ties to industry, more on-line courses, and enhanced career advising in order to speed students' time to graduation and provide career education to retain students until graduation (Building American Skills Through Community Colleges, 2014). The Department of Education, responding to rising tuition, has issued Gainful Employment Rules, which tie federal aid eligibility for vocational programmes to the earnings and debt of their former students. The policy covers all vocational programmes at for-profit colleges and vocational, certificate programmes at public and private non-profit colleges (Stratford and Fain, 2014).

In sum, the concept of employability is driving higher education policy worldwide as governments see their economies inextricably linked to a trained workforce. The McKinsey report 'Education to Employment' based on a survey of youth, educators and employers in nine countries captures the universality of concern concerning the university-workplace transition: '[If] education does not enable youth to have skills to obtain employment, we have a problem' (in Sharma, 2013, p. 1).

Mismatch – and alignment – between higher education, skills and employer expectations

If the goal for policy makers is to better link education with development of skills required by employers in order to promote economic growth, there is not always agreement among universities, employers and students about how successfully this happens. One study found that 50% of US employers reported having trouble finding qualified graduates to fill positions at their company and nearly a third rated colleges fair to poor for producing successful employees. Employers were particularly critical that students graduating with a bachelors degree lacked basic workplace proficiencies, like adaptability, communication skills and the ability to solve complex problems (Fisher, 2014). These criticisms of the job readiness of graduates are repeated by employers around the globe (Tse, Esposito and Chatzimarkakis, 2013). The McKinsey Global Institute's survey of employers in nine countries (Brazil, Germany, India, Mexico, Morocco, Turkey, Saudi Arabia, the United Kingdom and the United States) found that only 43% of employers agreed that they could find enough skilled entry-level workers. The report highlighted the disconnect between employers, universities and students about how well graduates were prepared for entry-level jobs (Mourshed, Farrell and Barton, 2012). Only 42% of employers and 45% of students said that new graduates are adequately prepared for entry-level jobs, in contrast with 72% of universities. Fewer than 50% of youth reported they had a good understanding of the job market when they chose their course of study.

What, then, makes a graduate employable? During the last two decades, several studies have been conducted to investigate graduate skills sought after by employers. An early study of skills valued by US employers conducted by Bikson and Law (1994) identified four categories of human resource needs most sought after by employers: domain knowledge, cognitive, social and personal skills, prior work experience and/or on-the-job training, and cross-cultural competence (also see Spitzberg and Changnon, 2009; Deardorff, 2006; Hunter, White and Godbey, 2006). A later study published by the RAND Corporation broadened the skills expected by employers in multinational companies to include general cognitive skills (problem solving, analytical ability); interpersonal and relationship skills; ambiguity, tolerance and adaptivity; cross-cultural competence; and personal traits (character, self-reliance, dependability) (Bikson et al., 2003).

Yorke and Knight (2006b) cautioned against reducing employability to a fixed set of skills or traits. They instead propose the 'USEM' account of employability that includes four broad, interrelated components:

- (U) Understanding of subject discipline and other matters pertinent to employability;
- (S) Skills practised in context;
- (E) Students' efficacy beliefs; and
- (M) Metacognition, subsuming elements of 'learning how to learn' and a capacity for self-regulation.

The attraction of their model is that it presents employability as a product of students' holistic learning and not as a set of attributes which are separate and removed from their higher education experience. In fact, York and Knight (2006b) stress that the extent to which a curriculum exploits the interrelatedness of these constructs will increase chances of student employability.

In other studies, employers stress the need for graduates who demonstrate so-called soft or interpersonal skills. Harvey et al. (1997) found that employers wanted graduates with knowledge, intellect, willingness to learn, self-management skills, ability to work in teams and interpersonal skills. Brennan et al. (2001) highlighted the significance of initiative, working independently, working under pressure, oral communication skills, accuracy, attention to detail, time management, adaptability, working in a team, taking responsibility and decision making. International study experiences – especially those linked to internships which build practical skills – are often associated by employers with the development of desired soft skills such as tolerance, open-mindedness, creativity, initiative and the ability to take on responsibility, empathy and respect. In the largest global survey of hiring managers and CEOs, representing responses from 10,000 people in 116 nations, 60% of respondents reported they valued the attributes that international experiences can confer to students (Moloney, Sowter and Potts, 2011).

Employers from diverse countries have found common ground with the soft skills they desire in new graduates. Playfoot and Hall (2009) surveyed 2,000 employers, employees, learners and training providers in 25 nations and found much commonality in all nations. For example, Chinese employers reported they seek graduates who can encourage others, demonstrate an ability and willingness to learn, foster positive relations with others and are flexible enough to work in different ways. South African employers indicated they seek graduates who demonstrate responsibility for themselves and others, are team workers, possess good communication skills and are risk takers and problem solvers. Brazilian employers valued adaptability, problem solving, relationship skills, an ability to manage peers, teams and processes and receptiveness to others and change.

Stephenson's (1998) concept of capability, which informed early research on employability, may best capture the characteristics that make a graduate employable. 'Capable' people have confidence in their ability to take effective and appropriate action; explain what they are seeking to achieve; live and work effectively with others; and continue to learn from their experiences, both as individuals and in association with others, in a diverse and changing society.

Response of higher education institutions to employability agenda

Systems of higher education have responded to the employability agenda in four interconnected ways: changes to the curriculum, closer engagement with industry, improved information to students about the labour market and enhanced measures to link employability with measures of quality assurance. These efforts are intended to make more explicit the acquisition and development of skills associated with graduates' employability. They also add value to the credentials a graduate earns from a particular institution and helps the institution gain a competitive edge in the increasingly competitive higher education market.

The first impact of the adoption of employability as an educational aim is with the curriculum (Mason et al., 2009). Yorke (2004, p. 410) poses the question: 'Does the curriculum contain enough opportunities for students to develop the range of skills, understandings and personal attitudes that they are likely to need in employment?' Referencing their USEM model, Yorke and Knight (2006b) see employability and learning as highly correlated. They note that work-based or work-related learning can be embedded into the whole curriculum, the core curriculum, as employability-related module within the curriculum or as work-based or work-related learning in parallel with the curriculum.

The following are examples of how institutions have addressed employability within the curriculum:

- Roehampton University in the United Kingdom established a Classical Civilization degree using non-traditional forms of assessment and delivery of its curriculum tied to specific employability skills, such as oral presentations or website design (Barrow, 2010).

- The Youth Economic Participation Initiative of the Talloires Network supports the National University of Malaysia's requirement for all first-year students, from every discipline, to take a compulsory entrepreneurship course that is designed to reduce graduate unemployment and provide a direct link between the university and business (Sharma, 2014).
- The Turku University of Applied Sciences, the second largest polytechnic in Finland, focuses its curriculum on working life, entrepreneurship and organization development. Students participate in a 'virtual enterprise' programme in which they set up practice business or enterprises that simulate the work of real companies (Supporting graduate employability, 2011).

As a second strategy to address employability of graduates, higher education has sought to more closely align with industry. The term 'employer engagement' refers to the collaborative relationship between employers and universities to meet both academic needs and the practical needs of the industry, It encompasses collaboration regarding research, knowledge transfer, placements and internship, workplace learning and the design and delivery of academic programmes. To governments, this engagement aligns the curriculum with needs of employers. To employers, it ensures that they interview well-prepared graduates. To universities, it ensures that their graduates are prepared to meet the needs of employers. And to students, it enhances their career opportunities (de Weert, 2011).

The OECD points out that employers value the introduction of a period of practical experience in higher education, for example through internships or cooperative education, and that workplace learning can significantly increase graduates' labour market success (OECD, 2013). Van Rooijen (2011) refers to learning-integrated work to describe the educational process in which employers are integral and equal partners with universities in the educational process, particularly aligning curriculum that has practical, experiential and 'real world' relevance.

Here are selected examples of how industry and higher education are partnering (for further discussion on the partnerships between industry and higher education, see Tillman, 2012):

- The University of Cooperative Education (UCE), established in 1972 by Bosch, Daimler Benz and Standard Elektrik Lorenz and the Baden-Württemberg Chamber of Commerce, enrols over 19,000 students across 11 campuses and combines semesters of academic study at the university with phases of on-the-job training and work-integrated experiences in companies (Reinhard, Osburg and Townsend, 2008).
- Some US colleges are adopting the German dual system of education and training. Ivy Tech established a programme through which students spend

three days a week in class and two at companies where they are paid for apprenticeships in electronics, advanced automation and robotics (Marcus, 2014).

- The Intel Vietnam Scholars Program created a privately funded scholarship programme for a small cohort of Vietnamese engineering students to complete an undergraduate degree in Mechanical or Electrical and Computer Engineering at Portland State University in the United States in order to address the workforce needs of an emerging economic sector in Vietnam (Intel Vietnam Scholars, 2014; Latz, 2009).
- Alcoa Foundation's Global Internship Program for Unemployed Youth is a two-year initiative that provides workforce development opportunities in the manufacturing sector for more than 500 unemployed youth (ages 18–24) in Australia, Brazil, Canada, France, Russia, Spain, the United Kingdom and the United States (Justian, 2014).

As a third initiative, universities are paying greater attention to how students learn about the labour market through career advising. The OECD advises that higher education has a responsibility to keep students informed of labour market risks and opportunities, cautioning that many students choose study fields that lead to poor employment prospects. Their report notes that although it is difficult to predict changes in the labour market or to match short-term labour market needs with long-term higher education outcomes, colleges and universities should help students become as informed as possible about how their choice of study fields will affect their employment options in the labour market (OECD, 2013).

Here are two examples of how universities have responded to demands that they strengthen how they advise students about the labour market:

- In 2005, 74 Centres for Excellence in Teaching and Learning (CETLs) were established in universities in England, several of which focused on employability. The University of Reading established a Centre for Career Management Skills (CCMS), which developed a Career Management Skills module that is compulsory for all undergraduates. The Centre also produced an online career management portfolio of tools called Destinations, which provides undergraduate and postgraduate students with access to a wide range of career management resources and information (Supporting graduate employability, 2011).
- The US Agency for International Development has funded several projects in the developing world (The Philippines, Egypt, Algeria) to build capacity of universities to design and manage career service offices to assist students in their transition to the workforce and train staff to administer appropriate services (career coaching, resume development, building sustainable

relationships with employers) (AUC Establishes Career Centers in National Universities, 2012).

Finally, institutions are challenged by public mandates for transparency and accountability in higher education that are often linked with measures of graduates' employability. Stakeholders at all levels – governments, employers, students – are demanding to see a return on investment, which increasingly includes evidence that graduates are employable once they complete their degrees (Ferns, 2012). In the United Kingdom, for example, websites such as Unistats allow prospective students to compare institutions, using the 'Key Information Set' (KIS) data, items of information which students have said that they find most useful when making choices about which course to study such as the likelihood of getting a job after graduation in specific fields, the type of job they might get and typical salaries (Purcell, 2014).

Harvey (2001, p. 101), however, cautions that such metrics risk making employability synonymous with simply getting a job, what he calls the 'magic bullet' approach to measuring employability:

> The assumption implicit in this is that the higher education institution pro-vides employability-development opportunities that enable the graduate to develop "employability" and hence get employed...There is a presupposed causal link between the employability-development opportunities and the individual employability of the graduate. This link is, invariably, used as a post hoc legitimation for using (convenient) graduate employment rates as a measure of an institution's employability rating.

He identifies factors that can mediate the employment process and distort this as a measure of employability: the type of higher education institution a student attends; whether a student is enrolled full or part-time; a student's location and mobility associated with employment opportunities; the student's area of study; previous work experience; and a student's age, ethnicity, gender and social class. Harvey (2001, p. 106), instead, argues for an employability audit, which identifies the 'work-experience opportunities' and the 'attribute-development opportunities' embedded in the curriculum. The focus is on assessing the process for how institutions prepare students to be employable, rather than simply measuring the output of whether they get a job.

Here are two examples of institutional strategy for measuring employability:

- The Tuning Project is an alternative methodology used by European and some US universities to measure for employability as an educational out-come. It assumes that any higher education programme should be of relevance for society, lead to employment, prepare for citizenship, be recognized by academia and be sufficiently transparent and comparable to facilitate mobility and recognition. It should also be sufficiently attractive to appeal to significant numbers of students, either in a national or international context. According to the Tuning methodology, learning outcomes should be expressed in terms of measurable competencies: what a learner is expected to know, understand or be able to demonstrate after completion of learning, and be established through a consultation process of relevant stakeholders, including employers. The competencies-based approach, it is assumed, makes it possible to consult with stakeholders, including employers, about the specific goals for each academic programme and establish appropriate assessment measures (Gonzalez, 2008; Tuning USA, n.d.).

- A private-sector effort in India aimed at assessing and evaluating the employability of candidates using a standardized employability test suggests an alternative approach to measuring a graduate's employability. The flagship product developed by Aspiring Minds is an Aspiring Minds Computer Adaptive Test that assesses skills including English-language proficiency, aptitude and learnability, personality, managerial competencies and domain knowledge across various industries such as IT and IT-enabled services, banking, financial services, insurance, retail and hospitality. The developers anticipate that the test will permit students in India to skirt traditional educational institutions and gain the knowledge they need from MOOC platforms such as Coursera or EdX (Knowledge@Wharton blog, December 12, 2014).

Critiques of the employability agenda

The employability agenda has not been without its critiques from within the academy. The chief concerns about employability as the primary performance measure for higher education are that it reduces a college or university degree to vocational training, promotes anti-intellectual, erodes academic freedom and diminishes academic standards and objectives (Morley, 2001; Tran, 2014). Some academics complain that the focus on teaching skills associated with employability comes at the expense of time spent on the academic subject itself, and even more damning, free and critical thinking that should define a college degree (Sarson, 2013). Morley (2001, p. 132) captured the essence of the debate: 'Do universities exist simply to meet the needs of modern capitalism and are students being constructed solely as future workers, rather than fully rounded citizens?'

Other critics argue that despite cautions that employability not be conflated with employment, the number of graduates who successfully find work remains a key measure for how universities are ranked (Knight and Yorke, 2006; Marope, Wells, and Hazelkorn, 2013; Yorke, 2004). In the United Kingdom, the Higher Education Funding Council for England (HEFCE) has developed measures of

university performance that include indicators of graduate labour market outcomes, such as the probability of new graduates finding employment after a
specified time interval (HEFCE, 2003). US law schools must report whether
their graduates are unemployed, in a job that requires a law degree or in a job
funded by the university, and provide salary information (Curtis, 2011). These
measures create very real disincentives to encourage students to travel, choose
an unconventional career, work in the non-profit sector or simply take time to
make a career choice (Sarson, 2013).

Still other critics claim the employability agenda distorts the real issues, a mismatch between the educational requirements for various occupations and the
amount of education obtained by workers (Vedder, 2007). The problem, these
critics argue, should really be viewed as one of 'underemployment'. College
graduates are underemployed, performing jobs which require vastly less educational tools than they possess. It can also be viewed as an 'overinvestment'
problem. Universities are churning out far more college graduates than required
by labour-market imperatives. Vedder (2007) sees the issue of employability as
seriously conflated with credential inflation, such that college graduates are
crowding out secondary graduates in blue-collar, low-skilled jobs such as taxi
driver, firefighter and retail sales clerks. He has questioned the 'college for all'
movement and, indeed, suggests that the education-work connection should be
reconsidered such that employability is not defined as the exclusive domain of
those with a post-secondary degree (Vedder, 2007; Vedder, Denhart and Robe,
2013).

Conclusion

The recent global recession and resulting economic stagnation, rising university tuition costs and questions about inequality of access to higher education
have raised new questions concerning the 'worth' or value of a university
degree in both developed and developing nations. The mismatch of training
and education of college graduates with the skills employers are demanding
has created disruptive social conditions and unrealistic expectations for tens of
millions of college-age graduates throughout the world. Labour market actors,
including governments, companies and workers, need to ensure that occupational requirements are matched through adequate education and training. The
extent to which this process is successful is a major factor shaping labour market outcomes, economic growth, productivity and competitiveness for nations,
states and communities.

Universities play a key role in mitigating the disruption graduates face in
successfully making the transition from classroom to the workforce. With an
estimated 75 million college-age youths unemployed, representing almost 13%
of all global youth, their loss to the labour market means the delayed pursuit of

careers, loss in wages and lack of skilled labour available to fill jobs in important technical and professional fields (Mourshed, Farrell and Barton, 2012).

An additional consequence of this disruptive pattern is the greater workforce 'mobility' or migration of well-educated talent seeking employment outside their home country. This pattern is especially harmful to the economic development of undeveloped nations whose labour force is perpetually seeking educated and skilled talent. Dobbs et al. (2012, p. 10) observe:

> To create better outcomes for workers and economies, policy makers and business leaders across the globe need to find ways to vastly improve the capacity to provide job-relevant education and training. And, in both developing and advanced economies, new approaches to job creation for low-and middle skill workers will be required.

We do not support the so-called vocationalization of higher education, however, given the global scale of the disconnect between obtaining a degree and finding gainful employment upon graduation, there is a clear need for all actors – government, industry and academic institutions – to advance alternative models of learning and skill development which enhance prospects for student employability. National policies will inevitably address different needs in different regions. As the AAU points out, the agenda for reforming higher education in Africa must prioritize a goal of graduating students skilled and prepared to address issues of poverty reduction, improving infrastructure, strengthening medical research and other development problems.

Employers will increasingly need to become active partners with higher education institutions to collaboratively develop periods of practical experience for students, for example, through internships or cooperative education programmes. Institutions need to strengthen student career development resources to assist students make informed career choices and selection of fields of study with appropriate and accurate knowledge about job prospects in their local, regional or national labour market.

The 'employability agenda' will likely impact the curriculum, impact the assessment of educational outcomes and shape the overall global higher education system for the foreseeable future.

References

Asian Development Bank (ADB) Improving transitions from school to university to workplace (Rep.) (2012, June). Retrieved December 5, 2014, from Asian Development Bank website: http://www.adb.org/publications/improving-transitions-school -university-workplace.

Association of African Universities (AAU) (2013) Transforming African Higher Education for Graduate Employability and Socio-Economic Development.

Retrieved November 5, 2014, from http://www.aau.org/sites/default/files/announce/GC13%20Proceedings%20-%20final.pdf.

AUC Establishes Career Centers in National Universities. (2012) Retrieved December 5, 2014, from http://www.aucegypt.edu/news/aucinthenews/Pages/ECDCCoverage.aspx.

Barrow, R., Behr, C., Deacy, S., Mchardy, F. and K. Tempest (2010) 'Embedding employ-ability into a classics curriculum: The classical civilisation bachelor of arts pro-gramme at Roehampton University', *Arts and Humanities in Higher Education*, 9(3), 339–352.

Becker, G. S. (1993) *Human Capital: A Theoretical and Empirical Analysis, with Special Reference to Education* (Chicago: The University of Chicago Press).

Bikson, T. K. and S. Law (1994) Global preparedness and human resources (Rep.). Santa Monica, CA: RAND Institute on Education and Training.

Bikson, T., Treverton, G. F., Moini, J. S. and G. Lindstrom (2003) New challenges for international leadership: Lessons from organizations with global missions (Rep.). Santa Monica, CA: Rand Corporation.

Brennan, J, Johnston, B, Little, B, Shah, T and A. Woodley (2001). *The Employment of U.K. Graduates: Comparisons with Europe and Japan* (London: CHERI/HEFCE).

British Council (2014). Can Higher Education Solve Africa's Job Crisis? Retrieved December 10, 2014, from http://www.britishcouncil.org/sites/britishcouncil.uk2/files/graduate_employability_in_ssa_final-web.pdf.

Building American Skills Through Community Colleges (2014) Retrieved December 5, 2014, from http://www.whitehouse.gov/issues/education/higher-education/building-american-skills-through-community-colleges.

Cai, Y. (2013) 'Graduate employability: A conceptual framework for understanding employers' perceptions', *Higher Education*, 65(4), 457–469.

CEDEFOP (2014) *Terminology of European Education and Training Policy* (Luxembourg: European Centre for the Development of Vocational Training).

Curtis, D. (2011, July) Law Schools May be Forced to Disclose Grads' Job Prospects. Retrieved November 24, 2014, from http://www.calbarjournal.com/july2011/topheadlines/th7.aspx.

Deardorff, D. K. (2006) 'Identification and assessment of intercultural competence as a student outcome of internationalization', *Journal of Studies in International Education*, 10, 241–266.

DeWeert, E. (2011, December) Perspectives on Higher Education and the Labor Mar-ket (Rep.). Retrieved November 24, 2014, from Center for Higher Education Policy Studies website: http://www.utwente.nl/mb/cheps/publications/Publications%202011/C11EW158%20Final%20version%20Themarapport%20onderwijs%20-%20arbeids markt.pdf.

Department of Work and Pensions (2004) *U.K. National Action Plan for Employment* (London: Department of Work and Pensions).

Dobbs, R., Madgavkar, A., Barton, D., Labaye, E., Manyika, J., Roxburgh, C., Madhav, S. (2012) The world at work: Jobs and skills for 3.5 billion people (Rep.). Retrieved November 5, 2014, from McKinsey Global Institute website: http://www.mckinsey.com/insights/employment_and_growth/the_world_at_work.

European Commission/EACEA/Eurydice (2014) Modernisation of Higher Education in Europe: Access, Retention and Employability 2014 (Rep.). Luxembourg: Publications Office of the European Commission.

Ferns, S. (2012) Graduate Employability: Teaching Staff, Employer and Graduate Perceptions (Rep.). Retrieved December 5, 2014, from Australian Collaborative

Education Network website: http://acen.edu.au/2012conference/wp-content/uploads/2012/11/84_Graduate-employability.pdf.

Fisher, K. (2014, November 13) The Employment Mismatch. Retrieved November 24, 2014, from http://chronicle.com/article/The-Employment-Mismatch/137625/#id=overview

Gibney, E. (2013, October 24) Robbins: 50 Years Later. Retrieved November 24, 2014, from http://www.timeshighereducation.co.uk/features/robbins-50-years-later/2008287.article.

Gonzalez, J. and R. Wagenaar (2008) Universities' contribution to the Bologna process (Rep.). Bilbao: La Universidad de Deusto.

Harvey, L. (2001) 'Defining and measuring employability', *Quality in Higher Education*, 7(2), 97–109.

Harvey, L., Moon, S., Geall, V. and R. Bower (1997) *Graduates' Work: Organisational Change and Students' Attributes* (Birmingham: Centre for Research into Quality).

Higher Education Funding Council for England (HEFCE) 2003. Performance indicators in higher education 2000–2001 and 2001–2002. Working Paper 59, Higher Education Funding Council for England, Bristol.

Hillage, J. and Pollard, E. (1998) Employability: Developing a Framework for Policy Analysis. Research Report RR85, Department for Education and Employment. Retrieved October 15, 2014, from http://www.employment-studies.co.uk/resource/employability-developing-framework-policy-analysis.

Hunter, W. D., White, G. P. and G. C. Godbey (2006) 'What does it mean to be globally competent?' *Journal of Studies in International Education*, 10(3), 267–285.

Intel Vietnam Scholars (n.d.) Retrieved December 3, 2014, from http://www.pdx.edu/cecs/intel-vietnam-scholars.

Justian, E. (2014, November 21) Global Internship Program Combats Youth Unemployment. Retrieved December 5, 2014, from http://www.triplepundit.com/2014/11/global-internship-program-combats-youth-unemployment/.

Kerr, C. (1963) *The Uses of the University* (Cambridge, MA: Harvard University Press).

Knight, P. and M. Yorke (2006) *Employability: Judging and Communicating Achievements* (Heslington, York: The Higher Education Academy).

Knowledge@Wharton, Assessing Employability Is Disrupting India's Higher Education Model (2014, December 12). Retrieved January 9, 2015 from http://knowledge.wharton.upenn.edu/article/assessing-employability-disrupting-indias-higher-education-model/.

Kok, W. (2004) *Facing the Challenge: The Lisbon Strategy for Growth and Employment* (Lisbon: High Level Group).

Latz, G. (2009). Cross-Border Capacity Building: Selected Examples of Portland State University's Involvement in Tertiary Level Educational Reform in Vietnam. Retrieved November 20, 2014, from http://www.pdx.edu/sites/www.pdx.edu.eli/files/media_assets/ingle/Cross-Border%20Capacity%20Building%20in%20Vietnam.pdf.

Marcus, J. (2014, August) How to Educate Americans for Jobs? Ask the Germans, Employers Urge. Retrieved December 4, 2014, from http://www.pbs.org/newshour/updates/educate-americans-jobs-ask-germans-employers-urge/.

Marope, P., Wells, P. J. and E. Hazelkorn (2013) *Rankings and Accountability in Higher Education: Uses and Misuses* (Paris: UNESCO).

Mason, G., Williams, G. and S. Cranmer (2009) 'Employability skills initiatives in higher education: What effects do they have on graduate labour market outcomes?' *Education Economics*, 17(1), 1–30.

Mcquaid, R. W. and C. Lindsay (2005) 'The concept of employability', *Urban Studies*, 42(2), 197–219.

Moloney, J., Sowter, B. and D. Potts (2011) QS Global Employer Survey Report 2011: How Employers Value an International Study Experience. Retrieved December 4, 2014, from QS Intelligence Unit: http://content.qs.com/qs/qs-global-employer-survey-2011.pdf.

Morley, L. (2001) 'Producing new workers: Quality, equality, and employability in higher education', *Quality in Higher Education*, 7(2) 131–138.

Mourshed, M., Farrell, D. and D. Barton (2012) *Education to Employment: Designing a System that Works* (McKinsey Center for Government).

OECD (1996). *Employment and Growth in the Knowledge Based Economy* (Paris: OECD).

OECD (1998). *Human Capital: An International Comparison* (Paris: OECD).

OECD (2013). *The State of Higher Education 2013* (Paris: OECD).

Playfoot, J. and R. Hall (2009, April) Effective Education for Employment: A Global Perspective. Retrieved December 5, 2014, from EdExcel: http://www.eee-edexcel.com/xstandard/docs/effective_education_for_employment_web_version.pdf.

Purcell, W. (2014, June 13) Employability is our job. *Inside HigherEd*, Retrieved January 9, 2015, from https://secure.timeshighereducation.co.uk/comment/opinion/employability-agenda-isnt-working/2002639.article.

Reinhard, K., Osburg, T. and R. Townsend (2008) 'The sponsoring by industry of universities of cooperative education: a case study in Germany', *Asia-Pacific Journal of Cooperative Education*, 9(1), 1–13.

Sarson, S. (2013, March 21) 'The employability agenda isn't working', *Times Higher Education*. Retrieved January 9, 2014 from https://secure.timeshighereducation.co.uk/comment/opinion/employability-agenda-isnt-working/2002639.article.

Scottish Government (2011) Putting learners at the centre: Delivering our ambitions for post-16 education (Rep.). Edinburgh: The Scottish Government.

Sharma, Y. (2014, September 5) Universities and Employability: Preparing for the Demands of Work. Retrieved December 5, 2014, from http://www.universityworldnews.com/article.php?story=20140904154515222.

Sharma, Y. (2013 January 6) A Focus on Skills Increasingly Links Higher Education with Employment. Retrieved December 4, 2014, from http://www.universityworldnews.com/article.php?story=20130103154436919.

Spitzberg, B. and Changnon, G. (2009) 'Conceptualizing Intercultural Competence', *The SAGE Handbook of Intercultural Competence* (pp. 2–52) (San Francisco, CA: SAGE Publications, Inc.).

Stephenson, J. (1998) 'The concept of capability and its importance in higher education', in Stephenson J. and M. Yorke (eds) *Capability and Quality in Higher Education* (pp. 1–13) (London: Kogan Page).

Stratford, M. and P. Fain (2014, May 28) Many Comments, Few Surprises. Retrieved December 3, 2014, from https://www.insidehighered.com/news/2014/05/28/public-comments-flood-us-department-education-gainful-employment-proposal.

Supporting graduate employability: HEI practice in other countries (Rep. No. 40) (2011) London: Department for Business, Innovation, and Skills.

Tillman, M. (2012) *Employer Perspectives in International Education in the SAGE Handbook on International Higher Education* (Thousand Oaks, CA: SAGE Publications, Inc.).

Tran, T. T. (2014) *Graduate Employability in Vietnam: A Loose Relationship between Higher Education and the Employment Market* (Hamburg: Anchor Academic Publishing).

Tse, T., Esposito, M. and J. Chatzimarkakis (2013, July–September) 'Demystifying youth unemployment', *World Economics*, 14(3). Retrieved December 5, 2014, from http://institut-innovation-competitivite.eu/sites/default/files/demystifying_youth _unemployment_tse_esposito_chatzimarkakis_sept_2013_0.pdf.

Tuning USA (n.d.) Retrieved December 4, 2014, from http://www.iebcnow.org/OurWork/ Tuning.aspx.

UN Youth Employment Network (n.d.). Retrieved December 4, 2014, from http://www .yefafrica.org/about-us/youth-employment-network

Van Rooijen, M. (2011) 'Transforming 21st century engagement: From work-integrated learning (WIL) to learning-integrated work (LIW)', *Journal of Cooperative Education and Internships*, 45(1), 5–10.

Vedder, R. (2007) *Over Invested and Overpriced: American Higher Education Today* (Washington, DC: Center for College Affordability and Productivity).

Vedder, R., Denhart, C. and J. Robe (2013) 'Why are recent graduates unemployed?' *University Enrollments and Labor-Market Realities* (Washington, DC: Center for College Affordability and Productivity).

Wiseman, A. and. N. H. Alromi (2007) *The Employability Imperative: Schooling for Work as a National Project* (New York: Nova Science Publishers).

Working Group on Employability (2009) Report to Ministers, Bologna Conference, Leuven/Louvain-la Neuve 28–29 April. (Rep.). Retrieved November 11, 2014, from http: //www.ehea.info/Uploads/LEUVEN/2009_employability_WG_report.pdf.

World Bank (2011) *Thailand Social Monitor: Towards a Competitive Higher Education System in a Global Economy* (Washington, DC: World Bank).

Wright, J. B. (2010) *Employability and Skills in the U.K.: Redefining the Debate* (London: London Chamber of Commerce).

Yorke, M. and P. T. Knight (2006a) 'Curricula for economic and social gain', *Higher Education*, 51(4), 565–588.

Yorke, M. and P. Knight (2006b) *Embedding Employability into the Curriculum.* (Heslington: The Higher Education Academy).

Yorke, M. (2004) 'Employability in the undergraduate curriculum: Some student perspectives', *European Journal of Education*, 39(4), 409–427.

Yorke, M. (2006) *Employability and Higher Education: What It Is – and What It Is Not* (Heslington: The Higher Education Academy).

Youth Employment Network (2014) The Youth Employment Network. Retrieved December 3, 2014, from http://www.ilo.org/public/english/employment/yen.

17
Internationalization of Higher Education

Yuan Gao, Chi Baik and Sophia Arkoudis

Internationalization of higher education (HE) is not a new concept. Universities have always been international in character in terms of 'the universality of knowledge' (Brown, 1950; cited in Knight and de Wit, 1995, p. 6) and by being an international community of scholars (Block, 1995). Despite being an old phenomenon, new mechanisms and patterns of cooperation and competition between universities have emerged in the past three decades and there has been a growing focus on exploring various aspects of internationalization within higher education institutions (HEIs). Most of the research has been rather general and broad in nature, discussing the 'what' of internationalization. This has included various definitions of the term, rationales and strategies resulting in often vague and abstract conceptual models that can be difficult to put into practice in universities. Recent attention has shifted more towards practical application of approaches, the 'how' of internationalization that aims to identify, measure and improve HEIs' policies and practices.

This chapter provides a review of the body of work on university internationalization in order to reveal the complexities and controversies of the phenomenon in the increasingly globalized era. The discussion includes the changing global setting, the definition and evolution of university internationalization and institutional strategies for internationalization. The last section highlights the less explored area of measurement of university internationalization. The chapter concludes with a brief discussion of the emerging body of literature on internationalization in non-English-speaking countries. This is an important topic as university internationalization has, until recently, focused mainly on Western universities' perspectives, while universities in non-English-speaking countries have largely been positioned as consumers of English-medium universities' internationalization strategies, rather than producers.

The changing drivers for internationalization

A number of global forces have influenced the emergence of internationalization as a key component of strategic priority in HEIs. These include regional competitiveness cross-border linkages, the new knowledge economy based on Information and Communication Technology (ICT), the pursuit of world-class research universities, the cuts in public budget for universities and the entrepreneurial nature of modern universities. These have resulted in HEIs reinventing their management structures and institutional systems in ways that place internationalization as a key strategic priority, and as such influencing the traditional cornerstones of universities – namely research and teaching.

The influence of globalization on HEIs has been well researched (e.g. see Huang, 2007; Marginson, 2011a, 2011b; Scott, 1998). Through university rankings and international comparisons, it is no longer possible for nations or for individual universities to seal themselves off from global effects (Marginson and van der Wende, 2007). As Scott (1998, p. 122) argues, 'not all universities are (particularly) international, but all are subject to the same process of globalisation – partly as objects, victims even, of these processes, but partly as subjects, or key agents, of globalisation'. Globalization has created opportunities for HEIs to reposition themselves in global, national and local landscapes via developing effective international strategies (Marginson and van der Wende, 2007), but with Western English-speaking universities dominating it is not an even playing field.

In the 'new global context', besides fierce competition, institutions are recognizing the need to partner with one another to better serve students, enhance research and meet public needs (Kinser and Green, 2009). As Van Ginkel (1997) claims, universities that want to be global players must focus their attention on the field(s) in which they are excellent and have to find co-makers, other universities and role players, in order to keep offering a broad variety of high-quality courses and research. Strategic partnerships in research, teaching and transfer of knowledge, between universities and industries beyond national borders, are seen as important in helping HEIs manage the challenge that globalization places on them (de Wit, 2002). Overall, there is growing importance placed on cross-border linkages and networks in research, teaching and knowledge production that makes contemporary academic mobility distinctive from past patterns (Wescott, 2005).

Regionalization of HE or creating a regional HE 'space' is an emerging approach that can increase competition and cooperation across international boundaries. The European case serves as a vivid illustration for the positive role that regional building can play in increasing the visibility of a regional HE system on the global map and raising considerable interest in other parts of the world for similar processes (Beerkens, 2004; Verger and Hermo, 2010). Regional building emphasizes both competition and cooperation of HEIs within a more integrated system that goes beyond national boundaries (Verger and Hermo, 2010). It suggests the potential for small-sized or medium-sized HE systems to cooperate with each other and act as a bloc to compete with dominant larger systems (Marginson, Murphy and Peters, 2010). As such, regionalization is here to stay as a feature of the global HE landscape.

These drivers have led university administrations to enact policies aimed at elevating institutions to the status of 'world-class' since policy makers and university leaders are convinced that world-class HE is the key to attracting global talent and being competitive in the high-tech global economy (Cantwell and Maldonado-Maldonado, 2009). Efforts to establish world-class universities have also influenced some emerging countries to narrow the gap with developed countries in the quality of education and research. For example, in China an important government strategy in promoting internationalization of HE has been to establish several large-scale comprehensive universities and support them with substantial funding (Huang, 2007).

The new global context is forcing universities to reconsider their mission, goals and responsibilities as well as to develop innovative strategies to improve their relevance and competitiveness. A major emerging trend commonly found among university systems is the adoption of corporate or business ideas, principles and strategies in reforming and operating HEIs (Healey, 2008; Yang, 2004). The transformation into entrepreneurial universities is partly due to decreased funding from governments and neoliberal governance structures, which have progressively set the context for the internationalization of HEIs (Huang, 2007; Marginson and van der Wende, 2007; Ng, 2012).

The definition and evolution of university internationalization

What is meant by university internationalization? Over the years, there have been various interpretations of the concept, and it is unlikely that there will ever be a universally accepted definition of the term. Three main phases in the evolution of the concept can be identified from the literature in the last three decades. Several representative definitions are summarized in Table 17.1.

Early understandings of internationalization were based on the institutional level and stressed a set of activities such as student and faculty mobility, international academic programmes and international projects. Arum and Van de Water (1992)'s definition is a good example. The focus of 'internationalization' then shifted from a set of activities to encompass all aspects of university life. A process perspective was introduced in defining university internationalization to illustrate the dynamic and changing nature of the phenomenon (e.g. see de Wit, 1995; Knight, 1994). Later, Knight (2004) updated her definition into a more comprehensive one that is widely used today. Most recently, Arkoudis

Table 17.1 Definitions of university internationalization

Periods	Definitions	Keywords/Foci
Early 1990s	'A process by which the teaching, research and service functions of a higher education system become internationally and cross-culturally compatible' (Ebuchi, 1990, p. 109).	Activities Course Programmes
	'The multiple activities, programmes and services that fall within international studies, international educational exchange and technical cooperation' (Arum and Van de Water, 1992, p. 202).	
	'It is faculty with an internal commitment striving to internationalize its own course offerings. It is the presence of an obvious institution-wide positive attitude toward understanding better other cultures and societies' (Harari, 1992, p. 75).	
Mid-1990s to early 2000s	'The process of integrating an international and intercultural dimension into teaching, research and service functions of the institution' (Knight, 1994, p. 7).	Process Institution/ Organization International dimension
	'The complex of processes whose combined effect, whether planned or not, enhances the international dimension of the experience of higher education in universities' (de Wit, 1995, p. 28).	
	'A process of organizational change, curriculum innovation, staff development and student mobility for the purpose of attaining excellence in teaching, research and the other activities which universities undertake as part of their function' (Rubzki, 1998, p. 16).	
Late 1990s to mid-2000s	'Any systematic effort aimed at making higher education responsive to the requirements and challenges related to the globalization of societies, economy and labour market' (van der Wende, 1997, p. 18).	Multilevel focus Systematic process Changes
	'The process of integrating an international, intercultural or global dimension into the purpose, functions or delivery of post-secondary education' (Knight, 2004, p. 11).	
	'The totality of substantial changes in the context and inner life of higher education relative to an increasing frequency of border-crossing activities amidst a persistence of national system' (Teichler, 2004, p. 22).	

et al. (2012, pp. 11–12) investigated internationalization from the perspective of the student experience and defined it in terms of both process and outcomes relating to students.

Over the years, the definitions of internationalization have become broader and more comprehensive as almost all aspects of university life have become internationalized. There has also been increased awareness that the meaning of internationalization is highly sensitive to the specific contexts of institutions, countries and cultures. Until recently, the majority of studies have conceptualized the phenomenon from a Western perspective and focused on internationalization in developed English-speaking regions and countries, including Europe, North America and Australia. It is fair to say that those regions have been the leaders of contemporary HE internationalization. When it comes to the 'followers' such as Eastern Asia, Latin America and Africa, however, the issue is more controversial and complicated.

Recent studies exploring HE internationalization in non-English-speaking countries, particularly in Eastern Asian countries, have revealed that internationalization in emerging countries means something different to how it is understood in developed Western countries (e.g. see Mok and Yu, 2013; Palmer et al., 2011). For example, in China, internationalization of HE means connecting China's educational practice with the mainstream of international trends (Yang, 2002). This could also be true for universities in Japan (e.g. see Arimoto, 2011; Le Phan, 2013), Malaysia (e.g. see Sidhu and Kaur, 2011), Taiwan (Ching and Chin, 2012) and Korea (see Kim and Choi, 2011). These emerging countries aspire to build their own world-class universities and research capacities, as well as to become a regional education hub. In this regard, internationalization has been treated as an effective strategy to improve the global competence of universities and the HE systems in these nations.

Marginson (2011a) argues that this could be regarded as a kind of synchrony that takes the form of one-way adjustment, imitating and following others, and may result in one-sided adaption to education practice in economically more advanced countries and the ignorance of one's own national characteristics. This is a much-debated point in the discourse on internationalization in non-English-speaking countries. Compared to the 'leader' countries, the followers have to face the tension between internationalization and the maintenance of their own national identities. This is not only a major challenge facing emerging Asian countries but also a concern of countries in Africa and Latin America (see Beigel, 2013; Jowi, 2012; Xiu-lan and Geo-JaJa, 2013).

Motives for internationalizing

As there are a variety of ways to describe and define internationalization, there are also a number of different motivations for university leaders to increasingly strive to internationalize their institutions. In the light of existing studies on university internationalization, the rationales driving the effort towards internationalizing HE are related to four aspects: political, economic, academic and social/cultural. They are not mutually exclusive or distinctively different.

Throughout history, universities have strived to gain knowledge and understanding of other cultures (Johnston and Edelstein, 1993; Kahane, 2009; Knight, 2004; Knight and de Wit, 1995; Marginson, 2011a; Maringe and Foskett, 2010), and during the process of colonial expansion, political rationales became increasingly influential in driving internationalization of HE. HE was seen as a tool for expressing the dominance of colonial powers (de Wit, 1998).

Since the end of the Cold War, economic imperatives, instead of political ones, have increasingly driven the internationalization agenda (de Wit, 1998; Harris, 2009; Tian and Lowe, 2009; Turner and Robson, 2008). The international student market is to a large degree, determined by a climate of 'do more with less' and decreased funding of HE (Welch, 2002). Universities can increase their income substantially through the export of educational service and high fees charged to international students (Altbach and Knight, 2007; Harris, 2008; Jiang, 2008). The economic rationale includes developing human resources for the international competitiveness of a nation in the global knowledge economy (Harris, 2009; Knight, 1997), which means preparing graduates who are internationally knowledgeable and competent to live and work in the global society of the 21st century (Coelen, 2009; Hser, 2005; Welch, 2002).

In terms of the academic motive, internationalization has become integral to institutional competition, worldwide reputation and brand building (Marginson, 2011b), enhancing research quality and academic standards (Taylor, 2010b), contributing to the resolution of global problems (Fielden, 2006; cited in Foskett, 2010, p. 38) and alerting societies to major emerging issues (Scott, 2005).

Universities also strive to retain their wider social missions. For example, they act as key cultural mediators in the encounter between world culture and national cultures (Scott, 2005) and aim to build international values, cross-cultural understanding, tolerance and the creation of democratic communities and citizenship (Chan, 2008; Knight, 1997; Meiras, 2004). Kreber (2009) asserts that, in terms of the social mission, the universities' goals in internationalization are to enhance international awareness, empathy, social action as well as to address the development needs identified by certain communities.

Ideologies on internationalization

Universities are guided by competing ideologies in embracing internationalization. Ideology suggested by Stier (2004, p. 85) refers to 'a set of principles, underpinnings, desired goals and strategies that structure actions and beliefs of international educators, groups, organisations or societies'. Three main ideologies that influence universities' actions and decisions on international-ization are referred to as *idealism, instrumentalism* and *educationalism*. These are not mutually exclusive categories and universities and policy makers do not adhere to one of these ideologies alone but often vacillate between them.

The idealists believe that through international academic cooperation, HE can contribute to the creation of a more democratic, fair and equal world. This particular type of ideology underpins the cultural/social rationales for internationalization, which stems from the normative assumption that 'inter-nationalization' is good per se. To learn about another culture is to increase tolerance. This leads to the utopian view that such education will reduce the likelihood of conflict between nations and cultures. The idealist perspec-tive connects internationalization with outside world rather than narrowing it within academic settings. Paradoxically, while the idealism standpoint advo-cates respect for plural values, the 'better world' assumed by idealists to be created through internationalization is largely based on Western value systems.

From the instrumentalist perspective, internationalizing HE is assumed to meet the demands of the capitalist world. The primary objective is to ensure a sufficient workforce. University education, according to the instrumental-ist's viewpoint, should be seen as a global commodity. Policy makers therefore aim to increase the level of transparency and transference between national education systems, to facilitate the mobility of labour force and homogenize university degrees and grading systems.

Although internationalization may be a response to the labour marker's demands for a globally competent workforce, for educationalists its purposes extend beyond the idealistic and professional aspirations of policy makers. Educationalists argue that being exposed to and having to adapt to an unfa-miliar academic setting will enrich the overall academic experiences of both students and teaching staff. The focus of educationalists on internationalization is personal growth and self-actualization. Aligned with educationalism, the pur-suit of academic excellence becomes the dominant motivation for universities to be internationalized (Stier, 2004).

Institutional strategies for internationalization

A large number of studies have explored the various strategies that different universities develop for internationalization[1] and a review of the literature (see David, 1992; Dewey and Duff, 2009; Knight, 1994, 2004; Overton, 1992; Scott, 1992) reveals a number of generic components that constitute inter-national strategies across institutions. These components are related to three broad aspects: governance, academic and service, which are summarized in Table 17.2.

Table 17.2 Key components of institutional internationalization strategies

Governance	• A supportive policy framework/organizational structure • International presence in leadership • Existence of an international office • Staff development of international awareness and skills • Budget for internationalization initiatives • Monitoring/evaluation system for internationalization performance/process
Academic	• International institutional agreements/networks/partnership • Outgoing and exchange opportunities for student/faculty • International research cooperation • Joint degrees/projects • International students recruitment • International visiting scholars • International conference and seminar • Internationalized curricula • Published papers on international journals • International/intercultural extracurricular activities • Interaction of international and domestic students
Service	• Infrastructure investment and construction • Orientation programmes • Language support • Consultancy • Libraries and computing services • Pastoral and tutorial arrangement • Support of families • Student security and welfare provision

The governance dimension

The governance component focuses mainly on administrative systems, leadership and the organizational mechanisms, financial budgets for internationalization initiatives and monitoring and evaluation systems (e.g. see David, 1992; Dewey and Duff, 2009; Knight, 1994, 2004; Overton, 1992; Scott, 1992). The managerial dimension plays an important role in establishing an institution-wide environment for promoting internationalization as well as in constructing a policy framework for developing international strategies. It is often argued that the more HEIs view internationalization from a holistic perspective, the more likely it is that administration processes will be put in place to support the activities (AIEA, 1989; Brandenburg et al., 2009; David, 1992; Liu, 2012; Papp, 2008; Taylor, 2010a).

In some parts of the world, the internationalization of university management may require a fundamental change in regulation. For example, Gao (2014a) argues that universities in China are neither fully independent nor autonomous and have to operate under strict regulations. Chinese universities encounter greater challenges in internationalizing their governance than their counterparts in Western countries. In China, the ownership of degrees does not belong to individual universities but the central government, which hampers the development of joint degree programmes with overseas institutions. It is also difficult to recruit international professors because salary levels are tightly controlled (Gao, 2014b).

The academic dimension

The academic dimension involves teaching, learning and research, which are the core functions of a university. There is a range of activities within this dimension, including, for example, recruiting international staff and students, providing outgoing and exchange opportunities for students and faculty, international institutional agreements, networks and partnerships, joint degree programmes, joint research projects and internationalized curricula and so on (AIEA, 1989; Knight, 2008; Liu, 2012; Stockley and de Wit, 2011; Taylor, 2010a; Weck and Denman, 1997).

It is worth noting that academic mobility has risen in prominence as a critical aspect of university internationalization. Over the past three decades, the number of students enrolled outside their country of citizenship has risen dramatically, from 0.8 million worldwide in 1975 to 4.5 million in 2012, a more than fivefold increase. G20 countries attract 82% of foreign students worldwide while some 75% of foreign students are enrolled in tertiary education in an Organisation for Economic Cooperation and Development (OECD) country. Europe is the top destination for students at the tertiary level of education enrolled outside their country of origin, hosting 48% of these students, followed by North America, which hosts 21%, and Asia hosts another 18%. The number of international students in Oceania has almost tripled since 2000, though the region hosts less than 10% of all foreign students. Other regions, such as Africa and Latin America and the Caribbean, are also seeing growing numbers of international students, reflecting the internationalization of universities in an increasing number of countries. Students from Asia represent 53% of foreign students enrolled worldwide. The largest numbers of foreign students from this continent are from China, India and Korea (OECD, 2014).

In the last 15 years, there has been a remarkable increase in short-term movement across borders for academic purposes, varying by nation and academic field (OECD, 2014). For example, under Europe's Erasmus Programme more than 46,000 staff from 33 European countries had spent time abroad by 2012, and more than 4,000 HEIs in 33 countries have participated in staff exchange and more are willing to join (Valiulis, 2013). Partly related to this increased academic mobility, international collaboration has grown considerably in academic research. This is reflected in the growth of internationally co-authored (or collaborative) scientific articles, the increased citations of foreign scientific articles, the rise of foreign funding for Research and Development (R&D) (Vincent-Lancrin, 2009), the large number of participants in international conference and the frequent international research visits (Trondal, 2010).

Another trend in terms of internationalizing university's academic activities is the internationalization of the curriculum aimed at integrating the intercultural or global dimension into the teaching and learning activities (Altbach, 2006). An international curriculum is deemed to develop graduates' intercultural competence as well as a sense of political responsibility, turning them into defenders of democratic principles of their society and true architects of social change (Leask, 2001; Welch, 2002). There has been a growing focus on developing curricula with an international focus, leading to internationally recognized professional qualifications. This includes interdisciplinary approaches and instruction in a foreign language in different universities (Liu, 2012).

The service dimension

The service dimension refers to both facilities that institutions provide and the services offered to support international students. It could include infrastructure construction, academic advice and guidance, language support, technical assistance, welfare provision and accommodation (Arum and Van de Water, 1992; Knight, 2008; Marginson, 2011a; Rubzki, 1995; Taylor, 2010a). Numerous authors have written about the impact of the wider university environment on students' satisfaction and academic achievement. This is, perhaps, especially apparent in the case of international students studying in an unfamiliar country and often using an unfamiliar language. Universities, therefore, invest in infrastructure to attract foreign students and provide effective support services as part of their internationalization strategy to help students adapt to the new environment.

Approaches to implementing internationalization strategies

Universities may stand at different stages in the process of internationalization and implement their internationalization strategies in different ways. Almost two decades ago, David (1992, p. 187) developed a two-dimensional model to describe the possible pathways that different universities may go through in the process of internationalization. As he projected:

- Some universities will take aboard international elements in a sporadic, irregular, often knee-jerk way, with many loose ends in terms of procedure structure. Others will develop precise explicit procedures from ad hoc to the highly systematic. There is thus a spectrum from the ad hoc to the highly systematic;

- For some universities, internationalisation is essentially a relatively marginal activity-an interesting and stimulating addendum to a predominantly regional or national focus. For others, internationalisation is highly central to their work and permeates every aspect of institutional life. There is thus another spectrum from marginality to centrality.

Most universities start their international endeavours from sporadic and marginal activities. If external pressures towards international entrepreneurialism are strong and finances precarious, internationalization will move to the central concern of the university quickly and continue to develop in an ad hoc way until firm leadership leads the institutional internationalization towards a highly systematic approach. In other cases, without severe external circumstances, internationalization activities are more likely to evolve from sporadic to systematic first, and then become one of the core missions of the institution with careful planning (David, 1992).

The shift in approach towards internationalization has been shown by Gao's (Gao, 2014a) study of internationalization in flagship universities in three different countries. Most universities in her study experienced a change in their internationalization approach from a one-dimensional model to an integrated model, and from developing superficial cooperation with overseas partners to more in-depth collaborations.

The way in which HEIs implement internationalization is not fixed and may change over time. The differentiation of HE provision means that institutions vary in missions, priorities and strategies. As a result, there can be significant differences in the path towards internationalization.

Monitoring and measuring university internationalization

As mentioned earlier, much of the published work on internationalization has focused on exploring how it is conceptualized and the strategies for implementing internationalization at an institutional level. Little is known about the measurement of universities' performance in relation to internationalization. Internationalization has evolved from being seen as an aggregation of dispersed activities within HEIs, to a comprehensive strategy that should be approached in a holistic way. This shift has added to the complexity of university internationalization and created a need for better data.

Universities require reliable information to monitor and assess their performance, and precise measures of achievements will help reduce the vagueness in each university's self-reports (Knight, 2008; Stier and Borjesson, 2010). The information that relevant indicators provide can help universities to distinguish between strategic aspiration and strategic reality and to recognize that, for some of the institutions, there is a 'gap' between the two (Foskett, 2010).

This information also enables universities to proceed to the more important step of identifying priority areas for improvement and maintaining their areas of strength (Arkoudis et al., 2012; Knight, 2008; Maringe, 2010).

The international ranking of universities is a widely debated example of how measurements have influenced institutional management and operation in a way that differs from the past (Marginson, 2011a; Marginson and van der Wende, 2009). Because of the increased global competition and the importance of rankings and league tables, HEIs need indicators to profile themselves and to show the international impact of their research and their appeal with international students (Beerkens et al., 2010).

In addition, there is a need to provide the public with reliable information. This is not only a matter of enhancing university reputation but, more importantly, about increased transparency. Indicators have the potential to help universities inform students, academics and other members of the public to what level an institution is internationalized. In recent years, the emergence of an accountability culture in HE that is based on evaluations has pushed this agenda (Beerkens et al., 2010; de Wit, 2010).

Current instruments for measuring university internationalization performance

Considerable endeavours have been made to develop various instruments to help universities assess their internationalization performance in the past two decades. The first international endeavour was the International Quality Review Programme (IQRP) developed by the Institutional Management in Higher Education,OECD, together with the Academic Cooperation Association (Knight and de Wit, 1995). The purpose of the IQRP is to provide universities with a tool to conduct self-evaluation in relation to internationalization. There are two main components of the tool: a self-assessment report and an external review by an international review team.

Following this endeavour, there has been a considerable growth in the number of projects that have attempted to construct appropriate indicators of internationalization in the decade thereafter. Not surprisingly, the first sets of indicators that were developed came from countries where internationalization had gained more importance because of an increasing flow of foreign students. In 2001, the American Council on Education (ACE) simplified the review process of the IQRP and further developed it into a five-point scale measurement to classify research universities in the United States within two groups: highly active and less active in internationalization (Green, 2005). Later Horn et al. (2007) designed a new instrument that included 19 indicators for research universities in America. The new measure allows the designers to generate an overall score of internationalization for each university, and the score is used to determine the position of a given institution in the ranking system.

In the United Kingdom, Ayoubi and Massoud (2007) identified three variables to examine the achievement of British universities in internationalization. The scores for the three variables were consolidated into a single international factor for each institution and compared with the international strategy intent factor of the institution. Universities could be classified into four groups: international winners, international actors, international speakers and international losers.

Instruments have also been developed in European countries. In the Netherlands in 2007, a tool was designed by the Netherlands Organisation for International Cooperation in Higher Education (Nuffic) to help universities map internationalization. Constituents of the Mapping Internationalization (MINT) tool include goals of internationalization, international activities, facilities, quality assurance and key figures (de Wit, 2009). In 2006, the Centre for Higher Education Development in Germany developed an instrument that included 186 key figures and indicators for HEIs to assess their performance in internationalization (Brandenburg and Federkeil, 2007). Later in 2010, another set of indicators was established by the German Academic Exchange Service to enable institutions to evaluate their level of internationalization and to compare themselves with peers (DAAD, 2010).

Most recently, more cross-border instruments have been established to serve a variety of types of HEIs in the European region. For example, the Indicators for the Mapping and Profiling Internationalisation (IMPI) project resulted in a set of transferable indicators, which captured 22 components of nine dimensions of university internationalization. This indicator set aimed to meet the needs of different types of institutions in Europe for monitoring and assessing their internationalization performance (Beerkens et al., 2010).

In addition, there has been growing interest in internationalization indicators in East Asia. In Japan, Osaka University set up a study to develop evaluation criteria for internationalization for Japanese HEIs. As a result, an 'a la carte menu' of indicators was established for both self-review and benchmarking purposes (Furushiro, 2006). Paige (2005) provided a list of more than 80 indicators for assessing whether certain realities of internationalization are present in Japanese universities. In Taiwan, efforts have been made by Chin and Ching (2009) to build three lists of indicators based on the perspectives of practitioners, experts and students. The issue of measuring university internationalization has also drawn the attention of Chinese scholars who developed a set of 18 indicators for ranking HEIs in Mainland Chinese (Chen et al., 2009).

Questioning internationalization: The unintended consequences

In the past three decades, we have seen intense developments in the scope, scale and importance of university internationalization. There is no doubt that this has changed the global HE landscape fundamentally. While much of the discussion has been on the importance and benefit of internationalization, in more recent years, serious questions have been raised about the unintended consequences of internationalizing, including commercialization, the danger of foreign degree mills and the brain drain of academic talent (Knight, 2013).

According to the 4th International Association Universities Internationalization Survey, the number one risk identified in relation to internationalization is the commodification and commercialization of education programmes. This concern was widely shared among respondents from both developing and developed countries (Egron-Polak and Hudson, 2014). At the heart of the debate is the impact of commodification and commercialization on the role and mission of universities. Traditionally, universities' contributions to society were achieved through their roles in education and research (Boulton and Lucas, 2008). Universities have been remarkably successful in seeking the practical application of discovery, reinvigorating and carrying forward the inherited knowledge of earlier generations and preparing students with both general and specific skills necessary to contribute to society (ibid.). However, the increasing commercial cross-border education is primarily focused on profit and cost-effectiveness, and there is a concern that the cultural values and civic mission that HE used to promote are gradually diminishing (Ng, 2012).

To meet the soaring demand for international education, the number of commercial companies that are proving educational programmes to students based in their home countries has been accelerating at an unprecedented rate. The new forms of cross-border education have led to concerns about the quality of the academic offerings, the integrity of the new types of providers and the recognition of credentials (Knight, 2013). Varghese (2009) argues that where profit-making takes precedence over academic standards and integrity, and when education is seen as an investment opportunity rather than a public service, cross-border education may be diverted from its essential objective of providing high quality education. In the case of online education, there are concerns around the quality of cross-border provision and the quality of the providers themselves (Ezell and Bear, 2012; Youssef, 2014).

Student mobility has always been conceived as one of the paramount aspects of HE internationalization. Human resources and a high-quality workforce have been recognized as the most valuable assets propelling a nation's economic growth (Gopinathan, 2007). Given this, the 'war for talent' (Gattoo and Gattoo, 2013) has been intensified to attract international students and academics for 'brain power'. As Knight (2013, p. 87) argues, 'the original goal of helping developing country students to complete a degree in another country and then return home to contribute to national development is fading fast as nations compete in the 21st century brain race'. Indeed, many countries are tailor-making their immigration policies to retain international students

(Gattoo and Gattoo, 2013) and recruiting foreign students is increasingly a priority for traditional source countries. For example, Singapore aims to attract 150,000 international students by 2015 and Malaysia is seeking 100,000 foreign students. China, which already has 196,000 foreign students, is aiming to enrol 300,000 overseas students by 2020 (Gattoo and Gattoo, 2013).

These unanticipated consequences illustrate the complexity of internationalization and highlight the need for more research on the effects and consequences of university internationalization in developed and developing nations.

Where to from here?

A review of the literature on internationalization of HE reveals that for the most part, internationalization has been conceptualized and constructed from a theoretical perspective. Far less attention has been paid to the various ways individual universities approach internationalization. The motives and priorities in relation to internationalization may vary greatly across different institutions and different contexts. Contextual factors can greatly affect the internationalization of universities in different countries. However, there is little empirical evidence to illustrate in what ways these institutional and national characteristics influence how internationalization is understood and how it is implemented.

In addition, the body of work on internationalization remains highly dominated by researchers in English-speaking Western countries. While there has been a recent increase in the number of studies exploring the phenomenon in non-English-speaking counties, emerging economies and less developed regions, most of these studies are case based and have not yet been systematically theorized. More focus should be placed on understanding internationalization and its significance from the perspectives of universities in countries and regions that have, to date, been largely neglected by researchers.

Last but not the least, for many practitioners and policy makers, internationalization is simply regarded as a 'good thing' and 'right thing' to do without questioning the real benefits it can reap. Apart from the revenue that overseas students can generate, other benefits of internationalization have yet been well demonstrated, particularly the cultural rewards. More empirical data are needed to help illustrate the benefits of 'being internationalized'; otherwise, the investment in internationalizing HE cannot be fully justified.

Note

1. Here, the term 'strategies' refers to a planned, integrated and strategic approach towards internationalization at an institutional level (Knight and de Wit, 1995).

References

AIEA (1989) *Guidelines for International Education at U.S. Colleges and Universities: Final Draft* (Durham, NC: Association of International Education Administration).

Altbach, P. G. (2006) 'Globalization and the university: realities in an unequal world', in J. J. F. Forest and P. G. Altbach (eds) *International Handbook of Higher Education* (pp. 121–139) (Dordrecht: Springer).

Altbach, P. G. and J. Knight (2007) 'The internationalization of higher education: motivations and realities', *Journal of Studies in International Education*, 11(3–4), 290–305.

Arimoto, A. (2011) 'Japan's internationalization of higher education: a response to the pressures of globalization', in D. W. Chapman (eds) *Crossing Borders in East Asian Higher Education* (pp. 195–210) (Dordrecht: Springer).

Arkoudis, S., Baik, C., Marginson, S. and E. Cassidy (2012) *Internationalising the Student Experience in Australian Tertiary Education: Developing Criteria and Indicators* (Melbourne: University of Melbourne, Centre for the Study of Higher Education).

Arum, S. and J. Van de Water (1992) 'The need for a definition of international education in U.S. universities', in C. B. Klasek, B. J. Garavalia, K. J. Kellerman and B. B. Marx (eds) *Bridges to the Future: Strategies for Internationalizing Higher Education* (pp. 191–203) (Carbondale, IL: Association of International Education Administrators).

Ayoubi, R. M., & Massoud, H. K. (2007) 'The strategy of internationalization in universities: a quantitative evaluation of the intent and implementation in UK universities', *International Journal of Educational Management*, 21(4), 329–349.

Beerkens, E. (2004) 'Global opportunities and institutional embeddedness: higher education consortia in Europe and Southeast Asia', Retrieved December 14, 2015, from http://doc.utwente.nl/50803/1/thesis_Beerkens.pdf.

Beerkens, E., Brandenburg, U., Evers, N., van Gaalen, A., Leichsenring, H. and V. Zimmermann (2010) *Indicator Projects on Internationalisation: Approaches, Methods and Findings: A Report in the Context of the European Project 'Indicators for Mapping & Profiling Internationalisation' (IMPI) Indicators for Mapping & Profiling Internationalisation* (Gütersloh: CHE Consult GmbH).

Beigel, F. (2013) 'The internationalization and institutionalization of research and higher education in Latin America: The emergence of peripheral centers', in F. Beigel (eds) *The Politics of Academic Autonomy in Latin America* (pp. 31–45) (Farnham: Ashgate Publishing Ltd).

Block, P. (1995) *Policy and Policy Implementation in Internationalisation of Higher Education* (Amsterdam: European Association for International Education).

Boulton, G. and C. Lucas (2008) 'What are universities for?' Retrieved May 9, 2012, from http://www.leru.org/index.php/public/publications/publications-2002-2009/.

Brandenburg, U. and G. Federkeil (2007) *How to Measure Internationality and Internationalisation of Higher Education Institutions! Indicators and Key Figures* (Gütersloh: Centre for Higher Education Development).

Brandenburg, U., Ermel, H., Federkeil, G., Fuchs, S., Groos, M. and A. Menn (2009) 'How to measure the internationality and internationalisation of higher education institutions: indicators and key figures', in H. de Wit (eds) *Measuring Success in the Internationalisation of Higher Education* (Vol. EAIE occasional paper. 22) (pp. 65–76) (Amsterdam: European Assoc. for Internat. Education).

Cantwell, B. and A. Maldonado-Maldonado (2009) 'Four stories: confronting contemporary ideas about globalisation and internationalisation in higher education', *Globalisation, Societies & Education*, 7(3), 289–306.

Chan, D. K. K. (2008) 'Revisiting post-colonial education development: reflections on some critical issues', *Comparative Education Bulletin: Special Issue: Education and Development in Post-colonial Societies*,11, 21–36.

Chen, C.-G., Zeng, M.-C., Wen, D.-M., Weng, L.-X., and Z. Yu (2009), 'The establishment of indicator system for the evaluation of internationalisation of reserch universities in China', *Peking University Education Review*, 7(4), 116–135 (in Chinese).

Chin, J. M.-C., and G.S. Ching (2009) 'Trends and indicators of Taiwan's higher education internationalization', *Asia-Pacific Education Researcher*, 18(2), 185–203.

Ching, G. S. and J. M.-C. Chin (2012) 'Managing higher education institution internationalization: contemporary efforts of a university in Taiwan', *International Journal of Research Studies in Management*, 1(3), 3.

Coelen, R. J. (2009) 'Ranking and the measurement of success in internationalisation: are they related?' in H. de Wit (eds) *Measuring Success in the Internationalisation of Higher Education* (Vol. EAIE occasional paper 22) (pp. 39–47) (Amsterdam: European Association for International Education).

DAAD (2010) *Internationalität an deutschen Hochschulen – Konzepte und Erhebung von Profildaten* (German: German Academic Exchange Service (DAAD)).

David, J. L. (1992) 'Developing a strategy for internationalization in universities: towards a conceptual framework', in C. B. Klasek, B. J. Garavalia, K. J. Kellerman and B. B. Marx (eds) *Bridges to the Future: Strategies for Internationalizing Higher Education* (pp. 177–190) (Carbondale, IL: Association of International Education Administrators).

de Wit, H. (1995) 'Education and globalization in Europe: current trends and future developments', *Frontiers: The Interdisciplinary Journal of Study Abroad*, 1, 28–53.

de Wit, H. (1998) 'Rationales for internationalisation of higher education', Retrieved April 5, 2012, from http://www.ipv.pt/millenium/wit11.htm.

de Wit, H. (2002) *Internationalization of Higher Education in the United States of America and Europe: A Historical, Comparative, and Conceptual Analysis* (Westport, CT: Greenwood Press).

de Wit, H. (2009) 'Measuring success in the internationalisation of higher education: an introduction', *European Association for International Education Occasional Paper*, 22, 1–8.

de Wit, H. (2010) *Internationalisation of Higher Education in Europe and Its Assessment, Trends and Issues* (The Hague, Netherland: NVAO).

Dewey, P. and Duff, S. (2009) 'Reason before passion: faculty views on internationalization in higher education', *Higher Education*, 58(4), 491–504.

Ebuchi, K. (1990) 'Foreign students and the internationalisation of the university: a view from the Japanese perspective', in K. Ebuchi (eds) *Foreign Students and the Internationalisation of Higher Education* (Hiroshima: Research Institute for Higher Education).

Egron-Polak, E. and Hudson, R. (2014) *Internationalization of Higher Education: Growing Expectations, Fundamental Values: IAU 4th Global Survey* (Paris: International Association of Universities).

Ezell, A. and Bear, J. (2012) *Degree Mills: The Billion-Dollar Industry that Has Sold Over a Million Fake Diplomas*, 2nd edn (Amherst, NY: Prometheus Books).

Foskett, N. (2010) 'Global markets, national challenges, local strategies: The strategic challenge of internationalization', in F. Maringe and N. Foskett (eds) *Globalisation and Internationalisation in Higher Education: Theoretical, Strategic and Management Perspectives* (London: Continuum).

Furushiro, N. (2006) 'Developing Evaluation Criteria to Assess the Internationalization of Univerisities', *Final Report Grant-in-Aid for Scientific Research* (Osaka: Osaka University).

Gao, Y. (2014a) 'Constructing internationalisation in flagship universities from the policy-maker's perspective', *Higher Education*, Doi: 10.1007/s10734-014-9834-x.

Gao, Y. (2014b) 'Toward a set of internationally applicable indicators for measuring university internationalization performance', *Journal of Studies in International Education*, Doi: 10.1177/1028315314559030.

Gattoo, M. H. and M. H. Gattoo (2013) 'The internationalization of higher education and its effect on student mobility', *International Journal of Research in Commerce, Economics and Management*, 3(10), 126–131.

Green, M. F. (2005) *Measuring Internationalization at Research Universities* (Washington, DC: American Council on Education).

Gopinathan, S. (2007) 'Globalisation, the Singapore developmental state and education policy: A thesis revisited', *Globalisation, Societies and Education*, 5(1), 53–70.

Harari, M. (1992) 'The internationalization of curriculum', in C. B. Klasek, B. J. Garavalia, K. J. Kellerman and B. B. Marx (eds) *Bridges to the Future: Strategies for Internationalizing Higher Education* (pp. 52–79) (Carbondale, IL: Association of International Education Administrators).

Harris, S. (2008) 'Internationalising the university', *Educational Philosophy and Theory*, 40(20), 346–357.

Harris, S. (2009) 'Translation, internationalisation and the university', *London Review of Education*, 7(3), 223–233.

Healey, N. (2008) 'Is higher education in really "internationalising"?' *Higher Education*, 55(3), 333–355.

Horn, A. S., Hendel, D. D., and G.W. Fry (2007) 'Ranking the international dimension of top research universities in the United States', *Journal of Studies in International Education*, 11(3–4), 330–358.

Hser, M. P. (2005) 'Campus internationalization: A study of American universities' internationalization efforts', *International Education*, 35(1), 35–48.

Huang, F. (2007) 'Internationalisation of higher education in the Era of globalisation: What have been its implications in China and Japan?' *Higher Education Management and Policy*, 19(1), 47–61.

Jiang, X.-P. (2008) 'Towards the internationalisation of higher education from a critical perspective', *Journal of Further and Higher Education*, 32(4), 347–358.

Johnston, J. and Edelstein, R. (1993) *Beyond Borders: Profiles in International Education* (Washington, DC: Association of American Colleges and American Assembly of Collegiate).

Jowi, J. O. (2012) 'African universities in the global knowledge economy: The good and ugly of internationalization', *Journal of Marketing for Higher Education*, 22(1), 153–165.

Kahane, D. (2009) 'Learning about obligation, compassion, and global justice: The place of contemplative pedagogy', *New Directions for Teaching and Learning*, 2009(118), 49–60.

Kim, E. Y. and S. Choi (2011) 'Korea's internationalization of higher education: Process, challenge and strategy', in D. W. Chapman, W. K. Cummings and G. A. Postiglione (eds) *Crossing Borders in East Asian Higher Education* (pp. 211–229) (Hong Kong: Comparative Education Research Centre, Hong Kong University).

Kinser, K. and M. F. Green (2009) *The Power of Partnerships: A Transatlantic Dialogue* (Washington, DC: American Council on Education).

Knight, J. (1994) *Internationalisation: Elements and Checkpoints CBIE Research No.7* (Ottawa: CBIE).

Knight, J. (1997) 'Internationalisation of higher education: A conceptual framework', in J. Knight and H. de Wit (eds) *Internationalisation of Higher Education in Asia Pacific Countries* (Amsterdam: European Association for International Education).

Knight, J. (2004) 'Internationalization remodeled: Definition, approaches, and rationales', *Journal of Studies in International Education*, 8(1), 5–31.

Knight, J. (2008) *Higher Education in Turmoil: The Changing World of Internationalization* (Rotterdam: Sense Publishers).

Knight, J. (2013) 'The changing landscape of higher education internationalisation – for better or worse?' *Perspectives: Policy and Practice in Higher Education*, 17(3), 84–90.

Knight, J. and H. de Wit (1995) 'Strategies for internationalization of higher education: Historical and conceptual perspectives', in J. Knight and H. de Wit (eds) *Strategies for Internationalization of Higher Education: A Comparative Study of Australia, Canada, Europe, and the USA* (pp. 5–32) (Amsterdam: European Association for International Education).

Kreber, C. (2009) 'Different perspectives on internationalization in higher education', *New Directions for Teaching & Learning*, 118, 1–14.

Le Phan, H. (2013) 'Issues surrounding English, the internationalisation of higher education and national cultural identity in Asia: A focus on Japan', *Critical Studies in Education*, 54(2), 160–175.

Leask, B. (2001) 'Bridging the gap: Internationalizing university curricula', *Journal of Studies in International Education*, 5(2), 100–115.

Liu, J. (2012) 'On the internationalization of higher education institutions in China', *Higher Education Studies*, 2(1), 60–64.

Marginson, S. (2011a) 'Imagining the global', in R. King, S. Marginson and R. Naidoo (eds) *Handbook on Globalization and Higher Education* (pp. 10–39) (Cheltenham: Edward Elgar Publishing).

Marginson, S. (2011b) 'Strategizing and ordering the global', in R. King, S. Marginson and R. Naidoo (eds) *Handbook on Globalization and Higher Education* (pp. 394–414) (Cheltenham: Edward Elgar Publishing).

Marginson, S., Murphy, P. and M. Peters (2010) *Global Creation: Space, Mobility and Synchrony in the Age of the Knowledge Economy* (New York: Peter Lang).

Marginson, S. and M. van der Wende (2007) *Globalisation and Higher Education: OECD Education Working Papers, No. 8* (OECD Publishing).

Marginson, S. and M. van der Wende (2009) 'Europeanisation, international rankings and faculty mobility: Three cases in higher education globalisation', in OECD, Centre for Educational Research and Innovation (eds) *Higher Education to 2030, Volume 2: Globalisation* (pp. 109–144) (Paris and Washington, DC: Organisation for Economic Co-operation and Development).

Maringe, F. (2010) 'The meanings of globalization and internationalization in higher education: findings from a world survey', in F. Maringe and N. Foskett (eds) *Globalisation and Internationalisation in Higher Education: Theoretical, Strategic and Management Perspectives* (London: Continuum).

Maringe, F. and N. Foskett (2010) 'Introduction: Globalization and universities', in F. Maringe and N. Foskett (eds) *Globalisation and Internationalisation in Higher Education: Theoretical, Strategic and Management Perspectives* (pp. 1–13) (London: Continuum).

Meiras, S. (2004) 'International education in Australian Universities: understandings, dimensions and problems', *Journal of Higher Education Policy & Management*, 26(3), 371–380.

Mok, K. H. and K. M. Yu (2013) *Internationalization of Higher Education in East Asia: Trends of Student Mobility and Impact on Education Governance* (Hoboken: Taylor and Francis).

Ng, S. W. (2012) 'Rethinking the mission of internationalization of higher education in the Asia-Pacific Region', *Compare: A Journal of Comparative and International Education*, 42(3), 439–459.

OECD (2014) *Education at a Glance: OECD Indicators* (OECD Publishing) http://dx .doi.org/10.1787/eag-2014-en'.

Overton, J. L. (1992) 'The process of internationalization at minority institutions', in C. B. Klasek, B. J. Garavalia, K. J. Kellerman and B. B. Marx (eds) *Bridges to the Future: Strategies for Internationalizing Higher Education* (pp. 164–176) (Carbondale, IL: Association of International Education Administrators).

Paige, R. M. (2005) 'Internationalization of higher education: performance assessment and indicators', 名古屋高等教育研究 (5), 99–122.

Palmer, J. D., Roberts, A., Cho, Y. H., and G. S. Ching (2011) *The Internationalization of East Asian Higher Education: Globalization's Impact* (Basingstoke: Palgrave Macmillan).

Papp, D. S. (2008) 'Strategic perspectives on internationalizing a university', *Presidency*, 11(3), 22–22.

Rubzki, R. E. J. (1995) 'The application of a strategic management model to the internationalization of higher education institutions', *Higher Education*, 29(4), 421–441.

Rubzki, R. E. J. (1998) *The Strategic Management of Internationalization: Towards a Model of Theory and Practice* (Ph.D. Diss.) (University of Newcastle upon Tyne).

Scott, P. (1998) 'Massification, internationalization and globalization', in P. Scott (eds) *The Globalization of Higher Education* (pp. 108–129) (Buckingham: The Society for Research into Higher Education/Open University Press).

Scott, P. (2005) 'Universities and the knowledge economy', *Minerva: A Review of Science, Learning and Policy*, 43(3), 297–309.

Scott, R. A. (1992) *Campus Developments in Response to the Challenges of Internationalization: The Case of Ramapo College of New Jersey (USA)* (Springfield: CBIS Federal).

Sidhu, G. K. and S. Kaur (2011) 'Enhancing global competence in higher education: Malaysia's strategic initiatives', *Higher Education Dynamics*, 36, 219–236.

Stier, J. (2004) 'Taking a critical stance toward internationalization ideologies in higher education: Idealism, instrumentalism and educationalism', *Globalisation, Societies and Education*, 2(1), 83–97.

Stier, J., & Borjesson, M. (2010) 'The internationalised university as discourse: institutional self-presentations, rhetoric and benchmarking in a global market', *International Studies in Sociology of Education*, 20(4), 335–353.

Stockley, D. and H. de Wit (2011) 'The increasing relevance of institutional networks', in H. de Wit (ed) *Trends, Issues and Challenges in Internationalisation of Higher Education* (Amsterdam: Centre for Applied Research on Economics and Management Hogeschool van Amsterdam).

Taylor, J. (2010a) 'The management of internationalization in higher education', in F. Maringe and N. Foskett (eds) *Globalisation and Internationalisation in Higher Education: Theoretical, Strategic and Management Perspectives* (pp. 97–107) (London: Continuum).

Taylor, J. (2010b) 'The response of governments and universities to globalization and internationalization in higher education', in F. Maringe and N. Foskett (eds) *Globalisation and Internationalisation in Higher Education: Theoretical, Strategic and Management Perspectives* (pp. 83–96) (London: Continuum).

Teichler, U. (2004) 'The changing debate on internationalisation of higher education', *Higher Education*, 48(1), 5–26.

Tian, M. and J. Lowe (2009) 'Existentialist internationalisation and the Chinese student experience in English universities', *Compare: A Journal of Comparative & International Education*, 39(5), 659–676.

Trondal, J. (2010) 'Two worlds of change: on the internationalisation of universities', *Globalisation, Societies and Education*, 8(3), 351–368.

Turner, Y. and S. Robson (2008) *Internationalizing the University: An Introduction for University Teachers and Managers* (London: Continuum).

Valiulis, A. V. (2013) 'Students and academic staff international mobility – a supplementary tool for better learning', *World Transactions on Engineering and Technology Education Canada*, 11(3), 204–208.

M. Van der Wende (1997) 'Missing links: the relationship between national policies for internationalization and those for higher education in general', in T. Kalvemark and M. Van der Wende (eds) *National Policies for the Internationalization of Higher Education in Europe* (Stockholm: National Agency for Higher Education).

van Ginkel, H. (1997) 'Networking and strategic alliances: Dynamic patterns of organization and cooperation', *Cre-Action*, (109), 91–105.

Varghese, N. V. (2009) 'GATS and transnational mobility in higher education', in R. Bhandari and S. Laughlin (eds) *Higher Education on the Move: New Developments in Global Mobility* (pp. 17–27) (New York, NY: Institute of International Education).

Verger, A. and J. P. Hermo (2010) 'The governance of higher education regionalisation: Comparative analysis of the Bologna Process and MERCOSUR-Educativo', *Globalisation, Societies and Education*, 8(1), 105–120.

Vincent-Lancrin, S. (2009) 'What is changing in academic research? Trends and prospects', in OECD, Centre for Educational Research and Innovation (eds) *Higher Education to 2030. Volume 2: Globalisation* (pp. 145–178) (Paris and Washington, DC: Organisation for Economic Co-operation and Development).

Weck, A. and B. Denman (1997) 'Internationalization of higher education: retrospect and prospect', *Forum of Education*, 52(1), 14–29.

Welch, A. (2002) 'Going global? Internationalizing Australian universities in a time of global crisis', *Comparative Education Review*, 46(4), 433.

Wescott, C. (2005) 'Promoting knowledge exchanges through diasporas', *G-20 Workshop on Demographic Challenges and Migration*, Sydney, August 27–28.

Xiu-lan, W. and M. A. Geo-JaJa (2013) 'Internationalisation of higher education in Africa: characteristics and determinants', *World Studies in Education*, 14(1), 79–101.

Yang, R. (2002) 'University internationalisation: its meanings, rationales and implications', *Intercultural Education*, 13(1), 81–95.

Yang, R. (2004) 'Openness and reform as dynamics for development: a case study of internationalisation at South China University of Technology', *Higher Education*, 47(4), 473–500.

Youssef, L. (2014) 'Globalisation and higher education: From within-border to cross-border', *Open Learning*, 29(2), 100–115.

B. Organizing Higher Education

18
Differentiation without Diversity: The Political Economy of Higher Education Transformation

Fadia Dakka

Introduction

Over the past 20 years the field of higher education (HE) has become a crucial site of multidisciplinary investigation. Its perceived strategic function as linch-pin of and catalyst to the fullest development of a knowledge-based economy has propelled a vivid academic debate – encouraged and summoned by national political establishments – over how to better harness its potential in order to gain competitive advantages and best compete in the global economy *arena*.

This chapter will explore differentiation and convergence as sectoral dynam-ics propelled by the interplay of policy interventions, path dependency and institutional response. Whichever the national recipe adopted, in fact, differ-entiation currently stands out as a crucial policy goal in many HE systems and national strategic agendas: from Ireland to Finland, through to the Netherlands and Spain – to name but a few countries with significantly different higher edu-cation systems and traditions. Diversification is regarded as the golden standard to achieve in order to better harness the economic and cultural potential of our learning societies. This commitment is also evident in the European Com-mission's communication on supporting growth and jobs – an agenda for the modernization of Europe's higher education system:

> There is no single excellence model: Europe needs a variety of higher educa-tion institutions, and each must pursue excellence in line with its mission and strategic priorities. With more transparent information about the spe-cific profile and performance of individual institutions, policymakers will be in a better position to develop effective higher education strategies and institutions will find it easier to build on their strengths.
>
> (European Commission, 2011, pp. 2–3)

The chapter will first look at a series of scholarly conceptual contributions aimed at theorizing differentiation and diversity (and its opposites) within higher education systems. It will then examine the English case to illustrate the saliency of the conceptual theorizations emerged in the preceding section. Exemplifying a common trend in Western (and increasingly non-Western) higher education, the English sector has been, and is being, reformed – structurally and ideologically – along neoliberal, market-oriented lines (Hill and Kumar, 2009; Huisman, 2009). Its latest reforms (2012), aimed at further diversifying the sector via enhanced institutional competition, efficiency and responsiveness, offer in this sense an interesting analytical take on the meanings of differentiation and diversity, as well as on the paradoxes and risks associated to policy formation and outcomes.

Differentiation, diversity and convergence in higher education systems

Comparative analyses (Altbach, 2007; Altbach and Forest, 2007; Arnove and Torres, 2007) have shown how the transition from elite to mass higher education is a universal phenomenon characterizing a wider social change that began in the Western mature capitalist economies in the second half of the 20th century. As a widely recognized point of reference for subsequent studies about massification, Trow (1970) defines the transition from elite to mass provision as a system enrolling from 15% to about 40% of the relevant age group. Many studies (Brown, 2009, 2010; Kogan and Hanney, 2000; McNay, 2006; Scott, 1996, 2005, 2012) offer a systematic treatment of massification and current restructuring with particular emphasis on Anglo-Saxon (US, UK, Australia) experiences. According to them, the expansion of the systems was partly led by policy, partly produced by demographic changes and partly the result of shifts in economic and social attitudes. Besides, crucial developments in the nature and modality of transmission of knowledge and the rise of the neoliberal ideology across the public sector constituted both contextual, intervening factors and triggers for further change. Expansion itself was the result of these combined forces and a prime agent of later change.

The progressive expansion of tertiary education can be seen as a global phenomenon arising from the interplay of inner forces shaping education systems and evolving trends in the organization of state, society, economy and culture. In that it confirms the massification thesis. However, the drift from binary to unified systems[1] by no means reflects a universal trend: in many European countries (such as Germany and, more recently, Austria, Finland and Switzerland) binary systems have been established as an organizational response to mass demand and national economic needs. Historically, whether unified or divided, the extended systems created since the 1970s were developed as a response to the raising social demands for a higher level of education and to the needs of a highly skilled labour force. Claims that still exist today. Each country performed the restructuring in a different way and at a different pace. Yet the presence of common socio-economic pressures deriving from the *impetus* of modernization created a general convergence in the direction of change.

After connecting historically and conceptually massification to the structuring and re-structuring of Western mature higher education systems, a trend towards internal stratification and polarization has emerged, providing the necessary context to the second part of this analysis. Focusing on a system-level perspective, it is now possible to look at the ways in which the literature explains differentiation and convergence in higher education.

What is differentiation and what are the related concepts?

Changes in the governance of the sector (from centralized government planning to steering at a distance), increased institutional accountability and a greater osmotic relation between HE and the broader society (emphasis on economic relevance) brought forcefully to the fore the need to understand the evolution of HE systems into increasingly diversified fields of social interaction. Yet the literature has exhibited a discomforting lack of theoretical *consensus* on differentiation and the mechanisms that allegedly promote it or hamper it.

In *The Mockers and the Mocked: Comparative Perspectives on Differentiation, Convergence and Diversity in Higher Education* (Meek et al., 1996), a collection of contributions provided a first coherent and integrated attempt at theorizing (and then empirically testing) and predicting movements in higher education either towards differentiation or homogenization (Meek et al., 1996, p. 3). Within the latter (Meek et al., 1996) Huisman offers a useful definitional distinction between diversity and differentiation by locating the origin and use of these terms in biological sciences. While differentiation refers to a process whereby several new parts emerge in a system to function as an integrated whole, diversity is the static measurement of the characteristics of different species/individuals in a given environment at a certain point in time. In other words, it expresses the variety or number of species and their relative proportions. When transferred and applied to the social sciences, these distinctions prove problematic and ideal typical for a number of reasons. What is important to retain, for operationalization's sake, is the distinction between dynamic processes (differentiation[2] and diversification[3] as opposed to convergence) and static dimensions (diversity vs. homogeneity).

Another useful clarification, as far as higher education is concerned, is Birnbaum's (1983) distinction between systemic, structural and programmatic diversity. The first one points to the different types of institutions that constitute a system. The second specifies inter-institutional differences (external diversity) that are caused by historical and legal foundation or differences within institutions (division of authority). Finally, programmatic diversity refers to differences in programmes and services between institutions within a system (horizontal differentiation). However, prominence will be given to institutional differentiation and convergence as opposing categories.

Differentiation and convergence: Concepts and theories

Drawing a parallel with Darwin's[4] natural selection principle – survival of the fittest – Meek et al. (1996) interrogate the social sciences in search for an equivalent principle explaining processes of differentiation. With the exception of Durkheim's[5] and Parsons'[6] early sociological landmarks on society and structural functionalism, there is less *consensus* on the causes of differentiation than on the mechanisms responsible for it. Crucially, economic (market) theories are presented as the counterpart to natural selection in the process of system differentiation. The market naturally produces differentiation leading to desired levels of diversity by fuelling competition among actors. In analogy to natural selection, competition will select and reward the strongest actors while penalizing the weaker and less adaptable ones. Simultaneously, actors will be encouraged to find niches in markets wherein they can excel or improve their chances of survival. This adaptive behaviour, nevertheless, expresses a contradictory logic: competition brings about not only differentiation and niche-seeking but also convergence, as a result of a *macro* logic of socialization.

Economic theory and neo-institutional organizational sociology illustrate somewhat countervailing tendencies as both originating from competitive dynamics. Therefore the market not only encourages differentiation but also unintentionally inhibits it by producing competitive and institutional isomorphism at the level of the organization.

Higher education literature emphasizes the same lack of theoretical *consensus* on differentiation and the mechanisms that allegedly promote or hamper it. A useful distinction can be made between politics/policy of higher education and research on higher education. From a political point of view, in fact, differentiation has been proactively sought after by governments: they deemed it not only intrinsically good and desirable per se but also essential to nationally restructure mass higher education. In this sense, the increasing marketization of the system has propelled a strong political and economic push towards stratification. More market in higher education means more choice for students, more institutional specialization to serve different socio-economic needs and more competition to achieve national and international excellence and recognition. Such a normative position is inevitably abandoned when researching the field to explain system dynamics. Here a variety of positions and levels of analysis are contemplated. Institutional diversity is generally considered fundamental to guarantee a responsive system, a system that can be especially attuned to the needs of the labour market in the context of a knowledge-based economy.

Shavit et al. (2007) find empirical correlation between expansion, differentiation and marketization and the stratification of individual educational opportunities. The main critique levelled to their study stresses the nature of higher education as a positional good (Hirsch, 1976), implying that the value of educational credentials is determined by its relative ordering on a hierarchy of credentials. Therefore, to the extent that education *is* a positional good, expansion will not affect the opportunity structure that individuals and classes face in the labour market, which can only be affected by a change in the relative educational inequalities between classes (Bourdieu, 2005; Comaroff and Comaroff, 2000; Giroux, 1983; Hill and Kumar, 2009).

According to Kogan (1997) specialization is the basis of differentiation in HE. The most important aspect of differentiation is institutional diversification and its irresistible propensity to stratification. In explaining dynamics of institutional stratification, the author identifies four main drivers: massification, policies of stratification, research-teaching divide and stratification based on students' entry-level qualification. Institutional diversification in massified systems of higher education comprises two significant dimensions: quality and function or mission.

With respect to policies of stratification at the *macro* level, the forces operating towards stratification are, for instance, national decisions to create a binary divide, to stratify and concentrate research resources and attempts by governments and other sponsors to elevate certain kinds of study and mission. Later, binary systems attempted to broaden provision[7] by creating high-level, non-university higher education institutions (HEIs). Finally, it has also been a means of containing the growth of higher education in its most expensive and prestigious forms by creating separate institutions that cost less than universities to maintain.

Stratification by quality[8] has been used for instance by the UK government to reinforce differentiation. On the research and teaching divide front, research selectivity/concentration promotes a clear institutional division between research-intensive and teaching-intensive missions. Still, it is research that determines the place of an institution within the hierarchy of esteem. Moreover, in recent times, the unity of research, teaching and study has been substantially challenged: the divisive potential inherent to massification and the proliferation of academic territories are both cases in point. The pure logic of research primacy contains a disruptive tendency which is aggravated by national policies that enforce a separation between research and teaching.

Yet again, Kogan (1997) sheds light on the coexistence of counter tendencies, within stratification, that produce convergence alongside differentiation.

Stratification may in fact reinforce conformity to the norms, values and practices of the leading traditional institutions. An empirical analysis of the mission statements of 178 UK institutions has confuted the assumption that the main point of differentiation was an emphasis on research *against* teaching. Most of them, including the old polytechnics, regarded themselves as being good at research, even though many of these self-rating statements could be contradicted by external assessment of quality. Signs of convergence are detected in the recently unified systems, wherein formerly different sectors show commonalities or signs of de-differentiation, also known as academic and vocational drifts (Codling and Meek, 2006; van Vught, 2008). The former characterizes the tendency and aspiration, among vocationally oriented institutions, to emulate – drifting upwards – prestigious universities, typically by developing research capacity to enhance their institutional profile. The latter, on the other hand, represents a move away from the pure academic, theoretic *curricula* of the more traditional universities towards more vocational programmes, viewed both as a contingent institutional response to the needs and vagaries of the labour market and as a signal of the new role and identity that universities fulfill in the knowledge-based economy. These tendencies of mission creep and horizontal vocational drift have been registered in several studies (Bleiklie, 2004; Clark, 1983; DiMaggio and Powell, 1983; Horta, Huisman and Heitor, 2008; Neave, 2005; Rhoades, 2007; Teichler, 2004; van Vught, 2008).

Academic drifts are an epiphenomenon of what Di Maggio and Powell call isomorphism: that is, the tendency that leads organizations to become similar in structure, culture and output by modelling themselves on institutions perceived to be more successful or legitimate. Strong entry barriers to the sector and the presence of professional staff moving between organizations also contribute to homogenization and convergence. Not only prestige-seeking institutions compete in the same field by offering similar products, but also less prestigious institutions try to emulate the elite in an academic procession that Brown (2011, p. 35), quoting Riesman (1958), imagines like a head turning back upon itself while the middle part seeks to catch up to where the head once was. So, paradoxically, lower-status, reputation-seeking institutions try to innovate and meet the educational and social needs that are not being met by the elite. This, in turn, creates not only more differentiation and responsiveness but also a sense of threat for those institutions that are at the bottom of the status hierarchy.

On the other side of the *spectrum*, horizontal vocational drifts are also common, especially under conditions of tight graduate labour markets and generalized pressure for a growing practical relevance of HE (Williams, 1995). Horta, Huisman and Heitor (2008) capture these contradictions by observing how the presence of the two types of drifts blurs the formal boundaries between universities and non-university institutions, undermining the foundations of binary systems.

These converging trends are considered as side effects or unintended consequences of marketization. Ironically, the very mechanism that is supposed to produce differentiation of products to meet a variety of needs, might end up producing uniformity (Brown, 2011). The former polytechnics might develop microclimates of research within largely teaching-intensive institutions in a double effort to differentiate their offer from that of further education colleges and improve their position *vis-à-vis* the research-intensive institutions. By offering some academic, theoretical programmes and research – at a lower price – they secure that substantial share of students who cannot afford the higher fees set by the traditional universities, and – at the same time – they develop similar internal characteristics, thus confirming the convergence hypothesis.

Traditional research-intensive universities not only promote vocationally oriented courses, but also are forced to be more responsive to and tailored around the needs of an empowered student-consumer-customer (Collini, 2012). Even though the system is functionally differentiated in segments that serve different markets (local, national, global), seek different students and have different missions, it is nevertheless financially sustained through one common funding regime based on the competitive allocation of scarce public resources. It is then legitimate to hypothesize that a stronger programmatic stratification might potentially coexist with the development of similar commercial strategies and client-seeking behaviours.

Converging tendencies are not just the unintended consequence of increased marketization, but also the result of idiosyncratic, cultural traditions. Analising the turning point of transition from elite to mass system of HE in late 1980s Britain, Parry (2003, p. 309) describes it as an arrested pattern of development due to the British reluctance to come to terms with diversity – diversity of mission, costs, standards, expressed both within and between institutions. For an American observer like Trow (1970), the British ambivalence towards differentiation acted like a powerful brake on the expansion. Underlying this ambivalence was a set of values and assumptions, endorsed by both the academic and policy community that would reassert the unity of the British system of higher education and therefore produce a commitment to high and uniform degree standards across the system including its (then) binary institutions and the open university.

van Vught (2008) has convincingly explained the concurrent presence of processes of differentiation and convergence within HEIs by developing a comprehensive conceptual framework based on the existing literature on differentiation and convergence. On the one hand, there are arguments in favour of *external* diversity, showing that differentiation is considered to be a worthwhile target to aim for. Diversified higher education systems are thought to produce higher levels of client orientation, social mobility, effectiveness, potential for innovation and flexibility. That is why many governments have designed and implemented policies geared towards increasing the level of differentiation in their higher education systems. On the other hand, there are studies that seek to investigate whether or not complex organizations such as HEIs harbour an immanent drive towards differentiation. Parsons and Platt(1973) and Clark(1983) illuminate processes of differentiation in the United States that occur, for instance, when new functions emerge in the system, such as the development of graduate schools as distinct from undergraduate colleges (Parsons and Platt, 1973). Clark (1983) maintains that the growing complexity of knowledge and knowledge specialization brings about ever-increasing fragmentation within and between HEIs. The major complexity of higher education systems and of the new functions associated with them derives from three related forces: the increasing variety of the student population, the growth of the labour market for academic graduates and the emergence and growth of new disciplines. The effects are ongoing differentiation processes and increasing levels of diversity (Clark, in van Vught, 2008, p. 6). Among the factors responsible for processes of convergence, contrariwise, academic drifts are viewed as a counterbalancing differentiation (Neave, 1979; Riesman, 1958), based on their analysis of the American HE system. But other significant and unintended obstacles to diversity are given by governmental policies, especially in the case of centralized state-planning and rigid controls on the introduction of new programmes or institutions (Birnbaum,1983). This is particularly interesting when applied to the English case considering the inner tension produced by a tight state-led policy regulation and the concomitant push towards the commodification of HE provision (Holmwood, 2011, 2014). Finally, Rhoades(1990) explains convergence as the result of a political struggle between academic professionals (i.e. their norms and values) and external lay groups (government policies structuring the competition). The defence of academic standards, norms and values can prevent processes of differentiation within HEIs.

After reviewing the existing literature on differentiation and convergence, van Vught (2008) argues that convergence is the product of a combination of *structural* isomorphism caused by competition and of *institutional* isomorphism produced by coercive, normative and mimetic pressures. The dialectic between external environmental conditions (such as government policies and regulation) and internal organizational characteristics highlights a crucial aspect of higher education structures. They are dynamic and prone to contradictions and tensions arising from multiple exogenous and endogenous factors.

Along the same lines are the observations made by Teichler (2004) who defines the structures of HE systems (their shape and size) as the result of external expectations and internal dynamics and as being moulded by influences and interests of society, governments, HE staff and learners. This gives rise to a perennial instability of these structures, whereby the extent of convergence or differentiation is constantly on the move through overall structural changes, as well as through the repositioning of the individual institutions on the map of higher education. He explains dynamics of change and the alternation of differentiation and convergence by referring to the institutional division of labour arising from the expansion of the systems, to drift theories, flexibilization[9] and cyclical[10] concepts.

Finally, Bleiklie (2004) interprets the relationships between different types of HEIs (universities, vocational and liberal art colleges) as an expression of the social order concepts 'hierarchy' and 'organism'. According to hierarchy, institutions are supposed to occupy different positions on a pecking order. A formal hierarchy will entail some kind of standardization or rationalization. *Organism* is a functional order. Within an organic totality institutions perform different tasks. Each function is unique and must be fulfilled to assure the smooth and adequate functioning of the whole. Such tasks may involve the education of people to specific occupations that society needs, such as engineers, doctors, nurses, and teachers. For Bleiklie (2004), hierarchy and organism are not mutually exclusive. They combine to different degrees generating systems that are more or less hierarchical and/or specialized. Besides, considering the often contradictory nature of government policies sustaining both elite and mass education, not only systems develop an inherent instability, but the contrast between convergence thesis and path dependency could prove misleading. Neither assumption can explain the future development of HE systems, because most probably the development will depend on how the systems manage to balance opposing tensions.[11]

van Vught, Teichler and Bleiklie's analyses on the dynamic morphology of higher education structures echo Codling and Meek's (2006) Twelve Propositions on Diversity in Higher Education. They explore the impact of five key factors – the environment, funding, policy intervention, competition and cooperation, and ranking – on the level of diversity within higher education systems. They examine in particular Australia and New Zealand, where the historical evolution of the sector has seen the progressive coexistence and amalgamation of traditional universities with more technical/vocational institutions. In a similar vein, the unification of the sector in the United Kingdom in 1992 has urged debates surrounding the notion and desirability of diversity. Before evaluating the impact of the aforementioned factors on the level of systemic diversity, however, Codling and Meek (2006) reflect on the different interpretations of and ensuing difficulty in measuring diversity. The meaning of system diversity/differentiation varies according to the different stakeholders. For instance, governments consider diversity as the level of institutional variety present in a system: here the parameters are institutional in that they are broadly defined as mission, student number, programme level and research activity (in a reprise of the Darwinian biological model, governments are concerned with institutional types, or genera). Yet, interestingly, when the student perspective is taken into consideration, diversity becomes associated with individual choice and tends to be based on different parameters such as reputation, cost, pro-gramme, location and access. Moreover, because students will isolate a segment of universities among which they are likely to choose, systemic diversity as a whole becomes, in this case, irrelevant. Having said that, the 12 proposi-tions advanced on diversity, which result from the assessed impact of sector ecology, funding structure, ranking, competition/cooperation and policy inter-vention, reinforce the hypothesis that institutional convergence (by mimetic pressures) will be the most likely result unless very specific conditions pre-vail. Geographic unevenness or regional variation might lead for instance to a greater institutional differentiation (such as the United States), while small countries with little regional variation to the economy (such as New Zealand) are not conducive to the development of institutional diversity. Politically, the best example of a direct intervention that imposes diversity is the creation of a binary system, which limits – through rigid regulation – natural isomorphic tendencies otherwise common in unitary systems. Economically, higher educa-tion systems that promote diversity *via* financial incentives will be more likely to be internally differentiated.

Differentiation or convergence? Unpacking the state-market-university relationship

The literature reviewed so far allows to draw two preliminary conclusions. First, differentiation and convergence are concomitant processes that define trends or movements within the perennial – albeit imperceptible – movement of higher education structures. To recall Bleiklie (2004), hierarchy and organism are far from being incompatible features of higher education systems. Second, when the analytical focus shifts from a process (or its responsible mechanism) to an intrinsic quality of the system such as diversity, a certain degree of interpretive elusiveness seems inescapable.

However, considering the worldwide trends towards marketization *in* and *of* higher education and the consequences it bears on the governance of the sec-tor, a more pertinent question would perhaps be the following: to what extent does marketization of higher education give rise to processes of differentiation and/or convergence?

The existing literature has cumulatively pointed to the emergence of a shifting, complex and dynamic governance that, acting as a mechanism of coordination of coordination (Dale, 2011) subsumes and re-organizes state and market *qua* institutions of coordination in the funding, ownership, provision and regulation of education at different scales (local, national, global).

Theoretical and conceptual analyses have demonstrated that marketization is a powerful restructuring mechanism responsible for both differentiation *and* convergence within the HE system. However, the ways and modalities in which it brings about those outcomes remain at times elusive and therefore need to be explored empirically (Rossi, 2010; Scott, 2005; van Vught, 2008). The English system has been purposefully selected because of its progressive exposure to market forces since the end of the 1980s. It therefore represents the ideal site to explore these mechanisms and their impact on sectoral differentiation and convergence.

Differentiation without diversity: The complex ecology of the English higher education

Scott (Scott and Callender, 2013) and Shattock (2012) highlighted incessant series of policy interventions since the Robbins report (1963), the significant continuities and ruptures across the political *spectrum* in the developing of a grand narrative – or the lack thereof- for an expanding HE system facing funding *dilemmas*, and the complex issues surrounding policy formation, delivery and implementation within New Public Management (NPM). All these developments should be read both as the expression of a macro narrative of socio-economic change, with higher education expressing and absorbing the tensions of a broader agenda of modernization and post-war state restructuring and as describing the peculiar English evolutionary thrust. In this sense, the marketization of the English higher education (Williams, 1995) represents only in part a response to the urgent financial and organizational demands of an expanding sector. Nevertheless, the rapid expansion of HE systems that begun in the 1960s encouraged a greater state intervention aimed at both the coordination of growing systems[12] and at the emerging necessity to adjust, synchronize and reorient higher education's outputs towards national needs (skilled workforce, applied research, widened participation). With the rise of the learning society and the knowledge-based economy, the intensification and internationalization of competition accentuated the need to boost the research mission of universities, together with a growing interest towards the Mode two knowledge (Gibbons et al., 1994).

More recently, the Browne report and, *a fortiori*, the White Paper, have impressed a significant acceleration to the pace of the English reform. A trajectory of change that Holmwood (2012) described as the fundamental obliteration of the social right to and of higher education to the altar of a neoliberal knowledge regime aimed at the structural reproduction of inequality.

From Browne to the White Paper: A more diverse sector?

The Independent Committee on Student Fees and Funding chaired by Lord Browne reported that fees should be uncapped but a progressive levy should be collected from those institutions charging more than £6,000 and paid into a scholarship fund. What was fully accepted and then implemented was the idea that a certain degree of cost-sharing between students/graduates and tax-payers was in order to guarantee the extra resources and the high standards of quality that the system needed, especially in light of the announced cuts in public expenditure. Next, investment in higher education was to be judged and justified primarily in economic terms, being it regarded as a private invest-ment producing higher lifetime earnings (graduate premium). As a corollary, the concentration of research funding to protect and foster research excellence in world-class institutions appeared almost as a stratagem to turn necessity into virtue. In other words, it was the result of contingency (austerity) and also a programmatic choice, one that would surely mean enhancing institutional (and social) stratification. Finally, a commitment to revive and enhance the teaching function emerged from the tripling of student fees and the subse-quent desire to empower the student-consumer, whose experience needed to prove worthy of the conspicuous investment. Centres of Excellence in Teach-ing and Learning, the Higher Education Academy, National Teaching Fellows were, for instance, policies designed to this end. Likewise, the National Stu-dent Survey (NSS), Key Information Sets (KIS) and Unistats were among the measures deployed to improve the information available to prospective stu-dents, thus introducing consumerist tools to serve the costumers/consumers of higher education. In sum, student's choice was to become the key driver of both funding/expansion and, by spillover effect, of quality improvement.

The White Paper extended in this sense Browne's financial prerogative to cre-ate a more dynamic and responsive system. Securing a sustainable system of funding was a paramount necessity and one that logically preceded the other two critical goals, respectively oriented to placing the students at the heart of the system (BIS, 2011) and to promote greater institutional diversity. The latter – in combination with student choice and research funding – is particu-larly relevant as it represents the government's attempt to significantly alter the configuration of the system.

A competitive system was to be created by freeing a pool of 65,000 con-testable places for students with entry-level qualifications equivalent to A-level grades of AAB+. The student number controls for the elite universities were therefore fully liberalized. An additional 20,000 places (the so-called margin) were made available, on a competitive basis, to those institutions charging fees less than £7,500. The purpose of the core and margin policy was to incentivize price differentiation among institutions, thus producing a natural (re-)stratification according to performance, prestige and institutional market positioning. These quasi-market *dispositifs* were intended to counteract the real-ity of rigidly state controlled student numbers and fee ceiling. The promotion of competition at the top end (AAB+ policy) and at the bottom end of the spec-trum (core and margin policy), proposed to differentiate more starkly the type of providers according to mission and student recruitment, was accompanied by a second proposal aimed at further diversifying the system *via* a lowering of the institutional entry barriers to the sector for the alternative provide. This category included smaller/monotechnic institutions, private and for-profit providers and further education colleges offering higher education degrees. The government set out to ease the rules and procedures to acquire university title and degree awarding powers, promoting franchising agreements that would uncouple the degree award from teaching and encourage Further education (FE) colleges to offer more HE programmes (to drive down costs of provision).

Finally, diversity required tackling the issue of widening participation, which the White Paper framed in terms of increasing social mobility for the students who are able and willing to benefit from it (echoing Robbins' commendable axiom). To the favourable repayment terms of the student loans[13] the government added full grants for living expenses available to students from disadvantaged backgrounds (family income less than £25,000 per year) and established a National Scholarship Programme that would reach its £150 million target in 2014. Moreover, institutions deciding to charge fees above £6,000 should negotiate a plan with the Office for Fair Access (OFFA) to put in place bursaries and scholarships for the less advantaged. Finally, the Higher Education Funding Council for England was to become the lead regulator for the sector, promoting competitiveness, protecting the interests of the students and allocating the quality research funding and the remaining direct grants during the transitioning phase.

Institutional response to change

The implementation of the White Paper revealed the contradictions and shortfalls of what has been variously termed a half-baked reform (Scott, 2013) or a work in progress that led, more often than not, to contradictory outcomes. The first paradox being the unrealized government desire to see variation in tuition fees, reflecting the different types of providers. The unintended consequence of the financing mechanism put in place was in fact a reduction in price sensitivity among the students and the consequent inability of the HEIs to charge variable fees (Bekhradnia, 2012; Scott and Callender, 2013).

This view is both compatible with the concept of higher education as a positional good (Hirsch, 1976) and the idea of higher education as a Veblen good, that is a luxury good whose high price signals quality. In 2012/2013, some English middle to low-tariff universities were in fact penalized (McGettigan, 2014), in terms of student admissions, for consciously making the decision to charge differential fees. A decision borne out of fairness and integrity concerns resulted in the distorted perception that the university was charging lower fees because it was running a deficiency model (Dakka, 2014).

The impact of the quasi-market on institutions, student numbers and the sector at large has been comprehensively evaluated by Gill Wyness (Scott and

Callender, 2013), who looked at student admissions in 2012–2013, when the reform came to effect. The numbers revealed a *polarized* outcome: Russell Group institutions generally benefitted from the AAB+ policy, while maintaining or expanding student intake. Further education colleges, at the opposite end, took advantage of the core-margin policy,[14] gaining more than 10,000 places from the pool of the contestable margin and resulting to be the only net gainer, with a 47% increase in student numbers on the previous year.

The mid-tier universities, attended by the majority of students, were negatively affected: they lost students to cheaper providers and were not well equipped to compete for AAB+ students, thus struggling to remain financially viable, facing departmental closures and internal radical reshuffling and/or enhanced competition with other universities in the squeezed middle. These outcomes are compatible with a qualitative, empirical study conducted on six public English HEIs in 2013 (Dakka, 2014). Its conclusions pointed to an odd case of *polarized convergence*. An increased cross-segment fragmentation reflected in steeper reputational stratification (elite vs. teaching institutions) was offset by a substantial and increasing convergence in organizational culture: here, the surprising resilience of academic drifts in a context of increasing research concentration was a strong case in point.[15]

If competition and mimetic behaviours go hand in hand with differentiation, the propensity to a cultural convergence around the corporate university model seems somewhat irresistible.

Conclusions: 'A distinction without a difference?'

Fourteen years ago, Brown (2000) maintained that the expansion in the size of the English higher education system and the consequent diversification of student body and undergraduate curricula were processes that had not been fully understood. The reason for this lack of understanding was to be found in the absence of a clear political debate about the nature and purpose of British higher education and in a fundamental difficulty to come to terms with the idea – and practice – of diversity.

Fourteen years later, everything has changed so that everything can be the same. Differentiation and diversity have been tied up with the marketization agenda in an effort to make the system more responsive to the needs of the wider economy, to improve student choice and quality of provision. Diversity and innovation have been promoted as twin concepts that mutually reinforce each other and thrive on competitiveness. However, this analysis has suggested that the system is currently being reshaped as a polarized sector with increasingly reduced levels of systemic diversity.

The literature reviewed and the empirical study conducted by the author have clarified that institutional differentiation is inhibited by policies that damage diversity, such as the Research Assessment Exercise or the academic threshold standards imposed by the Quality Assurance Agency or indeed by the institutionalization of metrics predicated upon uniformity of standards, procedures and desired goals (NSS, league tables, KIS). Institutional differentiation is also fundamentally undermined by academic drifts, innovation drifts and, perhaps *fatally*, by the positional nature of higher education (increasingly perceived as a luxury good).

Different policy alternatives have been advanced – in England – to try and lift such hindrances: in 1988 the Advisory Board for the Research Councils had proposed a threefold categorization of universities into R, T, X, where R stands for publicly funded research intensive institutions, T for teaching-only universities and X for universities focusing on both. In 1997, Watson (in Brown, 2000) advanced a more refined classification of the English institutions that produced six types: the international research university; the modern professional formation university; the curriculum innovation university; the distance, open learning university; the university college; and, finally, the single subject, specialized college.

Both ideas were discarded in favour of a different approach, ideally based on a combination of rationalization of provision and HEFCE-targeted initiatives to promote diversity such as the Higher Education Innovation Fund (HEIF) or other initiatives aimed at encouraging excellence in teaching and learning. The results yielded in this respect were not impressive. One way to discipline the plurality of contemporary institutional missions and aspirations could be *via* the reprise of the so-called Wisconsin model: a regional system of networked institutions under which each university or college has a particular role enabling it to specialize, while all students benefit, through credit transfer and pathways, from access to the whole system (Brown, 2000, p. 3).

In light of the recent policy changes and targets, this model of provision could square the circle by providing simultaneously more specialization and flexibility, more student choice and access for a greater cohort of students. However, I would argue that this is unlikely to happen for three major and connected reasons: first, because real institutional differentiation cannot happen without a full and shared understanding of what diversity is and means for the development of a system of mass higher education; second, because the connection between diversity and innovation has been taken for granted without unpacking the core – philosophical – assumptions that build their connection; and, last but not least, because the necessary debate about the meanings and purposes of higher education in the 21st century has failed to happen.

Notes

1. A transition that has historically characterized the British and Australian higher education systems.

2. By which is meant the emergence of new entities in the system under scrutiny.
3. The processes leading to an increase of the number of entities of the subject under survey.
4. As enunciated in Darwin's *Origin of Species* (1859).
5. *The division of Labor in Society* (1893).
6. *Societies: Evolutionary and Comparative Perspectives* (1966).
7. Absorbing the bulk of the second wave of massification.
8. Selective, competitive funding.
9. In contrast to clear patterns of institutional segmentation according to institutional types, it will be more likely to see permeability of educational ladders and soft patterns of diversity: no decision in one's educational career is definite or permanent, and rapid adaptations to changing conditions are the norm.
10. Certain patterns and policies come and go in cycles: opening up educational roots and reduction of the differences between varied types of higher education institutions and course programmes might be on the agenda at times where shortage of graduates is felt; whereas segmentation and hierarchization of higher education might be favoured and actually might take place, when fears of over-supply of graduates and 'over-education' dominate the scene (Teichler, 2004, p. 8).
11. Bleiklie proposes an interpretive framework centred on the notion of *knowledge regimes* as dynamic pillars explaining the integration of contemporary HE systems.
12. With formal articulation of issues of differentiation and stratification and/or their opposites.
13. Students would start to repay their debt once earning at least £21,000 per annum (paying 9% of their income above £21,000); the interest rate on their loans would be limited to inflation; graduates earning between £21,000 and £41,000 would be charged progressively a higher interest rate up to a maximum of inflation plus 3% when annual earnings exceeded £41,000; and any outstanding debt would be written off after 30 years.
14. However, due to a failure of this policy to generate a sufficient incentive for price variation among the HEIs, core-margin policy was phased out in 2013 (e.g. margin reduced to 5,000 places to be distributed formulaically among the HEIs).
15. For a thorough analysis of the evolution of the English Research Assesment Exercise (RAE) from its inception in 1986 until the latest iteration (Research Excellence Framework 2014) and the gradual shift from research selectivity to research concentration and impact, see Palfreyman and Tapper (2014)

References

Altbach, P. G. (2007) *Traditions and Transitions: The International Imperative in Higher Education* (Rotterdam, Netherlands: Sense Publishers).

Altbach, P. G., and J. J. F. Forest (eds) (2007) *International Handbook of Higher Education* (18) (pp. 246–280).

Arnove, R. F., and C. A. Torres (eds) (2007) *Comparative Education: The Dialectic of the Global and the Local*, 3rd edn (Lanham, Maryland: Rowman & Littlefield Publishers, Inc.).

Bekhradnia, B. (2012) Higher education reforms: future implications, from https://www.youtube.com/watch?v=IOAUhClCcyI.

Birnbaum, R. (1983) *Maintaining Diversity in Higher Education* (San Francisco: Jossey-Bass).

BIS (Department for Business, Innovation and Skills) (2011) *Higher Education: Students at the Heart of the System.* Retrieved February 10, 2015, accessed online at https://www.gov.uk/government/uploads/system/uploads/attachment_data/file/31384/11-944-higher-education-students-at-heart-of-system.pdf.

Bleiklie, I. (2004) Organizing higher education in knowledge society. UNESCO Forum Occasional Paper Series. Paper No. 6. In: *Diversification of Higher Education and the Changing Role of Knowledge and Research*.(ED-2006/WS/44).

Bourdieu, P. (2005) *The Social Structures of the Economy* (Cambridge: Polity Press).

Brown, R. (2000) 'Diversity in higher education: do we really want it?' *Perspectives: Policy and Practice in Higher Education*, 4(1), 2–6.

Brown, R. (2009) Where the US goes today, HEPI [Online]. Retrieved February 1, 2015, from http://www.hepi.ac.uk/484-1579/Where-the-US-goes-today.html.

Brown, R. (2010) What future for UK Higher Education? Research & Occasional Paper Series: CSHE.5.10. http://cshe.berkeley.edu/.

Brown, R. (ed) (2011) *Higher Education and the Market* (London: Routledge).

CHE (Committee on Higher Education) (1963) *Higher Education: A Report by the Committee Appointed by the Prime Minister under the Chairmanship of Lord Robbins, 1961–63 (The Robbins Report)* (London: HMSO).

Clark, B.R. (1983) *The Higher Education System: Academic Organization in Cross-National Perspective* (Berkeley: University of California Press).

Codling, A., Meek,V.L. (2006) 'Twelve propositions on diversity in higher education', *Higher Education Management and Policy*, (OECD), 18(3),1–26.

Collini, S. (2012) *What Are Universities For?* (London: Penguin Books).

Comaroff, J. and J. L. Comaroff, (2000) 'Millennial capitalism: first thoughts on a second coming', *Public Culture*, 12(2), 291–343.

Dakka, F. (2014) 'Unpublished doctoral thesis' *Discourses and Strategies on Institutional Competition, Differentiation and Convergence in the English Higher Education* (Bristol: University of Bristol).

Dale, R. (2011) 'Globalising Education and Governance' (lecture), Summer school on regionalization, globalization and privatization in education, accessed online at http://vimeo.com/35134410.

DiMaggio, P. J. and W. W. Powell (1983) 'The iron cage revisited: institutional isomorphism and collective rationality in organizational fields', *American Sociological Review*, 48(2), 147–160.

European Commission (2011) 'Supporting growth and jobs – an agenda for the modernisation of Europe's higher education systems', accessed online at https://www.cun.it/uploads/3329/commissioncommunication20settembre2011.pdf?v=.

Gibbons, M., Limoges, C., Nowotny, H., Scott, P., Schwartzman, S., and M. Trow (1994) *The New Production of Knowledge: The Dynamics of Science and Research in Contemporary Societies* (London: Sage).

Giroux, H. (1983) 'Theories of reproduction and resistance in the new sociology of education: a critical analysis', *Harvard Education Review*, 55(3), 257–293.

Hill, D. and R. Kumar (eds) (2009) *Global Neoliberalism and Education and its Consequences* (New York: Routledge).

Hirsch, F. (1976) *Social Limits to Growth* (Harvard: Harvard University Press).

Holmwood, J. (ed) (2011) *A Manifesto for the Public University* (London: Bloomsbury Publishing).

Holmwood, J. (2012) *The Higher Education Experiment in England*. Retrieved January 8, 2015, accessed online at http://andreasbieler.net/wp-content/files/Holmwood.pdf.

Holmwood, J. (2014) 'From Social rights to the market: neoliberalism and the knowledge economy', *International Journal of Lifelong Education*, 33(1), 62–76.

Horta, H., Huisman, J. and M. Heitor (2008) 'Does competitive research funding encourage diversity in higher education?' *Science and Public Policy*, 35(3), 146–158.

Huisman, J. (ed) (2009) *International Perspectives on the Governance of Higher Education: Alternative Frameworks for Coordination* (New York: Routledge).

Kogan, M. (1997) 'Diversification in higher education: differences and commonalities', *Minerva*, 35(1), 47–62.

Kogan, M. and S. Hanney (2000) *Reforming Higher Education* (London: Jessica Kingsley Publishers).

Meek, L. V., Goedegebuure, L., Kivinen, O., and R. Rinne (eds) (1996) *The Mockers and the Mocked: Comparative Perspectives on Differentiation, Convergence and Diversity in Higher Education*, Issues in Higher Education (Emerald Group Publishing Limited: UK).

McGettigan, A. (2014) Article. Retrieved January 7, 2015, accessed online at http://www.timeshighereducation.co.uk/features/uncontrolled-expansion-how-private-colleges-grew/2016579.article

McNay, I. (ed) (2006) *Beyond Mass Higher Education: Building on Experience* (Berkshire: The Society for Research into Higher Education & Open University Press).

Neave, G. (1979) 'Academic drift: some views from Europe', *Studies in Higher Education*, 4(2), 143–159.

Neave, G. (2005) 'The supermarketed university: reform, vision and ambiguity in British higher education', *Perspectives: Policy and Practice in Higher Education*, 9(1), 17–22.

Palfreyman, D., and T. Tapper (eds) (2014) *Reshaping the University: The Rise of the Regulated Market in Higher Education* (Oxford: Oxford University Press).

Parry, G. (2003) 'Mass higher education and the English: wherein the colleges?' *Higher Education Quarterly*, 57(4), 308–337. https://www.gov.uk/government/uploads/system/uploads/attachment_data/file/32425/12-905-understanding-higher-education-in-further-education-colleges.pdf.

Parsons, T. and G. M. Platt (1973) *The American University* (Cambridge: Harvard University Press).

Riesman, D. (1958) *Constraint and Variety in American Education* (Lincoln: University of Nebraska Press).

Rhoades, G. (1990) 'Political competition and differentiation in higher education', in J. C. Alexander, and P. Colony (eds) *Differentiation Theory and Social Change* (New York: Columbia University Press), 187–221.

Rhoades, G. (2007) 'Distinctive choices in intersecting markets: seeking strategic niches', in R. L. Geiger, C. L. Colbeck, R. L. Williams, and C. K. Anderson (eds) *Governing Knowledge: A Study of Continuity and Change in Higher Education. A Festschrift in Honour of Maurice Kogan* (Dordrecht: Springer).

Rossi, F. (2010) 'Massification, competition and organizational diversity in higher education: evidence from Italy', *Studies in Higher Education*, 35(3), 277–300.

Scott, P. (1996) 'Markets in post-compulsory education – rhetoric, policy and structure', in N. Foskett (ed) *Markets in Education: Policy and Practice – Volume 2: Markets in Post-compulsory Education* (Southampton: Centre for Research in Education Marketing, University of Southampton).

Scott, P. (2005) 'Mass higher education – ten years on', *Perspectives: Policy and Practice in Higher Education*, 9(3), 68–73.

Scott, P. (2012) *The Political Economy of Mass Higher Education: Privatisation and Nationalisation* (Nottingham: University of Nottingham/Nottingham Jubilee Press).

Scott, P., and C. Callender (eds) (2013) *Browne and Beyond: Modernizing English Higher Education* (London: Institute of Education Press).

Scott, P. (2013) Article. Retrieved January 2015, accessed online at http://www.theguardian.com/education/2013/feb/04/higher-education-university-student-decline.

Shavit, Y., Arum, R., Gamoran, A., and G. Menahem (eds) (2007) *Stratification in Higher Education: A Comparative Study* (Stanford, CA: Stanford University Press).

Shattock, M. (2012) *Making Policy in British Higher Education 1945–2011* (England: Open University Press).

Teichler, U. (2004) Changing Structures of the Higher Education Systems: The Increasing Complexity of Underlying Forces. UNESCO Forum Occasional Paper Series. Paper No.6. In *Diversification of Higher Education and the Changing Role of Knowledge and Research* (ED-2006/WS/44).

Trow, M. (1970) 'Reflections on the transition from mass to universal higher education', *Daedalus*, 99, 1–42.

van Vught, F. A. (2008) 'Mission diversity and reputation in higher education', *Higher Education Policy*, 21(2), 151–174.

Williams, G. (1995) 'The "marketization" of higher education: reforms and potential reforms in higher education finance', in D.D. Dill, and B. Sporn (eds) *Emerging Patterns of Social Demand and University Reform: Through a Glass Darkly* (Oxford: Pergamon Press).

19
How Information and Communication Technology Is Shaping Higher Education

Arne M. Fevolden and Cathrine E. Tømte

Introduction

Information and communications technologies (ICTs) have had a tremendous impact on science (Selwyn, 2014). They have enabled scientists from fields as diverse as physics and economics to carry out studies that would have been inconceivable half a century ago, and they have brought forth a significant amount of new knowledge. Nevertheless, these technologies have so far only had a moderate effect on higher education and higher education institutions (HEIs) (Bates, 2014). Although educators have made use of presentation software and made teaching material available online, and administrators have made use of learning management systems and used the Internet to recruit new groups of students, the HEIs themselves and the teaching methods they employ have remained largely the same (Bates, 2014; Daniel, 1996). However, this might be about to change.

There has recently been a series of ICT-based developments that might have a more profound impact on higher education, which have appeared under headings such as 'MOOCs' (Massive Open Online Courses), 'Big Data', 'learning analytics' and 'adaptive learning'. Although these ICT-based developments have only recently reached the public eye, they have already generated much public controversy about what their consequences might be. Optimistically inclined commentators have argued that these developments will make higher education free (or cheap) and available for everyone (see *Economist*, 2014; Ng, 2013), whereas pessimistically inclined commentators foresee the end of HEIs and the destruction of vital research infrastructure (see de Freitas, 2013). Others have maintained that the impact of the developments will be more subtle and gradual and that their effects on higher education will only be marginal or moderate.

Perhaps the reason why these new ICT-based developments have generated so much debate is that they seem to usher in something essentially new, while introducing little novelty in terms of new technologies, pedagogies or institutional arrangements. As some commentators have pointed out, the 'pioneering' MOOCs make use of nothing more than standard Internet applications and function as nothing more than traditional distance learning institutions (Bates, 2014). Nevertheless, as other commentators have argued, the ICT-based developments that we are witnessing today operate on a scale that is new and unprecedented (see discussion in Young, 2013). We agree with both sides of this discussion. The individual elements that make up these ICT-based developments are not necessarily new, but at the same time the scale and combination of these elements constitute something truly novel, which might bring along substantial changes in higher education.

In this chapter, we will examine these ICT-based developments and discuss their possible implications for higher education governance. We will not focus on the impact of new ICTs, but on the impact of new ICT-based developments. In fact, we are interested in the consequences of ICT for teaching and learning ('where', 'when' and 'how') as well as for the system and its institutions. We will distinguish between two groups of ICT-based developments – those developments that mainly affect *where* and *when* we learn, and those that affect *how* we learn. In the first group, we find ICT-based developments that enable students to follow courses off-campus, at a time and pace of their choosing, such as online learning, Open Educational Resources (OER) and MOOCs. In the second group, we find ICT-based developments such as adaptive learning and Big Data that can be used to identify the issues that students struggle with and how their learning outcomes can be improved. Although the ICT-based developments from both groups are interlinked, we would argue that this distinction can help us uncover important analytical dimensions, such as whether computers with broadband access will replace traditional campuses or whether new pedagogies will replace traditional classroom and lecture-based teaching.

This chapter is organized in the following way. In the second and third sections, we present the two groups of ICT-based developments that are mentioned above. In the fourth section, we look at how these developments again might affect higher education. Finally, we conclude by discussing implications of these ICT-based developments for higher education governance.

The *where* and *when* of teaching and learning

There have been several attempts to characterize e-learning in terms of 'where' and 'when' (Allen and Seaman, 2014; Gaebel et al., 2014b; Means et al., 2010). In the following paragraphs we introduce key terms such as e-learning, blended/hybrid learning, online learning and MOOCs and how these concepts have been understood. A first step might be to explore how these terms respond to 'where' and 'when' with regard to the flexibility of higher education.

Classifications of online learning

When the US Department of Education conducted a review and meta-analysis of online learning studies, it defined online learning as 'learning that takes place partially or entirely over the Internet' (Means et al., 2010, p. 9). Two purposes of online learning were promoted: learning conducted online as a substitute for, or alternative to, face-to-face-learning, and online learning components combined/blended with face-to-face instructions to provide learning enhancement (Means et al.). We find a similar approach in the survey of online learning in the United States, conducted annually since 2006 by the Babson Survey Group (Allen and Seaman, 2014). In this survey, four categories represent degrees of flexibility concerning the use of Internet in various types of courses. Also here, the 'where' and 'when' emerge as indicators. The first category includes traditional courses that are not using online technology. In the second category, the Internet supports traditional face-to-face learning, for example, by posting syllabuses on a learning management platform. The third category concerns hybrid or blended forms and involves substantial online content deliveries, such as online discussions and video tutorials. The last category comprises an entirely online learning environment in which mostly all content is delivered online (Allen and Seaman, 2014, p. 6). E-learning thus serves as an overall term that includes teaching and learning activities supported by ICT. Variations of 'where' and 'when' are associated with blended learning and online learning (Gaebel et al., 2014b). Table 19.1 illustrates how various ICT-based teaching and learning activities relate to the 'where' and 'when' approach.

Over the years, there has been a shift in the uptake of 'where' and 'when' in e-learning in HEIs. For example, Bates (2014) states that e-learning *activities* have changed. From being a supplement to traditional teaching, also defined as blended learning, to the use of flipped classroom models, where the learning activities moved out of the classroom to the Internet, towards what he

Table 19.1 E-learning according to 'where' and 'when'

		Where		When	
E-learning		Campus based (classroom)	Distance (wherever)	Synchronous (real time)	Asynchronous (whenever)
	Blended	×	×	×	×
	Online		×	×	×
	MOOCs		×		×

characterizes as 'a "re-design of campus-based classes" where the teaching on campus is reconsidered due to the use of technology' (Bates, 2014). He describes this development as moving from a fixed 'where' and 'when' solution, such as face-to-face interaction at campus or in classrooms, towards flexible solutions, including online learning at a distance. The flexibility involves both students and teachers (Bates, 2014).

Bacow et al. (2012) suggest to distinguish four axes that group content and approach in online learning in order to understand the diversity. These axes are (1) purely online versus blended approaches that also include face-to-face interaction; (2) self-paced systems versus systems where all students participate simultaneously in teaching and learning within established schedules; (3) systems that rely on social games and a peer-based approach versus systems oriented towards individual learners; and (4) massive open online courses (MOOCs), that is, large-scale teaching generated by hardware, versus approaches that require significant effort by teaching staff to ensure interaction with students.

The emergence of e-learning

Although e-learning, and online learning in particular, is considered as an important trend in contemporary higher education (Allen and Seaman, 2014; Bates, 2014), it is still a rather new development. In its earliest days, online learning was introduced by a few dedicated institutions, such as The Open University in the United Kingdom, but these initiatives had little direct impact on teaching and learning activities in conventional universities (Bates, 2014). Moreover, the HEIs that promoted online learning, such as technical and open universities, have not always been leading in other e-learning activities such as various ICT-supported teaching or digitalization of educational resources (Gaebel et al. 2014).

The first online courses that emerged in the mid-1990s derived their online content from extensive experience with distance-based education and learning, which again existed long before the introduction of modern ICT (Casey, 2008). In such courses, diverse sources of media and information were adopted, such as print-based correspondence education, broadcast television and radio, along with videoconference and video systems and educational software programmes delivered on CDs or the like. They did not, however, include any Internet-based components (Means et al., 2010).

For example, the UK Open University (OU) was founded in 1969 to provide international distance education by making (college) learning available for everyone. Over the years, the OU has adopted emerging technologies in its educational systems, such as radio, television and finally the Internet. In 2014, the OU had 200,000 students studying online. Other colleges, on the other hand, have offered online education that mirrors their traditional courses – with class sizes and student numbers that are more modest in size. These colleges first started to offer online education based on asynchronous collaboration tools such as e-mail and digital learning platforms. However, as bandwidth and software improved, they began to include synchronous elements such as real time audio, video and communication.

MOOC

The term 'MOOC' seems to have originated as a description of a course on 'Connectivism and Connective Knowledge', which was taught in 2008 by two professors at the University of Manitoba in Canada for a group of 30 students officially enrolled on campus (Young, 2013). What separated this course from other courses was that the professors encouraged everyone on the Web to contribute to the course by giving comments and joining in the discussions. About 2,300 people answered the call and signed up for the course as informal participants. The result was an almost overwhelming number of blog posts and online commentaries, and the two professors had to help the students to manoeuvre and absorb the information. The sheer magnitude of the event led to a name search that would describe this new type of course adequately. The suggestion that swiftly gained acceptance was MOOC: massive open online course.

Although the professors at the University of Manitoba came up with the first official MOOC, professors at American Ivy League universities brought MOOCs into the limelight (Baggaley, 2013; Young, 2013). In 2011, when Sebastian Thrun of Stanford University announced on YouTube that he would teach an open, online course on artificial intelligence, he tapped into a new 'market': by the time the course started, he had a staggering 160,000 registered pupils. Another professor at Stanford, Andrew Ng, achieved similar results. Inspired by this success, both professors established companies that had the ambition of providing access to online courses across the globe (Coursera (Thrun) and Udacity (Ng)). Others soon followed: for example, the joint effort of Massachusetts Institute of Technology (MIT) and Harvard University (edX).

Although edX, Coursera and Udacity attracted much media attention as MOOCs, they were in many ways different from the MOOC at the University of Manitoba. The Manitoba MOOC relied extensively on user-produced content, while edX, Coursera and Udacity provided a platform for students to access ready-made lectures. Some commentators argue that the difference between them runs deeper and involves different learning philosophies (Baggaley, 2013). They started to refer to the MOOCs established at Manitoba as 'Connectivist MOOCs' or 'cMOOCs' and to edX, Coursera and Udacity as 'xMOOCs'. Despite the merits of the cMOOCs, it was the xMOOCs that the *New York Times* referred to when it declared 2012 'the year of the MOOC' (Pappano, 2012). And it is the xMOOCs that capture the interest of an overwhelming number of students.

There is an ongoing discussion whether the MOOCs actually represent a distinctly new type of e-learning (Wiley, 2014; Young, 2013). One distinction that is highlighted is how MOOCs have been flagged by their technology providers such as Coursera and edX. In conventional online learning courses, other aspects such as the content/subject is highlighted more than the technological platform on which it is based (Wiley, 2014). In terms of 'when' and 'where', the MOOCs provide a form of asynchronous distance learning that is quite similar to traditional online learning. Nevertheless, the MOOCs seem to provide these courses on a scale that is unprecedented and in a format that is unfamiliar to most universities and colleges.

The *how* of higher education

This section contains two parts. The first part concerns the 'how' question as regards ICT-based developments influence teaching and learning. The second part explores how ICT-based developments may discover new ways of learning.

ICTs' influence on the 'how' of teaching and learning

Whereas e-learning comprises various ways of adopting ICT in teaching and learning processes, the concept of the 'flipped classroom' has emerged as a new method of teaching that exploits the possibilities of the Internet. In this way, technology developments also influence 'how' teaching and learning are practised. Lage, Platt and Treglia (2000, p. 32) define a flipped classroom as follows: 'Inverting the classroom means that events that have traditionally taken place inside the classroom now take place outside the classroom and vice versa.' This often means that students themselves go through subject materials prior to a teaching session. This methodology has gradually been adopted in primary, secondary and tertiary education (Hamdan et al., 2013).

Flipped classrooms have various aims. First, students should be able to prepare for teaching. Second, teaching is adapted to the students' skill level. And third, teachers have (more) time to keep closer track of each student. The subject matter is available as digital learning resources, often as videos or interactive tasks via the Internet as students go through the learning process on their own. The fact that students themselves must take responsibility for their learning may contribute to a more student-active teaching instead of teacher-led instruction. The Kahn Academy was one of the first content providers that initially published instructional video clips on algebra on YouTube. Currently, it is providing instructional video clips in several subjects.

To complete the flipped classroom concept successfully, studies demonstrate the need for structural changes. Hamdan et al. (2013) point out four measures as essential to the success of the flipped classroom. The four include awareness of the importance of (1) flexible learning environments, (2) the learning culture, (3) the subject matter and (4) a competent teacher. The four points describe a student-centred learning process where cooperation and communication are the premises for learning activities. The teacher's main role is to facilitate learning for each student based on his or her existing knowledge. The teacher must also be able to assess which parts of the subject are suitable for self-study and which for the communal learning. Teachers who use inverted classroom pedagogy would also benefit from an ongoing dialogue with colleagues for continuous skills development. They also must accept constructive criticism from colleagues and reflect on improvement opportunities in their own practice (Hamdan et al., 2013).

How ICT-based developments may enhance/discover new ways of learning

ICT-based developments might also alter 'how' we learn (European Commission, 2014; Gaebel et al., 2014b). Currently, ICT-based developments have mostly been directed towards providing students with access to various digital learning resources and improving the communication between students, teachers and HEIs. Nevertheless, there are reasons to believe that a new era or paradigm, based on developments in ICT, is emerging. We introduce and discuss below why this might be the case. In making increasing use of digital learning resources, HEIs (as well as other stakeholders) generate data and network activity logs that can, for example, be used to analyse how students learn and to improve their educational results. Three important ICT-based developments that have emerged in this regard are 'Big Data', 'learning analytics' and 'adaptive learning systems'.

The term 'Big Data' indicates large datasets that are so complex that they challenge traditional methods of analysis. As our lives are connected increasingly to the Internet, numerous data logs are being generated. These data logs raise both opportunities and challenges for society, including higher education. Such opportunities and challenges are, for example, ethical dimensions (privacy) and literacy dimensions (such as methods and skills in how to use these data for improving existing teaching and learning practices, or even develop new practices).

'Learning analytics' has emerged as one term to understand how to analyse Big Data deriving from the educational context and, if possible, to improve learning systems through adaptive technologies (UNESCO, 2012). Learning analytics covers several analytical approaches. One way to group these approaches concerns the level they focus on. Macro analytics enables cross-institutional analytics, for example, by collecting data from learning management systems from several HEIs and comparing these data or by collecting and analysing data deriving from MOOCs. The latter will be discussed in more detail in the following paragraphs. The meso-level analytics operate at an institutional level, by operating in the same fashion as at the macro-level, but solely within a single institution. Micro-level analytics might include tracking and analysing data from individual learners and teachers (UNESCO, 2012).

Another approach to understanding these levels of learning analytics is to split the term into learning analytics and academic analytics (Long and Siemens, 2011). Long and Siemens identify learning analytics at micro levels; both course level – involving social networks, discourse analysis, conceptual development and the like – and departmental level, including predictive modelling and patterns of success and failure. For the meso and macro levels, Long and Siemens (2011) introduce the term 'academic analysis', which embraces learner profiles, performance of academics and knowledge flow. Academic analysis includes comparisons within and between higher education systems that (supra)national governments and education authorities might consider useful (Long and Siemens, 2011, p. 34).

In the remainder of this section, we focus on the micro-level analytical approaches. There are a number of such micro-level approaches: learning platforms, predictive, social network, discourse and adaptive learning analytics (Long and Siemens, 2011). What we refer to as 'basic learning analysis' or 'learning platform analytics' involves using analysis functions, such as activity patterns of the users inherent in most learning platforms in use today. This includes, for example, simple visualizations of the data logger that can give each participant a quick overview of their results compared with others (benchmarking) and give the teacher an overview of the participants' activities.

A more advanced form of learning analytics at the micro level is predictive analytics. This involves combining statistical data, such as demographics and previous study results, with dynamic data, such as logs indicating user patterns in learning platforms, meaning which documents participants work with or the extent of their participation in the online discussion. The goal of such analyses is to predict each participant's learning, by identifying distinctive learning patterns for different groups and directing them into appropriate action at an early stage.

Analysis of social networks can visualize relationships. The goal is to identify if participants are not socially and academically involved in an educational programme or if teachers interact with participants in a study group. The Social Networks Adapting Pedagogical Practice (SNAPP) is an example of applied technology to analyse learning behaviour. SNAPP analyses the social network and forum activity in the learning management systems, the so-called LMS, providing teaching staff diagnostic instruments to evaluate the digital participant activity towards learning. Recent research shows that there is strong correlation between 'online activities' (collaboration with other participants or with others who knew the subject well) and test results. Participants who collaborate with peers achieve better results than those who work alone (Breslow et al., 2013).

Discourse analysis is considered as the most complex form of learning analytics. This approach comprises systems that log and enhance participants' and teachers' contributions or activities and the quality of what is being written. The system will then be able to provide specific feedback to teachers and learners about the quality of their contributions. Although there is already technology that can analyse certain qualitative aspects of a text, as it stands at the moment it is not good enough for advanced learning purposes (UNESCO, 2012).

Adaptive learning systems are (Web-based) technologies that ensure a personalized or customized learning environment for students. The technology adapts content to correspond with the student's learning activities. These systems are different from regular digital learning resources, because they adjust content to each individual's skills or learning style. Each student can learn at a different pace and have different levels of knowledge within the current subject (Brusilovsky and Peylo, 2003; Romero et al., 2009).

Learning styles, cognitive styles or learning achievements have been the most common information sources on which adaptive learning systems have been based. In recent years, we have witnessed the development of adaptive learning systems that include more than single-person-based sources. We have seen systems that include both learning styles and learning behaviour (Ozyurt et al., 2013; Tseng et al., 2008). Findings from these studies indicate that such systems contribute to a better experience of the learning situation of the learner and also contribute positively towards improving learning achievement and learning outcomes (Tseng et al., 2008).

The implications of ICT-based developments for higher education

A wide range of new ICT-based developments have emerged that can potentially affect higher education. What kind of implications these ICT-based developments will actually have is still an open question. This section addresses some debates about potential effects of these new ICT-based developments.

The end of higher education as we know it?

Opinions about the consequences of ICT-based developments for HEIs differ greatly (Selwyn, 2014). Although most commentators believe that these developments will, to some extent, help to re-invent HEIs, others have argued that the impact of these developments will be even more profound. The latter have argued that the successful 'institutionalization' of MOOCs may be so unsettling that traditional HEIs will cease to exist (*Economist*, 2014; Pappano, 2012). We will discuss two concepts that have been used to justify such views: the concept of 'disruptive innovations' (Bower and Christensen, 1995; Christensen,

1997) and the concept of 'cost disease' (Baumol and Bowen, 1966). We explore the extent to which these concepts apply to higher education.

The concept of 'disruptive technologies' (later, disruptive innovations) was coined by Bower and Christensen (1995), Christensen (1997) and Christensen and Raynor (2003). This (refined) concept aims to explain a paradoxical pattern of industrial evolution where leading companies are suddenly and abruptly replaced by smaller competitors providing low-range niche products. Christensen (1997, 2003) found this pattern repeated in several industries and were wondering whether this pattern emerged because the industry leaders were not sufficiently innovative or adequately responsive to customers' needs. They discovered, however, that innovativeness and customer sensitivity were not the reasons why these industry leaders failed. On the contrary, by catering to the needs of their mainstream customers, the leading companies tend to ignore down-market opportunities for cheaper and lower-performing products. These smaller and less profitable markets were often left to newcomers, who provided cheap and tawdry products that often offered added advantages such as 'portability' (for the first transistor-based radios) or smaller size (for successive generations of hard disks).

Leading companies tended to outperform their market by providing products that offered greater performance than was needed by mainstream customers. At the same time, newcomers improved their products rapidly and became competitive in mainstream markets, but with added advantages that they learned from competing in the low-range markets. In this sense, the newcomers' products became disruptive by replacing and pushing out the leading companies, despite their innovative attitude.

There are certainly similarities between Christensen's (1997) theories of disruptive innovations and MOOCs. MOOCs provide services that in many areas lag behind conventional HEIs. They offer neither the same number of courses as universities nor the same opportunity to obtain academic degrees. MOOCs also lack effective ways of testing students' learning outcomes, and their courses are not accredited in the same way as university degrees. Nevertheless, MOOCs might – as the newcomers in Christensen's theories – remedy these shortcomings over time. In addition, MOOCs offer increased flexibility and might in the future include adaptive functionalities that could give them a competitive edge over conventional teaching. For the moment, they appear to be cheaper and could behave as 'price busters'. Other shortcomings are likely be more difficult to remedy. MOOCs cannot, by definition, provide the same sort of interaction between teachers and students, or the same type of learning environment, as university or college campuses. Prospective students, however, might – as the customers in Christensen's theories – see this interaction and learning environment as beneficial, but not strictly necessary for completing their studies or gaining knowledge and competence that the labour market requires.

Baumol's concept of cost disease is also used to project the end of traditional HEIs. The central idea in Baumol's theory is that productivity grows at different rates in different sectors of the economy: capital-intensive sectors such as manufacturing tend to experience a great deal of productivity growth, while labour-intensive sectors such as nursing tend to experience less productivity growth. When a sector of the economy experiences productivity growth, the salaries of workers both in this sector and sectors that did not experience similar growth tend to increase. While an increase in salaries for workers in the capital-intensive sectors is offset by the increases in productivity, the same increase results in higher costs in the labour-intensive sectors. The result is, for example, that buying a sound system is much cheaper today than 20 years ago, while attending a classical music concert is much more expensive.

Higher education is a sector that typically suffers from cost disease, because there are limited opportunities to improve the productivity of teaching. Higher education has, as a result, seen large cost increases. In some countries, such as the United States, this has translated into higher student tuition costs and in other countries, such as Norway, it has led to higher public sector expenditure (Bowen, 2013). Although Baumol and Bowen (1966) pointed out that if countries that experience such cost increases can afford them (as increased productivity results in increased wealth), then they are seldom willing to fully compensate the sectors that lag in productivity. Arguably, lagging productivity among the HEIs leads to a cost pressure on the HEIs that paves the way for 'more productive' MOOCs.

The extent to which the concepts of disruptive innovation and cost disease will hold in higher education's future is unclear. There are some reasons why MOOCs as newcomers will not become competitive against traditional HEIs. First, MOOCs may not be able to provide an education of comparable quality to that of traditional HEIs. Second, students and governments may be willing to pay for the additional education costs that accrue due to cost disease. And third, it is also possible that HEIs adopt some of the same digital tools that the MOOCs apply and thereby increase their productivity (and lower their costs). If any of these assumptions hold, then MOOCs and open education initiatives become more of a supplement to traditional education than full-blown educational institutions in their own right.

From mass education to personalized learning?

ICT-based developments can also have implications for pedagogy. For example, Big Data and learning analytics can have a broad range of positive implications for higher education (Hollands and Tirthali, 2014a). These rich sources of information can transform pedagogical approaches in HEIs. For example, at the micro level, learning analytics can provide learners with improved and personalized ways of learning. Moreover, learning analytics may also identify at-risk students and provide them with personalized interventions.

More demanding learning analytic approaches, such as adaptive learning systems, will in the future give more insight into how students interact with course materials and correlate student actions with learning processes and outcomes. Although the systematic adoption of learning analytics is still in its initial phase, it is likely that it will lead to course designs that contribute higher levels of student success.

MOOCs represent an interesting case in this respect. They generate numerous and diverse data that might be analysed by various approaches in the learning analytic regime. This will influence both HEIs offering these MOOCs and HEIs that involve MOOCs from external providers for educational purposes. The most demanding forms of such analysis are still in an exploratory phase. In analysing data from institutions that offered MOOCs in 2012 and 2013, Ho et al. (2014) had the aim of identifying the learning patterns that gave good results for participants. They concluded that such patterns are hard to identify, because, although the study contained data from nearly 850,000 participants, even more data are required to detect clear patterns. The reason is that learning in MOOCs takes so many forms, which again need even greater amounts of data to identify learning patterns. Another conclusion was that learning analytics seems to require extensive cooperation between the many institutions that own data from MOOCs. Ho et al. (2014) believe that institutions must enter into binding collaboration and data sharing among themselves to realize the potential of learning analytics (ibid.).

Even if learning analytics in the future contribute to solving complex decisions and to providing learners with personalized feedback and improved learning contexts and outcomes, critical voices highlight the risk of trusting only technology-based findings, which mainly derive from generalization and simplification. They point to a risk in considering findings from learning analytics as objective and neutral. How should one ensure that important details are not ignored? Will automated research change our understanding of knowledge? Will more data provide better information (UNESCO, 2012)? Such questions come to the fore in contemporary debate.

The new technological developments also touch upon ethical issues. Proponents of learning analytics argue that proper use will provide students, teachers and institutions with new tools that can enhance learning. Opponents, however, are concerned about privacy issues. As countries around the world hold different policies on privacy, the privacy issue is a complicated matter. It seems that data from MOOC participants are considered as the property of the MOOC providers (Ho et al., 2014). Any future collaboration agreements between MOOC providers and HEIs, for example to conduct and use learning analytics, are expected to include privacy issues.

Nonetheless, commercial technology providers, even in this initial phase, are about to gain ground within the field of adaptive learning systems. Like MOOCs, these providers have ambitious goals to expand their activities to an international educational context. It would be reasonable to address challenges related to privacy and legislation on privacy to educational governance around the world.

Education for everyone?

The emergence of MOOCs and open education initiatives in particular, and e-learning more generally, raises several questions about access to education and accreditation of qualifications. Several MOOCs and open education initiatives have the explicit aim of making education free and available for everyone (see section 'The *where* and *when* of teaching and learning'). It raises, however, questions about both its ideological underpinnings and the motivation of the actors involved in realizing it. Is there a democratic principle such as an equal right to equal education, or should students carry some of the cost associated with their education? Are universities that act as the MOOCs' content providers motivated by an ambition to make education free and available to all, or do they use MOOCs as a means to market their traditional educational programmes? Is e-learning about reducing costs and increasing access to higher education, or is it about providing better education and developing new ways or methods of learning? Recent research findings suggest, for example, that in Europe HEIs seem to share the same motives for expanding e-learning, namely to improve the use of classroom time and to promote flexibility in learning provision 'regardless of whether learners are on or off campus, recent school leavers or adult learners' (Gaebel et al., 2014, p. 71). As for MOOCs in particular, administrators and faculty members have highlighted MOOCs as reaching and giving access to new groups of students on a global scale; but recent findings indicate that so far this has not been accomplished, mainly due to available bandwidth and technological infrastructure across countries around the globe (Hollands and Tirthali, 2014b). Moreover, in improving economics by reducing costs, the development of MOOCs is still in its initial phase, and therefore it is too early to tell whether MOOCs will contribute to cost reduction. Researchers suggest that sharing MOOC content and resources across faculties and institutions might, however, in the future contribute to cost savings (ibid.).

Another important question is what type of education MOOCs and open education initiatives will provide. On the one hand, there are students who want to complete a university or college degree, and it is unclear to what extent MOOCs can serve those students. On the other hand, there are students following MOOC courses who already have a higher education degree and take these courses primarily to add to or extend their existing knowledge (Hollands and Tirthali, 2014a). In Web and mobile industries, professionals are urged to constantly learn and update their competence, and in this MOOCs are reported as offering an accessible and flexible way to acquire such job-specific skills (Canals and Mor, 2014). This is likely to be the case in more sectors.

MOOCs and open education initiatives provide academic courses that primarily contribute to non-formal and informal learning. It remains an open question if they will provide degree-based education in the future, or whether their activities will primarily be directed towards continuing education for employees that already have a university or college degree. An important issue in this regard is accreditation of the education provided by MOOCs and open education initiatives.

MOOCs and open education initiatives can help their students acquire new knowledge, but this new knowledge will be of little help if the students cannot convince potential employees or other HEIs that they have acquired sufficient proficiency in their field of study (NOU 2014–2015, 2014). In the United States, there is an ongoing debate about online education and accreditation (Gaebel, 2014a; NOU 2014–2015, 2014). A student can already get a type of informal acknowledgment for MOOC courses – often called 'badges' – certifying completion of the course. Some universities, such as Colorado State University, have allowed certain MOOC courses – such as Stanford's course on artificial intelligence (Udacity) – to count as transfer credits towards a degree (NOU, 2014). Nevertheless, there is still a continuing debate about the extent to which online and MOOC-based courses should be accredited at the federal level and an even bigger debate about the extent to which employees will consider MOOC courses as a serious equivalent to campus-based education. In Europe, there has so far been less discussion about credit earning at MOOCs (Gaebel, 2014; NOU, 2014).

Conclusion and implications for governance

In this chapter, we have looked at how ICT-based developments influence higher education and their potential implications. New ICT-based developments can affect 'where', 'when' and 'how' students learn, and in the following paragraphs we discuss the consequences of these technological developments for students, teachers and HEIs.

If e-learning technologies are widely adopted, students are likely to benefit in terms of increased flexibility and improved learning outcomes. OERs, online videotaped lectures, MOOCs and the like will enhance student access to educational resources independent of campus (OECD, 2012). Moreover, students' communication with HEIs and with peers will be facilitated by technological developments.

In the future, a student's identity as campus student and/or online student may become blurred as both groups are offered the same learning resources without making a distinction of what it takes to be either of these. Moreover, even if recent developments in terms of 'how', such as 'Big Data' and 'learning analytics' creates new opportunities for new pedagogical approaches, such as student-centred learning and personalized learning, issues related to privacy, however, remain unresolved.

Similar opportunities and challenges are identified for teachers, in particular in terms of 'where' and 'when'. However, research has demonstrated that not all teachers are interested in changing their ways of teaching or in replacing existing teaching methods with new ICT-based tools and resources. Furthermore, not all teachers have the necessary skills and competencies to adopt digital learning resources for subject syllabuses in teaching (Prestidge, 2012). This might constitute a challenge for their job position as well as for the institution, if e-learning turns out to be an institutional strategy, an idea which is about to gain ground throughout Europe (Gaebel et al., 2014).

HEIs can benefit from these new technological developments in various ways. For example, they are able to reach out to new groups of students by means of online educational programmes and MOOCs. In addition, collaboration is feasible across institutes and faculties. Moreover, MOOCs and other online participation might contribute to innovate pedagogy in various ways, and Big Data generated from MOOCs and online resources may enhance research on teaching and learning based on various forms of learning analytics (Hollands and Thirtali, 2014b). However, quality frameworks for e-learning would need to be developed – there have been some initial initiatives such as the EFQUEL-framework (2011) mainstreaming of e-learning, but researchers suggest that a mainstream approach might be more appropriate, for example, to integrate e-learning within the Bologna Process goals on convergence in higher education (Gaebel et al., 2014b, p. 72).

References

Allen, I. E. and J. Seaman (2014) *Grade Change. Tracking Online Education in the United States* (Wellesley, MA: Babson College/Sloan Foundation).

Bacow, L. S., Bowen, W. G., Guthrie, K. M., Lack, K. A. and M. P. Long (2012) Barriers to Adoption of Online Learning Systems in U.S. Higher Education. Retrieved from http://www.sr.ithaka.org/sites/default/files/reports/barriers-to-adoption-of-online-learning-systems-in-us-higher-education.pdf.

Baggaley, J. (2013) 'MOOC rampant', *Distance Education*, 34(3), 368–378.

Bates, T. (2014) *Teaching in a Digital Age*. Open Textbook. Retrieved from http://opentextbc.ca/teachinginadigitalage/

Baumol, W. and W. Bowen (1966) *Performing Arts, The Economic Dilemma: A Study of Problems Common to Theater, Opera, Music, and Dance* (New York: Twentieth Century Fund).

Bowen, W. G. (2013) *Higher Education in the Digital Age* (Princeton: Princeton University Press).

Bower, J. and C. M. Christensen (1995) 'Disruptive technologies: Catching the wave', *Harvard Business Review*, 73(1), 43–53.

Breslow L., Pritchard, D., E., DeBoer, J., Stump, G, S., Andrew, Ho, D. and D., T. Seaton (2013) 'Studying Learning in the Worldwide Classroom: Research into edX's First MOOC', *Research and Practice in Assessment*, Volume Eight.

Brusilovsky, P. and C. Peylo (2003) 'Adaptive and intelligent web based educational systems', *International Journal of Artificial Intelligence in Education*, 13, 156–169.

Canals, E. and Y. Mor (2014) *MOOCs for Web Talent Network. Final report*. European Commission. http://openeducationeuropa.eu/sites/default/files/Final%20Report_Web skillsMOOCs.pdf.

Casey, D. M. (2008) 'A Journey to Legitimacy: The Historical Development of Distance Education Through Technology', *TechTrends: Linking Research and Practice to Improve Learning*, 52(2), 45–51.

Christensen, C. M. (1997) *The Innovator's Dilemma: When New Technologies Cause Great Firms to Fail* (Boston, MA: Harvard Business School Press).

Christensen, C. M. and M. E. Raynor (2003) *The Innovator's Solution: Creating and Sustaining Successful Growth* (Boston, MA: Harvard Business School Press).

De Freitas, S. (2013) *The Final Frontiers for Higher Education?* Coventry University. Retrieved http://benhur.teluq.uquebec.ca/ted/Ressources/mooc.pdf

Daniel, J. S. (1996) *Mega-Universities and Knowledge Media. Technology Strategies for Higher Education* (London: Kogan Page).

The Economist (2014, June 28), 'Creative destruction,' Leader.

EFQUEL (2011) Unique. *European Universities Quality in e-Learning*. Information Package. EFQUEL, Brussels.

Gaebel, M., Kupriyanova, V., Morais, R. and E. Colucci (2014) *E-learning in European Higher Education Institutions: Results of a Mapping Survey Conducted in October–December 2013* (Brussels: European University Association).

Gaebel, M. (2014) MOOCs – *Massive Open Online Courses* (Brussels: European University Association).

Hamdan, N., McKnight, P., McKnight, K. and K. M. Arfström (2013) *A Review of Flipped Learning*, Flipped learning network 2013.

Ho, A. D., Reich, J., Nesterko, S., Seaton, D. T., Mullaney, T., Waldo, J. and I. Chuang (2014) HarvardX and MITx: The first year of open online courses (HarvardX and MITx Working Paper No. 1).

Hollands, F. and D. Tirthali (2014a) 'Why do institutions offer MOOCs?' *Online Learning* (formerly *Journal of Asynchronous Learning Networks*), 18(3), 1–19.

Hollands, F. M. and D. Tirthali (2014b) *MOOCs: Expectations and Reality. Full Report*. Center for Benefit-Cost Studies of Education, Teachers College, Columbia University, http://cbcse.org/wordpress/wp-content/uploads/2014/05/MOOCs_Expectations _and_Reality.pdf.

Kahn Academy, https://www.khanacademy.org/.

Lage, M. J., Platt G. J. and M. Teglia (2000) 'Inverting the classroom. A gateway to creating an inclusive learning environment', *Journal of Economic Education*, Winter, 30–43.

Long, P. and G. Siemens (2011) *Penetrating the Fog: Analytics in Learning and Education*. EDUCAUSE Review, 46(5), 30–32, from http://www.educause.edu/ero/article/ penetrating-fog-analytics-learning-and-education.

Means, B., Toyama, Y., Murphy, R., Bakia, M. and K. Jones (2010) *Evaluation of Evidence-Based Practices in Online Learning: A Meta-Analysis and Review of Online Learning Studies* (Washington, DC: U.S. Department of Education. Office of Planning, Evaluation, and Policy Development Policy and Program Student Service).

Ng, A. (2013) Learning From MOOCs *Inside Higher Ed* 24.1.2013. Retrieved at https:// www.insidehighered.com/views/2013/01/24/essay-what-professors-can-learn-moocs.

NMC Horizon Report: *2014 Higher Education Edition*. Retrieved at: www.nmc.org.

NOU 2014: 5 *MOOCs for Norway – New Digital Learning Methods in Higher Education*, The Ministry of Education and Research. Retrieved from https://www.regjeringen

.no/contentassets/ff86edace9874505a3381b5daf6848e6/en-gb/pdfs/nou20142014000
5000en_pdfs.pdf.
OECD (2012) *Connected Minds: Technology and Today's Learners*, Educational Research and
Innovation (Paris: OECD Publishing).
Özyurt, Ö., Özyurt, H., Baki, A. & Güven, B.(2013) 'Integration into mathematics
classroom of an adaptive and intelligent individualized e-learning environment:
implementation and evaluation of UZWEBMAT', *Computers in Human Behvior*, 29,
726–738.
Pappano, L. (2012) 'The year of the MOOC', *New York Times*, November 4, Retrieved from
http://www.nytimes.com.
Prestidge, S. (2012) 'The Beliefs behind the teacher that influences their ICT practices',
Computers and Education, 58, 449–458.
Romero, C., Ventura, S., Zafra, A. and P. de Bra (2009) 'Applying web usage mining for
personalizing hyperlinks in web-based adaptive educational systems', *Computers and
Education*, 53, 828–840.
Selwyn, N. (2014) *Distrusting Educational Technology. Critical Questions for Changing Times*
(Abingdon: Routledge).
Tseng, J., C., R., Chu, H-C., H., G-J. & Tsai, C-C. (2008) 'Development of an adaptive learn-
ing system with two sources of personalization information', *Computers & Education*, 51,
776–786.
UNESCO (2012) *Learning Analytics. Policy Brief*. UNESCO Institute for Information
Technology in Education, November 2012, available at http://iite.unesco.org/policy
_briefs/.
Wiley, D. (2014) *Koller, Thicke, and Noble: The 'Blurred Lines' Between Traditional Online
Courses and MOOCs*, from http://opencontent.org/blog/archives/3703.
Young, J. R. (2013) *Beyond the MOOC Hype: A Guide to Higher Education's High-Tech
Disruption* (Washington, DC: The Chronicle of Higher Education).

C. Governing Higher Education

20

The Rise of 'Higher Education Regionalism': An Agenda for Higher Education Research

Meng-Hsuan Chou and Pauline Ravinet

Introduction

Nation states have traditionally played central roles in the governance of higher education policies, but in recent decades the world's regions and organizations are seen to be increasingly involved in this process. The rise of this phenomenon that we depict as 'higher education regionalism' is related to two different dynamics: (1) the renewal of regional cooperation – in all fields – following the emergence of a multipolar world since the end of Cold War and (2) the international competition to transition towards 'knowledge-based' economies and the role that research and higher education sectors play in this process.

In Europe, the Bologna Process towards a European Higher Education Area (EHEA) has attracted much attention. But this is not the only regional initiative in the higher education sector. There have been consistent efforts in building 'common areas' in Africa, Latin America and Asia that predate or follow Europe's Bologna. While various mechanisms have been introduced, with diverse range of institutionalization and collaboration, these initiatives all emphasize the importance of establishing intra-regional mobility, degree recognition and the participants' ambition to compete on the global higher education market vis-à-vis other regions. How do we account for these regional initiatives? What drives the dynamics? Who are the central actors in developing regional higher education policy arrangements? And what are the effects on national higher education systems, policies and institutions?

These questions should not be confined only to practitioners and researchers interested in the globalization of higher education (King, Marginson and Naidoo, 2011). Regionalism is related, if not central, to many higher education reforms. For instance, we cannot extract regionalism from any of the following contemporary controversial debates: international student flows and the implications for fostering national civic responsibilities; competition between universities and the utility/futility of global rankings; transnational education whereby students remain home and receive foreign degrees; the mushrooming of branch campuses around the world; and the digital revolution in higher education.

This chapter introduces regionalism in the higher education sector. We first survey studies of regionalism in higher education in political science and higher education to highlight the disciplinary divide. While there may be gaps, we argue that political science and higher education studies have much to offer to one another. We show this by offering a novel definition of 'higher education regionalism' bridging their respective insights before proposing a framework for comparative analysis. By defining a research agenda for exploring a variety of 'higher education regionalisms', we give attention to the comparative dimension and explain how and why comparisons are useful. Finally, we show the framework's value-added through an exercise of examining higher education initiatives from around the world.

The current state of research on (higher education) regionalism

To map the current state of research on regionalism in higher education, we examined the political science and higher education literature. So far very little analytical or empirical cross-fertilization has taken place between these subdisciplines, which we consider as a missed opportunity because both subdisciplines have much to offer in enhancing our understanding of regionalism.

Political science contributions: What is regionalism?

The political science literature has wrestled to come up with a unified definition for 'regionalism' that has 'region' at its core. The most cited introductory pieces (Caporaso and Choi, 2002; Fawcett and Gandois, 2010; Hettne, 2005; Mattli, 2012) reveal that 'region' has been defined in at least two different ways. Firstly, a *dimensional approach* that defines a 'region' as a physical and sociopolitical space characterized by geography, politics, economics, society, culture, language or function (Hettne, 2005). Secondly, a *density approach* that emphasizes the cohesion of the 'space' and promotes the investigation of 'region' according to degrees of 'region-ness' (Warleigh-Lack and Van Lagenhove, 2010, p. 547). In the latter, research interest lies in the emergence and consolidation of a regional space, regional complex, regional society, regional community or the 'region-state' from a loosely to a closely integrated entity. It follows that for political scientists the examination of the regional phenomenon is about questioning the *processes* of its creation and subsequent institutionalization through a variety of policy instruments and initiatives. Put differently, it is not about giving a fixed definition of what constitutes a region.

'Regionalism', according to Fawcett and Gandois (2010), can be defined as a 'political project of region creation' whereby policy instruments and mechanisms are introduced to manage *political* cooperation (cf. Hettne, 2005; Caporaso and Choi, 2002; Mattli, 2012). In this way, 'regionalism' relates to statehood through the reference of role and scope of political devices beyond the national level, and the pooling or delegation of national prerogatives to some supranational level. Furthermore, it implies some administrative structure essential for this regional political project. By contrast, Fawcett and Gandois (2010) define 'regionalization' as a process of 'region formation that may be bottom up'. We can further differentiate 'regionalism' and 'regionalization' from 'regional integration', which is a broader and far more complex process of economic, social and political transformation involving multiple sectors.

Contrasting 'regionalism' from 'regionalization' or 'regional integration' allows us to categorize the dynamics taking place in the higher education sector. 'Higher education *regionalism*' would thus refer to a 'top-down' political project designated to region creation in which political instruments and mechanisms are introduced to organize higher education cooperation. 'Higher education *regionalization*' would suggest 'bottom-up' or 'horizontal' higher education cooperation involving, for instance, networks instead of 'top-down' political leadership. To continue, 'higher education *regional integration*' would refer to the role of higher education in the formation of a regional identity, elite or workforce that involves economic, social and political steering from multiple governance levels. As we shall see below, this simple differentiation enables us to make sense of the distinct political science approaches that have been introduced and revived in the last decade to examine regional initiatives.

The rise of the 'new regionalism' literature (Hettne, 2005; Hettne and Söderbaum, 2000) in political science seeks to analyse the renewal of 'regionalization' dynamics throughout the world following the first wave in the 1950s and 1960s. (Here, as the reader will see, 'regionalism' and 'regionalization' are used interchangeably.) The constructivist thinking from international relations infuses the 'new regionalism' approach, which goes beyond a strict definition of geographical regions based on free trade or security alliance. This way of thinking reflects the contemporary international political context of multipolarity and globalization rather than bipolarity and the Cold War.

Scholars of the European Union (EU) and European integration who have advocated abandoning its 'sui generis myth' have been the most receptive of the 'new regionalism' approach (cf. Mattli, 2012; Warleigh-Lack and Van Langenhove, 2010; Warleigh-Lack, 2014). Indeed, in promoting a comparative regionalism research agenda, Warleigh-Lack and Van Langenhove

(2010, p. 545) urge EU scholars to 'consider phenomena which are actually more widespread, such as the links between subnational mobilisation and macro-region-building, as unique to the EU/European context'. This is because, according to Warleigh-Lack and Van Langenhove (2010, p. 553), regional cooperation may constitute a 'real web of regional integration schemes that partly overlap in membership and/or mandate'. Issues of inter-regionalism, and the relations between regions as a defining feature of international relations, signal a new area of research (cf. Mahant, 2007; Baert, Scaramagli and Söderbaum, 2014). Similarly, integration scholars such as Börzel and Risse (2009) call for examining the circulation of 'regional integration' models around the world.

Interestingly, the proliferation and renewed interest in 'regionalism' approaches have not resulted in systematically examining regional cooperation in the higher education sector by political scientists. Higher education remains an underexplored area for regional integration and lacks a regionalism research agenda, which has traditionally been more focused on foreign and security issues, trade and diplomacy (cf. Acharya 2009; Jetschke and Murray, 2012). This is unfortunate, because the different waves of 'regionalism' have much to offer for assessing the potential varieties of 'higher education regionalisms'. Indeed, from the founding works of regional integration theory (cf. Haas and Schmitter, 1964; Etzioni, 1965), the following questions are still relevant: why do some regional processes succeed while others do not take off? How do we explain the differences in regional set-ups, with some having extensive supranational institutional governance structures while others have the skeletal minimum? Are regional processes more internally driven (i.e. by socio-economic exchanges, interstate bargaining, supranational institutions) or externally driven (as a reaction to external threat or pressure)?

Similarly, the questions at the heart of the 'new regionalism' research agenda about the relationship between regional cooperation and globalization are also highly relevant. For instance, shall we understand the development of higher education regional initiatives as a driver of the emerging globalized knowledge economy? Or should we interpret it as a response to, or a way to accommodate, globalization for a policy sector that is still considered a defining feature of state sovereignty? These questions suggest that a more systematic research agenda on 'higher education regionalism' may hold the key to understanding higher education developments in the era of globalization. From EU scholars who promote the 'new regionalism' approach, we are asked to consider the uniqueness of the European model (i.e. the Bologna Process) and its supposed diffusion around the world. Inter-regionalism may also find a place in studies of higher education: are there overlapping regional initiatives in the higher education sector? In the next section, we shall turn to the current state of research in higher education about regional initiatives.

Higher education studies contributions: What do we know about regional initiatives?

Higher education observers[1] and specialists have commented extensively on regional initiatives. We differentiate two strands of this broad scholarship: (1) *European* 'higher education regionalism' and (2) other occurrences of 'higher education regionalism' from around the world. It is in the latter set of literature that we find attempts to systematically examine and even theorize the rise of 'higher education regionalism'.

Studies of European higher education cooperation and governance are well developed and have been dominated by strong interest in, unsurprisingly, the Bologna Process. Indeed, we can argue that European 'higher education regionalism' constitutes its own veritable field of study even within higher education studies. Three thematic issues can be identified in this strand of literature: the role of the European Commission in the construction of the EHEA (cf. Capano and Piattoni, 2011; Corbett, 2011; Gornitzka, 2010; Keeling, 2006); the nature of the EHEA (cf. Chou and Gornitzka, 2014; Ravinet, 2007, 2008; Scott, 2012); and the effects of the EHEA (cf. Vukasovic, 2013; Witte, 2006). At the same time, these three themes have rarely been approached as a case of 'regionalism' or even 'regionalization'. Similarly, while there is growing interest in the external dimension of the Bologna Process, it is uncommon that other instances of 'higher education regionalism' are conceptualized as units of comparison. Instead, developments in other world regions are studied in light of how Europe's Bologna Process has influenced their emergence and evolution[2] (Huisman et al., 2012). This reflects the way in which EU studies in general operates within its own conceptual universe, overlooking commonalities of other regional projects in the world.

There are, however, exceptions to the Eurocentric approach to higher education studies. For instance, in her research on the role of the Council of Europe in European higher education governance, de Melo (2013) questions the various actors and factors behind overlapping regional initiatives. In the 2010 special issue in *Globalisation, Societies and Education*, we find a critical perspective on the 'regionalization' of higher education and its connection with globalization (Jayasuriya and Robertson, 2010). In this volume, Verger and Hermo (2010) gave the first comparative overview of Bologna and the MERCOSUR-Educativo in Latin America. Similarly, in a recent article, Woldegiorgis, Jonck and Goujon (2015) compare Bologna with Africa Union's (AU) Higher Education Harmonisation Strategy using Knight's (2012, 2013) framework, which remains the most developed approach among higher education studies.

Introducing a toolkit for investigating 'regionalization'[3] in higher education, Knight (2012, pp. 11–13) begins with a 'continuum of intensity' with two endpoints: 'cooperation' (less intense) and 'integration' (more intense). For her, 'cooperation' is present when there is a multitude of bilateral and multilateral collaborative activities within a geographical region. Next, 'coordination' takes place when we observe an emergence of more organized networks and joint programmes. 'Higher education regionalism' is at the 'convergence-harmonization' stage when we see the introduction of instruments such as regional quality assurance schemes and credit systems. At the 'integration' stage, we would find a robust and sustainable common higher education space. Knight (2012, p. 11) warns, however, that one should not use this continuum as a yardstick for measuring the 'successfulness' of 'higher education regionalization'. It is possible that states may not desire deeper integration and consider the smooth functioning of agreed mechanisms to be a success already. Knight (2012, pp. 14–16) then delineates six sets of characteristics, each constituting its own continuum, of a 'higher education regionalization' process: informal/formal; ad hoc/intentional; bottom-up/top-down; internal/external; incremental progression/quantum leap; and reactive/proactive/strategic.

Finally, Knight (2012, pp. 17–20) distinguishes three approaches to 'higher education regionalization'. Firstly, the *functional* approach that relates to the 'practical activities of higher education institutions and systems', specifically, the alignment of system through agreed quality assurance schemes, credit transfer systems, qualification frameworks, mobility programmes and so on. Secondly, the *organizational* approach that refers to the development of a bureaucratic structure to steer the regional initiatives (e.g. networks). Thirdly, the *political* approach that addresses the political will essential to make the regionalization of higher education a political priority (e.g. the declaration of intent, binding conventions, agreements).

Political scientists would find Knight's framework engaging, but would raise these questions: why does she not engage with the classic regional integration literature, where the exercise of defining the scale of integration and relevant dimensions has been de rigueur? Similarly, her characteristics of 'regionalization' are useful in structuring an exploratory empirical mapping, but are these characteristics specific to higher education? Can they be fruitfully connected to more generic concept development in the comparative regionalism field? Are her functional, organizational and political 'approaches' merely dimensions for comparison? If so, could they be collapsed? For instance, the first dimension (functional approach) would be concerned about the substance, that is, which aspects of higher education are subject to 'regionalization' forces and through which instruments? The second dimension (combining organizational and political approaches) would refer to the institutional structure shoring up diverse forms of 'regionalization': institutional architecture, formal and informal routines and working culture, professionalization, formal and informal procedures governing rule-making and so on.

To sum up, studies of regionalism in higher education are scattered across multiple disciplines. We summarized those from political science and higher education studies and showed how there has been very little empirical and analytical cross-fertilization between them. In the next section, we will propose how they may begin to do so.

A comparative approach

We bridge the insights from political science and higher education studies for examining 'higher education regionalism' by first giving our definition of regionalism. We then introduce a 'three dimension' framework as an alternative to the 'continuum' framework.

Defining 'higher education regionalism'

We define a 'region' as follows. Firstly, a 'region' must have a visible geographical contour at the supranational level (continental, subcontinental, transcontinental). Secondly, a 'region' is to be identified inductively. We accept that a 'region', a 'regional area', a 'regional network', a 'regional project' is what the participating actors designate at the outset. This inductive approach implies that actors may not have the same definition of the region to which they belong, or that they may believe they belong to more than one, and that different regional projects may be competing and/or overlapping for a given geographical territory. We see this perspective as essential for capturing multiple empirical manifestations of the phenomenon.

As a 'political project of region creation', we argue that to be identified as a case of regionalism, there must be some involvement of a state authority, whether it is under the form of governmental bodies from different countries (such as education ministries and quality assurance agencies) and/or international organizations (an emanation of state authority). A regional project, or network, or partnership led and managed solely by particular higher education institutions such as universities without any involvement or steering from national or international public policy actors are not an instance of regionalism. Involvement, of course, does not imply that the state authority is the initiator or the 'pilot' of the regional project. In some instances where supranational institutions are lacking or governmental resources are low, it is often those non-governmental actors who promote and drive regional cooperation. This brings to mind the question concerning diverse patterns of relationships between governments, international organizations and non-governmental organizations within processes of regionalism. Empirically, we expect to observe a variety of relationship patterns – which we call 'constellations' – in each instance of 'higher education regionalism', especially across time.

For political scientists, our 'higher education regionalism' approach promotes a sector-based approach to studying regionalism. This differs from the classical international relations approach towards regional processes, which queries the motivations of states in pooling sovereignty and the creation and consolidation of regional organizations (Caporaso and Choi, 2002). Following this classic approach, the usual starting point for studying regionalism would be the formal multipurpose regional organization such as the EU and AU. We believe, however, that there is an alternative strategy to gaining more insights into regional developments. Reflecting our inductive approach towards regionalism, our understanding of the phenomenon not only refers to large-scale formal regional organizations but also encapsulates a variety of regional political arrangements and projects that may be more or less formal.

The policy sector, we argue, is an excellent entry point for examining regionalism because it allows researchers and practitioners to assess a variety of political projects and cooperation at the same time and without prior assumptions about the supposed 'regional model'. This is important because studying regionalism is not only about delineating the main features of the regional organisations but also about the concrete regional policy instruments and devices and how the policy actors activate them to achieve their respective objectives. We believe that studying regionalism in any given policy sector requires researchers to address at least the following questions: what are the different processes present? What are the mechanisms leading to their emergence, institutionalization, de-institutionalization or re-institutionalization? What are the institutional forms and policy instruments adopted for these processes? Who are the actors involved? How do they strategize to achieve their aims? By posing these questions, which we elaborate below, our approach to regionalism is equally inspired by comparative public policy and the extant regional integration literature.

Thus, we define the concept of 'higher education regionalism' as referring to a 'political project of region creation' involving at least some state authority (national, supranational, international), who in turn designates and delineates the world's geographical region to which such activities extend, in the higher education policy sector. This process of region building entails the adoption of a variety of mechanisms and instruments that would amount to a discernible policy (action as well as inaction).

Comparing 'higher education regionalisms'

In reflecting upon the more recent literature in both political science ('new regionalism') and higher education studies (comparing regional experiences in higher education cooperation), we will outline how to organize a comparative regionalism research agenda in higher education studies by answering the following questions: why compare? Which aspects should be compared to generate fruitful analytical, empirical and policy discussions across different world regions?

A comparative approach is important for identifying meaningful generalizations. Comparisons challenge the assumption of 'uniqueness' of any single case study and are especially crucial in rigorous exercises of concept formation

(Gerring, 1999). As EU scholars who have embraced the 'new regionalism' approach, most research on the EU (ours included) would benefit from going beyond the 'sui generis myth' and take the claim that European integration is merely 'one regionalization among many' seriously (Warleigh-Lack, 2014). A *comparative* 'higher education regionalism' approach explicitly eschews the European case as a 'model' and considers it as only one among multiple rationales behind regional initiatives.

Our proposed concept of 'higher education regionalism' aims to capture the diverse political processes, arrangements, mechanisms and instruments facilitating regional higher education policy cooperation throughout the world. This may include a variety of regional initiatives, both within a geographical region and between regions. The general approach taken in comparative regionalism revolves around the depth of integration ('region-ness'). Instead of using an 'integration continuum' as a yardstick to assess the relative success/failure of 'higher education regionalism', or position certain regional initiatives along this continuum, it is far more revealing to consider these three aspects of 'higher education regionalism': (1) *constellation of actors* central and active in these processes, (2) *institutional arrangements* adopted or even abandoned for this undertaking and (3) the *ideas and principles* embedded in and operationalized by these regional initiatives.

Studying the *constellation of actors* means identifying the individual and collective actors involved and characterizing their patterns of interaction. In particular, attention needs to be paid to the relative role of the different categories of actors. For instance, are government officials the initiators with transnational actors being the implementers? What is the logic of action driving state actor participation? Do they embrace the idea that their state sovereignty is threatened and/or higher education is a vital sector for a globalized knowledge economy? Or, do they follow an appropriate idea prevalent at the time (e.g. the need to establish *regional* 'Erasmus', such as the 'Arab Erasmus', to remain competitive amidst knowledge economies)? Or, do we instead find actors representing international organizations or even academia, in the driver's seat? For instance, is the World Bank or UNESCO promoting the emergence of regional initiatives in Asia or Africa and dictating their institutional arrangements? Alternatively, do national and international conferences (between foreign ministers, rectors) play a role in this process? What about actors who wear 'different institutional hats'? How do they navigate between these different higher education arenas?

The *institutional arrangements* refer to the institutional form and rules, and the instruments adopted for regional higher education initiatives. Examining institutional arrangements allows us to identify how and why the regional cooperation emerged, as well as how it subsequently evolves. We expect institutional forms to vary across the world's geographical regions, especially if they are embedded into the region's multipurpose associations such as the EU, which already proposes particular institutional blueprints and acceptable 'ways of doing things'. If they are not linked to existing regional associations, to what extent are they 'networked' into the region? And what is the network size (only among selected higher education institutions or open to all eligible universities in the region)? Concerning instruments, it would be essential to first compare the overall 'set' (quality assurance mechanism; degree recognition; mobility schemes?) before identifying similarities and differences in detail.

Ideas and principles refer to the paradigms, policy ideas and programmatic ideas guiding 'higher education regionalisms'. Does the 'knowledge-economy/society' discourse drive the regional cooperation? Indeed, is it about becoming more 'competitive' or 'excellence' vis-à-vis another leading region(s) through attracting the 'best-and-brightest' and/or fostering regional 'talents'? How then do the respective geographical regions differentiate their initiatives? For instance, are the ideas and principles embedded in that region's higher education cooperation coupled with grander schematic ideas such as the 'Rise of Asia' or the 'free movement of knowledge'?

The expected outcome of a comparison across these three aspects is likely to be *varieties* of 'higher education regionalism'. We believe that such an approach offers more value-added than one advocating measuring *degrees* of regionalism. Firstly, an inductive approach is more likely to produce unexpected findings that may contribute to the broader globalization debate. Secondly, this approach is also less normative than one that considers regionalism along a 'developmental continuum'. We depart clearly from the (more or less explicit) assumption that there is a 'better' regional model as indicated by the 'degree' of integration or level of 'region-ness' perspective.

We have argued that a more systematic comparative approach to 'higher education regionalism' represents a stimulating agenda for higher education research, but we are fully aware that definitive and exhaustive findings are still emerging. We believe that the 'three dimension' comparative framework introduced here requires intensive fieldwork. From our perspective, most key data and mechanisms in each dimension are unlikely to be found in official documents. The approach demands in-depth qualitative data collection through interviews with key actors ('snowballing' after several interview rounds), process tracing, archival work and, ideally, participant observation of negotiations. Yet, as we shall show next what can be done at this stage is a synthetic compilation of instances of regionalism and a first application of the framework using the example of the Bologna Process.

Examples from around the world

A first comparative analysis of 'higher education regionalisms' reveals that there are many examples, which can be categorized either as 'intra-regionalism' (cooperation between entities *within* the same geographical region) or 'inter-regionalism' (cooperation between entities *across* two or more geographical regions). This overview shows that there are many overlapping features between instances of 'higher education regionalisms', as well as differences. To encourage future research in this area, we conclude with an application of our 'three dimension' framework to an instance of 'higher education regionalism' in Europe.

Intra-regionalism

The most prominent example of regional higher education cooperation is Europe's Bologna Process, launched in 1999, that aims to establish a European Higher Education Area (Ravinet, 2007). Bologna is a coordination process of national higher education policies around a set of common objectives (such as common degree structure and quality assurance mechanisms). Considered very 'soft' and voluntary in the beginning, Bologna quickly institutionalized from a process of voluntary participation into a system of monitored coordination (Elken and Vukasovic, 2014; Ravinet, 2008). While 'European', the Bologna Process is not a EU process. From a regionalism perspective, what is fascinating about Bologna is that it exhibits features of *overlapping* regionalism (Bologna currently has 49 members, while the EU has 28) and *competing* regionalism. Concerning the latter, the momentum for its emergence came from participating governments in Bologna, but the European Commission has repeatedly attempted to incorporate more higher education issues into EU's Lisbon Strategy (now Europe 2020 Strategy) (Corbett, 2011; Keeling, 2006;) and, the idea goes, 'absorb Bologna' (Chou and Gornitzka, 2014). The 'models' behind Bologna objectives and discourse and the Commission's discourse on higher education are different, with the latter exhibiting more 'neoliberal' features. While not a EU instrument, the Bologna Process has exerted an unprecedented effect on European higher education policy, being the driver and lever for reforms within and beyond the continent (Vukasovic, 2013; Witte, 2006). From the late 2000s onwards, Bologna became more abstract and ambiguous, with Scott (2012) arguing that it has become a 'branding strategy' for many higher education institutions that sought to pitch its programme as Bologna 'compliant'.

In Africa, there is also a variety of continental and subcontinental initiatives and agreements. For instance, within the framework of the 1981 Arusha Convention, the African Union launched the Strategy of Harmonisation of Higher Education Programmes in 2009 (Hoosen, Butcher and Njenga, 2009). The Harmonisation Strategy aims to create the foundation for pan-African academic integration and student and faculty mobility. To do so, participating member states believe that they need to enable the comparability of qualifications as well as quality assurance – two core themes also in the Bologna

Process. With inputs from the Association for the Development of Education in Africa (consisting of donor countries, international organizations and non-governmental organizations), the AU also oversees the adoption and implementation of several Action Plans in the area of higher education with activities ranging from gender parity in higher education to teacher training (see Annex of activities in African Union, 2006). At the subcontinental level, we note the adoption of the Protocol on Education and Training of the Southern African Development Community Region in 1997, and the agreement between African French-speaking countries within the African and Malagasy Council for Higher Education (CAMES) framework. From a regionalism viewpoint, what is interesting about African higher education developments are their *breadth* and *depth*. More than Europe, African higher education initiatives are multiple and 'boundary-spanning': at the level of subregional and pan-continental, as well as between countries constituting the same linguistic community. In practice, the depth of regional cooperation is also impressive: the level of intra-regional mobility is high even in comparison to EU levels. Furthermore, there has been a common 'tenure' procedure between countries of French-speaking western Africa and Madagascar since 1982. Indeed, *les concours d'intégration interafricains du CAMES* in the medical sciences, law, economics and management sciences have since recruited more than 1,300 academics (assistant professor level) from across the region.

Looking at Asia, there are also several initiatives that predate the Bologna initiative. For instance, in 1965 following a meeting between several education ministers from Southeast Asian countries, the UNESCO Commission in the Philippines and a US official, the South East Ministers of Education Organisation was created (SEAMEO.org). After establishing several Regional Centres on various themes (such as public health, tropical medicine), the members institutionalized the Regional Centre for Higher Education in 1993 to lead projects between 11 South Asian countries. Several European countries (e.g. France and the United Kingdom) are associated members. Within the Association of Southeast Asian Nations (ASEAN) framework, the ASEAN University Network was established in 1995 to facilitate: '(1) youth mobility, (2) academic collaboration, (3) standards, mechanisms, systems and policies of higher education collaboration, (4) courses and programmes development and (5) regional and global policy platforms' (AUNSEC.org). In 2012, China, Japan and South Korea launched the Collective Action for Mobility Programme of University Students in Asia – CAMPUS Asia. Modelled after the EU's successful student mobility programme (Erasmus), CAMPUS Asia seeks to improve mobility between these three countries via quality assurance and degree recognition. From the regionalism perspective, what stands out about higher education developments in Asia are the extent to which they are generally ad hoc (one-off), specialized (i.e. only applicable to certain academic disciplines), many (see number of

AUN-endorsed activities) and 'networked'. Instead of being an instance of *over-lapping* regionalism, we see these initiatives as amounting to a case of *networked* regionalism (Rathus, 2011; Yeo, 2010), which eschews *formal* institutions and prefers *informal* ones. Indeed, this preference extends to the region's collaboration with Oceania: the 2006 Brisbane Communiqué brings together the 27 countries across the Asia-Pacific region in the higher education sector, with the aim of improving the recognition and quality of education and training across the region.

Finally, turning to Latin America, we see the 2008 Latin America and the Caribbean Area for Higher Education (ENLACES) initiative for supporting collaborative project on the continent has attracted attention. This initiative, however, emerged from a series of actions dating back to early 1990s. In 1991, members of Mercado Común del Sur (MERCOSUR), Common Market of the South, adopted a Protocol of Intention confirming the importance of the (higher) education sector in achieving their objectives; the signatories indicated that one of the aims was to 'harmonise education systems'. Since 1992, the MERCOSUR ministers met repeatedly on these issues with one commission organized explicitly for higher education. In 2003, the region's mechanism for programme accreditation (MEXA) and mobility scheme (MARCA) were created (cf. Gomes, Robertson and Dale, 2012). These developments led some observers to note the 'mercosurisation' of higher education in the region (Solanas, 2009). From a regionalism viewpoint, higher education cooperation in Latin American differs from other world regions: for them, evident in the discourse accompanying these actions, it has always been about sustaining the economic development in the region. Implementation has been, however, slow. Only some 150 students went on exchange through the MARCA scheme in the same year that 150,000 Erasmus students went abroad (Verger and Hermo, 2010, p. 117). Similarly, we see *overlapping* regionalism: the Inter-American Organization for Higher Education (IOHE), which Canada initiated in 1980, connects more than 300 institutions and national university associations in 26 countries to 'support the development of common Inter-American areas of higher education'. In short, intergovernmental cooperation devices in Latin America are old with some instruments, but very few outcomes.

Inter-regionalism

Regionalism also occurs through regional associations and umbrellas, which we briefly discuss here. It is useful to note that the most common, yet debated, narrative about the circulation of higher education regionalism models worldwide is the influence of the Bologna Process (see Huisman et al., 2012). While several initiatives mentioned above did refer to Bologna as a departure point, the Bologna 'claim' is still at best an assumption to be tested. Through the EU institutional framework, however, European ministers and the European

Commission have extensively sought to engage other regional associations in higher education issues. For instance, at the Third EU-League of Arab States (LAS) foreign affairs ministerial meeting held in Athens in June 2014, the ministers encouraged LAS academic institutions and students to 'fully use the potential of the new Erasmus+ Programme and Horizon 2020' (EU, 2014, p. 4). Similarly, under Framework Programme 7 (predecessor of Horizon 2020), the EU financially supported the Nyerere programme, which awarded scholarships to enable academic exchanges between African universities, through its Intra-ACP University Mobility Programme (Africa-EU-partnership.org). In the same way, the European Commission funded initiatives that aimed to deepen inter-regionalism between Latin America, the Caribbean (LAC) and the EU ('Towards the EU-LAC Knowledge Area'). These initiatives point to Europe as an active 'regional node' in 'higher education inter-regionalism', but we caution that this should not be construed to imply that there is a 'European model' at work or that such a model determined operations in partner regions.

We conclude our brief empirical overview with a table synthesizing an instance of 'higher education regionalism' in Europe – the Bologna Process (see Table 20.1). This simple application shows how researchers interested in

Table 20.1 'Higher education regionalism' in Europe – the case of the Bologna Process

Europe	
Bologna Process	
Actor constellations (Who? Patterns of interaction?)	Governments (initiators of the Bologna Process) European Commission (supporter; modernization agenda) Council of Europe Stakeholder organizations
Institutional arrangements (Form, rules, instruments?)	Common degree structure (Bologna Process) ECTS system (Bologna Process; EU) Qualification Framework (EU) Quality assurance (Bologna Process; EU) Funding schemes (EU) Mobility programmes (EU)
Ideas and principles (Paradigm, policy ideas, prog. ideas)	'Europe of Knowledge' 'Competitiveness' 'Employability' 'Twenty-first century skills'

↑ Intra-regional dynamics ↓
(Articulation of three dimensions? Overlap of regional initiatives?)

(Africa) ← **Inter-regional dynamics** → (Latin America)
(Articulation between regions for each dimension? Circulation of regional models?)

regionalism in the higher education sector can embark on a comparison of different 'higher education regionalisms' from around the world.

Conclusions

In this concluding section, we briefly summarize 'what we know' to point to 'what remains to be answered'. We know that 'higher education regionalism' is an important phenomenon for those wishing to understand the changing governance of higher education in a globalization context and the transformation of states' traditional steering role. At first glance, it appears that Europe's Bologna Process has been the 'gold standard' in accounting for the rise and spread of 'higher education regionalism' globally, but our short overview of other regional higher education initiatives challenges this claim. Many non-European regional cooperation, while sharing concerns and having similar mechanisms, predate the launch of Bologna, and thus indicate that the emergence and evolution of 'higher education regionalism' is a more complex story, with subtle relationships with the momentum undoubtedly unleashed by the Bologna Process. We know that only a comparative approach to studying 'higher education regionalism' could generate meaningful accounts of these processes.

There is still much we do not know about 'higher education regionalism'. For instance, we have very little empirical analysis and data on inter-regionalism. Indeed, are there more inter-regional cooperation in the higher education domain that excludes Europe? How do the existing inter-regional initiatives connect with one another and with ongoing regional or national ones? Could regional models be identified that encompass similarities as well as differences? And could these regional models be used to predict future developments? A more basic question is: how did Bologna evolve from a regional initiative into the European 'model' for higher education cooperation? Did this branding process require purposeful actors and, if so, who are they? Did they devise some 'export' strategy and, if so, how did this approach evolve over time? Did the 'European model' experience competition when presented abroad? How was it appropriated, resisted or accepted? Indeed, many questions remain to be answered about 'higher education regionalisms' before we have a more profound understanding of regionalism in the higher education sector.

Notes

1. See *Globalhighered*, *University World News*, or *Times Higher Education*.
2. See Huisman et al. (2012) chapter where higher education regional initiatives taken in Asia, Latin America, Africa and the United States are presented as 'responses [to the Bologna Process] from other regions' and characterized as 'Bologna-type' initiatives.
3. Knight (2012, p. 4) defines 'regionalization' as the 'intentionally building connection and relations among higher education actors and systems in a region'.

References

Acharya, A. (2009) *Constructing a Security Community in Southeast Asia* (New York: Routledge).

African Union (2006) *Second Decade of Education for Africa (2006–2015) Plan of Action* (Addis Ababa: African Union).

Baert, F., Scaramagli, T. and F. Söderbaum (2014) *Intersecting Interregionalism Regions* (Dordrecht: Springer).

Börzel, T. A. and T. Risse (2009) 'Diffusing (Inter-)Regionalism: The EU as a model of regional integration', *KFG Working Paper Series*, No. 7, Kolleg-Forschergruppe 'The Transformative Power of Europe': Free University Berlin.

Capano, G. and S. Piattoni (2011) 'From Bologna to Lisbon: The political uses of the Lisbon "script" in European higher education policy', *Journal of European Public Policy*, 18(4), 584–606.

Caporaso, J. A. and Y. J. Choi (2002) 'Comparative regional integration', in W. Carlsnaes, T. Risse and B. A. Simmons (eds) *Handbook of International Relations* (pp. 480–500) (London: Sage).

Chou, M.-H. and Å. Gornitzka (eds) (2014) *Building the Knowledge Economy in Europe*, (Cheltenham: Edward Elgar).

Corbett, A. (2011) 'Ping pong: competing leadership for reform in EU higher education 1998–2006', *European Journal of Education*, 46(1), 36–53.

Elken, M. and M. Vukasovic (2014) 'Dynamics of voluntary coordination: Actors and networks in the Bologna Process', in M.-H. Chou and Å. Gornitzka (eds) *Building the Knowledge Economy in Europe* (pp. 131–159) (Cheltenham: Edward Elgar).

Etzioni, A. (1965) *Political Unification: A Comparative Study of Leaders and Forces* (New York: Rinehart and Winston).

EU (2014) 'Declaration: Third European Union-League of Arab States, foreign affairs ministerial meeting', *Athens, Greece*, June 10–11, 2014.

Fawcett, L. and H. Gandois (2010) 'Regionalism in Africa and the Middle East: Implications for EU studies', *Journal of European Integration*, 32(6), 617–636.

Gerring, J. (1999) 'What makes a concept good? A critical framework for understanding concept formation in the social sciences', *Polity*, 31(3), 357–393.

Gomes, A. M., Robertson, S. L. and R. Dale (2012) 'The social condition of higher education: Globalisation and (beyond) regionalisation in Latin America', *Globalisation, Societies and Education*, 10(2), 221–246.

Gornitzka, Å. (2010) 'Bologna in context: A horizontal perspective on the dynamics of governance sites for a Europe of Knowledge', *European Journal of Education*, 45(4), 535–548.

Haas, E. and P. Schmitter (1964) 'Economics and differential patterns of political integration: Objections about unity in Latin America', *International Organization*, 18(3), 705–735.

Hettne, B. and F. Söderbaum (2000) 'Theorising the rise of regionness', *New Political Economy*, 5(3), 457–472.

Hettne, B. (2005) 'Beyond the "New" regionalism', *New Political Economy*, 10(4), 543–571.

Hoosen, S., Butcher, N. and B. K. Njenga (2009) 'Harmonization of higher education programmes: A strategy for the African Union', *African Integration Review*, 3(1), 1–36.

Huisman, J., Adelman, C., Hsieh, C.-C., Shams, F. and S. Wilkins (2012) 'Europe's Bologna process and its impact on global higher education', in D. K. Deardorff, H. de Wit, J. Heyl and T. Adams (eds) *The Sage Handbook of International Higher Education* (pp. 81–100) (Thousand Oaks: Sage).

Jayasuriya, K. and S. L. Robertson (2010) 'Regulatory regionalism and the governance of higher education', *Globalisation, Societies and Education*, 8(1), 1–6.

Jetschke, A. and P. Murray (2012) 'Diffusing regional integration: The EU and Southeast Asia', *West European Politics*, 35(1), 174–119.

Keeling, R. (2006) 'The Bologna process and the Lisbon Research Agenda: The European Commission's expanding role in higher education discourse', *European Journal of Education*, 41(2), 203–223.

King, R., Marginson, S. and R. Naidoo (eds) (2011) *Handbook On Globalization And Higher Education* (Cheltenham: Edward Elgar).

Knight, J. (2012) 'A conceptual framework for the regionalization of higher education: application to Asia', in J. N. Hawkins, K. H. Mok and D. E. Neubauer (eds) *Higher Education Regionalization in Asia Pacific* (pp. 17–36) (New York: Palgrave Macmillan).

Knight, J. (2013) 'Towards African higher education regionalization and Harmonization: functional, organizational and political approaches', *International Perspectives on Education and Society*, 21, 347–373.

Mahant, E. (2007) 'Interregionalism and International relations', *Canadian Journal of Political Science*, 40(3), 777–778.

Mattli, W. (2012) 'Comparative regional integration: Theoretical developments', in E. Jones, A. Menon and S. Weatherill (eds) *The Oxford Handbook of the European Union* (Oxford: Oxford University Press).

de Melo, S. (2013) 'Regionalising higher education transformation in Europe: What kind of positionality for the Council of Europe in relation to the Bologna Process, 1999–2010?', Bristol: University of Bristol.

Rathus, J. (2011) *Japan, China and Networked Regionalism in East Asia* (Basingstoke: Palgrave Macmillan).

Ravinet, P. (2007) 'La genèse et l'institutionnalisation du processus de Bologne: Entre chemin de traverse et sentier de dépendance', Paris: Ecole Doctorale de Sciences Po.

Ravinet, P. (2008) 'From voluntary participation to monitored coordination: Why European countries feel increasingly bound by their commitment to the Bologna process', *European Journal of Education*, 43(3), 353–367.

Scott, P (2012) 'Going beyond Bologna: Issues and themes', in A. Curaj, P. Scott, L. Vlasceanu and L. Wilson (eds) *European Higher Education at the Crossroads* (pp. 1–14) (Dordrecht: Springer).

Solanas, F. (2009) 'El impacto del MERCOSUR en la educación superior: Un análisis desde la "Mercosurización" de las políticas públicas', *Archivos Analíticos de Políticas Educativas*, 17(20), 1–18.

Verger, A. and J. P. Hermo (2010) 'The governance of higher education regionalisation: Comparative analysis of the Bologna Process and MERCOSUR-Educativo', *Globalisation, Societies and Education*, 8(1), 105–120.

Vukasovic, M. (2013) 'Change of higher education in response to European pressures: Conceptualization and operationalization of Europeanization of higher education', *Higher Education*, 66(3), 311–324.

Warleigh-Lack, A. (2014) 'EU studies and the new Regionalism', in K. Lynggaard, K. Löfgren and I. Manners (eds) *Research Methods in European Union Studies* (Basingstoke: Palgrave Macmillan).

Warleigh-Lack, A. and L. Van Langenhove (2010) 'Rethinking EU Studies: The Contribution of Comparative Regionalism', *Journal of European Integration*, 32(6), 541–562.

Witte, J. (2006) *Change of Degrees and Degrees of Change: Comparing Adaptations of European Higher Education Systems in the Context of the Bologna Process* (Enschede: CHEPS/Universiteit Twente).

Woldegiorgis, E. T., Jonck, P. and A. Goujon (2015) 'Regional higher education reform initiatives in Africa: A comparative analysis with the Bologna Process', *International Journal of Higher Education*, 4(1), 241–253.

Yeo, L. H. (2012) 'Institutional regionalism versus networked regionalism: Europe and Asia compared', *International Politics*, 47(3/4), 324–337.

21
Institutional Governance Structures

Nicoline Frølich and Joakim Caspersen

Defining and approaching institutional governance structures

A great deal of effort has been undertaken to structure and organize higher education institutions in line with national policies, often inspired by international policy shifts. The influence of these policy shifts has been interpreted in several ways, with two dominant arguments prevailing (see, for example, Amaral, Jones and Karseth, 2002; Amaral, Meek and Larsen, 2003; Amaral et al., 2009; Huisman, 2009; Paradeise et al., 2009). On the one hand, studies focus on the similarities of the reforms and their similar influence on higher education institutions. On the other hand, national path dependencies and reform trajectories are emphasized. To provide an update on the influence of reforms on higher education institutions, a global literature review is presented. The review examines one key feature of higher education reforms: the changes in institutional governance structures.

This chapter presents an overview of studies around the globe addressing institutional governance structures in light of the policies and policy tools that governments have designed and implemented with the aim to reorganize institutional governance structures. The review includes literature from the past decade, structured around the following questions:

- What are the rationales for introducing policies aimed at restructuring institutional governance structures?
- How have higher education institutions responded to the policies?
- What are the implications of the introduced policy changes at the university level?

Institutional governance structures can be seen as an umbrella term that 'refers to all relevant dimensions of the way higher education institutions are governed, for example, developments concerning the formal and informal institutional decision-making procedures and structures; changes in the composition, tasks and functioning of institutional governance bodies; and the growing involvement of external stakeholders in institutional governance issues' (Amaral and Maassen, 2002, p. xii). In this chapter, we focus on reforms that aim to change institutional governance structures in line with this broad definition so as to be able to *review* the international literature. How have institutional governance structures been described, conceptualized and studied in the international literature? This approach leads us to focus on how higher education institutions are internally structured, what the governing bodies are, what the composition and responsibilities of these governing bodies are, how decisions are made, what kind of leadership is exercised and what kind of policy instruments are used.

Institutional governance structures can, nevertheless, be a slippery term. This term refers not only to formal *organizational* structures but also to these structures' *institutional* aspects, providing 'the central forum for the struggle over what these institutions are or should be, and the complex and evolving relationships between academics, students, and external interests' (Reed, Meek and Jones, 2002, p. xv). Furthermore, institutional governance structures can be seen in relation to state-imposed reforms and changes in the relationship between state and higher education more generally (Reed et al., 2002, p. xv). Across the globe, governance reforms and policy tools vary. However, they arguably share similarities in the sense that they focus to some extent on legal and financial policies and instruments, internal and external organizational changes in higher education, and the introduction of systems for accreditation and quality assurance.

Methodology

The analysis is based on a systematic literature review of key journals in higher education in the past decade (2004–2014). The search was performed through EBSCO*host* and the databases Academic Search Premier, Business Source Elite, ERIC and SocINDEX. Together, these databases cover a range of journals within education, social science and business studies. Only peer-reviewed articles in scientific journals were included. The search strategy was to find articles within the above-mentioned frameworks that contained the term *higher education* or the term *universities* (and all singular and plural forms of these terms) in the abstracts. In addition, the articles contained one of the following terms in their key words or subject specifications: *board, boards, neo-Weberian, new public management, NPM, governance, leadership, policy, policies, reform, reforms, strategy, strategies* and *autonomy*.

This broad search produced more than 50 000 hits, but a large share of these hits were from what we consider to be irrelevant journals in the context of our review study (such as *Science, Nature* and *Lancet*). To narrow down our search, we extracted journals within the findings that were relevant and cross-checked this list with the average impact factor of the journals.[1] As a result, the following journals were included: *Studies in Higher Education, Research in Higher Education, Journal of Higher Education, Quality in Higher Education, Journal of Education Policy, Higher Education Quarterly, Tertiary Education and Management, Review of Higher Education, Higher Education, Harvard Educational Review, Higher Education Policy* and *European Journal of Education*. We would argue that these journals represent our field of study well.

All abstracts of the resulting 3,000 articles were scanned, read and checked for relevance by both authors. This step reduced the list to 422 articles. Next, both authors examined the 422 abstracts in greater detail and decided which articles explicitly addressed one or more of the research questions. This final round further reduced the list to 53 articles. These articles form the foundation for our review.

The articles cover a range of themes. In the first round of analysis, we organized the literature in four categories – namely, studies focusing on (1) legal and funding instruments, (2) internal organization, (3) external organization (e.g. relationships with external world/stakeholders) and (4) evaluation/quality assurance. Moreover, to carry out a global comparison, we also organized the literature according to the geographical scope of the studies. Next, we concentrated on similarities and differences within and across regions. Each of the 53 articles was assessed for the three research questions we posed: what are the rationales for introducing government-induced policies aimed at restructuring institutional governance structures? How have higher education institutions responded to these policies? What are the implications of the introduced policy changes at the university level?

The results of our analyses are summarized in Table 21.1 and will be discussed throughout the rest of the chapter.

Europe

In our review, we found several studies with a comparative perspective across Europe. For example, in their 2013 study, Kretek, Dragšić and Kehm compared university boards across Europe and included changes in institutional governance structures. They took as a point of departure that new public management (NPM) has been the most significant driver for a profound process of organizational transformation in European public universities. The university responses have been formalization, standardization, the strengthening of internal hierarchies and the promotion of organizational identity. The changes have involved a reconfiguration of internal governance structures, such as stricter hierarchies, more powerful chief executives and the introduction of university boards that are composed of external members and are involved in decision-making at the top level. University boards are expected to oversee university leadership. They observed the following patterns across Europe: most higher

Table 21.1 Main themes in institutional governance studies across the globe

	North America	Asia	Africa	South America	Australia	Europe
Legal/financial	The use of performance indicators in strategic planning (Lewis, Hendel and Kallsen, 2007) Strategies to cope with financial challenges (Deering and Sá, 2014)	n/a	n/a	n/a	n/a	The financial autonomy of universities (Kohtamäki and Lyytinen, 2004)
Internal structure and organization	The characteristics of higher education leadership (Jones, 2011) The characteristics of higher education leadership (Bryman, 2007) – The characteristics of boards (Taylor and de Lourdes Machado, 2008)	The impact of human relation (HR) reforms in universities (Lai, 2010) Factors influencing the governance paradigm of universities (Christopher, 2012)	n/a	Collective decision making in universities (Durand and Pujadas, 2004) –	Leadership and management in the case of widening participation (Devlin, 2013) – The development of effective governance cultures (Baird, 2006) The characteristics of effective boards (Rowlands, 2013b) Factors influencing the governance paradigm of universities (Christopher, 2012) The characteristics of higher education leadership (Bryman, 2007)	Academics' commitment to mergers (Puusa and Kekäle, 2013) The role of university board members (Kretek, Dragšić and Kehm, 2013) Shared governance (Stensaker and Vabø, 2013) The characteristics of boards (Taylor and de Lourdes Machado, 2008) Tensions between marketization and academization (Ek et al., 2013) The role of university board members (Kretek et al., 2013) Distributed leadership and its effectiveness (van Ameijde et al., 2009) The characteristics of higher education leadership (Bolden, Petrov and Gosling, 2008; Breakwell and Tytherleigh, 2010; Bryman, 2007; Jameson, 2012) Characteristics of supervisory boards (de Boer, Huisman and Meister-Scheytt, 2010)

External structure and organization	n/a	Integration among academic staff in merged institutions (Cai, 2006) The impact of neoliberalism on university management (Mok, 2010) Stakeholders' perceptions of national policies for internationalization (Cho and Palmer, 2013)	The level of autonomy of the university with regard to the state (Arikewuyo and Ilusanya, 2010)	n/a	The factors impacting on the functioning of merged institutions (Locke, 2007) Factors influencing the governance paradigm of universities (Christopher, 2012) The characteristics of strategic planning (Lillis and Lynch, 2014) Board members' influence on the boards' identity and work (Meister-Scheytt, 2007; Rytmeister, 2009) The factors affecting the decision to merge among higher education institutions (Kyvik and Stensaker, 2013)
Evaluation and accreditation – quality assurance	n/a	n/a	n/a	The implementation of systems for quality assurance (French et al., 2014; Shah and Nair, 2011) The board's role in quality assurance (Rowlands, 2012, 2013a, 2013c)	The implementation of systems for quality assurance (Askling, Lycke and Stave, 2004) The implementation of systems for quality assurance (Csizmadia, Enders and Westerheijden, 2008) The introduction of quality management (Papadimitriou, 2011)

education laws across Europe provide for university boards with either external members only or a combination of internal and external members. There has been a gradual strengthening of the power of these bodies. Since the introduction of governing boards, criticism from students and the scientific community has been directed at these governing bodies. Kretek et al. (2013) argued that the governance practices depend on how board members enact their board member role. This in turn depends on a number of organizational factors such as the organizational coupling between the scope of strategic management, the formal composition of the board and the board members' role expectations.

De Boer et al. (2010) examined governing boards across the Netherlands, Austria, and the United Kingdom. They found the main drivers of governance reforms to be NPM; stakeholders in society outside the universities, such as the public, the professions and the market; and the increasing importance of universities in the knowledge society. The boards differ in their composition, independence, transparency and accountability. The board composition in all three countries reveals that the board members belong to established networks (old boys' networks). The composition of the Dutch and Austrian boards raises questions regarding the extent to which expertise and representativeness are well served; whereas in the United Kingdom, substantial consideration has already been given to balancing different types of expertise. The Austrian boards seem to be based on political steering in appointments, and some of the Austrian and Dutch cases have strong linkages with business; both raise questions about the independence of boards. In Austria, the board is not accountable to anybody – neither to the minister nor to the parliament or to the university or its bodies, and in Netherlands the accountability relationships are primarily formal. By contrast, in the United Kingdom, accountability is addressed regarding both funding and transparency. The authors discussed the balance between composition, independence, transparency and accountability, as well as the implications for the legitimacy and efficiency of the board.

Several studies in our sample examined the situations in the Netherlands and Switzerland. Huisman, de Boer and Goedegebuure (2006) revealed a mixed picture regarding different higher education actors' views on the implementation of a new governance act in 1997 based on NPM in Dutch universities. Fumasoli and Lepori (2011) investigated strategy processes in Swiss universities. They argued that university strategies can be seen as attempts to create organizational coherence. The coherence depends on the ability of university governance structures to balance centralization and bottom-up processes through good communication. Kallenberg's (2007) study, which is also from the Netherlands, developed a framework for exploring the role of middle managers in strategy processes.

Some studies in our sample dealt with universities in the Scandinavian countries. Interestingly, these studies focused on the internal organization of universities (Ek et al., 2013; Puusa and Kekäle, 2013; Stensaker and Vabø, 2013), as well as the external organizational relationships among universities (Kyvik and Stensaker, 2013). Ek et al. (2013) explored how heads of departments across all faculties of a university deal with the tension between marketization and academization. Heads of departments have to cope with pressures from external reforms and internal forces like traditions and power relations inside academia. The drivers of external pressures are the Bologna Process, with increased focus on employability and quality assurance and the call for improvement to academic and scientific education by linking education closer to research. They found that the responses to such pressures vary across disciplines and professions. The 'problem' of adjusting to increased demands for market relevance is more prominent in the academic disciplines, but the academization of professional educational programmes requires attention as well. Stensaker and Vabø (2013) analysed how a sample of Nordic universities perceives the place and role of governance in the strategic development of universities. They found that most universities emphasize leadership and leadership development as key instruments in strengthening their governance capacity. Nevertheless, the cultural and symbolic aspects of governance, internal legitimacy and trust seem to be at stake. The main drivers of changes in institutional governance are argued to be institutional autonomy reforms in exchange for stronger accountability claims.

Puusa and Kekäle (2013) investigated a merger process between two Finnish universities. The widespread rationale for mergers in higher education involves a maximization of economies of scale and the hope of achieving administrative, economic and academic benefits. The study suggested that the leadership of the merged university was weaker than the leadership of the two former universities, owing to the lack of time and grounding of the top-down administratively run merger process. However, the merged university seemed to have gained efficiency in administration and realized financial savings. Interestingly, the study found that despite resistance towards the merger, the academics became even more committed to their work and to their close colleagues during the merger process. Kyvik and Stensaker (2013) examined the factors that impact the decision to merge among higher education institutions. In general, mergers are often imposed by government, with the aims of addressing institutional fragmentation, lack of financial and academic vitality, low efficiency and low quality. In other cases, mergers have been voluntary, based on a change in rationale from a system effectiveness perspective to a market competition perspective. In the latter, a merger can be described as a strategic choice that is aimed to enhance the competitive advantage of the merged institution at the national or international level. A successful merger process can be characterized by the fact that the initiative for the merger came from the institutions themselves and included only two institutions. The unsuccessful merger process is characterized by a slightly more complex merger, consisting of three institutions, which would result in multi-campus institutions. In addition, none of the partners would have the power to dominate the merged institution.

The characteristics of higher education leadership have been dealt with in a number of studies on universities in the United Kingdom (Bolden et al., 2008; Breakwell and Tytherleigh, 2010; Bryman, 2007; Jameson, 2012). As we note in the subsequent section on North America, Bryman (2007) discussed how policy changes in the past few decades have placed new demands on leadership and searched for indications of effective leadership based on studies in the United Kingdom, the United States and Australia. Bolden et al. (2008) explored tensions in higher education leadership and teased apart its multilevel nature at the individual, group and organizational levels. Breakwell and Tytherleigh (2010) investigated whether the personal characteristics of the head of an institution are related to university performance. They found little support for the existence of this type of relationship. Most of the variation in performance was explained by non-leadership factors. Jameson (2012) took as a point of departure that the multiple uncertainties about the future of English higher education may lead to a decrease of trust in the values, collegial ethos and civic role of universities. The main theoretical concept that Jameson used was negative capability, and she argued that 'if leaders are able to focus, listen, act with discretion and skilfully contain negative emotions arising from uncertainties rather than rush to implement imprudently deterministic solutions; they are more likely to inspire trust within their institutions' (p. 395). Jameson's study indicates that challenging 'performative, managerial cultures that lessen self-organising egalitarian potentials for excellent collegial scholarship' is necessary (p. 412). Moreover, the implication of skilful leadership is the ability to listen and reflect, which may contribute to maintaining trust in the purpose of universities.

Taylor and de Lourdes Machado (2008) compared the governing boards of universities in the United States and Europe (focusing on the Netherlands, Austria, Norway and Sweden). In Europe, NPM has promoted the adoption of management practices that are imported from the private sector. Governing boards in the United States previously enjoyed a relatively quiet situation, as well as anonymity. However, these bodies have come under great pressure recently. Governing boards are increasingly expected to function properly and professionally with the needed expertise to oversee the success of the institution. Governing boards are not an exclusively 'new' feature in Europe; lay boards have existed in Italy, the Netherlands and England. Whereas governing boards in the United States have been constructed within a state control model, the European boards have been put in place in accordance with a state supervision model. The US boards are intended to lessen and prevent government intervention in the institutions. In the European context, attempting to strike a balance between market forces and the heritage of the academe and its values could create governance challenges.

A study by Christopher (2012), with its focus on universities in Australia, the United Kingdom, the Netherlands, Belgium and Malaysia, allows for comparisons between Europe and a more global selection of countries. The driving forces of university reforms that have been identified are neoliberal government ideas and corporate managerialism, which have influenced European and Australian universities. A second factor is the changed role of funding bodies, and a third factor is increased global competition. However, as Christopher (2012) argued, the academic culture and internal administrative management structures or cultures of universities also shape and reshape policy reforms. Huisman's (2009) observation is that despite the unique blend of drivers and internal responses of the universities, European and Australian universities seemingly show more similarities in responses compared with Malaysian universities, which are predominantly government controlled with little or no resistance from collegiality, autonomy and the internal management culture.

North America

Two different studies by Lewis et al. (2007) and by Deering and Sá (2014) discuss the introduction of performance indicators in higher education institutions as a response to external changes in the United States and Canada. However, in the Canadian case, the changes are not directly linked to increased accountability, as is the case in the United States, but rather are the consequence of decreased public funding. In the Canadian case, the introduction of incentive-based budgeting systems is an internal, strategic response to challenges, whereas in the US case, the implementation of these systems is part of an accountability-enhancing strategy. Taylor and de Lourdes Machado (2006) also argued that the increased focus and attention on the role of governing boards in the United States must be interpreted within a state supervisory model, whereas challenges from NPM models of governance place not only pressure on autonomy but also emphasis on decreased direct government intervention. The underlying rationale is that any monopolization of power endangers the public good; thus, higher education is too important to society to be governed exclusively by the faculty. As pointed out in the studies by Lewis et al. (2007) and by Deering and Sá (2014), the introduction of performance indicators and incentive-based budgeting systems not only challenges the balance between accountability and institutional autonomy but also seems to be an efficient measure for allocating resources within the institutions. However, doing so can also lead to different strategic responses: an increase in contingent faculty, the generation of more alternative funding through fees and paid services and cost-cutting by reducing or eliminating nonessential programmes. In the Canadian case, the introduction of incentive-based budgeting systems in 3 (of 97) universities is also interpreted as a strategic response in itself, with potential intended and unintended consequences. Based on a comparison across the United Kingdom, Australia and the United States, Bryman (2007) discussed how policy changes in the past few decades have placed new demands on leadership and searched for indications of effective leadership. New policies demand new leadership styles. Although efficient styles can be identified, it is important to be aware of the contextual contingency of leadership in higher education.

Asia

As Cai (2006) pointed out, it is somewhat paradoxical that most of the literature on mergers in higher education is from Western Europe, considering that the largest mergers have taken place in China. According to Cai, there have been over 300 mergers in China since 1992, involving over 700 colleges or universities. Mok (2012) described how the development in China is a process of privatization in a neoliberal policy tradition. However, as costs have risen for the citizens in this system, there has been a need for new state interventions and control in higher education, and more emphasis has been given to government funding. Lai (2010) described how control of academic work in China has taken the form of academic managerialism, relying on accountability and steering at a distance. Chinese state efforts to create world-class universities have reinforced tensions between academic staff and management. This situation has led to a double-entry bookkeeping strategy among academic staff as a way in which to adapt to external demands and quantitative measures of quality. It also created a context where administrative domination within the universities had to be handled, as there was a lack of influence in university decision-making by academics in favour of the administrative staff. The processes were believed to harm the academics' commitment to the university. Cai (2006) also described five factors at the institutional level that are important for a positive outcome of mergers: (1) cultural integration (cultural differences between the pre-merger institutions negatively influence this factor), (2) intensive interaction between members in the different pre-merger groups so as to promote integration, (3) good management so as to accommodate change, (4) a shared understanding of the mission of the merged organizations and (5) high academic prestige of the post-merger organization (this factor is related to the effectiveness of academic staff integration). Overall, the academic managers must support and develop close contact between the academic staff in the pre-merger institutions so as to provide a good foundation for academic staff integration.

Christopher (2012) noted that changes in higher education in Malaysia are predominantly government controlled, with little or no resistance from collegiality, autonomy and the internal management culture. Changes are also driven by global competition. Reforms inspired by neoliberalism are a strong driver in this development, a point also made by Mok (2010). In Singapore and Malaysia, there exists an imbalance between state centralism on the one hand and neoliberal politics of privatization and decentralization on the other (Mok, 2010). This means that academic managers such as deans are given a great deal of freedom; however, their institutions rely on state funding. Hence, they work in what is described as a regulated – deregulated environment. According to Mok (2010), the development implies that international drivers for organizational change in higher education institutions, such as international policy trends, are important but should not be overstated vis-à-vis the national context of steering and governance. Mok (2010) also argued that the particular socio-economic and socio-political contexts of the countries and systems be taken into consideration in research. Furthermore, in a neoliberal and privatized system, academics do not feel emancipated or empowered; they instead feel burdened by control and accountability measures.

Australia

In Australia, many contributions describe how the development of external quality audits in universities is part of a larger movement that includes most parts of the world. It is argued that the introduction of quality audit systems can provide institutions with a tool for improvement (if effectively implemented) on various education quality measures (Shah and Nair, 2011). Christopher (2012) argued that Australian universities show a resemblance to European universities in their response to such changes, with a mix of governance control mechanisms at the board, operational and assurance management levels.

A great deal of attention has been given to the role of governing boards in the development of external quality audits in Australia. Rowlands (2012, 2013a, 2013b, 2013c) described the introduction of quality assurance systems as part of the globalization of policies and practices associated with neoliberalism, the knowledge economy, managerialism and quality improvement. Rowlands (2012) particularly highlighted the role of boards in higher education institutions, arguing that the introduction of an audit-based accountability culture has transformed the role of boards. The power and significance of the boards have gradually diminished, and more attention is given to systems of quality assurance rather than to the de facto execution of management by the board. This means that academic boards hold more symbolic than real power and that they are the key site of struggle for the balance between managerialism and academic work. However, with higher education institutions under pressure, it should be emphasized that academic boards also hold latent or tacit functions, such as information dissemination, visibility among academic leaders, support building and networking. Thus, board effectiveness is a broad concept, and boards play an important role in developing academic standards that emphasize enhanced learning outcomes and academic quality rather than compliance.

Baird (2006) argued that the support functions for Australian boards have been highly professionalized but that different board models have different innate tensions. The corporate model, which is promoted by the government and legislation, and the participatory model, which some universities consider to be worth fighting for, are, by nature, partly conflicting. The normative frameworks for boards and university management advocated by government fail to address such tensions, or even actively suppress them. To develop a quality culture of governance among board members, board members should do the following: discuss the tensions that exist, explicate their ideas of what it implies to be a university in terms of prioritizing and consider how different visions of what constitutes a university relate to strategic planning and practices. In summary, the development of a quality culture of governance should be seen as more than the implementation of prescribed quality measures. Instead, boards should be able to develop their own culture and discursive practices.

Africa

The only study from the African continent included in our review is an article by Arikewuyo and Ilusanya (2010). The issue of autonomy and interference is more direct than in many of the other studies, with descriptions given on the role played by nepotism in admission to universities, the dismissal of academic staff involved in strikes and the direct interference in university matters by political authorities. Similar problems are argued to characterize many African countries. The study in question examines the level of autonomy in a third-generation university in Nigeria, meaning that it was developed during the Second Republic (1979–1983). According to the empirical results, the Nigerian government often influences the membership of the governing councils, the quality control of academic standards, the number of students in particular fields and the level of tuition fees. There is also considerable government intervention in the admissions quotas for minority groups, the establishment of new fields of teaching, the control of the governing councils, the standards of academic disciplines and the accreditation of courses. Some of the areas where the government exercises influence can be seen as similar to what is found in other systems and countries, such as staff recruitment. However, unlike most other systems, there are virtually no government interventions in terms of curriculum decisions, teaching and quality assessment procedures. In the areas of governance, administration and finance, the level of state interference is higher in Nigeria than other countries. Appointments to governing councils are often steered according to *national interests*. The overall perception of the situation is that a struggle towards full autonomy is ongoing. However, it is also noted that the international literature suggests that there is no such thing as a fully autonomous university.

South America

The only study from the South American continent included in our review is the article by Durand and Pujadas (2004) on how governance teams in Argentine universities assess their own functioning. In Argentina, the financial crisis between 1998 and 2002 struck harder than in many other countries experiencing a recession at the same time, leaving the state practically bankrupt. It is argued that Argentine universities have responded passively to the political and economic crises and exhibited a reluctance to change. Thus, drivers for reform are not found explicitly in international reform policies and trends, although the national crisis had partly international causes. In this policy environment, universities must establish new leadership paths and practices so as to promote community building and value-oriented behaviour. Academic leadership must be seen as a collective task, with the capacity for team building and teamwork. This implies the stimulation and development of a non-utilitarian culture and behaviour at the institution. Temporary appointments to leadership positions and rotations in these positions are seen as essential tools for developing the 'real university', which is described as not 'one of the market substitutes proposed in the last years' (p. 41).

Geographical divisions or regime patterns?

As stated in the introductory section of this chapter, previous studies have shown that two dominant perspectives on reforms prevail. An alternative way to reflect upon the outcomes of our review is to see to what extent changes in institutional governance structures are related to politico-administrative regimes. The structural characteristics in which policy processes take place could affect the governance reforms and, hence, the institutional governance structures. We argue that this alternative way of comparing reforms from different countries add to the understanding of institutional governance structures.

Bleiklie and Michelsen (2013) developed such a conceptual framework for comparative analysis of higher education policies in Europe. Their assumption was that policy change in higher education may be better understood in terms of the structural characteristics through which policy processes take place. They observed that three major trends have characterized higher education policies since 1990: stronger institutional hierarchies, stronger interinstitutional networks and standardization and formalization. However, there is considerable variation across countries regarding the degree and form of the actual changes that have taken place. Based on contributions in the public administration literature (Lijphart, 1999; Painter and Peters, 2010; Pollitt and Bouckaert, 2004; Verhoest et al., 2010), Bleiklie and Michelsen developed a typology of politico-administrative regimes across Europe. The different regime types that they distinguished are public interest (e.g. England[2]), social democratic/consensual (e.g. Norway), Napoleonic (e.g. France, Italy and Portugal) and *Rechtsstaat* (rule of law; e.g. Germany, Switzerland and the Netherlands). As revealed in our literature review, the European politico-administrative regimes show some interesting features with regard to variation across Europe. Several studies concentrated on the Napoleonic regime, and some studies focused on reforms in the Scandinavian regime, the public interest regime and the *Rechtsstaat* regime. Moreover, only a few studies are comparative across regimes, and those studies include mostly data or research that allows for comparison between the public interest regime and the *Rechtsstaat* regime.

Despite the differences in politico-administrative regimes, Kretek et al. (2013) managed to focus on the similarities across regimes regarding university responses. Formalization, standardization and the strengthening of internal hierarchies, as well as the power of chief executives and external board members, are common features across the regimes. However, governance practices depend on how board members enact their board member role (Kretek et al., 2013). The university responses also depend on the features of the academic culture such as the influence and resistance embedded in collegiality and the internal management culture (Christopher, 2012). Nevertheless, a few differences between the regimes can be seen. In the Scandinavian context, mergers have attracted the interest of higher education researchers, while leadership practices have been more of interest in the public interest regime. Studies on strategies and middle managers have been conducted within the *Rechtsstaat* regime.

Regarding the implications of the institutional governance reforms, these articles also point to similarities across regimes. Most higher education laws across Europe provide for university boards with either external members only or a combination of internal and external members. A gradual strengthening of the power of these bodies can be observed. Moreover, when these bodies introduce laws, increasing criticism of these bodies from students and the scientific community is noted (Kretek et al., 2013). Across regimes, potential governance challenges also exist with regard to striking a balance between market forces and the heritage of the academe and its values (Taylor and de Lourdes Machado, 2008). However, regarding the public interest regime and the *Rechtsstaat*, the composition, transparency, accountability and independence of boards vary, and questions regarding their legitimacy can be raised (de Boer et al., 2010). The implications of the reforms seemingly depend on the mix of academic culture, autonomy and collegiality of individual universities (Christopher, 2012).

Our review of the literature on institutional governance structures across European political regimes shows that the literature relates mainly to internal structures and organization or to external structures and organization. Few studies in our sample examined policy reforms from the perspective of the higher education institutions with regard to legal and financial reforms or evaluation and accreditation. This pattern can also be seen in other geographical areas of the world. The review also indicates that few studies have examined university responses in the Napoleonic regime and in the continents of Africa and South America. However, studies from these areas identified in our review are not likely to represent the real development of research or policy changes. Rather, it reflects a publishing tradition related to a particular group of countries, as well as a particular research tradition with nodes and networks across the aforementioned countries. Many of the studies on institutional governance are also from English-speaking countries (the United Kingdom, the United States and Australia). Finally, we note that only a small number of studies compare institutional governance across Europe and North America or across Europe, Australia and Asia. Such comparisons would enhance the understanding of how regimes differ in their institutional governance structures.

Reform drivers and responses

Regarding the rationales for introducing policies aimed at restructuring institutional governance structures, all the studies included in this review refer more or less to similar descriptions of reforms – new managerialism, NPM, accreditation and quality assurance. Hence, despite the differences between the politico-administrative regimes, they all point to the importance of NPM as a driver of university reforms (de Boer et al., 2010; Kretek et al., 2013; Taylor and de Lourdes Machado, 2008). In addition, De Boer et al. (2010) include the growing importance of stakeholders in higher education and the knowledge society in terms of rationales for governance reforms focusing on the public interest regime and the *Rechtsstaat*. Other driving forces of university reforms identified global competition and the changed role of governing bodies (Christopher, 2012).

However, few studies discuss the content of the reforms in detail and refer only to the broader concept of the reforms. This vagueness might cover up specific peculiarities of more concrete reform packages. Without aiming to explain the similarities and differences observed further, we suggest – in line with Frølich and Sahlin (2013) – that reforms are themselves carriers of mixed and blended logics and ideas. Thus, reforms carry ambiguous templates of institutional governance models. Reforms emerge from and carry new institutions; institutions mix and blend in the idiosyncratic organizational setting. The overall vagueness of the discussion on new managerialism inhibits more contextualized analysis of institutional governance structures.

Conclusion

Based on an extensive review, comparisons between Europe, North America, South America, Australia, Africa and Asia have been made. Across European politico-administrative regimes, as well as around the world, NPM reforms are still seen as the main driver of institutional governance reforms in higher education. The introduction and functions of governing boards are major themes when university responses are examined both in different European political-administrative regimes and in North America and Australia. Privatization and financial constraints seem to be the main types of policy reform tools in Asia. However, in South America, Africa and, to some extent Asia, the drivers of reforms appear to be more specifically related to the local political situation such as post-Mao China and the financial crisis in Argentina, although the literature from these parts of the world is harder to include in a systematic review.

In higher education and public administration studies in general, two main arguments for understanding policy development, policy tools and institutional responses prevail. One main argument refers to the rapid spread of policies across the globe and emphasizes policy borrowing and coping with policies. The other main argument repeatedly points out how national trajectories and path dependencies influence implementation processes, the choice and effectiveness of policy tools and the proposed policy solutions. Our contribution has been to view institutional governance structures in a systematic way as we examined how institutional governance structures have been developed, implemented and responded to around the globe. This lens has enabled us to systematize the literature on institutional governance structures published in the past decade. Based on the review, both global similarities and geographical differences clearly come to the fore. However, through the lens of politico-administrative regimes, the similarities within Europe are still more evident than the differences. This would lead us to conclude that the national trajectories are perhaps less distinct than they were previously. Yet, clear differences in the scope and influence of the reforms around the world should not be understated, and this diversity should be examined and conceptualized in future studies.

Notes

1. For some journals, four-year impact factors were available; for others, five-year impact factors were available. To control for this difference, we divided the impact factor by 'number of years' before we sorted the journals.
2. The typology was developed within the framework of the Transforming Universities in Europe (TRUE) project; the data for the countries that were mentioned as examples came from this project.

References

Amaral, A., Jones, G. A. and B. Karseth (eds) (2002) *Governing Higher Education: National Perspectives on Institutional Governance* (Dordrecht: Kluwer Academic).

Amaral, A. and P. Maassen (2002) 'Preface', in A. Amaral, G. A. Jones and B. Karseth (eds) *Governing Higher Education: National Perspectives on Institutional Governance* (pp. xi–xv) (Dordrecht: Kluwer Academic Publishers).

Amaral, A., Meek, V. L. and I. M. Larsen (eds) (2003) *The Higher Education Managerial Revolution?* (Dordrecht: Kluwer Academic).

Amaral, A., Neave, G., Musselin, C. and P. Maassen (eds) (2009) *European Integration and the Governance of Higher Education and Research* (Dordrecht: Springer).

Arikewuyo, M. O. and G. Ilusanya (2010) 'University autonomy in a third-generation university in Nigeria', *Tertiary Education and Management*, 16(2), 81–98.

Askling, B., Lycke, K. H. and O. Stave (2004) 'Institutional leadership and leeway – important elements in a national system of quality assurance and accreditation: experiences from a pilot study', *Tertiary Education and Management*, 10(2), 107–120.

Baird, J. (2006) 'Beyond professionalisation: enhancing the governance culture for Australian university governing boards', *Tertiary Education and Management*, 12(4), 297–309.

Bleiklie, I. and S. Michelsen (2013) 'Comparing HE policies in Europe: structures and reform outputs in eight countries', *Higher Education*, 65(1), 113–133.

Bolden, R., Petrov, G. and J. Gosling (2008) 'Tensions in higher education leadership: towards a multi-level model of leadership practice', *Higher Education Quarterly*, 62(4), 358–376.

Breakwell, G. and M. Tytherleigh (2010) 'University leaders and university performance in the United Kingdom: Is it "who" leads, or "where" they lead that matters most?' *Higher Education*, 60(5), 491–506.

Bryman, A. (2007) 'Effective leadership in higher education: a literature review', *Studies in Higher Education*, 32(6), 693–710.

Cai, Y. (2006) 'A case study of academic staff integration in a post-merger Chinese university', *Tertiary Education and Management*, 12(3), 215–226.

Cho, Y. H. and J. D. Palmer (2013) 'Stakeholders' views of South Korea's higher education internationalization policy', *Higher Education*, 65(3), 291–308.

Christopher, J. (2012) 'Governance paradigms of public universities: an international comparative study', *Tertiary Education and Management*, 18(4), 335–351.

Csizmadia, T., Enders, J. and D. F. Westerheijden (2008) 'Quality management in Hungarian higher education: organisational responses to governmental policy', *Higher Education*, 56(4), 439–455.

de Boer, H., Huisman, J. and C. Meister-Scheytt (2010) 'Supervision in "Modern" university governance: boards under scrutiny', *Studies in Higher Education*, 35(3), 317–333.

Deering, D. and C. M. Sá (2014) 'Financial management of Canadian universities: adaptive strategies to fiscal constraints', *Tertiary Education and Management*, 20(3), 207–224.

Devlin, M. (2013) 'Effective university leadership and management of learning and teaching in a widening participation context: findings from two national Australian studies', *Tertiary Education and Management*, 19(3), 233–245.

Durand, J. and C. Pujadas (2004) 'Self-assessment of governance teams in an Argentine private university: adapting to difficult times', *Tertiary Education and Management*, 10(1), 27–44.

Ek, A.-C., Ideland, M., Jönsson, S. and C. Malmberg (2013) 'The tension between marketisation and academisation in higher education', *Studies in Higher Education*, 38(9), 1305–1318.

French, E., Summers, J., Kinash, S., Lawson, R., Taylor, T., Herbert, J., Fallshaw, E. and C. Hall (2014) 'The practice of quality in assuring learning in higher education', *Quality in Higher Education*, 20(1), 24–43.

Frølich, N. and K. Sahlin (2013) 'University Organization as Bridging: Ambiguous, Competing and Mediated Institutions'. Paper presented at the 29th EGOS Colloquium, Montreal, 4–6 July 2013.

Fumasoli, T. and B. Lepori (2011) 'Patterns of strategies in Swiss higher education institutions', *Higher Education*, 61(2), 157–178.

Huisman, J. (ed) (2009) *International Perspectives on the Governance of Higher Education: Alternative Frameworks for Coordination* (London: Routledge, Taylor & Francis Group).

Huisman, J., de Boer, H. and L. Goedegebuure (2006) 'The perception of participation in executive governance structures in Dutch universities', *Tertiary Education and Management*, 12(3), 227–239.

Jameson, J. (2012) 'Leadership values, trust and negative capability: managing the uncertainties of future English higher education', *Higher Education Quarterly*, 66(4), 391–414.

Jones, D. G. (2011) 'Academic Leadership and Departmental Headship in Turbulent Times', *Tertiary Education and Management*, 17(4), 279–288.

Kallenberg, T. (2007) 'Strategic innovation in HE: the roles of academic middle managers', *Tertiary Education and Management*, 13(1), 19–33.

Kohtamäki, V. and A. Lyytinen (2004) 'Financial autonomy and challenges to being a regionally responsive higher education institution', *Tertiary Education and Management*, 10(4), 319–336.

Kretek, P. M., Dragšić, Ž. and B. M. Kehm (2013) 'Transformation of university governance: on the role of university board members', *Higher Education*, 65(1), 39–58.

Kyvik, S. and B. Stensaker (2013) 'Factors affecting the decision to merge: the case of strategic mergers in Norwegian higher education', *Tertiary Education and Management*, 19(4), 323–337.

Lai, M. (2010) 'Challenges to the work life of academics: the experience of a renowned university in the Chinese mainland', *Higher Education Quarterly*, 64(1), 89–111.

Lewis, D. R., Hendel, D. D. and L. Kallsen (2007) 'Performance indicators as a foundation of institutional autonomy: implications for higher education institutions in Europe', *Tertiary Education and Management*, 13(3), 203–226.

Lijphart, A. (1999) *Patterns of Democracy: Government Forms and Performance in Thirty-Six Countries* (New Haven: Yale University Press).

Lillis, D. and M. Lynch (2014) 'New challenges for strategy development in Irish higher education institutions', *Higher Education Policy*, 27(2), 279–300.

Locke, W. (2007) 'Higher education mergers: integrating organisational cultures and developing appropriate management styles', *Higher Education Quarterly*, 61(1), 83–102.

Meister-Scheytt, C. (2007) 'Reinventing governance: the role of boards of governors in the New Austrian university', *Tertiary Education and Management*, 13(3), 247–261.

Mok, K. H. (2010) 'When state centralism meets neo-liberalism: managing university governance change in Singapore and Malaysia', *Higher Education*, 60(4), 419–440.

Mok, K. H. (2012) 'Bringing the state back In: Restoring the role of the state in Chinese higher education', *European Journal of Education*, 47(2), 228–241.

Painter, M. and B. G. Peters (2010) 'The analysis of administrative traditions', in M. Painter and B. G. Peters (eds) *Tradition and Public Administration* (pp. 3–16) (Basingstoke: Palgrave MacMillan).

Papadimitriou, A. (2011) 'Reforms, leadership and quality management in Greek higher education', *Tertiary Education and Management*, 17(4), 355–372.

Paradeise, C., Reale, E., Bleiklie, I. and E. Ferlie (eds) (2009) *University Governance: Western European Comparative Perspectives* (Dordrecht: Springer).

Pollitt, C. and G. Bouckaert (2004) *Public Management Reform: A Comparative Analysis*, 2nd edn (Oxford: Oxford University Press).

Puusa, A. and J. Kekäle (2013) 'Commitment in the context of a merger', *Tertiary Education and Management*, 19(3), 205–218.

Reed, M. I., Meek, V. L. and G. A. Jones (2002) 'Introduction', in A. Amaral, G. A. Jones and B. Karseth (eds) *Governing Higher Education: National Perspectives on Institutional Governance* (pp. xv–xxxi) (Dordrecht: Kluwer Academic Publishers).

Rowlands, J. (2012) 'Accountability, quality assurance and performativity: the changing role of the academic board', *Quality in Higher Education*, 18(1), 97–110.

Rowlands, J. (2013a) 'Academic boards: less intellectual and more academic capital in higher education governance?' *Studies in Higher Education*, 38(9), 1274–1289.

Rowlands, J. (2013b) 'The effectiveness of academic boards in university governance', *Tertiary Education and Management*, 19(4), 338–352.

Rowlands, J. (2013c) 'The symbolic role of academic boards in university academic quality assurance', *Quality in Higher Education*, 19(2), 142–157.

Rytmeister, C. (2009) 'Governing university strategy: perceptions and practice of governance and management roles', *Tertiary Education and Management*, 15(2), 137–156.

Shah, M. and S. Nair (2011) 'The influence of strategy and external quality audit on university performance: an Australian perspective', *Tertiary Education and Management*, 17(2), 139–150.

Stensaker, B. and A. Vabø (2013) 'Re-inventing shared governance: implications for organisational culture and institutional leadership', *Higher Education Quarterly*, 67(3), 256–274.

Taylor, J. and M. de Lourdes Machado (2006) 'Higher education leadership and management: from conflict to interdependence through strategic planning', *Tertiary Education and Management*, 12(2), 137–160.

Taylor, J. S. and M. de Lourdes Machado (2008) 'Governing boards in public higher education institutions: a perspective from the United States', *Tertiary Education and Management*, 14(3), 243–260.

van Ameijde, J. D. J., Nelson, P. C., Billsberry, J. and N. van Meurs (2009) 'Improving leadership in higher education institutions: a distributed perspective', *Higher Education*, 58(6), 763–779.

Verhoest, K., Roness, P. G., Verschuere, B., Rubecksen, K. and M. MacCarthaigh (2010) *Autonomy and Control of State Agencies: Comparing States and Agencies* (Basingstoke: Palgrave MacMillan).

22
From Collegial Governance to *Boardism*: Reconfiguring Governance in Higher Education

Amélia Veiga, António Magalhães and Alberto Amaral

Introduction

Until the last quarter of the 20th century, many European universities had been primarily governed by academics, and the state acted as a buffer protecting higher education institutions and academics from the interference of external interests (Neave, 2012) and held ruling power over non-academic matters. From a normative stance, less than half a century ago, Moodie and Eustace still considered that in universities, 'the supreme authority...must...continue to rest with the academics' (Moodie and Eustace, 1974, p. 233), and Burton Clark (1983) argued that the adoption of models based on the metaphor of *organized anarchy* would be more appropriate for allowing individuals and research teams to liberate their inventive capacity and to produce innovative ideas.

Over the last decades, higher education reforms were grounded in the shift from state control to supervisory models and to quasi-market regulation inducing corporate-like models of governance (Meek, 2003). This shift relied on increased institutional autonomy, based on the assumption that the more autonomous institutions were, the better they would respond to changes in their organizational environment (Amaral and Magalhães, 2001; Magalhães et al., 2013), and the better they would perform (Aghion et al., 2009; Ritzen, 2011). The increasing use of markets as instruments for regulating public domains was an additional argument for enhancing institutional autonomy as a condition to compete in a market (Dill et al., 2004; De Boer, Enders and Leisyte, 2007). However, 'more muscular executive/managerial prerogative within universities, in response to increased external government regulation...ironically reduces the relative autonomy of universities (including senior managements) in relation to government' (Blackmore, Brennan and Zipin, 2010, p. 6). Under the influence of New Public Management (NPM), governance reforms introduced private sector management tools, emphasizing market-based competition, efficiency, performance and value for money, concentrating decision power in the central administration, while weakening the representation of academics (Ferlie, Musselin and Andresani, 2009). The configuration of universities as corporations (Marginson and Considine, 2000) enhanced managerial modes of coordination (Blackmore et al., 2010) and corporate-like features in universities (Meek, 2003).

The re-conceptualization of universities as organizations and, more recently, as 'complete organizations' (Brunsson and Sahlin-Andersen, 2000; De Boer, Enders and Leisyte, 2007) can be seen as an effect of these reforms. However, the degree of the universities' organizational 'completeness' varies to very different extents and 'cannot be reduced to the complete-incomplete dichotomy, neither can the study of organizational responses be limited to the adoption-resistance axis' (Seeber et al., 2014, p. 25). The idea of universities as 'complete organizations' induced their shift from a 'republic of scholars' to a 'stakeholder organization' (Bleiklie and Kogan, 2007) and empowered boards in university governance as key structures in defining the organization's strategies (Amaral, Tavares and Santos, 2013; Shattock, 2012) and reshaping structures and processes in higher education governance (Amaral et al., 2013; Magalhães et al., 2013; Paradeise, Reale and Gostellec, 2009).

Managerialism triggered the rise of *boardism* as a distinctive governance praxis in higher education as it involves both normative assumptions and technical and practical elements. In this sense, *boardism* impinges on and legitimizes the structure of governance and influences its practices. Thus, the shifting balance of power between academics on the one hand and managers/administrators and representatives of external interests on the other affects university governance and plausibly the nature of teaching and research activities (Magalhães and Veiga, 2013). Rather than the setting up of governing boards (such as a board of governors, administration council, supervisory council), *boardism* in higher education concerns the incorporation of normative and technical elements stemming from corporate-like organizations in the governance processes in interaction/tension with academic self-governance. In our view, *boardism* refers to a shift in internal power balances, and, in this sense, academic boards reflect *boardism* when the governance rationale increases the influence of managerial concerns over academic endeavours, resulting in the loss of power of academics in the structures and processes of decision-making. For example, in the United Kingdom, the subordination of the academic board to the board of governors can be interpreted as an example of *boardism* as, in the case of conflict, the power of the executives prevails over the will of academics. Another example is given by the loss of decision-making power of senates in the Portuguese case.

This chapter starts by identifying *boardism* in Europe and beyond, signalling out its features in higher education governance. Shared governance will be discussed under this concept by using the perspective of balance and tensions of power between academics and managers/administrators. Our analysis focuses on a number of European countries as well as Australia, Canada and the United States and aims to explore the rise of *boardism* in higher education and its various forms and effects. In Europe, NPM-inspired higher education reforms have affected higher education systems and the institutional governance structures at different rates and paces. Also in Australia, Canada and the United States, *boardism* has been a core feature of higher education reforms. According to Fisher, Locke and Cummings,

> in mature systems, shared governance is an important 'touchstone' for academics, but is under threat, significantly circumscribed, or has already been replaced by stronger institutional management and corporate governance, even in public institutions (for example, in Australia, Norway, the UK, and the USA).
>
> (2011, p. 378)

Boardism in higher education governance

What is *boardism*?

We consider the concept of *boardism* as representing the decrease of academic self-governance and the decline of the power of academics in university decision-making processes. The reinforcement of managerial powers became an important ingredient of *boardism* under the influence of NPM. Research indicates that reforms in higher education that intend to enhance institutional autonomy emphasize managerial powers, while the power of academics and students in higher education management processes and structures tends to decrease (Amaral et al., 2013).

Another ingredient of *boardism* is the role of external stakeholders in governing higher education institutions. This role results from the combined influence of NPM-inspired reforms, pointing out the need for the university's responsiveness to their external environment and the accountability pressures as a counterpart of more institutional autonomy. These features of *boardism*, that is, the shift in internal power balance and more external representation, will be analysed with the aim of identifying how managerial and academic self-governance interact in Europe and beyond.

Why *boardism*?

To understand the rise of *boardism* as a governance praxis, it is necessary to take into consideration the constellation of concepts and discourses within which it is emerging. The argument is that the hegemonic influence of the NPM approach, the assumption of market regulation, the discourses on the autonomy of universities and their re-conceptualization as 'complete organizations' are configuring *boardism* as a governance praxis. *Boardism* emerges from concepts and discourses based on narratives as policy and management stories aimed at making sense of policy and action, melting normative and ideological ingredients with technical elements as pointed out by Ferlie et al. (2009). In the last decades, under the influence of NPM, discourses on the enhancement of institutional self-regulation have reinterpreted the meaning of institutional autonomy in public policy-making. In spite of its theoretical fluidity (Boston, 2011), the NPM narrative represents the idea that efficiency and effectiveness are to be achieved through management instruments used in the private sector, specifying goals and emphasizing competition for clients, performance measurement and the use of markets as instruments of regulation for the public sector (Meek, 2003).

Previous research has focused on the influence of narratives such as NPM and Network Governance (Paradeise et al., 2009) and New Governance (Magalhães et al., 2013). These narratives induce and legitimize policies and expectations influencing national and institutional strategies. In each country narratives 'can be linked to specific conceptions and theories regarding the relationship between the state and the society' (Ferlie et al., 2009, p. 13).

The NPM perspective is visible in the stimulation of competition; in the vertical steering of the system through the setting of explicit targets and the signature of performance contracts; in the development of a 'management must manage' perspective; in the focus on efficiency and value for money; and in the reduction in the representation of academics and students in higher education management processes and structures. At different paces, European higher education systems appear to converge on the need to develop a managerial approach (Paradeise et al., 2009) to the detriment of the bureaucratic narrative of administration and the collegial governance narrative.

The emphasis on the managerial approach is the ground on which *boardism* finds explanation and is central to understanding its key features in Europe. The increase of managerial governance implies the reinforcement of hierarchical steering inside universities with emphasis on stronger managerial and executive roles for rectors, deans and heads of department, configuring *boardism* as a distinctive governance praxis. In other words, it is more than the mere introduction of new structures, such as the university boards, boards of trustees or other supervisory boards. Rather, it is a praxis involving decision-making and action and their legitimating discourses on efficiency and effectiveness.

Since the 1980s, markets have become increasingly used in Europe as a means to politically steer public sectors, promoting the implementation of governance models that allow for adequate responses to competitive environments. NPM, by stressing the superiority of the market as a mode of coordination, emphasizes the advantages of managerial-based governance models over academic self-governance. Where academic self-governance relies on the major influence of collegial structures and processes, managerial governance refers to the reinforcement of hierarchies and organizational top-down decision-making. The enhancement of managerial-based governance models feeds *boardism* and is fed by it.

Shared governance through the lens of *boardism*

While in the United Kingdom and Continental Europe academics had, until the last decades, a strong role in the governance of their institutions under collegial models, in the United States there has been a tradition of strong leadership, with an important role of the executive and the board of trustees. Kells (1992) argues that in the 1970s and 1980s executives gained power relative to the academics, but from the 1990s onwards there have been signs of decreasing executive power. This shift in the United States is embodied in the concept of shared governance, which underlines the representation of academics in the structures and decision-making processes. However, in practice this concept can range from academic involvement in all decision-making issues to no involvement at all (Minor, 2004). Notwithstanding, we would argue that in general, governance reforms in Europe are decreasing the academics' power in governance practices, while in the United States a shift in power balance is moving in the opposite direction.

Schuetz (1999) defines shared governance as a system of self-governance where all those affected by a decision assume responsibility in decision-making. Shared governance models are in permanent adaptation and should consider inputs and concerns of three groups – the governing board, the president and the faculty ('faculty' in the American meaning) – 'while ultimately serving the needs of the broader society' (Stoessel, 2013, p. 1). Stoessel (2013) underlines that the shared governance model is aimed at curbing excessive powers of faculty members by introducing an external lay board of trustees composed of local citizens, industrialists and clerical staff. The role of the governing board is to achieve short and long-term goals while respecting the university's core values and mission and upholding the interests of society and students, thus incorporating the value of social consciousness (Stoessel, 2013). The president is a leader in charge of maintaining the course of the institution in a positive direction (Trow, 1985), and Kerr (2001) argues that a contemporary university president is mainly a mediator between the different stakeholders. Stoessel (2013, p. 5) considers that

> the faculty plays an integral role in the model as the actors in charge of disseminating the core principles of an institution, to the customer...The faculty sees their value as being a deliberate buffer against the encroachment

of political influence, controversial policies, and diminished educational quality.

From the point of view of academics, shared governance represents the idea that they delegate governance powers to managers, enabling them as key decision-makers. From the perspective of managers and administrators, shared governance ultimately assumes academics to be contributors to the decision-making processes. As *boardism* relates to power relationships between academics and managers/administrators, the concept of shared governance brings forward an interesting discursive tension, as pointed out by Olson (2009). Shared governance is an empty or floating signifier, implying that it describes the inter-group structures and processes, but it is too vague with regard to power relationships (Olson, 2009). From this perspective, the meaning of shared governance shows a means to ends reversal depending on the constituency voicing the argument:

> [S]hared governance is both a means to an end and an end to be maintained and valued; it is a collaborative process while also an outcome of collegiality; it is steeped in tradition yet concerns itself with change and innovation in the academy, and most of all, it seeks to bridge difference and yet curiously exacerbates it.
>
> (Crellin, 2010, p. 80)

Elaborating on the relationship between managerial and executive functions and academic self-governance, Shattock (2012) underlines the risks for universities to have governing structures centred on the governing boards and their executive branches hindering the importance of academic guidance in higher education governance. Following Clark's (1983) assumption that the core business of the universities is the production and dissemination of knowledge, Shattock (2012, p. 61) attributes an important role to academics and their views on institutional strategies while underlining that 'academic self-governance alone with no external involvement would fail a public accountability test and will be unlikely to flourish outside the special Oxbridge context'. In his view, 'good governance' models incorporate and enact the interaction between governing bodies and academic self-governance.

Shared governance appears as illustrating the tension between academic and managerial governance as underlined by the concept of *boardism*. The relationship between academics and managers emerges in a dynamic field of forces that ultimately represents the idea of the prevalence of the latter over the former. Hence, our focus is not on the shared character of governance but rather on the changes of power balances in the internal governing relationships induced by *boardism*.

Boardism in European higher education

In this section, the analysis of the changes in academic self-governance and managerial governance is based on previous research (e.g. CHEPS, 2007). As to the influence of external stakeholders in the governance structures of higher education institutions, the identified changes focused on the composition of the governing boards (Magalhães, Veiga and Amaral, 2014). We made use of the outcomes of the research project 'Transforming Universities in Europe' (TRUE), which involved eight different countries and data collected on 26 institutions of different types (comprehensive research universities, specialized universities and newly established universities) (Bleiklie, Enders and Lepori, 2013).

In exploring *boardism* in Europe, we have used a number of dimensions to cluster the various countries. First, in investigating the influence of NPM on the governance reforms at the national level, we looked at the degree of its influence. As suggested by Seeber et al. (2014), the influence of the NPM narrative can be high, medium or low. Second, the timing of the reforms is taken into account: there are NPM front-runners, latecomers or slow-movers (Paradeise et al., 2009). Third, the different countries are also clustered on the basis of the influence of external stakeholders in governing universities.

The United Kingdom and the Netherlands

In the late 1970s, the United Kingdom and the Netherlands emerged as determined reformers and widely reorganized their higher education governance system. The governance reform in the United Kingdom is described as a 'shift of substantial significance and scale' (Ferlie and Andresani, 2009, p. 195). While a post-NPM policy rhetoric and some remains of the bureau-professional model are visible in the role ascribed to peer review and professional collegiality, the research and funding policies, the enhancement of managerialism and the emergence of a professionalized bureaucracy were inspired by NPM (Ferlie and Andresani, 2009). These policies led to a more top-down management attitude towards academic issues (Shattock, 2006) with an impact on internal settings, namely on leadership and on the development of managerial norms and values. In the last decades, there were no significant changes with regard to 'the strong role of the top management in all fields of internal governance' (CHEPS, 2007, p. 221). In the United Kingdom, the influence of external stakeholders is high as reflected in the composition of the board of governors in the universities surveyed in the TRUE project. The 'main changes were the establishment of a small executive board, half of whom must be from outside the university' (Amaral et al., 2013, p. 663), and the subordination of the academic board to the board of governors. The academic board represents academia, and the board of governors includes the external stakeholders and substantiates the corporate governance approach aiming 'to ensure that governing bodies can meet their obligations to their wider constituencies inside and outside the institution' (Shattock, 2006, p. 52).

The influence of the NPM narrative in the Netherlands is reflected in the reinforcement of managerial governance over the last decade (CHEPS, 2007). The room for manoeuvre of Dutch universities to draw up, for instance, strategic plans increased by strengthening the roles of the executives and managers (Westerheijden, de Boer and Enders, 2009), and '[e]xecutive powers have grown at the expense of representative bodies' (CHEPS, 2007, p. 156). The influence of external stakeholders is also high, at least formally. Boards are externally dominated, as all their members are external to the university, and they are appointed by the Ministry of Education, Culture and Science. Boards are accountable to the ministry, suggesting that governance accountability is to multiple external stakeholders.

In the United Kingdom and the Netherlands, *boardism* was related with the decrease of academic self-governance and became stable in the last years (CHEPS, 2007). In the Netherlands, the increase of managerial governance and the influence of external stakeholders are evident features of *boardism*. The members of the supervisory board are all external and appointed by the minister, and '[t]raditional bodies of academic self-governance have been abolished or have been disempowered by having a consultative function mainly' (Enders, de Boer and Weyer, 2013, p. 12). While in the United Kingdom the interaction between academic self-governance and managerial governance is counterbalanced by the network governance perspective (Paradeise et al., 2009) and practices, in the Netherlands this interaction is marked by a large increase in the influence of managerial governance.

In both countries, a strong version of *boardism* as a governance praxis is visible in the decrease of academic self-governance, the increase of managerial governance and in the high proportion of external members in the composition of the boards.

Norway and Portugal

Norway and Portugal are latecomers to NPM and its influence over higher education reforms is medium. In Norway, the NPM influence can be traced back to the 1990s, but it assumed a more comprehensive influence with the Quality Reform introduced in 2002–2003, along with the influence of other governance narratives and practices. For instance, the new degree structure 'lend considerable support to a neo-Weberian narrative that emphasises continuity regarding the strong role of the state in the regulation of higher education' (Bleiklie, 2009, p. 152). However, the NPM narrative has become increasingly influential, namely by the introduction of tougher competition for research funding (Bleiklie, 2009). Academic self-governance decreased as reflected in the fact that 'since 2003 academic leaders could be appointed rather than elected' (CHEPS,

2007, p. 165). In turn, managerial governance has increased: 'since 2003 and 2005 the law gives the authority to determine internal governance to the institutions themselves' (CHEPS, 2007, p. 165). The Norwegian legal framework imposes 'a certain balance of powers of the different estates, by establishing that all should be represented in the board without any group having the majority' (Amaral et al., 2013, p. 13). The influence of the external stakeholders might be high, as the governing board may decide, by a majority of at least two-thirds of its members, to have a majority of external members. However, in the universities surveyed in the TRUE project this is not the case; the percentage of external members in the university boards range from 14% to 36%.

In Portugal, the managerial and the NPM governance narrative also played a central role in public policies, higher education included. The Law 62/2007, on the new legal framework for Portuguese higher education institutions, was elaborated under the influence of NPM. This law is grounded in political and managerial assumptions on governance that give predominance to managerial governance over academic self-governance, enhancement of the role of external stakeholders in decision-making bodies and the possibility to constitute higher education institutions as private foundations.

In 2007, an analysis of the extent and impact of the higher education governance reform in Portugal showed that managerial governance had increased (CHEPS, 2007). The introduction of the Law 62/2007 weakened the role and power of academics and students in governing bodies such as senates, and these governing bodies became not obligatory and can now only have an advisory role. The Law also set a maximum number of 25 membership seats in scientific councils of faculties, irrespective of faculty size. This reflects the prevalence of managerial governance over academic self-governance. However, the Law also allows universities to establish advisory bodies that can be seen as elements of the enhancement of academic networks to 'mitigate this effect and to counterbalance the underrepresentation of faculties/schools/departments in the governance bodies' (Magalhães et al., 2013, p. 304). The fact that external board members are chosen by the internal members of the governing board might indicate the limited range of influence of external stakeholders in the governance of Portuguese higher education institutions. The external members represent about one-third of the members of the boards.

Both in Norway and Portugal, *boardism* is being shaped by the increase of managerial governance and the influence of external stakeholders to some extent, but it is less penetrating than in the United Kingdom and the Netherlands. *Boardism*, based on decreased academic self-governance, is more visible in Norway than it is in Portugal.

France, Germany and Italy

In France, Germany and Italy, the influence of the NPM narrative is low, and these countries are slow-movers. In France, it is hard to recognize a direct influence of NPM in higher education reforms (Musselin and Paradeise, 2009). The changing relationship between the state and the universities resulted mainly from the policy of contracts initiated in 1988. The contracts do not echo the NPM narrative as they were 'aimed at reducing inequalities within the French system rather than differentiating and developing competition among universities' (Musselin and Paradeise, 2009, pp. 45–46). Moreover, the contracts are not seen as instruments for budget allocation linked to objectives. The emphasis has been put on their negotiation, 'rather than on their evaluation' (Musselin and Paradeise, 2009, pp. 45–46). This policy has empowered French universities by enhancing the supremacy of presidents in governance structures and processes (Musselin and Paradeise, 2009). These dynamics reinforced the role of rectors/presidents as strong actors in higher education institutions and have strengthened managerial governance in an attempt to improve the effectiveness of management structures. Simultaneously, they also induced academic self-governance as 'presidents of HEIs [higher education institutions] are elected by representatives of three Councils consisting of scientific and administrative staff, students and external stakeholders' (CHEPS, 2007, p. 83). The French contractual policy model can be seen as a shift from direct national administration 'in the direction of a more "evaluative state"' (Musselin and Paradeise, 2009, p. 30), and an attempt to limit the range of influence of external stakeholders in university decision-making as reflected in the proportion of one-fourth of external members in the university councils surveyed in the TRUE project.

In Germany, NPM approaches related to governance reforms were introduced in debates on public management in the mid-1980s. Only in the mid-1990s did they enter the debates in higher education. As the result of the governance reforms, hybrid arrangements of traditional university governance and NPM-inspired models of governance can be identified, together with the introduction of mission-based contracts as a regulation tool (Schimank and Lange, 2009). The reason for the delayed emergence of NPM in German higher education was that ministries distrusted universities, due to both the limitations university leadership had in negotiating general goals with faculties and institutes and the frailties of the reporting process of universities with regard to their achievements of targets and missions (Schimank and Lange, 2009). These obstacles reflected on the institutions' internal settings and on the perceived need that general boards had to be 'educated' about how a university works (Schimank and Lange, 2009). Apparently, this indicates the presence of a significant collegial power in place, resisting the decrease of academic self-governance. The decrease of academic self-governance has become visible in the loss of competencies of academic governance bodies such as senates, councils and faculty boards (CHEPS, 2007). The managerial powers of presidents and rectors have increased, echoing the NPM narrative element that 'managers must manage'. The presence of external stakeholders in university governance has been shaped by conflicting arguments between those supporting the traditional strong influence of academics and those in favour of NPM-inspired governance. Currently, there are contradictory views about the presence of external stakeholders in institutional governance, as it may lead 'to a more utility oriented opening of the universities for the needs of the greater public or on the contrary to an exclusion of public and academics for the sake of a strengthened influence of a small elite of industry and business representatives' (Schimank and Lange, 2009, p. 73). Interestingly enough, the conflicting perspectives on the representation of external interests in German university boards are not reflected in the three universities surveyed in the TRUE project as the proportion of external members is half and in one university the university council consists of external members only.

In Italy, the NPM market-oriented and competitive-driven policies (such as funding and resource allocation based on outcome evaluation) neither penetrated the governing of the system nor the governance of institutions. In spite of the fact that the 1997 Bassanini law introduced some measures inspired by the NPM narrative, the legalist governance culture continued to stress uniformity and national procedural homogeneity, combined with a low management capacity of the public sector. This might explain 'the gap between the rhetoric of the reforms and the effectiveness of their implementation' (Reale and Potí, 2009, p. 78). Additionally, the long-standing existence of an 'academic oligarchy' also challenged NPM-inspired decision-making procedures, seen as lacking decentralization of power to the basic units, self-evaluation routines and appropriate management tools (Reale and Potí, 2009, p. 78). Since the 1990s, the resistance of the academic community with respect to managerial governance has not allowed the government to accelerate the process of modernization (Moscati, 2009). The limited range of influence of external stakeholders is linked to the attempt to 'reduce the number of components of both the *Senato* and the *Consiglio*' (Reale and Potí, 2009, p. 90). The mitigated influence of external stakeholders appears to reflect the fact that 'NPM ideas were introduced but in coexistence with local practices' (Reale and Potí, 2009, p. 78), as reflected in the proportion of external members in the universities surveyed that hardly reaches one-third.

The ingredients of *boardism* in France, Germany and Italy, in terms of the shifting power balance between academics and managers in university decision-making have resulted in relatively low levels and protracted NPM influence in higher education. The power of academics and their governance practices counteracted the hegemonic discursive NPM influence, mitigating the conflicting role attributed to external stakeholders as voicing the external interest only 'requiring them ... to simply approve the proposals the leadership makes' (Kretek, Dragšić and Kehm, 2013, p. 52). In these countries, we witness a mitigated version of *boardism*, which is mainly the result of successful resistance of advocates of the academic self-governance model. However, there are hints that may lead to further versions of *boardism* induced by the managerial role of French university presidents and the decrease of academic-self-governance in Germany.

Boardism beyond Europe

The United States

In the United States, higher education, the involvement of academics in institutional governance 'has not always been the norm' (Jones, 2011, p. 119). Unlike in the European context, where governance is moving from traditional academic collegiality to managerialism, in the United States it was only in 1966 with the 'Statement on Government in Colleges and Universities' that the participation of academics in institutional governance was clearly introduced and that the concept of shared governance gained momentum.

The idea of increasing managerial governance, from the perspective of *boardism*, dominated college and university governance until the mid-1960s, and the role of the executive increased in the 1960s and 1970s (Kells, 1992). Boards of trustees and appointed presidents/chancellors were common for central governing bodies, and these appointed leaders were the main source of institutional decision-making power (Jones, 2011). The focus on the 'shared' character of governance, the complexity of universities as organizations and public expectations for efficiency and accountability reinforced the weight of managerial governance at all levels. Gallos (2009, p. 137), referring to faculty senates in the United States, underlines that academics have been seen as both advocates of their own interests as well as 'watchdogs to guard turf and prevent what faculty see as "bad" administrative decisions'. However, these reactive stances paradoxically opened the way to legitimize corporate-like governance models, which developed in the United States based on the assumption that the performance of the organization depends on the performance of its boards. As a consequence, there has been an emphasis on the definition of purpose and direction of institutional strategies, plans of activities and budgetary plans and management of human resources, let alone the reinforcement of decision-making and implementation chains. However, despite many obstacles, shared governance continues to play an important role in institutional decision-making (Jones, 2011).

The debate on shared governance is illustrative of boardism in the United States

> Although trustees should view the faculty as the principal resource for informed oversight of academic policies and programmes, faculty should

recognize the boards responsibility to govern and welcome responsible strategic oversight of the faculty's prerogatives

(Dennis, Bhoendradatt Tewarie and Quinton White, 2003, p. 59)

On the one hand, the debate on shared governance brings forward the 'academy's' ability to meet escalating external changes... [and the] introduction of new principles of intergroup leadership' (Crellin, 2010, p. 72) underlining the power of managers over academics. On the other hand, shared governance also implies adding more stakeholders to the university governance structures, contributing to translating *boardism* into a governance praxis. The tension between academic governance and the influence of external stakeholders, namely the trustees, underlines the need for academics to comply with external guidance. This reflects the contrast identified by Dennis et al. (2003) between the *academic* culture and the *corporate* and the political culture.

Australia

The corporate-like models prevail in the English-speaking world (e.g. the United States, Australia, Canada). Managerial governance enhances *boardism*, as corporate governance models are seen as the best solutions to cope with economic and social changes. Additionally, academic governance is reshaped under managerial forms that decrease academic self-governance. On the relationships between corporate and academic governance, the Australian case presents interesting features. Meek and Davies describe the situation as

> a primary example of where NPM and market competition have replaced many traditional forms of academic governance. Within this changed policy context, many responsibilities have been devolved to individual universities... Moreover, institutions are now placed in a much more highly competitive environment, and considerable pressure has been placed on universities to strengthen management, to become more entrepreneurial and corporate-like.
>
> (Meek and Davies, 2009, p. 44)

A document issued in 2013 by the Australian Conference of Chairs of Academic Boards and Senates (CABSS Working Party on Corporate and Academic Governance) to inform the Tertiary Education Quality and Standards Agency (TEQSA) reflects a clear separation between corporate and academic governance, similar to the bicameral UK system of a governing board and a university/education council (CABSS Working Party on Corporate and Academic Governance, 2013). From the perspective of *boardism*, the presence of academic self-governance decreases as it is reframed under the influence of managerial governance.

Assuming that academic governance is a subset of the overall governance system of an educational organization, CABSS recommends that

> the overall governance of an institution comprises its corporate governance, encompassing the corporate governing body and executive management, and its academic governance. There should be a clear distinction between the responsibilities of the different governance and management components, including a clear and discernible separation between corporate and academic governance.
>
> (CABSS Working Party on Corporate and Academic Governance, 2013, p. 3)

The emphasis on the encompassing character of corporate governance and on the separation between corporate and academic governance might be interpreted as a diminishment of academic self-governance in favour of managerial governance.

Canada

In Canada, public universities are legally defined as private not-for-profit corporations, and

> [t]he charter legislation of most Canadian universities implies at least three sources of decision making. The governing board is assigned the responsibility for administrative matters while the senate is assigned responsibility for academic matters. The third source of decision-making is the central administration of the university.
>
> (Jones, 2002, p. 218)

Jones refers to the importance of policy networks in the governance of Canadian universities. Mainly, student's organizations and faculty associations appear to play an important role in institutional decision-making (Jones, 2002). However, the structure and balance of representation that emerged in the reform processes of the 1960s and 1970s is being challenged, and the 'boundaries between academic and administrative policy matters are often ambiguous, but given the superior authority of the board, disputes on these boundaries issues are often resolved in favour of the "administrative" perspective' (Jones, 2002, pp. 228–229). Additionally, Trakman (2008) pointed out that academic staff must be (re)trained as university administrators in a business-like organization. Such training 'often involves developing and understanding of the relationship between governance and management, including the responsibility of managers to carry out delegated governance functions' (Trakman, 2008, p. 68). The influence of external stakeholders in the corporate university governance model is not as large as it could be expected. 'Even if university governors are subject to corporate responsibility to diverse stakeholders, it is necessary to determine to which stakeholders they are primarily responsible to and if those responsibilities are corporate' (Trakman, 2008, p. 70). Similarly, in Australia and Canada, the influence of the external stakeholders appears to be mitigated as their role is mediated by academic boards 'responsible for managing external relationships and engaging with external stakeholders' (Vilkinas and Peters, 2013, p. 24).

Conclusion

Higher education governance reforms are often associated with a redistribution of decision-making authorities and the reorganization of decision-making structures in order to achieve greater organizational efficiency and effectiveness in high-quality service delivery. However, *boardism* in higher education governance reforms affected the relationship between academics and managers in organizational governance, triggering tensions and resilience. These tensions make the issues of power, interests and conflicts relevant to explain institutional responses as underlined by Gornitzka, Kyvik and Stensaker (2005). While shared governance induces a normative stance towards university governance promoting a 'desirable' balance of powers, *boardism* as a praxis refers to the actual tension between academic self-governance and managerial governance. It allowed for tracing power balances and identifying 'who the winners and losers are in the process of shaping government policies and reforms' (Gornitzka et al., 2005, p. 54). From this perspective, the reforms in Europe suggest that from a general point of view managers can be regarded as winners, although the picture is quite nuanced if we take a closer look.

Comparing *boardism* in Europe and beyond contributed to clarify that in Europe, *boardism* has been developed with eroding academic self-governance models, while in the United States it reflects an attempt to integrate elements of academic self-governance in the existing governance structures and processes. Where the United States shared governance models may reflect an utter version of *boardism* as a praxis, governing models in Europe appear to display a more nuanced picture.

With regard to the influence of external stakeholders, it could be argued that both their presence and guidance are associated with the prevalence of managerial governance. Their presence in the boards suggests that NPM had an impact on university decision-making, but the effectiveness of their roles has not been analysed in this chapter. Rather, in the analysis it has been interpreted as a normative ingredient of *boardism*. Further research could enlighten the consequences of the role of external stakeholders in higher education governance, but it could be argued that, depending on the actual powers they possess, the higher the proportion of external board members, the higher their potential influence is. In Europe, the United States, Canada and Australia, the external stakeholders' role is subsumed by governing structures and institutional leadership as a socially desirable assumption legitimized by the influence of NPM.

The concept of *boardism* allowed for identifying the dynamics of power relationships between academics, managers/administrators and external stakeholders. As a praxis, it contributes to looking at the governance arrangements as an arena of political action involving governance narratives and national and institutional ethos.

Acknowledgement

The present chapter was financed by FEDER funds through the Operational Competitiveness Programme – COMPETE and by national funds through FCT – Foundation for Science and Technology, under the project FCOMP-01-0124-FEDER-027445.

References

Aghion, P., Dewatripont, M., Hoxby, C. M., Mas-Colell, A. and A. Sapir (2009) The governance and performance of research universities: evidence from Europe and the U.S. (Vol. Working Paper 14851): National Bureau of Economic Research.

Amaral, A. and A. Magalhães (2001) 'On markets, autonomy and regulation the Janus Head revisited', *Higher Education Policy*, 14(1), 7–20.

Amaral, A., Tavares, O. and C. Santos (2013) 'Higher education reform in Portugal: A historical and comparative perspective of the new legal framework for public universities', *Higher Education Policy*, 26, 5–24.

Blackmore, J., Brennan, M. and L. Zipin (2010) 'Re-positioning university governance and academic work: an overview', in J. Blackmore, M. Brennan and L. Zipin (eds) *Re-positioning University Governance and Academic Work* (pp. 1–16) (Rotterdam: Sense Publishers).

Bleiklie, I. (2009) 'Norway: from tortoise to eager beaver', in C. Paradeise, E. Reale, I. Bleiklie and E. Ferlie (eds) *University Governance: Western European Comparative Perspectives* (pp. 127–152) (Dordrecht: Springer).

Bleiklie, I. and M. Kogan (2007) 'Organization and governance of universities', *Higher Education Policy*, 20(4), 477–494.

Bleiklie, I., Enders, J. and B. Lepori (2013) 'Special Issue: transforming universities in Europe', *Higher Education*, 65(1).

Boston, J. (2011) 'Basic NPM ideas and their development', in T. Cristensen and P. Laegreid (eds) *The Ashgate Research Companion to New Public Management* (pp. 17–32) (Surrey: Ashgate Publishing).

Brunsson, N. and K. Sahlin-Andersen (2000) 'Constructing organizations: the example of public sector reform', *Organization Studies*, 21, 721–746.

CABSS Working Party on Corporate and Academic Governance (2013) Corporate and Academic Governance in the New Regulatory Environment. University of Western Sydney: Conference of Chairs of Academic Boards and Senates.

CHEPS (2007) The extent and impact of higher education governance reform across Europe – final report to the Directorate-General for Education and Culture of the European Commission (Vol. 1) (Enschede).

Clark, B. (1983) *The Higher Education System* (California: University of California Press).

Crellin, M. A. (2010) 'The future of shared governance', *New Directions for Higher Education*, 2010(151), 71–81. doi: 10.1002/he.402.

de Boer, H., Enders, J. and L. Leisyte (2007) 'Public sector reform in Dutch higher education: the organizational transformation of the university', *Public Administration*, 85(1), 27–46.

Dennis, J. G., Bhoendradatt Tewarie, A. and J. Quinton White (2003) 'Governance in the twenty-first-century university: approaches to effective leadership and strategic management', *ASHE-ERIC Higher Education Report*, 30(1).

Dill, D., Teixeira, P., Jongbloed, B. and A. Amaral (2004) 'Conclusion', in P. Teixeira, J. Jongbloed, D. Dill and A. Amaral (eds) *Markets in Higher Education: Rhetoric or Reality?* (pp. 327–353) (Dordrecht: Springer).

Enders, J., de Boer, H. and E. Weyer (2013) 'Regulatory autonomy and performance: the reform of higher education re-visited', *Higher Education*, 65(1), 5–23. doi: 10.1007/s10734-012-9578-4.

European Students' Union (ESU) (2012) Bologna with Student Eyes. Brussels: ESU.

Ferlie, E., Musselin, C. and G. Andresani (2009) 'The governance of higher education systems: a public management perspective', in C. Paradeise, E. Reale, I. Bleiklie and E. Ferlie (eds) *University Governance: Western European Comparative Perspective* (pp. 1–19) (Dordrecht: Springer).

Fisher, D., Locke, W. and K. Cummings (2011) 'Comparative perspectives: emerging findings and further investigations', in W. Locke, K. Cummings and D. Fisher (eds) *Changing Governance and Management in Higher Education. The Perspectives of the Academy* (pp. 369–379) (Dordrecht: Springer).

Gallos, J. V. (2009) 'Reframing shared governance: rediscovering the soul of campus collaboration', *Journal of Management Inquiry*. doi: 10.1177/1056492608326326

Gornitzka, Å., Kyvik, S. and B. Stensaker (2005) 'Implementation analysis in higher education', in A. Gornitzka, M. Kogan and A. Amaral (eds) *Reform and Change in Higher Education* (pp. 35–56) (Dordrecht: Springer).

Jones, G. A. (2002) 'The structure of university governance in Canada: a policy network approach', in A. Amaral, G. A. Jones and B. Karseth (eds) *Governing Higher Education: National Perspectives on Institutional Governance* (pp. 213–234) (Dorderecht: Kluwer Academic Publishers).

Jones, W. A. (2011) 'Faculty involvement in institutional governance: a literature review', *Journal of the Professoriate*, 6(1), 117–135.

Kells, H. R. (1992) *Self-Regulation in Higher Education* (London: Jessica Kingsley Publishers).

Kerr, C. (2001) *The Uses of the University* (Cambridge, MA: Harvard University Press).

Kretek, P., Dragšić, Ž. and B. Kehm (2013) 'Transformation of university governance: on the role of university board members', *Higher Education*, 65(1), 39–58. doi: 10.1007/s10734-012-9580-x

Magalhães, A. and A. Veiga (2013) 'What about education in higher education?' in L. Smith (ed) *Higher Education: Recent Trends, Emerging Issues and Future Outlook* (pp. 57–72) (New York: Nova Science Publishers).

Magalhães, A., Veiga, A., Amaral, A., Sousa, S. and F. Ribeiro (2013) 'Governance of governance in higher education: practices and lessons drawn from the Portuguese case', *Higher Education Quarterly*, 67(3), 295–311, doi: 10.111/hequ12021

Magalhães, A., Veiga, A. and A. Amaral (2014) *The Changing Role of External Stakeholders: Effective Actors, Imaginary Friends or Non-Interfering Friends?* Paper presented at the International Research Society for Public Management (IRSPM), Ottawa, Canada.

Marginson, S. and M. Considine (2000) *The Enterprise University: Power, Governance and Re-invention in Australia* (Cambridge: Cambridge University Press).

Meek, L. (2003) 'Introduction', in A. Amaral, V. L. Meek and I. M. Larsen (eds) *The Higher Education Managerial Revolution?* (pp. 1–29) (Dordrecht: Kluwer Academic Publishers).

Meek, L. and D. Davies (2009) 'Policy dynamics in higher education and research: concepts and observations', in V. L. Meek, U. Teichler and M. L. Kearney (eds) *Higher Education Research and Innovation: Changing Dynamics* (Kassel: UNESCO Forum on Higher Education).

Minor, J. T. (2004) 'Understanding faculty senates: moving from mystery to models', *Review of Higher Education*, 27(3), 343–+. doi: 10.1353/rhe.2004.0004

Moodie, G. C. and R. B. Eustace (1974) *Power and Authority in British Universities* (Oxford: Allen and Unwin).

Moscati, R. (2009) 'The implementation of Bologna process in Italy', in A. Amaral, G. Neave, C. Musselin and P. Maassen (eds) *European Integration and the Governance of Higher Education and Research* (pp. 207–225) (Dordrecht: Springer).

Musselin, C. and C. Paradeise (2009) 'France: from incremental transitions to institutional change', in C. Paradeise, E. Reale, I. Bleiklie and E. Ferlie (eds) *University Governance: Western European Comparative Perspective* (pp. 21–49) (Dordrecht: Springer).

Neave, G. (2012) 'Change, leverage, suasion and intent: an historical excursion across three decades of change in higher education', in Western Europe *Managing Reform in Universities – The Dynamics of Culture, Identity and Organizational Change* (pp. 19–40) (Basingstoke: Palgrave Macmillan).

Olson, G. A. (2009) 'Exactly what is "Shared Governance"?' *The Chronicle of Higher Education*, July 23, 2009, http://chronicle.com/article/Exactly-What-Is-Shared/47065/

Paradeise, C., Reale, E., Bleiklie, I. and E. Ferlie (2009) *University Governance: Western European Comparative Perspectives* (Dordrecht: Springer).

Paradeise, C., Reale, E. and G. Gostellec (2009) 'A comparative approach to higher education reforms in western European countries', in C. Paradeise, E. Reale, I. Bleiklie and E. Ferlie (eds) *University Governance: Western European Comparative Perspectives* (pp. 197–225) (Dordrecht: Springer).

Reale, E. and B. Potí (2009) 'Italy: local policy legacy and moving to an "in between" configuration', in C. Paradeise, E. Reale, I. Bleiklie and E. Ferlie (eds) *University Governance: Western European Comparative Perspective* (Dordrecht: Springer).

Ritzen, J. (2011) *A Framework for Scoring the Empowerment of Universities in the EU Member States*. Paper presented at the University Policy for Strengthening Competitiveness and Social Cohesion, Maastricht.

Schimank, U. and S. Lange (2009) 'Germany: a latercomer to new public management', in C. Paradeise, E. Reale, I. Bleiklie and E. Ferlie (eds) *University Governance: Western European Comparative Perspectives* (pp. 51–76) (Dordrecht: Springer).

Schuetz, P. (1999) 'Shared governance in community colleges', *Eric Digests*, 4.

Seeber, M., Lepori, B., Montauti, M., Enders, J., de Boer, H., Weyer, E., Bleiklie, K., Hope, S., Michelsen, G., Mathisen, N., Frølich, L., Scordato, B., Stensaker, E., Waagene, Z., Dragsic, P., Kretek, G., Krücken, A., Magalhães, F., Ribeiro, S., Sousa, A., Veiga, R., Santiago, G., Marini, and E. Reale (2014) 'European universities as complete organizations? understanding identity, hierarchy and rationality in public organizations', *Public Management Review*, 1–31. doi: 10.1080/14719037.2014.943268

Shattock, M. (2006) *Good Governance in Higher Education* (Berkshire: Open University Press).

Shattock, M. (2012) 'University governance', *Perspectives: Policy and Practice in Higher Education*, 16(2), 56–61. doi: 10.1080/13603108.2011.645082

Stoessel, J. W. (2013) 'Conceptualizing the shared governance model in American higher education: considering the governing board, President and faculty', *Student Pulse*, 5(12). http://www.studentpulse.com/a?id=818

Trakman, L. (2008) 'Modelling University Governance', *Higher Education Quarterly*, 62(1–2), 63–83. doi: 10.1111/j.1468-2273.2008.00384.x

Trow, M. (1985) 'Comparative reflections on leadership in higher education', *European Journal of Education*, 20(2/3), 143–159.

Vilkinas, T. and M. Peters (2013) 'Academic governance provided by academic boards within the Australian higher education sector', *Journal of Higher Education Policy and Management*, 36(1), 15–28. doi: 10.1080/1360080X.2013.825419

Westerheijden, D., de Boer, H. and J. Enders (2009) 'An "Echternach" Procession in different directions: oscillating steps towards reform', in C. Paradeise, E. Reale, I. Bleiklie and E. Ferlie (eds) *University Governance: Western European Comparative Perspectives* (pp. 103–125) (Dordrecht: Springer).

23

Global University Rankings, an Alternative and Their Impacts

Don F. Westerheijden[1]

Rankings have been debated in higher education since more than two decades, when the *US News & World Report* made an impact on the higher education community with its first college ranking. The debate reached new heights of intensity since global university rankings appeared, shortly after the turn of the century. This chapter will focus on the rise of those global university[2] rankings, and as I am a member of the team that developed U-Multirank (full disclosure), I will present U-Multirank as an alternative to the first three global university rankings: the Shanghai Academic Ranking of World Universities, the *Times Higher Education* (THE) World University Rankings and the QS World University Rankings. Besides methodological issues, in this chapter I will give attention to the impacts these rankings have, including U-Multirank. As the findings regarding impacts turn out to be not unequivocally positive, should we stop producing or reading them – will there be a fall of rankings?

The first section will first explain why rankings could arise in higher education. In the second section, I will describe the rise of the global university rankings, while a short description of the main indicators used is given in the following section. The critique of these rankings makes up the fourth section, and in the fifth section, I present U-Multirank as an alternative. Both in fourth and fifth sections I will briefly go into impacts or users' views. Finally, the sixth section contains some concluding remarks.

Concepts: Diversity and rankings in higher education

The several tens of thousands of higher education institutions across the world differ from one another: some have perhaps less than a hundred students while others tens of thousands of students; some offer one or very few degrees in a single area of knowledge or in a profession while others offer hundreds of different degrees in many areas; some are heavily engaged in internationally published research while others focus on teaching only. We live in a globalizing world, where people's horizon of attention has expanded from traditional geographical areas of interest (the town where one lives, the region, the country's capital, or perhaps – if it is not too large – the whole country) to the whole world – or at least to the parts of the world that figure in the worldwide media. The global flow of information made many people around the world aware of the existence of many more higher education institutions than just the local or national ones. At the same time, higher education grew in importance in society: enrolment rates rose from elite to mass or even universal levels, higher education is increasingly seen as an asset in the (also increasingly global) economic competition and so forth. Accordingly, many have reasons to be interested in higher education institutions from farther afield. But what is relevant information?

Diversity: Vertical and horizontal

If all higher education institutions were exactly similar, there would be no need for information about individual ones; it is diversity that drives the interest in university rankings.

Similar entities can be compared along a single dimension; one is higher, bigger, faster, better or in another way more valuable than the other. We call this *vertical* diversity.[3] The metaphor comes to mind of a mountain where it is 'best' to be at the top. The other understanding is *horizontal* diversity, that is, of entities being not quite similar, showing differences along different dimensions (size, colour, function, age, etc.), without judging whether one is more valuable than another. Interestingly if one has university rankings in mind, in searching the internet definitions of diversity in this horizontal sense come out on top of the search machines. For instance, '[t]he concept of diversity encompasses acceptance and respect. It means understanding that each individual is unique, and recognizing our individual differences' (University of Oregon, 2015). A main theme in this chapter will be that most university rankings measure – or construct – vertical diversity and ignore the significant horizontal diversity among higher education institutions.

Diversity of users: The need for different rankings

Diversity of the horizontal type equally applies to the persons who might be interested in higher education institutions. Prospective students may want to consider different fields of study, as well as different locations to study their chosen field. University leaders may want to find benchmarking partners from whom they can learn about better performance of a certain function (such as getting better at the 'third mission'). Higher education ministers may want to find better mechanisms to distribute funds, or more effective international scholarship programmes. The upshot is that different stakeholders have different information needs for different decisions they may want to take, and we contend that it takes different rankings to satisfy those needs.

Information, credence goods, ranking and classification

In a comprehensively rational theory of behaviour, one would expect persons to search all the necessary information before choosing the option that best fulfils their utility function (Kreps, 1990). What many theories of rational behaviour seemed to forget is that collecting information is a costly behavioural option in itself, so that bounded rationality theories may give better models of human behaviour (Allison and Zelikow, 1999; Becker, 1976; De Vree, 1982; Simon, 1957; Stigler, 1961).

The information problem is particularly pertinent regarding (higher) education. The standard assumption is that the quality of a good (in the sense of the degree to which a given purpose can be fulfilled) can be known in advance. Those are 'search goods'. While that assumption may apply to material goods, most services do not fulfil it: only upon experiencing the service can a person judge its quality; those are called 'experience goods'. For some services, though, even after consuming them the quality may not become clear, because effects materialize only after a long time or because effects remain uncertain to the consumer, for instance because other events may compound effects. Those are called 'credence goods'. A good case can be made that education, just like a physician's consult, is a credence good (Bonoma, Tedeschi and Lindskold, 1972; Dulleck and Kerschbamer, 2006): one's career – clearly a long-term effect – may depend on many circumstantial events and factors besides the degree or the learning outcomes gained from education. For an individual's health, another factor that correlates with one's level of education, the same applies perhaps even stronger. To make a somewhat reasoned choice for a particular credence good, actors must rely on proxy information that is available in advance.

This is where rankings come into play. A university ranking, in these terms, can be defined as a concise instrument providing prima facie readily interpretable information on vertical diversity among higher education institutions. For reasons to be explained below, we should add: or among entities within higher education institution such as study programmes. A similar instrument to inform about horizontal diversity in a concise manner could be called a classification, after the Carnegie Classification that set the standard for such instruments since the 1970s in the United States. Since both classifications and rankings intend to inform stakeholders in the credence-good area of education, as an umbrella term 'transparency instruments' has come into use especially in the European context.

Rise of global university rankings

Information on higher education may not have been much of a problem for stakeholders when higher education systems were elite, in Trow's terms (Trow, 1974): a few universities, mostly based on the same model, catering for a small proportion of society whose families often had had experience with the country's universities since generations. This changed with access to higher education becoming more democratized ('first-generation students'), and with the increasing (horizontal) diversity of higher education institutions when polytechnics and similar institutions were added to the traditional ones to accommodate the growing demand for higher education efficiently. This happened in different countries at different moments of time, though in general it started after the Second World War and sped up around the 1960s–1980s.

University rankings have been traced back to the interbellum (Dill, 2009), and first gained ground in a higher education system so large that it could not be understood in detail by stakeholders while there was sufficient uniformity to make system-wide information interesting, that is, the United States. The *US News & World Report* ranking of colleges in the United States has appeared annually since 1983 (Dill, 2009), ostensibly to assist students in finding 'the best' college across all 50 states of the United States. For aspiring students, the United States was a relevant area, because of the similarity of language of instruction and degrees (four-year undergraduate and two-year graduate degrees being the most common model), because of the nation-wide career-inspired mobility they would contemplate and because of the costs college choice involves especially in prestigious private universities.

The recent rise to prominence of rankings across the world goes associated with the idea that mobility in the 21st century is no longer just national – not even in large nations like the United States, India or China – but global. The best and brightest of all students now take universities across the world into consideration when deciding how to start their careers. There can be little doubt that this is connected to globalization: information about universities can travel instantaneously around the globe; students from anywhere can fly to a university anywhere in the world in little more than a day; and in ever more countries affluent classes can afford to do so. At least for some, the world is getting ever flatter, to paraphrase the metaphor from Friedman's highly debated book (Friedman, 2005). For others, going abroad for study may be the only way out of a dismal future at home. Either way, international student mobility has almost doubled in the decade since the turn of the century to reach three million (Shields, 2013), and informing students is the major aim that global rankings profess to pursue.

The first global university ranking was the Shanghai Academic Ranking of World Universities (ARWU), which was published first in 2003. A year later, the THE ranking appeared. When the *Times Higher Education* changed its methodology in 2009 and dismissed its provider of data, the latter, Quacquarelli Symonds (QS), began to publish its own ranking. European higher education institution respondents mentioned these three as the most influential rankings, even above national ones (Hazelkorn, Loukkola and Zhang, 2014). To this trio a fourth was added in 2014, U-Multirank, which follows a very different approach to the idea of ranking.

Besides these rankings of universities worldwide, dozens of other university rankings exist. Some of these are also global in nature, but are less prominent in the public view because they have more limited aims. The Leiden ranking is an example: it provides information about the research performance of the 750 most research-productive higher education institutions in the world. The main difference with for example the Shanghai and THE rankings is that the Leiden ranking does not use any other indicators than research publications and citations, and that it does not pretend to give a picture of 'the' quality of the universities; its stays close to its data base: 'the ranking aims to provide highly accurate measurements of the scientific impact of universities and of universities' involvement in scientific collaboration' (http://www.leidenranking .com/#sthash.tzsnUp7l.dpuf). Another example is the Webometrics ranking, which wants to stimulate internet use: 'We intend to motivate both institutions and scholars to have a web presence that reflect accurately their activities...university authorities should reconsider their web, open access and transparency policy, promoting substantial increases of the volume and quality of their electronic publications' (http://www.webometrics.info/en/node/ 21). It collects information about, in 2015, around 20,000 higher education institutions across the world.

Another category of global rankings is made up of specialized rankings, providing information not about comprehensive universities, but specialized schools. The *Financial Times's* ranking of business schools is a prominent example of this category.

The largest number of university rankings, though, are not global but national. On the one hand, it may be easier to find more, comparable information about higher education institutions within the same national context. On the other hand, it recognizes that for most students the national horizon is a more relevant horizon of consideration when choosing where to study even in an era of globalization. These rankings include more indicators aiming to show quality of education, as this is what prospective students are most interested in.

Some years ago, Hazelkorn counted almost a dozen global rankings, some regional ones (e.g. in Southeast Asia), and more than 50 national ones (Hazelkorn, 2011) – the number certainly has not reduced since then.

Main indicators in global university rankings

Rankings use different sources of information to construct their rankings. Always, the aim is to construct quantitative data, enabling calculations and ranking in an objective way – criticism of those ways will follow in the next section.

The Shanghai ARWU is, from this perspective, the simplest of the major global rankings, relying purely on information external to the universities ranked (www.shanghairanking.com): it includes indicators on publications and academic awards associated with each university, which it interprets as indicating quality of research (50%) and quality of education (50%). However, a university's quality of education is indicated by having Nobel Prize and Fields Medal (the mathematics equivalent of Nobel Prizes) winners among its former graduates, and highly cited researchers and Nobelists and Fields Medal holders among current staff members, which in fact tilts the balance of information heavily towards a university's research. The ARWU selects for its ranking only universities with Nobelists or Fields Medal winners, highly cited researchers, with publications in *Nature*, or achieving a threshold of publication numbers. Obviously then higher education institutions not involved heavily in research do not qualify. Similar criteria in the other two global rankings also limit the ranked universities to less than 1% of all higher education institutions around the world.

The THE ranking (www.timeshighereducation.co.uk) uses more varied information sources than the ARWU, some from separate databases, some from the universities ranked. It too aims to get a balance between indications of education and of research, but again research-based indicators predominate. To measure research (I do not see a valid reason to separate citations from research as the THE does; together they make up 60% of the ranking weight), it uses in 2014–2015: publication and citation indicators, corrected for size of the university to give small highly publishing and highly cited universities also a chance; research income; and an international reputation survey among academics. The survey is split between the research and education parts of the THE, but in total weighs in for about one-third of the final ranking. The remainder of the indicators (less than 5% each on average) for education are the staff–student ratio (as THE says: 'as a simple (and admittedly crude) proxy for teaching quality'; 4.5%); the ratio of PhD to undergraduate degrees to indicate knowledge-intensiveness (2.25%); the number of PhDs awarded, normalized for institutional character and size (6%); and income level of the university, also normalized for size (2.25%). Internationalization is indicated by the proportions of international staff, international students and international co-publications (each 2.5%). Finally, THE measures income from industry to indicate innovation (2.5%).

The data going into the QS ranking in 2014 (www.topuniversities.com) include citation data (size-normalized, 20%); two surveys, one among academics, the other among employers; and staff and student ratios. The academic survey is the most important indicator (40%), while the employers' survey adds another 10%. International survey data therefore make up half the ranking in the QS. QS is the only one among the three to aim at the employment dimension. Citation data and the staff – student ratio each count for 20%. The proportions of international students and international staff together determine the last 10% of the ranking.

Besides the ranking, QS offers an opt-in star system, allowing universities to showcase strengths in a wider range of dimensions: research, teaching, employability, internationalization, facilities, online/distance learning, social responsibility, innovation, arts and culture, inclusiveness and specialist criteria. About 150 universities have chosen to take part in this additional feature.

What is the business model of the rankers? The Shanghai ranking is linked to a publicly funded university, the Shanghai Jiao Tong University, although the ranking itself became an independent enterprise in 2009. The THE ranking is focused on sales of the Times Higher Education. The QS case is more complex: its income starts with the stars, and as the QS website and media activity show, all of this is connected to its organizing fairs (presumably particularly interesting to those in the QS stars system) where universities recruit overseas students, especially held in South Asia and East Asia.

Critiques of university rankings

In the book that the U-Multirank development team published, much space was devoted to summarizing and analysing the criticism of global university rankings and their basic characteristics (van Vught and Ziegele, 2012). Another source of bringing much of the criticism of the global university rankings together can be found in Hazelkorn (2011). A fruitful way to organize the criticism was given by the U-Multirank publication, which will be followed here.

The problem of unspecified target groups

As appeared above, students are often portrayed as an important target group for university rankings. Rankings intend to assist them in making a more rational choice of where they are going to study. As shown above (section 'Diversity of users: The need for different rankings'), there are different groups of stakeholders. According to Hazelkorn, governments, parents and industry are using rankings more than expected (Hazelkorn, 2011). These different categories of users may want to take quite different decisions to which a university ranking might contribute relevant arguments. Obviously, for such different decisions, different actors need different information on different objects: students would want to know about the learning experience in a certain study programme and whether there is a good chance of employment; university leaders might want to know if another institution would be a good benchmarking partner to learn how to organize knowledge transfer; research councils might want to know if a university already had a strong research performance; and so forth. The case for a multidimensional transparency tool is obvious once this is realized. Until recently, however, it was simply assumed implicitly that a single ranking must be relevant to any user. Target groups' information needs were not analysed, and target groups were not distinguished in the rankings. In fact, especially the global rankings were not user-oriented, but were supply-driven: they used available information (see also section 'The problem of narrow range of dimensions').

It is contested, however, to what extent existing transparency tools reach the groups among students most constrained by social factors (Cremonini, Westerheijden and Enders, 2008; Hazelkorn, 2011). Rankings might thus continue and even strengthen social stratification of students rather than help widen access to high-performing higher education institutions.

Such sociological worries apply less to, for example, institutional leaders; for them, the lack of credible and comparable information on other universities is the main reason for their interest in transparency tools. Research universities especially have begun to reference themselves worldwide (Marginson, 2008), urging decision-makers in these universities to think bigger and set the bar higher. A consequence of this worldwide phenomenon is a global 'reputation race' (van Vught, 2008) among research-oriented universities. Reputation is an efficient and therefore attractive indicator of 'quality' for actors who do not have the time, need or other resources to delve deep for detailed information (Stigler, 1961), or to worry about what makes up 'quality'. Hence also the remark that '[r]ankings enjoy a high level of acceptance among stakeholders and the wider public because of their simplicity and consumer-type information' (AUBR Expert Group, 2009, p. 4). Reputation is 'good' for institutional managers (van Vught, 2008), because a high reputation is what many stakeholders act upon. A good reputation helps gain better access to funds, highly performing staff members, well-prepared first-year students, and so on, all of which might result in measurably better performance in later years. It does not follow that repeating existing reputations is helpful, since persons' shortcuts to form a reputation can be anything: rather than on the actual quality of education, university reputation probably depends on hearsay (in academic terms: previous reputation), and as Marginson wrote, on being located in a well-known major city or on establishing a university brand (Marginson, 2008), which in turn partly depends on institutional age.

The problem of ignoring diversity within universities

Global university rankings were designed to inform about *whole* institutions, ignoring internal variance in qualities among academic fields within an institution. However, only very few 'world class' universities perform highly in (almost) all of their departments. The most appropriate and realistic strategy for most universities around the world is to focus their efforts on being outstanding in a limited number of fields. The majority of higher education institutions thus have both high and low(er) performing departments or schools. Besides, although for some purposes it may be desirable to have institution-wide information, for many others – such as a student's choice to study a certain programme – it is necessary to know about the diversity within the university.

In many, especially global, league tables treating the institution as a whole used to be an unquestioned assumption. Having come to realize this shortcoming, the three major global rankings started to add field-level rankings to their publications and websites. However, their field-level rankings were limited by the fact that the universities were the ones pre-selected for the whole-institution rankings. These field-level rankings amount to reshufflings of the same set of institutions, they are not rankings of the (potentially) best examples in the field of, for example, economics, which might be found in non-ranking universities.

The problem of narrow range of dimensions

Global league tables tend to concentrate their actual data collection to where measurable data are publicly available at a worldwide scale, which limits the dimensions to bibliometric databases, or lists of Nobel Prize winners, and perhaps some basic university statistics like student numbers. Global league tables create the impression among readers, however, that they address the universities' *overall quality*. However, institutional quality is a much more encompassing concept. Even if a number of rankings seem to correlate, putting the same universities in their top ten, this may be a measurement artefact rather than an indication of an underlying 'true' quality across different dimensions of performance. For instance, there are only two major suppliers of publication and citation databases, which to a large extent cover the same publications.

To complement the bibliometric indicators, the ARWU ranking adds research-related rewards achieved by scientists from the universities, that is, Nobel Prizes and Fields Medals. QS and THE include other indicators as well, and in both cases the largest weight next to bibliometric indicators is given by reputational surveys. The size of their worldwide samples of university teachers (THE and QS), or of employers (QS) seems impressive, but that does not make the indicators more valid. Academic researchers may know individual colleagues, but rarely do they know about the performance of a whole department or field in another university. If they do, it is in most cases because of knowledge of research, for example through having read their publications, or having done research projects with them. Knowledge of colleagues' quality of teaching is very rare. Moreover, actual knowledge of other universities is mostly limited to other universities in the respondents' own country. Knowledge about foreign universities is mostly very limited – globalization is far from complete and for insider knowledge about universities, the world certainly is not flat yet. Reputation is an individual shortcut, but not a valid source of scientific information, as explained above. The rankers doing those worldwide surveys cannot know how to value the different shortcuts taken by their respondents. What reputation surveys measure, is therefore highly uncertain; they are 'prone to being subjective, self-referential and self-perpetuating' (Hazelkorn, 2011, p. 75). Moreover, there are incentives to lie in reputation surveys: by answering that one has a low esteem for other universities, one's own scores better in the ranking. Several incidents in (especially US) national rankings show that this is not purely hypothetical.

By focusing on publications and how they are received by academic colleagues (as measured through citations in yet other scientific publications) the global rankings emphasize the research function of universities. The other functions of higher education institutions – education, the 'third mission' (whether defined as knowledge transfer or as community outreach) – and other characteristics making up the quality of higher education institutions – for example, international orientation – are hardly valued in the conceptual frameworks that in fact underpin the indicators used in those global rankings.

The limitation in dimensions does not apply as strongly to national rankings: these often include information from universities about elements intended to indicate quality of education. They tend to provide more relevant information directed at students than the global rankings. This can be done more easily at the national level than internationally. For instance, selectivity or SAT-scores[4] might be an indicator in the United States, but does not have meaning in higher education systems with open access as in many European countries. Still, the indicators used are often only distant proxies of quality of the students' learning experiences: Is fewer students per class by definition better? Are PhD holders always better teachers? One class of information that actually would inform about students' learning experiences are surveys: in Europe, often satisfaction surveys are available, either institutionally or nationally. The US focus on students' engagement rather than satisfaction in the NSSE (National Survey of Student Engagement; see http://nsse.iub.edu) makes an at least equally valid alternative. Such national surveys cannot, however, be used for international comparison as they use different methods, items and scales.

The problem of composite overall indicators

The major global university rankings, as well as most national rankings (e.g. *US News and World Report*) aggregate their indicators into a composite overall score by assigning particular weights to the single indicators. Composite indicators are used in many performance indicators systems and rankings. In the course of growing complexity of many social systems, they can be seen as an instrument of 'distilling reality into a manageable form'. But at the same time they carry the danger of oversimplifying complex social realities and calculating misleading averages out of opposite indicators. Presenting results in the form of one composite overall indicator, although very common, at the same time is one of the 'main courses for the institutional unease' with league tables in higher education (Usher and Savino, 2006).

Two major problems of this practice must be mentioned here. First, assigning weights to individual indicators implies a conceptual model. However, there is no scientific theory of the quality of a university, nor are there empirical arguments for assigning particular weights to indicators (Dill and Soo, 2005). Weights are therefore arbitrary. At the same time, the chosen weights define the university model actually supported by the ranking. In the Shanghai as well as THE rankings, the ideal university is a natural science research-oriented, large institution, because that is the type of institution producing large numbers of publications and citations in the bibliometric databases (Filliatreau and Zitt, s.a.).

Second, I come back to the different target groups of rankings: users have different priorities and preferences, that is, they would need different weights even if the available indicators were relevant to them. A composite indicator with fixed weights inevitably means patronizing users of rankings by deciding about the importance and relevance of different indicators. In recent years, some rankings introduced (in their Web-based tools) interactive elements to leave the decision about the relevance of indicators to the users. Some rankings (e.g. the *Guardian* ranking in the United Kingdom) are doing this by allowing the user to assign their own weights to a number of individual indicators as the basis for the calculation of a composite indicator. Others like the German CHE university ranking allow users to choose a limited set of indicators and having a personalized ranking of universities fulfilling those user-set criteria.

Besides, the methodology of global rankings to construct their composite indicator is statistically problematic. Saisana and D'Hombres (2008) demonstrated that the final rank of a university in those rankings was not robust. Based on a sensitivity analysis and simulations using a multitude of possible weighting systems, they showed that the rank position of 67% of universities in the THE ranking and of 60% in the Shanghai ARWU were highly sensitive to the composition of the overall score. Variation were larger in the lower ranks, but even, for example, the Massachusetts Institute of Technology (MIT) could be classified anywhere between the 10th and the 25th positions with the THE data.

The problem of league tables

The global university rankings, and many national ones as well, consist of league tables, ordering universities on a single scale from numbers 1 to *x*. This model supposes that each difference in a rank position of an institution marks a difference in quality – number 32 is better than number 33, is better than 34, and so on. In league tables, 'minimal differences produced by random fluctuations may be misinterpreted as real differences' (Müller-Böling and Federkeil, 2007). In statistical terms, the league table approach ignores the existence of standard errors in data. Hence league tables tend to exaggerate differences between institutions and push vertical stratification to the extreme. Meaningful rankings should be confined to establishing ranges (as the NRC ranking of PhD programmes in the United States does), or groups, or clusters of institutions with similar profiles and/or programmes.

League tables are also highly sensitive to changes in the methodology to compile tables, in particular with regard to methods of standardization of original scores. For instance, the introduction of z-score aggregation as a new method of standardization in the THE ranking in 2008 led to a drop for the London School of Economics from 17th to 59th – yet in the THE publications the year-on-year change was highlighted as if the same thing was measured.

The problem of field and regional biases in publication and citation data

The problem of field and regional biases regards the challenge of existing rankings to address diversity related to cultural, language and contextual factors, especially when it comes to data on research performance.

First, the two major databases on publications and citations that are used for bibliometric ranking data, Thomson Reuters' *Web of Science* and Elsevier's *Scopus*, mainly include journal articles published in peer-reviewed journals. Yet publication cultures and modes vary considerably between different fields (e.g. Hicks, 2004; Leeuwen et. al., 2001; Moed, 2005). Peer-reviewed international journals are the prime vehicles for knowledge dissemination in the natural sciences, medical sciences and life sciences. Building rankings on those journal articles implies a bias in favour of these fields. In many applied sciences and in engineering, conference proceedings are more important than journal articles. In the social sciences and humanities, book publications (both monographs and book chapters) play an important role in knowledge dissemination. In recent years, both bibliometric databases have begun to widen their coverage of under-represented domains of knowledge production. Thus, numbers of journal increased and conference proceedings are now being indexed as well. Still, coverage is likely to remain unsatisfactory in the arts and humanities in particular.

Second, the sets of journals in these two databases are biased against non-English speaking countries. This flaw too is recognized and has started to be addressed in recent years, by widening the databases to include some journals in, for example, French, German, Chinese and Japanese languages.

The problem of unspecified and volatile methodologies

The early league tables were published with little or no information on the methodology used to compile them. Thus, a 2009 report complained: 'Research has found that the results of the Shanghai Jiao Tong Academic Ranking of World Universities (ARWU) are not replicable, thus calling into question the comparability and methodology used' (AUBR Expert Group, 2009, p. 51). The major rankings now give an explanation of their methodology, though it appears be hard to replicate the exact rankings (e.g. AUBR Expert Group, 2009).

In addition, magazines publishing annual league tables have been accused of changing their methodology in order to achieve changes in their top positions, as there would be little news value in repeatedly having the same universities at the top and this could affect magazine sales (Dill and Soo, 2005).

Some changes are also meant to improve the methodology; thus, THE expands its number of indicators almost yearly as more sophisticated data and analyses became available. Nevertheless, comparability over the years is limited and statements like 'University X has now risen to number N' may be due to methodical changes as much as to any change in reality in research or education, even at the very top of the rankings.

The problem of impacts

Hazelkorn (2011) has devoted quite some effort to show the intended and unintended, the desirable and perverse impacts of especially the global rankings on universities and on higher education system authorities. Students also seem to be increasingly influenced by rankings, although mostly at graduate level, in international mobility choices, and with students from higher socio-economic strata (Cremonini et al., 2008). Moreover, in the college choice process, rankings remain only one of many sources for decision-making (e.g. Nora, 2004; Reay, Davies, David and Ball, 2001; Vossensteyn, 2005).

At the level of national decision-making, the drive towards 'world class' is the most prominent effect of global university rankings (Hazelkorn, 2011). Large countries with well-developed economies and well-developed higher education systems like France, Germany and Japan have started 'excellence initiatives' to make some universities gain a higher place in the global rankings – perhaps as a side effect of increasing their research and innovation capacities, but it is an explicit and intended side effect (Cremonini, Westerheijden, Benneworth and Dauncey, 2014). Less well-developed countries are doing the same: China's policies to boost the development of high-quality universities, like its 'Project 985', may even have sparked off the Shanghai ranking in the first place. Russia has a '5/100' policy, explicitly aimed at getting five Russian universities in the 'top 100'. But even many small (e.g. Finland) or low-income countries (e.g. Vietnam) want to achieve a university getting mentioned in the global rankings' top 200s.

In this framework, the World Bank coined the term 'world-class university'; Salmi (2009) gave the recipe: freedom to organize itself, concentration of talent and abundant resources. Saudi Arabia's King Abdullah University of Science and Technology (KAUST) was purpose-built following this recipe. Critics have seen especially resources condition as endangering the rest of the higher education system, because money might be channelled from socially more productive investment in, for example, community colleges (in European terms, level-five degrees) into a would-be 'world-class university'. As an alternative, 'world-class higher education *systems*' have been promoted – also by Salmi (2009), by the way.

Within higher education institutions, the global rankings are at the same time criticized and despised, and followed avidly: the wide publication of rankings is getting too important to risk one's reputation. Hazelkorn found, for instance, that 71% of her respondents want to be in the top 25% internationally (Hazelkorn, 2011). In internal management, ranking results have become subject of management contracts and strategic plans, sometimes affecting resource reallocation between departments (Hazelkorn mentioned an example of arts departments losing money to sciences), but have also boosted marketing efforts.

U-Multirank as the alternative to global league tables

Criticizing rankings does not make them disappear. On the contrary, it has been recognized that they are here to stay, as people actually use them; there is a demand for rankings. Around 2009, the international European U-Multirank team therefore took the bold step of developing an alternative ranking that would not suffer from the weaknesses of the other global university rankings. They found a willing ear at the European Union, which at the same time was looking for opportunities to highlight the strengths of European universities that were, in its view, underestimated by the three global rankings.

Design of U-Multirank

To design a different ranking that avoided the problems mentioned in the previous section (and others), the design principles for what became U-Multirank included (van Vught and Ziegele, 2012):

- It is not a single ranking, but *user-driven*, individual rankings for each user developed through a process with continuous stakeholder involvement;
- The ranking is *multidimensional*, valuing all areas of *performance* of higher education institutions (education, research, knowledge transfer, community outreach and internationalization);
- While striving to accommodate a large variety of higher education institutions (not just the traditional research universities), comparisons should

only be made of institutions with similar activity profiles (*compare like with like*);

- The ranking is *multi-level*: some users are interested in institution-level rankings, others in rankings of fields within universities; and
- Methodological soundness:

  - Indicators should be reliable, valid, feasible (for data collection) and internationally comparable;
  - The ranking should not include arbitrary procedures like adding up or averaging incomparable indicators; and
  - It should minimize incentives and possibilities for strategic behaviour of participating universities.

Validity meant first of all that the indicators in U-Multirank should inform as directly as possible about a university's *performances* (outputs) rather than concentrating on more readily available information on inputs and conditions (income, staff numbers, etc.).

Comparability was a serious limiting condition, since a balance had to be found between using common definitions and adapting to national or local realities. That was not so much a problem when using international databases of publications and citations, or of patents – a new data source not used by other rankings – but when it came to using data delivered by universities themselves, a multiple-round verification process became necessary to arrive at numbers of, for example, teaching staff that were comparable internationally while accommodating to who were actually teaching students in the different universities, and to the figures that universities could actually produce from their administrations.

Methodological limitations made inclusion of some of our desired indicators impossible; for example, employment levels of graduates. Employment is too dependent on local, regional and national employment levels, it differs per study field of knowledge, and it is recorded differently in different countries.

The methodological considerations on reliability and validity also led to not aiming for spuriously precise measurements, but to use robust ratings: for each indicator we used a five-point scale spanning the actual values found among the participating universities. The cut-off points between the categories were in principle 20-percentile groups, from top 20% ('A' score) to bottom 20% ('E') with adjustments if there were, for example, a number of (almost-)tied institutions at the border. In such cases, we tried to shift the cut-off to a meaningful gap, so that we may have, for example, a top 17% on a certain indicator, but with a visible difference to the second-rate institutions in that indicator.

To avoid composite scores, it was decided to show all separate indicators in the ranking. Whereas the THE composes a ranking out of some 15 indicators, U-Multirank shows all of its 30-odd indicators at the institutional level; if one drills down to field-based information, the total number of (partly same, partly different) indicators is some three dozen. It includes novel indicators like art-related output (to re-balance the science bias in publication databases), patents achieved, interdisciplinary publications and co-publications with regional non-university authors. At the field level, student satisfaction survey data are included as well, hence the larger number of indicators.

The large number of indicators, together with the principle of user-driven, individualized rankings necessitated using a Web tool (www.umultirank.org); U-Multirank does not lend itself easily to presentation in a journal or magazine. The website has separate entry points for students (guiding them directly to the field and programme level) and for decision-makers more interested in universities as a whole. Realizing that this customisable information system takes getting used to, ready-made rankings are available as well.

Some first-year results

In its first year, U-Multirank included extensive information on over 500 universities regarding its five dimensions of performance (education, research, knowledge transfer, internationalization and regional engagement), and it included publicly available data about some 300 additional, well-known research universities. The latter sample was included to provide a comparison with the established global rankings, for example in the ready-made ranking of research and research linkages. At the level of fields, four fields were included (to be extended in later years, eventually becoming a cyclical roster with updates every three years).

The universities in U-Multirank were located in 70 countries all over the world, although the sample had better coverage of European than of international universities: 62% of U-Multirank universities were from Europe, 17% from North America, 14% from Asia and 7% from Africa, Latin America and Oceania. The volunteers in this first year included traditional research universities and also many higher education institutions that had not been represented in other global rankings; the latter group included many specialized universities, universities of applied sciences and similar 'polytechnic'-type institutions. In all, U-Multirank included some 300 universities that were new to global rankings. Around 30 of these institutions showed top-group ('A') scores on more than ten indicators; at the same time, not a single university among the total of more than 800 showed top scores across all institutional-level indicators. Talking about a number-one university therefore does not make sense in the U-Multirank methodology; in fact, the lack of universities with top scores in all indicators proves empirically the need for multidimensional rankings. These results prove as well that U-Multirank taps different kinds of excellence than the other global rankings.

Participants' views of U-Multirank in Europe

The funder of the development and start-up phase of U-Multirank, the European Commission, appreciated the first round of U-Multirank and as a consequence granted the second half of its project support, reaching until 2017.

How the traditional research universities in Europe reacted to the first round of U-Multirank was studied by their umbrella organization, the European University Association (EUA). From its sample (126 responses, with 85 universities that participated in U-Multirank actively by providing institutional data), more than 60% found collecting the institutional data for U-Multirank hard work and an even larger majority agreed it took more work than expected, but at the same time more than 60% found it worthwhile because it effectively captured institutional activities (Loukkola and Morais, 2015). Over 85% of the universities planned to continue their participation in U-Multirank; also the large majority of respondents that did not participate in the first round said they anticipated joining later. Sixty per cent of the respondents also said they would use the U-Multirank results in one way or another; 11% said they would not, while the remaining 30% were not yet sure (Loukkola and Morais, 2015).

Concerns of the institutions – apart from the effort needed to gather data – focused on cross-country comparability of the information (Loukkola and Morais, 2015).

As the EUA pointed out, a number of these results reflected results that a previous study by the same organization had uncovered about the other global rankings (Hazelkorn et al., 2014) – especially that universities are divided about rankings and about participating in them. A similar study among the higher education institutions in U-Multirank that were not in the membership range of the EUA, such as universities of applied science, would make an interesting complement to the EUA report.

Fall of university rankings?

The chapter's title evokes the metaphor of 'rise and fall', but will rankings ever fall? Probably, 'rise and fall' is the wrong metaphor at least for a long time to come. Rankings are here to stay, because they satisfy a need for information that many categories of stakeholders experience regarding higher education. The question – and among some the wish – of a fall is largely due to the weak answer that most current university rankings give to stakeholders' demands. The global university rankings did not do a valid and reliable job; many national rankings suffer from the same weaknesses, although examples of better practice may be found (the CHE ranking in Germany is often cited as a best-practice example). At the global level, U-Multirank tried to respond to some of the other rankings' weaknesses, even at the cost of increasing complexity for users, following not only the first (as the other global rankings do) but also the second part of

Einstein's adagium 'to make the irreducible basic elements as simple and as few as possible without having to surrender the adequate representation of a single datum of experience' (Calaprice, 2010). According to the information about participant universities now available, U-Multirank was partially successful in that respect in its first year, although further development is certainly necessary.

At least, U-Multirank helped to shift the game of ranking already since its announcement. I have the impression that part of the improvements in the methodology of the other global rankings since 2009 would not have happened without U-Multirank entering the scene. A better metaphor than 'rise and fall' could be, therefore, the dialectic development of thesis – antithesis – synthesis: rankings as the thesis, criticism as their antithesis and U-Multirank as a first example of the synthesis of global rankings, or in a currently more popular expression: ranking 2.0. Let us see what next versions will bring.

Notes

1. The responsibility for the current text, including any remaining errors, lie with the author. The chapter, in particular the section on U-Multirank, could not have been written, however, without the work of his colleagues on the U-Multirank team, especially Frans van Vught, Frank Ziegele, Jon File, Frans Kaiser and Gero Federkeil.
2. For brevity, I will use the term 'university', although unless explicitly stated otherwise I intend all higher education institutions.
3. I use 'diversity' as a state of being different, while 'differentiation' denotes the process of becoming more different.
4. It was first introduced in 1926 and its name and scoring have changed several times, being originally called the Scholastic Aptitude Test, then the Scholastic Assessment Test, then the SAT Reasoning Test and now simply the SAT.

References

Allison, G. and P. Zelikow (1999) *Essence of Decision* (2nd ed) (New York: Longman).

AUBR Expert Group. (2009). *Assessing Europe's University-Based Research – Draft*. s.l. [Brussels]: European Commission – DG Research.

Becker, G. S. (ed) (1976) *The Economic Approach to Human Behavior* (Chicago/London: University of Chicago Press).

Bonoma, T. V., Tedeschi, J. T. and S. Lindskold (1972) 'A note regarding an expected value model of social power', *Behavioral Science*, 17, 221–228.

Calaprice, A. (ed) (2010) *The Ultimate Quotable Einstein* (Princeton University Press).

Cremonini, L., Westerheijden, D. F., Benneworth, P. and H. Dauncey (2014) 'In the shadow of celebrity? World-Class university policies and public value in higher education', *Higher Education Policy*, 27, 341–361.

Cremonini, L., Westerheijden, D. F. and J. Enders (2008) 'Disseminating the right information to the right audience: Cultural determinants in the use (and Misuse) of rankings', *Higher Education*, 55, 373–385.

De Vree, J. K. (1982) *Foundations of Social and Political Processes: The Dynamics of Human Behaviour, Politics, and Society* (Bilthoven, NL: Prime Press).

Dill, D. D. (2009) 'Convergence and diversity: The role and influence of university rankings', in B. M. Kehm and B. Stensaker (eds) *University Rankings, Diversity, and the New Landscape of Higher Education* (pp. 97–116) (Rotterdam; Boston; Taipeh: Sense Publishers).

Dill, D. D. and M. Soo (2005) 'Academic quality, league tables, and public policy: A cross-national analysis of university ranking systems', *Higher Education*, 49, 495–533.

Dulleck, U. and R. Kerschbamer (2006) 'On doctors, mechanics and computer specialists: The economics of credence goods', *Journal of Economic Literature*, 44 (1), 5–42.

Filliatreau, G. and M. Zitt (s.a.). *Big Is (made) Beautiful Some Comments about the Shanghai Ranking of World-Class Universities*. s.l. [Paris]: OST.

Friedman, T. L. (2005) *The World Is Flat: A Brief History of the Twenty-First Century* (New York: Farrar, Straus and Giroux).

Hazelkorn, E. (2011) *Rankings and the Reshaping of Higher Education: The Battle for World-Class Excellence* (London: Palgrave Macmillan).

Hazelkorn, E., Loukkola, T. and T. Zhang (2014) *Rankings in Institutional Strategies and Processes: Impact or Illusion?* (Brussels: EUA).

Hicks, D. (2004). The Four Literatures of Social Science, in Moed, H. F., Glänzel, W. & U. Schmoch (eds.), *Handbook of Quantitative Science and Technology Research: The Use of Publication and Patent Statistics in Studies of S&T Systems* (pp. 473–496) (Dordrecht etc.: Springer).

Kreps, D. M. (1990) *A Course in Micro-Economic Theory* (New York: Harvester Wheatsheaf).

Loukkola, T. and R. Morais (2015) *EUA Members' Participation in U-Multirank: Experiences from the First Round* (Brussels: EUA).

Marginson, S. (2008) *Global, Multiple and Engaged: Has the 'Idea of a University' Changed in the Era of the Global Knowledge Economy?* Paper presented at the Fifth International Workshop on Higher Education Reforms 'The Internationalization of Higher Education and Higher Education Reforms', Shanghai.

Moed, H. F. (2005). *Citation Analysis in Research Evaluation* (Dordrecht: Springer).

Müller-Böling, D. and G. Federkeil (2007) 'The CHE-Ranking of German, Swiss and Austrian Universities', in J. Sadlak and L. N. Cai (eds) *The World-Class University an Ranking: Aiming Beyond Status* (pp. 189–203) (Bucharest: CEPES).

Nora, A. (2004) 'The role of habitus and cultural capital in choosing a college, transitioning from high school to higher education, and persisting in college among minority and nonminority students', *Journal of Hispanic Higher Education*, 3(2), 180–208.

Reay, D., Davies, J., David, M. and S. J. Ball (2001) 'Choices of degree or degrees of choice? class, "Race" and the higher education choice process', *Sociology*, 35, 855–874.

Saisana, M. and B. D'Hombres (2008) *Higher Education Rankings: Robustness Issues and Critical Assessment. How Much Confidence Can We Have in Higher Education Rankings?* (Luxembourg: Office for Official Publications of the European Communities).

Salmi, J. (2009) *The Challenge of Establishing World-Class Universities* (Washington, DC: World Bank).

Shields, R. (2013). 'Globalization and international student mobility: A network analysis', *Comparative Education Review*, 7(4), 609–636.

Simon, H. A. (1957) *Models of Man* (New York: Wiley).

Stigler, G. J. (1961) 'The economics of information', *Journal of Political Economy*, LXIX, 213–225.

Trow, M. (1974) 'Problems in the transition from elite to mass higher education', in OECD (ed) *Policies for Higher Education* (pp. 51–101) (Paris: OECD).

University of Oregon (2015) 'Definition of Diversity', http://gladstone.uoregon .edu/~asuomca/diversityinit/definition.html, accessed 2015-03-14.

Usher, A. and M. Savino (2006) *A World of Difference: A Global Survey of University League Tables* (Toronto: Educational Policy Institute).

Van Leeuwen, T. N., Moed, H. F., Tijssen, R. J. W., Visser, M. S., & A. F. J. van Raan, (2001). 'Language biases in the coverage of the Science Citation Index and its consequences for international comparisons of national research performance', *Scientometrics*, 51, 335–346.

van Vught, F. A. (2008) 'Mission diversity and reputation in higher education', *Higher Education Policy*, 21(2), 151–174.

van Vught, F. A. and F. Ziegele (eds) (2012) *Multidimensional Ranking: The Design and Development of U-Multirank* (Dordrecht etc.: Springer).

Vossensteyn, J. J. (2005) *Perceptions of Student Price-Responsiveness: A Behavioural Economics Exploration of the Relationships Between Socio-Economic Status, Perceptions of Financial Incentives and Student Choice* (Enschede: CHEPS).

D. Funding Higher Education

24

The Funding of Research in Higher Education: Mixed Models and Mixed Results

Ben Jongbloed and Benedetto Lepori

Introduction

This chapter will look into the question of how governments have organized the public funding of research and how that funding has changed in recent years. To make their national economies more knowledge driven, innovative and competitive, many governments have introduced reforms in their national research system. This is the case in Europe – the prime focus of this chapter – as well as in the rest of the world.

The reason why governments fund research is that research – in particular when it does not have obvious commercial applications – has important spillovers into society. Private investors in search for innovation will normally not take these benefits into account and, therefore, will underinvest in basic (fundamental) research. To correct an insufficient level of private investment, governments therefore will be prepared to invest in their national research systems (Geuna, 2001). Of all public and private expenditure on research and development (R&D) in Europe, almost a quarter is performed by the higher education (HE) sector. In 2012, total higher education spending on R&D (HERD) accounted for 0.47% of the Gross Domestic Product (GDP) in the 28 member states of the European Union (OECD, 2014), a share that has increased in most countries over the last decade.

Funding is a critical issue for Higher Education Institutions (HEIs), as it provides for the salaries of researchers, it enables the training of new researchers and it helps HEIs in building research laboratories. Unprecedented massification in higher education (HE) has enormously benefited European society, but it also causes budgetary challenges for governments and HEIs alike. As a result, there is a growing awareness of the costs of research. These concerns, as well as the reduced fiscal capacity of governments due to the economic crisis, are driving the search for new sources of income and efficiencies. Governments are rethinking the size and shape of higher education systems and calling into question the sustainability of current funding models. This has induced changes in the nature and form in which funding – including the funding of research – is provided to their HEIs.

Apart from the size of the public research budget, the nature and form in which it is provided to HEIs is also discussed. It is felt that research budgets increasingly are being subjected to conditions for their allocation and accompanied with growing accountability requirements (Dill and van Vught, 2010). HEIs are facing increasing expectations about how they undertake their role – in terms of the core missions of teaching and research, as well as in how they engage with their many stakeholders from the public and private domains. For HEIs this implies a greater focus on measuring institutional performance, with associated implications for strategy, resource management and relationship management.

Against this backdrop we will be discussing three main questions: first, we discuss the underlying policy rationales that led countries to implement reforms in research funding and the related changes in the allocation mechanisms. Second, we present some data on the funding situation of European HEIs: the changes in funding levels and the balance between core funding and other (third-party) funds. Third, we review the evidence of the impacts of research funding on performance and the behaviour of researchers and HEIs and whether this type of funding increases performance and/or leads to any unintended effects. In the course of this chapter, it will turn out that some of the more challenging questions, such as whether funding really matters, can only be partially answered.

In presenting our case, we will mainly look at the European experience over time. The reader is referred to Chapter 25 by Li and Zumeta for a discussion on research funding in the United States, as the United States represents a contrasting approach to supporting higher education research (see also Feller, 2009).

Funding streams and allocation models

Main funding streams

Research funding in higher education is a complex and multifaceted issue, which deals with two different issues: on the one hand, how the state governs and supports higher education institutions (HEIs) and their activities, and, on the other hand, the specific policy goals and instruments to support research, not necessarily only in the higher education sector. Accordingly, a high diversity concerning funding sources, purposes and allocation modes is found. As we discuss later, most of the recent funding reforms in European

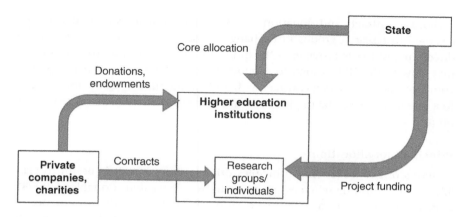

Figure 24.1   The main funding streams to HEIs

countries significantly altered the criteria for allocation and the composition of funding streams with the goal of improving efficiency and system performance.

Figure 24.1 identifies the main funding streams for research in HEIs (excluding financing from families and students for educational purposes; Jongbloed, 2004; Lepori, 2011).

In most countries, the core public allocation represents the largest part of the HEIs' research budget (Lepori et al., 2007a). This is a yearly contribution from the state (national, as well as regional, particularly in federal countries like Germany, Spain and Switzerland), which is attributed for the day-to-day operations of HEIs, such as the payment of staff, infrastructure and maintenance. Whereas in the past these funds were attributed for specific activities and items, like personnel or travel, today in most cases the core funds are attributed as a lump sum payment, leaving the HEI free to decide on their use within the institution (Lepori et al., 2013b) depending on their priorities. Usually, this lump sum is one block grant for the carrying out of education and research.

Project funding relates to funds allocated to research groups and/individuals in HEIs, allowing them to conduct specific research activities that are limited in scope and time (Lepori et al., 2007b). An example is funds awarded by research councils after an evaluation by peers of the project proposals submitted by researchers. Other examples are projects funded by European Framework Programmes (EU-FP) and contracts awarded by government departments or innovation agencies. Project funding allows more targeted support to research groups and individuals based on their excellence or topicality (Lepori, 2011). In most European countries, project funding covers between a quarter to one-third of public research funding. It displays wide differences between countries in terms of organization and its focus on scientific excellence versus policy or economic relevance (Lepori et al., 2007b; van Steen, 2012).

Grants, contracts and donations from private companies and charities are awarded to research groups in exchange for specific research and services of direct interest to the provider of the funds. Donations and endowment income may flow to the HEI as such to support its general activities. When a private company signs a research contract with an HEI, the funds usually flow directly to a research group – taking into account some of the overhead related to the project.

Principles for allocation

In terms of the underlying principles driving allocation, it is useful to classify research funding schemes according to two dimensions (Jongbloed, 2008): first, the level of centralization of decision-making versus the importance of distributed market mechanisms; second, the reliance on activities and inputs versus the use of output and performance (or outcome) measures as criteria for allocating funding. In Figure 24.2, these two dimensions form the axes, producing four quadrants.

It is generally believed that in recent decades higher education funding systems in many countries moved from a centralized and input-oriented allocation (Q1) towards a more outcome-oriented allocation (Q2) or a decentralized allocation based on output measures (Q3), often incorporating a variety of project funds awarded competitively (Q3 and Q4). Many reforms of funding systems were inspired by the New Public Management (NPM) doctrine in government

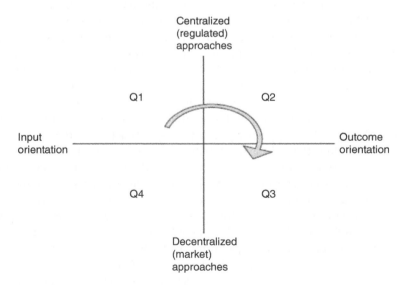

Figure 24.2   Classifying funding mechanisms

(Pollitt and Bouckaert, 2000) and were driven by the assumption that introducing competition and performance-based funding (PBF) would increase the performance of the HE system, as well as of individual HEIs (Teixeira et. al., 2004; Paradeise et. al., 2009). As we shall review in the following sections, empirical evidence in this respect is more nuanced (CHEPS, 2010; Nieminen and Auranen, 2010).

When the HEIs' core funds (for teaching and research) are based on institutional performance measures, budgets can be based on actual (i.e. realized) outcomes, for example according to a formula driven by the number of research publications and/or the acquisition of project funds (Q2; Jongbloed, 2011). Alternatively, budgets can be based on future (i.e. expected) outcomes, when public funding is allocated according to a performance agreement (Q4) between the individual HEI and the relevant funding authority, which defines institution-specific (or 'mission-based') objectives.

It is common to see a combination of funding options used in practice, with every country having its own mix, reflecting historical and political developments.

Complementarities between funding streams

Funding instruments for research differ, depending on their policy goals and their underlying rationale for steering HEIs and research groups. This implies that building on their respective complementarities is becoming increasingly crucial for authorities and HEIs. It also means we are witnessing the emergence of mixed funding models (Lepori, 2011). In terms of the policy goals, three main types of research strategies can be distinguished (CREST, 2009), namely promoting capacity building in research, promoting autonomy and competition within the research system, and prioritization of research groups and fields in alignment with the strategic goals of the country.

Institutional funding allocated in the form of block grants provides HEIs with some stability in the support of their research, allowing them to set up and develop their research infrastructure and capabilities. HEIs can allocate resources as they see fit, supporting research in line with their own strategic goals and research agenda. This is compatible with the idea that HEIs act as strategic entities in developing their own research portfolio (Bonaccorsi and Daraio, 2007) and to let excellence emerge from competition between HEIs. Leveraging on institutional funds, HEIs strategically act to build on their capabilities and to compete for project funds following their own strategic priorities.

Project funding allows governments to target the best research groups and individuals within HEIs (Lepori et al., 2007a); an important function since HEIs generally consist of groups with different levels of quality and not all HEIs are willing to be selective in their internal research funding. However, a heavy reliance on project funds affects an institution's ability to make strategic choices in the internal allocation of its funds as it brings the risk of research fragmentation. Furthermore, success in generating revenue from project funding tends to correlate with research reputations and status. This may bring the risk of promoting conservative research and hamper innovation in research (Laudel, 2006).

A central difference in this respect with the United States is that, while in the American system research grants usually cover the full research costs, in most European countries they only cover direct research costs – for example, personnel hired specifically for the project – plus some fixed overhead rate (e.g. 20% of the direct costs). This implies that the general research costs of the European university are primarily borne by the institutional budget. This model is clearly rooted on the notion that project funds are additional and complementary to the core funds received from the state (Figure 24.1). In Europe, the adoption of full costing for research is very diverse (Estermann and Claeys-Kulik, 2013) and to this day the discussion still continues, in particular with relation to project funds administered through the large-scale European research funding programmes, such as the EU-FP and the European Research Council.

The previous paragraph illustrates the context in which HEIs are deciding on their research portfolio. Where new funding streams – some project based, others more investigator driven – are emerging, research groups and institutional leaders find themselves in a position where they have to balance the various demands and priorities and seek complementarities and substitution opportunities across the different funding streams.

Some empirical evidence on funding

This section provides some empirical evidence of changes to the funding of higher education research in the last decades. This analysis is unfortunately compounded with data issues: national aggregates on research funding are available at OECD and EUROSTAT, but they are affected by the problematic distinction between educational and research funding (OECD, 2002). Data at the level of individual HEIs are provided by projects like the European Microdata (EUMIDA) and the European Tertiary Education Register (ETER, 2015), but disaggregated data on research funding are not always available (Bonaccorsi et. al., 2007) and do not allow for the investigation of temporal changes. In turn, a number of recent studies relied on ad hoc data collections (CHINC project; Lepori et. al., 2007b) and on expert assessment (CHEPS, 2010), but this information is dependent on subjective assessment and only covers a limited number of cases.

How did levels of funding change?

It has often been argued that, from the 1990s onwards, universities have been confronted with changing funding conditions for their research. This includes tightening budgets, growing inequality in allocations per institution and a concentration of funds in a selected number of institutions (Geuna, 2001).

In absolute terms, Eurostat data show that in European countries, public funding for R&D in higher education steadily increased in recent decades if expenditures are expressed per inhabitant and in euros that have the same purchasing power over the whole of the European Union (Figure 24.3). This leads us to conclude that the financial crisis after 2008 seems to have only had a limited impact on the institutions' research resources, except for countries like Greece and Spain (Skrbinjek and Lesjak, 2014).

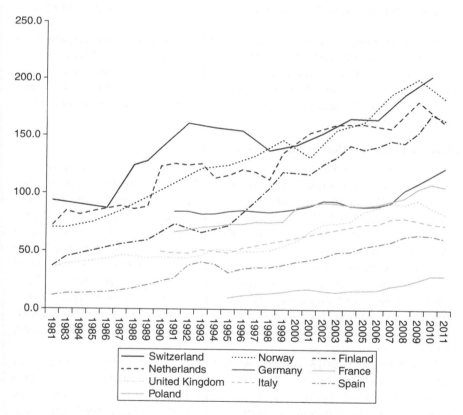

Figure 24.3 Higher education R&D expenditure financed by the government in purchasing power standards (PPS) per inhabitant at constant 2005 prices
Source: Eurostat.

The data point to a distinction between three groups of countries in terms of their spending on higher education research: (1) medium-sized high-investing countries, including Switzerland, Norway, Finland, the Netherlands, Sweden, Austria and Denmark; (2) most large Western European countries, with a medium level of funding (Germany, France, the United Kingdom); and (3) central/eastern/southern European countries, characterized by a much lower level of public support to their universities' R&D. Only very few countries have over time managed to move from one group to another (Finland and Norway). This reflects two major structural determinants of public investment in university R&D: (1) the level of national wealth, as public expenditures for research and higher education are strongly correlated with GDP and (2) the positioning of universities in the national research (and innovation) system, since in countries like France or Germany and in Central and Eastern Europe much of the public research is traditionally performed outside universities (Larédo and Mustar, 2001).

Placing the trends next to developments in the number of students provides a slightly more nuanced picture. Over the last 15 years, research funds per student increased in most countries, but there also were cases of stagnation or reduction. In the 1980s and 1990s, many European countries experienced declines as their higher education systems were confronted with a strong increase in student numbers.

Has the concentration of funding increased?

The distribution of resources across HEIs sometimes may reveal more than aggregate funding volumes, as aggregates will conceal situations where a few HEIs are well funded and others face a scarcity of research funds, especially when confronted with increasing numbers of students. Next to the degree of competition, the structure of higher education systems plays a key role in this respect: in countries with a binary higher education system, the higher vocational education sector normally enrols a large share of students, while receiving comparatively few resources for research (Lepori and Kyvik, 2010). Therefore, doctorate-awarding HEIs in binary systems tend to enjoy better resourcing conditions for research compared to unitary systems where undergraduate students are all enrolled in PhD-awarding institutions (Bonaccorsi, 2009).

ETER data (ETER, 2015) on the distribution of research funds point to high levels of concentration in a few HEIs. For example, in 2012, the average national-level Gini coefficients of HEIs' R&D expenditures for a selection of countries for which reasonably complete data are available (see Figure 24.4) was 0.69, indicating a fairly high level of concentration.

When normalizing R&D expenditures by means of the number of undergraduate students to account for the (education-related) size of the HEI, a

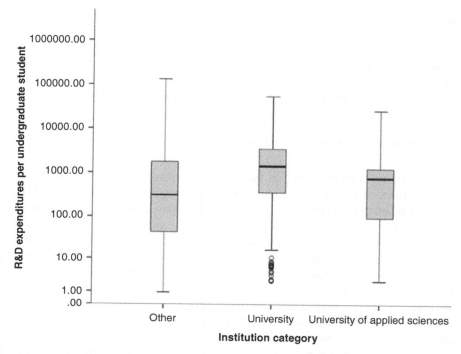

Figure 24.4 R&D expenditures per undergraduate student, year 2012 (in purchasing power parities)
Coverage: CH, CY, DK, FI, GR, HR, LT, LV, LU, NO, PL, SE. N = 315.
Source: ETER.

similar pattern of inequality in the distribution of research resources emerges (Figure 24.4). The level of research funds is generally lower outside the university sector, but the distribution is skewed also for doctorate-awarding universities.

It is generally believed that the concentration of research funding increased in recent decades as an outcome of a more competitive resource allocation and of the introduction of funding schemes that support research excellence. Empirical evidence is however more nuanced: in the United Kingdom, a strong concentration of funds in some research universities already characterized the system in the 1980s, and the main function of competitive allocation was to avoid spreading out resources throughout the whole system after the integration of polytechnics in 1992 (Stiles, 2000). Of the £1.6 billion allocated annually by English Funding Council (HEFCE), 10 out of the 130 institutions receive one-half of the funding, while the top four institutions receive 30% (De Boer et al., 2015). In Switzerland, the establishment of a binary system allowed the number of students to more than double, while essentially maintaining a situation where 90% of the research resources flow to universities (Lepori et al., 2013a).

One may conclude that, while the size of the higher education system increased strongly in the last decades, research funding remained largely concentrated in research-oriented universities. The widespread perception of an austerity situation might well reflect this skewedness rather than an overall scarcity of funds.

Are allocation mechanisms changing? Is funding becoming more competitive?

In Europe, the mechanisms for the public funding of research underwent many reforms. Incremental funding in many countries has been replaced by formula-based approaches, and contract approaches have been introduced – often on top of formulae (de Boer et al., 2015). Input- and cost-related factors remain very important nevertheless. A 2010 study of funding reforms in Europe (CHEPS, 2010) concluded that, over the period 1995–2008, there was a decline in the relative share of the core operational grant that institutions receive from their public authorities, although the change was rather modest. In 2008, almost half (47%) of the public research funds made available in Europe were allocated to institutions in competition or as targeted funds, usually with an eye upon improving research quality. In other words, we see a move towards more market-type mechanisms in resource allocation.

The rise of funding allocated by means of competitions and targeted funding has led to a diversification of funding sources for institutions, with one-third of European countries having more than a quarter of their revenue coming from third party funds (see next section).

Due to this variety of funding streams, there is no simple dichotomy between institutional core funding and project funding – say, between non-competitive funding and competitive funding. Nowadays, the first funding stream exhibits many characteristics of the other, particularly now that governments tend to introduce performance criteria in the mechanisms that underlie the allocation of core funding (Nieminen and Auranen, 2010; de Boer et al., 2015).

A well-known example is found in the United Kingdom, where results from periodic national research assessments drive part of the core funds of the university. These research assessment exercises (RAEs; Barker, 2007) provide a post hoc evaluation of research units within universities (approximately corresponding to departments), each of which is given a numerical score.

In recent years, quite a few countries introduced performance contracts of some sort as a condition for the core funding awarded to an institution (Jongbloed, 2011; de Boer et al., 2015). Performance contracts between individual higher education institutions and their relevant funding authorities define institution-specific (or 'mission-based') objectives in line with national strategic priorities. Such contracts may focus on specific areas of performance – in education, research, technology transfer and so on. The funding authority may attach financial consequences to the realization (or non-realization) of the agreed performances.

Did the composition of funding change over time?

Reducing the HEIs' dependency on core government allocations has been a second major driver of funding reforms in the recent past. This was partly a response to calls for injecting market incentives in higher education, while at the same time increasing the autonomy of the higher education institutions (Massy, 2004). The resulting diversification of funding sources comprised two elements: an increase in the share of project funds and an increase in the share of funds from the private sector.

Data display a moderate process of differentiation, but a lasting importance of core funding, which still represents the largest share of the budget of public HEIs in most countries, the main exceptions being the United Kingdom and Ireland. Among the 117 universities covered by the CHINC project, only 10% had a share of core budget below 50% in 2003, most of them located in the United Kingdom (Lepori et. al., 2007b). More recent (2012) data from the ETER project (ETER, 2015) show that the situation did not change in the following years. Among the 1083 HEIs for which data were available, only about 10% derived less than 50% of their total budget from core government budgets, while for some two-thirds the core budget represents more than 75% (see Figure 24.5; the data do not include the United Kingdom). What can be observed is a convergence towards a funding mode where about three quarters of the budget is provided by the state as core funds, which are complemented by third-party funds and student fees. This pattern reflects the move towards a more diversified higher education funding system, but changes have not been as extensive as the UK case.

Concerning project funding, country-level studies display large differences between countries and a moderate tendency to increase the project funds' share in national research funding (Lepori et. al., 2007b; van Steen, 2012). In 5 out of the 17 countries covered in the latest OECD study, the share of project funding exceeded 50% of public research funding (including Belgium, Finland and Ireland), whereas for 12 it ranged between 23% and 50% (van Steen, 2012). In most European countries, project funding therefore remains a complementary stream to core funding.

At the level of individual HEIs, data normalized by the number of professors support the finding that third-party funds are more concentrated than the core budget and that most of these kinds of project funds are in fact acquired by research universities (see Figure 24.6), thus confirming these institutions'

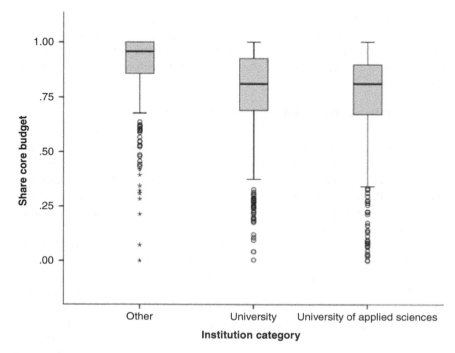

Figure 24.5 Fraction of the core government allocation in the total HEI's budget in the year 2012 (N=1083)
Countries covered: Belgium, Switzerland, Cyprus, Czech Republic, Germany, Denmark, France, Croatia, Ireland, Italy, Lithuania, Luxembourg, Malta, the Netherlands, Norway, Poland, Portugal, Sweden and Slovakia.
Source: ETER.

function of targeting high-quality research (the median score for universities is about eight times the one for universities of applied sciences).

An analysis of the participation of universities in EU-FP confirms this high level of concentration and provides some evidence on the factors determining it. Among the 1376 research-active HEIs included in the EUMIDA database (i.e. nearly the full population of European HEIs that are actively involved in research), 152 accounted in 2009 for 70% of the total participation in the EU-FP (Lepori et. al., 2014). Furthermore, the number of EU-FP participations is proportional to the organizational size and is strongly influenced by the institution's international reputation (approximated by citation impact) and its status. The latter is often the result of the cumulative effects in terms of winning competitive research funding.

Finally, public policies are aimed at increasing the share of private funds – to replace public funds, or to encourage HEIs fulfilling their so-called third mission and providing relevant knowledge to society (Gulbrandsen and Slipersaeter,

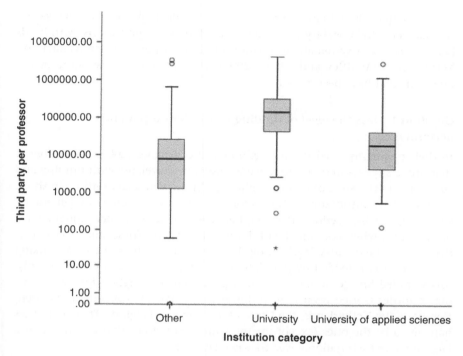

Figure 24.6   Third-party funds per professor, year 2012 (N=687)
Countries covered: Switzerland, Cyprus, Germany, Croatia, Ireland, Italy, Lithuania, Luxembourg, Malta, the Netherlands, Norway, Portugal and Sweden.
Source: ETER.

2007; Jongbloed, 2010). If we leave aside private funding in the shape of tuition fees for educational services, data (ETER, 2015) display that private funds for HE research are, at most, complementary to public funds. Out of 834 HEIs for which data on private funding are available for the year 2012, only 5 had a share exceeding 20% of their total revenues and for 66 the private share exceeded 10%. The HEIs for which this share exceeds 20% includes three business schools and one theological institution. This clearly illustrates that a high share of private funds is very much linked to the specific character and specialization of the institution. On a similar note, shares of private funds between 10% and 20% are found in cases of technical HEIs such as the Polytechnic of Milan or Delft University of Technology.

Evidence of impacts

Since the 1980s, concerns about a new funding climate and rationale for higher education research, as well as its possible negative consequences, have been raised (Geuna, 2001). In line with the NPM rationale, higher education research was subjected to budgetary cuts and increased market-type reforms, with funds being linked to a systematic evaluation of research performance (Geuna and Martin, 2003; Whitley and Glaser, 2007). We will now discuss some of the questions that have been raised.

Question 1: Does the level of funding matter for output and performance?

In their frequently cited studies, Aghion and colleagues (2007, 2009) suggest that university research performance is positively correlated with funding and autonomy in the areas of finance, buildings, hiring and salary setting. In short: money is key; autonomy is also important; and the two are complementary, suggesting an interaction effect: higher levels of funding per student have more impact when combined with budget autonomy. These studies were carried out on the country level, using the sum of a country's Shanghai ranking scores (reversed) divided by population. Looking at European countries only, this so-called Bruegel index of research performance is highest for the following countries (sorted from high to lower performance): Switzerland, Sweden, Denmark, the Netherlands, the United Kingdom and Belgium. These countries happen to be the ones (except for the United Kingdom) that are investing a large share of their national wealth (say GDP) in research.

At the level of the individual HEI, van Vught (2012) suggests that there is a relationship between a university's revenue per student and its scientific impact score (Figure 24.7). Larger annual budgets, whatever the way these are created (whether through more public funding, higher tuition fees, mergers or otherwise), combined with modest student enrolment levels, appear to correlate strongly with higher scientific impact scores. In a sample of about 30 universities from across the world, three American universities (MIT, Harvard, Stanford), two Swiss universities (EPF Lausanne and ETH Zürich) and both Oxford and Cambridge University combine a high scientific impact score with high funding levels per student.

Question 2: Does competitive funding increase performance?

Competition is believed to be the key to research excellence (van den Besselaar, Hemlin and van der Weijden, 2012). Surely, there are various forms of competition that can take place within the research sector, namely a competition to attract the best researchers, to attract PhD candidates, to attract funding and to reach a higher position in the research rankings. National governments often introduce competitive funding in their effort to encourage research excellence (OECD, 2014).

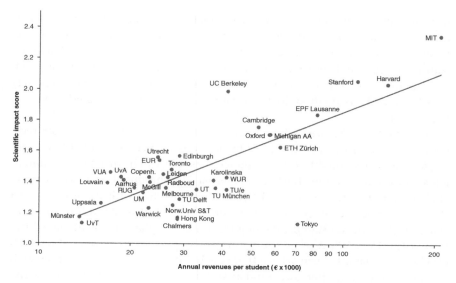

Figure 24.7 Institutional scientific impact vs. annual revenues per student: a comparison of 13 Dutch and 25 non-Dutch universities
Source: van Vught, 2012.

In their study on reforming European universities, Aghion and colleagues (2009) detect a positive effect of competition for research grants on university output. The authors state that excellence requires three factors: resources, autonomy and incentives. They point to the need for European universities to increase funding (public and private), autonomy and to increase international mobility and competition for faculty and funding. The combination of more autonomy and putting incentives in place is expected to contribute to universities specializing in particular areas of strength.

Auranen and Nieminen (2010) analyse the degree of competition across countries by combining two measures, namely the ratio between project-based and core funding and the level of competition in the allocation of core funding. Their analysis on eight European countries suggests that countries with a more competitive funding environment (e.g. the United Kingdom, Finland, Australia and Denmark) are more productive in terms of publication performance. However, the relationship is not as straightforward as it seems because some countries that have made their research funding more competitive do not exhibit a clear improvement in research productivity, while some of the European countries that are clearly in the lead in terms of research performance (Switzerland, Denmark, the Netherlands) do not (yet) have a very competitive funding environment (see also Himanen et al., 2009). This lack of a clear relationship between competitive funding and research performance – at least on the country level – was also found by others (e.g. Liefner, 2003; Daraio et al., 2011). This may be caused by the fact that other features of national research systems are more important – levels of funding, openness of systems, contextual differences – while also questions may be asked about the methodology (causality, time lags) used for studying these relationships.

Concerns have also been raised that a university's ability to realize its strategic research ambitions can be restricted by an over-reliance on competitive funding sources, while the shift towards project-based research with more utilitarian aims and the increase in short-term external funding might weaken the more challenging, investigator-driven basic research. To deal with these risks, both the amount and the drivers of the core 'internal' institutional funding appear as essential elements for supporting long-term strategic planning by higher education institutions. While some stress competitive pressure as a driver of research excellence, it has also been argued that collaboration is a key feature of research excellence and, that, therefore, funders will need to think carefully about striking the right balance between collaboration and competition and the funding instruments that will lead to these two seemingly contrasting goals (van den Besselaar et al., 2012).

Question 3: Does performance-based funding really matter for research performance?

A parallel trend to the increase in the share of competitive project funding is one where institutional funding is becoming performance based. This trend may be regarded as a complementary policy tool aimed at improving the outcomes from institutional funding streams. Performance-based funding (PBF) is expected to enhance efficiency and quality (Hicks, 2012): if money is given to the best performers, it will most likely produce better results. This belief is then translated into a funding mechanism where the core funding of universities is based on earlier results. Indeed, we have witnessed a trend of institutional budgets becoming more tied to specific teaching and research outcomes via formula-based funding systems (Jongbloed and de Boer, 2012). In contrast to the 1990s, when only a few countries used output-related criteria in funding, almost 20 European countries now use elements of performance to drive budgets of HEIs.

As a matter of fact, two approaches can be distinguished in the introduction of evaluation and performance assessment of HEIs (Whitley and Gläser, 2007). In some countries, like the Netherlands, performance assessments were introduced but without having a direct impact on the allocation of (core) public funds – they rather act through normative pressures and reputational effects or through the institution's internal resource allocation system (Jongbloed, 2009).

In other countries, performance assessment is directly linked to allocation of funding. One of these countries is the United Kingdom.

The United Kingdom was one of the first countries to introduce (in 1986) PBF on the basis of periodic Research Assessment Exercises (RAEs). In RAEs, the quality of research conducted by UK university departments is assessed and block funding for research has since been dependent on the university department's RAE rating. In 2014, the RAE was replaced by the Research Excellence Framework, which now also takes into account the impact a department's research has had on society. Poland and Italy are some of the other countries where research funding is performance driven (Hicks and Katz, 2011). And more recently, some of the Nordic countries have made research funding dependent on the number of research publications. There exists quite some variety in the way countries have shaped their particular type of PBF. Sivertsen (2014) states that the trend is towards more complex and composite PBF approaches, with countries adopting methodologies from other contexts to their own system. Yet, he concludes, it is difficult to see a clear relation between PBF and national research performance. It may very well be that it is not PBF as such that drives performance, but accompanying elements like the increased transparency or a more rich dialogue between universities and funding authorities.

Whether output-based funding succeeds in raising research quality and/or quantity also depends on how the output of research activities are assessed and ultimately rests on the quality of the output measures. Several imperfections of research output measures (e.g. bibliometric indicators, like the number of publications, citations or the share of publications that are highly cited) have been identified in the literature (van Raan, 2004). When part of the research output is not measurable, funding based on objective indicators may induce researchers to concentrate their efforts on the measurable outputs of research. Output-based indicators are necessarily based on past research accomplishments, which may favour older, more experienced researchers and research units at the cost of young researchers and new research units. However, the latter may be more productive in the future, but have had less possibility to express their potential (Viner, Green and Powell, 2006). A similar reasoning applies to new research areas and new approaches versus established ones.

Universities are also engaged in education and the transfer of research findings to the general public. If incentives to engage in the three activities are unevenly balanced, this may lead to one of them being crowded out. When education funding does not depend on education output and the effort academics put into education is hard to verify, strong financial rewards for research output may come at the expense of the quality of education. The same applies to knowledge transfer activity, which often is a legal task but hardly rewarded explicitly by public funders (Smith, Ward and House, 2011).

Whether the positive effects of PBF will actually occur depends on several factors, including on how the PBF system is designed. Any incentives created by a PBF system have to trickle down to the shop floor level, where research actually takes place. Therefore, the decisions made within the university will determine whether the organization of funding makes a difference in terms of research excellence (Jongbloed, 2009).

In the United Kingdom, one can observe an increasing selectivity in institutional research funding since the introduction of the RAE in 1986. The RAEs are believed to have driven an improvement in the number of staff being assessed as undertaking internationally excellent work, and have contributed to an increase in the United Kingdom's overall publication levels by embedding a culture of research management across all universities (de Boer et al., 2015). However, the process has brought with it a high cost burden, and questions remain about the proportion of outputs which represent an improvement in research quality, and those that represent undesirable side effects (game playing, over-publication). Nevertheless, there is no serious discussion in the United Kingdom about abandoning it, and in 2008–2009, a detailed policy discussion about replacing it with a bibliometric-based system came to the conclusion that such an approach would be more arbitrary and less useful than the current system. It is clear that, in its own terms, the RAE has succeeded in delivering the long-standing science policy goals of the government – initially to improve excellence, then to build critical mass and, more recently, to create impact and socio-economic benefits from that research (Barker, 2007; Himanen et al., 2009; Smith, Ward and House, 2011).

All in all, PBF systems seem to have strong effects on universities, even if they involve a small share of the total funding. Hicks (2012), quoting other researchers, argues that it is mainly claims for prestige that universities can derive from a favourable RAE score that make the systems work and not so much the financial rewards.

Question 4: Does the concentration of research funding lead to a higher research performance?

A policy of concentration of research funding was introduced in quite a few countries, like in the United Kingdom as an outcome of the RAE, based on the expectation that this produces higher quality research. This policy is based on the assumption that a high concentration of talent is an important driver of research excellence. This may be true in particular in those disciplines which are resource intensive or where physical proximity of others in their field is important. The notion of critical mass may vary significantly across subject areas. Larger research groups are common in experimental disciplines while theorists tend to work in smaller teams or even individually. Kenna and Berche (2011) show that the dominant driver of research quality is the quantity of researchers that an individual researcher is able to communicate with (ibid., p. 529). They conclude that, if external funding becomes available, it is most beneficial to support medium-sized groups – and to optimize research performance in a given discipline, these groups should be promoted – while small ones must endeavour to attain critical mass.

Opinions on the relative merits of big or small research groups will continue to exist. Some will argue for an integration of units and more breadth, while others favour smaller groups, specialization, diversity and competition. Larger units may be able to reap economies of scale and economies of scope, while smaller groups may be more agile and more rapid to respond to change. Crucial in this discussion is, once again, the concept of performance and quality. Research groups will normally be engaged in a variety of activities and it is critical how the diversity of their 'products' is assessed – both in terms of quantity and quality. In their analysis of research performance on the level of the research group (and not on the university level), researchers from SPRU (von Tunzelmann et. al., 2003) state that in many scientific fields, productivity seems to rise as the team size increases to about six or eight persons, above which there is usually little or no extra gain per capita. Some studies find a lower 'threshold' beyond which additional economies do not arise, while a few (e.g. in arts and humanities) find no threshold at all. Where present, the threshold has been found to be somewhat higher in applied subjects such as clinical medicine, and it is probably lower in more theoretical subjects such as mathematics. If the unit of analysis is not the research group but the department or the university as a whole, then the evidence for any critical mass is less clear. Since departments are collections of research groups and universities may be seen as collections of departments, the evidence base for a government policy that will result in increasing the concentration of research resources on large departments and large universities appears to be lacking (von Tunzelmann et. al., 2003).

Much of the above discussion rests on evidence from the United Kingdom, where the quality of research appears to have increased, and, therefore, it is unclear if increasing productivity is due to concentration or through better targeting of the best research groups thanks to the RAE.

Conclusions

Data presented in this chapter highlight the importance of funding arrangements both for higher education policies and for HEIs, as well as the complexity of their mechanisms of actions. In most European countries, governments followed New Public Management recipes that higher education institutions should (and could) be steered at a distance through economic incentives. Accordingly, from the 1990s, public funding systems in most countries have been reformed by moving from core budgets based on historical and input-related conditions to an allocation based on performance and a higher share of project funds. The move has however been rather gradual, and differences between countries are quite large. The United Kingdom is one case where most funding is linked to performance, while some continental European countries have introduced some competitive elements alongside a system of core funding that still is very much based on inputs. Two important characteristics of countries need to be considered in this respect: first, the overall level of resources, as wealthier countries can to some extent afford to distribute funding more widely, in order also to reach regional goals and to maintain diversity in the system; second, in the structure of higher education systems, as in binary systems, a large part of selectivity is achieved through the distinction between types of HEIs, with Universities of Applied Sciences receiving a much lower share of research funding.

As a matter of fact, changes in how public research funding to HEIs is allocated can also be interpreted as a response to the need to keep a level of concentration of research resources within rapidly expanding HE systems (due to the massification of higher education). Two broad types of responses can be identified in this respect: the creation of a second HE system receiving much less resources for research and the introduction of performance-based approaches to institutional funding.

Empirical evidence on the effects of these responses are, at best, partial. Indeed, there is some evidence that economic incentives do influence HEIs and scientists' behaviour and that, for example, linking funding to levels of research outputs leads to an increase in the latter. Whether this reflects changes in research practices and long-term impact is however contested; at the same time, increasing concerns have been raised that focus on short-term outputs might turn detrimental to sciences, as this also requires a focus on long-term results and undertaking risky projects. Indeed, it is increasingly recognized that the effects of funding reforms are mediated through social and institutional structures at the higher education institution- and research group levels and that, therefore, their impact will depend on how the system is organized.

One of the few established facts is that, for research performance, the level of funding is more important than how funds are allocated and that most of the differences in international reputation of countries and HEIs are driven by different levels of resources. Differences in this respect between European countries – or indeed between the United States and Europe – may last over several decades (European Commission, 2011).

Following these insights, there are no straightforward relationships between funding mechanisms and research activities, rather funding policies are moving away from the somewhat simple NPM recipes to a more complex design, which reflects the multiple actors and the multiple goals in national – and increasingly international – research systems. Increasing emphasis is placed on the complementarity between funding mechanisms in order to fulfil a mix of often-competing goals – like concentrating funding in the best HEIs, while keeping opportunities for new entrants in the R&D system, respectively finding a balance between the relevance of research for society and economy and the promotion of long-term investigator-driven research (Radosevic and Lepori, 2009). Furthermore, incentive systems are evolving in terms of the choice of performance measures incorporated. In particular we are witnessing a tendency where countries start considering the diversity of institutional missions represented in their HE systems, whereas other countries start to include indicators of the societal impact of academic research next to the bibliometric indicators. Finally, path dependency and the institutional embeddedness of national research systems implies that there is no best practice for the funding of research that can be easily transferred from one country to the other, even if a particular country's experiences might provide useful lessons. Reforming national funding systems is more an art of taking into account local conditions and political realities than a straightforward application of some textbook recipes describing how economic incentives work and in what mix they should be administered.

References

Aghion, P., Dewatripont, M., Hoxby, C. M., Mas-Colell, A. and A. Sapir (2009) *The Governance and Performance of Research Universities: Evidence from Europe and the US*, Cambridge MA: National Bureau of Economic Research, Working Paper.
Aghion, P., Dewatripont, M., Hoxby, C., Sapir, A. and A. Mas-Colell (2007) Why reform Europe's universities? Bruegel Policy Brief Issue #04 (Brussels: Bruegel).
Barker, K. (2007) 'The UK research assessment exercise: The evolution of a national research evaluation system', *Research Evaluation*, 16(1), 3–12.
Boer, H. de., B. Jongbloed, P. Benneworth, L. Cremonini, R. Kolster, A. Kottmann, K. Lemmens-Krug and H. Vossensteyn (2015) *Performance-Based Funding and Performance Agreements in Fourteen Higher Education Systems. Report for the Ministry of Education* (Enschede: CHEPS).
Bonaccorsi, A. and C. Daraio (2007) *Universities and Strategic Knowledge Creation. Specialization and Performance in Europe* (Cheltenham: Edward Elgar).
Bonaccorsi, A., Daraio, C., Lepori, B. and S. Slipersaeter (2007) 'Indicators on individual higher education institutions: addressing data problems and comparability issues', *Research Evaluation*, 16(2), 66–78.
Bonaccorsi, A. (2009) 'Division of academic labour is limited by the size of the market. Strategy and differentiation of European universities in doctoral education', in M. McKelvey and M. Holmén (eds) *Learning to compete in European universities* (pp. 90–127) (Cheltenham, UK: Edward Elgar).
CHEPS (2010) *Progress in Higher Education Reform across Europe. Funding Reform* (Brussels: European Commission).
CREST OMC Working Group (2009) *Mutual Learning on Approaches to Improve the Excellence of Research in Universities* (Brussels: European Commission).

Daraio, C., Bonaccorsi, A., Geuna, A., Lepori, B. and et. al. (2011) 'The European university landscape: a micro characterization based on evidence from the Aquameth project', *Research Policy*, 40(1), 148–164.

Dill, D. D. and F. A. van Vught (eds) (2010) *National Innovation and the Academic Research Enterprise: Public Policy in Global Perspective* (Baltimore: The Johns Hopkins University Press).

Estermann, T. and A. Claeys-Kulik (2013) *Financially Sustainable Universities. Full Costing: Progress and Practice* (Brussels: European University Association).

ETER (2015) 'European tertiary education register', http://eter.joanneum.at/imdas-eter/ (retrieved 7 January 2015).

European Commission (2011) *Innovation Union Competitiveness Report* (Brussels: European Commission).

Feller, I. (2009) 'Performance measurement and the governance of American academic science', *Minerva*, 47(3), 323–344.

Geuna, A. (2001) 'The changing rationale for European university research funding: are there negative unintended consequences?' *Journal of Economic Issues*, XXXV(3), 607–632.

Geuna, A. and B. Martin (2003) 'University research evaluation and funding: an international comparison', *Minerva*, 41, 277–304.

Gulbrandsen, M. and S. Slipersaeter (2007) 'The third mission and the entrepreneurial university model', in A. Bonaccorsi and C. Daraio (eds) *Universities and Strategic Knowledge Creation. Specialization and Performance in Europe* (pp. 112–143) (Cheltenham: Edward Elgar).

Hicks, D. and J. S. Katz (2011) 'Equity and excellence in research funding', *Minerva*, 49, 137–151.

Hicks, D. (2012) 'Performance-based university research funding systems', *Research Policy*, 41(2), 251–261.

Himanen, L., Auranen, O., Puuska, H. and M. Nieminen (2009) 'Influence of research funding and science policy on university research performance: a comparison of five countries', *Science and Public Policy*, 36(6), 419–430.

Jongbloed, B. (2004) *Funding Higher Education: Options, Trade-Offs and Dilemmas* (Enschede: CHEPS).

Jongbloed, B. (2008) 'Creating public-private dynamics in higher education funding. A discussion of three options', in J. Enders and B. Jongbloed (eds) *Public-Private Dynamics in Higher Education Funding* (pp. 113–138) (Bielefeld: Transcript).

Jongbloed, B. (2009) 'Steering the Dutch academic research enterprise: universities' responses to project funding and performance monitoring', in P. Clancy and D. D. Dill (eds) *The Research Mission of the University. Policy Reforms and Institutional Response* (pp. 79–94) (Rotterdam: Sense Publishers).

Jongbloed, B. (2010) 'The regional relevance of research in universities of applied sciences', in Kyvik and B. Lepori (eds) *The Research Mission of Higher Education Institutions Outside the University Sector* (pp. 25–44) (Dordrecht: Springer).

Jongbloed, B. (2011) 'Funding through contracts', in J. Enders, H. F. de Boer and D. F. Westerheijden (eds) *Reform of Higher Education in Europe* (pp. 173–191) (Rotterdam: Sense Publishers).

Jongbloed, B. and H. de Boer (2012) 'Higher education funding reforms in Europe and the 2006 modernisation agenda', *The Modernisation of European Universities: Cross-National Academic Perspectives*, 1, 127.

Kenna, R. and B. Berche (2011) 'Critical mass and the dependency of research quality on group size', *Scientometrics*, 86(2), 527–540.

Larédo, P. and P. Mustar (2001) Research and Innovation policies in the new global economy. An international comparative analysis.

Laudel, G. (2006) 'The art of getting funded: how scientists adapt to their funding conditions', *Science and Public Policy*, 33(7), 489–504.

Leisyte, L., Enders, J. and H. de Boer (2009) 'The balance between teaching and research in Dutch and English universities in the context of university governance reforms', *Higher Education*, 58(5), 619–635.

Lepori, B. (2011) 'Coordination modes in public funding systems', *Research Policy*, 40(3), 355–367.

Lepori, B., Benninghoff, M., Jongbloed, B., Salerno, C. and S. Slipersaeter (2007a) 'Changing models and patterns of higher education funding: some empirical evidence', in A. Bonaccorsi and C. Daraio (eds) *Universities and Strategic Knowledge Creation. Specialization and Performance in Europe* (pp. 85–111) (Bodmin, Cornwall: MPG Books Limited).

Lepori, B., van den Besselaar, P., Dinges, M., van der Meulen, B., Poti, B., Reale, E., Slipersaeter, S. and J. Theves (2007b) 'Indicators for comparative analysis of public project funding: concepts, implementation and evaluation', *Research Evaluation*, 16(4), 243–255.

Lepori, B., Dinges, M., Reale, E., Slipersaeter, S., Theves, J. and P. Van den Besselaar (2007c) 'Comparing the evolution of national research policies: what patterns of change?' *Science and Public Policy*, 34(6), 372–388.

Lepori, B. and S. Kyvik (2010) 'The research mission of universities of applied science and the future configuration of higher education systems in Europe', *Higher Education Policy*, 23, 295–316.

Lepori, B., Huisman, J. and M. Seeber (2013a) 'Convergence and differentiation processes in Swiss higher education: an empirical analysis', *Studies in Higher Education*, 39(2), 197–218.

Lepori, B., Usher, J. and M. Montauti (2013b) 'Budgetary allocation and organizational characteristics of higher education institutions. A review of existing studies and a framework for future research', *Higher Education*, 65(1), 59–78.

Lepori, B., Heller-Schuh, B., Scherngell, T. and M. Barber (2014) Understanding factors influencing participation to European programs of higher education institutions. *STI 2014, Leiden*.

Liefner, I. (2003) 'Funding, resource allocation, and performance in higher education systems', *Higher Education*, 26(4), 469–489.

Massy, W. F. (2004) 'Markets in higher education. Do they promote internal efficiency?' in P. Teixeira, B. Jongbloed, D. Dill and A. Amaral (eds) *Markets in Higher Education* (pp. 13–36) (Dordrecht: Springer).

Nieminen, M. and O. Auranen (2010) 'University research funding and publication performance – an international comparison', *Research Policy*, 39, 822–834.

OECD (2002) *Frascati Manual. Proposed Standard Practice for Surveys on Research and Experimental Development* (Paris: OECD).

OECD (2014) *Promoting Research Excellence. New Approaches to Funding* (Paris: OECD).

Paradeise, C., Reale, E., Bleiklie, I. and E. Ferlie (2009) *University Governance. Western European Comparative Perspectives* (Dordrecht: Springer).

Pollitt, C. and G. Bouckaert (2000) *Public Management Reform: A Comparative Analysis* (Oxford: Oxford University Press).

Radosevic, S. and B. Lepori (2009) 'Public research funding systems in central and eastern Europe between excellence and relevance', *Science and Public Policy*, 36(9), 659–666.

Sivertsen, G. (2014) Performance-based funding. Workshop on national research funding systems. *Dialogic/EC DG Research/ERC*.

Skrbinjek, V. and D. Lesjak (2014) Changes in higher education public funding during economic and financial crisis. Conference paper, 1377–1386.

Smith, S., Ward, V. and A. House (2011) ' "Impact" in the proposals for the UK's research excellence framework: Shifting the boundaries of academic autonomy', *Research Policy*, 40(10), 1369–1379.

Stiles, D. R. (2000) 'Higher education funding patterns since 1990: a New Perspective', *Public Money & Management*, 20(4), 51–57.

Teixeira, P., Jongbloed, B., Dill, D. and A. Amaral (2004) *Markets in Higher Education. Rhetoric or Reality?* (Dordrecht: Kluwer Academic Publishers).

van den Besselaar, P., Hemlin, S. and I. van der Weijden (2012) 'Collaboration and competition in research', *Higher Education Policy*, 25(3), 263–266.

van Raan, A. F. J. (2004) 'Measuring science', in H. F. Moed, W. Glänzel and U. Schmoch (eds) *Handbook of Quantitative Science and Technology Research* (pp. 19–50) (Dordrecht: Kluwer Academic Publishers).

van Steen, J. (2012) *Modes of Public Funding of Research and Development: Towards Internationally Comparable Indicators* (Paris: OECD Publishing).

van Vught, F. A. (2012) *University Profiles. International Rankings, Institutional Maps and the Need to Discuss the Structure of Dutch Higher Education. Opening of Academic Year 2012/13* (Maastricht: Maastricht University).

Viner, N., Green, R. and P. Powell (2006) 'Segmenting academics: resource targeting of research grants', *Science and Public Policy*, 33(3), 166–178.

von Tunzelmann, N., Ranga, M., Martin, B. and A. Geuna (2003) *The Effects of Size on Research Performance: A SPRU Review* (Brighton: SPRU).

Whitley, R. and J. Glaser (2007) *The Changing Governance of the Sciences. The Advent of Research Evaluation Systems* (Dordrecht: Springer).

25
State Support for Higher Education

Amy Y. Li and William Zumeta

The purpose of this chapter is to describe and analyse the current environment of governmental support and related policies for higher education in the United States in the context of patterns in other developed countries. The primary focus on the United States here is designed to illuminate in a contemporary, yet historically, conscious way the most salient features of – as well as challenges facing – the American model. Its key components are increasingly influential in animating governmental policies towards higher education in many OECD countries.

Most basically, college and universities still depend heavily on governmental appropriations, yet ample and stable public funding is no longer the norm in the United States as elsewhere. This chapter explores how the prioritization of higher education funding has been affected by economic, political and structural factors across time. Individual states are the governmental entities primarily responsible for higher education in the United States, a federal state. The chapter considers the impacts of diminishing core state support for public higher education, including the impact on tuition charges to students. Both state and federal governments in the United States also fund higher education indirectly through financial aid to students to a greater extent than most other countries – although others are clearly moving in this direction – so an overview of financial need- and 'merit'-based student aid is provided, specifically focused on how these programmes evolved and how they relate to student access and degree completion.

As a result of decreasing public funding support, American colleges and universities, much like those in other OECD nations, have also increasingly sought alternative sources of revenue. The major sources are private donations, research grants and associated spinoff technology transfer enterprises, and extended learning courses and programmes that charge full cost or more. The chapter includes an examination of state-enacted policies that seek to more efficiently and accountably distribute higher education funding, specifically the renaissance of outcomes-based funding models. All of these themes have some parallels in other countries and these are noted where relevant. The chapter concludes with some suggestions for profitable lines of future research.

Contextual background

Governance

The governance structure of higher education within the United States is relevant in understanding how finance policies are made, so we explain it briefly here, and then offer some comparison with European governance structures. In decreasing order of power and influence over academic institutions, the standard typology of state governance includes the following categories: *consolidated governing board* with line authority over campuses and their spending; *regulatory coordinating board* with authority over new programme approval but usually not over budgets; *weak coordinating board*, and *planning agency* with the latter two limited largely to advisory roles (McGuinness, 2003). There has been a slight movement in the direction of governing boards in recent decades (though a few states have moved in the opposite direction), but the balance remains fairly close. In 2012, 26 states had governing boards and 24 had coordinating or planning boards (Education Commission of the States, 2012).

Governance structure affects how a state handles tuition and student aid policy, the oversight of private colleges and assessment of institutional performance (Tandberg, 2013). However, the direction of the governance structure effect on postsecondary appropriations found depends on the study and its methodology. Some researchers find that a consolidated governing board is associated with increased state funding (McLendon, Tandberg and Hillman, 2014), while others find the opposite result (Tandberg, 2009). Instability in the political regime in a state may also cause the adoption of governance legislation that can alter structures (and ultimately finance policies), with chances increased by a change in legislative party control. In particular, an increase in Republican legislators is associated with a higher likelihood of trying new policies and greater state oversight in general. Thus, governance reform in higher education is responsive to cycles of political change (McLendon, Deaton and Hearn, 2007).

As in America, forms of governance in Europe today are intended to make universities more efficient and accountable to national policy priorities. A comparison to European approaches is helpful here. A recent classification of European higher education governance has a three-category typology, identifying state-centred, self-governing and market-oriented governance arrangements (Dobbins, Knill and Vögtle, 2011). *State-centred* models are somewhat similar to the US consolidated governing boards, where the state (similar to the national ministry) closely supervises many aspects of institutional functioning including academic personnel, curriculum and admissions. In many such countries, the government is also ultimately responsible for quality assurance. In US governing board states, the board has quality assurance responsibilities but may delegate these to a greater or lesser degree to individual campuses. Boards also give considerable weight to the judgments of independent accrediting bodies. In the Dobbins et al. state-centred model, finances are also determined and allocated by the state. In the United States, governing boards allocate what they get from the state and may influence how much it is, but they do not determine it. This responsibility falls on the legislature and governor.

Among the European models, the *self-governing* model sees the university as a self-determining community of scholars (the Humboldt model) and functions with weak administrative management, collegial control by the professoriate and strong faculty autonomy in research and teaching. In such cases, there often exists today a growing divergence between governmental political and economic development goals for higher education and the aims of self-governing academics. Such historic governance models are found with declining frequency. The closest analogue in the US context may be the few states with very weak coordinating boards or even weaker planning boards. The most prominent example of this is the state of Michigan, where the public universities do not have oversight boards above the campus level.

Finally, in the *market-oriented* model, universities compete for students and for financial resources from the state, which are in turn linked to students and competitive research proposals. Entrepreneurial behaviour is rewarded. Higher education is considered primarily a commodity and strategic state investment (Dobbins et al., 2011). These types of approaches are increasingly prominent in American policy-maker thinking, as they are elsewhere. While they are perhaps more prevalent in coordinating board states, similar ideas also play a role in some states with governing board arrangements, although governing boards, with direct responsibility for public colleges and universities, are not well suited to taking private institutions fully into account in structuring incentives and competition.

Historical context

Unlike many other nations, in the United States the national government plays no direct role in the oversight or basic funding of institutions of higher education, leaving this role to the 50 states.[1] Yet, today's structure of public higher education finance began to take shape after the federal government took an important step in enacting the Morrill Act in 1862. This act authorized land grants to states designed to stimulate the development and growth of public universities to advance learning in 'agriculture and the mechanic arts' (Heller, 2002, p. 225). In the 20th century, college enrolments expanded rapidly once mass secondary schooling was in place, and this occurred decades before Europe began to follow suit (Goldin and Katz, 2008). During this time, tuition and fees were low, approximately $80 per year when the Second World War began (Cheslock and Hughes, 2011, p. 372). Although episodic across time and states, there has also been an expansion of federal- and state-supported student financial aid programmes, programmes that were for the most part initiated in the 1960s and 1970s.

In addition to the fact that states are the primary governmental players in American higher education, the United States differs from Western Europe and many other countries in that it has a substantial private non-profit academic sector (Levy and Zumeta, 2011). Indeed, this sector contains many of the universities that make the top 20 in world rankings of universities, such as Harvard, Stanford, MIT and the like, and is marked by a 'true privateness' in relation to much of government regulation that is not seen elsewhere (Aghion et al, 2007). The private sector, together with the decentralization of governance to the state level, has allowed for a large and diverse set of academic institutions to emerge in the United States, totalling some 7500, according to the federal IPEDS data set (2013). This total includes about 1,900 private non-profit colleges and universities, 2,200 public institutions of which more than half are two-year colleges, and close to 3,400 for-profit colleges (ibid.). The United States is a large country, but these numbers are, in relation to the population, considerably greater than are seen elsewhere (Goldin and Katz, 2008). The public institutions tend to be much larger on average than the private schools as evidenced by the fact that about 70% of all US higher education enrolments are in public institutions, nearly 20% are in private non-profits, and around 10% are in for-profit schools (a share that has grown greatly since the mid-1990s).

Federal roles

After the Morrill Act, the American federal government paid little attention to higher education for many decades. Its next big step was the 'GI Bill' of 1944, which began the 'massification' of higher education in the states (Trow, 1994). The GI Bill paved the way for one major federal role – to provide large amounts of financial aid to students through grants, loans and work-study support (Zumeta, 2015). The second major role of the federal government in American higher education is the funding of academic research, which also emerged out of the nation's Second World War experience. The total amount of federal research funding awarded to colleges and universities in 2009 reached $33 billion, accounting for 60% of all separately budgeted academic research and development by universities (Association of American Universities, 2011). Organizations such as the National Institutes of Health, the National Science Foundation and a variety of smaller provider agencies including the US Department of Education propagate the advancement of knowledge conducted by research institutions that compete for grant funds. The subsidization of research by the US government emphasizes its interest in the country's scientific and technological relevance – albeit with considerably more steering as to areas of inquiry than has been seen in Europe – which it decided after the War to accomplish primarily through universities (see Chapter 24 by Jongbloed and Lepori on funding streams for research in European higher education institutions).

Research-intensive universities now spend more on federally supported research than they do on instruction. More often in recent years, though, federal grants require a matching contribution from institutions, which are increasingly hard-pressed to provide it. Also, federal contributions to university research-related overhead have been squeezed down in recent years. Although untangling internal university finances is complex, it is commonly believed by analysts now that universities use undergraduate tuition revenue to subsidize other operations, including research (Ehrenberg, 2012; Fowles, 2013). This is one way that pressures to contain government (in this case federal) expenditures on higher education have been felt.

Private sectors

The United States is below the international average in the proportion of students enrolled in the private higher education sector (31.3% including for-profits), while Latin America has the highest share (at 48.6%) and Europe has a comparatively low private share (16% with most of that in Eastern Europe) (Levy and Zumeta, 2011). There is considerable variation in US private sectors by region and state with the older eastern states tending to have proportionally large and prestigious private sectors while western states depend much more on public colleges (Goldin and Katz, 2008). In the former states, the public sectors are often somewhat underdeveloped and forced to charge relatively high tuition while private institutions get the benefit of generous state student aid programmes that can help students bear their high charges. In the west, public tuition tends to be lower and student aid programmes underdeveloped.

In the United States, private institutions are free to set their own prices and admissions policies and in all but a couple of states offer what academic programmes they choose without state involvement. Moderately selective private colleges may serve as substitutes for public institutions in some regions and for some subgroups of students, such as the religiously oriented. When public institution prices increase substantially, some student demand may be redirected towards private colleges, as long as need-based student aid follows (Thompson and Zumeta, 2001). Aid that follows the student, such as federal Pell grants and most state student aid, allows flexible options for students to choose where to study among accredited institutions. The United States made the key policy decisions about providing federal and substantial state support for higher education through students, who can choose where to attend, during the period from the mid-1940s through the 1970s. Other countries have recently adopted important parts of this market-oriented financing model.

Components of higher education finance

Next we consider the major components of the financing of US higher education, which are: state appropriations and state-level factors that affect them, tuition, student financial aid, and the emergence of alternative revenue sources.

State appropriations

As mentioned, states are the governmental entities that provide the core of support for public higher education institutions in the United States. In many states, local governments also provide some support for public community colleges. In 2013, $81.6 billion in state and local support was provided to colleges and universities, which is slightly more than half of the total educational revenue of these institutions (SHEEO, 2013). State and local support (excluding appropriations for capital, research and medical education) per full-time-equivalent (FTE) student was $6,105 in 2013, which, although slightly higher than the prior year, remains lower than any year prior to 2009 among the last 25 (SHEEO, 2013). Higher education is the largest discretionary[2] item in state budgets and, therefore, a vulnerable target for budget reductions during hard times (Burke, 2002), such as the recent 'Great Recession'. Universities are also capable of generating their own, non-state revenue, and therefore are seen as capable of absorbing financial setbacks more readily than other programmes. Higher education has tools as well to decrease expenditures by increasing student–faculty ratios and hiring more part-time lecturers, limiting course availability, and increasing faculty teaching loads, whereas other state agencies have stricter, less flexible spending requirements. Most crucially, there exists the impression that universities can mitigate the effects of economic downturns by passing on costs to students in the form of higher tuition. Indeed, students have shown that they are willing to pay more, however much they may complain. In sum, policy makers believe that universities have the capacity to balance budgets through techniques unavailable to other state-funded programmes (Lasher and Sullivan, 2004).

Tuition

As mentioned, tuition is an important source of revenue for US colleges, often spiking during times of recession. States have been increasingly slow to restore higher education support even when times improve, so tuition at public institutions has continued to climb (Figure 25.1). The overall trend towards greater student contribution to university finances applies elsewhere, but the United States led the way and did so from the states rather than from the national policy level. In 2013, public institutions collected net (after discounts and

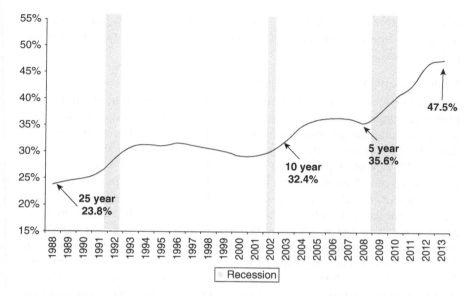

Figure 25.1 Net tuition as a percentage of public higher education total educational revenue, US, fiscal years 1988–2013

Note: Net tuition revenue used for capital debt service is included in net tuition revenue, but excluded from total educational revenue in calculating the above figures.

Source: State Higher Education Executive Officers, *State Higher Education Finance FY 2013* report, page 22, 'Figure 4'. Reprinted with authors' permission.

waivers) tuition revenues of $61.8 billion, compared to $81.6 billion in state appropriations (SHEEO, 2013). Plenty of focus has been placed on the rising price of college in the United States. However, the steep published price represented by tuition is not always the actual price paid; rather, it is *net prices* paid by students after aid is considered that primarily determine college affordability. For 2013–2014, the estimated average published in-state tuition and fee price at a public four-year institution was $8,893, while the hypothetical average student pays a net price of $3,120 after all financial aid and tax benefits are considered; the average published tuition at a public two-year college was $3,264 (although after aid the net price was negative, allowing something towards other costs); while private four-year colleges charged an average of $30,094 (net price of $12,460) (College Board, 2013a). Note that none of these figures includes other college-related costs, such as books and supplies, or living expenses. Regardless of these student costs and their escalation in recent years, most economists still assess a college education to be a very good investment on average (Baum and Ma, 2013; Carnevale, Strohl and Melton, 2011).

Public tuition levels vary considerably by state, and there are notable regional patterns. Prices tend to be high in the older eastern states where private colleges have long dominated. In the west, there are fewer private colleges and public tuition rates are substantially lower. The south and midwest regions tend to be in between these two extremes, both in private sector representation and public tuition levels.

Student financial aid

In addition to state appropriations to institutions, government funding for higher education comes directly to students in the form of financial aid. Here, we discuss financial aid specifically in the United States and point the reader to Barr (2012) for an economic comparative analysis of financial aid that includes the OECD, as well as the United States. Federal financial aid is available for use at any type of accredited higher education institution, public or private, although students attending for-profit institutions are not eligible for many state aid programmes. In the 2012–2013 academic year, $238.5 billion in financial aid was awarded to undergraduates and graduate students in the form of grants (state funded and federally funded), federal loans, tax credits and deductions and work-study support (College Board, 2013b). In academic year 2011–2012, 85% of first-time, full-time undergraduate students at four-year degree granting institutions received some form of financial aid[3] (National Center for Education Statistics, 2014). Federal loans are the most common source of student borrowing as these are subsidized (interest does not accumulate while the student is attending school) (US Department of Education, 2014). The largest federal student grant programme, Pell Grants, provides up to $5,730 (average of around $3,650) to financially needy students for the 2014–2015 award year.

As for state-provided student aid, a key milestone occurred in 1972, when the federal Higher Education Act was reauthorized, creating the State Student Incentive Grant (SSIG) programme (now called Leveraging Educational Assistance Partnership, or LEAP). The SSIG provided federal matching funds to states that developed scholarship programmes to help students with financial need. By 1979, every state was operating at least one need-based grant programme, many in response to this incentive (Heller, 2004). In both the major federal and state grant programmes, the basic idea was to provide help to students with demonstrated financial need. State student aid programmes now provide close to $10 billion per year in grants to students (National Association of State Student Grant and Aid Programs, 2013), although there is wide variation in the scale of states' student aid efforts.

In 1993, a new era of financial aid emerged with the creation of the Georgia HOPE scholarship programme. This programme was the first so-called 'merit-based' student aid programme as it awarded funds based on students earning at least a B-average in high school with a similar grade average in college required for renewal. The student's annual family income had to be below $66,000 to be eligible. The scholarship covered the full cost of tuition at any Georgia public college for two years (Heller, 2002). In its first year of operation, 1993–1994, $21.4 million was given out to 43,000 students (Heller, 2002), funded by ticket sales from a newly created state lottery. Other states also developed merit-based programmes, and at least 15 states now operate what is considered a broad-based merit programme (Doyle, 2006). Most are concentrated in the southern region of the United States and are similarly funded by profits from state-run lottery games.

The idea behind merit aid programmes is to motivate high school and college student achievement, since college scholarships and their renewal are based on marks or grades and performance on standardized tests. Merit aid is also intended to combat 'brain drain', whereby high-potential students move out of state for college and often end up staying in the receiving state for employment (Cohen-Vogel, Ingle, Levine and Spence, 2007). Yet, merit aid support goes disproportionately to affluent and middle-class students, most of whom would otherwise have attended college anyway, and researchers and advocates for equity worry about their overshadowing of programmes that help low-income students access higher education (Heller and Marin, 2004). Indeed, few states with merit programmes offer much need-based aid.

The type of financial aid received may affect a student's decision to attend college. Empirically, grant aid has the most influence on the likelihood of enrolment, followed by loans and work-study aid, as would be expected (St. John, 2003). Grant aid (but not loans) increases persistence rates among low- and middle-income students (Alon, 2011). Aid also affects degree completion rates. After controlling for student and institutional variables, college completion rates were found to be positively predicted by the proportion of state appropriations allocated for student aid grants (Titus, 2006). Unmet financial need contributes to a lower likelihood of student college completion (ibid.).

Despite the widely accessible information about financial aid on websites and in books, brochures and the like, many students and families are poorly informed about the cost of college and how to pay for it (Perna, 2006). They tend to overestimate cost and underestimate available aid, which discourages attendance. Lack of information is more common among low-income, Latino and black students and among first-generation (i.e. first in family to attend college) students. Knowledge gaps can perpetuate the educational gaps between the wealthy and the poor and among racial minorities. Greater understanding about college pricing and aid leads to greater chances of application, enrolment and willingness to borrow (Perna, 2006). How to improve the usability and use of financial and other college information, particularly with regard to underrepresented populations, is a key area for research and policy experimentation as the success of market-oriented models for financing higher education and access to it depend on students making well-informed decisions. What policy analysts call 'information asymmetry' – students have problems accessing and processing information about their college choices – is a key area of current research and policy experimentation, and this is not limited to the United States (Brown, 2012).

Factors affecting state funding

Researchers have become especially interested in how higher education is funded during periods of recession, given the far-reaching implications of the 2007–2009 'Great Recession' and its aftermath. In periods of scarce and uncertain resources, states have demonstrated limited commitment to higher education compared to other public needs such as health care and primary/secondary education. Harold Hovey (1999) posited that in flush economic times higher education is treated more generously (funded at a higher rate of annual increase) than other budget categories, since it is seen as a worthy investment in the state's future economic future and human and social capital. By contrast, during difficult economic times, for reasons already mentioned, higher education is disproportionately cut, even after controlling for economic, political and higher education factors such as enrolments, leading to ongoing volatility in the sector's finances. Once funding is cut, the more recent recessions have also instigated a more extended period for appropriations to recover to previous levels; indeed, they have recently failed to do so before the onset of the next recession. Slow recovery from serious cuts in the early and late 2000s downturns is compared to swifter recoveries after recessions in the 1980s and 1990s (Doyle and Delaney, 2011). Comparative research across developed nations on the cyclical ups and downs of higher education funding, within the context of long-term stagnation or decline, would be a valuable contribution to the literature.

As mentioned, funding for higher education is influenced by various economic, demographic and political factors (Tandberg and Griffith, 2013), although there is some disagreement as to which variables matter most. Previous research has pointed to a positive relationship between per capita income and state higher education funding, yet gross state product does not appear to affect appropriations (Delaney and Doyle, 2011). A state's available tax revenues and its tax effort, or willingness to tax, do affect the overall appropriations level for higher education (Archibald and Feldman, 2006). Some analysts find that, in the United States, the presence of a Republican-controlled legislature and Republican governor diminishes state spending on higher education (McLendon, Hearn and Mokher, 2009). More liberal states are more generous towards higher education, as well as to other Democratic-leaning ideals about government and education support (Tandberg, 2009, 2010). Other researchers, using different methods, claim instead that Republicans are more generous towards higher education and also tend to support two-year colleges as opposed to research universities (Weerts and Ronca, 2012). Again, comparative research would be interesting here, to shed light on whether left- or right-leaning governments in general tend to treat higher education (and particular sectors of it) more or less generously, considering their overall attitudes towards public spending.

Different sectors of American higher education are affected differently when it comes to volatility in state support. Research universities are viewed as most independent, able to secure external funds such as competitive federal grants, and also are more expensive and thus generally less accessible to students of modest means compared to other sectors. On the other hand, two-year colleges are open access, inexpensive and most dependent on public funds. Thus, research universities have experienced the most fluctuations in state funding with the ebbs and flows in the health of the national economy, whereas two-year college funding has been less volatile in general (Weerts and Ronca, 2012). Two-year colleges are able to gather political support when they are broadly accessible and train students for the perceived workforce needs of the state. They also enrol the most students in many states and are usually widely distributed geographically, which tends to increase their legislative support. In much of the world, higher education subsectors are less clearly defined than in the American case. Still, to the extent distinct subsectors exist, it would be of interest for researchers to compare across countries how differently they have been treated during recent economic downturns.

Alternative revenue sources

Due to decreasing or unreliable state appropriations, public colleges all over the world are looking increasingly to other sources of revenue. 'Academic capitalism' is the idea that universities and faculty engage increasingly in market-like behaviours to compete for funds from external grants and contracts, specialized endowments, industry partnerships and spinoff companies (Slaughter and Leslie, 2001). Non-governmental sources are seen as more needed than ever to provide the funding for prolific research, as well as to help compensate for flagging state support. Increased 'privatization' and commercialization are in part a result of the university seeking such alternative revenue streams.

Fundraising. American universities today place more emphasis on their development or advancement offices as well to bring in private donations and cultivate relationships with external funders, who can often help with a new building or an endowment, but nearly always in return for having their priorities addressed. Fundraising has become an expected task within the public university as it has long been in the private institution, and development officers facilitate an environment where long-term financial support can be achieved for certain purposes via privately funded endowments (Vogel and Kaghan,

2001). A recent trend has been to seek more current use gifts rather than endowments because the former can more readily substitute for missing state funds for some purposes. Gifts should ideally be an appropriate match between the donor and the recipient's priorities, but there is a risk that the priorities of donors will distort those of academe if it is sufficiently starved for general-purpose funds. In 2009, $304 billion of philanthropic support was given to American higher education, with 75% from individual donors, 5% from family foundations and the remaining amount from corporations and broader-based foundations (Drezner, 2011, p. 2). Growth in giving to higher education has increased substantially, from around $2 billion in 1965 (in 2009 dollars) to $40 billion in 2009 (Drezner, 2011, p. 11). Policy makers and academic leaders in other nations looking to the American model for guidance in seeking new funding sources would do well to study the problems with, as well as the successes of, the aggressive approach of its universities to private fundraising.

Non-resident tuition. Many universities have also revamped their recruitment efforts to generate more revenue from students. A growing source of income is international students, as is also apparent in Australia and the United Kingdom. In 2012–2013, international students composed 7.2% of all US higher education enrolments, a record high, and contributed an estimated $27 billion to the national economy (Institute of International Education, 2014). International students are typically ineligible for scholarships and government funding, pay higher tuition rates at public colleges and tend to come from wealthier families (Harding, 2014). More institutions are changing recruitment foci to attract domestic out-of-state students, who pay 'full cost' or higher prices, as well.[4] Of course, not all institutions can be successful in competition to attract students who would formerly have been likely to attend their home state school at much lower tuition rates. Thus, international students are especially attractive.

Continuing education. More public and private universities are creating divisions of continuing education that largely attract older students who attend part time for certificates or lifelong learning goals and sometimes for degrees earned outside the standard structure. The courses offered can be credit bearing or non-credit. These divisions most often do not receive permanent direct institutional support and therefore operate to earn back their costs or more, drawing on existing faculty or adjuncts from the community (Breneman, 2005). These college 'offshoots' function more similarly to for-profit colleges in their tendency to offer vocationally oriented courses and promote distance learning. Almost 75% of four-year college continuing education programmes generated revenues that exceeded costs, as did 56% of those at two-year institutions, according to Pusser, Gansneder, Gallaway and Pope (2005, p. 38). The offering of self-sustaining, and even profitable, continuing education divisions is simply another example of entrepreneurial behaviour in higher education (Pusser and Doane, 2001) and one that is available to all types of institutions.

Technology transfer. Beginning with a shift in federal policy in 1980 that allowed universities to seek patents on products of their federally funded research (the Bayh-Dole Act), the large American research universities have shown increasing interest in commercializing research discoveries and their downstream products (Slaughter and Rhoades, 2004). This interest is not motivated entirely by financial considerations – universities recognize a mission to serve society by making the fruits of knowledge and discovery useful in the form of new medicines, software and other products (Dill, 2010). Yet, recent fiscal strains have certainly reinforced the motivation to supplement institutional (and individual faculty) income with revenues from patents, licenses and equity in spinoff companies (ibid.), and this interest is not unique to the United States (Dill and van Vught, 2010). In the interest of local economic development, some states have subsidized these efforts (Geiger, 2010; Zumeta, 2010).

Although there have been some 'blockbuster' academic patents generating large income streams for a few institutions, in a purely financial sense the results of sizeable university investments in such 'technology transfer' have been disappointing for most institutions. University leaders and staff are unlikely to have the expertise to make efficient decisions regarding start-ups and other technology transfer ventures to produce substantial revenue (Feller, Feldman, Bercovitz and Burton, 2002). According to recent analyses, relatively few universities actually make more money than they spend on these activities (Bulut and Moschini, 2009), a finding also true internationally (Dill and van Vught, 2010). In that sense the pursuit is similar to intercollegiate sports, where major American universities spend a great deal of money in pursuit of on-field and financial success that only a few achieve (Cheslock and Knight, 2015).

Performance accountability

Fuelled in part by the increasing cost of higher education, a new accountability movement that is not limited to the United States has focused attention on the efficient use of resources by colleges. Accountability in the American context has long looked different from accountability in most other countries by virtue of the role of its somewhat autonomous accrediting entities. Many other countries utilize government ministries to define academic quality and enforce standards of excellence (Zumeta and Kinne, 2011). King discusses accountability and performance measurement (see Chapter 26), as well as autonomy; Williams and Harvey discuss quality assurance (see Chapter 27). As evidenced by recent recessionary periods, in the United States there exists a correlation between resource scarcity and the call for greater accountability of higher education to its governmental sponsors (Hou, Lunsford, Slides and Jones, 2011). A traditional focus on inputs (e.g. enrolments) has shifted to an emphasis on the outputs (e.g. degrees, job placements in high-demand fields) and outcomes of interest to state policy makers. States are demanding that universities report on student outcomes and improve institutional performance.

The accountability culture in the United States has emerged in part from reports on the graduation outcomes of college students. For instance, the *Measuring Up* reports by the National Center for Public Policy and Higher Education (2008) graded state higher education systems on categories such as access, participation, graduation, affordability, societal benefits and learning outcomes but found evidence of learning outcomes to be scarce. The OECD has published articles on the topic of US higher educational competitiveness in relation to its peers, and the State Higher Education Executive Officers as well as the Educational Testing Service have published reports on using evidence to improve institutional results (Bogue and Johnson, 2010). Institutions have always been evaluated by accreditation standards, the external peer-based process of ensuring degree programmes are of sound quality. The public and those they elect are no longer willing to accept a peer review process alone, however, to ensure satisfactory delivery of instruction (Sanford and Hunter, 2011).

Performance funding policies

Within the United States, incentive structures have emerged that link some of state appropriations to state-desired performance outcomes (Dougherty and Reddy, 2013) and are referred to as outcome-based funding or performance funding. These forms of state budgeting for higher education can be categorized into three different but related funding schemes as follows. *Performance funding* is a strategy that links state funding 'directly and tightly to the performance of public campuses on individual indicators' (Burke and Minassians, 2003, p. 3). There is a specific formula used to allocate a percentage of state funding conditional on a college's achievement of output thresholds, with this percentage varying from around 1% of the overall budget to (very recently) approaching 100%, depending on the state. Alternatively, *performance budgeting* allows the legislature 'to consider campus achievement on performance indicators as one factor in determining allocations for public campuses' (ibid., p. 3). In this approach, the state has discretionary power to determine funding levels and takes performance into account but not formulaically. Finally, the third option, *performance reporting*, does not formally link appropriations to outcomes but rather depends upon 'information and publicity' based on specified performance reports to 'encourage colleges and universities to improve their performance' (ibid., p. 5). The majority of states today operate, at minimum, a performance reporting policy, and about 25 states have instituted some form of performance funding (Snyder, 2014), although many of the models in use are limited in scope. These budgeting models are part of what is called the performance accountability movement in American higher education and, of course, it has parallels in other sectors and other countries (see Jongbloed and Vossensteyn, 2001; Jongbloed, 2010). As in other areas of higher education policy and finance, United States' ideas in this sphere have been influential outside its boundaries (see Chapter 24 by Jongbloed and Lepori, for funding allocation models in Europe).

Performance funding has experienced a rather unstable history in the United States, often getting abandoned during difficult fiscal times. Researchers have been interested as well in whether the direct linking of state funds to college outcomes effectively incentivizes better performance. The evidence on effects to date of performance funding is less than impressive in achieving the targeted ends. At both two-year and four-year institutions, the policy appears to have had little impact on degree attainment rates, for example, where it has been in place long enough to evaluate (Tandberg, Hillman and Barakat, 2014; Tandberg and Hillman, 2014). Explanations for these findings are that impacts are at best lagged years after the policy is in place, given the average time-to-degree and the learning period that institutions must got through to change their outputs. Often, performance funding programmes have not survived long enough to produce results. The percentage of funding tied to performance is also a factor in the effectiveness of policies – states that allocate 5% or less of their appropriations based on performance, as has generally been the case until recently, may well see little impact, whereas states that allocate 25% or more could plausibly have a very considerable impact.

A challenge of performance funding also is the unclear connection between student outcomes and the college's behaviours. A well-thought-out implementation plan, as well as internal assessment and vigilance, must be present to connect the creation of new programmes or advising structures to the improved progress of students, or results will likely be disappointing. Additionally, incentive funding regimes could tempt colleges to engage in perverse tactics to increase measured performance, such as lowering academic standards or 'cream skimming', that is, admitting students who will likely bolster retention and graduation rates while limiting access to students who would not. The latter group tends to be of lower income and from under-represented groups (Dougherty and Reddy, 2013).

In the past 20 years, accountability has evolved from a topic of academic discourse to one through which influential stakeholders demand the assessment of higher education outcomes in comparable and quantitative ways. Performance funding is simply one policy to emerge from this movement, and one that has gained popularity in the United States. Other countries are also subject to similar accountability pressures and could follow a similar path, so it is important that empirical research address the full range of potential impacts. In any case, ongoing institutional assessment and data collection are needed to respond to external oversight.

Conclusion

In summary, this essay has sought to illuminate how higher education governance, finance and policy are, in one influential nation, the United States, interrelated through the dynamics of state oversight, public appropriations, tuition policy, student financial aid and performance accountability. This historical overview of these topics in the context of American federalism emphasizes the importance of these complex finance and governance matters to the functioning of higher education across the 50 American states, but the implications are not restricted to the United States. Many, if not most, developed countries face similar challenges, and some are trying policies influenced by American models. Clearly, there is a need for research on how well such models work and how they can be adapted to different national contexts.

With a recent past and likely future of scarce public resources, an accelerated interest in efficiency and a need for institutions to generate increased revenue from non-tax and non-tuition sources is apparent nearly everywhere. American colleges and universities have stepped up to these challenges in creative and innovative ways. However, some of these moves have proven more productive than others and some have potential for mission distortion. This is another area ripe for research and analysis. An environment of limited resources also catalyzes policies that call for greater transparency and justification of institutions' actions, results and spending patterns, as is seen in recent performance accountability schemes tied to public funding. Yet, plausible as performance accountability seems to be on the surface, much remains to be learned about how to design schemes that do more good than harm over time.

Universities must be increasingly creative in securing funding and vigilant in substantiating what they do with their money. The future promises to be a challenging one as academic institutions everywhere are called upon to produce more of what policy makers want with resources that will continue to be constrained and volatile. And, of course, we do not want to sacrifice the many benefits of academic autonomy and creativity too heavily for the supposed gains from accountability either.

Notes

1. There are other federal states of course, including Australia, Canada, Germany and the United Kingdom, to name a few, but the limited role of the national government in higher education in the United States was altogether unique until after the Second World War. Interestingly, as the central government's role in US higher education has expanded, other countries have shown interest in adopting a more federal approach to higher education policy and finance, employing policy tools long in use in America such as tuition, student aid grants and loans, and competition for research grants.
2. 'Discretionary' expenditures are not mandated by federal or state law, regulation or court order. Other large state expenditure categories such as primary and secondary

education, Medicaid (the federal-state health care program for the indigent) and prisons are subject to spending mandates of various kinds.
3. This figure includes institutional aid to students, which is a large item in private, non-profit institutions' budgets in particular.
4. The European Union, it might be noted, does not permit such differential pricing, at least for students from member countries. Still, institutions in EU countries may benefit from enrolments of international students in both financial and other ways.

References

Aghion, P., Dewatripont, M., Hoxby, C., Mas-Colell, A. and A. Sapir (2007) 'Why reform Europe's universities?' *Bruegel Policy Brief,* (4).

Alon, S. (2011) 'Who benefits most from financial aid? The heterogenous effect of need-based grants on students' college persistence', *Social Science Quarterly,* 92(3), 807–829.

Archibald, R. B. and D. H. Feldman (2006) 'State higher education spending and the tax revolt', *Journal of Higher Education,* 77(4), 618–644.

Association of American Universities (2011) University Research: The Role of Federal Funding. Retrieved February 8, 2015, from http://www.aau.edu/WorkArea/DownloadAsset.aspx?id=11588.

Barr, N. (2012) *The Economics of the Welfare State,* 5th edn (New York: Oxford University Press).

Baum, S. and J. Ma (2013) *Education Pays* (Princeton, New Jersey: The College Board).

Bogue, E. G., and B. D. Johnson (2010) 'Performance incentives and public college accountability in the United States: a quarter century policy audit', *Higher Education Management and Policy,* 22(2), 9–30.

Breneman, D. W. (2005) 'Entrepreneurship in higher education', *New Directions for Higher Education,* (129), 3–9.

Brown, R. (2012) 'The myth of student choice', *VISTAS: Education, Economy and Community,* 2(2), 7–20.

Bulut, H. and G. Moschini (2009) 'US universities' Net returns from patenting and licensing: a quantile regression analysis', *Economics of Innovation & New Technology,* 18(2), 123–137.

Burke, J. C. (2002) *Funding Public Colleges and Universities for Performance* (Albany, NY: Rockefeller Institute Press).

Burke, J. C. and H. P. Minassians (2003) 'Reporting higher education results: missing links in the performance chain', *New Directions for Institutional Research* (116) (San Francisco, CA: Jossey-Bass).

Carnevale, A. P., Strohl, J. and M. Melton (2011) *What's It Worth? The Economic Value of College Majors* (Washington, DC: Georgetown University Center on Education and the Workforce).

Cheslock, J. J. and D. Knight (2015) 'Diverging revenues, cascading expenditures, and cascading revenues: The unbalanced and growing financial strain of intercollegiate athletics on universities and their students', *Journal of Higher Education,* 86(3), 417–447.

Cheslock, J. J. and R. P. Hughes (2011) 'Differences across states in higher education finance policy', *Journal of Education Finance,* 36(4), 369–393.

Cohen-Vogel, L., Ingle, W. K., Levine, A. A. and M. Spence (2007) 'The "Spread" of merit-based college aid: politics, policy consortia, and interstate competition', *Educational Policy,* 22(3), 339–362.

College Board (2013a) Trends in College Pricing. Retrieved November 1, 2014, from http://trends.collegeboard.org/sites/default/files/college-pricing-2013-full-report.pdf.

College Board (2013b) Trends in Student Aid. Retrieved November 1, 2014 from http://trends.collegeboard.org/sites/default/files/student-aid-2013-full-report.pdf.

Delaney, J. A. and W. R. Doyle (2011) 'State spending on higher education: testing the balance wheel over time', *Journal of Education Finance*, 36(4), 343–368.

Dill, D. D. (2010) 'The United States', in D. D. Dill and F. A. van Vught (eds) *National Innovation and the Academic Research Enterprise: Public Policy in Global Perspective* (pp. 387–437) (Baltimore, MD: Johns Hopkins University Press).

Dill, D. D. and F. A. van Vught (eds) (2010) *National Innovation and the Academic Research Enterprise: Public Policy in Global Perspective* (Baltimore, MD: Johns Hopkins University Press).

Dobbins, M., Knill, C. and E. M. Vögtle (2011) 'An analytical framework for the cross-country comparison of higher education governance', *Higher Education*, 62(5), 665–683.

Dougherty, K. J. and V. Reddy (2013) 'Performance funding for higher education: what are the mechanisms? What are the impacts?' in K. Ward and L. E. Wolf-Wendel (eds) *ASHE Higher Education Report*, 39(2) (San Francisco, CA: Jossey-Bass).

Doyle, W. R. (2006) 'Adoption of merit-based student grant programs: an event history analysis', *Educational Evaluation and Policy Analysis*, 28(3), 259–285.

Doyle, W. R. and J. A. Delaney (2011) *Bouncebacks in Higher Education Funding: Patterns in Length of Time to Recovery Following Cuts in State Appropriations* (Madison, WI: WISCAPE Policy Brief).

Drezner, N. D. (2011) 'Philanthropy and fundraising in American higher education', *ASHE Higher Education Report*, 37(2), 1–155.

Education Commission of the States (2012) 50-State Analysis: State-Level Coordinating and/or Governing Agency. Retrieved October 30, 2014, from http://ecs.force.com/mbdata/mbquestU?Rep=PSG01&SID=a0i700000009vZI&Q=Q0667.

Ehrenberg, R. G. (2012) 'American higher education in transition', *Journal of Economic Perspectives*, 26(1), 193–216.

Feller, I., Feldman, M., Bercovitz, J. and R. Burton (2002) 'Equity and the technology transfer strategies of American research universities', *Management Science*, 48, 105–121.

Fowles, J. (2014) 'Funding and focus: resource dependence in public higher education', *Research in Higher Education*, 55(3), 272–287.

Geiger, R. L. (2010) 'Pennsylvania', in D. D. Dill and F. A. van Vught (eds) *National Innovation and the Academic Research Enterprise: Public Policy in Global Perspective* (pp. 438–479) (Baltimore, MD: Johns Hopkins University Press).

Goldin, C. and L. F. Katz (2008) *The Race between Education and Technology* (Cambridge, MA: Harvard University Press).

Harding, J. T. (2014) 'Follow the campus money', *Phi Kappa Phi Forum*.

Snyder, M. (2014) *Driving Better Outcomes: Typologies and Principles of Outcomes-Based Funding Models* (Washington, DC: HCM Strategists).

Heller, D. E. (2002) 'The policy shift in state financial aid programs', in J. C. Smart and W. G. Tierney (eds) *Higher Education: Handbook of Theory and Research*, 27 (pp. 221–262) (New York, NY: Agathon Press).

Heller, D. E. (2004) 'The changing nature of financial aid', *Academe*, 90(4), 36–38.

Heller, D. E. and P. Marin, P (2004) *State Merit Scholarship Programs and Racial Inequality* (Cambridge, MA: The Civil Rights Project at Harvard University).

Hou, Y., Lunsford, R. S., Slides, K. C. and K. A. Jones (2011) 'State performance-based budgeting in boom and bust years: an analytical framework and survey of the states', *Public Administration Review*, (June), 370–388.

Hovey, H. A. (1999) *State Spending for Higher Education in the New Decade: The Battle to Sustain Current Support* (Washington, DC: National Centre for Public Policy and Higher Education).

Institute of International Education (2014) Open Doors Presentation. Retrieved November 1, 2014, from http://www.iie.org/en/Research-and-Publications/Open-Doors.

Jongbloed, B. and H. Vossensteyn (2001) 'Keeping up performances: an international survey of performance-based funding in higher education', *Journal of Higher Education Policy and Management*, 23(2), 127–145.

Jongbloed, B. (2010) 'Funding higher education: a view across Europe', *European Centre for Strategic Management of Universities*, Retrieved February 4, 2015, from http://www.utwente.nl/bms/cheps/publications/Publications%202010/MODERN_Funding_Report.pdf.

Lasher, W. F. and C. A. Sullivan (2004) 'Follow the money: the changing world of budgeting in higher education', in J. C. Smart (ed) *Higher Education: Handbook of Theory and Research*, 19 (pp. 197–240) (Dordrecht, Netherlands: Kluwer).

Levy, D. C. and W. Zumeta (2011) 'Private higher education and public policy: a global view', *Journal of Comparative Policy Analysis: Research and Practice*, 13(4), 345–349.

McGuinness, A. C. (2003) *Models of Postsecondary Education Coordination and Governance in the States* (Denver, CO: Education Commission of the States).

McLendon, M. K., Deaton, R. and J. C. Hearn (2007) 'The enactment of reforms in state governance of higher education: testing the political instability hypothesis', *The Journal of Higher Education*, 78(6), 645–675.

McLendon, M. K., Hearn, J. C. and C. G. Mokher (2009) 'Partisans, professionals, and power: the role of political factors in state higher education funding', *The Journal of Higher Education*, 80(6), 686–713.

McLendon, M. K., Tandberg, D. A. and N. W. Hillman (2014) 'Financing college opportunity: factors influencing state spending on student financial aid and campus appropriations, 1990 through 2010', *The ANNALS of the American Academy of Political and Social Science*, 655(1), 143–162.

National Association of State Student Grant and Aid Programs (2013) 44th Annual Survey Report on State-Sponsored Student Financial Aid: 2012–2013 Academic Year. Retrieved September 1, 2014, from http://www.nassgap.org/viewrepository.aspx?categoryID=3#.

National Centre for Education Statistics (2014) Fast Facts: Financial Aid. Retrieved November 6, 2014, from http://nces.ed.gov/fastfacts/display.asp?id=31.

National Centre for Public Policy and Higher Education (2008), Measuring Up, Retrieved November 6, 2014, from www.highereducation.org.

Perna, L. W. (2006) 'Understanding the relationship between information about college prices and financial aid and students' college-related behaviors', *American Behavioral Scientist*, 49(12), 1620–1635.

Pusser, B. and D. J. Doane (2001) 'Public purpose and private enterprise: the contemporary organization of postsecondary education', *Change*, 33(5), 18–22.

Pusser, B., Gansneder, B. M., Gallaway, N. and N. S. Pope (2005) 'Entrepreneurial activity in nonprofit institutions: a portrait of continuing education', *New Directions for Higher Education*, (129), 27–42.

Sanford, T. and J. Hunter (2011) 'Impact of performance-funding on retention and graduation rates', *Education Policy Analysis Archives*, 19(33), 1–30.

SHEEO (2013) State Higher Education Finance FY 2013. Retrieved September 1, 2014, from http://www.sheeo.org/sites/default/files/publications/SHEF_FY13_04292014.pdf.

Slaughter, S. and L. L. Leslie (2001) 'Expanding and elaborating the concept of academic capitalism', *Organization*, 8(2), 154–161.

Slaughter, S. and G. Rhoades (2004) *Academic Capitalism and the New Economy: Markets, States and Higher Education* (Baltimore, MD: Johns Hopkins University Press).

St. John, E. P. (2003) *Refinancing the College Dream: Access, Equal Opportunity, and Justice for Taxpayers* (Baltimore and London: Johns Hopkins University Press).

Tandberg, D. A. (2009) 'Interest groups and governmental institutions: the politics of state funding of public higher education', *Educational Policy*, 24(5), 735–778.

Tandberg, D. A. (2010) 'Politics, interest groups and state funding of public higher education', *Research in Higher Education*, 51(5), 416–450.

Tandberg, D. A. (2013) 'The conditioning role of state higher education governance structures', *The Journal of Higher Education*, 84(4), 506–543.

Tandberg, D. A. and C. Griffith (2013) 'State support of higher education: data, measures, findings, and directions for future research', in M. B. Paulsen (ed) *Higher Education: Handbook of Theory and Research*, 28 (pp. 613–685) (Dordrecht, Netherlands: Springer Science+Business Media).

Tandberg, D. A. and N. W. Hillman (2014) 'State higher education performance funding: data, outcomes, and policy implications', *Journal of Education Finance*, 39(1), 222–243.

Tandberg, D. A., Hillman, N. W. and M. Barakat (2014) 'State higher education performance funding for community colleges: diverse effects and policy implications', *Teacher's College Record*, 116(12), 1–31.

Thompson, F. and W. Zumeta (2001) 'Effects of key state policies on private colleges and universities: sustaining private-sector capacity in the face of the higher education access challenge', *Economics of Education Review*, 20(6), 517–531.

Titus, M. A. (2006) 'No college student left behind: the influence of financial aspects of a state's higher education policy on college completion', *The Review of Higher Education*, 29(3), 293–317.

Trow, M. (1994) 'Federalism in American higher education', in A. Levine (ed) *Higher Learning in America: 1980—2000* (pp. 39–66) (Baltimore, MD: Johns Hopkins University Press).

US Department of Education (2014) Federal Student Aid. Retrieved November 1, 2014, from https://studentaid.ed.gov/types/loans/plus.

Vogel, A. and W. N. Kaghan (2001) 'Bureaucrats, brokers, and the entrepreneurial university', *Organization*, 8(2), 358–364.

Weerts, D. J. and J. M. Ronca (2012) 'Understanding differences in state support for higher education across states, sectors, and institutions: a longitudinal study', *The Journal of Higher Education*, 83(2), 155–185.

Zumeta, W. (2010) 'California', in D. D. Dill and F. A. van Vught (eds) *National Innovation and the Academic Research Enterprise: Public Policy in Global Perspective* (pp. 480–526) (Baltimore, MD: Johns Hopkins University Press).

Zumeta, W. (2015) Il finanziamento dell'istruzione superiore statunitense: diversità e decentramento in prospettiva storica, fino al recente declino ('US higher education finance: Historical decentralization and diversity, recent decline'), *Memoria E Ricerca*, 49, 55–70.

Zumeta, W., and A. Kinne (2011) 'Accountability policies: directions old and new', in D. E. Heller (ed) *The States and Public Higher Education Policy: Affordability, Access, and Accountability* (pp. 173–199) (Baltimore, MD: Johns Hopkins University Press).

E. Accountability and Quality

26
Institutional Autonomy and Accountability

Roger King

Introduction

A key feature of higher education governance arrangements around the world is their apparent convergence, at least in formal terms. Certain global models, such as the so-called New Public Management (NPM), appear to have considerable traction (King, 2009, p. 41). Nonetheless, we need to be careful. Models – such as those configured around the preference by higher education policy-makers for increased institutional freedoms and performance accountability – are dynamic entities. They change in the processes of adoption and implementation, as negotiation by affected groups, the historical path 'dependencies' of particular nations, and as varying cultural interpretations come to exert their influences. Formal governance arrangements that emphasize institutional autonomy and accountability in one country, for example, may look very different in practice to those found in other countries with apparently similar policies and structures.

The objective of this chapter is to examine the changing notions of institutional autonomy and accountability over recent decades and also to discuss origins, comparative and cultural variations and changing interpretations. In particular, the chapter seeks to situate these concepts in wider contexts of dynamic change, including those associated with globalization and the recent technological revolution, and within broader developments in the state associated with risk and delegation. The rise of digital higher education and the applications of Big Data analytics particularly have considerable scope for changing long-held notions of academic autonomy.

Parts of this chapter are condensed versions of extracts drawn from King (2007, 2011).

Institutional autonomy

In higher education reform over recent decades, the idea of institutional autonomy has moved from that predominantly associated with 'community' self-governance and professional and academic freedom – effectively licensed by the state, if not necessarily explicitly part of any formal 'compact' – to that defined by the organizational autonomy of the university as a unitary actor in its own right.

There are theoretical antecedents to such a development. Functionalist sociological accounts of modernization, not least those of Talcott Parsons (Parsons and Platt, 1973), have regarded the organizational autonomy of the university as part of wider social processes of differentiation and effectiveness of sectors found in advanced societies. Others, such as Merton (1942) and Popper (1945), have been concerned to promote university (and academic) freedoms to help protect scientific and creative powers – by shielding institutions particularly from state and commercial incursions. More recently, Bourdieu (1990) has seen the important elite reproductive role for higher education (and the necessity to disguise this through emphases on meritocracy and intellectual achievement) as necessitating the apparent formal autonomy of the university from wider elite integration and social inequalities (Naidoo, 2004).

Public service reforms

State delegation of increased powers to universities and colleges, as part of wider public service reforms in recent decades, have seemed especially pertinent to Continental European systems. In the United Kingdom, universities have long enjoyed freedoms as institutions, captured in legal charters of incorporation, although the post-1992 'new universities' generally have had their powers comparatively more defined, circumscribed and shaped by Higher Education Acts and similar national state legislation. Their European counterparts, however, have been part of higher education sectors shaped by both a strong state and powerful professional associations (Clark, 1983). As Enders, de Boer and Wayer (2013, pp. 7–8) note:

> On the one hand, the state functioned as a strong regulator and funder of universities, exercising bureaucratic control over procedural matters. On the other hand, the state protected the autonomy of the university as a social institution; academic freedom as well as academic self-governance, and substantial matters, were delegated to academics within a broad state framework. The protection of academic freedom and guaranteed funding by the state enabled universities to establish normative and constitutive principles without being subject to strong external design (Olsen, 2007). The university as an organization developed, however, very limited authority and capacity to regulate itself.

In recent years, this state of affairs has changed, encouraged by models of state supervision rather than state control, with focus on the managerial and regulative capacities of university leaders and on performance output evaluations rather than the micro control by the state of input factors.

Before discussing these evaluative processes, however, we turn to the concept of accountability.

Accountability

In contemporary parliamentary democracies (and their functional equivalents), the traditional form of exercising accountability by the principal over its agent is usually quite direct. This largely takes the form of regular parliamentary scrutiny of ministers. In the modern age of large-scale administration, however, a compelling view is that accountability, including within government, is discharged through bureaucratic hierarchies and rational decision-making. Here, incumbents holding clearly specified and authorized positions – particularly in those organizations such as civil services pursuing the public good – both demand accountability from subordinates and, in turn, provide it to their superiors. This occurs according to processes of formal rule-application. These are intended to severely reduce individual arbitrariness in decision-making, yet they also constrain the wayward, sometimes corruptible and spasmodic accountability of electoral politics (Dowdle, 2006).

Nonetheless, the notion of public accountability itself is contestable and subject to a range of competing interpretations. For example, lawyers often regard it as constituted by the processes of legal enforcement or interpretation (including against governments), although theorists of democracy tend to see it as better exercised through direct forms of political participation, such as elections. Neoliberal and market policy reformers, however, are inclined to view accountability as spontaneously generated through the disciplines arising from the multitude of well-informed individual consumer decisions found in competitive markets.

For some, these more private forms of governance and accountability should allow public interest goals to be imposed on (or contracted on) private actors. So, for example, in return for public funding and delegated freedoms, in some jurisdictions universities are required to promote social and 'fair' access in their admissions. More broadly, they are accountable and funded according to performance outputs and other evaluations. In such processes, private actors 'increasingly commit themselves to traditionally public goals as the price of access to lucrative opportunities to deliver goods and services, and to perform functions that might otherwise be provided directly by the state' (Freeman, 2006, p. 84).

Accountability regimes in higher education systems, nonetheless, tend to be hybrids or combinations of types of accountability principles and processes.

They involve state, market and professional (self-governing) forms and reflect the different control systems that are laid upon institutions. The different mechanisms of governance – state hierarchy, markets and networks – are associated with different accountability principles and features. Governance through public law, for example, involves control based on the state's ability to promulgate rules, to monitor for compliance and to apply sanctions when necessary. It is a hierarchical model of accountability. On the other hand, governance through markets results in accountability flowing from the discipline exercised on prices and quality from the aggregation of individual decisions by buyers and sellers in competitive conditions. However, governance by networks tends to operate through mutual monitoring, and accountability processes are organized through essentially self-regulatory mechanisms (Scott, 2006).

Nonetheless, accountability is considerably aided by the growth of explicitness, codification and formality as key governance principles. When processes and procedures, along with goals, plans and targets are written down, then it becomes more possible to evaluate and monitor activities and to take corrective action where compliance is not occurring. This action may be undertaken in a variety of ways, from legal sanctions to persuasion (Carey, 2010; Stensaker, 2011).

Finally, the practices of the university classroom, historically exercised in splendid isolation – and unchallenged authority – by individual academics, is giving way to forms of digital and online learning which strongly conduces team teaching and accountability. As McClusky and Winter (2012, p. 75) note, 'the digital classroom leaves a fingerprint of the activities of an entire class inside a public document in a way that the physical, traditional classroom was never capable of accomplishing'.

Digital courses map all interactions between academic and student that enables outside evaluation and appraisal, not least comparatively over many courses. Moreover, academics are becoming 'prisoners' of an electronic, software/hardware-driven administrative regime in institutions – integrating virtually all student related information requirements – that has a driving compulsion of its own. Rather than being undermined solely by managerialism, individual academic autonomies are also being gradually whittled away by the digital reorganization of university and college administrations and their data requirements.

Principal–agent approaches to organizational autonomy and accountability

Recent moves in higher education systems to an emphasis on institutional, rather than individual or communitarian, autonomy and the concomitant developments of formal accountability requirements, have found explanation in principal–agent theory. Enders, de Boer and Weyer (2013), for example, point out the advantages to governments (as principals) of devolving more autonomy to universities (as agents) as part of a new modality of strengthened principal control.

In this view, the local knowledge possessed by institutions is beyond the capacity of the state. Consequently, universities are better placed to exercise effective internal controls (not least over their staff) than are governments, provided, of course, universities and colleges develop the managerial and other capacities to enable them to do so.

In return, governments can shed responsibilities and delegate risks to universities, provided again, of course, that institutions are incentivized to exercise such responsibilities. As principals lack the full knowledge to tightly control agents – and always face the often conflicting interests of their agents, underpinned by the latter's ability 'at a distance' to operate more for themselves than their principals – financial, quality and general performance monitoring of the agent by the principal is necessary. Increasingly, market-based accountabilities also are encouraged or mandated in support of principals' control objectives. Competitive status and market dynamics between universities, for example, reinforce more bureaucratic or legalistic types of accountability being exercised by principals.

At the same time, however, principals have become more fragmented as governments have devolved functions to semi-independent regulatory and executive agencies. The state has become more disparate than before. Ministries other than for higher education, for example, start to become regulators of higher education (such as the Home Office in the United Kingdom for student immigration rules and related volume flows). Intermediary agencies, including for accreditation, funding and quality assurance also act on behalf of the government in a more pluralistic governing arrangement than found with a tightly cohesive unitary state.

University autonomy compared: Europe

As university leaderships have gained more autonomy, it is not surprising that they have supported calls that it be increased. The European Universities Association (EUA), for example, in its 2009 Prague Declaration, states that such developments would enable universities and colleges to respond more efficiently and effectively to the multiplying needs of knowledge economies. In a subsequent report on institutional autonomy in the same year, it stated that 'EUA strongly believes that increasing institutional autonomy is key to enabling universities to respond to these new demands... EUA reaffirms the crucial role of autonomy as a success factor for European universities in the next decade' (Estermann and Nokkala, 2009, p. 4).

Moreover, the European Commission (2006) and the European Council of the European Union (2007) support such views, with the former marking 'as a priority the creation of new frameworks for universities, characterized by improved autonomy and accountability'. Yet the report by Estermann and Nikkola reveals a rather patchwork development of such notions, with considerable diversity in framework conditions, regulation and implementation processes. As they remark, 'Although many studies have identified a trend away from direct state control towards indirect steering mechanisms (such as financial or quality assurance) public authorities still retain a central role in the regulation of the higher education system and, in a large number of countries, still exert direct control' (Estermann and Nikkola, 2009, p. 6).

Moreover, in their consideration of the various dimensions of autonomy – organizational, financial, staffing and academic – it is clear that while the study observes a movement in general terms towards university autonomy throughout Europe, this is uneven. Additionally, even where formal autonomy exists, there are often major disconnects with the actual practices on the ground, including where increased accountability requirements have blunted university freedoms.

Scientific autonomy and its impact on regulatory governance in higher education

A key organizing feature for universities and colleges found historically, perhaps more in the United States, the United Kingdom, Australia and New Zealand than Continental Europe, is the notion that the role of the state should be sufficiently liberal democratic and pluralist to enable the higher education sector to operate relatively autonomously (as should other sectors, particularly those with strong professions). Particularly, a domain understanding in political culture in such democracies is that world-class research and science require social and political conditions that provide the individual and institutional freedoms essential for creativity and innovation.

Among influential mid-20th century advocates of such a position have been the philosopher Karl Popper (1945), with his notions of the necessity for 'open' or non-totalitarian societies to enable scientific progress to be made, based on refutation as a scientific method, and the social scientist Robert Merton (1942/96). For both Merton and Popper, there was an historical affinity between the critical rationalism ('organized scepticism' and 'disinterestedness') that underpins both well-conducted science and the processes of a properly functioning democracy (King, 2011, p. 423).

As a sociologist, Merton regarded science predominantly as a social institution. It involves recognized methods and accumulated knowledge, but above all it comprises interacting individuals and networks reproducing norms and standards that effectively are self-regulating and self-producing. Specifically, Merton asserts that the conditions of individual freedom, institutional autonomy and scientific and other forms of pluralist self-regulation that constitute key value systems in liberal democracies, are functional for reproducing high-quality science. The market as well as the state, if both become overly intrusive and prescriptive, can threaten the ideal of normative self-regulation.

The required academic community for both Merton and Popper resembles what Polanyi (1962) calls the political system of 'republics'. That is, it is not subverted or cramped by an over-intrusive state regulation or by commercialization and private objectives. Rather academic authority is determined by mutual, self-regulatory association.

As Ferlie, Musselin and Andresani (2008) note, even in contemporary times, where the state has become a major funder of the higher education system, the sector is still characterized by 'a high degree of autonomy and insulation from governmental steering...The German idealist tradition built around the Humboldtian model, and the American functionalist sociology of professions, both idealized this tradition' (p. 327). Ferlie et al. suggest that this conception relies on an ideology of academic freedom and strong faculty control over key work practices in both domains of research and teaching.

The United Kingdom

State-backed professional autonomy characterized the British system of higher education until well into the 1980s. Rather than government action and market forces, the major driver of the institutional framework of rules and incentives was the tradition of collegial governance and academic autonomy, in which the collective actions designed to assure academic standards were professional self-regulation, as found, for example, in the external examining system (Dill, 2005).

In comparison with Continental European societies, however, university self-regulation and state support for the professions was based more on close ties between institutional leaders and government, than formal incorporation of a professional academic occupation (King, 2007). Moreover, as chartered and mainly charitable bodies, universities were formally independent of government in a way not always found in Continental Europe.

The introduction of a body of higher education law in the 1980s and 1990s, however, which introduced stronger governmental regulatory frameworks for higher education, based on accountability to government, taxpayers, students and other perceived stakeholders, helped to reduce the formal autonomy of the universities (although, arguably, it increased the corporate freedoms of the newly created universities – the former local authority-maintained polytechnics). New legislation in the 1988 and the 1992 Education Acts created a more prescriptive instrument for government funding and provided for the external quality quality assessment of the university output by government-backed funding and oversight agencies (such as the Higher Education Funding Council for England – HEFCE – and, eventually, the Quality Assurance Agency – QAA – in particular).

Greater formal external accountability for universities was inevitable in the UK political climate of the 1980s and 1990s, when there was a broad turn away generally from governance reliance on professional and elite regulation and culture, to more transparent and numerical forms of public evaluation and democratic holding to account (King, 2007; Kogan and Hanney, 2000). Moreover, the UK system of higher education during these decades moved from being predominantly an elite to a much more mass sector, involving substantial increases in public expenditure and student numbers. This more costly taxpayer-funded environment also made it unlikely that traditional self-governing approaches could survive and be regarded as sufficient for accountability purposes.

Subsequently, statutory provisions, associated especially with funding, have given greater means of direction and influence to ministers. The longstanding discretions allowed to universities and their collegiate systems of academic governance have been whittled away by the introduction of external and often highly codified accountability procedures by government, funding agencies, the Research Councils and QAA. Consequently, relationships between the universities and the state have become increasingly formalized and 'regulated', replacing previous self-governance controls which operated mainly through informal networks. Now the relationship is characterized by greater wariness, procedure and transparency.

Nonetheless, the development of the higher education regulatory state in England, especially in recent years, has not been a straight line progression away from professional self-regulation to external state intervention. It is best characterized by regulatory oscillation and often patchwork design. The regulation regime contains both hierarchical and vertical controls, on the one hand, and continued reliance on self-regulation and normative professional codes on the other.

Despite the apparent intensification of the higher education regulatory state in England, the picture still reveals ambiguity and doubt about the appropriate balance between state direction and recognition of institutional autonomy. Although government administrations in the last two decades or so have sought to increase market competition, managerial authority and corporate identity for universities, ministers have shown no real inclination to abdicate responsibility for the provision of higher education within their territory. Indeed, scientific knowledge and high level skills are increasingly regarded as essential for a nation's general prosperity.

The higher education regulatory state in England is ambiguous because the government constantly recognizes that levels of creativity, innovation and scientific development upon which the state and economy rely would atrophy with over-formalistic, command-and-control regulation, unless it is tempered by the incorporation of professional peer review. Academic incorporation into such processes has been a key methodology for establishing the credibility of the overall approach.

Evaluative state

As we have noted, the direction of travel for higher education systems in Continental Europe has been rather different, as more direct forms of state interventionism have diminished and have become replaced by broader 'steering mechanisms' associated more with an 'Evaluative State' than a command-and-control one (Neave, 1988). It has been described as moving 'from dirigisme to supervision, from ex-ante control to ex-post evaluation, from rules to regulation' (Ferlie et al., p. 328). Moreover, in countries such as France, the state may have developed more, and stronger, relationships with the representatives of the academic profession than with higher education institutions... leading to a co-management of the system by the ministry and representatives of the profession (Ferlie et al., p. 329).

Nonetheless, Dill (in press) notes that the strong influence of the EU tradition of associating professional control and self-regulation with national associations in higher education governance studies, leads to an underplaying of the model of academic and collegial control at the institutional level found in the United Kingdom and the United States. Although managerialism in many countries has rather diminished the force of such a model, there are countries that have sought to encourage academic collegial control at the institutional level. Dill (2015) also makes the point that there are signs that the dominant individual professor role in some EU research universities is not precluding a voluntary relocation of academic authority in research doctoral education to the collegial university level.

The rise of the 'Evaluative State' (Neave, 2006, 2008) in the 1980s in Continental European countries, has been regarded as a 'pre-conditioner' for institutional autonomy, a transition stage where many issues concerning delegated responsibility are first tried out. Gradually institutional responsibility – leading to more 'corporate self-hood' by universities – becomes part of new contract, rather than an entitlement, undertaken with the state (Neave, 2009). The transition from well-established personal and positional autonomy, which was well-established in Western Europe, was 'to a formally expanded interpretation, as institutional autonomy was largely accompanied within the workings of the Evaluative State' (Neave, 2009, p. 4). The establishment of macro steering systems – based on goals of increased performance, quality of output and efficiency – is key to this change.

The Evaluative State, and more formalized corporate management and institutionalized freedom of universities, characterize the promulgation in the 1980s and 1990s of a form of governance good practice applicable to a wide range of public service systems and not just higher education (King, 2009).

The New Public Management

We have referred to some of the 'special' features of higher education, not least its history of academic collegiality, and individual and professional freedom, that distinguish its relationship to the state in comparison to most other public sectors. We have also described the state's reliance on universities for scientific innovation and creativity. Yet changes in these state-university relationships have occurred and we have suggested that these are informed by broader regulatory and governance dynamics in the wider society. In this sense, the NPM and its impact on higher education systems, is an example of a governance model that has become both globally and comparatively institutionalized (see also the chapter by Broucker and De Wit).

Marginson and van der Wende (2007) suggest that the techniques of the NPM reflect the processes of systemic and institutional reform generally being conducted throughout the world in response to globalization. In their view,

> the templates of the new public management include the modelling of national systems as economic markets; government-steered competition between institutions, and executive-steered competition between academic units; part devolution of responsibility for administering and often for raising finances; incentives to link with business and industry; performance measures and output-based funding; and relations with funding agencies and managers based on quasi-corporate forms such as contracts, accountability and audit.
>
> (2007: 8–9)

Broadly, the NPM refers to the greater application of private sector instruments across a range of public services (not just higher education). This occurs in the context of reduced governmental scope and size, including reshaped bureaucracies that generally demarcate operational from strategic functions. Additional characteristics include more quasi-independent and independently managed agencies, the introduction of competition through internal markets, the growth of public–private partnerships and the more powerful use of performance management and evaluation techniques.

Apart from broader efforts to reduce an overburdened welfare state and to resist ever-accumulating responsibilities accruing to it, the NPM may be regarded as part of a wider regulatory effort by governments to restrict the power and influence of 'producer' groups, including professional associations, seen as at least potentially inimical to wider consumer, client and public interests. Consequently, increased managerial controls and institutional autonomy aim to reduce the political and policy powers of organized academics by enrolling a new cadre of managerial leaders in universities and colleges to assume responsibility for internal control and for taking key strategic and funding decisions.

Nonetheless, it could be argued that professional self-regulation has been weakened by individual competitiveness and in-fighting, as well as a reluctance to strengthen the processes of collegial and peer review at departmental and institutional levels. Hood (2004: 198), for example, notes that the debilitation of 'mutuality' or self-regulation in higher education is not solely down to governmental reforms, but rather has changed its form. That is, there has been a move away from 'mutual co-existence' among autonomous scholars to more 'peer review of performance in teaching and research'.

In similar vein, Enders, de Boer and Wayer (2013) argue that increased autonomy policies are not aimed at weakening the state but relieving it of myriad micro responsibilities. This enables it to broadly steer while delegating responsibility for herding academic and others into line through strengthened local managerialism. They refer to 'regulatory autonomy' as capturing 'the use of organizational autonomy as a tool of a new regime of control' (Enders et al., 2013: 9).

In the Dutch case, for example, 'autonomy policies for strengthening managerial discretion and internal control of universities are combined with regulatory policies for external control that steer organizational choices...and aimed at aligning universities more closely with government goals' (p. 9). Rather than the state stepping back, in this view there is a marked move away from longstanding beliefs in university autonomy 'that are built on institutional trust and linked to professional autonomy...to a new organizational autonomy (p. 5)'. Consequently, rather than the state directly threatening individual or personal autonomy, it is a new breed of corporate managers and administrators who provide the greatest challenges to it.

Governmentality

A key social science understanding of the causes and purposes of the NPM is found in the 'governmentality' literature that has developed around the work of Foucault, and this focuses attention on the many different ways in which power is exercised in society through a host of agencies, apparatuses, institutions and architectures. The term 'governmentality' fuses the idea of government and mentality and focuses particularly on the view that any act of governance is itself self-governing and must take account of the self-regulating order of things (O'Malley, 2004, 2008).

In this view, the aim of government gradually has shifted away from a focus simply on command and obedience, towards exploring how self-regulating capabilities may be harnessed to wider governmental goals. On the one hand, this makes government more difficult, dealing with more complex levels than with straight-line command and control instruments, and requires recognition of the limits to its influence; yet, on the other hand, enrolling society's self-regulatory capabilities offers more knowledgeable and efficient forms of state authority.

In this way, liberal governance is no longer understood as constraining or constituting forms of natural liberty but as enabling a new yet artificial liberty. Individuals and organizations, such as universities, are empowered to manage themselves – but as a technique of government.

Accountability and the risk university

The 'Better Regulation' agenda that has strongly influenced governments and policy-makers internationally, particularly encouragement of risk-based approaches for regulating universities, may be regarded as further recent evidence of increased formalism in higher education governance. Risk-based regulation, for example, is regarded by some governments as a way of rebalancing institutional autonomy and accountability processes within a context of also encouraging university entrepreneurialism, especially on the global (competitive) stage. For example, 'less risky' institutions are expected to experience lighter-touch quality accountability, in return for which they should feel freer to focus more intently on enterprise and innovation.

Risk-based frameworks for the external quality assurance of universities in Australia and England, too, are examples where increased explicitness is introduced to enable the risk appetites of regulators to be more transparent than hitherto and to constrain any 'red-tape' or over-bureaucratic tendencies by regulatory agencies.

Although all governments profess full commitment to transparency and accountability, in some instances approaches to higher education have evidenced a more nuanced perspective by Ministers. The UK Coalition Government for example, formed in 2010, in devising policies for higher education in England has been wary of some of the consequences of accountability demands for entrepreneurial risk-taking in universities and colleges. That is, the rise of the 'risk university' heightens the possibility that institutions will respond to wider accountability demands and performance judgements by recoiling from taking any risk at all and losing global competitiveness and innovation appetite.

In this view, universities appear more challenged by risks than ever – legal, reputation, funding. security, ethical – and particularly by extending processes of external evaluation, such as rankings, quality assurance and professional accreditation. These growing external constraints on institutions – which positively are aimed at improving accountability, not least in the eyes of the public – nonetheless have the potential to make universities highly risk averse. There is a danger for policy-makers that universities will become increasingly reluctant to undertake the entrepreneurialism and innovation that governments wish them to adopt, and for which institutional autonomy is intended. That is, accountability, rather than being complementary to institutional autonomy, always contains the perverse danger of being antithetical to it.

To counteract this negative consequence, managed risk-taking, rather than mere risk avoidance, has become the governmental policy objective in England. This is captured by the government's introduction of a policy of risk-based external quality assurance. The aim of risk-based regulation is to optimize risk tolerance and regulatory proportionality in both universities and their regulators – accepting that some risk is inevitable and can be ignored – rather than seeking to eliminate all adverse organizational outcomes. The assumption is that it is sub-optimal for the sector, and for the universities, if regulators and governors try and eliminate all risk – including the reputation risk that arises from accountability processes imposed in the interests of taxpayers and students/consumers.

Consequently, risk-based regulation aims at focusing regulatory attention on those parts of the sector that are regarded as the riskiest. In this way, regulatory attention on well-attested good performers can be reduced, allowing more enterprising (and autonomous) activity to occur without universities constantly looking back at the accountability consequences.

The aim is not to apply a fixed set of rules in a standardized manner, as through standard and cyclical institutional review visits to institutions, but to be selective and focused on risk. In turn, the external regulation of institutions is intended to be of a higher quality, not least as regulators such as external quality assurance agencies are required to be more transparent in their approach. Essentially, governments introduce risk-based regulation to regulate the regulators – to constrain administrative or bureaucratic power and to prevent them passing on their 'red tape' proclivities to their regulated clients – and to get them more formally to justify what they do and thus to improve their decision-making.

Accountability overload and an attempt to rein back on its demands, at least for high performers, by releasing them from at at least some regulatory constraints, reflects a desire by some governments to constrain external bureaucracy in higher education. It may be regarded as part of a broader European and worldwide public policy movement over the last decade or more to improve regulation by placing accountability demands into a wider consideration of public policy goals for higher education.

Asian universities

So far, we have discussed the relationships between institutional autonomy and the state – and notions of accountability – through US and western European perspectives, although recognizing key differences between countries, not least between those of the United Kingdom and some major Continental ones. Marginson (2010) describes how many of the 'Confucian' nations, notably those in East Asia, are helping to make the Asia Pacific a global force in higher education, as student numbers and research grow dramatically to match those levels found in the region's leader – Japan – and elsewhere since the 1970s.

In terms of governance, however, academic freedom and autonomy appear strongly constrained by a Party-led state in a number of these countries, raising doubts about the ability of such countries to generate cultures of openness and criticality. Nonetheless, Marginson observes a striking expansion in scientific output in the Confucian systems in recent years. A number of major Asia-Pacific countries, such as China, Singapore, Taiwan, Hong Kong and South Korea, appear to take the view that resources, rather than type of governance system, count for more in facilitating high-quality research. Kim (2011), in her discussion of South Korea, for example, despite the granting of formal enhanced autonomy to institutions, including a capacity to offer more differentiated salaries and the creation of an entrepreneurial culture and visionary leadership, notes the strong reluctance of governments in South Korea to actually let go of important areas of institutional decision-making, despite repeated promises to do so.

In China, there has been considerable governmental resources for research, yet a culture of institutional and individual autonomy in the universities has barely developed. The influence of the Communist Party-led state remains strong, not least in appointments to senior administrative positions, including university presidents, and in the authorization of institutional evaluation plans, funding allocations, curricula and faculty size (McGregor, 2010). Publications and research activities can be closely inspected by the state. In China, 'shared governance' between academics and university leaders is weakly practiced in comparison with other countries (Cummings et al., 2010).

Undoubtedly China's higher education development in recent years is not remarkably different from that found in many other countries, including liberal democracies. That is, mass expansion accompanied by privatization, decentralization and institutional concentration has been the order of the day (Liu and Wang, 2010). Nonetheless, although central government in China is moving away from strict command-and-control of its leading research universities and towards utilization of some of the meta-evaluations and accountabilities found in the NPM forms of governance found in the West, particular difficulties are presented in responding to demands for institutional autonomy and academic freedom within a system that has been traditionally strongly Party-controlled. Even so, swapping state control for the managerial direction associated with the NPM may not provide the conditions for scientific freedom desired by many academics in China.

Global science

The apparent subjugation, if not actual elimination, of academic processes of coordination and self-governance by formalized state policies of institutional autonomy and moves to more regulative interventions is nonetheless challenged by aspects of globalization. Global science especially remains strongly characterized by self-regulatory and collaborative processes found in networks that stretch across time and space. 'Global science occurs largely behind the back of the nation state, despite powerful political rhetoric espousing the competitive economic necessity of scientific nationalism in the knowledge economy' (King, 2011: 418).

Despite the claims of Popper, Merton and others that an open meritocratic society, based on institutions of freedom, allows processes of empirical refutation to dispel tendencies to orthodoxy and dogma, resources and relationships in global science appear to be subject to forms of cumulative inequality and preferential attachment that benefit elite scientists through traditional processes of reproductive hierarchy (Wagner, 2008). National states have difficulty in shaping or steering such hierarchies or exercising much influence over the autonomies of individual scientists, whose freedoms appear to have been enormously reinforced by the communications and technology revolutions that have underpinned globalization.

Emergent global science enhances the opportunities for researchers to undertake collaborative projects across territorial boundaries outside the direct control of national governments. As such it reinforces the individual autonomy and self-governing features of an earlier academic age. A feature of global forms of governance is often their private and self-regulatory nature. In science, global networks and their associated processes of standardization have begun to exceed the power of governmental scientific nationalism.

While the latter model regards scientific outcomes as national assets to benefit a country's economic and military objectives – an approach that emerged strongly in the decades after the ending of the Second World War in 1945 – global science is characterized by a self-governing and self-reproducing form of coordination that is highly unequal in its national consequences. It has developed strongly in the last two decades or so, not least with the ending of the Cold War between the United States and the Soviet Union (including their respective allies) and the widespread communicative use of the Internet. Wagner (2008) notes that, in the sixteenth and seventeenth centuries, as well as now, scientific coordination and discovery are characterized by scientists exchanging ideas as part of a shared search for knowledge. However, in the current age networks have a technical dimension (the Internet) as well as a social one.

Governments exercise less control over science now than a few decades ago, when high-cost 'big science' predominated. A preponderance of worldwide scientific joint ventures is formed by person-to-person projects rather by trans-ministerial agreement. Mainly, these are arranged collectively by individuals through well-established professional and disciplinary linkages. The object is to create a research project of discovery founded on complementary capabilities and shared curiosities. Finance, however, is usually derived from national and similar public funding agencies that are unable or unwilling to exercise too strong a constraint on who is enrolled to work on the project, especially when elite scientists are involved, once projects have been approved.

National priorities set by governments also appear to aid networked global science of a more informal kind in that national research and innovation agendas display a remarkable convergence around a few areas, such as biochemistry, nanotechnology, genetics and the environment, rather than reflecting local concerns and circumstances, thus facilitating worldwide scientific 'clustering'. Modern science is thus an emergent transnational system (it reproduces itself through the interdependence of countless individual actions rather than by sovereign direction).

Wagner (2008: 1) provides considerable evidence to support the view that the focus of science has moved from the national to global level and that 'self-organizing networks that span the globe are the most notable features of science today'. Scientists are collaborating across the globe not because they are ordered by government to do so but because this is often the best way to utilize different perspectives, resources and knowledge to conduct the high-quality science that satisfies both individual curiosity and the career desire for esteem, reputation and also scientific community.

Such a picture contrast sharply with the dominant paradigm for knowledge and innovation in most of the advanced countries in the second half of the 20th century, which Wagner terms 'scientific nationalism' and where science is conceived as both governmental and national property. In the United States, Europe and Japan, large federal and regional agencies came into existence after 1945 to manage the relationship between the scientific and political communities and to introduce regulations, standards, funds and institutions to govern such relationships.

However, the recent movement to a globally based, networked science is controlled effectively by researchers rather than by governments. Global science is self-reproducing in that its structure is formed by interacting and communicative researchers who use such structures as the basis for their own action as autonomous agents and who, through their scientific collaborations founded on worldwide views as to how science should be governed and with what precepts, thereby sustain such self-governing structures. The global alliances of scientists, like university league tables, provide reputation and informational short-cuts within a world of exploding knowledge and potential contacts. They are 'status-signalling' devices, creating a basis of trust that facilitates confidence in exchanging information on the foundation of common norms.

Global science is thus both open and bounded. Reputation provides a heuristic to 'order' rapidly growing knowledge, and disciplinary and institutional rankings help do this by reinforcing existing worldwide patterns of scientific opportunity and inequality. Although scientific networks remain collegiate, insider-understood and protected (Kealey, 2009; Wagner, 2008), and while obscure processes and the high levels of tacit knowledge found in scientific experimentation and outputs continue to maintain strong exclusionary tendencies, these are not the only mediating characteristics. Strong norms of autonomy, objectivity, testability and peer judgement provide key standardizing features across the global scientific network.

New developments

The role of ideas, policy learning and modelling – and processes of dialogue and deliberation – appear increasingly significant in a globalizing world. Such processes, in discussing the higher education regulatory state, not least the changing relationships between the state and universities based around notions of institutional autonomy and accountability, appear to lead to a convergence or even an isomorphism between national systems. A variety of institutional processes help to account for such apparent homogeneity across the world. The role of international organizations in shaping debate over best-practice governance arrangements are influential, as are undoubtedly meetings of national policy-makers in various bilateral and other forums.

Nonetheless, as models travel and become adopted by others, they also become domesticated and adapted, not least as political leaders meet objectors with vested interests in the status quo. Moreover, notions such as autonomy and accountability are interpreted rather than simply adopted and, in turn, various global templates are always undergoing revision and modification. As we have seen with various Asian higher education systems, such as in South Korea, formal adoption of a governance model is not quite the same thing when it comes to substantive implementation and delivery.

Nonetheless, some models, such as the NPM, attract and build-up a kind of 'network power'. 'Network power' characterizes the 'pulling' power of universalizing or dominant models or standards (Grewal, 2008). That is, some norms such as those around institutional autonomy, transparency and accountability may reach levels of adoption by a critical mass of countries and others, particularly in the global age, such that a 'tipping point' is reached and widespread agreement to follow by current non-adopters quickly ensues.

There is an increasing tendency for certain standards and governance models to displace competing and incompatible models by exercising a 'magnetizing' or 'snowballing' effect that generates an increasing global dominance. These effects take place as a certain level of adherents to a model is reached. This makes it increasingly difficult for non-adopters to resist. If they do so, they feel increasingly marginalized from the international policy community that provides the critical social networking that they value.

Nonetheless, states and national control cultures retain the ability to shape and reinterpret models that nonetheless they feel strongly pressured internationally to adopt. Institutional autonomy and accountability appear globally unstoppable normative apparatuses on the surface – in practice, however, myriad national variations remain.

Also, models of autonomy and accountability in higher education are likely to be disrupted by the digital revolution. Technological innovation has the capacity to sharply change individual and collective behaviour in organizations and sectors (Ostrom, 1990). Recent developments in online and blended learning are impacting on the traditionally integrated skills of university and college teachers ('unbundling'), with important consequences for local and wider collegial governance systems. Traditional concepts of autonomy and accountability, at both the individual and collective level, undoubtedly will continue to be marked by dynamism and change (Bowen, 2013).

Conclusion: Future research directions

In considering fruitful future research directions, which would enhance the study of institutional autonomy and accountability in higher education, two particular, and to date rather overlooked, themes would be invaluable.

First, examining the consequences of the new technology, including its associated data management systems and analytics, for higher education governance. Bowen (2013) provides an exemplary account of the possibilities for such enquiries but more research work, not least in countries other than the United States, is needed. Key questions are: Which public policies help to proactively shape technological innovation and benefit learning? How best can we understand both the governance of change in higher education and the implications of socio-technical change for governance arrangements, not least the self-regulatory and autonomous practices of university academics?

Second, considerations of institutional autonomy, accountability and state 'supervision' of universities and colleges in a globalized age must take fuller account of science and research activities and practices. Whatever may be happening in learning and teaching, there is evidence that individual and peer control of science may be increasing at the expense of state direction, not least because of the impact of the Internet. Higher education research has often neglected scientific activity and left it to the curiosity of other social sciences. This impoverishes our understanding of autonomy and accountability in higher education and requires remedying as soon as possible.

References

Bourdieu, P. (1990) Homo Academicus (Cambridge: Polity Press).
Bowen, W. (2013) Higher Education in the Digital Age (Princeton, NJ: Princeton University Press).
Carey, K. (2010) Accountability in American Higher Education (Basingstoke: Palgrave Macmillan).
Clark, B. (1983) The Higher Education System: Academic Organization in Cross-National Perspective (Berkeley: University of California Press).
Commission of the European Communities (2006) Delivering on the Modernization Agenda for Universities: Education, Research and Innovation. COM 208 final, May.
Commission of the European Universities (2007) The European Research Area: New Perspectives. COM 161 final, April.
Cummings, W., Locke, W. and D. Fisher (2010) 'Faculty perceptions of government and management', International Higher Education, 60(Summer), 3–5.
Dill, D. D. (in press) 'Academic quality and academic responsibility: a critical reflection on collegial governance', in P. John and J. Fanghanel (eds) Dimensions of Marketization in Higher Education (New York and London: Routledge).
Dill, D. D (2005) 'The degradation of the academic ethic: teaching, research and the renewal of professional self-regulation', in R. Barnett (ed) Reshaping the University: New Relationships between Research, Scholarship and Teaching (Maidenhead: SRHE/Open University Press).
Dowdle, M. (2006) 'Introduction', in M. Dowdle (ed) Public Accountability: Designs, Dilemmas, and Experiences (Cambridge: Cambridge University Press).
Enders, J., de Boer, H. and E. Weyer (2013) 'Regulatory autonomy and performance: the reform of higher education re-visited', Higher Education, 65, 5–23.
Estermann, T. and T. Nokkala (2009) University Autonomy in Europe 1: Exploratory Study (Brussels: European Universities Association).
Ferlie, E., Musselin, C. and L. Andresani (2008) 'The "Steering" of higher education systems: a public management perspective', Higher Education, 56(3), September, 325–348.
Freeman, J. (2006) 'Extending public accountability through privatization: from public law to publicization', in M. Dowdle (ed) Public Accountability: Designs, Dilemmas, and Experiences (Cambridge: Cambridge University Press).
Grewal, D. (2008) Network Power: The Social Dynamics of Globalization (New Haven, CT and London: Yale University Press).
Hood, C. (2004) 'Conclusion: making sense of controls over government', in C. Hood, O. James, B. G. Peters and C. Scott (eds) Controlling Modern Government: Variety, Commonality and Change (pp. 185–205) (Cheltenham: Edward Elgar).
Kealey, T. (2009) Sex, Science and Profits (London: Vintage Books).
Kim, T. (2011) 'Globalization and higher education in South Korea: towards ethnocentric internationalization or global commercialization of higher education?', in R. King,

S. Marginson and R. Naidoo (eds) Handbook on Globalization and Higher Education (pp. 286–305) (Cheltenham: Edward Elgar).

King, R. (2007) The Regulatory State in an Age of Governance: Soft Words and Big Sticks (Basingstoke: Edward Elgar).

King, R. (2009) Governing Universities Globally: Organizations, Regulation and Rankings (Cheltenham: Edward Elgar).

King, R. (2011) 'Governing knowledge globally', in R. King, S. Marginson and R. Naidoo (eds) Handbook on Globalization and Higher Education (pp. 415–437) (Cheltenham: Edward Elgar).

Kogan, M. and S. Hanney (2000) Reforming Higher Education (London: Jessica Kingsley).

Liu, J. and X. Wang (2010) 'Expansion and differentiation in Chinese higher education', International Higher Education, 60(August), 7–8.

Marginson, S. (2010) 'Confucian values', Times Higher Education, 17 June.

Marginson, S. and M. van der Wende (2007) Globalization and Higher Education (Paris: OECD).

McCluskey, R. L. and M. L. Winter (2012) The Idea of the Digital University: Ancient Traditions, Disruptive Technologies and the Battle for the Soul of Higher Education (Washington, DC: Westphalia Press).

McGregor, R. (2010) The Party: The Secret World of China's Communist Rulers (London: Penguin).

Merton, R. (1942/1996) On Social Structure and Science (Chicago: University of Chicago Press).

Naidoo, R. (2004) 'Fields and institution strategy: Bourdieu on the relationship between higher education, inequality and society', British Journal of Sociology of Education, 25(4), 457–471.

Neave, G. (1988) 'On being economical with university autonomy: being an account of the retrospective joys of a written constitution', in M. Tight (ed) Academic Freedom and Responsibility (pp. 31–48) (Buckingham: Open University Press).

Neave, G. (2006) 'The evaluative state and Bologna: old wine in new bottles or simply the ancient practice of coupage', Higher Education Forum, 3(March), 27–46.

Olsen, J. (2007) 'The institutional dynamics of the European university', in P. Maassen and J. Olsen (eds) University Dynamics and European Integration (pp. 25–54) (Dordrecht: Springer).

Neave, G. (2008) 'From guardian to overseer: trends in institutional autonomy, governance, and leadership', in A. Amaral (ed) Reforma do Ensino Superior (Lisbon: Conselho Nacional de Educacao).

Neave, G. (2009) 'Institutional autonomy 2010–2020. A tale of Elan – two steps back to make one very large leap forward', in B. Kehm, J. Huisman and B. Stensaker (eds) The European Higher Education Area: Perspectives on a Moving Target (Rotterdam: Sense Publishers).

O'Malley, P. (2004) Risk, Uncertainty and Government (Oxon: Routledge-Cavendish).

O'Malley, P. (2008) 'Governmentality and risk', in J. Zinn (ed) Social Theories of Risk and Uncertainty (Oxford: Blackwell).

Ostrom, E. (1990) Governing the Commons (Cambridge, MA: Cambridge University Press).

Parsons, T. and G. Platt (1973) The American University (Boston: Harvard University Press).

Polanyi, K. (1962) 'The republic of science: its political and economic theory', Minerva, 1, 54–74.

Popper, K. (1945) The Open Society and Its Enemies (London: Routledge).
Scott, C. (2006) 'Spontaneous accountability', in M. Dowdle (ed) Public Accountability: Designs, Dilemmas and Experiences (Cambridge: Cambridge University Press).
Stensaker, B. (2011) Accountability in Higher Education: Global Perspectives on Trust and Power (London: Routledge).
Wagner, C. (2008) The New Invisible College: Science for Development (Washington, DC: Brookings Institution Press).

27
Quality Assurance in Higher Education

James Williams and Lee Harvey

Introduction

Since the 1980s, quality assurance in higher education has grown dramatically, has come to affect every level of the sector and has become an accepted and integral part of academic life. Saarinen (2010, p. 55) has observed that 'quality has turned from a debatable and controversial concept to an everyday issue in higher education'. Concomitantly, quality assurance has become, as Rosa and Amaral (2014, p. 9) describe it, a 'professionalized' and internationally networked activity. However, as higher education faces increasingly difficult challenges of globalization and marketization, so too quality assurance becomes increasingly complex. At the same time, the literature on quality assurance has also increased in scale and complexity. How are we to make sense of it all? This chapter reviews the key research relating to quality assurance in higher education. The focus of the chapter will be research conducted since the early 1990s, when quality became a key concern of the sector, what Newton has referred to (2002) as the 'quality revolution'. However, earlier work, will be cited where relevant.

The chapter will inevitably range widely but build on work by Harvey and Williams (2010a, 2010b) that explored key themes of research published in the journal *Quality in Higher Education*. This was the first time that such a broad range of research on aspects of quality and quality assurance had been thematized. The review identified a wide range of themes, notably researchers' frequent attempts to define quality in the sector; external quality assurance processes; internal quality assurance processes; stakeholder perceptions of quality processes; and the overall impact of quality assurance. That this review provided a useful framework for understanding the broad range of research in the field is indicated by the number of references to it, although it was really intended as a stock-taking exercise on the journal's fifteenth anniversary.

Key to understanding quality assurance in higher education is how quality is defined and this issue is at the heart of much work in the field. The chapter begins with an analysis of the ways in which commentators have defined quality in higher education with a view to identifying the extent to which quality assurance and enhancement are dichotomized. The section builds on the seminal definition of quality in higher education by Harvey and Green (1993) and explores the extent to which the notions in this work have influenced following definitions and understanding of quality. The notion of quality as transformation is clearly important here and will inform analysis of the literature on quality processes at every level from module evaluation to institutional development.

The chapter explores how researchers see such definitions playing out in practice. Following Harvey and Williams (2010a, 2010b), existing research largely falls into two categories: those focusing on external quality monitoring processes and those that examine internal mechanisms to assure and improve quality. This takes account of work in different countries, work that crosses international boundaries and explores how quality models cross cultural boundaries. While there is a huge amount of material relating to quality assurance procedures, researchers seem reticent to question their wider impact. This chapter identifies and analyses research that explores the impact of quality assurance regimes. It identifies the different ways in which commentators measure the impact of quality assurance. It explores whether commentators believe that the huge expansion and investment in quality assurance has been worthwhile.

Finally, the chapter explores the extent to which commentators believe a 'quality culture' has been developed in contemporary higher education. It identifies different understandings of the term and whether this is useful as a way of monitoring and improving what we do in higher education. It explores the extent to which existing research indicates that academic staff and students themselves actually engage with quality assurance processes in a meaningful way and whether quality is in any way regarded as a tool for transformation of the sector.

Defining quality

Underpinning any understanding of quality assurance is our chosen understanding of quality itself and so we must start with definitions. For Harvey (2006a), defining quality is integral to understanding quality assurance: 'quality is the conceptual tool through which [quality assurance is] implemented'. It is therefore vital to underpin any discussion of quality assurance with a definition of quality in higher education and much space has, unsurprisingly, been given to it. Defining quality in higher education is, of course, fraught with difficulties: the discourse of quality tends to associate quality with assessment and produces and reproduces received ideas of quality (Saarinen, 2005).

The search for a working definition of quality in higher education

Early attempts to define quality explicitly largely appear to have failed, following Pirsig, who famously stated in *Zen and Art of Motorcycle Maintenance*, which largely focused on quality in higher education, 'even though quality cannot be defined, you know what it is' (Pirsig, 1974). For many years, academic commentators were content to accept this implicit understanding of quality. Indeed, Vroejenstijn, for example, argued (1991), that 'it is so hard to define quality in higher education that we should stop bothering'. However, defining quality in a way that was both explicit and operationalizable was vital in the early 1990s because quality assurance was developing rapidly.

Harvey and Green (1993) were the first to reach a workable definition of quality in higher education. Their argument that quality in higher education can be categorized as exception, perfection, value for money, fitness for purpose and transformation highlighted the multifaceted nature of quality in the sector. Harvey's later (2006a) refinement of the earlier categorization emphasizes that transformation is at the heart of quality assurance. This definition has proved influential and many articles that deal specifically with issues around defining quality in the context of higher education all build on it. In some cases, these categories are tested against contemporary perceptions and remain. Even where new definitions are posited, the Harvey and Green (1993) definition remains the central reference point for many researchers.

Quality in higher education: a contested definition

However, several authors, while positive about the Harvey and Green (1993) definition, have argued that quality remains a contested concept in the context of higher education: for Tam (2001), the split was between production models versus total quality experience approach. Van Kamenade *et al.* (2008), attempted to draw key themes from all the many definitions of quality in higher education, including those of Harvey and Green. Some researchers on quality in higher education contexts even fail to mention Harvey and Green at all, suggesting either, at best, lack of familiarity with their work or, at worse, pure dismissal of a social science approach.

Research has consistently indicated that stakeholders tend to identify three particular categories as dominant over many years: value for money, fitness for purpose and transformation (Cheng, 2014; Melrose, 1998). Interestingly, very little research, if any, has been conducted into the extent that the Harvey and Green categorization has actually affected quality assurance policy at institutional, national or even supranational levels.

Whose quality?

A key issue that the Harvey and Green definition highlights is the different perspectives that different stakeholders have on quality. Harvey's early research in the field (Harvey *et al.*, 1992) explored student's perceptions of quality and the principle that all stakeholders should contribute to the quality assurance process underpinned much further work on student satisfaction surveys. A large amount of research has since been conducted by a range of scholars that explores the perceptions of students on various aspects of the quality of their higher education experience. Attention has also turned to academic staff and their perceptions of the quality process. Newton's work (2000, 2002) on academic resistance to quality processes that has been influential ever since. More recently, Cheng (2014) has identified similar resistance to quality processes and for similar reasons: they feel no ownership for the quality assurance process (see Harvey, 2007b).

Different stakeholders have different perceptions of what quality actually means (Iacovidou, Gibbs and Zopiatis, 2009). Those people responsible for implementing quality assurance may not be aware of an underlying philosophy of quality assurance but they are nonetheless affected by it (Melrose, 1998). While there has been much research that explores the perceptions of quality and quality assurance of students and academic staff, there has been remarkably little that looks at those of administrative staff responsible for the implementation of quality processes at institutional level. What is clear is that stakeholder perspectives are recognized as being important but that they are not static: it is important that researchers continue to explore the changing perspectives of different stakeholders in the light of changing socio-political context.

Defining quality assurance and quality enhancement

While much has been done to define quality in higher education, the term 'quality assurance' is used frequently without definition. Harvey (2006a) observes that quality assurance is 'about checking the quality of a process or outcomes. Purposes of quality assurance include compliance, control, accountability and improvement'. Blackmur (2010) argues that quality assurance has not 'been adequately conceptualised', arguing that 'it means to guarantee, to give comfort that, ex ante, some defined result will happen if certain antecedents are in place and, *ex post*, that, if it has happened, this is because these antecedents were in place'.

Similarly, the term 'quality enhancement' is used frequently but without clear definition. Indeed, it is often used interchangeably with the term 'quality improvement'. For Brown (2014), quality enhancement 'describes the improvement of pedagogy through information and ideas from research, benchmarking, quality assurance, and other exchanges of experience and practice'.

Quality assurance: A neo-colonialist activity?

Quality assurance models are well known for being transplanted from one country to another with surprisingly little adaptation. This approach assumes that definitions of quality are generic but very little work has explored the veracity of this assumption. Some of the research already undertaken indicates western cultural dominance of quality assurance. For example, Idrus (2003) highlighted negative reactions in some developing countries to the importation of quality models, while noting an assumption that quality assurance models are frequently transplanted from 'developed' countries to 'developing' countries. Others, such as Lemaitre (2002), have argued that the importation of quality assurance models is little more than a facet of cultural imperialism. It is important to reflect, with Singh (2010), on whether dominant quality assurance models are those of the current globally economic powers, whether we should see worldwide quality assurance in terms of 'centres' and 'peripheries'.

History and development of external quality assurance

While definition of quality has exercised many scholars, the general history and development of quality assurance in higher education has attracted limited attention. The development of the earliest quality assurance system in higher education, which is the external examiner system in the United Kingdom, has been explored by Silver (1996). There has been important work on the development of quality assurance worldwide (e.g. Campbell and Rosnayi, 2002), of quality assurance agencies (Woodhouse, 2004) and of national quality assurance systems (Brown, 2014). However, descriptions of the general history and development of quality assurance are largely descriptive and rather limited as historical studies. Much more serious historical study of quality assurance is needed in which documentary sources are fully analysed and critically interpreted.

Theoretical and political origins of external quality assurance

The theoretical and political origins of external quality assurance have been explored to an even lesser degree. An early work that sought to explain the universities apparent acquiescence in the new quality assurance regime (Harker, 1995) argued that quality assurance (understood as controlling and challenging institutional autonomy) was a result of the prevailing Lyotardian postmodernism that took hold of the contemporary academy. The political origins of quality assurance in the United Kingdom have been identified by Harvey (2005), who placed them firmly in the neoliberal policies of the governments of the 1980s: for him, the concern of the Thatcher governments was with making universities accountable for public money and reducing the influence of local authorities. These studies are important in making a serious attempt at critiquing external quality assurance in historical and sociological contexts but only highlight the limited nature of systematic research in this area.

Dichotomizing quality assurance and enhancement

Over the last two decades, some scholars have identified a dichotomy between quality assurance and quality enhancement. Swinglehurst *et al.* (2008) provides a dichotomized view of quality assurance and enhancement in which quality assurance appears negatively as a top-down, teacher-focused system in opposition to a democratic, collaborative, learning-focused process. Arguably, this may be using the term 'quality assurance' as a proxy for the term 'quality compliance'. While it is arguable that it is easy to over emphasize this dichotomy, it is clear that such a distinction exists both in the minds of individual academic staff and at institutional level. For example, Filippakou and Tapper (2008) imply that there has been a split by arguing that a transition has been made from a focus on quality assurance to quality enhancement at institutional level.

However, other authors do not agree that there is a dichotomy between these two activities. Indeed, for authors such as Raban (2007), quality assurance and the quality enhancement are simply two elements in the same process and cannot be disconnected. As we have seen, Harvey (2006a) is clear on the matter: quality assurance is a process that includes both accountability and improvement. However, he does not make reference to quality enhancement. The implication here is that quality enhancement cannot take place without assurance. Further research is needed to explore the relationship between the two activities: both the perceptions of stakeholders and the performance of quality assurance itself.

Tension between accountability and improvement

Much clearer is the tension between accountability and improvement, and much of the critical work on quality assurance reflects on this tension. Amaral (2007) argues that accountability is traditionally more of a concern for governments, whereas universities have been more concerned with improvement. However, it is usually recognized as outlined by Harvey (2006a) that quality assurance is a process that includes accountability and improvement. The tension between the two was clearly of concern in the 1990s and much research recommended keeping accountability and improvement roles of external quality assurance agencies separate (Harvey and Williams, 2010a). The relationship between accountability and improvement has since become more nuanced. Massy *et al.* (2007) argued that enhancement and accountability can be combined and ensure quality assurance. Indeed, Danø and Stensaker (2007) argued that while much of the rhetoric has suggested a tug of war between accountability and improvement, they are not two ends of a single dimension but two dimensions that can be developed autonomously.

Not surprisingly, much work focuses on quality audit as a key activity of quality assurance agencies. The work in this area has highlighted positive aspects of the audit process. Dill (2000) argued that, as an accountability mechanism, it has forced institutions to take quality assurance seriously and put teaching and learning at the top of institutional agendas. Similarly, Woodhouse (2003) argued that external quality audit can augment an institution's ability to improve. However, Cheng (2009) is less positive, having found that some academics (in a UK-based study) perceive audit as a symbol of distrust of their professionalism.

Work on quality assurance around the turn of the millennium noted a concern with accreditation, which is one of the major outcomes of many national quality assurance systems (Van Damme, 2000). In the main, research has tended to highlight the cumbersome, controlling effect of accreditation systems (Faber and Huisman, 2003). In particular, early work has highlighted the threat posed by accreditation to improvement-focused quality assurance processes (Haakstad, 2001; Westerheijden, 2001). Indeed, Haakstad (2001) argued that if one must have accreditation it should be at the institutional not programme level, based on a flexible, but reinforced, audit method. This wise analysis, however, has subsequently been ignored in much of Europe and there have been costly and unnecessary programme accreditation schemes imposed, primarily by politicians, on the higher education sector in many countries (Harvey and Williams, 2010a). There is clearly much evaluation to be done to establish the extent to which early fears have been realized.

A shift towards transformative and experiential learning?

Several commentators have argued that there is a need for and shift towards transformative and experiential learning (Bramming, 2007; Harvey and Knight, 1996). Authors have explored a range of activity to inform effective improvement processes: engaging students in the improvement process; collecting student feedback on programmes; and explored potential for student engagement with curriculum design (Harvey and Williams, 2010b). However, these positive developments are overshadowed by increasingly instrumental attitudes of students (Dolnicar, 2005), teaching overload (McInnis, 2000) and increasing class size (Fearnley, 1995).

Trust and quality assurance

While the key appears to be balance between accountability and improvement, an essential element of this is the apparent dissolution of trust: an issue that recurs (Amaral and Rosa, 2010). Some of the work argues that external quality assurance needs to foster 'social capital' in and between academic institutions (Dill, 1995), an idea that has informed work by Leeuw (2002) that highlights the damage that game-playing among auditors can do to the quality assurance process. Arguably, however, the notion of trust is antithetical to quality assurance: Raban (2007) argues that audit culture in higher education, as in other public organizations, has attempted replace a system based on trust between professionals and public with one based on accountability and transparency. While this may be true, the issue has not been resolved and as quality assurance procedures continue to develop, the issue of trust will remain a core concern for further research at every level of the sector.

For some authors, the key to engaging academic staff with and improving quality is an institutional respect for their autonomy, through self-evaluation and highlighting the need for ownership of quality assurance by academic staff (Harvey and Williams, 2010a). A recurrent concern among commentators on quality assurance is that the processes do not match the expectations of academics. There have been repeated concerns about the artificiality of quality assurance processes in higher education. There is a need to replace a 'name and shame' approach with continuous quality improvement (Gosling and D'Andrea, 2001). Much research indicates that academic staff preference is for flexibility over control culture (Harvey and Williams, 2010a). This reinforces how important internal processes are and how, ultimately, it is what goes on routinely in institutions that impacts on quality.

For many academics, quality assurance is often seen as a burdensome extra, to be responded to through ritualized compliance, famously referred to by Newton (2000) as 'feeding the beast'. Indeed, Barrow (1999) argued that academics perform in ways they feel are required (what he calls 'dramaturgical performances') during peer-review events. Quality assurance fails to be a part of the everyday activity of academics because they perceive no real link between the quality of their academic work (teaching and research) and the performance embodied in quality assurance processes. Ownership of quality assurance is a concern here (Jacobs and Du Toit, 2006). Without this, so some commentators suggest, academic staff are likely to resist quality assurance processes within universities (Anderson, 2006; Newton, 2002).

The role of management

In all of this, the role of management and leadership in the development of effective quality assurance has been a consistent focus of research. Authors have argued that the response to the demands of external quality assurance requires strong leadership at all levels along with effective strategy rather than simply responding to audit findings (Gordon, 2002; Middlehurst, 1997). However, empowerment of academic staff is a key component in this (Tam, 1999). Harvey (2007b) observes, 'Leadership in a quality culture is inspirational rather than dictatorial. Leadership is at all levels in the institution and does not refer to just senior managers.'

Purposes of measuring

The role of performance indicators as quality instruments has been a consistent concern of commentators for many years. It is now well established that performance indicators are tools of accountability and are used for various political ends (Yorke, 1998). The use of unverifiable 'soft' data as tools for allocating resources was long ago critiqued by Ewell (1999) for being, simply, too vague a measure. Since then, much research has critiqued the use of indicators such as students' evaluations of their experience and graduate employment. In both these cases, several key issues have emerged and are key areas for further reflection.

Student feedback as a source of data

Student feedback on their own experience has been identified as a significant source of data for quality assurance. Several commentators have reflected on the value of student feedback surveys as a valid source of up-to-date information from students to inform continuous quality improvement (Harvey, 2003; Hill, 1995; Popli, 2005). Many different approaches to gathering student feedback have been identified and tested (Richardson, 2005). However, being clear on the purpose of student feedback is essential (Williams and Cappuccini-Ansfield, 2007). While institutional surveys can be useful, students' evaluations of their classroom experience, is often critiqued as an ineffective measure of anything: it does not identify what the students have learned and highlights the students' perceptions of the teacher (Harvey and Williams, 2010b). The other major problem with the use of student experience surveys is that they tend to be used to the exclusion of all other data rather than being used as part of a process of triangulation.

Graduate employment data

Graduate employment data tends only to show whether graduates have actually found employment rather than saying anything more nuanced (Little, 2001). The UK Destinations of Leavers from Higher Education survey shows only whether graduates have found work within six months of leaving university. The development of discipline knowledge and generic skills is a fundamental focus of quality assurance and much attention has been given to employability. Employment rates of graduates is a core concern of students the world over (Harvey and Williams, 2010a). However, key to much of the work on employability and its relation to quality assurance is the notion that it should not be simply about students getting a job but something deeper (Gibbs, 2009). Harvey (2001) noted that 'any evaluation of employability needs to indicate areas for internal improvement rather than simply ranking institutions'.

In general, researchers seem to view national performance indicators with suspicion, especially when they simply measure the easily measurable, rather than being carefully designed to evaluate the underlying issues. The key underlying issue, ultimately, is that of individual learning: one of the biggest changes in the discussion of quality assurance is the shift from focusing on teaching quality to quality of learning experience, reflected in the subtle change in language often used from 'teaching and learning' to 'learning and teaching'. This indicates that the emphasis of many researchers and other commentators in the field is on the student learning experience.

Quality assurance and the consumerization of higher education

Alongside accountability has developed what is often referred to as the consumerization of higher education and this, arguably, affects much of the research on quality assurance in the sector. Quality assurance, as a notion, emerged first in the industrial sector and concepts have inevitably transferred over. At the same time, higher education has increasingly been influenced by market models, with students increasingly expecting to pay fees for their studies, institutions finding themselves having to compete with other institutions, both nationally and internationally. Quality assurance has had to take account of these challenges and it would perhaps be surprising if researchers did not address these issues.

Industrial models of quality assurance

The origins of quality assurance are largely in the industrial sector and much work has been done to apply industrial models to the higher education sector. Many scholars have been critical of movements such as Total Quality Management as being inappropriate for a higher educational setting (Harvey and Williams, 2010a) although approaches such as 'Six Sigma' are still being applied in places with varying degrees of success (Kumi and Morrow, 2006). The continuing interest in applying industrial and business models of quality assurance to higher education is problematic because there is little effort to make clear what the parallels are between the sectors.

Students as customers?

As an adjunct to this debate is a concern among commentators with the development of marketization and consumerism in the sector and its impact on quality assurance. There has been a huge amount written that critiques the notion of a higher education market but the focus in the quality assurance debate has tended to be on the role of students as customers or consumers. This debate has been sharply defined over the use of student satisfaction surveys as quality monitoring tools. Popli (2005) discussed the notion of 'customer delight'. At the heart of this debate is the notion of the consumer: much space has been given to discussion whether students (as fee payers) are in fact consumers or not. This focus ignores the possibility that other stakeholders have a claim on the role of consumer: few studies have yet resolved this issue.

The marketing of higher education does not come easily to academic staff and despite the ubiquitous marketing departments in universities that seem to clash with academic values and perspectives. The rhetoric of students as consumers does not sit comfortably. Most marketing efforts appear, rather to be selling what already exists rather than responding in any radical way to market demand, which is just as well given the fickleness of passing fads in higher education. An increasingly popular approach to engaging students as partners has, as yet, failed to attract much rigorous research but is potentially a rich vein for further work (Little, 2011; Nygaard *et al.*, 2013).

The learning institution

Several commentators have highlighted the role of internal quality assurance processes as methods to develop what Meade (1995) described as 'learning institutions'. Research has highlighted the ways in which institutions and staff can shift from compliance to developing engagement with quality improvement (Harvey and Williams, 2010a). Harvey's (2007a) analysis of the epistemology of quality is a rare attempt to explore the conceptual nature of quality and how different approaches to quality assurance fragment and compartmentalize elements of quality and fail to link it to quality learning. The only other paper of a similar nature is Mauléon and Bergman's (2009) analysis of quality within service industries.

Teaching quality

There has been a consistent concern about the quality of teaching, not least the relationship between quality assurance and the assessment of pedagogy. Harvey and Williams (2010b) identified three main concerns of research in the field. First, research on teaching assessment has suggested different ways of assessing teaching, including scorecards, peer review, student evaluation and peer mentoring. Second, commentators have argued that teaching quality improvement needs to be more closely linked with staff development. Third, this goes hand in hand with reward and recognition of teaching improvement. Ewell (2010) argues that 'on the whole, quality review has helped redress this imbalance because it tends to focus its lens most heavily on teaching'.

However, 'the elephant in the room' as Ewell (2010) reflects, 'remains the fact that we don't really know how all of this has affected how much or how well students learn'. Assessment of student learning is a major focus of concern, constituting a core element in the quality of the student experience. Commentators have argued for a shift from traditional method-led examination-oriented systems to motivational and transparent assessment that directly tested specified learning outcomes. More effort and resources, it is argued, should be directed at staff development enabling and encouraging appropriate assessment practices (Knight, 2002). Of course, it is debatable about how much quality assurance encourages this shift from teaching to learning and to what Biggs (1999) calls 'constructive alignment'.

Impact of quality assurance

There is surprisingly little work on overall impact of quality assurance. Many studies have focused on national situations rather than taking a general view of the impact of quality assurance. Harvey and Williams (2010b, p. 102) argue that this 'reflects the general paucity of significant research into the impact of quality assurance processes'.

Early attempts to weigh up the impact of external quality monitoring

Baldwin (1997) argued that a combination of external and internal processes had resulted in three main areas of gain: more rigorous course approval procedures; increased awareness of students' perspectives on teaching and learning; and a perceptible shift in the climate, with a new attention to teaching issues and an intensification of debate about effective learning. On the deficit side were four key issues: an excessive bureaucratization of procedures, with associated pedantry and legalism; a greatly increased administrative workload for academic staff taking them away from their 'core business'; a formalism that can stifle creativity and individuality, the very qualities that universities should foster; and a de-professionalization of academic staff, associated with a policing mentality and a lack of trust. These themes of bureaucratization, administrative burden, stifling of creativity and lack of trust have been recurring concerns ever since.

Much of the research on the impact of external quality assurance since then indicates that implementation of quality assurance systems has had a positive impact on different national sectors by promoting greater concern for quality within institutions (Harvey and Williams, 2010a). Quality assurance audits have contributed to the enhancement of learning and teaching but there is a question of sustainability, which is dependent on effective resourcing. There is some debate about the relative effectiveness of external quality monitoring and internal quality processes in encouraging continuous quality improvement. This raises the question of the need for external process and has led to the perpetual claim by external agencies and governments that without the external process there would be no incentive for developing internal processes. This reflects growing distrust and raises the question of how universities maintained such high standards for 800 years!

Cause and effect?

Less positive is Stensaker's (2003) article in which he identified areas in higher education where changes have taken place. He asked whether quality improvement is actually the result of external quality monitoring. He suggested that the data is ambiguous and highlighted typical side effects of current external quality monitoring systems. He argued that lack of effects directly attributable to external quality monitoring should not be seen as a design error alone but as a misconception of how organizational change actually takes place. A more dynamic view on organizational change, highlighting the responsibility of the institutional leadership as 'translators of meaning', would contribute to a more useful process.

There are many other more significant factors impacting on student learning than external quality monitoring, which are not concerned with either the complexity of a whole teaching programme or the issues such as leadership or the culture in which students learn. Social, economic, political and personal contexts are powerful influencers and for quality monitoring to have an impact on student learning, the emphasis must be on curriculum, learning, teaching and assessment (Horsburgh, 1999).

Need for rigorous impact research

Impact research is difficult because it is impossible to control all relevant factors to be able to map causal relationships (Harvey and Newton, 2004). However, impact studies reinforce the view that quality assurance is about compliance and accountability and has contributed little to any effective transformation of the student learning experience. Where changes to the student experience have taken place, this has arguably been the result of factors other than the external quality monitoring: at best the existence of the latter provides a legitimation for internally-driven innovation. Instead of politically acceptable methods, quality evaluation needs to adopt appropriate research methodologies rather than taken-for-granted assurance approaches.

Worldwide, quality assurance processes have been implemented, modified, replaced or augmented with more stringent policies and procedures. While the pace and intensity of quality assurance and enhancement activities has accelerated greatly, its impact on the improvement of programmes and students remains less clear (Ratcliffe, 2003). Equally unclear is whether the current investments in quality reviews have delivered the political and social assurances that reputedly promulgated them, or whether the time and resources devoted to them are warranted given their uncertain benefits.

Developing a quality culture?

One of the underlying concerns of much of the research on quality assurance is that quality assurance is, or at least, should be, about more than quality control or compliance. Indeed, much of the research explores ways in which processes can stimulate greater commitment to quality processes. This is a desire to build what is usually referred to as 'quality culture'. Most importantly, developing a real culture of quality through effective learning means moving away from preserving what higher education already is towards an aspiration towards what it could be (Gordon and Owen, 2009).

The term 'quality culture' has often been mentioned but seldom defined satisfactorily (Harvey, 2007b). Harvey and Stensaker (2008) argue that the term 'quality culture' is ambiguous: quality culture is a set of group values that guide how improvements are made to everyday working practices and consequent outputs. A quality culture is, arguably, a set of taken-for-granted practices that encapsulate the ideology of the group or organization. Vlăsceanu *et al.* (2004) states that quality culture refers to 'a set of shared, accepted, and integrated patterns of quality ... to be found in the organizational cultures and the management systems of institutions'.

'Quality culture' was early recognized as core to assuring and improving quality in the sector. Harvey and Green (1993) observed, following industrial models, that everyone in an institution needed to be responsible for quality, not just the quality assurance managers. In his reflection on the first European Quality Assurance Forum, Harvey (2007b) emphasizes the need for academic ownership of the quality process and Naidoo (2013) emphasizes the need for a focus on empowerment of academics. Quality culture is fundamental for so many writers on quality assurance because it is primarily about engaging stakeholders in a continuous quality improvement process.

Conclusion

A review of the state and scale of research and reflection on quality assurance is clearly fraught with difficulties and is inevitably going to be incomplete. However, this review indicates above all that quality assurance has developed hugely since the early 1990s as a subject of serious academic study and one that is multifaceted. Research on quality assurance has been important in a range of ways. In particular, it has challenged long-held implicit understandings of quality in the sector and has highlighted the important and complex role that quality assurance processes play in higher education. The research has highlighted the need for continuous evaluation as part of a quality improvement process in the sector and has challenged those responsible for quality assurance to be both more explicit about their aims and more transparent in their approaches. The review also indicates that reflection and research go hand in hand with policy and implementation. The relationship between quality assurance practitioners and researchers is not one of subject and researcher but more of a conversation that takes place not only in academic journals but also through international networks.

There is, however, little research evidence identifying the extent to which the burgeoning body of research in the field actually influences quality assurance at institutional level. It is not, significantly, clear how far individuals who are responsible for aspects of the implementation of quality assurance processes are affected or even aware of theoretical underpinnings of what they do. While we understand much more clearly the perceptions of students and academic staff of quality assurance processes, there is almost nothing about the experiences of support staff. This is important because this group of staff are responsible for the implementation of institutional processes.

Concomitantly, there is little research into the differences between national quality assurance agencies and their priorities. The notion that quality assurance is a unified concept in practice is clearly incorrect. Only a relatively few studies have critiqued the uncritical import of quality assurance principles from one country or group of countries to another (mainly the United Kingdom and the United States). Research on quality assurance in different national contexts tends to accept the rightness of imported models rather than questioning their appropriateness for their own cultural traditions. This is not helped by the continuing tendency for research into quality assurance to fall into disciplinary silos. Research into quality assurance in higher education is multidisciplinary but there is little cross-referencing between disciplines.

While there are large numbers of studies of specific processes and approaches, there is little research into the overall impact of quality assurance on the sector. Much still takes a normative approach, projecting perceptions of what should be in place rather than what actually is in place. There is a tendency for research to focus on teaching and learning, whereas research is given much less attention and facilities are given even less. Much more research is required that explores the impact of quality assurance on institutional facilities and the relationship between the quality of facilities and the student experience. Indeed, much work provides descriptions of processes without fully evaluating them. This appears to be part of a continuing problem. As Harvey long ago noted (1999), what is needed is much more critical evaluative approach to quality assurance.

The development of quality assurance has resulted in clear documentation and transparency, although external processes could be better aligned to everyday academic activity. Internal processes are still developing and the link between external processes, internal processes and improvements in teaching and learning seem to be tenuous and patchy. What is remarkable is the internationalization of quality assurance and the standardization of procedures, even though they leave a lot to be desired. Attempts to push a consumerist approach to higher education have met with indifference and while there are increasing social demands being placed on higher education there remains a strong commitment to autonomy, independence and academic freedom, which quality assurance procedures sometimes rub up against. As Ewell reflects (2010), 'Twenty years of continually evolving quality review, however, has at least given us a vocabulary to begin to talk about this most important question. And that too is a form of progress.'

References

Alperin, J. P. (2013) 'Brazil's exception to the world-class movement', *Quality in Higher Education*, 19(2), 158–172.

Amaral, A. (2007) 'The many rationales for quality', in L. Bollaert, S. Brus, B. Curvale, L. Harvey, E. Helle, H. Toft Jensen, J. Komljenovič, A. Orphanides and A. Sursock (eds) *Embedding Quality Culture in Higher Education* (pp. 6–10) (Brussels: European Universities Association).

Amaral, A. and M. J. Rosa (2010) 'Recent trends in quality assurance', *Quality in Higher Education*, 16(1), 59–61.

Anderson, G. (2006) 'Assuring quality/resisting quality assurance: Academics' responses to "quality" in some Australian universities', *Quality in Higher Education*, 12(2), 161–173.

Baldwin, G. (1997) 'Quality assurance in Australian higher education: The case of Monash University', *Quality in Higher Education*, 3(1), 51–61.

Barrow, M. (1999) 'Quality-management systems and dramaturgical compliance', *Quality in Higher Education*, 5(1), 27–36.

Biggs, J. B. (1999), *Teaching for Quality Learning at University* (Buckingham: SRHE and Open University Press).

Blackmur, D. (2010) 'Does the emperor have the right (or any) clothes? The public regulation of higher education qualities over the last two decades', *Quality in Higher Education*, 16(1), 67–69

Blanco Ramírez, G. (2014) 'Trading quality across borders: Colonial discourse and international quality assurance policies in higher education', *Tertiary Education and Management*, 20(2), 121–134

Bramming, P. (2007) 'An argument for strong learning in higher education', *Quality in Higher Education*, 13(1), 45–56.

Brown, R. (2004) *Quality Assurance in Higher Education: The UK Experience since 1992* (Abingdon: RoutledgeFalmer).

Brown, R. (2014) *What Price Quality Enhancement?* (York: Higher Education Academy).

Campbell, C. and C. Rozsnyai (2002) *Quality Assurance and the Development of Course Programmes* (Bucharest: UNESCO).

Cheng, M. (2009) 'Academics' professionalism and quality mechanisms: Challenges and tensions', *Quality in Higher Education*, 15(3), 193–205.

Cheng, M. (2014) 'Quality as transformation: Educational metamorphosis', *Quality in Higher Education*, 20(3), 272–289.

Crozier, F., Costes, N., Ranne, P. and M. Stalter (2013) *ENQA: 10 Years (2000–2010): A Decade of European Co-Operation in Quality Assurance in Higher Education* (Brussels: European Association of Quality Assurance Agencies).

Danø, T. and B. Stensaker (2007) 'Still balancing improvement and accountability? Developments in external quality assurance in the Nordic countries 1996–2006', *Quality in Higher Education*, 13(1), 81–93.

Dill, D. D. (1995) 'Through Deming's eyes: A cross-national analysis of quality assurance policies in higher education', *Quality in Higher Education*, 1(2), 95–110.

Dill, D. D. (2000) 'Designing academic audit: Lessons learned in Europe and Asia', *Quality in Higher Education*, 6(3), 187–207.

Dolnicar, S. (2005) 'Should we still lecture or just post examination questions on the web?: The nature of the shift towards pragmatism in undergraduate lecture attendance', *Quality in Higher Education*, 11(2), 103–115.

European University Association (EUA) (2006) *Quality Culture in European Universities: A Bottom-up Approach* (Brussels: European Universities Association).

Ewell, P. T. (1999) 'Linking performance measures to resource allocation: Exploring unmapped terrain', *Quality in Higher Education*, 5(3), 191–209.

Faber, M. and J. Huisman (2003) 'Same voyage, different routes? The course of the Netherlands and Denmark to a "European model" of quality assurance', *Quality in Higher Education*, 9(3), 231–242.

Fearnley, S. (1995) 'Class size: The erosive effect of recruitment numbers on performance', *Quality in Higher Education*, 1(1), 59–65.

Filippakou, O. and T. Tapper (2008) 'Quality assurance and quality enhancement in higher education: contested territories?' *Higher Education Quarterly* 62(1–2), 84–100.

Gibbs, G. (2010) *Dimensions of Quality* (York: Higher Education Academy).

Gibbs, P. (2009) 'Quality in work-based studies not lost, merely undiscovered', *Quality in Higher Education*, 15(2), 167–176.

Gordon, G. (2002) 'The roles of leadership and ownership in building an effective quality culture', *Quality in Higher Education*, 8(1), 97–106.

Gordon, G. and C. Owen (2009) SHEEC Theme on the Management of Quality: Cultures of enhancement and quality management systems and structures. Final Report November 2008, Published January 23, 2009, SHEEC. Retrieved February 25, 2015, from http://www.enhancementthemes.ac.uk/docs/report/the-management-of-quality-cultures-of-quality-enhancement.pdf?sfvrsn=18.

Gosling, D. and V.-M. D'Andrea (2001) 'Quality development: A new concept for higher education', *Quality in Higher Education*, 7(1), 7–17.

Haakstad, J. (2001) 'Accreditation: The new quality assurance formula? Some reflections as Norway is about to reform its quality assurance system', *Quality in Higher Education*, 7(1), 77–82.

Harker, B. (1995) 'Postmodernism and quality', *Quality in Higher Education*, 1(1), 31–39.

Harvey, L. (1999) *Evaluating the evaluators*, paper presented at the Fifth Biennial Conference of the International Network of Quality Assurance Agencies in Higher Education (INQAAHE). Santiago, Chile.

Harvey, L. (2001) 'Defining and measuring employability', *Quality in Higher Education*, 7(2), 97–109.

Harvey, L. (2003) 'Student feedback', *Quality in Higher Education*, 9(1), 3–20.

Harvey, L. (2005) 'A history and critique of quality evaluation in the UK', *Quality Assurance in Education*, 13(4), 263–276.

Harvey, L. (2006a) 'Understanding quality', Section B 4.1–1 of 'Introducing Bologna objectives and tools', in L. Purser (ed) *EUA Bologna Handbook: Making Bologna work* (Brussels: European University Association and Berlin, Raabe).

Harvey, L. (2006b) 'Impact of quality assurance: Overview of a discussion between representatives of external quality assurance agencies', *Quality in Higher Education*, 12(3), 287–290.

Harvey, L. (2007a) 'The epistemology of quality', *Perspectives in Education*, 25(3), 1–13.

Harvey, L. (2007b) 'Quality culture, quality assurance and impact: Overview of discussions', in L. Bollaert, S. Brus, B. Curvale, L. Harvey, E. Helle, H. Toft Jensen, J. Komljenovič, A. Orphanides and A. Sursock (eds) *Embedding Quality Culture in European Higher Education* (pp. 81–84a) (Brussels: European University Association).

Harvey, L., Burrows, A. and D. Green (1992) *Total Student Experience: A First Report of the QHE National Survey of Staff and Students' Views of the Important Criteria for Assessing the Quality of Higher Education* (Birmingham: University of Central England).

Harvey, L. and D. Green (1993) 'Defining quality', *Assessment and Evaluation in Higher Education*, 18(1), pp. 9–34.

Harvey, L. and P. Knight (1996) *Transforming Higher Education* (Buckingham: Open University Press and Society for Research into Higher Education).

Harvey, L. and J. Newton (2004) 'Transforming quality evaluation', *Quality in Higher Education*, 10(2), 149–165.

Harvey, L. and B. Stensaker (2008) 'Quality culture: Understandings, boundaries and linkages', *European Journal of Education*, 43(4), 427–42.

Harvey, L. and J. Williams (2010a) 'Fifteen years of *quality in higher education* (Part One)', *Quality in Higher Education* 16(2), 3–36.

Harvey, L. and J. Williams (2010b) 'Fifteen years of *quality in higher education* (Part Two)', *Quality in Higher Education* 16(2), 79–113.

Hill, R. (1995) 'A European student perspective on quality', *Quality in Higher Education*, 1(1), 67–75.

Horsburgh, M. (1999) 'Quality monitoring in higher Education: The impact on student learning', *Quality in Higher Education*, 5(1), 9–25.

Iacovidou, M., Gibbs, P. and A. Zopiatis (2009) 'An exploratory use of the stakeholder approach to defining and measuring quality: The case of a Cypriot higher education institution', *Quality in Higher Education*, 15(2), 147–165.

Idrus, N. (2003) 'Transforming quality for development', *Quality in Higher Education*, 9(2), 141–150.

Jacobs, G. J. and A. Du Toit (2006) 'Contrasting faculty quality views and practices over a five-year interval', *Quality in Higher Education*, 12(3), 303–314.

Kumi, S. and J. Morrow (2006) 'Improving self-service the six sigma way at Newcastle University Library', *Program* 40(2), 123–136

Leeuw, F. L. (2002) 'Reciprocity and educational evaluations by European Inspectorates: Assumptions and reality checks', *Quality in Higher Education*, 8(2), 137–149.

Lemaitre, M. -J. (2002) 'Quality as politics', *Quality in Higher Education*, 8(1), 29–37.

Little, B. (2001) 'Reading between the lines of graduate employment', *Quality in Higher Education*, 7(2), 121–129.

Little, S. (ed) (2011) *Staff-Student Partnerships in Higher Education* (London: Continuum).

Loukkola, T., Zhang, T., Sursock, A. and A. Vettori (2012) *Examining Quality Culture in Higher Education Institutions* (Brussels: European Universities Association). Retrieved December 3, 2014, from http://www.eua.be/eqc.

Massy, W. (2003) *Honoring the Trust: Quality and Cost Containment in Higher Education* (Bolton, MA: Anker Publishing).

Massy, W., Graham, S. and P. M. Short (2007) *Academic Quality Work: A Handbook for Improvement* (Bolton, MA: Anker Publishing).

Mauléon, C. and B. Bergman (2009) 'Exploring the epistemological origins of Shewhart's and Deming's theory of quality: Influences from C.I. Lewis' conceptualistic pragmatism', *International Journal of Quality and Service Sciences* 1(2), 160–171.

McInnis, C. (2000) 'Changing academic work roles: The everyday realities challenging quality in teaching', *Quality in Higher Education*, 6(2), 143–152.

Meade, P. (1995) 'Utilising the university as a learning organisation to facilitate quality improvement', *Quality in Higher Education*, 1(2), 111–121.

Melrose, M. (1998) 'Exploring paradigms of curriculum evaluation and concepts of quality', *Quality in Higher Education*, 4(1), 37–43.

524 Themes: Accountability and Quality

Middlehurst, R. (1997) 'Reinventing higher education: The leadership challenge', *Quality in Higher Education*, 3(2), 183–198.

Naidoo, D. (2013) 'Reconciling organisational culture and external quality assurance in higher education', *Higher Education Management and Policy*, 24(2), 85–98.

Narasimhan, K. (2001) 'Improving the climate of teaching sessions: The use of evaluations by students and instructors', *Quality in Higher Education*, 7(3), 179–190.

Newton, J. (2000) 'Feeding the beast or improving quality? Academics' perceptions of quality assurance and quality monitoring', *Quality in Higher Education*, 6(2), 153–163.

Newton, J. (2002) 'Views from below: Academics coping with quality', *Quality in Higher Education*, 8(1), 39–61.

Nygaard, C., Brand, S., Bartholomew, P. and L. Millard (eds) (2013) *Student Engagement: Identity, Motivation and Community* (Farringdon: Libri Publishing).

Pirsig, R. K. (1974) *Zen and Art of Motorcycle Maintenance* (London: Bodley Head).

Popli, S. (2005) 'Ensuring customer delight: A quality approach to excellence in management education', *Quality in Higher Education*, 11(1), 17–24.

Raban, C. (2007) 'Assurance versus enhancement: Less is more?' *Journal of Further and Higher Education*, 31(1), 77–85.

Ratcliff, J. L. (2003) 'Dynamic and communicative aspects of quality assurance', *Quality in Higher Education*, 9(2), 117–131.

Richardson, J. T. E. (2005) 'Instruments for obtaining student feedback: A review of the literature', *Assessment & Evaluation in Higher Education*, 30(4), 387–415.

Rosa, M. J. and A. Amaral (2014) *Quality Assurance in Higher Education Contemporary Debates* (Houndsmills: Palgrave Macmillan).

Rowley, J. (1996) 'Measuring quality in higher education', *Quality in Higher Education*, 2(3), 237–255.

Saarinen, T. (2005) 'From sickness to cure and further: Construction of "quality" in Finnish higher education policy from the 1960s to the era of the Bologna process', *Quality in Higher Education*, 11(1), 3–15.

Saarinen, T. (2010) 'What I talk about when I talk about quality', *Quality in Higher Education*, 16(1), 55–7.

Silver, H. (1996) 'External examining in higher education: A secret history', in R. Aldrich (ed) *History and Education: A Tribute to Peter Gordon* (London: The Woburn Press).

Singh, M. (2010) 'Quality assurance in higher education: Which pasts to build on, what futures to contemplate?' *Quality in Higher Education*, 16(2), 189–194.

Stensaker, B. (2003) 'Trance, transparency and transformation: The impact of external quality monitoring on higher education', *Quality in Higher Education*, 9(2), 151–159.

Swinglehurst, D., Russell, J. and T. Greenhalgh (2008) 'Peer observation of teaching in an online environment: An action research perspective', *Journal of Computer Assisted Learning* 24(5), 383–393.

Tam, M. (1999) 'Managing change involves changing management: Implications for transforming higher education', *Quality in Higher Education*, 5(3), 227–232.

Tam, M. (2001) 'Measuring quality and performance in higher education', *Quality in Higher Education*, 7(1), 47–54.

van Damme, D. (2000) 'Accreditation in global higher education: The need for international information and cooperation. Outline of an IAUP approach', Memo for the Commission on Global Accreditation of the International Association of University Presidents New York.

Van Kemenade, E., Pupius, M. and T. W. Hardjono (2008) 'More value to defining quality', *Quality in Higher Education*, 14(2), 175–185.

Vlăsceanu, L., Grünberg, L. and D. Pârlea (2004) *Quality Assurance and Accreditation: A Glossary of Basic Terms and Definitions* (Bucharest: UNESCO-CEPES). Retrieved February 25, 2015, from http://www.aic.lv/bolona/Bologna/contrib/UNESCO/QA& A%20Glossary.pdf.

Vroeijenstijn, A. I. (1991) *External Quality Assessment: Servant of Two Masters?*, paper presented at the Council for Academic Accreditation Conference on '*Quality Assurance in Higher Education*', Hong Kong, July 15–17, 1991.

Westerheijden, D. F. (2001) 'Ex oriente lux?: National and multiple accreditation in Europe after the fall of the Wall and after Bologna', *Quality in Higher Education*, 7(1), 65–75.

Williams, J. and G. Cappuccini-Ansfield (2007) 'Fitness for purpose? National and institutional approaches to publicising the student voice', *Quality in Higher Education*, 13(2), 159–172.

Woodhouse, D. (2003) 'Quality improvement through quality audit', *Quality in Higher Education*, 9(2), 133–139.

Woodhouse, D. (2004) 'The quality of quality assurance agencies', *Quality in Higher Education*, 10(2), 77–87.

Yorke, M. (1998) 'Performance indicators relating to student development: Can they be trusted?', *Quality in Higher Education*, 4(1), 45–61.

28
Student Involvement in University Quality Enhancement

Manja Klemenčič

Introduction

Calls to improve the quality of higher education have become more prominent in recent years everywhere. The quality of higher education has been gaining attention around the world, especially in view of 'massification' and the rising cost of higher education. An ever-larger share of population in individual countries is enrolled in higher education. This situation offers immense opportunities for human capital development through quality higher education. Equally, poor educational conditions incur significant costs in terms of missed learning opportunities and unsatisfactory student experience. As higher education has increasingly become linked to economic progress and social well-being, governments demand accountability and evidence for quality in return for public money invested into higher education (Klemenčič, Ščukanec and Komljenović, 2015). The increase in higher education enrolments puts pressure on the quality of higher education provisions, as it becomes more difficult to give students the educational treatment that they tend to value most: personalized, with flexibility in terms of modes of learning and materials, and ample one-on-one time with teachers and advisors (McCormick, Kinzie and Gonyea, 2013). The pressure is greater in mainstream, non-elite institutions that have often expanded beyond their capacities, and that cater for the majority of students within national higher education systems. The increased diversity of student populations, with different backgrounds, expectations and learning needs, present further challenges for institutions to develop conditions that enable quality higher education for all.

Massification, marketization and demands for accountability have brought student experience and student learning to the centre of quality assurance policies and practices in higher education. Accordingly, students' influence

The author would like to thank David Dill for his most helpful feedback on this chapter and guidance to additional literature.

on – and involvement in – university[1] structures and processes towards quality enhancement have become a more noticeable trend. This chapter is specifically concerned with student involvement in quality enhancement of their universities. The key questions here are what roles do the students play in university quality enhancement and how these roles are conditioned by the institutional context. In other words, this chapter explores the institutional conditions and organizational culture that shape student agency in structures and processes towards university quality enhancement. The proposed framework presents a shift from the traditional focus on how institutions can assure educational quality to how students can be co-responsible for and contribute to the well-being and advancement of their university The discussion in this chapter contributes to the broader theme of how human agency – individual and collective – shapes higher education policies (Marginson and Rhoades, 2002), and specifically how universities as organizations enable or hamper student agency in quality assurance as part of university governance.

The chapter consists of four sections. Taking the concept of student agency as the starting point (Klemenčič, 2015), and drawing from Sen's capability approach (Sen, 1999), Swidler's cultural kit (1986), March and Olsen's (2009) logic of appropriateness and Hirschman's (1970) theory of exit, voice and loyalty, this chapter first conceptualizes student involvement in quality enhancement from the point of view of student capital, agentic possibilities and agentic orientations. The next section on students' power focuses on both the formal rules and procedures and the informal cultural schemas that have an influence on students' capabilities to be involved in and influence university quality. The third section turns to individual students and their willingness and motivation to be involved in university quality processes and structures. The focus here is on loyalty and the different underlying relational ties between students and their universities (belonging, mattering and needs fulfilment) and how these play out in students' agentic orientations. The concluding section discusses the different modes and practices of student involvement in university quality enhancement.

Conceptualizing student involvement in university quality enhancement

Conceptualizing student involvement in university quality enhancement can be built on the theory of student agency. Student agency is defined as students' self-reflective and intentional action and interaction with their environment (Klemenčič, 2015). This encompasses variable notions of agentic possibility (*power*) and agentic orientation (*will*) in a specific context – here university governance and specific policies, structures and processes towards university quality enhancement.

There are three distinct modes of student agency in university quality structures and processes, each of which is founded in students' beliefs that they can influence their environment by their actions: personal, proxy and collective (Klemenčič, 2015; cf. Bandura, 2001). Personal agency is students' solitary actions that can be directed at changing their own circumstances or also those of others. Students exert proxy agency when they ask their student representatives or student government to act on their behalf to solve a particular problem or secure a particular outcome (Klemenčič, 2015). This can happen for a number of reasons. Students would exercise proxy agency in areas in which they cannot exert direct influence, typically because they feel they do not have direct control over institutional conditions or practice. For example, if an individual student is provoked by the university's decision to discontinue a particular study programme, he or she may turn to the student government to try to overturn this decision (proxy agency). Also, students who are worried about the possible risks associated with filing a complaint against a particular professor or administrator often prefer to file a complaint via student representatives. Students also exercise proxy agency when they do not wish to invest time and resources, or when they believe student representatives can tackle the problem more effectively (Klemenčič, 2015). Whereas student proxy agency relies heavily on the perceived efficacy of student government and elected student representatives, students exercise collective agency when they believe in their collective efficacy as a group to secure a mutually desired outcome (Klemenčič, 2015; cf. Bandura, 2001). Student protests and sit-ins are the most notable form of student collective agency, and there are ample examples of students protesting against poor study conditions.

The guiding question of this chapter revolves around students' agentic possibility and agentic orientation towards self-reflective and intentional action within university context towards quality enhancement. The emphasis here is not on students' behaviour to maximize their self-interests, which is indeed students' expected default behaviour, but rather on the questions when and under what conditions students can and are willing to act to contribute to university quality even if they do not have any immediate direct benefits from that action. In other words: how can universities enable and elicit in their students' intentional and conscientious responses to contribute to university quality? The implied desired outcome is thus the collective well-being of the university and quality education for all students. To illustrate: if a student complains that she does not receive sufficient advisory support in preparing her senior thesis and asks for more support, she is only trying to enhance the quality of her own educational experience and outcomes. If the same student would raise the issue with her student representative and alert that there might be a problem in how advising is administered at her department and the school, she would be trying to improve the situation also for her peers. Responding to student satisfaction surveys is one example of involvement where personal and communal interests overlap, since negative feedback may result in timely improvements. When students provide feedback on future curriculum planning, they are contributing to the university quality enhancement beyond their immediate self-interest.

Student capital

The starting point of this discussion is in recognizing that students possess resources – *student capital* – that are salient for the purposes of enhancing university quality. Students have first-hand experience of, and thus valuable insights into, educational processes and learning environments. As such, students – individually, by proxies, or collectively – can bring to university administrators information and expertise for the purposes of quality enhancement. Individual students can be a source of raw data on experience, satisfaction or behaviour, which is collected through student surveys. Students can act as expert advisors to university administrators in advisory committees. They obtain such roles either by being elected student representatives or by being handpicked by administrators to play this role, or simply by offering input even if they do not participate in student representation. Student representatives participate in university governing bodies in strategic planning and policy making.

The legitimation of policy processes and outcomes is another resource students possess. Regardless of whether students are considered an internal constituency, as in democratic collegiate governance regimes, or stakeholders or customers as in corporate universities, having students involved in decision processes is perceived to be important for the legitimation of decision processes and outcomes. This is so even when student involvement was only conceived as 'window dressing' and students had no effective influence.

Finally, students can offer student services, such as tutoring, counselling, organizing student events and managing student groups, all of which complement the formal university operations and can help implement specific institutional quality objectives. While students thus have various *resources* that they can employ towards university quality enhancement, the question arises whether they have the *possibilities* and *motivations* to do so.

Student agentic possibilities (students' power) to influence university quality enhancement: Sen's (1999) capability approach and Swidler's (1986) cultural kit

Student agentic possibilities (students' power) to influence university quality enhancement can be explained by drawing from Amartya Sen's (1999) capability approach, which emphasizes persons' real opportunities and positive freedoms to intervene in and thus influence the environmental context. The capability approach is a theoretical framework that 'entails two core normative claims: first, the claim that the freedom to achieve well-being is of primary moral importance, and second, that freedom to achieve well-being is to be understood in terms of people's capabilities, that is, their real opportunities to do and be what they have reason to value' (Stanford Encyclopaedia of Philosophy, 2011, introduction). This framework can be transposed to the university quality context because universities care, or should care, about the well-being of students in a higher education context, and about the quality of the education experience of their students.

The capability approach highlights the effective freedoms, in the sense of what students are able to do and to be within their university, to achieve well-being. So, it is not only the question of *what* resources students have that is important but also the question of the opportunities the student has to *employ* whatever resources they have towards well-being and self-formation. A primary concern of students in a university is, of course, related to enjoying a rewarding academic experience and gain credential achievement. Their capability to control and influence their learning processes and environment is directly related, indeed an implicit condition, to achieve these objectives.

In applying the capability approach to student involvement in university quality enhancement, we should distinguish between (1) the equality of *outcomes* of student involvement and (2) the equality of *opportunity* among students to influence university quality. The equality of outcomes, that is, improvement of university quality to the benefit of all students, bridges the potentially self-interested – instrumentalist – involvement in university quality with the involvement based on principles of social justice – enhancing quality for all (Nussbaum, 2006). The emphasis here is thus on student involvement in institutional quality processes, which may lead to the improvement of conditions for all students (as opposed to improvements only for oneself or for one's own in-group.). The equality of opportunity refers to the 'freedoms' of students, that is, their real opportunities to act – opportunities 'that do not exist only formally or legally but are also effectively available to the agents' (Stanford Encyclopaedia of Philosophy, 2011, section 2.7).

It is these freedoms that are in the centre of the discussion in the next section on students' power, which focuses on institutional pathways and institutional cultures of student involvement. Institutional pathways are directly linked to the legal status of students within a university and the specific structures, rules and procedures of decision-making within that university's governance arrangements. University cultures also influence students' behaviour – including engagement with matters of university quality – by shaping a repertoire or 'tool kit' of habits, skills, symbols, world views and styles from which students construct 'strategies of action' (Swidler, 1986, p. 273). In other words, university culture defines among other things how students interact with their university. For example, these interactions could be under-pinned by authoritarian–paternalistic, democratic–collegiate or managerial–corporate behaviour schemata, each of which invokes different conceptions (or metaphors) of students, such as students as pupils, as constituency or as customers.

Student agentic orientations to influence university quality: March and Olsen's (2009) logic of appropriateness and Hirschman's (1970) exit, voice and loyalty

Student agentic orientations – or students' will – to intentionally contribute to university quality enhancement are another and equally important part of the discussion. In a university context, students face competing demands on their time from academic requirements, extracurricular opportunities and the straightforward enjoyments of student life already celebrated in the 13th-century *Carmina Burana*. The latter should not be underestimated. As Grigsby (2009, p. 86) points out in her study of college life at a US university, '[h]aving fun is viewed...as an important responsibility that [students] must fulfil in order to claim the genuine college experience'. Furthermore, the cultural val-ues in post-modern Western societies increasingly emphasize individualism and choice (Grigsby, 2009), which do not always align with altruistic motivations to engage with the university beyond the instrumental logic of action based on a cost-benefit analysis. There is obviously a difference if you ask students to comment on the library opening hours because university administration is planning to change these or if you ask them to comment on changes in the curricula that will be implemented only after they graduate.

There are two ways to go about answering the question of students' will-ingness and motivation to influence institutional quality beyond their own immediate self-interest. One lies in the 'logic of appropriateness' as defined by March and Olsen (2009, p. 2):

> The logic of appropriateness is a perspective that sees human action as driven by rules of appropriate or exemplary behaviour, organized into institutions. Rules are followed because they are seen as natural, rightful, expected, and legitimate. Actors seek to fulfil the obligations encapsulated in a role, an identity, a membership in a political community or group, and the ethos, practices and expectations of its institutions. Embedded in a social collectiv-ity, they do what they see as appropriate for themselves in a specific type of situation.

The willingness of students to be actively involved in institutional quality depends on whether such involvement is considered 'appropriate', that is, natural, expected and legitimate for each and every student. Universities can communicate to their students that by being part of the university community and 'a good citizen of the university' it is natural (and expected) that they respond to surveys, participate in planning committees, volunteer for tutoring and so on. The logic of appropriateness effectively presents a conceptual bridge between the notions of students' agentic possibilities and agentic orientations. It means that students have effectively internalized the university culture and the formal rules (agentic possibilities) described above and use them as personalized normative prescriptions. However, whether university culture and rules become students' 'internalized prescriptions of what is socially defined as normal, true, right or good, *without, or in spite of,* calculation of consequences and expected utility' (March and Olsen, 2009, p. 3 [*emphasis added*]), requires more than mere structural possibilities for action and the sense of duty. The norms of appropriate behaviour lead to dutiful observance of rules and norms to avoid sanctions or shaming, but do not necessarily motivate students to act beyond their self-interest.

For genuine, conscientious students' involvement, students need to feel a certain degree of 'loyalty', defined as a strong feeling of allegiance and attachment to one's university or indeed to a collectivity or group of people within that university. The concept of loyalty within organizations has been developed in relation to a person's action to address dissatisfactions by Hirschman (1970) in his classic work on 'Exit, Voice, and Loyalty'. Hirschman argues that in organizations employees react to dissatisfaction with either exit or voice. Which of the two is chosen depends to some extent on loyalty. Loyalty, according to Hirschman, may drive a dissatisfied employee to voice complaints because he or she would wish to change the organization from within, rather than simply quit and look for job opportunities elsewhere. At the same time, as emphasized by Leck and Saunders (1992), loyalty may also mean that employees simply persist in an organization, passively waiting for conditions to improve by themselves. Thus, loyalty may have active and passive behavioural dimension depending on which interpretation is considered.

While recognizing that students are not employees of universities and that their time span with the university is much shorter than employees' tenure, the concept of loyalty is relevant to conceptualizing students' investment in university quality matters. Like employees, students too are tied to the university, and their exit option is fairly costly considering time, effort, financial cost of transfer to another programme or institution. Developing Hirschman's concept, there are basically two alternative ways that students can react to dissatisfaction with university quality: 'exit' means withdrawal from the university or switching to another programme within the same university, and 'voice' means that they agitate and try to influence positive changes. However, this chapter seeks to pursue the matter further by exploring not only how students react to dissatisfaction but also under which conditions students voluntarily seek to make a positive impact on their university, both for their own personal benefit and for the benefit of the entire academic community. This leads us to the various relational ties between universities and students that comprise the concept of loyalty and thus influence students' motivations for involvement in university matters: belonging, mattering and psychological ownership. These will be addressed in the section on students' will to influence university quality enhancement.

Students' power in students' legal status and university governance arrangements

The formal rules, procedures and norms that regulate student involvement in university governance in general, and in quality assurance in particular, are derived from the legal position of students in the university and the particular university governance model.

The legal position of students differs significantly across higher education systems. There are two overarching approaches, each of which provides a variety of national and institutional interpretations. One approach suggests that there exists an implied contract between the student and the university of which the implication is that the university has obligated itself to provide a certain standard of quality of education provision to which student has been admitted upon payment of necessary fees (Buchter, 1973). Even if no specific contract document is signed at the time of admission of the student to the university, the admission itself can be regarded as a formation of contractual relationship between an individual student and the university as a corporate body. This contractual relationship is implied in the various university publications, such as course catalogues, policies and promotional material used for recruitment. These publications include disclaimers of obligations of university towards students and also the terms describing the process leading to conferral of degrees. This approach also implies that access to higher education is not granted to all in the sense that a student may not be accepted to a university without the institution having to give any reason (Farrington, 2000). Common initially to the Anglo-American context and to the private higher education sector worldwide, this model is slowly diffusing also into public higher education sector elsewhere.

The second approach is common to countries which conceive higher education as a public good and thus hold it a right (in some countries even constitutional right) for students to access it. There is an implicit social contract between state and students evident in higher education legislation, which stipulates that access is largely granted to all that are academically apt and aspire to higher education with expectation that these will upon graduation contribute to the economy and societies. The state thus establishes, owns and provides funding to public higher education institutions. Public universities are accountable for quality education not only to students but also to the state and other interested stakeholders, such as employers. Accordingly, the state requests from the universities to show responsible use of public funds and of quality education provisions through various quality assurance frameworks, performance evaluations and participation of external stakeholders in governing bodies of universities. In European countries, student unions have played a prominent role in political processes instigating the quality reforms in the framework of the intergovernmental Bologna Process. The resulting European Standards and Guidelines for Quality Assurance in Europe essentially made student involvement in external and internal higher education quality assurance mandatory (ENQA, 2009; Klemenčič, 2012a).

These two different approaches to state–student relationship are reflected also in the different university governance arrangements, which are a reflection of governmental steering and institutional autonomy. There are basically two main overarching university governance models which differ in terms of in whose hands power is located. The democratic governance model, which emerged from the 1960s protests, divides decision-making powers among academic staff and students as university's primary constituencies. Both groups are represented in, and typically also have, voting rights in governing bodies of universities. Autonomous student governments, whose primary aim is to organize, aggregate and mediate the interests of the collective student body (Klemenčič, 2012b, 2014), play a prominent role in university politics.

At present, the most predominant model is the managerial–corporatist model in which all stakeholders are involved in the university decision processes run by academic managers with considerable executive powers. The managerial–corporatist model tends to invoke conception of students as stakeholders and increasingly of students as customers. Regardless of the metaphor used, in this governance model students are also involved in decision-making, but tend to be invited through advisory and service roles, rather than political roles with decision-making powers as in the democratic model (Krücken and Meier, 2006).

The conceptualization of students as consumers, and consumerist discourse in higher education in general, has been linked to the introduction or strengthening of competitive elements in higher education along with changes in funding arrangements (decrease in public funding, rising tuition fees, recruitment of foreign fee-paying students) and institutional governance (towards applying management principles from business to higher education governance structures and procedures) (Naidoo, Shankar and Veer, 2011). The designation of students as customers in policy discourse has elicited significant debate in scholarly circles (McCulloch, 2009; Molesworth, Nixon and Scullion, 2009; Naidoo and Jamieson, 2005; Redding, 2005; Riesman, 1998; Schwartzman, 1995). The main point of controversy is whether students conceived as customers gain or lose influence in higher education processes and structures, a question that has so far not been adequately empirically explored in the literature (Van Andel, Botas and Huisman, 2012).[2]

Market-driven reforms have certainly accelerated institutional attention to quality, thus creating new opportunity structures and processes for student involvement (Klemenčič, 2012b): in offering advice and feedback, performing student services and managing student facilities. Student governments tend to adapt to these new opportunities and expectations, resulting in changes in their organizational structures, practices, priorities and orientations (Klemenčič, 2012b). As Stensaker and Michelsen (2012, p. 29) report for the case of Norwegian students unions, '[s]tate reforms moving in the direction of a more integrated and marker-oriented higher education field have provided important conditions for a more encompassing student union and a stronger re-institutionalization of student interest', which indeed is characterized by the co-existence of democratic and consumer dimensions of student interests. Student unions are both invited to be involved and invent new pathways of involvement in quality assurance.

Elsewhere, such as in the United Kingdom, the consumer orientation of students has been associated with the increases in the number of complaints raised by students to their universities.[3] The United Kingdom's political commitment to student charters[4] has been attributed not only to a general concern about quality and standards in universities but also to the emerging role of the student as a 'consumer' (Cooper-Hind and Taylor, 2012). Scholars critical of political discourse that casts students as customers point out that students who identify as customers change their expectations and relationships to teachers whom they see more as providers of educational services and credentials and are expected to serve students in transactional relationships. Students as consumers are inclined to demand more vocationalist orientations in the curriculum, that is, courses and topics that are directly relevant to employability. The notion of students as consumers arguably implies students' passivity in classroom: students increasingly expect to be provided with knowledge and to be assisted to develop competences rather than assume responsibility for own learning (Van Andel, Botas and Huisman, 2012). The opposing view, promulgated also in policy initiative such as the United Kingdom's 'Students at the Heart of the System' (BIS, 2011), contests the assumption that conceptualizing students as consumers leads to such consequences. The argument is that, with more choice, clearly set standards to help students know what to expect from the institution and clear procedures to complain when these expectations are not met, students are granted more control over their education, which in turn makes them more responsible for own learning and more engaged (Van Andel, Botas and Huisman, 2012). The assumption here is that students will apply pressure on the institutions to strive towards high-quality provision, thus reinforcing the institutional attention to quality of teaching and learning, support service and overall learning environment (Naidoo, Shankar and Veer, 2011).

An important implication of conceiving students as customers rather than as democratic constituents or stakeholders is in the role of student proxy agencies – representative student associations to which individual students turn to act on their behalf to solve a particular problem or secure a particular outcome (cf. Klemenčič, 2015). Universities that conceive students as internal constituency or stakeholders tend to be supportive of organized student interests and create formal channels of involving student representatives in institutional quality processes. In the consumer student conception, the stress is more on individual (rather than collective) student feedback on quality. Institutional complaint procedures are put in place as part of students' contractual rights. Student satisfaction surveys are administered to collect responses from the student body. Given the transactional nature of student–university relationships, the emphasis is perhaps more on students' involvement in view of guaranteeing their individual (and thus collective) satisfaction rather than student involvement in a collective sense for the well-being and development of the entire academic community. This distinction lies at the centre of the discussion in the next section.

Students' will and mattering, needs fulfilment and the sense of collective belonging

The nature and context of the relationships between students and universities are in constant flux not only due to changes in government steering of higher education and overall market conditions in higher education but also because student expectations towards higher education institutions are changing. In the context of these developments, the university-student relationships are also changing. The previous section addressed the formal rules, procedures and informal cultural schemas of university–student relationship as depicted through students' capabilities to be involved in institutional processes and structures. This section turns to individual students and their willingness and motivation to be involved in university quality processes and structures.

Students' agentic orientations are developed in the context of multiple demands on their time derived from the academic requirements, extracurricular opportunities and social and economic circumstances, such as the family obligations, personal relationships and work arrangements. Students' decisions on 'strategies of action' (cf. Swidler, 1986) are also influenced by the broader societal values. The individualist versus collectivist societal value make-up, as depicted in Hofstede's (1997) cultural dimension theory, is inevitably present also in a higher education setting. The question here is whether and to what extent students are willing to act in the interests of the entire university community, when this means acting beyond or even despite of their immediate self-interests.

A university is built on strong interdependencies among its internal constituencies, and this naturally enables collective behaviour. However, the consumerist metaphors of students which have been evoked in corporatist universities may be seen as inhibiting a sense of civic commitment to ones' own university and to collective well-being. The expressive individualism in consumerist culture and choice-based values may indeed undermine the collective spirit which could be seen as inherent in educational establishments and puts in question – or significantly alters – the pathways to social integration that have been for long held as essential for student retention and college success (Astin, 1985). So, the question here is not whether the university can change students' personal preferences towards self-formation. Rather, the question is whether it can also instigate in students a sense of duty towards the university and a sense of belonging, indeed collective belonging, which will in turn lead to commitment to and involvement in university quality enhancement.

To answer this question, this section explores the normative side of the university–student relationship, exposing the variety of theoretically distinct relational ties that comprise the concept of loyalty as discussed earlier. In organizational theory, Materson and Stamper (2003) organized relational ties into three dimensions: need fulfilment, mattering and belonging, and these can be adapted to student-university relationships. Need fulfilment refers to students' perception that their university is providing important benefits to them, and that their individual expectations are compatible with the university's aims. In other words, the student feels that studying at this university is a good for him or her. Mattering refers to the student's perception that the university cares about the well-being of its students. Students' satisfaction with education provisions, learning environments and support services comes to the fore here, as do the institutional policies and practices to enhance student engagement in educationally purposeful activities which are seen as critical for students' success (McCormick, Kinzie and Gonyea, 2013). Belonging refers to students' perceptions of intimate association with the university as demonstrated through perceived insider status, psychological ownership and organizational identification.

Students who have come to feel a strong sense of insider status perceive that they are a central and important part of the university ('I am an important part of my university') (cf. Stamper and Masterson, 2002). This sense fills human needs for inclusion, agency and control, consequently increases students' sense of responsibility to be involved in and support university functions (cf. Stamper and Masterson, 2002). Psychological ownership is when students have come to feel a strong sense of ownership of their university and perceive it as 'my university' ('I own my university'), which fulfils their need for efficacy and the sense of place and consequently leads to an expectation of having more voice in institutional processes and structures (cf. Stamper and Masterson, 2002). Organizational identification – when students define themselves in terms of their university ('I am defined by my university') (cf. Stamper and Masterson, 2002) – is especially strong when students perceive their university as distinct (fulfilling particular purpose) and/or prestigious. For example, the European Humanities University, which became 'university-in-exile' in Kaunas, Lithuania, after the shutdown by Belarusian authorities in 2004, renders a distinct organizational identification. Collectively, these three concepts have been characterized as representing a sense of belonging in that individuals have invested themselves in the organization and consider it to be a personalized space (Masterson and Stamper, 2002).

Students' sense of belonging is essential for students' positive student experience and academic engagements (Astin, 1985; Thomas, 2012), student retention (Reay et al., 2010; Thomas, 2012; Tinto, 1993) and – more generally – for a person's subjective sense of well-being, intellectual achievement, motivation and even health (Walton and Cohen, 2007). The sense of belonging may be challenged by a perceived mismatch between a student's background and the institution's culture, such as, for example, in cases when first-generation students or minority students join elite institutions and feel that their social and cultural practices are inappropriate to those of the university (Reay et al., 2001; Thomas, 2012).

Researchers have argued that higher education officials can intervene in the institutional 'habitus' to create conditions that strengthen the sense of students' belonging to the institution and consequently their integration and agency (Strayhorn, 2012; Thomas, 2012). As Thomas (2012, p. 69) suggests: 'The commitment to a culture of belonging should be explicit through institutional leadership in internal and external discourses and documentation such as the strategic plan, website, prospectus and all policies' and 'Staff capacity to nurture a culture of belonging needs to be developed'. According to Thomas (2012), particular care should be devoted to first-year students, to the monitoring of students' behaviour and progress and to a holistic approach to student engagement, including meaningful interactions between staff and students and supportive peer relations, which at least to some extent could be institutionally facilitated.

The interventions to strengthen students' sense of belonging are often closely linked to the institutional efforts to build a sense of collective identity. Universities use sports events, artefacts with university crests, university magazines, online news and student newspapers, graduation ceremonies, alumni events and more as instruments of collective identity building. The institutionally supported activities towards developing a sense of community are perhaps more pronounced in institutions that rely on philanthropic donations as a part of their funding model. If an institution expects alumni donations and other forms of in-kind alumni support (e.g. arranging internships and career advising for students), the administration tends to pay attention to students' sense of belonging to the university, as opposed to belonging to a particular peer group that facilitates social integration.

None of the existing literature on student belonging and university community building has specifically targeted the question of students' motivation to contribute to institutional quality. The argument here is that students' involvement in university quality is conditioned by the students' sense of belonging, mattering and need fulfilment to and by the university. However, this sense of belonging should not be based on individualistic and consumerist notions of higher education as a 'set of consumer choices' (Grigsby, 2009, p. 88), but indeed as shared – communal – processes, in which students' self-formation is facilitated by their communal commitment in quality and advancement of the academic communities and the university to which they belong. Universities thus need to cultivate and communicate communal values and facilitate communal processes. There is a difference if students' sense of collective belonging rests on entertainment and private enjoyment – such as sports games, as Grigsby (2009) observes at an American university – or when students volunteer to clear snow on campus or when they participate in town hall meetings to discuss future curricular reforms. Nathan (2005, p. 56) observes that '[r]ather than being located in its shared symbols, meetings, activities, and rituals, the university for an undergraduate was more accurately a world of self-selected people and events'. To enable student agency in university quality assurance, the task for university is to offset the situation where the 'the ego-centred networks were the backbone of most students' social experience in the university' (Nathan, 2005, p. 55).

Conclusion

Several principles emerge from the above discussion that can strengthen student agency in university quality assurance and enhancement. Student engagement in quality needs to be embedded in a sustainable culture of partnership between students – individual or as represented by proxy agencies – and university administration. This implies reciprocity in relationships, a sense of shared responsibilities and collective commitments to mutually agreed goals. Such culture would not only *offer* students spaces and pathways of involvement but also grant them a leadership role, in which they have the freedom to *invent* new spaces and pathways of involvement, as well as to redefine and introduce new parameters of institutional quality (Ashwin and McVitty, 2015).

Some scholars, like MacFarlane (2012), perceive student inclusion in quality assurance as the 'domestication of the student voice'. He points to a number of incidents where universities, to protect their reputation, have implicitly and sometimes explicitly encouraged students to over-score their perception of quality in national student surveys or favourably assess the university when interviewed by external review panels. Indeed, when student involvement in quality is used as a means of marketing and reputation building in rankings, this not only skews the validity of student feedback but has potentially adverse effects on how students internalize their own role and relationship to the university: do students frame their relationship to the university mostly in terms of expectations as to what the university will provide them with or they also consider their own contribution, civic engagement within university community and indeed leadership for the purposes of improving the university quality for all? This personal contribution is valuable even if it is not genuinely altruistic, that is, if students get involved to build their CV and social network. Even such involvement might yield positive outcomes.

Furthermore, student surveys have become one of the largest and most frequently used data source for quality assessment in higher education (Klemenčič and Chirikov, 2015). The student satisfaction and engagement surveys have been hailed as a driver of institutional reforms towards improvement in students' experience, for example through improvements in student support services and student facilities and in teaching and assessment (Richardson, 2013). Student surveys and similar instruments signal to students what their university cares about and implicitly what aspects of quality students should be concerned about. Indeed, universities are 'value-based organizations' (Long, 1992) or 'culturally loaded' organizations (Clark, 1983), in which values and norms guide their members' behaviour. Therefore, universities need to actively manage 'meanings' implicit in its structures, procedures and instruments (Dill, 1982, 2012) in view of the implications these have on students' and their relationship to the university. Building on Dill's argument, the proposition here is that universities need to attend to the language and symbols that help clarify and give meaning to student involvement in quality enhancement (cf. Dill, 2012).

This chapter has argued that one of the central students' capabilities in higher education includes influence over university quality in the sense of educational provisions, learning environments and support services. But the kind of involvement advocated here is one where students act to improve a certain aspect of university without, or even in spite of, personal self-interest. To elicit students' will for such involvement, more is needed than formal pathways of involvement, and even more than a sense of duty or social pressure for involvement. A strong collective university identity and of collective belonging is a necessary condition for genuine and conscientious student involvement in university quality assurance and enhancement.

Notes

1. In the reminder of the chapter, the term 'universities' is used in generic form referring to all types of higher education institutions, not only research universities.
2. A notable example is Van Andel, Botas and Huisman (2012), who explore students' choice in curricular matters and their sense of empowerment through the exercising of their choice as customers in higher education.
3. See, for example, 'University complaints by students top 20,000' by Fran Abrams, BBC News, 3 June 2014.
4. https://www.gov.uk/government/news/student-charter-group-gets-down-to-work.

References

Ashwin, P. and D. McVitty (2015) 'The meanings of student engagement: implications for policies and practices', in R. Pricopie, P. Scott, J. Salmi and A. Curaj (eds) *Future of Higher Education in Europe* (Dordrecht, Netherlands: Springer).

Astin, A. W. (1985) *Achieving Educational Excellence* (San Francisco: Jossey-Bass).

Bandura, A. (2001) 'Social cognitive theory: an agentic perspective', *Annual Review of Psychology*, 52, 1–26.

BIS (Department for Business Innovation and Skills) (2011) Higher education: Students as the heart of the system. Report for Department for Business Innovation and Skills (BIS) (London), Retrieved January 15, 2015, from https://www.gov.uk/government/uploads/system/uploads/attachment_data/file/31384/11-944-higher-education-students-at-heart-of-system.pdf.

Buchter, J. F. (1973) 'Contract law and the student-university relationship', *Indiana Law Journal*, 48(2), 253–268.

Clark, B. R. (1983) *The Higher Education System: Academic Organization in Cross National Perspective* (Berkeley: University of California Press).

Cooper-Hind, H. and J. Taylor (2012) 'Student complaints: an accurate measure of student dissatisfaction?', *Higher Education Review*, 44(3), 54–80.

Dill, D. D. (1982) 'The management of academic culture: notes on the management of meaning and social integration', *Higher Education*, XI, 303–320.

Dill, D. D. (2012) 'The Management of academic culture revisited: integrating universities in an entrepreneurial age', in B. Stensaker, J. Välimaa and C. Sarrico (eds) *Managing Reform in Universities: The Dynamics of Culture, Identity and Organisational Change* (Basingstoke, UK: Palgrave Macmillan).

ENQA (European Association for Quality Assurance) (2009) Standards and guidelines for quality assurance in the European higher education area Retrieved January 15, 2015, from http://www.enqa.eu/files/ESG_3edition%20(2).pdf.

Farrington, D. (2000) 'A study of student-institution relationships in selected member states of the Council of Europe', *European Journal for Education Law and Policy*, 4, 99–120.

Grigsby, M. (2009) *College Life through the Eye of Students* (Albany: SUNY Press).

Hirschman, A. O. (1970) *Exit, Voice, and Loyalty: Responses to Decline in Firms, Organizations, and States* (Cambridge, MA: Harvard University Press).

Hofstede, G. (1997) *Cultures and Organizations: Software of the Mind* (New York: McGraw-Hill USA).

Klemenčič, M. (2012a) 'The changing conceptions of student participation in HE governance in the EHEA', in A. Curaj, P. Scott, L. Vlasceanu and L. Wilson (eds) *European*

Higher Education at the Crossroads: Between the Bologna Process and National Reforms (Dordrecht, Netherlands: Springer).

Klemenčič, M. (2012b) 'Student representation in Western Europe: introduction to the special issue', *European Journal of Higher Education*, 2(1), 2–19.

Klemenčič, M. (2014) 'Student power in a global perspective and contemporary trends in student organising', *Studies in Higher Education*, 39(3), 396–411.

Klemenčič, M. (2015) 'What is student agency? An ontological exploration in the context of research on student engagement', in M. Klemenčič, S. Bergan and R. Primožič (eds) *Student Engagement in Europe: Society, Higher Education and Student Governance*, Council of Europe Higher Education Series No. 20 (Strasbourg: Council of Europe Publishing).

Klemenčič, M. and I. Chirikov (2015) 'On the use of student surveys', in R. Pricopie, P. Scott, J. Salmi and A. Curaj (eds) *Future of Higher Education in Europe* (Dordrecht, Netherlands: Springer).

Klemenčič, M., Šćukanec, N. and J. Komljenovič (2015) 'Decision support issues in Central and Eastern Europe', in K. Webber and A. Calderon (eds) *Institutional Research and Planning in Higher Education: Global Contexts and Themes* (New York: Routledge Press/Taylor&Francis).

Krücken, G. and F. Meier (2006) 'Turning the university into an organizational actor', in G. S. Drori, J. W. Meyer and H. Hwang (eds) *Globalization and Organization: World Society and Organizational Change* (Oxford: Oxford University Press).

Long, E. L. (1992) *Higher Education as a Moral Enterprise* (Washington, DC: Georgetown University Press).

Leck, J. D. and D. M. Saunders (1992) 'Hirschman's loyalty: attitude or behavior?', *Employee Responsibilities and Rights Journal*, 5, 219–230.

Macfarlane, B. (2012) 'Re-framing student academic freedom: a capability perspective', *Higher Education*, 63, 719–732.

March, J. G. and J. P. Olsen (2009) *The Logic of Appropriateness*, Arena Working Papers WP 04/09 (Oslo: ARENA).

Marginson, S. and G. Rhoades (2002) 'Beyond national states, markets, and systems of higher education: a glonacal agency heuristic', *Higher Education*, 43, 281–309.

Masterson, S. S. and C. L. Stamper (2003) 'Perceived organizational membership: an aggregate framework representing the employee-organization relationship', *Journal of Organizational Behavior*, 24, 473–490.

McCulloch, A. (2009) 'The student as co-producer: learning from public administration about the student–university relationship', *Studies in Higher Education*, 34(2), 171–183.

McCormick, A. C., Kinzie, J. and R. M. Gonyea (2013) 'Student engagement: bridging research and practice to improve the quality of undergraduate education', in M. B. Paulsen (ed) *Higher Education: Handbook of Theory and Research* (Vol. 28) (Dordrecht, The Netherlands: Springer).

Molesworth, M., Nixon, E. and R. Scullion (2009) 'Having, being and higher education: the marketisation of the university and the transformation of the student into consumer', *Teaching in Higher Education*, 14(3), 277–287.

Naidoo, R. and I. Jamieson (2005) 'Empowering participants or corroding learning? Towards a research agenda on the impact of student consumerism in higher education', *Journal of Education Policy*, 20(3), 267–281.

Naidoo, R., Shankar, A. and E. Veer (2011) 'The consumerist turn in higher education: policy aspirations and outcomes', *Journal of Marketing Management*, 27(11–12), 1142–1162.

Nathan, R. (2005) *My Freshman Year: What a Professor Learned by Becoming a Student* (Ithaca: Cornell University Press).

Nussbaum, M. (2006) *Frontiers of Justice: Disability, Nationality, Species Membership* (Cambridge, MA: Harvard University Press).

Reay, D., Davies, J., David, M. and S. J. Ball (2001) 'Choices of degree or degrees of choice? Class, "race" and the higher education choice process', *Sociology*, 35(4), 855–874.

Redding, P. (2005) 'The evolving interpretations of customers in higher education: empowering the elusive', *International journal of consumer studies*, 29(5), 409–417.

Richardson, J. T. E. (2013) 'The National Student Survey and its impact on UK higher education', in M. Shah and C. Nair (eds) *Enhancing Student Feedback and Improvement Systems in Tertiary Education*, CAA Quality Series (5) (Abu Dhabi: Commission for Academic Accreditation, UAE).

Riesman, D. (1998) *On Higher Education: The Academic Enterprise in an Era of Rising Student Consumerism* (New Brunswick, Transaction Publishers).

Schwartzman, R. (1995) 'Are students customers? The metaphoric mismatch between management and education', *Education*, 116(2), 215–222.

Sen, A. (1999) *Development as Freedom* (Oxford: Oxford University Press).

Stanford Encyclopaedia of Philosophy (2011) The capability approach, Retrieved January 15, 2015, from http://plato.stanford.edu/entries/capability-approach/.

Stensaker, B. and S. Michelsen (2012) 'Governmental steering, reform and the institutionalization of student interest in higher education in Norway', *European Journal of Higher Education*, 2(1), 20–31.

Strayhorn, T. L. (2012) *College Students' Sense of Belonging: A Key to Educational Success for all Students* (New York; London: Routledge).

Swidler, A. (1986) 'Culture in action: symbols and strategies', *American Sociological Review*, 51, 273–286.

Thomas, L. (2012) *Building Student Engagement and Belonging in Higher Education at a Time of Change: Final Report from the What Works? Student Retention & Success Programme* (United Kingdom: Higher Education Academy). Retrieved January 15, 2015, from https://www.heacademy.ac.uk/sites/default/files/What_works_final_report.pdf.

Tinto, V. (1993) *Leaving College: Rethinking the Causes and Cures of Student Attrition*, 2nd edn (Chicago; London: University of Chicago Press).

Van Andel, J., Botas, P. C. P. and J. Huisman (2012) 'Consumption values and empowerment of the student as customer: taking a rational look inside higher education's "Pandora's Box" ', *Higher Education Review*, 45(1), 62–85.

Walton, G. M. and G. L. Cohen (2007) 'A question of belonging: race, social fit, and achievement', *Journal of Personality and Social Psychology*, 92(1), 82–96.

F. Inequalities in Higher Education

29
Widening Participation in Higher Education: Policy Regimes and Globalizing Discourses

Penny Jane Burke and Yu-Ching Kuo

Introduction

This chapter presents an overview of the international policy regimes focused on widening participation (WP) in higher education (HE). Such policy regimes are related to complex questions of inequality in and beyond HE and contested discourses of social justice, quality and equity. At the same time, these policy regimes are also shaped by the wider politics and perspectives of globalization and neoliberalism, both creating and constraining possibilities for equity in HE (Burke, 2012; Rhoads and Szelenyi, 2013; Williams, 2013). Discourses of 'excellence' are increasingly foregrounded in HE policy, and this poses particular challenges for widening access and participation. The chapter will analyse different policy regimes and discourses across national contexts to examine the relationship and tensions between WP, discourses of excellence and the institutional and social positioning of HE in broader contemporary social structures and relations. Taking a comparative approach, the chapter will analyse policy statements and texts concerned with access and WP in China, the United States and England.

WP is largely concerned with redressing the historical and persistent under-representation of certain social groups in HE. The social groups targeted by policy have often been explicitly defined, although this is not consistently the case. Historically, China has been most concerned with targeting rural and remote groups; the United States with providing access to HE for people of colour; and England has been focused on those from lower socio-economic groups, low-participation neighbourhoods and those with disabilities. Yet in all three countries, questions over who should be targeted fluctuates and there are ongoing struggles over which groups are foregrounded and which are made invisible through different policy regimes. Questions of student mobility and its relation to WP have also been a concern of policy, and the inflation of international student fees together with tightened visa regulations has arguably reinforced inequalities in participation and international student mobility.

The different meanings circulating from policies of WP are often implicit, while assumptions are often made about a common or universal understanding of the term. We want to show that the meanings attached to 'WP' are not only highly contextual but are also connected to diverse and competing values and perspectives, as well as interconnected policy regimes. The formation of policy is a site of struggle over meanings, values and competing sets of interests. The concept of 'policy regime' is drawn on to illuminate the different and contested discursive strands that are brought together to form policy 'regimes' and the implications of this for enduring inequalities in and through HE.

Conceptualizing WP policy regimes and assemblage

Regime theory has been widely discussed and deployed in political science and, specifically, in the field of international relations. Stephen Krasner (1982) defines regimes as 'sets of implicit or explicit principles, norms, rules, and decision-making procedures around which actors' expectations converge in a given area of international relations' (p. 186). Krasner's view is consistent with Keohane and Nye (1989) who consider regimes as 'assets of governing arrangements (that includes) networks of rules, norms, and procedures that regularize behaviour and control its effects' (p. 5). Kratochwil and Ruggie (2001) also define regimes as governing arrangements 'constructed by states to coordinate their expectations and organize aspects of international behaviour in various issue-areas' (p. 347). Wilson (2000) identifies four key dimensions of a policy regime: (1) power or the arrangement of power; (2) policy paradigm; (3) organization within government, the policy-making arrangements and the implementation structure; and (4) the policy itself. Wilson (2000) explains that a paradigm is like a 'lens that filters information and focuses attention' (p. 257). Importantly, the paradigm operates to signify particular assumptions about the policy problem, including 'its cause, its seriousness, its pervasiveness, those responsible for creating it or ameliorating it, and the appropriate governmental response' (ibid.). As Wilson (2000) argues, researchers generate particular understandings of the problem which then shapes the ways that the policy problem might be defined.

We draw on these perspectives but want to further nuance them by paying closer attention to the messiness of policy formation, which is not simply created through sets of shared perspectives, agreement over principles and rational decision-making but through fluid processes that involve struggles over meaning and the negotiation and contestation of different values, positions and perspectives. The 'policy regime' might be considered as a set of governing arrangements that 'spans multiple subsystems and fosters integrative policies' (Jochim and May, 2010, p. 303), reconceptualizing WP as comprised of multiple dimensions, areas and agendas. The regime perspective provides us with a sophisticated viewpoint from which to investigate alignment and misalignments between (and within) the current governance structures, as different actors might position themselves in relation to competing policy agendas or priorities across complex power relations within and beyond the policy regime of WP. One possible alignment and misalignment might be between some discourses of excellence, which accentuate elitism and/or selectivity, and some discourses of WP, which focus on providing access and inclusion, although we argue that excellence and WP are not necessarily in opposition.

May and Jochim (2013, p. 18) suggest a shift in perspective 'from studying a particular legislative enactment and its implementation to studying the regime *contours* for a broader collection of policies' (emphasis added). We consider the WP policy regime as a constellation of institutionalized arrangements that constitute regulatory technologies and practices of WP. As such, WP might be understood as a set of (often contradictory) policies (May and Jochim, 2013; Wilson, 2000), which profoundly affect different students, staff and institutions, often in unequal ways depending on their social positioning and cultural histories. It is also important to understand that policy regimes are not fixed and solid entities but are fluid, complex and discursive, as well as highly contextual and interrelated with other policy regimes. A post-structural reworking of 'regime' helps to conceptualize the multiple, complex and non-linear formations that constitute policy. Foucault's concept of 'regimes of truth' illuminates the discursive processes and relations by which particular strands of policy become hegemonic 'truths' while others become marginalized and overshadowed. For example, within the regime of WP, certain strands of the policy have become increasingly foregrounded, shaped by neoliberal values and assumptions (Burke, 2012). These include a regime of truth that WP is necessary in order to maximize human capital as we move into the new social order of 'knowledge and information economies'. Within such perspectives, discourses of 'employability' are foregrounded, shaping the logic of WP policy regimes, while hierarchies of difference are sustained through moves towards a differentiated market of HE (Naidoo, 2010).

Furthermore, although policy formation might be located at the level of government, it is also formed through interconnecting local, regional, institutional and global contexts. The concept of 'assemblage' helps to further nuance the concept of a 'policy regime' to understand how within and across a policy regime 'global forms interact with local elements, and how the products of these interactions are contingent, uneasy and involve unstable relationships' (Ong and Collier, 2004, p. 7). As Rizvi and Lingard (2011, p. 8) explain:

> policy is not derived from a distinct and discrete value that has been accorded authority, but represents an assemblage of a diverse body of ideas, values, historical settlements and a particular understanding of the current conditions of political possibilities.

Rizvi and Lingard (2011) draw on the concept of assemblage to examine policies of 'equity' in the Australian HE context. 'Equity' could be used interchangeably with 'WP' as it signifies a similar policy agenda (Gale and Seller, 2013). Rizvi and Lingard argue that a commitment to equity in itself does not necessarily define a policy regime because its formation depends on interpretation and how equity is 'reconciled with a range of other values, such as excellence, justice, efficiency, democracy and autonomy' (2011, p. 9). They argue that 'policies need to be aligned to the political settings in which they are developed, allocated and implemented' (ibid.). Such insights are useful for analysing national policy regimes of WP in relation to multiple, competing and intersecting discourses, including, for example, discourses of 'excellence'.

Widening participation policy regimes and the discourse of excellence

A key contemporary discourse related to WP policy regimes is 'excellence', profoundly shaping possibilities and imaginaries in relation to challenging under-representation and exclusion in HE. The forces of neoliberal globalization have placed pressure on institutions to strive towards becoming 'global universities' and to position themselves as 'world-class', competing for the 'best students' in a stratified market driven by discourses of 'excellence' and league table rankings. Against this highly competitive and increasingly commercialized landscape, often contradictory policy concerns to widen participation (can we can change it to: the way that WP is to align with/in the realm of social policies) have become a well-established trope, including the need for institutions to illustrate their value through their diverse student bodies. Nations and institutions attempt to negotiate the regulatory demands of 'excellence' and 'equity' despite the often contradictory values attached to each. Although we do not consider excellence as opposed to equity, we do argue that discourses of 'excellence' in higher education institutions (HEIs) often overshadow discourses of WP (see e.g. Stevenson, Burke and Whelan, 2013), and we argue that different policy positions, perspectives and instruments play a significant role in this overshadowing.

Rostan and Vaira (2011) examine the ways in which discourses of excellence have become increasingly prevalent in HE. They argue that the concept of excellence has been incorporated with a 'so-called ranking movement which is both a manifestation of the new global competitive environment and a driver of change in the field of HE' (p. vii). They note that many countries:

> have been more and more engaged in promoting policies aiming at making respective systems and institutions to attain and/or maintain top-level, or world-class, quality. Excellence as a policy issue reflects the institutional and competitive pressures exerted by the global ranking movement on national systems and institutions.
>
> (Ibid.)

Excellence thus might pose some tensions for the aspirations of WP policy regimes. In seeking excellence, processes of selection and differentiation often become embedded in everyday practices and naturalized, sometimes seen as a necessary and inevitable dimension of HE. Maher and Tetreault (2007) argue that excellence has become associated with the notion of privilege, as exemplified in the idea of privileged access to high-status institutions and resources. Discourses of excellence associated with university prestige compel institutions to participate in performative and competitive practices in the race to be ranked as 'world-class'. However, Marginson (2007, p. 132) points out that competition is not only at the level of institutions but also between nations. He explains:

> Regardless of whether they are performing well or badly relative to economic capacity, all nations want to increase their number of ranked universities and to see their leading institutions move up the Jiao Tong and Times Higher tables. [...] There is a growing emphasis on institutional stratification and research concentration. All these responses have cemented the role of the rankings themselves and further intensified competitive pressures.
>
> (Ibid.)

Nixon (2013, p. 96) traces the ways that the drive for 'excellence' often undermines WP policy regimes. He warns that competition for funds and for students has led to institutional stratification and the self-protective groupings of institutions which lobbied intensively for their market niche. Within this context institutional prestige has itself become a marketable commodity.

What we see are levels of institutional sedimentation that provide the bases for structural inequalities that define, restrict and control the horizons of expectation and possibility. 'Competition between and within universities', as Stromquist (2012) points out, 'does not foster equity but instead creates "winners" and "losers"'.

(Nixon, 2013, p. 178)

Nixon argues that in the UK context, 'institutional prestige has itself become a marketable commodity'. This has reinforced institutional stratification, with the post-1992 universities well represented across the broad spectrum of second-league institutions and institutions that have gained university status more recently almost entirely occupying the bottom league. Similarly in the US context, Lazerson (2010, p. 23, also see Nixon, 2013) argues that HE has expanded in a segmented and hierarchical fashion in ways that might well be interpreted as having 'preserved the social structure of inequality... The overall effect was to leave the nation as socially divided as in the past'. Further research by Heller (2007, pp. 48–49, also see Nixon, 2013) shows that 77% of all high-income students attended a 4-year college, while only 33% of poorer students did, and that 62% of higher income students completed a bachelor's degree, with only 21% of their low-income peers obtaining this level of education. In the Chinese context, the impact of the 'excellence' discourse on WP is similarly observed:

> Elitism is being reinvigorated as neo-liberalism has taken hold. Paralleling this pattern of programmatic convergence, Chinese higher education institutions are being structured in a hierarchical way, according to their function and goals.
>
> (Zha, 2009, p. 55)

A critical analysis of policy regimes offers an important tool in uncovering tensions and contradictions. The counter-discourse we aim to promote through our analysis is principled and normative, multidimensional and comparative. As a normative discourse it is strongly anchored in moral and ethical principles: How should HE, as a scarce resource, be redistributed among competing constituents, both within the larger student population: socio-economically diverse groups of the welfare state and culturally, ethnically, racially and sexually diverse actors of civil society? As a multidimensional discourse, taking the policy regime perspective acknowledges that HE systems are subject to multiple and often conflicting expectations and demands such as equity, excellence, efficiency, trusteeship of cultural heritage and the advancement of problem solving via research and debate in the public sphere. We now turn to each of the country cases to apply an analysis of the WP policy regimes at play and their implications for equalities in HE.

A comparative approach: The cases of China, United States and England

In the next sections, we present the cases of China, the United States and England to consider the ways policy regimes play out in different contexts and how this sheds light on the contested and discursive nature of WP. These country cases were selected due to their different histories of and approaches to WP, the different groups being targeted and the different strategies, policies and approaches being taken. Each of these cases highlight differences between political ideologies: for example, the United States is often constructed as ideologically conservative and operationally liberal (Ellis and Stimson, 2012); the United Kingdom fluctuates between the political right and left and yet attempts to balance at the centre of this political spectrum; and China self-claims to be a 'socialist democracy' (People's Daily Online, 02 September, 2004). Such political and positional differences help us to trace policy regimes as fluid and dynamic formations that are also highly contextual and to show the implications of this for the discourse of WP which is often assumed to be a universally shared aspiration.

Widening participation in China

With vast regional differences in quality and access to universities, largely due to gaps in development and differences in population, China now aims to rework the HE system to support students from underdeveloped areas to compete on more equal terms with their peers from more affluent parts of the country (Ramo, 2004).

China's new development approach is driven by a desire to have equitable, peaceful high-quality growth; critically speaking, it turns traditional ideas like privatisation and free trade on their heads.

(Ramo, 2004, p. 4)

Yang Dongping (2008, cited in Yang Siwei, 2012, p. 102) designated the period between 1990 and 2003 as an era of 'economicism', mostly resulting from the impact of globalization, national skills formation to promote knowledge-based economic development, China's entry into the World Trade Organization (WTO) and its adherence to the General Agreement on Trade in Services (GATS) (in which education was considered as a purchasable service) in 2001. The idea of 'economicism' was adapted by the Chinese government, leading China to move towards the industrialization of HE. The Chinese Government is committed to a set of 'world-class university' initiatives that aim to cultivate talented elites for its national development. It is also invested in the development of a market socialist economy with Chinese characteristics, as a mechanism to provide educational opportunity to those from disadvantaged backgrounds. In 2001, *The Fifteen National Educational Enterprise Programme* was the first policy document comprising the virtue of educational equality, which stated:

> (the development of HE) must be consistent with socialism's educational principle: equity and justice, paying attention to the educational opportunities for those who live under disadvantaged conditions, making an effort to offer lifelong learning to enhance civic development.
>
> (Cited in Yang Siwei, 2012, p. 102)

Yet, we cannot be sure whether the aspiration of a 'harmonious socialist society' and what Ramo (2004) calls 'equitable growth' have been achieved in China, at least not from the current literature that might help to understand questions of equity in HE. Furthermore, in 2014, Chinese government announced an increase in tuition fees from 2015 for the first time in more than 10 years, although financial aids are promised to those from lower socio-economic backgrounds. For example, in Jiangsu province, tuition fees for majors, such as medicine, engineering and liberal arts, will increase from about 4,600 Yuan ($741) to 5,500 Yuan ($886) a year (Cang, 2014). Like its western counterparts, the marketization of HE and policy changes involving student tuition fees have reduced opportunities to access HE, particularly for socially and economically disadvantaged school leavers. The Bureau of China Statistics data released in 2010 suggested that the share of government appropriation for education in total funds dramatically declined (down from 80.3% in 1996 to 47.6% in 2008) and the ratio of tuition and fees to the total HE funds increased (up from 13.7% in 1996 to 33.7%) (Dong and Wang, 2012).

The World Bank's (2009) report synthesizes factors that have created barriers to access to HE, not limited to, but including family background, place of residence, gender inequality and monetary barriers. Access to HE is evidently influenced by both household income and parents' occupation (Zha and Ding, 2007; Zhou et al., 1998). This report points out that in comparison to students from wealthy urban areas, students from rural regions of China are under-represented in HE. For instance, the chance of a student from an urban area entering a Tier 1 institution is 1.48 times higher than that of a rural student (Ding, 2007). Less than 20% of rural students study at the two most prestigious universities (Tsinghua and Beijing) (Zhang and Liu, 2006), while in 2001, 18% of students registered with Tsinghua University were from Beijing (Rui Yang, 2007). Additionally, China's one-child policy has prioritized HE for male students over female students. Opportunities for female students living in rural regions are often considerably fewer than the educational opportunities available to male students (Wang, 2005).

Chinese HE has been developing rapidly in terms of both quality and quantity. As Yang Xiaoming (2011, pp. 127–128) examined, in economic terms, the supply is greater than the demand in the HE market. When making decisions about tuition and fee charges, the affordability for students and their parents is not fully taken into consideration by senior managers in HE. As the Peking University's research on Chinese family wealth and living habits released in July 2013 shows, the gap in income between the nation's top earners and those at the bottom is widening. Average annual income for a family in 2012 was 13,000 Yuan ($2,100), while the average for a Shanghai family was 29,000 Yuan ($4,700). Average family income in urban areas was about $2,600, while it was $1,600 in rural areas (Wong, 2013). Therefore, universities are inclined to charge higher fees as the tuition and fee charges are currently not being appropriately regulated by the Chinese government. The opportunities for those from socially and economically disadvantaged backgrounds are not sufficiently guaranteed, largely because the Chinese government's ability to promote social equality has been weakened. When examining the recent Chinese HE development and formation, social and economic equality has indeed not only declined but also worsened. Those who are from socially and economically disadvantaged backgrounds are more likely not to choose to study in lower status and less well-resourced HEIs. While HE is supposed to play a key role in enhancing and furthering social mobility, the overall tuition and fee-charging system in China has impeded social mobility for those from disadvantaged backgrounds (ibid.). Dong and Wang (2012) point out that most educational resources in China are distributed to HEIs in urban areas. Yet, the average university entrance examination score of students from rural areas is about 20 points higher than their urban peers. 'High-priced and rising tuition and fees has likely prohibited many outstanding students with low socio-economic status (SES) from accepting higher education opportunities' (p. 5). Dong and Wang argue further that unlike the US model, which has adapted 'high-charging and high financial support' policies since the 1990s, the Chinese model remains a 'high-charging and low subsidizing' university fee mechanism. The widening income inequality between rural and urban families and the rapid increase in tuition and fees beyond many students' affordability are thus significant factors that undermine education opportunity for those from low-income family backgrounds.

Discourses such as '(market) socialism with Chinese characteristics' and sometimes 'socialist market economy' have been adopted predominantly by the Communist Party of China (CPC) to describe the economic system deployed in China since the 1980s. Such discourses also run through HE-related policy documents since 1978 and have become connected to the diversification of HE and the massification of HE. The 1998 Higher Education Act states: 'HE must correspond with the overall goals of national development, and serve the modernization of socialism' (Yang Siwei, 2012, p. 103). Fan et al. (2012) note that the ways that the Chinese authority adapts and synthesizes the 'market' and 'socialism' do not appear to accord with some scholars' usages in political economy and finance. However, as Xing and Shaw (2013) demonstrate, 'Chinese economic reform contains many disembedding elements where the economy (market) is empowered to play its due and logical roles, [while] there has been a strong "visible" hand to embed market reform with the political establishment and with socio-cultural settings' (pp. 88–89).

The WP Policy Regime in China might be best understood as intersecting with the broader political project of developing a 'socialist market economy', as well as strong ambitions to compete as a major player in the global market of HE. In response to globalization and global competition, like its western counterparts, Chinese HEIs has moved in the direction of the corporatization and industrialization of HE. The 'visible hand' of Chinese government also appears in the context/market of HE by constantly emphasizing the concept of socialism with Chinese characteristics as if this concept is seen as a powerful ideological instrument for safeguarding social fairness and justice. For the CPC, social justice and equality are the core values of the Party (Constitution of Communist Party of China, March 23, 2013). The Chinese government clearly intends to develop the Chinese model of HE that incorporates Chinese socialism's core values, while developing world-class universities by adapting western market approaches.

Widening participation in the United States

The US Policy Regime of WP provides an illustrative example of the complexity of policy formation through the assemblage of different perspectives, values and positions across different geographic spaces and the contestations over meaning, values and perspectives that play out. The US policy aiming to WP has involved a relatively progressive agenda with affirmative action used as a mechanism to redress the social inequalities between historically disadvantaged and privileged groups. In his speech in 1965, President Johnson sets out this progressive and liberal agenda, arguably embedded in a social justice framework of redistribution:

> You do not wipe away the scars of centuries by saying: 'now, you are free to go where you want, do as you desire, and choose the leaders you please.' You do not take a man who for years has been hobbled by chains, liberate him, bring him to the starting line of a race, saying, 'you are free to compete with all the others,' and still justly believe you have been completely fair... This is the next and more profound stage of the battle for civil rights. We seek not just freedom but opportunity – not just legal equity but human ability – not just equality as a right and a theory, but equality as a fact and as a result.
> (Johnson, June 4, 1965)

However, the discourses of meritocracy and excellence have increasingly countered and undermined such values and perspectives. Those who advocate meritocracy argue that in a democratic society, all who work hard must be rewarded fairly on the basis of individual merit and that affirmative action is a form of 'reverse discrimination'.

> Those who oppose affirmative action argue that it defies the American ideal of meritocracy – that you will succeed if you work hard enough. The claim is that preference is given to those groups protected under the legislation while excluding innocent and deserving Whites by practicing 'reverse discrimination'. Such action can potentially benefit economically advantaged minorities, while members of disadvantaged minorities who gain power and wealth are stigmatized, and their qualifications are continually under scrutiny. Furthermore, in a democratic society, all people are viewed and judged without their skin color. From this perspective, affirmative action is seen as perpetuating racism and prejudice rather than rectifying and remedying discriminatory attitudes and beliefs.
>
> (Baptiste and Villa, 2012, p. 39)

Janet L. Yellen, the Chair Board of Governors of the Federal Reserve System, identifies HE as one of the cornerstones of opportunity in the United States (Yellen, 2014). She explains that the United States is one of the few advanced economies in which public education spending is often lower for students in *lower income households* than for students in *higher income households*. Furthermore, she notes that the costs of HE participation have risen much faster than income for the large majority of households since 2001 and have become especially burdensome for households in the bottom half of the earnings distribution. She argues that

> Rising college costs, the greater numbers of students pursuing higher education, and the recent trends in income and wealth have led to a dramatic increase in student loan debt. Outstanding student loan debt quadrupled from $260 billion in 2004 to $1.1 trillion this year. Sorting families by wealth, the SCF shows that the relative burden of education debt has long been higher for families with lower net worth, and that this disparity has grown much wider in the past couple decades. Higher education has been and remains a potent source of economic opportunity in America, but I fear the large and growing burden of paying for it may make it harder for many young people to take advantage of the opportunity higher education offers.
>
> (Yellen, October 17, 2014)

Financial aid is a major strand of the WP policy regime as most undergraduates need scholarships and/or loans to afford the cost of HE (Mohrman,

2009, p. 111). The preference for scholarships is fuelled by moves towards the marketization of HE and the race to be positioned at the higher ranks of the league tables, shaped by discourses of 'excellence'. Merit-based financial aid allows institutions to attract the students with strong academic records or special talents such as athletic or musical ability. Students and their parents, for their part, prefer to pay less money for college rather than more, so students often attend the institutions offering the highest amount of financial aid even if the school is not their top choice. The process escalates as students seek larger and larger scholarships and institutions spend more and more for the most desirable applicants. Mohrman argues that it is the market system working with a vengeance (ibid., p. 112).

> Since the 1960s, need-based aid has dominated the American HE landscape, but merit scholarships (awarded without regard to financial need) have grown rapidly in the last decade. In 1994, need-based grants from all sources totalled US$18.6 billion nationwide while merit scholarships provided US$1.2 billion. By 2004, need-based grants increased 110 percent to US$39.1 billion, while merit scholarships rose to US$7.3 billion – a 508 percent increase (Kahlenberg, 2006). Some of the new merit aid came from funds that had previously been allocated to need-based scholarship programmes, hence the current public policy debate about the best way to distribute limited financial aid dollars. Few analysts oppose scholarships for talented students as a matter of principle but many believe that need-based aid is a better policy choice for assisting students with the high cost of college.
>
> (Mohrman, 2009, pp. 111–112)

The contestations over merit-based or needs-based scholarships might be viewed in light of 'the rise of the student consumer', which is connected to the way that 'social mobility is considered to be brought about through the individualized economic function of HE'. Williams analyses policy texts from the United States to reveal the emergence of 'individualist discourses', which reinforce the notion that the beneficiaries of HE are mainly individuals, with HE being constructed largely as a private rather than a public good. She maps this in relation to the increasing significance employment plays in HE policy, leading to the perception of HE as a private investment for future employment prospects (Williams, 2013, p. 47).

Altbach (2011, p. 11) highlights the complex ways that different values are in contestation with particular policy regimes. The neoliberal perspective is driving the shift to the marketization and privatization of HE and is compelling nations and institutions to compete in a global market for the prize of being considered 'world-class'. Yet, the WP policy regime is also placing pressure on nations and universities to demonstrate how they are addressing equity and diversity and recruiting and retaining students from traditionally under-represented backgrounds. As national institutions, Altbach argues, research universities are elite and meritocratic in their culture and practices. They serve only a minority of undergraduate students, usually those who are deemed to represent the nation's 'best and brightest', and Altbach (2011) outlines the problematic tension between 'elite and meritocratic', linked to discourses of 'excellence' for WP policy regimes:

> However, terms like elite and meritocratic are not necessarily popular in a democratic age when access has been the key rallying cry of proponents of higher education for decades. Yet, for research universities to be success-ful, they must proudly pro-claim these characteristics. Research universities cannot be democratic; they recognize the primacy of merit, and their deci-sions are based on a relentless pursuit of excellence. At the same time, they are elite institutions in the sense that they aspire to be the best – as often reflected in a top ranking – in teaching, research, and participation in the global knowledge network. (p. 11)

Widening participation in England

Since Margaret Thatcher's conservative government came to power in 1979, neoliberalism has become a prevailing political ideology that led to the pro-motion of the marketization and privatization of public services, including universities (Williams and Kitaev, 2005). Tony Blair, the New Labour Prime Minister, took power from the Conservatives in 1997. Yet, as Heffernan (2011, p. 163) states, Tony Blair and his successor Gordon Brown never 'radically reformed the Thatcherite economic settlement' but aligned with Thatcher's pro-market approaches. Such approaches have been further reinforced and extended by the current Conservative-Liberal Democrat Coalition party. Like the United States and China (Zhao, 2010), the adaptation of this approach often results in a decrease in public spending on HE and an increase in university tuition (Carpentier, 2012).

When New Labour came to power in 1997, it placed WP at the heart of HE reforms, which included the introduction of student fees in 1998. The par-ticipation rates for young people entering HE in the United Kingdom were considered low by international standards (OECD, 2005), with further evidence to suggest that young people from lower socio-economic backgrounds were dis-proportionately less likely to access post-compulsory education (Blanden and Machin, 2004; Machin and Vignoles, 2004). More recent statistics made avail-able by the Higher Education Funding Council for Education (HEFCE, 2010) claim that the above trends are now less acute and the likelihood of those from the lowest participation areas taking up a place at university (e.g. areas where the participation rates for young people entering post-compulsory education is low) has increased by 30% over the last 5 years and by 50% over the last 15 years. University enrolment figures obtained by the Sutton Trust (2010), however, conclude that the proportion of children on free school meals enrolled at the 25 most academically selective universities in England over the 3-year period 2005/06, 2006/07 and 2007/08 is equal to only 2% (approximately 1300 pupils each year) compared with 72.2% of other state school pupils and 25.8% educated at independent schools.

The meanings of WP remain contested and shifting in England; there is a long history of struggles over who has access to HE and in what forms (see Burke, 2012 for a historical overview and analysis of the debates). The WP policy regime in England is often linked with social justice (HEFCE, 2014a). However, the social justice strands of the regime are usually overshadowed by neoliberal and meritocratic principles and a current dominant discourse is that WP should 'promote and provide the opportunity of successful participation in higher education to all who can benefit from it' (HEFCE, 2014b). HE has moved quickly towards a marketed framework and, as Ball (2008, p. 9) observes, New Labour's appeal to the superiority of markets (over welfare-bureaucracy regimes) and global competitiveness reflects the 'subordination of education to economic imperatives'. Such privileging of the market (and associated discourses of competition, consumerism and entrepreneurialism) as mechanisms for transforming education can be traced to the Thatcher years (1988 Education Act), with moves to vocationalize HE, integrate 'enterprise' into degree schemes and generate closer links between HE and industry and commerce (Trowler, 1998).

The Conservative-Liberal Democratic Coalition was formed in May 2010 cementing trends towards 'enterprise' and decentralization. WP continues to be a central tenet of HE policy under the Coalition government, attracting significant public and HEIs funding (BIS, 2014). HEIs spent £424 million on access measures in 2010–2011 (HEFCE, 2013), and governments have spent about £87 million on widening access over 2013/14, with an additional £224 million on retention, £15 million on disability, and £100 million on the National Scholarship Programme (Universities UK, 2013). This investment coincides with adjustments to how WP activities and strategies are governed with a shift from a centrally organized WP policy regime to a devolved management regime, in which universities run their own WP schemes made of bespoke, 'in-house' access initiatives. Under the current arrangement, the HEFCE for England make the continued receipt of the WP budget allocation conditional on the production of an annual Access Agreement that all HEIs charging tuition fees of more than £6000 (more than the basic level of graduate contributions) are required to submit to the Office for Fair Access (OFFA).

The WP policy regime in England emphasizes the imperative to develop human capital to create competitive knowledge economies via entrepreneurialism and a highly skilled workforce (Boden and Epstein, 2006). This in turn drives massification, which, because of financial considerations, can only be achieved by increasing student fees (Barr, 2004). Neoliberal individualization of responsibility and reward (Walkerdine, 2003, p. 239) rationalizes these fees in terms of the downstream financial return to the individual graduate – education is constructed as an investment in the project of the self (Barr, 2004). This, in a neat elision, makes charging full fees an important aspect of WP with positive ramifications for social justice. WP also increases student numbers and, therefore, grows the HEIs' market (Burke, Boden and Whelan, 2014).

WP discourses were explicitly interpolated with the reform of student fees from 2012 to 2013 onwards. HEIs wishing to charge home/EU students in excess of £6000 pa are now locked into a system for the control, accountability and regulation of WP. A tie-in between permission to charge fees above the £6000 baseline and WP constitutes a financial control mechanism for 'steering at a distance', which has the intent and capacity to substantially determine, through regulation, how WP is enacted. WP activity is tied to government performance indicators, creating a form of accountability (Burke, Boden and Whelan, 2014).

At national level, responsibility for WP strategy and funding in England lies with the Department of Business, Innovation and Skills (BIS), the HEFCE and OFFA. BIS, as the ministry responsible for HE, sets high-level policy and decides on WP-funding allocations, which are then distributed by the HEFCE. These funds have been termed the 'Student Opportunity Fund' since 2013. In 2013–2014, HEFCE distributed £332 million in WP funds for three key categories: students from disadvantaged backgrounds; students with disabilities; and retention. Institutions develop strategies, interventions and policies to make decisions about how to allocate their funding and so there are a range of diverse practices across the country. Institutions are now required to demonstrate the effectiveness of the ways they use WP funding through evaluation; however, there remains a problem of the fragmentation of WP, as different opportunities and mechanisms are put in place by different institutions. Individual students are left to decode the diverse range of different institutional forms of support on offer across the country. This raises potential weaknesses in the system; the instruments of evaluation might not be fit for purpose; and there is potential for inequity across the system, with some students receiving greater support by the mere coincidence of their geographical location or due to a more informed choice of university.

In addition, HEIs are required to use a portion of all Home/EU fees charged at over £6,000 to support student access, success and progression by developing dedicated WP infrastructure and activities. This has to be evidenced by their Access Agreements – detailed individual WP plans which must be approved by OFFA, the non-departmental public body responsible for safeguarding fair access to HE in England. OFFA, a regulatory body, has powers to direct HEFCE to fine a university or suspend part of its grant if it deems an Access Agreement unacceptable. A refusal by OFFA to approve an Access Agreement would prevent the institution from charging above the baseline fee. WP activities at organizational level are therefore funded through HEFCE's Student Opportunity Fund, a portion of the student fee income and other institutional funding sources. Overall, institutional expenditure on WP has been shown to vary greatly (OFFA, 2013), as does the nature of activity.

A number of recent changes in policy and funding have created financial uncertainties for HEIs and have implications for increasing levels of organizational stratification of and inequalities in HE. There is an ongoing policy tension between HEI autonomy and the current demand for more careful monitoring, evaluation and regulation of WP activities. For instance, measures have been taken to ensure that HEIs move away from using additional fee income to provide financial support directly to students in the form of bursaries and so on, and towards investment in infrastructure and activity designed to support student access, success and progression through an emphasis on the 'student lifecycle' (BIS, 2014). The logic is that, as the deferral and income-contingent nature of loan repayment means that no one is excluded by virtue of finance from participation in HE, efforts should be directed at 'correcting' information asymmetries among excluded potential students and supporting them practically through HE (Burke, Boden and Whelan, 2014). There is now a greater attention to progression to postgraduate level study and employment and an emphatic shift from generating activities to evaluating and demonstrating evidence of outcomes. HEIs are now required to demonstrate how they are also supporting mature and part-time students, as well as young people from disadvantaged backgrounds. The anticipated diminution of the Student Opportunity Funding will have implications for those HEIs that recruit larger proportions of students from disadvantaged backgrounds (Universities UK, 2013). In the context of the stratification of HEIs, WP activity may become associated with less prestigious institutions, with concomitant social justice implications for students (Burke, Boden and Whelan, 2014).

BIS, OFFA and HEFCE have collectively expressed concern over the efficacy of WP strategies, leading to increasing demands for evaluation. There is evidence that lower socio-economic groups are still not accessing or progressing through HE; Les Ebdon, director of OFFA, has claimed that 'children from the wealthiest families... [are] up to eight times more likely to win places than the most disadvantaged... at the most selective institutions' (Sutton Trust, 2013, p. 6). In March 2014 OFFA released research claiming that there was 'no evidence' that bursaries influenced retention rates (OFFA, March 6th, 2014). Many institutions have consistently failed to meet their key annual WP benchmarks over the last decade (Whelan, 2013).

Qualitative research highlights that WP structures, activities and support are variable and uneven across institutions, regions and localities (Burke, 2012). Harrison and Hatt (2009, p. 1) have questioned the targeting methodologies (which follow HEFCE guidance) used in institutions to determine allocation of resources and participation in WP activities, finding that these tend to 'miss learners from lower socio-economic groups in areas of wider affluence and those in rural areas'. The concentration of WP budgets on outreach and financial support has tended to ignore issues of participation (Burke, 2012), and HEFCE and OFFA have now redirected their expectations of institutions towards the development of activities that explicitly support the whole 'student lifecycle' from access to progression (BIS, 2014). Finally, stark disparities remain in access by institutional type (Whelan, 2013), and there is a lack of evidence to evaluate WP 'progress'.

Conclusions

We have argued that the current practices related to WP policy regimes in China, England and the United States have perpetuated a vicious cycle of structural inequalities and that discourses of excellence and meritocracy often play a significant part in reproducing this cycle. In England and in the United States, WP policy regimes might be characterized as occupying a peripheral position in relation to social welfare policy. That is, policy makers and state actors often treat WP policy regimes as one aspect of an overall package of income and opportunity redistribution policy instruments. These redistribution policy instruments are often translated into financial aids. The US case illustrates that when the discourse of excellence intertwines with the merit-based financial aid mechanism, structural inequalities become reinforced. The Chinese government has created a binary system, which aims to incorporate the core values of Chinese socialism and to prevent 'unethical' western market practices from tarnishing the Party's core values. However, our analysis suggests that the Chinese model has not sufficiently offered a better mechanism than the western one in WP in HE. The English case is firmly located in a meritocratic view and has embedded WP in its moves towards a marketized approach, including the introduction and more recently the inflation of student fees. However, this has arguably reinforced rather than challenged inequities in student access to HE.

Although we have argued that discourses of excellence often undermine WP, in the *Times Higher Education* in May 1998, Amartya Sen points out that

it is important to understand the complex connection between academic excellence and social equity. Rather than seeing the two as being in deep

tension, we have to appreciate more fully how academic excellence promotes social equality, and how the advancement of social equity in turn
may help the cause of academic excellence.

(Sen, 1998)

As Sen says, equity and excellence do not have to be in tension, and with careful
and sensitive policy formulation a connection might be made to enhance both
dimensions. However, we must not naïvely believe that academic excellence
and social equity can straightforwardly co-exist either. The potential tensions
between academic excellence and social equity require both facilitation and
intervention through carefully formulated polices and governance arrangements that are deeply sensitive to the complexities of power and inequality. For
example, while the correlation between educational and economic inequality
is difficult to break down, policy debate and reform are urgently required to
tackle the issue concerning the cost of weakening student financial support
mechanisms that brings about the fragmentation of WP policy regimes.

HE institutions also need to play a part in eliminating the structural inequalities often exacerbated by meritocratic assumptions and perspectives. We argue
that the complex connection Sen refers to above must be reinforced by the
quality of coordination within any WP policy regime. WP policy regimes must
create alignments between different and often conflicting policy areas, between
social actors, in order that concerns to redress inequalities do not become
overshadowed. It is thus crucially important to uncover the core values and
discourses that sustain – or undermine – WP policy regimes.

References

Altbach, P. G. (2011) 'The past, present and future of the research university', in P. G.
    Altbach and J. Salmi (eds) *The Road to Academic Excellence-the Making of World-Class
    Research Universities* (pp. 11–32) (Washington, DC: The World Bank).
Ball, S. J. (2008) *The Education Debate* (Bristol: Policy Press).
Baptiste, H. P. and E. Q. Villa (2012) 'Affirmative action', in J. A. Banks (ed) *Encyclopedia
    of Diversity in Education* (pp. 35–40) (Thousand Oaks, CA: SAGE Publications).
BIS (Department for Business, Innovation and Skills) (2014) National Strategy for
    Access and Student Success in Higher Education. Retrieved November 27, 2014,
    from https://www.gov.uk/government/uploads/system/uploads/attachment_data/file/
    299689/bis-14-516-national-strategy-for-access-and-student-success.pdf.
Blanden, J. and S. Machin (2004) 'Educational inequality and the expansion of UK higher
    education', *Scottish Journal of Political Economy*, 54, 230–249.
Boden, R. and D. Epstein (2006) 'Managing the research imagination: globalisation and
    research in higher education', *Globalisation, Societies and Education*, 4(2), 223–236.
Burke, P. J. (2012) *The Right to Higher Education: Beyond Widening Participation* (London
    and New York: Routledge).
Burke, P. J., Boden, R. and P. Whelan (2014) The Governance of Widening Participation.
    Unpublished work-in-progress.

Cang, W. (August 8, 2014) 'Tuition fees see first hike in 10 years', China Daily. Retrieved January 9, 2015, from http://www.chinadaily.com.cn/china/2014-08/08/content_18269714.htm.

Carpentier, V. (2012) 'Public-private substitution in higher education: has cost-sharing gone too far?' *Higher Education Quarterly*, 66(4), 363–390.

Constitution of Communist Party of China (2013) The News of Communist Party of China. March 29, 2013. Retrieved November 26, 2014, from http://english.cpc.people.com.cn/206972/206981/8188088.html.

Ding, Xiaohao (2007) 'Expansion and equality of access to higher education in China', *Frontiers of Education in China*, 2(2), 151–162.

Dong, Haiying and Xuehong Wan (2012) 'Higher education tuition and fees in China: implications and impacts on affordability and educational equity', *Current Issues in Education*, 15(1), 1–10.

Ellis, C. and J. A. Stimson (2012) *Ideology in America* (New York: Cambridge University Press).

Fan, J. P. H., Morck, R. and B. Yeung (2012) 'Translating market socialism with Chinese characteristics into sustained prosperity', in J. P. H. Fan and R. Morck (eds) *Capitalizing China* (pp. 1–34) (Chicago: University of Chicago Press).

Gu, Mingyuan and Zhongying Shi (eds) (2010) National Long-Term Education Reform and Development Plan 2010–2020. Retrieved October 4, 2014, from http://www.gov.cn/jrzg/2010-07/29/content_1667143.htm.

HEFCE (2010) Trends in Young Participation in Higher Education: Core Results for England. Retrieved November 15, 2014, from http://www.hefce.ac.uk/media/hefce/content/pubs/2010/201003/10_03.pdf.

Heffernan, R. (2011) 'Labour's new labour legacy: politics after Blair and Brown', *Political Studies Review*, 9(2), 163–177.

Heller, D. E. (2007) 'Financing public research universities in the United States: the role of students and their families', in R. L. Geiger, C. L. Colbeck, R. L. Williams and G. K. Anderson (eds) *Future of the American Public Research University* (pp. 35–54) (Rotterdam and Taipei: Sense Publishers).

Higher Education Funding Council for England (HEFCE) (2014a) Widening Participation Policy. Retrieved November 15, 2014, from http://www.hefce.ac.uk/whatwedo/wp/policy/.

HEFCE (2014b) Understanding the Impact of Widening Participation. Retrieved November 15, 2014, from http://www.hefce.ac.uk/whatwedo/wp/current/impact/.

Johnson, L. B. (June 4, 1965) Commencement Address at Howard University: To Fulfill These Rights. Retrieved November 20, 2014, from http://www.presidency.ucsb.edu/ws/index.php?pid=27021.

Keohane, R. O. and J. S. Nye (1989) *Power and Interdependence*, 2nd edn (Boston and London: Scott, Foresman and Co., Glenview).

Knapp, L. G., Kelly-Reid, J. E. and R. W. Whitmore (2007) Enrollment in Postsecondary Institutions, Fall 2005; Graduation Rates, 1999 and 2002 Cohorts; and Financial Statistics, Fiscal Year 2005. Retrieved November 15, 2014, from http://nces.ed.gov/pubs2007/2007154.pdf.

Krasner, S. (1982) 'Structural causes and regime consequences: regimes as intervening variables', *International Organization*, 36(2), 185–205.

Kratochwil, F. and J. G. Ruggie. (2001) 'International organization: the state of the art or an art of the state', in L. L. Martin and B. A. Simmons (eds) *International Institutions: An International Organization Reader* (Boston: The MIT Press).

Lazerson, M. (2010) *Higher Education and the American Dream: Success and Its Discontents* (Budapest: Central European University Press).

Machin, S. and A. Vignoles (2004) 'Educational inequality: the widening socio-economic gap', *Fiscal Studies*, 25, 107–128.

Maher F. and M. Tetreault (2007) *Privilege and Diversity in the Academy* (New York/London: Routledge).

Marginson, S. (2007) 'Global university rankings: implications in general and for Australia', *Journal of Higher Education Policy and Management*, 29(2), 131–142.

May, P. J. and A. E. Jochim. (2013) *Policy Regime Perspectives: Policies, Politics, and Governing*, paper presented at the International Conference on Public Policy, Grenoble, France, Retrieved June 26–28, 2013.

Mohrman, K. (2009) 'What world-class universities should not adopt from the American higher education model', in Jan Sadlak and Liu Nian Cai (eds) *The World-Class University as Part of a New Higher Education Paradigm: From Institutional Qualities to Systemic Excellence* (pp. 97–118) (Bucharest: UNESCO-CEPES).

Naidoo, R. (2010) 'Global learning in a neoliberal age: implications for development', in E. Unterhalter and V. Carpentier (eds) *Global Inequalities and Higher Education: Whose Interests Are We Serving?* (Hampshire: Palgrave).

News of the Communist Party of China (March 29, 2013) Communist Party of China in Brief. Retrieved September 25, 2014, from http://english.cpc.people.com.cn/206972/206981/8188401.html.

Nixon, J. (2013) 'The drift to conformity: the myth of institutional diversity', in Tero Erkkilä (ed) *Global University Rankings: Challenges for European Higher Education* (pp. 92–108) (London and New York: Palgrave Macmillan).

OECD (2005) *Education at a Glance* (Paris: OECD).

OFFA (2013) Access Agreement and Widening Participation Strategic Assessment 2011–12 and National Scholarship Programme 2012–13 (in-year) Monitoring Outcomes. Retrieved November 15, 2014, from http://www.offa.org.uk/wp-content/uploads/2013/06/HEFCEOFFA-Joint-Monitoring-Outcomes-Report.pdf.

OFFA (March 6, 2014) Research finds 'no evidence' of positive effect of bursaries on student retention. Retrieved November 15, 2014, from http://www.offa.org.uk/press-releases/offa-research-finds-no-evidence-of-positive-effect-of-bursaries-on-student-retention/.

People's Daily Online (September 2, 2004) The Political Spectrum of Asian Political Parties. http://en.people.cn/200409/02/eng20040902_155680.html.

Ramo, J. C. (2004) The Beijing Consensus. Retrieved October 4, 2014, from http://fpc.org.uk/fsblob/244.pdf.

Rhoads, R. and K. Szelényi (2011) *Global Citizenship and the University: Advancing Social Life and Relations in an Interdependent World* (Stanford, CA: Stanford University Press).

Rostan, M. and M. Vaira (2011) 'Questioning excellence in higher education: an introduction', in M. Rostan and M. Vaira (eds) *Questioning Excellence in Higher Education: Policies, Experiences and Challenges in National and Comparative Perspective* (pp. vii–xvii) (Rotterdam: Sense Publishers).

Salmi, J. (2011) 'The road to academic excellence: lessons of experience', in Philip G. Altbach and Jamil Salmi (eds) *The Road to Academic Excellence-the Making of World-Class Research Universities* (Washington, DC: The World Bank).

Sen, A. (2006) *The Argumentative Indian: Writings on Indian History, Culture and Identity* (London: Penguin).

Sen, A. (May 4, 1998) Excellence and Equity. Time Higher Education. Retrieved November 25, 2014, from http://www.timeshighereducation.co.uk/news/excellence-and-equity/107112.article.

Stevenson, J., P. J. Burke and P. Whelan (2014) *Pedagogic Stratification and the Shifting Landscape of Higher Education* (York: Higher Education Academy).

Sutton Trust (2010) Responding to the New Landscape for University Access. Retrieved November 12, 2014, from http://www.suttontrust.com/public/ . . . /access-proposals-report-final.pdf.

Sutton Trust (2013) Universities Summit Report. Advancing Access and Admissions, The Sutton Trust Summit, November 2013. Retrieved November 12, 2014, from http://www.suttontrust.com/news/publications/universities-summit-report/.

Trowler, P. (1998) *Education Policy* (East Sussex: The Gildredge Press).

Wang, W. (2005) 'Son preference and educational opportunities of children in China-I wish you were a boy!', *Gender Issues*, 22(2), 3–30.

Whelan, P. (2013) *The Discourse and Policy of Widening Participation in England*. Unpublished PhD thesis, Leeds: Leeds Metropolitan University.

Williams, J. (2013) *Consuming Higher Education? Why Learning Can't Be Bought* (London and New York: Bloomsbury Academic).

Williams, G. and I. Kitaev (2005) 'Overview of National Policy Contexts for Entrepreneurialism in Higher Education Institutions', *Higher Education Management and Policy*, 17(3), 125–141.

Wilson, C. A. (2000) 'Policy regimes and policy change', *Journal of Public Policy*, 20(3), 247–274.

Wong, E. (July 19, 2013) Survey in China Shows a Wide Gap in Income. *The New York Times*. Retrieved January 9, 2015, from http://www.nytimes.com/2013/07/20/world/asia/survey-in-china-shows-wide-income-gap.html?_r=0.

World Bank (2009) Literature Review on Equity and Access to Tertiary Education in the East Asia Region. Retrieved September 29, 2014, from http://siteresources.worldbank.org/EDUCATION/Resources/278200-1099079877269/547664-1099079956815/5476701276537814548/WorldBank_EAR_Equity_LitReview.pdf.

Xing, L. and T. M. Shaw (2013) 'The political economy of Chinese state capitalism', *The Journal of China and International Relations*, 1(1), 88–113.

Xinhu News (September 4, 2014) Xinhua Insight: China to Reform College Entrance Exam, Enrollment System. Retrieved September 28, 2014, from http://news.xinhuanet.com/english/indepth/2014-09/04/c_133621671.htm.

Xu, B. and E. Albert (November 17, 2014) The Chinese Communist Party. *Council on Foreign Relations*. Retrieved November 20, 2014, from http://www.cfr.org/china/chinese-communist-party/p29443.

Yang, Rui (2007) 'Urban–rural disparities in educational equality: China's pressing challenge in a context of economic growth and political change', in W. T. Pink and G. W. Noblit (eds) *International Handbook of Urban Education* (pp. 333–358) (Dordrecht: Springer).

Yang, Siwei (2012) 'Higher education', in S. W. Yang (ed) *The Education Development since the Reform and Opening Up in China* (Taipei: Wunan), ISBN: 9789571166407 (printed in traditional Chinese).

Yang, Xiaoming (2011) *The Research on Higher Education Policy* (Zhengzhou: Daxiang) (Printed in Simplified Chinese). ISBN:9787534760167.

Yellen, J. L. (October 17, 2014) Perspectives on Inequality and Opportunity from the Survey of Consumer Finances – Remarks by Chair Board of Governors of the Federal Reserve System at the Conference on Economic Opportunity and Inequality.

Retrieved November 13, 2014 from http://www.federalreserve.gov/newsevents/speech/yellen20141017a.pdf.

Zha, Q. (2009) 'Diversification or homogenization: how governments and markets have combined to (re)shape Chinese higher education in its recent massification process', *Higher Education*, 58(1), 41–58.

Zha, X. and S. Ding (2007) 'Can low tuition fee policy improve higher education equity and social welfare?' *Frontiers of Education in China*, 2(2), 181–190.

Zhang, Y. and B. Liu (2006) 'Social occupational classes and higher-education opportunities in contemporary China: a study on the distribution of a scarce social capital', *Frontiers of Education in China*, 1(1), 89–99.

Zhao, X. (2010) 'Market forces in higher education-Chinese and British experience between mid-1980s and mid-1990s', *International Education Studies*, 3(1), 66–72.

Zhou, X., Moen, P. and N. B. Tuma (1998) 'Educational stratification in urban China: 1949–94', *Sociology of Education*, 71(3), 199–222.

30
Gender in Higher Education: A Critical Review

Pat O'Connor, Teresa Carvalho, Agnete Vabø and Sónia Cardoso

Introduction

This chapter is concerned with describing and critically evaluating the literature on the existence of and explanations for gender imbalances in higher education (HE) focusing particularly on girls' increasing access to HE and women's limited access to senior positions there. These topics reflect a fundamental paradox in HE across Western society, namely that despite increases in women's participation at undergraduate and post-graduate levels (UNESCO, 2012) their access to senior positions remains limited (EU, 2013). It cannot simply be assumed that the latter will automatically increase, since the growth of girls' access to HE is not a recent phenomenon. Women, especially in Western Europe and North America, started to catch up with men in terms of enrolments in the 1970s and had surpassed them by the early 1980s, with the rate of women's enrolments growing almost twice as fast as men's rate (UNESCO, 2012). This raises fundamental problems for Western societies since educational achievements have been seen as a meritocratic basis for accessing senior positions in HE.

Senior positions in HE include those at (full) professorial level and in senior management at Rector/Vice Chancellor (VC)/Presidential level (EU, 2013). Several rationales for the promotion of gender equality in senior positions have been advanced. First, equality has been seen as an important element in contributing to social justice within democratic societies. Second, it has been seen as having economic benefits, with some studies showing a positive correlation between the presence of highly educated women in leadership positions and business performance (Smith, Smith and Verner, 2006). In national and international contexts, diversity (including gender) has been seen as contributing to research innovation (EU, 2012). Women's education, in general, and gender initiatives, in particular, have also been seen as contributing to economic growth (OECD, 2012). Third, in HE itself, an important rationale is that organizations that create a culture of equal opportunity (EO) are better able to attract, retain and motivate the most qualified individuals (McIntyre et al., 2002). Fourth, in a gendered society, it is suggested that women can bring distinct perspectives which facilitate effective representative leadership (Neale, 2011). Fifth, women's presence in the highest positions increases their opportunities to influence organizational and scientific decisions (Santiago, Carvalho and Vabø, 2012). Sixth, their occupancy of such positions provides role models for a new generation of HE students and faculty (EU, 2013).

In this chapter, the focus is on gender inequality from women's perspective. Gender is seen as a systemic phenomenon that is 'present in the processes, practices, images and ideologies, and distributions of power in the various sectors of social life' (Acker, 1992: 167) and is a crucial basis for inequality regimes (Acker, 2006). Gender does not simply differentiate between individuals; it is socially constructed and multi-level (Risman and Davies, 2013; Wharton, 2011). Thus, explanations for girls increasing access to HE and women's limited access to senior positions in HE are located at several levels. These include the following: the individual (e.g. socialization; entitlement); the interactional (e.g. 'Othering'; patronizing); the organizational (e.g. structure and culture); the systemic (e.g. the relationship with the state); and the wider institutional cultural level (e.g. cultural stereotypes). These levels are analytically distinct, although in practice they frequently interrelate. In this chapter, attention is mainly focused on European countries with broadly similar HE systems and patterns of student participation, but with rather different patterns as regards the proportion of women in senior positions (i.e. Norway, Ireland and Portugal).

Getting in but not getting on in higher education

Women's participation in HE, relative to men's, has increased, especially in Western Europe and North America. Across the EU 27, women constitute just under half (46%) of all PhD graduates and their rate of increase from 2002 to 2010 was more than twice that of their male counterparts (EU, 2013). Indeed, female PhD graduates equalled or outnumbered men in all areas except Science, Maths and Computing (where they nevertheless made up 40% of the PhD graduates) and Engineering, Manufacturing and Construction (where they constituted 26% of the PhD graduates) (EU, 2013: 5). Furthermore, such patterns have appeared not only in countries such as Norway (which typically is ranked highly on international gender equality indices) but also in countries, such as Portugal, which are ranked much lower on these indices. In Portugal, for instance, gender gaps in PhD attainment are reversing: from 2004 to 2011, 62% of all PhDs awarded went to females and the proportion of women was higher than men, even in PhDs in Science and Engineering (Scientific American, 2014). Both in the United States and Canada similar, although weaker, patterns exist (Bekhouch et al., 2013). However, rather than being welcomed, such patterns are seen as reflecting a 'dumbing down' of standards; 'easier' assessments that are assumed to test 'diligence rather than intelligence' (Leathwood and Read, 2009: 18), reflecting a wider pattern of female 'misrecognition' (Frazer, 2008).

The proportion of women in academic positions in universities has also increased steadily cross-nationally, although women remain under-represented in (full) professorial positions (i.e. grade A positions) in both the EU and elsewhere (e.g. Australia). Across the EU, although women constitute 44% of grade C academic staff, they constitute only 20% of grade A staff (i.e. the equivalent of full professor) (EU, 2013). The proportion of women in professorial positions also varies substantially between different disciplinary areas, being highest in the Humanities and lowest in Science and Engineering, with Medicine in an intermediate position (EU, 2013). However, despite their very different rankings on international inequality indices, the proportion of women at professoriate level in Ireland and Portugal is quite similar (19% and 24%, respectively) (Carvalho, Cardoso and Sousa, 2014; O'Connor, 2014a): reflecting a global pattern of under-representation of women in such positions (Husu, 2001).

Women are also poorly represented in university senior management cross-nationally. On average, throughout the EU 27, 16% of all HE organizations and only 10% of universities are headed by women (EU, 2013). There is a relationship between this and rank on international gender equality indices. For instance, Norway is ranked high on such indices and is among those having the highest proportion of women in these positions. However, there is no simple relationship between these patterns and the students' gender profile. Thus, for example, in Portugal, despite the high proportion of women at PhD level, only 7% of those leading universities are women. Furthermore, the similarity in the professorial profiles of Portugal and Ireland is not reproduced at this level. Thus, no woman has ever headed up an Irish public university.

Explanations for these gender imbalances will now be explored at several levels.

Individual level

Women's participation in HE is frequently the result of the interaction of diverse factors (individual, interactional, organizational, systemic and institutional) (UNESCO, 2010, 2012). Yet increases in that participation tend to be seen as an individual achievement, related to the fulfilment of personal expectations and individual social mobility (Schoon and Eccles, 2014). Internationally, there are persistent differences in the fields in which men and women predominantly enrol, indicating that horizontal segregation persists, particularly among undergraduates. For instance, women predominate (70%–75%) among graduates in Education and Health and Welfare in the overwhelming majority of countries (EU, 2013). Directly or indirectly, these patterns reflect an extension of women's caring role in the family. Similarly, undergraduate programmes involving technology are predominantly chosen by men. Indeed, in a wide range of countries, at most one-third of all graduates in the fields of Engineering, Manufacturing and Construction are women, despite many initiatives to reduce stereotypical gendered choices (OECD, 2013).

Explanations at the level of the individual for the under-representation of women in senior positions in HE (whether academic or managerial) are particularly attractive since they suggest that 'the problem is women' constructing them 'as a remedial group, with the emphasis on getting them into better shape in order to engage more effectively with existing structures' (Morley, 1994: 194). Much is made of women's lack of career planning and ambition, low self-esteem, poor political skills, poor ability to market themselves and their lifestyle choices (O'Connor, 2014a). Such explanations suggest that such patterns are 'natural' (reflecting essentialist views) or that they reflect underlying cultural constructions of femininity/masculinity. In both cases, they are depicted as inevitable, ignoring the wider social context (e.g. one in which there are often strong gendered cross-cultural norms surrounding modesty concerning individual achievements and a reluctance to 'self-promote': Bagilhole and Goode, 2001).

Elements of persisting male privileging can also be identified. In stratified HE systems, where different types of HE organizations co-exist, men tend to enrol in the more prestigious and well-resourced ones (Leathwood and Read, 2009). A focus on choices 'whether free or constrained' (Ceci and Williams, 2011) underplays the part played by the wider societal and cultural context. A gendered felt lack of entitlement in Western society reflects a wider gendered pattern of 'misrecognition' (Frazer, 2008), supported by the wider cultural institutional level (discussed later).

When stripped of their essentialist qualities, explanations at the level of the individual have an element of validity, reflecting as they do 'the psychological effects of living in a sexist society' (Husu, 2001: 38). To some extent they can be seen as effectively 'blaming the victim'. In so far as such attitudes reflect deeper constructions of femininity or gendered selves, they can be seen as constituting cultural limits to the possibilities for change at a particular moment in time. However, they can be eroded by challenging the assumptions on which they are based (Ridgeway and Correll, 2004). The dramatic increase in the proportion of women students in HE challenges assumptions that change cannot occur.

Interactional level

There is an ever-increasing recognition of the importance of day-to-day interaction or 'micro-politics' (Morley, 1999) as a way of perpetuating gender inequalities. It is reflected in homosocial behaviour and various kinds of 'Othering' including exclusionary or patronizing behaviour; differential informal evaluation of men and women and their competencies; and 'doing gender' (West and Zimmerman, 1987) in a way that organizes 'relations of inequality' (Wharton, 2011: 8).

Homosociability, the selection of others with similar characteristics to oneself (Kanter, 1977) and the 'Othering' (Acker, 1980) of those who are seen as different were early recognized as crucial interactional processes. Such processes, first, may constitute part of the explanation for the persistence of horizontal segregation in students' participation in HE (discussed earlier). Second they are relevant at the academic staff level since peer evaluation, networking, mentoring and sponsorship are crucial, with success reflecting evaluative (and often gendered) judgements (Lamont, 2009). Third, the gender of the person enacting the performance is in itself an important element in the evaluation of that performance. Thus, in Bourdieu's (2001) terms, the symbolic negative coefficient attached to being a woman affects the perceived value of that performance.

At an interactional level the impact of such a coefficient has been most clearly documented in the differential expectations and evaluations of men and women, reflecting unconscious bias (Valian, 1999). Such biases were reflected in the evaluation of Swedish medical research funding applications where: 'a female applicant had to be 2.5 times more productive than the average male applicant to receive the same [scientific] competence score as he' (Wenneras and Wold, 1997: 3). Gender gaps in citation patterns have also been identified, with male authors being less likely to cite publications by women (Mc Laughlin Michell et al., 2013).

At a day-to-day interactional level, the women senior managers in O'Connor's (2014a) study saw their gender as very visible to their male colleagues and not in a positive way. According to those women, their male senior management colleagues (particularly those who had not worked outside the Irish HE system) saw them as 'challenging', 'disruptive', 'irritating' and 'frightening'. Such attitudes were not peculiar to that context. The word 'frightening' which is evocative both of women's perceived power and unacceptability, was also used by Husu's Finnish respondents (2001:144). The women senior managers in the Irish study overwhelmingly saw their female colleagues' perception of them as supportive, capable and competent; while the men were much more likely to see their own gender as invisible to both men and women (reflecting the invisibility of the privileged characteristics of those in hegemonic positions). There was also evidence of a kind of paternalistic 'heroic masculinity' (Kerfoot and Whitehead, 1998: 451), a 'patronizing benevolent sexism' (Krefting, 2003: 269), among senior managers in Portugal and Ireland, which purported to protect women by not involving them in university management 'for their own good' (O'Connor, 2014a). Interactional patterns that erode women's sense of confidence, their evaluation of themselves and their desire to participate in such, often predominantly male, contexts are an important element in the informal creation of 'chilly' organizational cultures.

Explanations at the interactional level help us to understand the micro-processes through which gender inequality is maintained.

Organizational level

A good deal of research at this level has focused on the barriers to women's access to senior positions, with much less attention being paid to student access. This reflects the fact that, typically, although academic organizations can influence the number of students admitted to a particular course, the total number of students admitted to HE reflects wider systemic policies framed by the state (see the next section).

Explanations for the under-representation of women in senior positions (whether the professoriate or senior management) have focused on structural or cultural explanations or an amalgamation of these, reflected in a variety of metaphors such as the leaky pipeline (i.e. the disappearance of women as they move up the hierarchy), glass ceilings, glass cliffs, labyrinths and so on. In structural terms, explanations include a focus on the nature of recruitment/retention processes; the nature and transparency of procedures and career structures (Knights and Richards, 2003); and the predominantly male profile of academic gatekeepers (e.g. journal editorships; research funding organizations) (Husu, 2006).

Thus, for example, although the advertising of professorial posts was expected, other than in exceptional circumstances, the majority of university professorial positions in the Netherlands were not advertised (Van den Brink and Benschop, 2012). Sheltzer and Smith (2014) found that male academic leaders in elite laboratories were significantly less likely to hire female postdoctoral trainees than their female counterparts, with consequences for such women's subsequent career achievements. Despite the increasing presence of various bureaucratic procedures such as workload models, there has been a tendency for women to be disproportionately allocated responsibility for administrative tasks (Carvalho and Santiago, 2010). This can be seen as an obstacle to the development of their research profile and hence their career progress (Sax et al., 2002). The undervaluing of lecturing also has consequences for women who are disproportionately assigned such work (O'Connor, 2014a).

The pipeline explanation implicitly assumes that men and women will be equally likely to occupy senior positions in the professoriate and in senior management in the future (Carvalho, White and Machado-Taylor, 2013; Heijstra, O'Connor and Rafnsdottir, 2013). However, Norwegian (also Swedish) studies of recruitment patterns over time (Hovdhaugen and Gunnes, 2008; Silander,

2010) suggest that women will not inevitably progress to professoriate or senior management positions as they have a slower career progression than men across all disciplines (see also Heijstra, Bjarnason and Rafnsdottir, 2014).

Cultural explanations have particularly focused on organizational cultures that are unfriendly or unhelpful to women (Coleman, 2011; Morley, 2013). Reference has been made to the way in which the culture and criteria of excellence in HE are implicitly based on a male model, making it difficult for women to access power other than as 'pseudo males' where their position is essentially fragile (Cockburn, 1991). Several studies have shown the application of different standards to men and women, for example experimental studies of curriculum vitae showed that when both sexes had achieved the same objective level of performance, double standards were applied by men, with women being held to a higher level of competence (Foschi, 2006). In the United States, in a randomized double-blind experimental study, both female and male science faculty from research-intensive universities rated the male candidate as more employable, and worthy of a higher starting salary than the identical female candidate (Moss-Racusin et al., 2012). Van den Brink and Benschop (2012) found that in professorial appointment processes, women were expected to be metaphorical 'five legged sheep', while male 'four legged sheep' were acceptable. Constructions of excellence, which underpin recruitment/promotion processes although ostensibly gender neutral, are increasingly recognized as directly or indirectly privileging men or male-dominated disciplines (Lynch et al., 2012; O'Connor, 2014a; O'Connor and O'Hagan, 2015).

In some managerialist contexts, a tendency for Rectors/VCs/Presidents to be chosen from predominantly male areas such as STEM (Science, Technology, Engineering and Mathematics) has been noted (Bagilhole and White, 2011), with surprisingly little attention being paid to the greater availability of senior posts in these areas of predominantly male academic employment. Organizations' 'privileging and non-responsibility' as regards caring responsibilities (Grummell et al., 2009; Lynch et al., 2012) has also been seen as affecting women's access to senior positions, with attitudes to maternity being a particularly critical issue. However, such attitudes cannot explain the absence of single women from senior positions (Morley, 2013). For Valian (1999), it is the cumulative effect of small disadvantages that ultimately impacts on women's access to organizational power.

Managerialism, with its focus on performance indicators, appears to offer the hope that formalization of procedures will increase women's access to senior positions (Deem, Hilliard and Reed, 2008). Lamont's (2009) focus on the essentially subjective character of peer evaluations underlines the limitations of such strategies, although there is evidence from experimental studies that accountability does reduce the extent of gender bias (Foschi, 2004).

Much of the literature on organizational change ignores the importance of embedding such change in the gendered content of teaching, research and related structures so as to reduce the possibility of equality policies being 'tick box' exercises which do not challenge the gendered structures or culture of HE (Kjendal, Rindfleish and Sheridan, 2005; Wagner et al., 2008). In Europe, Zimmer (2003) found no link between Affirmative Action programmes (AA programmes) at universities and the number of women in top positions. However, studies evaluating a number of policies and procedures implemented in Australia, ranging from simple training initiatives directed at women to the establishment of positional quotas, indicate a positive impact on women's success rates in applying for middle and higher level positions (Winchester et al., 2006). With a small number of exceptions (such as the positive evaluations of mentoring at the Norwegian University of Science and Technology), other strategies such as mentoring, targets, quotas and various kinds of AA programmes have been widely discussed, but with few attempts at evaluating their impact in terms of increasing the proportion of women in senior positions.

Relatively little attention has been paid to identifying the key drivers of gendered change within organizations. O'Connor (2014b) presents a narrative of organizational change in a new university, where formal and informal leadership coalesced around gender equality with the proportion of women in the professoriate increasing from zero to 34% over a 15-year period. There have been accounts by individuals of their roles as change agents (Morley and Walsh, 1996) or 'tempered radicals' (Myerson and Scully, 1995). However, little consideration has been given to analysing the structural conditions and cultural contexts that facilitate moving a gender agenda forward in HE.

Overall, although explanations at the organizational level have demonstrated its importance, frequently the focus of intervention reverts to 'fixing the woman'.

Systemic level

Individual HE organizations exist in a wider systemic context and are impacted on by the state and other stakeholders. These actors shape the role (and sometimes the structures) of HE and intentionally or accidentally influence its gendered nature through the development and implementation of national state policies, including those related to student access. In some countries, such as Ireland and Portugal, increased participation by girls in HE has come about almost by accident, largely due to a selection process based on academic grades, in a context where the state has imposed no limits on the total number of students admitted to HE, in the context of other objectives (such as political popularity, regional development, etc.) (Carvalho and Santiago, 2010; O'Connor, 2014a).

Globalization and its gendered impact on women's access to senior positions in HE has been subject to relatively little empirical investigation, although international activity has become an integral part of academia (Fox and Mohapatra, 2007). Women academics face more barriers to international activities than men; are less likely to engage in international collaboration (Vabø et al., 2014), to publish internationally or with international co-authors (Padilla et al., 2011); or to be successful in accessing international research funding (Ledin et al., 2007). These gender differences may reflect women's position in society and the disproportionate assignment of family responsibilities to them. Global trends towards research intensive universities also disadvantage women even in countries such as Sweden and Norway (Lindgren et al., 2010). Research that is gender blind 'may often be bad science or of limited value' (Mavin and Bryans, 2002: 247), but this is literally unthinkable in many HE systems.

In the context of neoliberalism, research activities with a potential commercialization focus, particularly in specific areas of Biosciences and Information Technology, have been prioritized globally. Universities that are publicly funded are in effect using some of these resources to generate private profits, while at the same time reducing expenditure on front-line teaching (Slaughter and Rhoades, 2010). These policies have gendered implications since the areas that are targeted (and where both state and privately funded professorial chairs are most likely to be located) are areas of predominantly male academic employment in HE. Cuts to front-line teaching can disproportionately affect areas where women faculty are most likely to be located (e.g. Humanities and parts of the Social Sciences).

Relationships between HE and the state vary cross-nationally. Unusually in Austria, the state has been very involved in interventions to promote the advancement of women through legislative measures, monetary and non-monetary support, including programme measures (such as *Excellentia*), and through the establishment of coordinated units for gender research in selected universities (Wroblewski and Leitner, 2011). The introduction of a legally binding 40% gender quota for university decision-making structures in 2009, in that context, increased the proportion of women VCs from zero in 2009 to 19% in 2012 (Wroblewski, 2014). The proportion of women Rectors in Norway (at 32%) (EU, 2013) may also indirectly reflect the impact of gender quotas in publicly funded organizations.

In societies such as Norway and even Iceland, where for many decades much emphasis has been put on solid welfare arrangements (e.g. generous maternity leave, childcare, legislation and measures for gender equality), the speed of change has been slower and the proportion of women at full professorial level is unexceptional (21% and 25% respectively) (Heijstra, O' Connor and Rafnsdottir, 2013). This suggests that improvements in the wider societal context appear in most cases to have limited effects on the gender profile of professorial leadership in HE. However, the *Excellentia* programme in Austria, with state support and a substantial budget, increased the proportion of female professors from 8% in 2003 to 19% in 2010, in a context where a substantial minority of existing (male) professors were due to retire and where earlier initiatives had created a pool of appointment ready women (Wroblewski and Leitner, 2011).

Overall, however, at the systemic level there has been little concern by the state or other stakeholders with gender.

Wider cultural institutional level

HE organizations are also enmeshed within a wider institutional context characterized by underlying gender stereotypes or cultural beliefs which are part of the symbolic structure that classifies people into two groups (i.e. men and women) and normatively attributes different and 'natural' personal qualities to them (aggression or dominance to men and submissiveness or subordination to women). While the specific areas that are seen as appropriate or 'natural' for women/men vary over time and across national contexts, predominantly female areas are typically less well paid than areas where men predominate. Such trends reflect a wider pattern of 'misrecognition' (Frazer, 2008) of girls and a privileging of boys (Connell, 1995). Ideological control through stereotypes is important to persuade women that gendered qualities are natural and inevitable, with the implicit assumption that those who lack these qualities are unnatural. The fact that in most Western societies, the family perpetuates such stereotypes offers further institutional support. Gender stereotypes are also important in sustaining the differential value of men and women (Ridgeway, 2011), providing the ultimate ideological underpinning at individual, interactional, organizational and systemic levels. Although these beliefs are very resistant to change, under particular conditions change can happen (Ely and Myerson, 2010).

At the individual student level, such stereotypes seem to have had little effect, other than perhaps in affecting girls' willingness to choose STEM subjects in particular national contexts. 'Think manager–think male' (Schein et al., 1996) has been seen as a universal phenomenon, especially among men. A tension has been identified between leadership roles and female gender roles in Western countries: 'People's beliefs about leadership are thus more similar to their beliefs about men than women' (Ely and Padavic, 2007: 52; see also Fitzgerald, 2014). Models of leadership are not inclusive of women or other 'outsiders' (Blackmore and Sachs, 2007). Gender stereotypes effectively legitimate the gendered occupancy of senior positions (Acker, 1990) and include 'disparaging stereotypic public cultural representations' of women in such positions (Frazer, 2008: 14). They create potential difficulties for women in envisioning themselves in such positions (Powell, Butterfield and Parent, 2002) and have been seen as a key factor in perpetuating gender inequality (OECD, 2012; Coleman, 2011). The presence of women in such positions facilitates the erosion of such stereotypes (O'Connor and Goransson, 2015; see also O'Connor and Carvalho, 2014 for a similar effect on gendered management styles).

At this wider cultural institutional level, stereotypes legitimate men's access to senior leadership positions.

Conclusions

We have been concerned with looking at gender in HE, focusing particularly on girls' increasing access to HE and women's limited access to senior positions. Gender is perceived as a multi-level phenomenon. Although analytically distinct, these different levels interact and reinforce each other. Extensive change has occurred at student level, since, especially in Europe (and North America), girls have improved their participation at both undergraduate and postgraduate levels. It is suggested that the systemic level (and particularly the state) has played a key and often unintended role: frequently (as in Portugal and Ireland) without any legitimating logic, or even any awareness of the gendered consequences of such action. The most socially acceptable explanation for this is at the individual level, underpinned by the institutional cultural one. Such explanations fit with meritocratic individualism. However, the achievements of girls over boys do raise troubling issues for societies which are most comfortable with male achievement. Hence, girls' success has been accompanied by mutterings about the nature of HE assessments and a greater valuation of those areas where male students and faculty are most likely to be found (i.e. STEM). Stereotypical beliefs about women are used to explain their scarcity in these areas in most societies, although in some countries, such as Portugal, patterns have changed.

The individual level, underpinned by the institutional cultural level, is also attractive as an explanation for the scarcity of women in top leadership positions in HE. Such explanations imply that the under-representation of women in such positions is 'natural', inevitable or what women want (Connell, 1995). However, they ignore the demonstrated gendered nature of HE organizations; their impact on women's career progression; women's frequent marginalization in 'chilly' organizational cultures; as well as the devaluing of women through gendered constructions of excellence. While the organizational level (supplemented by the interactional one) seems particularly important in affecting the proportion of women in professorial positions, the systemic level is more relevant to their increasing proportion in senior management (i.e. at Rector/VC/Presidential level). Paradoxically, it is cross-national structures (e.g. OECD and EU), driven by a market ideology, which are becoming uneasy about the loss to society consequent on the exclusion or marginalization of highly educated women.

Trying to identify critical points of intervention in the context of the multi-level reality of gender is difficult. It is clear that individual behaviour can change. It is also clear that at the systemic level some degree of change can be driven by legislative enactments and structural initiatives. The support of senior leadership, particularly for fundamental cultural change at the organizational level is crucial, as is the embedding of such change in gendered research. The status of HE organizations as effectively expert organizations and the dominance of assumptions about the gender-neutral nature of constructions of excellence further complicates the issue and makes the achievement of organizational change, even in terms of such limited objectives as women's access to leadership positions, difficult. In the context of managerialism, one can expect the proliferation of initiatives aimed at 'fixing the woman' being used to effectively legitimate the persistence of male domination of senior positions.

HE plays a key role in perpetuating gender inequalities. There is a tension between girls' individual achievements in HE and the persistence of male-dominated leadership structures. It is still not clear how these tensions are to be resolved and what implications they have for the structure and culture of HE organizations; for related institutions such as the state; and for underlying issues concerned with the nature of expert authority and gender inequality. It is possible that pressure for changes in HE will increase, in a context where women's participation in HE is increasing and where such participation, in general, and gender equality initiatives, in particular, are seen as critical to economic growth (OECD, 2012) and research innovation (EU, 2012). The question as to whether it is in society's interest to perpetuate lack of diversity in senior leadership positions is now beginning to be raised at a systemic level. However, it seems possible that attempts will be made to devalue women's participation and achievements: predominantly male areas being seen as most strategically important (Frazer, 2008).

The use of a multi-level approach illustrates the importance of various levels in affecting specific gender patterns. Countries such as Norway which are highly ranked on international gender equality indices are more likely to have women in senior management positions (reflecting the involvement of the state). Countries with lower scores on gender equality indices (such as Portugal) have gender gaps favouring women at PhD level, even in STEM subjects. Organizational factors continue to affect the under-representation of women in professorial positions. The chapter thus illustrates the contextual complexity of gender patterns and the importance of looking at the issue cross-nationally.

References

Acker, S. (1980) 'Women, the other academics', *British Journal of Sociology of Education*, 1(1), 81–91.

Acker, J. (1990) 'Hierarchies, jobs, bodies: a theory of gendered organizations', *Gender and Society*, 4(2), 139–158.

Acker, S. (1992) 'New perspectives on an old problem: the position of women academics', *Higher Education*, 24(1), 57–75.

Acker, J. (2006) 'Inequality regimes: gender, class and race in organizations', *Gender and Society*, 20(4), 441–464.

Bagilhole, B. and J. Goode (2001) 'The contradiction of the myth of individual merit and the reality of a patriarchal support system in academic careers: a feminist investigation', *European Journal of Women's Studies*, 8(2), 161–180.

Bagilhole, B. and K. White (eds) (2011) *Gender, Power and Management: A Cross-Cultural Analysis of Higher Education* (Basingstoke: Palgrave Macmillan).

Bekhouch, Y., Hausmann, R., Tyson, L. D. and S. Zahidi (2013) *The Global Gender Gap Report, September 2013* (Geneva, Switzerland: World Economic Forum).

Blackmore, J. and J. Sachs (2007) *Performing and Reforming Leaders: Gender, Educational Restructuring and Organisational Change* (Albany, NY: State University of New York).

Bourdieu, P. (2001) *Masculine Domination* (California: Stanford University Press).

Carvalho, T., Cardoso, S. and S. Sousa (2014) 'Changes in the institutional context and academic profession: a case from Portugal', in I. Weijden, K. Prpic and N. Asheulova (eds) *(Re)searching Scientific Careers* (pp. 117–140) (S. Petersburg: Publishing House 'Nestor-Historia').

Carvalho, T. and R. Santiago (2010) 'New challenges for women seeking an academic career: the hiring process in Portuguese HEIs', *Journal of Higher Education Policy and Management*, 32(3), 239–249.

Carvalho, T., White, R. and M. L. Machado-Taylor (2013) 'Top university managers and affirmative action', *Equality, Diversity and Inclusion*, 32(4), 394–409.

Ceci, S. J. and W. M. Williams (2011) 'Understanding current causes of women's under-representation in science', *PNAS*, 108(8), 3157–3162.

Cockburn, C. (1991) *In the Way of Women: Men's Resistance to Sex Equality in Organizations* (London: Macmillan).

Coleman, M. (2011) *Women at the Top Challenges, Choices and Change* (Basingstoke: Palgrave Macmillan).

Connell, R. W. (1995) *Masculinities*, 2nd edn (Cambridge: Polity Press).

Deem, R., Hilliard, S. and M. Reed (2008) *Knowledge, Higher Education and the New Managerialism* (Oxford: Oxford University Press).

Ely, R. and D. Myerson (2010) 'An organisational approach to undoing gender: the unlikely case of offshore oil platforms', *Research in Organisational Behaviour* (30), 3–34.

Ely, R. J. and I. Padavic (2007) 'A feminist analysis of organisational research on sex differences', *Academy of Management Review*, 32(4), 1121–1143.

EU – European Union (2012) *Structural Change in Research Institutions: Enhancing Excellence, Gender Equality and Efficiency in Research and Innovation*, Retrieved December 2, 2012, from http://ec.europa.eu/research/science-society/document_library/pdf _06/structural-changes-final-report_en.pdf.

EU – European Union (2013) *She Figures 2012 – Gender in research and innovation*, Statistics and Indicators (Brussels: European Commission, Directorate-General for Research and Innovation), Retrieved April 12, 2013, from http://ec.europa.eu/research/ science-society/document_library/pdf_06/she-figures-2012_en.pdf.

Fitzgerald, T. (2014) *Women Leaders in Higher Education* (London: SRHE)

Foschi, M. (2004) 'Blocking the use of gender-based double standards for competence', in *EU Gender and Excellence in the Making* (pp. 51–57), Retrieved June 15, 2014, from http: //ec.europa.eu/research/science-society/pdf/bias_brochure_final_en.pdf.

Foschi, M. (2006) 'On the application files design for the study of competence and double standards', *Sociological Focus*, 39(2), 115–132.

Fox, M. F. and S. Mohapatra (2007) 'Social-organizational characteristics of work and publication productivity among academic scientist in doctoral-granting departments', *The Journal of Higher Education*, 78(5), 542–571.

Frazer, N. (2008) 'From redistribution to recognition? Dilemmas of justice in a "Post Socialist" Age', in K. Olson (ed) *Adding Insult to Injury Nancy Frazer Debates Her Critics* (London: Verso Books).

Grummell, B., Devine, D. and K. Lynch (2009) 'The care-less manager: gender, care and new managerialism in higher education', *Gender and Education*, 21(2), 191–208.

Heijstra, T., Bjarnanson, T. and G. L. Rafnsdottir, (2014) 'Predictors of gender inequalities in the rank of full professor', *Scandinavian Journal of Educational Research*, doi:10.1080/00313831.2014.904417

Heijstra, T., O'Connor, P. and L. G. Rafnsdottir (2013) 'Explaining gender inequality in Iceland: what makes the difference?', *European Journal of Higher Education*, 3(4), 324–331.

Husu, L. (2001) *Sexism, Support and Survival in Academia: Academic Women and Hidden Discrimination in Finland* (Helsinki: University of Helsinki Press).

Husu, L. (2006) *Gate Keeping, Gender and Recognition of Scientific Excellence*, Paper presented at 16th ISA World Congress of Sociology, July 23–30, 2006, Durban, SA.

Kanter, R. M. (1977) *Men and Women of the Corporation*, 2nd edn (New York: Basic Books).

Kerfoot, D. and S. Whitehead (1998) 'Boys' Own stuff: masculinity and the management of further education', *Sociological Review*, 46(3), 436–457.

Knights, D. and W. Richards (2003) 'Sex discrimination in UK academia', *Gender, Work & Organization*, 10(2), 213–238.

Krefting, L. A. (2003) 'Intertwined discourses of merit and gender: evidence from academic employment in the USA', *Gender, Work and Organization*, 10(2), 260–278.

Lamont, M. (2009) *How Professors Think* (Cambridge Mass/London: Harvard University Press).

Leathwood, C. and B. Read (2009) *Gender and the Changing Face of Higher Education: A Feminized Future?* (Berkshire: McGraw-Hill International).

Ledin, A., Bornmann, L., Gannon, F. and G. Wallon (2007) 'A persistent problem. traditional gender roles hold back female scientists', *EMBO Reports*, 8(11), 982–987.

Lindgren, G., Jansson, U., Jonsson, A. and T. Mattsson (2010) *Nördar, nomader og duktiga flickor – kön och jämställdhet i excellenta miljöer* (Stockholm: Delegationen for jämstaldhet i högskolan).

Lynch, K., Grummell, B. and D. Devine (2012) *New Managerialism in Education: Commercialisation, Carelessness and Gender* (Basingstoke: Palgrave).

Mavin, S. and P. Bryans (2002) 'Academic women in the UK: mainstreaming our experiences and networking for action', *Gender and Education*, 14(3), 235–250.

McIntyre, R. M., Bartle, S. A., Landis, D. and M. R. Dansby (2002) 'The effects of equal opportunity fairness attitudes on job satisfaction, organizational commitment, and perceived work group efficacy', *Military Psychology*, 14(4), 299–319.

McLaughlin, M. S., Lange, S. and H. Brus (2013) 'Gendered citation patterns in international relations', *International Studies Perspectives: Special Issue Feminism in International Relations*, 14(4), 485–492.

Morley, L. (1994) 'Glass ceiling or iron cage: women in UK academia', *Gender, Work & Organization*, 1(4), 194–204.

Morley, L. (1999) *Organising Feminisms: The Micropolitics of the Academy* (Basingstoke: Palgrave Macmillan).

Morley, L. (2013) *Women and Higher Education Leadership: Absences and Aspirations* (London: Leadership Foundation for Higher Education).

Morley, L. and V. Walsh (eds) (1996) *Breaking Boundaries: Women in Higher Education* (London: Taylor & Francis).

Moss-Racusin, C. A., Dovidio, J. F., Brescoll, V. L., Graham, M. J. and J. Handelsman (2012) 'Science faculty's subtle gender biases favour male students', *PNAS* 109(41) 16474–16479.

Neale, J. (2011) 'Doing senior management', in K. White and B. Bagilhole (eds) *Gender, Power and Management. A Cross Cultural Analysis of Higher Education* (pp. 140–167) (London: Palgrave Publishers).

O'Connor, P. (2014a) *Management and Gender in Higher Education* (Manchester: University Press).

O'Connor, P. (2014b) 'Understanding success: a case study of gendered change in the professoriate', *Journal of Higher Education Policy and Management*, 36(2), 212–244.

O'Connor, P. and T. Carvalho (2014) 'Different or similar? Constructions of leadership by senior managers in Irish and Portuguese universities', *Studies in Higher Education*, 6, 1–28. http://www.tandfonline.com/eprint/7YSQTUDKrnpEnKiV3hfy/full.

O'Connor, P. and A. Goransson (2015) 'Constructing or rejecting the notion of other in senior university management: the cases of Ireland and Sweden', *Educational Management, Administration and Leadership*, published online before print June 17, 2014. 43(2), 323–340, doi:10.1177/1741143214523015

O'Connor, P. and C. O'Hagan (2015) 'Excellence in university academic staff evaluation: a problematic reality?' *Studies in Higher Education*, doi:10.1080/03075079.2014.1000292.

OECD – Organisation for Economic Co-operation and Development (2012) *Closing the Gender Gap: Act Now*, Retrieved October 2014, from http://www.oecd.org/gender/closingthegap.htm.

OECD – Organisation for Economic Co-operation and Development (2013) *Education at a Glance*, OECD Publishing, Retrieved October 2014, doi:10.1787/eag-2013-en.

Padilla-González, L. E., Metcalfe, A. S., Galaz-Fontes, J. F., Fisher, D. and I. Snee (2011) 'Gender gaps in North American research productivity: examining faculty publication rates in Mexico, Canada, and the U.S.', *Compare: A Journal of Comparative and International Education*, 41(5), 649–668.

Powell, G. N., Butterfield, D. A. and J. D. Parent (2002) 'Gender and managerial stereotypes: have times changed?', *Journal of Management*, 28(2), 177–193.

Ridgeway, C. (2011) *Framed by Gender: How Gender Inequality Persists in the Modern World* (Oxford: Oxford University Press).

Ridgeway, C. and S. Correll (2004) 'Unpacking the gender system: a theoretical perspective on gender beliefs and social relations', *Gender and Society*, 18(4), 510–531.

Risman, B. J. and G. Davis (2013) 'From sex roles to gender structure', *Current Sociology Review*, 61(5–6), 733–755.

Santiago, R., Carvalho, T. and A. Vabø (2012) 'Personal characteristics, career trajectories and sense of identity among male and female academics in Norway and Portugal', in M. Vukasovic, P. Maassen, M. Nerland, R. Pinheiro, B. Stensaker and A. Vabø (eds) *Effects of Higher Education Reforms: Change Dynamics* (pp. 279–304) (Rotterdam: Sense Publishers).

Sax, L., Hagerdon, L., Arredondo, M. and F. Dicrisi (2002) 'Faculty research productivity: exploring the role of gender and family related factors', *Research in Higher Education*, 43(4), 423–632.

Schein, V. E., Muller, R., Lituchy, T. and J. Liu (1996) 'Think manager-think male: a global phenomenon?', *Journal of Organizational Behaviour*, 17, 33–41.

Schoon, I. and J. Eccles (eds) (2014) *Gender Differences in Aspirations and Attainment – A Life Course Perspective* (Cambridge: Cambridge University Press).

Scientific American (2014) 'How nations fare in PhDs by sex', *Scientific American*, 11(4), Retrieved October 24, 2014, from http://www.scientificamerican.com/article/how-nations-fare-inphds-by-sex-interactive/.

Sheltzer, J. M. and J. C. Smith (2014) 'Elite male faculty in life sciences employ fewer women', *PNAS*, 111(28), 10107–10112.

Silander, C. (2010) *Pyramider Och Pipelines. Om Högskolesystemets Påverkan på jämställhet i Högskolan*, Doctoral thesis (Växjö, Linneus: University Press).

Slaughter, S. and G. Rhoades (2010) *Academic Capitalism and the New Economy: Markets, States and Higher Education* (Baltimore, MD: Johns Hopkins University Press).

Smith, N., Smith, V. and M. Verner (2006) 'Do women in top management affect firm performance? A panel study of 2500 Danish firms', *International Journal of Productivity and Performance Management*, 55(7), 569–593.

UN (2014) Human Development Report. Retrieved December 28, 2014, from http://hdr.undp.org/en/content/human-development-index-hdi.

UNESCO – United Nations Educational, Scientific and Cultural Organization (2010) *Global Education Digest 2010. Special focus on gender* (Montreal, Quebec: UNESCO I), Retrieved September 11, 2014, from www.uis.unesco.org/publications/GED2010.

UNESCO – United Nations Educational, Scientific and Cultural Organization (2012) *World Atlas of Gender Equality in Education* (Paris: UNESCO).

Vabø, A., Padilla-González, L. E., Waagene, E. and T. Næss (2014) 'Gender and faculty internationalization', in Huang, Futao, Finkelstein, Martin J., Rostan, Michele (eds) *The Internationalization of the Academy* (pp. 183–205) (Springer: Netherlands).

Valian, V. (1999) *Why So Slow. The Advancement of Women* (Cambridge, MA: MIT Press).

Van Den Brink, M. and Y. Benschop (2012) 'Gender practices in the construction of academic excellence: sheep with five legs', *Organisation*, 19(4), 507–524.

Wagner, A., Acker, S. and K. Mayuzumi (eds) (2008) *Whose University is it Anyway? Power and Privilege on Gendered Terrain* (Toronto, Canada: Sumach Press).

Wenneras, C. and A. Wold (1997) 'Nepotism and sexism in peer review', *Nature*, 387 (6631), 341–343, Retrieved May 22, 2011, from http://sciencethatmatters.com/wp, content/uploads/2007/04/wenneras97nepotism.pdf.

West, C. and D. Zimmerman (1987) 'Doing gender', *Gender & Society*, 1(2), 125–151.

Wharton, A. S. (2011) *The Sociology of Gender: An Introduction to Theory and Research* (Oxford: John Wiley & Sons).

Winchester, H., Lorenzo, S., Browning, L. and C. Chesterman (2006) 'Academic women's promotions in Australian universities', *Employee Relations*, 28(6), 505–522.

Wroblewski, A. (2014) 'Female participation in management and cultural change: precondition or high expectations?' Paper presented at the *8th International Interdisciplinary Conference on Gender, Work and Organisation* June 24–26, 2014, Keele.

Wroblewski, A. and A. Leitner (2011) 'Equal opportunity policies at Austrian universities and their evaluation: development, results and limitations', *Brussels Economic Review*, 54(2), 317–339.

Zimmer, A. (2003) *Research and Training Network. Women in European Universities*, Final Report 2000–2003 (Brussels: European Union).

Index

604   *Index*

Printed and bound by CPI Group (UK) Ltd, Croydon, CR0 4YY